Getting Action from Organizational Surveys

THE PROFESSIONAL PRACTICE SERIES

The Professional Practice Series is sponsored by the Society for Industrial and Organizational Psychology (SIOP). The series was launched in 1988 to provide industrial/organizational psychologists, organizational scientists and practitioners, human resource professionals, managers, executives, and those interested in organizational behavior and performance with volumes that are insightful, current, informative, and relevant to organizational practice. The volumes in the Professional Practice Series are guided by five tenets designed to enhance future organizational practice:

1. Focus on practice, but grounded in science
2. Translate organizational science into practice by generating guidelines, principles, and lessons learned that can shape and guide practice
3. Showcase the application of industrial/organizational psychology to solve problems
4. Document and demonstrate best industrial and organizational-based practices
5. Stimulate research needed to guide future organizational practice

The volumes seek to inform those interested in practice with guidance, insights, and advice on how to apply the concepts, findings, methods, and tools derived from industrial/organizational psychology to solve human-related organizational problems.

Previous Professional Practice Series volumes include:

Published by Jossey-Bass

Customer Service Delivery
Lawrence Fogli, Editor

Employment Discrimination Litigation
Frank J. Landy, Editor

The Brave New World of eHR
Hal G. Gueutal, Dianna L. Stone, Editors

Improving Learning Transfer in Organizations
Elwood F. Holton III, Timothy T. Baldwin, Editors

Resizing the Organization
Kenneth P. De Meuse, Mitchell Lee Marks, Editors

Implementing Organizational Interventions
Jerry W. Hedge, Elaine D. Pulakos, Editors

Organization Development
Janine Waclawski, Allan H. Church, Editors

Creating, Implementing, and Managing Effective Training and Development
Kurt Kraiger, Editor

The 21st Century Executive
Rob Silzer, Editor

Managing Selection in Changing Organizations
Jerard F. Kehoe, Editor

Evolving Practices in Human Resource Management
Allen I . Kraut, Abraham K. Korman, Editors

Individual Psychological Assessment
Richard Jeanneret, Rob Silzer, Editors

Performance Appraisal
James W. Smither, Editor

Organizational Surveys
Allen I. Kraut, Editor

Employees, Careers, and Job Creation
Manuel London, Editor

Published by Guilford Press

Diagnosis for Organizational Change
Ann Howard and Associates

Human Dilemmas in Work Organizations
Abraham K. Korman and Associates

Diversity in the Workplace
Susan E. Jackson and Associates

Working with Organizations and Their People
Douglas W. Bray and Associates

Getting Action from Organizational Surveys

Getting Action from Organizational Surveys

New Concepts, Technologies, and Applications

Allen I. Kraut, Editor

Foreword by Allan H. Church
and Janine Waclawski

JOSSEY-BASS
A Wiley Imprint
www.josseybass.com

Published by Jossey-Bass
A Wiley Imprint
989 Market Street, San Francisco, CA 94103-1741   www.josseybass.com

Jossey-Bass books and products are available through most bookstores. To contact
Jossey-Bass directly call our Customer Care Department within the U.S. at 800-956-7739,
outside the U.S. at 317-572-3986, or fax 317-572-4002.

Jossey-Bass also publishes its books in a variety of electronic formats. Some content that
appears in print may not be available in electronic books.

Library of Congress Cataloging-in-Publication Data

Getting action from organizational surveys : new concepts, technologies, and applications
/ Allen I. Kraut, editor ; foreword by Allan H. Church and Janine Waclawski.
     p. cm. — (The professional practice series)
  Includes bibliographical references and index.
  ISBN-13: 978-0-7879-7937-9 (alk. paper)
  ISBN-10: 0-7879-7937-6 (alk. paper)
  1. Employee attitude surveys. 2. Organizational effectiveness—Evaluation.
3. Organizational change. I. Kraut, Allen I. II. Series.
  HF5549.5.A83G48 2006
  658.30072'3—dc22

                                                           2005026067

Printed in the United States of America
FIRST EDITION
HB Printing   10 9 8 7 6 5 4 3 2

The Professional Practice Series

*This book is dedicated to Richard A. Dunnington, a
founder of the Mayflower Group, the premier organizational
survey consortium. For a quarter of a century, as manager
of personnel research at IBM, he was a persevering and
effective advocate for organizational surveys, succeeding in
making them a "way of life" at IBM and creating a positive
example for other firms.*

Contents

Foreword

Welcome to the latest edition of the Society for Industrial and Organizational Psychology's (SIOP) contribution to enhancing professional practice. This focus of this volume, our first as incoming series coeditors, can be summed by the simple phrase "back to the future." Although a glance at the title might suggest to the uninitiated that this is yet another book on surveys, it is much more than that. In fact, it represents a significant leap forward in the way we think about and use survey methodology.

You hold in your hands the next generation of thinking on organizational surveys—one where people care about and do something with the data obtained to drive organizational change. Although surveys are popular as a methodology, not every survey results in action, and not all practitioners understand the critical importance of leveraging their data to make real changes. The chapters in this book go a long way to solving this gap in professional practice in all fields of applied survey work.

Organizational surveys are one of the most common forms of data collection at the disposal of practitioners and researchers in the social sciences. Whether you are in industrial/organizational psychology, organization development, or human resource development, surveys have always been a primary means of collecting data about a whole host of issues, including employee attitudes, perceptions, and behaviors. In fact, organizational surveys have become so popular over the past decade that we are now adding new words to the vernacular, such as *linkage, pulse, nonresponse, relative weights, oversurveying,* and *organizational health.* As you will see, this book explains them all—and adds *taking action* to the list as well. In short, this is a hot topic for practitioners.

Second, Allen Kraut and the outstanding collection of authors he has assembled for this book are widely known and well respected throughout the industry for their excellence in survey practice.

Anyone wanting to know what the best in class are doing in the survey arena need only review some of the chapters in this book. All of the chapters focus on doing something with survey results, not just creating excellent survey items. Between the introduction of new concepts to the survey arena, new methods of collecting and delivering results, and new applications to different organizational situations, this book really delivers. In addition, Kraut himself is a pioneer in the field of organizational survey, between his many years with IBM and his volume on surveys, *Organizational Surveys: Tools for Assessment and Change* (1996), which has become a classic. In other words, this book is full of important information from leading-edge practitioners and above all is about taking action from surveys.

This is a subject near and dear to our own hearts. As survey practitioners ourselves for the past fifteen years, we cannot help but be energized by the wealth of new survey-related knowledge, practice, and guidance that appears in this book. We were very pleased when Kraut agreed to bring his project forward as our first editorial contribution to SIOP's Professional Practice series. This is a contribution from the heart to our profession, and we offer our sincerest thanks to him and all of the contributors. This book has incredible material that anyone in any field interested in surveys will find informative and immediately useful.

Allen Kraut and his associates have recreated their magic from 1996. This book represents both a significant contribution to the current state of organizational surveys and takes us to entirely new places professionally. We are confident that you will come away from this book having learned something new about the importance, value, process, or outcomes to taking action from surveys.

This focus on action is a critical one, as this is typically where the survey process falls down and where we as practitioners may fail to deliver on our clients' expectations. Taking action from surveys, not the conduct of the survey itself, is what is vital to making surveys an effective tool in organizations. As practitioners, we need to be as action oriented as the client organizations we serve. The key message in this book is that organizational surveys are only as good as the actions that result from them. Enjoy—and survey well!

June 2005

ALLAN H. CHURCH
JANINE WACLAWSKI
Series Editors

Preface

The central theme of this book is getting action in response to organizational survey results. We know that the majority of medium and large firms use surveys, and there is a pressing need to use surveys well. And yet experienced survey professionals often point to the lack of meaningful action as the major downside of organizational surveys.

How do we get more and better actions from our surveys? What would it take for surveys to be such a valuable tool that they become a regular, ongoing measurement in all organizations, just as budgets and performance appraisals are done regularly to guide desired behaviors? I believe we can gain the answer by taking a fresh look at organizational surveys, in a way that builds on what we have learned in recent decades and uses our growing sophistication to build a new understanding of the power and use of surveys.

This book presents the latest views of expert contributors—people at the leading edge of best practices in the field of organizational surveys—on how to get action from organizational surveys. This book is not intended to be an update of the popular and well-accepted 1996 *Organizational Surveys: Tools for Assessment and Change,* which I edited. Rather, this book should be seen as a companion piece. It is more narrowly focused, primarily on the theme of getting action. And although a few chapters may overlap slightly with the earlier work, this book is a complement to it, not a newer version.

The Audience

The primary audience for this book will be survey practitioners and consultants and their clients, as well as most industrial/organizational psychologists. Human resource (HR) management professionals are also a major audience for this volume. All HR professionals who work with organizational surveys and want to improve their impact will benefit from a reading of its contents.

 Another strong audience will be instructors and graduate students in all related disciplines, such as industrial/organizational psychology, consulting psychology, HR management and organizational behavior, and organizational development.

Overview of the Book

The contributors' presentations showcase recent survey developments in thoughtful and far-reaching expositions. After an overview and introduction to the topic, the chapters are grouped into three major parts.

Part One, "New Concepts," covers new ways of looking at and understanding surveys and their role. The chapters examine the impact of employee attitudes and perceptions on organizational performance, customer satisfaction, and the role of organizational development in making surveys effective.

The chapters in Part Two, "New Technologies," report new techniques, including Web-based administration, the use of improved computer programs for dealing with write-in comments, innovative statistical approaches, and the use of "pulse" surveys.

The chapters in Part Three, "New Applications," show the variety of applications in which survey data play an exciting and important role. These include managing mergers and acquisitions, dealing with turnover, helping to drive change and organizational effectiveness, and dealing with the special needs of complex, global organizations. Some case studies are included.

May 2005   ALLEN I. KRAUT

Acknowledgments

Among the major contributors to this book are the dozens of reviewers who read and gave detailed feedback on the chapters. Their efforts greatly improved the caliber of the work. I owe thanks for their efforts to the following doctoral students and graduates of Baruch College, City University of New York, most of whom were in my seminar on organizational survey research: Jeanine Andreassi, Kira Barden, Corinne Donovan, Amorette Ferrante, Irene He, Daniel Hickey, Kristen Kirkland, Jessica Osedach, David Prottas, Brian Redmond, Yonata Rubin, David Youssefnia, and Angelique Shaydulova, who was also my research assistant, and reviewed a very large number of manuscripts.

Several of my faculty colleagues at Baruch gave generously of their time and thought, and I thank Moshe Banai, Judi Komaki, Richard Kopelman, Robert J. Lee, Harry Rosen, and Charles Scherbaum.

In addition, there were many knowledgeable colleagues from industry and consulting who gave helpful comments and feedback, often on more than one chapter. I appreciate the input from the following: Marc Berwald, Leo Brajkovich, Robert Burnaska, Harold Tragash, Lise Saari, Jerry Halamaj, Victoria Berger-Gross, Aiofe Brennan, Wendy Combs, Norman Costa, William Dodd, Michelle Ehler, Elaine Eisenman, Salvatore Falleta, Kris Fenlason, William L. Fuller, Andrea Goldberg, George Hollenbeck, Sherry Hoy, Edward Kahn, Steve Katzman, Stephanie Kendall, Angela Lynch, Steve Marcus, Mitchell Marks, Wayne McCullough, Nicholas Mills, Mathian Osicki, Maria V. Park, Patricia Pedigo, Tom Rauzi, Steve Rogelberg, Ben Schneider, S. Harold Simonetti, Scott Spera, Stephen Temlock, Marian Thier, Lori Foster Thompson, Saskia Trienen, Anna Marie Valerio, Vicki Vandaveer, and Bernard Witlieb.

Most of all, I appreciate the time, energy, and thought from our forty-three contributors, all of whom are busy and successful practitioners. While many come from academia and industry, and even more have such experience in their backgrounds, most are now in consulting firms. In these firms, survey practices are the core competencies. The majority of the authors have a mix of experience in academia, industry, and consulting. Taken together, the contributing authors are an extremely impressive group of leading-edge practitioners, and we are fortunate to have them share their best ideas and thinking with us.

The Authors

Allen I. Kraut is professor of management at Baruch College, City University of New York. In 1995, he received the Society for Industrial and Organizational Psychology's Distinguished Professional Contributions Award for his work in survey research. He managed U.S. and worldwide organizational surveys for the IBM Corporation for many years, until leaving in 1989. Jossey-Bass published his edited volume, *Organizational Surveys: Tools for Assessment and Change,* in 1996. Kraut earned a Ph.D. at the University of Michigan and was with the Institute for Social Research. He is a Fellow of the American Psychological Society and was awarded a Diplomate from the American Board of Professional Psychology. He also heads Kraut Associates, specializing in opinion surveys.

Peter Bachiochi is an associate professor and assistant chair of the psychology department at Eastern Connecticut State University. He held previous teaching positions at Bowling Green State University and Suffolk University. He also worked for four years at IBM in its human resource research group as a survey specialist and internal consultant. He continues to provide survey consulting services to several nonprofit organizations. He received his Ph.D. in industrial-organizational psychology from the University of Connecticut, and his research interests include minority employee recruiting and retention, affirmative action, job satisfaction, and team leadership.

Daniel Baitch is a vice president of organizational research at JPMorgan Chase in New York. He works with corporate and business unit staff to design and manage a wide variety of strategic employee research and measurement processes, including merger assessments, the global employee survey, and performance metrics. He previously worked with the research and consulting teams at Learning International, Towers Perrin, and Development Dimensions International. He is a coauthor of a number of research papers, as well as the book *High Performance Sales Organizations: Creating Competitive Advantage in the Global Marketplace* (1995). Baitch holds a Ph.D. in applied research from Hofstra University.

Karen M. Barbera is president of organizational assessment and research at Valtera Corporation (formerly PRA). For the past ten years, she has worked with the firm's clients in the design, development, execution, and follow-through of its survey programs. Her survey experience includes a large-scale process involving more than 800,000 employees. In addition to her client work, she has been involved in designing technological solutions to enhance survey processes. Prior to joining Valtera, she worked at IBM on the development, validation, and implementation of selection systems. She received her Ph.D. in industrial and organizational psychology from Bowling Green State University.

Ralph J. Bishop is global manager of qualitative research for ISR, an organizational research and consulting firm. Trained at Northwestern University, where he received his Ph.D. in cultural anthropology, he has over fifteen years' experience analyzing and interpreting open-ended responses from large-scale surveys. Before joining ISR, he worked as an independent researcher and consultant. He studied cultural diversity in Vicksburg, Mississippi, under a scholar-in-residence grant from the National Endowment for the Humanities and has taught at several Chicago-area colleges and universities. He was also a cofounder of the National Association for the Practice of Anthropology and served as general editor of the *NAPA Bulletin* series from 1983 to 1998.

Ingwer Borg is professor of applied psychological methods at the Justus-Liebig-Universität (Giessen, Germany), scientific director of the Zentrum für Umfragen, Methoden und Analysen (ZUMA, Mannheim, Germany), and partner of Human Resources Consulting (Munich, Germany). His main fields of research and development are employee surveys and data analysis. He has written or edited 14 books and more than 150 articles in journals or books.

He has extensive experience in practical survey work, surveying millions of employees in dozens of German and international companies over the past twenty years, and using these data to promote business goals in appropriate follow-up processes.

J. Thomas Bowler, Jr., has been vice president, human resources and organization, of Pratt & Whitney, a division of United Technologies Corporation (UTC), since 2001. He championed the creation of the Employee Fulfillment Center of Excellence and the company's Employee Fulfillment improvement process. Bowler joined UTC at Pratt & Whitney in 1979 and has held a variety of management positions at Hamilton, UTC Corporate Headquarters, the former UT Automotive business, and Carrier—including four years as head of human resources for Carrier Asia-Pacific Operations. He received a master's degree from Harvard University.

Scott M. Brooks is general manager of the West Coast region for Gantz Wiley Research, a consulting firm specializing in employee and customer surveys. Much of his consulting and research work focuses on leveraging linkages between employee surveys, employee turnover, customer satisfaction, and business results. This involves creating human resource metrics, balanced scorecard tools, and other frameworks to help clients use strategic input from surveys. He has over fifteen years of experience in survey research. He holds a Ph.D. in industrial and organizational psychology from the Ohio State University and has authored numerous presentations and publications on employee measurement topics.

W. Warner Burke is the Edward Lee Thorndike Professor of Psychology and Education at Teachers College, Columbia University. He was the first executive director of the OD Network. Burke's consulting experience has been with a variety of organizations in business and industry, education, government, religious, and medical systems. He is a past editor of both *Organizational Dynamics* and the *Academy of Management Executive.* His publications number over 150, and he has received the Public Service Medal from the National Aeronautics and Space Administration and the Distinguished Scholar-Practitioner Award from the Academy of Management. His latest book is *Organization Change: Theory and Practice* (2002).

Bruce H. Campbell is an executive consultant at Gantz Wiley Research, a survey research consulting firm. With over twenty years of employee survey research experience, Campbell is skilled in developing customized surveys to meet a variety of needs, including union vulnerability assessment, employer of choice analysis, and linkage research (a study of links among employee opinions, customer loyalty, and business performance). Previously Campbell was a consultant at a survey firm conducting large-scale employee surveys and prior to that led internal survey initiatives for Control Data (now Ceridian). He has five years of Ph.D. course work in social psychology at the University of Minnesota.

Allan H. Church is vice president of organization and management development for PepsiCo, where he is responsible for leading the talent management and people development agenda. Before he joined PepsiCo in December 2000, he spent nine years as an external consultant working for W. Warner Burke Associates and several years at IBM. He has served as adjunct professor at Columbia University and is currently a Visiting Faculty Scholar at Benedictine University. An active writer, he has authored four books (two on organizational surveys), twelve book chapters, and over one hundred articles. He received his Ph.D. in organizational psychology from Columbia University.

Joe Colihan is part of the workforce research team at IBM. His responsibilities include managing IBM's Global Pulse Survey program. He has conducted research in the areas of organizational culture and effectiveness, motivation and job satisfaction, leadership competencies, retention, teamwork, job stress, job families, diversity, work/life balance, and linking employee attitudes to customer satisfaction and business performance. He earned his doctorate in psychology from the University of Missouri-St. Louis.

Norman D. Costa is founder of eXpert Survey Systems, Inc. He has over thirty-five years of experience in organizational surveys, advertising and marketing research, statistical programming, work/family studies, and best company lists. He was director of Strategic Surveys for Wm. Schiemann & Associates (now Metrus) and general manager of the Metro New York Office of Genesee Survey Services. He worked for IBM for twenty-four years in the United States and Asia. He is an innovator in expert systems—a form of artificial intelligence—for employee surveys. He holds a certificate in software development in the UNIX/Linux environment from Pace University. He received a Ph.D. in educational psychology from the Graduate School of the City University of New York.

Anthony T. Dalessio is a consulting human resource professional in the IBM Workforce Research department. He has been a senior specialist at Bell Atlantic (now Verizon), a director at LIMRA International, and a consultant to the National Aeronautics and Space Administration. In his roles in these organizations, he has worked as a scientist-practitioner in the areas of employee surveys and selection. He received his Ph.D. from Bowling Green State University.

Michelle A. Donovan is a senior researcher in the human resources research group at Intel Corporation. In this position she manages the Global Employee Survey and consults on surveys and assessments conducted worldwide. Prior to Intel, she worked at Terranova Consulting Group and Personnel Decisions Research Institutes. Her research has been published in the *Journal of Applied Psychology* and *Personnel Psychology*. She has also served as an officer for the IT Survey Group and Bay Area Applied Psychologists. She earned her Ph.D. in industrial/organizational psychology from the University of Illinois at Urbana-Champaign.

Larry D. Eldridge, vice president of Consulting, and director, Genesee Survey Services, has worked in the field of employee opinion surveys for nearly thirty years. While at Eastman Kodak, he conducted surveys throughout the world and was chairman of the Mayflower Group. Since joining Genesee, he has consulted with premier U.S. corporations including GE, Raytheon, Johnson & Johnson, Xerox, Northwestern Mutual, PacifiCare, Cisco Systems and the Home Depot. He received his Ph.D. in business administration from the University of Rochester, majoring in organizational behavior. He is a member of the American Psychological Association and the Society of Industrial and Organizational Psychology.

Kristofer J. Fenlason is director of organization effectiveness at Data Recognition Corporation, where he is responsible for developing and providing consulting services in organizational surveys, multisource feedback, and customer satisfaction. He has over fifteen year's experience providing in-depth survey and multisource feedback consultation to a diverse mix of clients. He has conducted research, presented, and published on the challenges associated with dual-method (paper and Web) surveying, linkage research, the usability of Web-based surveys, job stress, and gender bias in the evaluation of women managers. He received his Ph.D. in industrial/organizational psychology from Central Michigan University.

James K. Harter is the chief scientist for the Gallup Organization's workplace management practice. Since joining Gallup in 1985, he has authored or coauthored more than a thousand research studies on employee satisfaction, engagement, individual differences, and well-being. Harter is the primary researcher and author of the first meta-analysis to investigate the relationships between work unit level employee satisfaction/engagement and performance results. Harter received his Ph.D. from the University of Nebraska-Lincoln and frequently serves as a guest lecturer at the University of Nebraska and other universities. He is a member of the American Psychological Association and the Academy of Management.

Jeff W. Johnson is a senior staff scientist at Personnel Decisions Research Institutes, where he has directed many applied organizational research projects for a variety of government and private sector clients. He developed relative weight analysis, a procedure for determining the relative importance of correlated predictor variables in a regression equation. His primary research interests are in the areas of personnel selection, performance measurement, research methods, and statistics. He frequently publishes in a variety of journals and is on the editorial board of *Personnel Psychology*. He received his Ph.D. in industrial and organizational psychology from the University of Minnesota.

Sarah Rassenfoss Johnson is a consultant with Genesee Survey Services, developing custom survey process and tools to create organization change. She was director of executive talent management and organization research at Eastman Kodak, managing worldwide employee research and executive recruiting, assessments, and succession planning. She was previously program director of worldwide human resource research at IBM, where she led a major redesign of the company's employee survey strategy. At Procter & Gamble she helped design the organization's first employee survey. She speaks frequently to professional groups on employee surveys. Johnson received her Ph.D. in industrial/organizational psychology from the Ohio State University.

Patrick Kulesa is global research director for ISR, an organizational research and consulting firm. He specializes in survey design and the application of advanced statistical analyses to employee survey data. His research focuses on the predictors of employee engagement and the links between employee attitudes and other measures of business performance, including customer satisfaction, occupational safety, productivity, and sales and profitability. He has conducted, presented, and published research on gender differences in the workplace leadership, and the nature and underlying causes of cross-national differences in employee opinion. He received his Ph.D. in social psychology from Northwestern University.

Kyle M. Lundby is a consultant and manager of norms and benchmarking at Gantz Wiley Research. He works with clients to develop and implement strategic employee and customer measurement systems. He is active in research and has numerous presentations and publications in the area of linkage research, as well as usability testing and the application of balanced scorecard metrics. Lundby is an adjunct professor at Augsburg College in Minneapolis and sits on the board of Minnesota Professionals for Psychology Applied to Work. His Ph.D. in industrial and organizational psychology is from the University of Tennessee.

William H. Macey is CEO of Valtera Corporation and has more than twenty-five years of experience in consulting with organizations to design and implement survey research. He has consulted with more than twenty-five of the Fortune 200 companies. Macey is a Society for Industrial and Organizational Psychology (SIOP) Fellow, SIOP past president, and a previous member of the editorial board of *Personnel Psychology*. He received his Ph.D. from Loyola University Chicago.

Mitchell Lee Marks is in the Department of Management of San Francisco State University. He leads JoiningForces.org and advises on team building, organizational effectiveness, leadership development, and the strategic planning and implementation of organizational change. He works extensively with firms planning and implementing mergers, restructurings, strategic changes, downsizings, and other major transitions. He is the author of five books, including *Charging Back Up the Hill: Workforce Recovery After Mergers, Acquisitions and Downsizings,* and *Joining Forces: Making One Plus One Equal Three in Mergers, Acquisitions, and Alliances,* as well as several articles in management and scholarly journals. He holds a Ph.D. in Organizational Psychology from the University of Michigan.

Paul M. Mastrangelo is a senior consultant at Genesee Survey Services, where he works with large-scale organizations in the design, implementation, and analysis of employee surveys for organization development efforts. Previously, he was a tenured associate professor at the University of Baltimore, where he directed the master's program in applied psychology. He received his Ph.D. in industrial and organizational psychology from Ohio University.

Brian S. Morgan is director of organization assessment services at Metrus Group. He has over twenty-five years of experience in employee surveys and follow-up action planning, with a focus on strategic uses of employee surveys. His articles have appeared in the *Harvard Business Review, Quality Progress, Strategy and Leadership, Personnel Journal, Public Relations Journal,* the *Journal of Applied Psychology,* and two edited volumes—*Handbook of Business Strategy (2nd Ed.),* and *Change Management Handbook.* He holds a Ph.D. in social psychology from Wayne State University.

Patricia L. Muldoon is the manager of the Employee Fulfillment Center of Excellence at Pratt & Whitney, a division of United Technologies Corporation. Pratt & Whitney designs, manufactures, and maintains commercial and military jet engines. She leads the company's employee fulfillment process, encompassing survey administration, goal setting, action planning, and follow-up. She has worked in a breadth of fields over her twenty-year career at Pratt & Whitney, including engineering, sales, and now human resources. She earned her M.B.A. at the University of Connecticut.

David H. Oliver is director of organization and management development for PepsiCo's International division, where he is responsible for organizational surveys, 360-degree feedback, performance management, and leadership development. He joined PepsiCo's Frito-Lay division in 2000 before moving to PepsiCo International in 2005. Prior to joining Frito-Lay, he spent five years at GTE (now Verizon), where he managed the employee selection group. He is a member of the Society for Industrial and Organizational Psychology and has published and presented articles in the areas of employee selection and organizational surveys. He received his Ph.D. in industrial/organizational psychology from the University of Southern Mississippi.

Sharon F. Parker is a senior consultant for Foresight International, where she manages many of Foresight's largest clients worldwide, leading the development and implementation of customized surveys and leadership assessments, which focus on employee engagement, customer satisfaction, leadership development, cultural change, and workplace improvement. She has coauthored two books on Web-based survey development and action planning. Parker received her master's degree in industrial/organizational psychology from Elmhurst College.

Robert J. Quinn is the development executive for the Treasury & Security Services business at JPMorgan Chase. He has worked at JPMorgan Chase, or one of its predecessor institutions, for over twenty-five years. He has held various positions in the corporate human resource area at JPMorgan Chase, including director of research and development, director of staffing and development, and director of organizational effectiveness. An organizational psychologist by background, he received his Ph.D. from Kansas State University. Quinn has taught in the M.B.A. programs at New York University and Baruch College and currently teaches in the Executive M.B.A. program at Baruch.

Steven G. Rogelberg is director of I/O psychology and organizational science at University of North Carolina–Charlotte. He has produced over fifty publications concerning organizational research methods, team effectiveness, employee well-being, meetings at work, and organization development. He serves as editor-in-chief of the two-volume *Encyclopedia of Industrial and Organizational Psychology*. He edited the *Handbook of Research Methods in Industrial and Organizational Psychology* (2004). He served as chair of education and training for the Society for Industrial and Organizational Psychology in 2004 and received a Professor of the Year Award and a Master Teacher Award. Rogelberg received nearly $300,000 of external grant funding. His Ph.D. in industrial/organizational psychology was completed at the University of Connecticut in 1994.

Tracey Carsten Roll is director of organization development at Insight Health Corp., where she is responsible for developing and providing consulting services in organizational surveys, leadership development, and customer satisfaction. She is experienced at managing the entire spectrum of activities for employee engagement and organizational effectiveness. She has designed and led survey initiatives that have included pulse, departmental, business unit, and organizationwide surveys. Roll also specializes in appreciative inquiry facilitation, leadership development, team effectiveness, change management, talent management, and culture formation. She received her Ph.D. in industrial and organizational psychology from the California School of Professional Psychology, San Diego.

William A. Schiemann is founder and CEO of Metrus Group, an organizational research and management consulting firm headquartered in Somerville, New Jersey. He is known for pioneering work in performance measurement, the emerging concept of "People Equity," and for linking employee behaviors with customer outcomes and financial performance. Schiemann is coauthor (with John Lingle) of *Bullseye! Hitting Your Strategic Targets Through High-Impact Measurement* (1999), and has written many articles for leading business publications. He has previously served as senior vice president at Sirota & Alper Associates and vice president of Opinion Research Corporation. He received his Ph.D. in organizational psychology from the University of Illinois.

Frank L. Schmidt is the Ralph L. Sheets Professor of Human Resources in the Tippie College of Business, University of Iowa. He was one of the two coinventors of validity generalization methods and has published over 150 journal articles and book chapters. He received the Distinguished Scientific Contributions Award (with John Hunter) from the American Psychological Association, the Distinguished Career Award from the Human Resources Division of the Academy of Management, and the Michael R. Losey Human Resources Research Award from the Society for Human Resource Management. He received his doctorate in industrial/organizational psychology from Purdue University.

Benjamin Schneider is senior research fellow at Valtera (formerly PRA). Previously he was the head of the industrial and organizational psychology program at the University of Maryland, where he received his Ph.D. in 1964 and where he is now professor emeritus. He has published more than 125 professional journal articles and book chapters, as well as eight books. His most recent books are (with Susan White) *Service Quality: Research Perspectives* (2004) and (with D. Brent Smith) *Personality and Organizations* (2004). Schneider has consulted on service quality issues with numerous companies, recently including Allstate, IBM, Toyota, Giant Eagle, Nextel, and Pepsico.

Michael J. Schroeder is president of Foresight Survey Support International, a survey consulting firm based in the Chicago area. For more than twenty years, he has designed and implemented large-scale employee engagement survey systems for some of the world's largest organizations. He has won international awards from *Human Resource Executive* and *Training* magazines for his contributions to the survey and training field. He is a frequent speaker and instructor at major conferences regarding surveys and post-survey action planning strategies. He holds a U.S. patent for hardware and software that accelerates collection and processing of survey data.

John C. Scott is vice president and cofounder of Applied Psychological Techniques, a human resource consulting firm. He directs consulting services in the areas of selection development and validation, 360-degree feedback, survey design, performance management, and executive assessment. Scott has served on the program committee for Division 14 of the American Psychological

Association and on the Society for Industrial and Organizational Psychology's Professional Practice Book Series editorial board and is a frequent presenter in the area of selection and assessment. He is coeditor (with Jack Edwards and Nambury Raju) of the *Human Resource Program Evaluation Handbook* (2003). He received his Ph.D. from the Illinois Institute of Technology.

Kathleen Suckow-Zimberg works at Microsoft as part of the on-boarding team, managing new employee orientation. She spent her first several years on the people research team managing the MS Poll (Microsoft's worldwide employee survey), exit survey, pulse survey, 360-degree feedback process, culture survey, and employee value proposition project. She was the Microsoft representative to the IT Survey Group, a survey consortia group of IT companies, holding the role of norms chair. Suckow-Zimberg previously worked for Lucent and AT&T in selection. She received her Ph.D. in industrial/organizational psychology from Purdue University.

Janine Waclawski joined the Pepsi Cola Company as a director of organization and management development in May 2002. In October 2003 she moved into a generalist role where she supports marketing. Previously she was a principal consultant at PricewaterhouseCoopers and a senior consultant at W. Warner Burke Associates. She has been an adjunct professor at Columbia University and has published over twenty-five articles and book chapters. She has also coauthored two books, *Designing and Using Organization Surveys* and *Organization Development: A Data Driven Approach to Organizational Change.* Waclawski received her Ph.D. in organizational psychology from Columbia University.

Sara P. Weiner is a consulting HR professional in IBM workforce research. She has been engaged in survey research for fifteen years in areas including attraction and retention of critical talent, career opportunity, client satisfaction, downsizing, navigating work and personal life demands, telecommuting, and transfer of training. She has published and presented in many of these areas. She received her doctorate in industrial and organizational psychology from the University of Connecticut.

Jack W. Wiley is president and CEO of Gantz Wiley Research, a consulting firm helping clients drive business performance through the strategic use of stakeholder input. With thirty years of survey research experience, Wiley's work has resulted in improved performance for organizations worldwide. Wiley developed the High Performance Model, demonstrating links among leadership practices, employee opinions, customer loyalty, and business performance. Previously Wiley was director of organizational research at Control Data and a personnel research consultant at Ford Motor Company. He is a licensed psychologist, achieved Senior Professional in Human Resources accreditation, and received his Ph.D. in organizational psychology from the University of Tennessee.

Scott A. Young is director of organizational assessment and diagnostics at Valtera Corporation (formerly PRA). He consults with the firm's employee survey clients in content development, survey administration, reporting, research, and action planning. He has also consulted with clients in the areas of multirater feedback and employee selection. He has managed Valtera's proprietary survey norms development and research and has conducted other research projects linking clients' employee survey results to business outcomes. He received his Ph.D. in industrial and organizational psychology from Northern Illinois University.

Matthias Zimmermann is founder and managing partner of LOGIT Management Consulting, a company specializing in strategic employee opinion surveys and based in Munich, Germany. He has long-time experience in organizational, evaluation, and survey research and has managed national and international survey projects for major companies in various industries. He has edited several books and published numerous articles. Prior to founding LOGIT, he was director and a member of the management board at HRC Human Resources Consulting, director of research and project management in a market research company, and project manager of human resources at American Express France. He received his Ph.D. in business education from the University of Mannheim, Germany.

Getting Action from Organizational Surveys

CHAPTER 1

Moving the Needle
Getting Action After a Survey
Allen I. Kraut

I have been doing organizational surveys for forty years, and a major concern during all that time has been how to get action after a survey has been completed. In fact, one of my first published articles was titled, "Opinion Surveys: Turning Results into Action" (Kraut, 1966). In this chapter, I push that interest further, reflect on what we have learned over the years, note some major changes in recent years, and consider how we can do better in the future.

Not long ago, while on a vacation safari in Africa, my interest in getting action from organizational surveys drifted into my mind as our guide described the behaviors of various jungle animals. I mused that efforts to produce action after a survey seemed very similar in some ways to what he said about the mating behavior of elephants. If asked, "In what ways?" a sardonic answer might be: "It seems that everything important takes place at a high level, it is accompanied by a great deal of sound and fury, and it takes at least eighteen months before you see any real results."

The frequent lack of action from surveys seems to fuel a streak of cynicism in many organizational cultures. This distrust pops up in an occasional "Dilbert" cartoon strip by Scott Adams, who can be seen as a contemporary commentator and philosopher. In one poignant drawing, the inept manager complains that the company survey says morale is low for the tenth year in a row, and this will have an impact on his bonus. In the next-to-last panel, he promises,

"You can be sure we'll make big changes . . .". In the last panel he adds, ". . . to the survey."

In this chapter, we review some of the major shifts in organizational survey practice in recent years and their implications for action. These include shifts in how we do surveys and their use to aid bottom-line organizational performance. We also examine specific organizational development practices, the relevant mind-sets, and behaviors that produce results. Overall, our aim is to see how we can best move the needle that registers important outcomes—how we can get meaningful action from the organizational survey.

Popularity of Surveys

Surveys of employees seem widespread, if not universal. No one seems to know just how many organizations do surveys, but a recent telephone poll of leading survey firms gives some idea (Kraut Associates, 2003). Their estimates vary but indicate that about three of four larger firms survey their employees—for example:

- Mercer Human Resource Consulting polled twenty-six hundred respondents in the U.S. workforce. Sixty-four percent said their firms did employee opinion surveys.
- In Watson Wyatt's 2002 survey of thirteen thousand employees in the U.S. workforce, 53 percent said their companies had conducted an employee survey in the past three years.
- Mercer Human Resource Consulting surveyed human resource (HR) leaders at three hundred U.S.-based organizations. Employee attitudes measures were used by more than three-quarters (78 percent).
- Watson Wyatt's 2001 Human Capital Index Survey of HR practices in five hundred publicly traded companies showed that 79 percent surveyed employees regularly.

Note that HR executives report a higher frequency of survey use than do samples of the national workforce. This suggests that survey use is higher among Fortune 1000 companies, as these larger firms are the most likely to be polled by consulting firms. It should be noted that these estimates of survey popularity tell us little about the frequency, regularity, or survival of surveys, or their quality or impact afterward.

Utility of Surveys

One way to assess the utility of surveys is to ask practitioners how they view the value and failings of the survey process. Although these professionals are hardly neutral, they are well informed and thus can offer useful insights. An opportunity to get practitioner views came a few years ago during a workshop with thirty survey researchers who worked for fifteen large high-technology firms. They were asked, "What do you see as the greatest *values* of doing organizational surveys?" Ninety-three comments were received and content analyzed. As shown in Table 1.1, the major themes describe various ways that surveys can "Improve Organizational Functioning," cited by 57 percent, and "Improve Communications," cited by 43 percent.

Table 1.1. Practitioner Views on Organizational Surveys

Greatest values of organizational surveys[a]

Improve organizational functioning	57%
Direct action toward improvement	21%
Facilitate assessment of current organizational programs/initiatives	12%
Aid in the development of strategy	11%
Help to identify organizational problems	9%
Efficient, systematic method to obtain large amounts of data	5%
Improve communication	43%
Facilitate information flow up: subordinates to managers	22%
Facilitate communication (general)	11%
Communicate values/concerns of management down to subordinates	10%

Greatest failings of organizational surveys[b]

No action taken on surveys' findings	42%
Questionable relevance—Surveys don't tap critical issues/concerns	19%
Survey process is too difficult	15%

(Continued)

Table 1.1. Practitioner Views on Organizational Surveys, Cont'd

Managerial disinterest/lack of concern about survey and findings	13%
Superficiality—Inability of survey to capture complexities	8%
Negative attitude among employees toward survey	3%

[a]A summary of ninety-three comments on the question, "What are the greatest values of organizational surveys?"

[b]A summary of eighty-nine comments on the question, "What are the greatest failings of organizational surveys?"

Source: Thirty survey researchers from fifteen high-technology firms.

The survey practitioners were also asked, "What are the greatest *failings* of organizational surveys?" Their eighty-nine comments were also content analyzed, and the resulting themes are shown in Table 1.1. Leading the list is "No action taken on survey findings," cited in 42 percent of the comments. Another 13 percent mention management's disinterest in or lack of concern about the survey findings. If there is any doubt that a lack of action is the Achilles heel of the survey process, this extraordinary indictment by survey practitioners themselves should convince us.

Major Changes in Survey Practice

Over the past decade or two, several major changes have taken place in the practice of doing and thinking about surveys in organizations (Kraut & Saari, 1999). These continuing changes have been caused by several forces, including computer technology, globalization, increased competition, and management understanding about the impact of employee behaviors on organizational performance. As we shall see, some of these changes overlap and intersect in fascinating ways. The observations made here are based primarily on my experiences in the field, interactions with other survey practitioners, published reports, and occasional benchmark studies. All the changes I describe have significantly enhanced the possibilities for, and desirability of, action to follow surveys. We now turn our attention to these changes in the purpose of surveys, conceptual models, Web technologies, and a deeper understanding of action planning used with organizational surveys. But first we examine changes in what management wants to know from surveys.

Focus of Surveys

Higgs and Ashworth (1996) were among the first to point out how the focus of surveys has changed, from individual workers in the 1930s to teams and business units in the 1990s. As they predicted, since the 1990s we have seen a further evolution as surveys look at broad organizational functioning and even how customers feel and think about the organization. As focus changed, so did the content of surveys. They have moved from preoccupation with morale and worker satisfaction to using respondents to report what they understand are the organization's goals and functioning, as well as to describe their own behavior and intentions.

The underlying role of surveys has shifted to reflect changes in survey practitioner and management concerns and perspectives; from concerns about morale and attitudes that might predict unionization to later concerns with turnover, absenteeism, stress, and implied links of satisfaction to productivity. More recently, we see greater interest in employees' views of their companies' strategies, such as those stressing customer satisfaction and product and service quality. In addition, there is greater emphasis on awareness of company mission and readiness for change. Finally, there is a growing trend for these perceptions to be linked, in one fashion or another, to bottom-line performance.

Performance, Not Just Satisfaction

Over time, environmental forces facing companies (Kraut & Korman, 1999) have fostered many changes. Shifting demographics and legislative changes have focused concerns about satisfaction onto issues like work/family life and equal opportunity. The drastically reduced rate (and fear) of unionization puts less of a premium on management concern with employee morale. Globalization and the increased competitive environment most firms face put an emphasis on organizational performance generally and on product quality and customer satisfaction specifically.

The emphasis on performance and not just satisfaction is obvious in the content of the questions themselves. Surveys are much less likely to ask about satisfaction with the cafeteria and parking lot, items that were staples of the past. Current surveys are even likely to omit items that ask about satisfaction with salary and benefits and instead add items about customer service. Companies reason that external compensation surveys can give them the objective data about their standing on pay and benefits, but employee surveys about customer service yield unique data from people who are close to the customer every day.

Subtler and more interesting to me are some of the changes in the way questions are asked in current surveys as compared to the past. Consider two questions asked by the Mayflower Group companies, a consortium of forty-one blue-chip companies that all use a core set of survey items (www.mayflowergroup.org). Both items ask employees about their training:

- 1970s item: "How satisfied are you with the training you received for your present job?" (Very Satisfied to Very Dissatisfied).
- 1990s item: "I have received the training I need to do a quality job" (Strongly Agree to Strongly Disagree).

The second question has substituted for the first by most of these companies. Consider the implications of this change. The concept of satisfaction has disappeared. The issue of training is reframed in terms of its impact on performance. So too a different message is being sent to people reading the questionnaire—one emphasizing performance rather than satisfaction.

There are also implications for the managers getting their unit's results to such items. In the first case, managers may throw up their hands and wonder what they should do to increase "satisfaction." In the second case, it is much harder to ignore employees who say they do not have the training they need to do a good job. Such replies compel the manager to find out what kind of training is needed to perform well. I believe we are seeing more of an effort to ask actionable questions. Practitioners are trying harder than ever before to reduce the chance for managers to be puzzled, or to evade action, due to poorly worded questions.

More Normative Data

The "granddaddy" of all survey consortiums, the Mayflower Group, continues to be alive and well. It remains at forty-one firms today, about the same as a decade ago (R. Johnson, 1996). However, it has undergone dynamic change in membership. About fifteen firms are no longer members, including those whose fortunes have declined, such as Honeywell and Unisys, and those that have continued to prosper, such as GE and J&J. An equal number have been added to the membership, including large retailers such as Home Depot and Target and high-tech firms like Sun Micro-systems and Siemens. (Mergers and name changes also affect the lists.)

The group's Web site says, "Normative data is available for the exclusive use of member companies on topics including general satisfaction, quality, training, and involvement, with new items on diversity and empowerment." It also notes that the group "provides a forum for the sharing of innovative best practices or bench-marking studies among member companies."

Other consortiums have been created to get the advantages of sharing best survey practices and comparative data norms. These include the Information Technology Survey Group (www.itsg.org), made up of eighteen firms in the high-tech arena, including five that are also members of the Mayflower group. Another group, founded in about the year 2000, is made up of a dozen firms in the financial services industry and calls itself the MIDAS Group. It has the same purposes of sharing data norms and best practices. These groups reportedly have been less strict than the Mayflower Group in insisting on identically worded survey items for comparison.

The desire for normative data has also led several large survey vendors to develop their own proprietary survey data norms, which they offer to clients. Some data norms are based on the re-sults of their clients, usually but not necessarily a broad set of com-panies. Others have tried to develop norms from national samples of employees and screened out respondents from small firms or nonrepresentative groups.

Top executives often desire a comparison of their results to norm data from other firms, although this is arguably a distraction from one's own results. Over time, most firms that actively pursue improvement seem to be guided more by comparison to their own historic results than to outside norm data.

Use of Models: A Conceptual Shift

An extraordinary shift over the past decade is the greater use of models linking employee attitudes and perceptions to an organization's bottom-line results. Of course, survey practitioners have had access to various models for some time. These include Nadler's organizational congruence model, based on open systems theory, which presents an organization as transforming various inputs to outputs (Nadler, 1977). Other models, such as the Burke-Litwin model (Burke & Litwin, 1992), have also been available.

A qualitative difference in models can be seen with the introduction of the Service–Profit-Chain model by Heskett and associates in an influential *Harvard Business Review* article (1994), which was later expanded to a book (Heskett, Sasser, & Schlesinger, 1997). In their view, a case can be made for understanding an organization's success, in profit, market share, and growth, as the outcome of customer behaviors such as purchases, repeat buying, and recommendations. These behaviors in turn are the product of the customers' interactions with a firm's employees.

Finally, the influence of employees on customers is based on a set of factors easily measurable by organizational surveys: employee skills, training, available resources, supervision, recognition and reward systems, and attitudes toward customers. These factors are all links in a chain going from employee beliefs and experiences to their interaction with customers, and then through customers' resultant behaviors to the firm's bottom line.

The importance of this model was furthered by a Sears Roebuck study published in the *Harvard Business Review* a few years later by Rucci and associates (Rucci, Kirn, & Quinn, 1998). Their research showed that improvements in employee attitudes of 5 points improved same-store customer attitudes by 1.3 points in the following quarter. Store revenues grew by 0.5 point in the quarter after that, leading to millions of dollars in profits. This study underlined the importance of measuring outcomes over time if we really want to think about cause and effect. It is not sufficient simply to correlate employee perceptions and unit performance at the same point in time. The direction of causation and consideration of the time between measures is critical to good research and proper understanding.

This way of thinking was furthered by the work described in Schneider and White (2004) on service quality and the linking research model of Wiley and Brooks (2000). In his writing, Wiley (1996) points out advantages of such models to the survey researcher, explaining that they make it easier to explain to managers the rationale for measuring employee views. The model also serves the researcher as a checklist of what concepts to measure. Survey items that do not measure a concept in the model must be challenged, or the model must be amended.

At the same time, measures of employee perceptions have joined the pantheon of other key issues, like customer satisfaction and financial results, on management's measurement "dashboards." These simultaneous postings have been furthered by the concept of a balanced scorecard, as popularized by Kaplan and Norton (1992), urging management to look at an organization's long-term effectiveness by going beyond financial measures.

Customized Models

Naturally, our understanding of organizational performance can be aided by systematic exploration and testing of the models that are proposed. Many of the authors noted above have already been doing that. Inspired by such models in the literature, some companies have been working with variants of their own making.

In my own experience, even "homemade" models can be remarkably useful in dealing with a firm's management. While they may not be systematically tested and scientifically validated, such a model can convey a way of thinking about what gets measured and why. As an example, Figure 1.1 shows a model created using concepts that were emerging from the literature a few years ago. It was used in a five-thousand-employee firm that sells information services.

The model proposes that a firm's performance, or results, such as market share, revenue growth, and success in new ventures, depends largely on client behavior, more specifically, clients'

Figure 1.1. The Survey Model

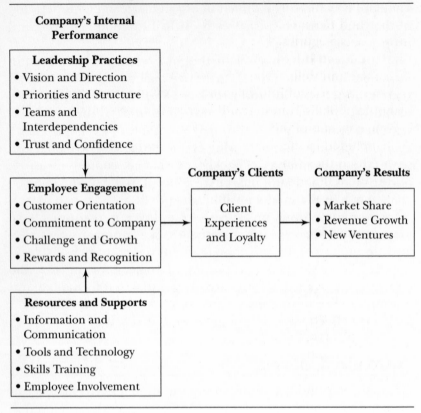

experiences and loyalty. Client behavior is greatly influenced by capable and enthusiastic employees. In this model, the umbrella term *employee engagement* was used to capture the underlying concepts of customer orientation, commitment to the company, feelings of challenge and growth, and a sense of rewards and recognition. (*Engagement* is a term that has been used, more or less similarly, by different writers, and seems quite popular now. As an example, one of the more fashionable works on the topic [Loehr & Schwartz, 2003] uses 108 words trying to define the concept. They convey the idea of an energetic, enthusiastic, focused employee, enjoying and dedicated to doing a good job. This reminds one greatly of what in the past would have been called a highly motivated employee.)

In our homemade model, the employee level of engagement is largely influenced by two major sets of forces, labeled *Leadership Practices* and *Resources and Supports*. Leadership Practices include the four subcategories of Vision and Direction, Priorities and Structure, Teams and Interdependencies, and Trust and Confidence. In the second umbrella term, Resources and Support, we cover the four subcategories of Information and Communication, Tools and Technology, Skills Training, and Employee Involvement.

The concepts of the model formed the basis for selecting items to be included in the survey and were a useful way of explaining why we used those survey items. Although not the basis for a scientific test, it did serve as a guide for testing relationships and was a useful practical tool for explaining results to managers. (The use of factor analysis with the collected survey data, to see how all the items actually hung together, led to some slight restructuring of the survey model.)

Technological Shift: Web Surveys

Over the past decade, we have seen an astonishing change in the number of surveys done using the Web. The great availability of personal computers makes it far easier to collect survey data by using the Internet or an organization's intranet. A review of several studies comparing Web-based studies to paper-and-pencil surveys shows virtually no difference in the response patterns to the two forms of surveys (Kraut, 2001). Respondents are just as favorable or unfavorable, make just about the same number of omissions, and researchers find measurement equivalence. The only difference is that Web surveys get at least 50 percent longer write-in comments. To the Web's credit, these comments are already in a computer-readable form and are much easier to process using text-handling programs.

Speed and Flexibility

One of the most obvious effects of Web-based surveys is the incredible speed with which data are processed and results are made available. Avoiding the need for printing and mailing survey forms and physically processing questionnaires has cut down on much effort and time. Only a decade ago, taking two or three weeks to process a survey and report the results would be considered fast. Now that time has shrunk to a period of just a few days or even hours.

While a survey researcher may see that as a fearsome expectation by a client, it is great for stimulating action. The data are clearly fresh, and there will have been little change in people or organizational structure. The shorter the time is for processing and reporting, the more the survey data will be seen as relevant and applicable.

Web-based surveys can also be more flexible. Questions can be changed, dropped, or added at the last minute. More important for the purpose of getting data on which to base action, branching can be used. Thus, if a question is answered unfavorably, the survey can branch to items that explore reasons for the negative response. Similarly, different and unique question sets can be introduced for people in selected functions or units. Questions tailored to the needs of different groups allow local rather than general topics to be measured. Such data will more likely be seen as relevant and spark action.

Reporting and Action Plan Management

In addition to collecting the data, Web-based survey systems are used to report data to relevant managers. Designated managers can get their data reports online, often in a choice of formats. Sometimes the managers can choose which comparison data they want, such as a prior year's results or data of higher-level units. The electronic data can be used for printed reports or presentations or converted into PowerPoint slides.

The development of action plans and the management of their execution are also being done online. Online systems are providing uniform formats for creating action plans and automatically reporting them to higher-level management and to HR staff. These plans include dates for completion and facilitate monitoring and follow-up. Such online action planning systems have tremendous potential for putting all managers "on the same page," helping to share good practices across an organization and making it easy for top management to follow action-taking steps.

More Frequent, Less Professional Surveys

Despite the advantages of Web-based surveys, we must recognize they have several dark sides. Ironically, one of these is the apparent ease of asking questions and collecting data. Web-based surveys look easy to do, but are often much more complex than they appear. Talking to survey vendors who offer Web-based surveys can reveal the complexities of the underlying processes. (See Chapter Eight, this volume, for more detail on that issue.) In addition, many do-it-yourself Web programs are available. With intriguing names like SurveyMonkey and Zoomerang, they make Web-based surveys seem easy. As a result, tales abound of poorly qualified people writing bad questionnaires and freely conducting surveys of dubious quality.

The apparent ease of administering surveys has also led to more frequent surveys. Many of these, sometimes called *pulse surveys,* are sample surveys. They can be done quarterly or as often as monthly. Often they are focused on a special topic or two.

Whether pulse surveys lead to action more than do general surveys is an open question. One suspects that when management gets and receives data back quickly on a topic of current interest, they are indeed more likely to act on the information. But when results on a general set of topics come in at frequent intervals, it may simply lull management into a "that's-nice-to-know" mind frame. Moreover, too frequent surveys may leave managers little time to act between administrations and leave survey staff racing from survey to survey. One already recognized cost of pulse or sample surveys is a reduction in response rates (Youseffnia & Berwald, 2004). It is not clear if this is due to reductions of the publicity and hoopla done for most census surveys or due to the lowered expectations that action will take place with pulse surveys, or to both.

Precoding

The so-called precoding done with Web surveys is both a great boon and a potentially great risk. The term *precoding* refers to using a respondent's electronic link (or URL, or pass code) to identify that person and tie his or her survey responses to company databases containing information on age, gender, promotability ratings, and performance appraisals, for example. Precoding does away with the need for asking demographic items and generally increases the accuracy of such data. It also allows wonderful opportunities for doing meaningful research, such as tying individual attitudes to later turnover.

Yet there appears to be a real danger of invading employees' presumed rights of privacy. In fact, precoding is prohibited in most of Europe because of privacy laws. Many employees would be shocked to find out that their responses will be connected to data in their personnel files. Where precoding is done, it is explained only in general terms. Employees are usually told that they are being identified and this is done for "research" purposes, but that they will remain completely anonymous, with the data being safe-guarded outside the company by a vendor. So far, I am unaware of this practice leading to any real problems; however, the ethical issues of precoding have yet to be fully explored.

From a practical stance, we might wonder if knowing one is being identified will have bearing on a person's responses. Ample data exist to show that more personal survey methods, such as face-to-face and telephone interviews, lead to more socially desirable responses on sensitive topics (Groves & Associates, 2004). It is reasonable to expect that employee awareness of precoding leads to more socially desirable responses on a close-to-home topic like "rate your manager" than it might on a general topic like "rate your overall satisfaction." Definitive research on this issue remains to be done.

Sophisticated Statistical Methods

Advances in computing have also encouraged some powerful new statistical advances. Many of these are far too technical to deal with here, other than to note their potential. Structural equation modeling and item response theory are among the techniques that are used to try to exploit survey data. They are rather complex and not to be used lightly or without a deep understanding. Moreover, management does not easily comprehend them. Another method, relative weight analysis, is an appealing and helpful method in looking at the drivers of key criteria. (See Chapter Fourteen, this volume, for more on this topic.)

Process That Gets Action

Most survey researchers are familiar with and have had training with many of the practices discussed so far. Survey technology, data processing, and statistical analysis are part of that kit of tools. These are necessary but not sufficient, in my judgment, to produce meaningful action from organizational surveys. Another set of tools is required. In a general sense, these can be described as organizational development tools. These are the concepts and practices by which we understand and are able to move an organization to make the most of its survey processes and results.

Doing a survey well is more complex than it seems. It can be compared to a well-played tennis game, where the winner has to be good at serving, forehand and backhand strokes, and offensive and defensive strategies. Winners have to do many things well to win, but failure may come from doing any one thing badly. The same may be said about surveys, successful and not. Surveys that succeed in their goals are all similar in that they do many things well. Unsuccessful surveys may fail for any one of dozens of reasons. But what are the right things done in the surveys that succeed? My answer comes more from long-time experience and countless discussions with other practitioners than from scientific studies. From these observations and conversations, a few practices stand out.

Begin with the End in Mind

This point is often associated with Covey (1989), who urges us, if we are to be successful, to "start with a clear understanding of your destination" (p. 98). Survey practitioners and management must foresee the end state of the survey. After the survey items are asked, the data collected and analyzed, and the results reported, then what? At that point, what will various people and groups in the organization do differently or better? What is the desired intent of the survey? How will we judge its success? Only when we have the end in mind can we start to guide the survey to achieving that purpose.

A key part of any survey's success is linking it to the organization's purpose. It is best if there is a clear and compelling need to do a survey. Both management and survey professionals must be clear on how the survey can help the business. Sometimes the catalyst is a current issue, such as key losses in staff, or the failure in a client project, or a poor product rollout. At other times, the need is created by organizational changes and restructuring, or by a merger or acquisition. Keeping the survey's purpose in mind helps one greatly to make the right decisions at several points during the survey process.

Purpose: Assessment *and* Change?

Surveys can serve many purposes, ranging from assessment to driving organizational change (Kraut, 1996). Knowing what one is trying to accomplish can make a huge difference in what and how surveys are done. An important basis for getting action after a survey is to be clear from the start on why it is being done. While some surveys try to accomplish several purposes, most tend to have only one or a few. The following typology is one way to think about survey goals:

- *To pinpoint areas of concern.* This is similar to an annual health checkup—a broad attempt to find out how things are going.
- *To observe long-term trends.* This is a follow-up to see if any changes have occurred since the previous survey. This can evolve into a way of life to continually seek organizational improvement.
- *To monitor program impact.* Here there is an attempt to see if attitudes changed in response to organizational changes, for example, in compensation, staffing workload, or training.
- *To gain input to future decisions.* Surveys can be used to make decisions by getting employee preferences on topics like training programs, flextime schedules, computer help systems, and other aspects of organizational life.
- *To add a communication channel.* We see surveys being used, especially in big firms, as a broad, disciplined, and periodic tool to aid in upward communications from employees. The types of questions asked in a survey also send a powerful message downward about management's concerns.

- *To conduct organizational behavior research.* Surveys aid our understanding of factors that have an impact on issues like employee turnover, commitment to good customer service, and achievement of service quality.
- *To drive and measure organizational change.* Surveys provide useful measures of success that can guide changes, such as work/family or quality initiatives, customer satisfaction emphasis, and mergers and acquisitions. Merely asking about certain concepts heightens their visibility and importance. The resulting survey data can assess progress and provide further leverage.

What Decisions Will Be Made?

One should always ask why the survey data are needed. Specifically, what decisions will be made based on the data obtained? Being aware of the potential issues makes it more likely that the right data will be collected. Of course, one should also ask if the survey is the only way, or even the best way, to collect such data. A related issue is to ask if the decision that might be made has been faced before, and if nothing happened before, what will be different now.

As part of the survey process, the practitioner has to build a readiness for management to make critical decisions. Selecting or creating compelling measures can do this. I have found that certain kinds of questions get much more attention than others. Some eye-openers include items like, "I [don't] have confidence in our top management to lead us," and, "If I have my way, I'll leave this company during the next year."

When the responses to key items are reported, appropriate benchmarks can be influential guides. Outside norm data are sometimes helpful, as in showing that items on pay and opportunity are almost always rated lower than feelings about one's job or manager. But previous internal data are often more powerful, as are comparisons among units or various employee sets, to show if a group is really high or low. Even rule-of-thumb guidelines are helpful, as when one points out that a result of less than 40 percent favorable on any item is usually disastrous.

Of course, it is helpful to check in advance, even before survey results are reported, what management believes or already knows. Asking executives at the start of a presentation to guess the identity of the high- and low-rated units on a chart is sometimes used to demonstrate to them what new information is coming out of the survey.

Ties to Organizational Goals

It should be clear that the survey purpose must be tied to organizational outcomes, either short term or long term. The survey content and process must be aligned with the organization's strategy and goals. The survey should also support the interests of its stakeholders, whether employees, customers, or stockholders. When a firm is undergoing or facing change, the survey should be tied to some vision of the future.

For example, a chemical company had recently developed a new statement of its vision and values. Soon after, it fielded a new survey asking questions only about its seven newly enunciated values, thereby putting those values into practical, operational terms and also measuring how well employees felt these seven values were being carried out. The values covered included topics like customer satisfaction, safety, and community citizenship, and the data provided useful feedback to management on how its new initiatives were going.

In order for management to take meaningful action, data must be seen as practical and useful. Therefore, the questions asked must be seen as actionable, not abstract. The item wording must be clear, not confusing. The respondents have to represent a large share of the employees who are invited to take part. The analysis and presentation must be crisp and cogent. Obviously a lot of things have to be done well.

One of these is to make sure that issues of interest to management are part of the survey content. The easiest way to accomplish this is simply to ask top management what they want to get out of the survey. What do they want to learn? What data will help them run the business better? If they cannot say, the survey practitioner can offer a menu of choices. Having such conversations with management is guaranteed to develop their interest in the outcomes and shape the survey content in useful directions. When such conversations do not happen or cannot be arranged, the survey practitioner should recognize the situation as raising a red danger flag.

Plan for the Entire Process

Many people see an organizational survey as an event, taking place at a certain point. It is more accurate and useful to see the survey as a longer-term process, from the early planning to follow-up action. When viewing it as a process, not an event, we recognize several critical steps that the survey practitioner must take to ensure that action will follow.

It may go without saying that action is unlikely to take place without a supportive top management. But even a willing executive team may need instruction and support to make things happen. One of the survey professional's main activities is to educate executives on their role in the survey process. Executives must be prepared to frame the survey as a positive act, not taken out of undue concern but rather as a sign of strength and intent to improve. It has to be portrayed as an earnest step in getting and using feedback. The executive's staffs have to understand that view and communicate it themselves.

The executive must also be prepared to talk up the survey and encourage his or her staff and organization to participate and actively use the data. Survey professionals have to share with top executives the survey timetable. Executives should be asked to sign and send relevant letters, use videotapes to encourage the survey at remote locations, and generally show their support and ownership of the survey. The effective practitioner will need to ghostwrite letters for management, provide them with updates on survey activities (such as informing them of pretests and survey launch schedules), keep executives informed on survey participation rates, and ask for time to be set aside for reviews of survey results and action planning.

When the data are being reported, practitioners may also have to help executives work through their emotional reactions to the data. Being able to do some hand-holding to help management accept and deal with the data is an important part of getting action after a survey (Nadler, 1996).

Develop a Commitment to Act

Many of the things suggested so far will build a commitment to act once the data are collected. Good practice always includes tapping issues of importance to the organization and its management. In some cases, forming a steering committee or advisory group will cement such commitment (Kraut, 1992). Members of such groups can represent different organizational units and interests, act as a liaison to different constituencies, anticipate reactions from different parts of the organization, and act as emissaries on behalf of the survey. Steering groups are especially helpful when a survey is being done for the first time, or in a complex organization, or to promote a particular firmwide initiative such as work/family life.

Several other reward activities also seem to work:

- Using incentives to act on the findings plays a powerful role. Recognition for getting good results or making improvements over prior years' results is an effective method. Even a simple "atta-boy" or "atta-girl" letter is useful reinforcement.
- Some firms give high-performing leaders recognition through a chance to talk about their actions in "internal best practices" sharing sessions.
- Financial incentives seem to be used by more and more firms to encourage improvement. To avoid crude gaming of the system by explicit scores, many firms use the results in a softer, indirect way regarding an executive's performance appraisal.

Have a Credible Survey

Simple as it sounds, the survey must seem credible to everyone in the organization. That means that the questions must be seen as clear, actionable, and organized into topic categories. These topics must be relevant to the business purpose. Communications leading up to the survey must paint the survey as an appealing opportunity for participants. An attractive image of the survey is needed to get high participation. The higher the response rates are, the more credible will be the results. Of course, the survey must be convenient and easy to complete, and the timing should not conflict with peak business periods.

The results and reports need to be processed quickly so data are seen as current. Presentations to management should be tied back to the reasons for the survey. The use of models during data feedback often reminds management of why the data are relevant to the firm's success. The analysis and presentation of results to management can be held up as a mirror, to show how key groups in the firm view their bosses. All of these considerations are needed to engage executive audiences and compel them to take meaningful action.

More Conversation, Better Diagnosis

A noticeable trend over the past two decades has been the use of shorter surveys. It is common to see many surveys of only fifty to seventy-five items in length, as opposed to far longer ones in years gone by. (Surveys are also done more frequently and often cover only selected issues.) In many ways, this is a welcome trend and reflects the concern to focus on performance-related issues rather than indulging in large fishing expeditions.

However, survey practitioners often run into managers who complain that the survey findings do not tell them enough, and they want to see more analysis or they lament that more questions were not asked. This complaint sometimes reflects a wrong-headed view of the survey as a device that will tell management all they need to know without having to talk to the people whose thoughts are being surveyed. In fact, perhaps the best view of a survey is that it should be used mainly as a platform for a meaningful dialogue between managers and other staff members. The most valid and valuable philosophy a manager can have about the organizational survey is to see it as a basis on which to have conversations about organizational performance. If managers do not already have such conversations, an organizational survey can jump-start a new and more productive way to interact on an ongoing basis.

SMART Action Plans

Action planning is sometimes rightly faulted for being poor, even when actions appear to be planned. For example, managers with evident problems of communication within their units sometimes create a simple action plan that says, "Improve communications." This reminds us of ineffective, if well-meaning, New Year's Eve resolutions. Fortunately, there are far better methods available to use. Perhaps the best is the so-called SMART approach to action planning (Locke & Latham, 1990). This is an acronym that stands for:

Specific—are identifiable, behavioral, and observable goals

Measurable—have outcome criteria and can be assessed objectively

Aligned—are congruent with the purpose and vision of the organization

Reachable—are realistic and can be attained

Time-Bound—have a clear timetable and deadline for achievement.

Using a SMART approach, our manager might formulate an action plan that meets all the criteria, by saying, "We will improve communications by having a weekly one-hour meeting of all department staff in the conference room on Monday morning, starting next month. The meetings will be run by me, on current topics, with time for questions and answers."

Good action plans assign accountability. The ownership for acting on different items will depend on the topic. For items under the local manager's control, such as his or her direct interaction with subordinates, the manager is obviously responsible. For topics like a firm's benefit plans, accountability may go up to a corporate level. Issues that require cooperation among groups might go to a higher-level manager or to a task force created to work out the various groups' interactions. Effective survey practitioners will push to have these accountabilities as clear-cut as possible. They will also play a supportive role in data interpretation, feedback of data, and facilitation of problem solving. They will prepare materials to guide managers in interpreting survey data and conducting meetings for feedback and action planning.

Survey professionals will best serve management if they urge them to limit the number of issues to take action on. Many firms find it best to have managers work on just one or two high-priority issues. This is much better than spreading oneself too thin and being overwhelmed by too many initiatives. I have always believed that managers benefit from a spillover effect—that is, an improvement in one area often spills over into improvements in other areas. Involving employees in planning and taking action can be a stylistic change that pays dividends later.

Emphasis on Action, Not Just Feedback

Over the past decade, there has been a decided shift to focusing on action after a survey, not simply providing feedback of survey results. Church and Oliver (2002) were among the first to point out how these two facets of the survey process, feedback and action, have different impacts on employee views of management responsiveness and employee satisfaction. In a nutshell, action is much more important than feedback. It also has a more positive impact on hard criteria, such as employee turnover, accidents, and missed workdays. (See Chapter Five for more details.)

In previous years, much attention was given to feedback techniques. Hinrichs (1996) provides a useful account of the early efforts of scholars at the University of Michigan to highlight survey feedback as critical. Beginning with Mann (1957), feedback was assumed to be a necessary, and presumably inevitable, precursor to action. Nadler (1977) took a similar stance, but distinguished the cascading "waterfall" model of data feedback, in which top management saw firmwide data first and became a role model for feedback meetings at lower levels, from the "bubble-up" methods, where lower-level units saw their data first and reported up on the actions they would take.

In one early study published in a serious journal, the focus was whether feedback was better when done by HR professionals or different levels of management, and if done in small or large groups (Klein, Kraut, & Wolfson, 1971). I read that piece now in wonder, realizing that "better" meant that employees liked it more or thought that action would be taken, without ever measuring if any action had actually been taken. The early emphasis on feedback methods has distracted many survey practitioners from the harder end result of actually getting action.

The importance of action, compared to feedback, can be seen in Table 1.2, drawn from my own research. In a large division of one company, employees were asked whether they "believe management will act on problems identified by this survey." The results were shown for four groups, sorted by whether they had gotten feedback or seen action taken in the previous year's survey. The proportion who thought management would now take action was highest (81 percent favorable) for those respondents who had gotten feedback *and* seen action from the previous survey. It was lower, as might be expected, for those who did not get feedback or see action (40 percent favorable). But the belief that management would act was the lowest of all for employees who said they had gotten feedback but did *not* see action taken (27 percent favorable)! (Similar relationships were found between the previous year's feedback and action and the next year's overall satisfaction levels.)

Table 1.2. Employees' Beliefs on Whether Management Will Act on Survey Results

		Saw Action Taken in Last Survey?	
		Yes	No
Got Feedback from Last Survey?	Yes	81% (N = 666)	27% (N = 246)
	No	48% (N = 27)	40% (N = 205)

Note: Percentage agreeing: "I believe management in my organization will act on problems identified by this survey."

Inevitably, surveys raise employees' expectations that responsible action will be taken. Viteles (1953) wisely quoted a company executive as saying, "An attitude survey is like a hand grenade— once you pull the pin you have to do something with it. Otherwise it may hurt you rather than help you" (p. 394). Of course, management may take actions and fail to credit the survey as stimulus. Actions taken must be effectively communicated to employees, or disappointment will result.

A Caution: Methodology Matters

While much of the discussion has dealt with organization development concepts, survey methodology itself matters in doing meaningful surveys. There are signs that more and more people coming into organizational survey work are not professionally trained in such methods. For example, Johnson and Paul (2005) report that the share of Mayflower Group members with master's or doctoral degrees in industrial/organizational psychology declined from 77 percent in 1992 to 52 percent in 2005. This may increase the risk that errors will be made due to lack of sophistication about surveys, and some of this is already apparent. A few examples will give an appropriate caution.

Without a doubt, question wording is important, and even highly similarly worded items can get vastly different responses. Sudman and Bradburn (1982, p. 137) report an interesting example of seemingly contrary wording giving surprising results. Matched samples were asked to agree or disagree with the following questions:

- "Do you think the United States should allow public speeches against democracy?" Twenty-one percent said yes.
- "Do you think the United States should forbid public speeches against democracy?" Thirty-nine percent said no.

When a firm tries to compare its findings to data from other organizations that ask almost the same question, it does so at its own risk, and with little clue as to whether to expect more or less favorable results.

Even the position of an item in a questionnaire can introduce order effects. Such effects can make comparisons of responses to the identical items over time somewhat chancy. Unexpected effects can come about from the content of intervening items affecting a respondent's answers to a later item. Or the effects can come from survey fatigue in a long questionnaire. One study of two equivalent groups found a question late in the survey could be five or more percentage points less favorable than the same item given early in the survey (Kraut, Wolfson, & Rothenberg, 1975). Making trend comparisons of items in varying placements across surveys can be hazardous, with mere artifact being the real cause of differences.

The increased use of sampling raises the importance of weighting respondents correctly. If different sampling fractions are used for different groups or if participation rates vary markedly, weighting must be used to avoid incorrect data when different subgroups are combined. (Many conversations lead me to believe weighting is often neglected.) An example from an actual case is shown in Figure 1.2.

Figure 1.2. Change in Attitudes for Weighted and Unweighted Responses

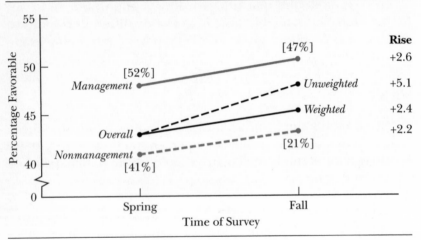

Note: Average of twenty-two items. Percentages in parentheses are response rates.

A client firm had asked me to analyze their data more fully. The staff told me that the overall results across two surveys had improved by 5.1 percentage points. But when I broke down the total into the two major groups (management and nonmanagement), they each had improved only by half that amount, a statistical impossibility. It turned out that a labor relations dispute had cut the nonmanagement response rates in half (from 41 percent to 21 percent). By simply adding all the respondents to tally the total, the now smaller number of less favorable nonmanagers had much less of a pull on the total, and the results showed a false improvement. Other firms that do not properly weight respondents for sampling and participation differences will expose themselves to similar distortions of their true results.

The term *drivers* takes us through another methodological swamp. It is typically used to refer to a cause-and-effect relationship, which would be appropriate. However, if the two variables being related actually occur at the same point in time, it is hard to reason that one causes the other. There we can merely say that the two are correlated. Only if we can believe that one measure occurs before the other, and influences it, can we use the term *driver.* If we can reasonably argue that attitudes toward one's pay or one's manager would predict an employee's intent to quit (and not vice versa), we can then talk about and assess those attitudes as drivers of the intent to quit. (The Sears Roebuck study by Rucci and associates discussed earlier is a good example of how to study drivers.)

Conclusion

Organizational surveys have become more a part of organizational functioning than ever before. In part, this is due to advances in computer technology, which make them easier to do. It is also due to the increased emphasis on performance rather than satisfaction and the recognition that employee perceptions can offer the key to better delivery of products and services and financial success. The increasing use of conceptual models that demonstrate these relationships is encouraged by growing global competition and a growing belief in their usefulness.

Someday we may see most organizations doing surveys on a regular annual basis, just as they now do performance evaluations and budget planning annually. (Special topic surveys will remain an exception.) None of these processes are done because they are fun, but because they are useful tools for enhancing effectiveness. But the frequency of a large organizational survey involves a paradox. Many firms prefer to do them every two years or so because, they say, "surveys are so much work" and it takes time to put actions in place. In fact, regular annual surveys may be relatively less work than biennial surveys, because greater organizational learning takes place. Management becomes more familiar with the ins and outs of the survey, and the lessons learned can be used while they are fresh in mind. The entire organization's survey maturity can be raised considerably, making each succeeding survey less arduous.

It is heartening to see that the pace of survey feedback and action taking has increased along with speedier Web-enabled surveys. The expectations for meaningful action following organizational surveys also seem higher. Survey practitioners should continue to encourage managers and executives to actively use the survey data from their employees and avoid the dangers of inaction. To be effective, survey practitioners must ensure that both they and management begin with the end in mind, are clear about the purposes and processes of the effective survey, and develop both the commitment and procedures that lead to responsive action taking. A clear understanding of the organizational development concepts, tools, and techniques that lead to action, and skill in applying this knowledge and skills, will ensure that surveys continue to be a meaningful device for organizational effectiveness in the future.

Acknowledgments

I am indebted to Angelique Shaydulova and Corinne Donovan for their extremely helpful comments on an earlier draft of this chapter.

References

Burke, W. W., & Litwin, G. H., (1992). A causal model of organizational performance and change. *Journal of Management, 18*(3), 523–545.

Church, A. H., & Oliver, D. H. (2002). *Does survey action planning really make a difference? The impact of taking action on employee attitudes and business outcomes.* Paper presented at the Practitioner Forum at the Annual Conference of the Society for Industrial and Organizational Psychology, Toronto.

Covey, S. (1989). *Seven habits of highly effective people.* New York: Fireside.

Groves, R. M., and Associates. (2004). *Survey methodology.* New York: Wiley.

Heskett, J. L., Jones, T. O., Loveman, G. W., Sasser, W. E., Jr., & Schlesinger, L. A. (1994, Mar.-Apr.). Putting the service profit chain to work. *Harvard Business Review*, 164–174.

Heskett, J. L., Sasser, W. E., & Schlesinger, L. A. (1997). *The service profit chain: How leading companies link profit and growth to loyalty, satisfaction and value.* New York: Free Press.

Higgs, A. C., & Ashworth, S. D. (1996). Organizational surveys: Tools for assessment and research. In A. I. Kraut (Ed.), *Organizational surveys: Tools for assessment and change.* San Francisco: Jossey-Bass.

Hinrichs, J. R. (1996). Feedback, action planning, and follow-through. In A. I. Kraut (Ed.), *Organizational surveys: Tools for assessment and change.* San Francisco: Jossey-Bass.

Johnson, R. (1996). Life in the consortium: The Mayflower Group. In A. I. Kraut (Ed.), *Organizational surveys: Tools for assessment and change.* San Francisco: Jossey-Bass.

Johnson S. R., & Paul, K. B. (2005). The changing role of the survey professional. In SIOP panel session, *Remembrance of Surveys Past: The Evolution of the Employee Survey,* at Annual Conference of the Society for Industrial and Organizational Psychology, Los Angeles, CA.

Kaplan, R. S., & Norton, D. P. (1992, Jan.-Feb.). The balanced scorecard: Measures that drive performance. *Harvard Business Review, 71–79.*

Klein, S. M., Kraut, A. I., & Wolfson, A. (1971). Employee reactions to attitude survey feedback: A study of the impact of structure and process. *Administrative Science Quarterly, 16,* 497–514.

Kraut Associates. (2003, Apr.). *The prevalence of employee opinion surveys among Fortune 1,000 Companies.* Unpublished report. Rye, NY: Kraut Associates.

Kraut, A. I. (1966). Opinion surveys: Turning results into action, *Personnel, 43,* 48–65.

Kraut, A. I. (1992). Organizational research on work and family issues. In S. Zedeck (Ed.), *Work, families and organizations* (pp. 208–235). San Francisco: Jossey-Bass.

Kraut, A. I. (1996). Planning and conducting the survey: Keeping strategic purpose in mind. In A. I. Kraut (Ed.), *Organizational surveys: Tools for assessment and change.* San Francisco: Jossey-Bass.

Kraut, A. I. (2001, Apr.) An e-mail to a friend (on Web versus paper surveys). *TIP (The Industrial-Organizational Psychologist), 38*(4), 37–39.

Kraut, A. I., & Korman, A. K. (1999). The "DELTA Forces" causing change in human resource management. In A. I. Kraut & A. K. Korman (Eds.), *Evolving practices in human resource management: Responses to a changing world of work.* San Francisco: Jossey-Bass.

Kraut, A. I., & Saari, L. M. (1999). Organization surveys: Coming of age for a new era. In A. I. Kraut & A. K. Korman (Eds.), *Evolving practices in human resource management: Responses to a changing world of work.* San Francisco: Jossey-Bass.

Kraut, A. I., Wolfson, A. D., & Rothenberg, A. (1975). Some effects of position on opinion survey items. *Journal of Applied Psychology, 60,* 774–776.

Locke, E. A., & Latham, G. (1990). *A theory of goal setting and task performance.* Upper Saddle River, NJ: Prentice Hall.

Loehr, J., & Schwartz, T. (2003). *The power of full engagement.* New York: Free Press.

Mann, F. (1957). Studying and creating change: A means to understanding social organization. In C. M. Arensberg & Associates (Eds.), *Research in industrial human relations: A critical appraisal* (pp. 146–167). New York: HarperCollins.

Nadler, D. A. (1977). *Feedback and organization development: Using data-based methods.* Reading, MA: Addison-Wesley.

Nadler, D. A. (1996). Setting expectations and reporting results: Conversations with top management. In A. I. Kraut (Ed.), *Organizational surveys: Tools for assessment and change.* San Francisco: Jossey-Bass.

Rucci, A. J., Kirn, S. P., & Quinn, R. T. (1998, Jan.-Feb.). The employer-customer-profit chain and Sears. *Harvard Business Review,* 82–97.

Schneider, B., & White, S. S. (2004). *Service quality: Research perspectives.* Thousand Oaks, CA: Sage.

Sudman, S., & Bradburn, N. M. (1982). *Asking questions: A practical guide to questionnaire design.* San Francisco: Jossey-Bass.

Viteles, M. S. (1953). *Motivation and morale in industry.* New York: Norton.

Wiley, J. W. (1996). Linking survey results to customer satisfaction and business performance. In A. I. Kraut (Ed.), *Organizational surveys: Tools for assessment and change.* San Francisco: Jossey-Bass.

Wiley, J. W., & Brooks, S. M. (2000). The high performance organizational climate: How workers describe top-performing units. In N. M. Ashkenasy, C.P.M. Wilderom, & M. F. Peterson (Eds.), *Organizational culture and climate* (pp. 177–191). Thousand Oaks, CA: Sage.

Youseffnia, D., & Berwald, M. (2004). *An exploratory look at the response rates of sample, census, special topic, and broad-based surveys.* Paper presented at Practitioner Forum at the annual conference of the Society for Industrial and Organizational Psychology, Chicago.

New Concepts

The chapters in this first part deal primarily with new concepts, or ways of thinking about and understanding survey data as they relate to organizational effectiveness. Major advances in several research areas provide new ideas about relating employee attitudes and perceptions to organizational outcomes, particularly to customer satisfaction and business unit financial performance. The importance of taking action to facilitate organizational development is also highlighted, with new results shedding light on the promise and potential of action taking after a survey.

James K. Harter and Frank L. Schmidt lead off in Chapter Two by proving a strong correlation between employee satisfaction and organizational performance when studied at the business unit or work group level. Still, their reanalysis of prior studies shows that the link between satisfaction and performance at the level of the individual employee is stronger than has been believed.

In Chapter Three, William H. Macey and Benjamin Schneider provide a set of concepts to guide survey development to gauge the ability to provide customers with a high-quality service experience. The concept of employee engagement, both attitudinally and behaviorally, is used to help understand what facets of organizational life should be measured to improve service climate.

William A. Schiemann and Brian S. Morgan in Chapter Four use the notion of the strategic survey to link employee perceptions to achieving critical organizational goals. They explain the desirable content of surveys as well as critical stages of the survey process: design, analysis, and implementation. They conclude with a list of best practices that define a strategic survey.

Allan H. Church and David H. Oliver show in Chapter Five the positive impact of taking action after a survey on employee perceptions and on employee turnover, accidents, and time missed from work. Data feedback alone adds little value; only the perception of action has a positive effect. They conclude with some practical tips to design and encourage action taking.

W. Warner Burke, a long-time expert in organization development, reviews in Chapter Eight the major concepts in the field to appreciate the role of surveys in enhancing organizational effectiveness. He reviews specific ways to sell the survey, help the organization prepare for the survey process, and use the feedback to create organizational change.

Jack W. Wiley and Bruce H. Campbell team up in Chapter Seven to illustrate the High Performance Model. They use a long-term case study to show how linkage research provides a conceptual and applicable framework to integrate the views of employees with customer and business performance measures. This is a case of organizational development at its best.

CHAPTER 2

Connecting Employee Satisfaction to Business Unit Performance

James K. Harter
Frank L. Schmidt

Employee satisfaction and its many facets and related constructs have been studied and discussed in over ten thousand articles and publications (in a search of PsychINFO). The concept of the satisfaction-performance relationship has intrigued researchers for decades, beginning with the Hawthorne studies (Roethlisberger & Dickson, 1939) and continuing with numerous reviews and large-scale syntheses of research. In this chapter, we review previous research on the satisfaction-performance relationship and various ways in which performance can be defined at the business unit level (as opposed to the individual level).

Unit-level analyses can provide a different perspective on the relationship between satisfaction and performance. For example, a restaurant chain may encompass six thousand employees and three hundred restaurants spread across various regions. Perhaps management keeps systematic measures of each employee's productivity through supervisory evaluations or other measures. One form of analysis might entail correlating individual employee job satisfaction with individual productivity (a sample size of six thousand). Or each restaurant can be thought of as a business unit and may have measures of employee satisfaction and performance (such as customer ratings, profit, and revenue) for the restaurant as a whole. The relationship between employee satisfaction and performance can also be estimated across the three hundred restaurants (or units). The analyses are conducted by treating business units as observations rather than individuals as observations (the sample size in this case is three hundred). We discuss advantages to the unit-level approach in this chapter. We also review the possible confounding variables that can be encountered in unit-level research and other methodological considerations. Next, we discuss the ways in which unit-level analyses can aid in estimating return on investment and areas in which science and practicality merge. Throughout the chapter, we discuss the unit-level research that is needed to test the theories to provide understanding that scientists and practitioners seek.

Conceptualizing the Satisfaction-Performance Relationship

Beyond academic interest, understanding the satisfaction-performance relationship is vitally important to organizational change initiatives. Employee satisfaction surveys can be used to initiate and assess change. What management is attempting to change should be important (that is, likely to create change on important outcomes) and actionable (that is, capable of being changed by actions of managers). To create change, the satisfaction facets measured (supervisory relations, coworker relations, benefits, and pay, for example) should be meaningful and performance related. Examples of actionable measures are provided later in this chapter.

Improving satisfaction may appeal to our human spirit as moral and altruistic. Being satisfied must be better for employee well-being than being disgruntled. But given that most organizations operate to make a profit, executives and managers want to know not only that satisfaction is altruistically appealing and better for employees, but also that satisfaction is related to other outcomes the organization is attempting to achieve, such as productivity, profitability, customer loyalty, employee retention, and safety.

This satisfaction-performance relationship has most frequently been conceptualized at the individual level. Judge, Thoresen, Bono, and Patton (2001) reviewed seven individual-level models of the satisfaction-performance relationship, which can also be considered relevant at the unit level:

1. Job satisfaction causes performance.
2. Performance causes job satisfaction.
3. Job satisfaction and performance are reciprocally linked.
4. The relationship between job satisfaction and performance is spurious (caused by some third variable that is related to both).
5. The relationship between job satisfaction and performance is moderated by additional variables.
6. There is no relationship between job satisfaction and performance.
7. Job satisfaction leads to performance only if we reconceptualize the variables.

In model 7, the theory postulates that particular facets of satisfaction, such as supervisory or coworker satisfaction, or related constructs, such as positive or negative emotion resulting from satisfaction, cause performance. Similarly, the relationship may hold only if one broadens the definition of performance to include all facets of performance. Organ (1988) suggested that the relationship between satisfaction and performance should be stronger once one broadens the definition of performance to include both task performance and organizational citizenship behaviors, such as volunteering for additional work, helping others with their work, and supporting organizational objectives. Defining performance at the unit level can be viewed as a broadening of the definition of performance. We will return to these theoretical propositions when we discuss causality.

Past Employee Satisfaction-Performance Research

The large majority of empirical studies on the satisfaction-performance relationship have focused on the individual-level relationship. Meta-analysis is a valuable statistical method that synthesizes the results of many different studies. Large-scale meta-analyses have been conducted, summarizing the extent of this relationship and its generalizability (Iaffaldano & Muchinsky, 1985; Judge et al., 2001). From a theoretical perspective, individual-level relationships are important to understand. However, when employee satisfaction is measured and reported organizationally, results are traditionally aggregated for work groups, organizational (business) units, or organizations (companies) as a whole.

The practical purpose of the typical employee survey is to gauge the climate of the organization to produce important and actionable survey results. To gain an accurate and representative picture of the climate, confidentiality is assured (providing another rationale for aggregate results, versus reporting individually).

When data are studied at the unit level, both the independent (satisfaction or its facets) and dependent (performance) variables change considerably. Ostroff (1992) argued that performance is too narrowly defined at the individual level and does not completely represent all of the behaviors and outcomes individuals influence when working with coworkers in their organization. Unit-level studies provide a summed view of the culture (or climate) and many of the ultimate outcomes the units are working to achieve.

For brevity, we use the term *satisfaction* to refer to the broad range of employee attitude measures that have been studied in unit-level analyses (for example, workplace climate, engagement, organizational commitment).

Validation research on employee satisfaction measures, if done appropriately, can create tremendous value to the organization as a whole, and to its individual managers and employees. It can create great efficiency in how workplaces are managed. If done inappropriately, it can create great confusion and inefficiency. The following sections describe factors that may influence where a survey falls on this continuum.

Individual-Level Research

In looking at past research, we will focus on the satisfaction-performance relationship from one particular angle, which is how the research on employee satisfaction-performance to date has influenced the value that researchers and managers have placed on employee satisfaction. This leads us to discuss how unit-level research may facilitate efficiency, utility, and change.

As we have already alluded to, the study of the satisfaction-performance relationship began with the Hawthorne studies (Roethlisberger & Dickson, 1939). After reviewing nine published studies of the satisfaction-performance relationship at the individual level, including studies of some behavioral outcomes such as accidents, absence, and turnover, Brayfield and Crockett (1955) concluded "minimal or no relationship" between satisfaction and performance (p. 405). This review was widely referenced until about 1985. Many additional qualitative reviews had been conducted prior to this time, with mixed conclusions, but all called for more theory-driven research in the area (Herzberg, Mausner, Peterson, & Capwell, 1957; Locke, 1970; Schwab & Cummings, 1970). Petty, McGee, and Cavender (1984) completed a meta-analysis of sixteen published studies on the satisfaction-performance relationship. Shortly after, Iaffaldano and Muchinsky (1985) conducted the first comprehensive quantitative meta-analysis of the satisfaction-performance relationship. They examined 217 correlations across 74 studies and concluded an average satisfaction-performance true score correlation of .17, indicating that satisfaction and performance were "only slightly related to each other" (p. 269). As such, much of the published research prior to the 1990s reinforced the notion that the satisfaction-performance relationship was weak at best.

Inferences made from early job satisfaction studies were problematic from several perspectives. First, many early reviews of research were based on significance tests from individual studies. Due to low statistical power, many results were nonsignificant. Second, there were some methodological problems with early meta-analyses, since corrected in Judge et al. (2001). Early meta-analyses included multiple studies from the same samples, thus violating assumptions of independence. They also used inappropriate forms of reliability estimation to correct the observed correlations for measurement error. When Judge et al. (2001) significantly expanded the meta-analysis (312 independent samples) and corrected the methodological concerns, the mean meta-analytic satisfaction-performance correlation was found to be .30 (76 percent higher than reported earlier by Iaffaldano and Muchinsky). The correlation is substantially higher (.52) in high-complexity versus medium- and low-complexity jobs (.29). These findings clearly rule out Judge et al. (2001) model 6, which postulates a zero relationship between job satisfaction and performance. Still, there is very little research on job satisfaction that has translated the relationship into practical value for managers and practitioners.

Unit-Level Research

Recent studies have estimated the relationship between job satisfaction (or related constructs) and performance at the unit (as opposed to individual) level. For instance, Schneider and his colleagues accumulated research on bank branches (Schneider, Parkington, & Buxton, 1980; Schneider & Bowen, 1992). They surveyed employee perceptions of the service quality of the bank branches and aggregated those responses at the branch level (unit level). They then surveyed customers of the same bank branches and aggregated their responses at the branch level. Next they studied the relationship between employee perceptions of service quality with customers' perceptions of service quality and found a positive correlation. (See Chapter Three, this volume.)

Early unit-level research focused primarily on cross-sectional studies. Studies found relationships between unit-level employee attitudes and performance outcomes, such as safety (Zohar, 1980, 2000), financials (Denison, 1990; Schneider, 1991), employee turnover (Ostroff, 1992), and customer experiences (Schneider et al., 1980; Ulrich, Halbrook, Meder, Stuchlik, & Thorpe, 1991; Schneider & Bowen, 1992; Schneider, Ashworth, Higgs, & Carr, 1996; Schmitt & Allscheid, 1995; Reynierse & Harker, 1992; Johnson, 1996; Wiley, 1991). Recently, Batt (2002) used multivariate analysis to study the relationship between human resource practices and sales growth. Findings from these studies have been mixed but generally are indicative of positive relationships between satisfaction and performance.

A large-scale meta-analysis (Harter, Schmidt, & Hayes, 2002), based on 7,939 business and work units, studied the relationship of employee attitudes (satisfaction and engagement) with safety, customer loyalty, financials, and employee turnover. The true score correlation of satisfaction and composite performance (composite of customer loyalty, financials, and employee retention) was .38 and highly generalizable across organizations. As in the case of the

Judge et al. (2001) individual-level meta-analysis, this unit-level meta-analysis has more firmly established a positive relationship between satisfaction and performance. There are positive concurrent and predictive relationships between satisfaction and various important business outcomes.

The practical effect of these relationships is substantial. For instance, in examples provided in Harter et al. (2002), top- and bottom-quartile business units on employee satisfaction represented an average difference of:

- 29 percent in annualized employee turnover for high-turnover companies (such as retail)
- 10 percent in annualized employee turnover for low-turnover companies
- 2.9 percent in terms of loyal customers
- 35 percent in sales and revenue

We discuss practical utility in more detail later in the chapter.

An updated meta-analysis (containing 13,751 business and work units) has recently been conducted, finding a true score correlation of satisfaction to composite performance (composite of safety, customer loyalty, financials, and employee retention) of .43 (Harter, Schmidt, & Killham, 2003). These findings provide empirical support for Ostroff's theory (1992) that performance defined at the individual level may not account for all of the combined effects of satisfaction, which can also influence the performance of others within the unit. Individual performance has frequently been measured with metrics that rely heavily on individual output, a concept of performance that may be too narrowly defined.

Additional unit-level studies have looked at longitudinal correlations (Ryan, Schmitt, & Johnson, 1996; Schneider, White, & Paul, 1998; Harter, 2000; Koys, 2001; Schneider, Hanges, Smith, & Salvaggio, 2003). Findings from these studies have been mixed, and causal implications have been inconclusive. A recent longitudinal meta-analytical study of 2,178 business units indicates stronger causal links from earlier satisfaction to later business unit outcomes than the reverse (Harter, Schmidt, Asplund, & Killham, 2004). These findings suggest that aggregate employee satisfaction is a cause of business outcomes (model 1 outlined earlier from Judge et al.) and tend to cast doubt on the opposite causal arrow (model 2 in Judge et al.). There is some evidence of reciprocal relationship (model 3 in Judge et al.), but to the extent this exists, the arrow appears to be stronger from satisfaction to performance than the reverse. Theoretically, it is likely this causal direction (supported with outcomes of customer loyalty, employee retention, and financials but still being tested with safety) means employee satisfaction causes employees to develop more productive intentions, which lead to behaviors that cause more positive organizational outcomes.

Researchers are just beginning to answer the question of causal direction, and more expansive theory and research is needed in this area. For instance, it is possible that a third variable (such as quality of management) explains the relationship between satisfaction and performance.

Early research on job satisfaction clearly reinforced interpretations that undervalued the importance of the satisfaction-performance relationship. More recent meta-analyses, including unit-level studies, provide a more concrete understanding of the magnitude and utility of the satisfaction-performance relationship. Given their importance, we turn to the technical aspects of unit-level analyses.

Defining Performance

As a first step in conducting unit-level analysis, it is important for the investigator to understand the nature of the organization under study. Organizations vary considerably across industries and geography. For instance, connecting satisfaction to performance for a health care organization may present a very different set of challenges from doing so for a financial institution or retail organization. Therefore, this first step is to assess the outcomes that are most important to the stakeholders in the organization, which requires a thorough understanding of the structure of the organization and how outcomes are measured and reported within it.

To conduct correlational analyses, satisfaction must be measured and aggregated at a level that aligns with the level in which relevant performance variables are measured. For a health care organization, that may be the department or hospital level, depending on which outcomes are measured. For instance, profitability (for example, earnings before interest, taxes, depreciation, and amortization) may be measured at the hospital level. Medical errors or employee turnover may be measured at a department level. A financial services organization may have two hundred bank branches. Across branches, there may be comparable measures of customer loyalty, employee turnover, sales, and profit. Similarly, retail organizations often have a very straightforward structure in which measures are the same in all stores.

Most outcomes measured within organizations can be classified as measures of efficiency, production, stability, quality, or safety:

Efficiency can include profit margin, costs, manufacturing efficiency, economic value added, sales per square foot, production per person, and return on investment.

Production (output) measures can include indexes of amount produced, such as number of units produced, sales, and revenue.

Stability measures can include employee retention rates, average length of service per person, part-time and full-time turnover, absenteeism rates, and theft.

Quality measures can include customer satisfaction, customer loyalty, customer return rates, patient loyalty, and number of defects. In addition to customer and patient satisfaction measures, there are also other ratings that can be used to assess the performance of units, such as supervisory ratings (completed by the supervisor of the unit manager).

Safety measures can include the number of safety incidents per hours worked, number of lost workdays due to safety incidents, injury rates, percentage of injury-free days, worker compensation claims, and malingering.

While these measures might be consistent within companies (between business units), their definition will vary widely across most companies. These circumstances make it impossible to pool data across companies. This problem can be solved by using meta-analysis techniques to synthesize research across studies. Correlations are computed separately within each company and are then combined across companies in the meta-analysis.

Time Periods

In addition to defining performance variables and aligning them at an aggregate level that coincides with the satisfaction measurement, aggregating the performance variables across appropriate time periods is also centrally important. This has implications for the reliability of the performance variables and their relevance to the research question at hand. Like individual performance, business unit performance measured over short periods of time is less stable than over longer periods of time. Performance fluctuates widely over short time intervals due to random variables, such as weather and other unexpected events. Averaging performance across time periods can reduce this noise in the data and increase reliability. In addition to fluctuating widely in short time intervals due to random and uncontrollable factors, performance variables can fluctuate (over both short and long time intervals) due to systematic variables that are outside the manager's and employee's control, such as the nature of local competition, population trends, and traffic patterns surrounding their business unit.

Other Confounding Variables

Prior to designing unit-level studies, scientists need to be aware that many variables external to satisfaction and performance can cause the relationship to be unrepresentative of reality. Employee length of service, the unit's competitive proximity, demographics of the location (socioeconomics, population density), age of the unit, size of the unit, capital investments, technology advances, and systematic seasonal weather patterns can all influence outcomes such as sales and profit. Control for these variables can take many forms. Technically, this can be done statistically through partial correlation or other general linear model methods. One can also control for these additional variables through comparison of current financial performance to past performance or to an expected performance (or goal). Retail organizations often generate targets based on factors such as location, competitive proximity, and past performance. Year-to-year sales are frequently used to control for seasonality (comparison of financials to same time period for previous years).

Employee turnover can vary based on the type of position (management versus nonmanagement or part time versus full time). The investigator can account for these differences by comparing only units with similar position types or comparing present turnover to past turnover (a difference score variable). It should be noted that difference score variables may contain substantial measurement error, but this is not a major consideration because the effects of measurement error are corrected for in meta-analysis.

Reliability of Performance Measures

The reliability of each performance measure should be calculated prior to conducting research. It is important to estimate the appropriate type of reliability to correct findings for measurement error. For variables where we anticipate real change (which includes most of the performance variables studied in unit-level analyses), there is a particular type of test-retest reliability that is appropriate (discussed in scenario 23 in Schmidt & Hunter, 1996; see Box 2.1).

Box 2.1. Test-Retest Reliability

The formula is $(r_{12} \times r_{23})/r_{13}$, where r_{12} is the correlation of the performance measure with itself (across units) from time 1 to time 2, r_{23} is the correlation of the performance measure with itself from time 2 to time 3, and r_{13} is the correlation of the performance measures with itself from time 1 to time 3.

Our experience is that unit-level performance variables are most reliable when accumulated for at least one quarter, and in many cases for six months or annually. Much as we would not expect one month's performance to be representative of an individual person's overall performance, we do not expect one month's data to be reliably indicative of a unit's performance. A variety of outside factors can influence performance for any one month. Only the accumulation of data over time will average out the random (or unpredictable) factors that influence performance for short time periods.

Reliability of Satisfaction Measures

The reliability and validity of the independent variable (satisfaction) can be increased by obtaining high response rates for each unit studied. Low response rates influence reliability because we then have less information on the satisfaction construct. From a validity perspective, low organizational response rates can be particularly problematic in unit-level research. If response rates vary widely by unit, it is possible that response rate presents itself as a confounding variable. Research on early and late responders (where substantial follow-up was used to obtain the responses of nonresponders) suggests that low response rates generally result in higher satisfaction scores that may not accurately represent the status of the business unit (Broberg, 2001), meaning the dissatisfied tend not to respond. This can create bias in the resulting effect sizes. It is always preferable to obtain high response rates (80 percent or above), but there are some alternatives that can be used when response rates are low or varying across units.

For example, the researcher can include only high response rate units in the analysis. However, this will reduce statistical power and potentially cause range restriction in the data on the performance variable. Lower-performing units have a higher tendency to obtain low response rates because they are less well managed. Another approach is to use partial correlation to remove the response rate effect from the analysis. (More information on how nonresponders differ from responders is provided in Chapter Thirteen, this volume.)

Obtaining multiple measures of satisfaction across time can also increase the reliability of the satisfaction measure. It is usually not feasible to obtain satisfaction measures more than two to four times per year, and many organizations collect such data only once per year. Each point in time is a representation of employee satisfaction for that time period and the recent past. However, obtaining and averaging multiple measures across time provides a more stable satisfaction measure that allows one to better calibrate the relationship between satisfaction and performance.

Time of Measure

Time itself is a critical design element that must be considered relative to the research question. Concurrent designs can include measurement of satisfaction at time 1 and measurement of performance variables at time periods just preceding and overlapping with time 1. Such a design is theoretically concurrent if one subscribes to the view that employee attitudes are a summary of the recent past. Whether this theory holds depends on the nature of the questions contained in the instrument. Questionnaires that contain more proximal time references (for example, "today") versus more distal references (for example, "the past six months") could differ widely.

Predictive designs measure satisfaction at time 1 and the performance variable during time periods following time 1. If the research question is, "Does satisfaction predict performance?" then this is the appropriate design. The time period of the satisfaction and performance variable measurement is centrally important to issues of causality. There are more elaborate designs that can be used to provide information on the nature of the causal relationship between satisfaction and performance. The most compelling answers to the causal questions will come from studies that integrate longitudinal data, meta-analysis, and path analysis (a correlational technique for testing the plausibility of competing causal models).

Only a thorough assessment of the nature of the organizations being studied will lead to a research design that allows the investigator to uncover true patterns of causality that exist in satisfaction-performance relationships.

Effect Sizes and Utility

Since unit-level research entails aggregation, sample size is often limited in any one organization, which limits the ability to obtain precise estimates of effect size. Any one study will contain potential distortion, caused by sampling error. In addition, systematic biases are caused by measurement error and range restriction. Meta-analysis (Hunter & Schmidt, 2004) can serve an important function in correcting for these biases. Accumulating many studies gives a sounder basis for calibrating the strength of the effect and its generalizability. As mentioned above, the predictive relationship between aggregate satisfaction and composite performance is approximately .40 (Harter et al., 2003) for units across organizations. This means that business units above the median on satisfaction have over double the probability of success (being above average on composite performance) in comparison to business units below the median.

But for many specific performance variables, the relationship is lower. For instance, the correlation between satisfaction and profit is .20 (Harter et al., 2003). Profit is a variable that is theoretically downstream from many shorter-term outcomes of satisfaction, such as customer loyalty, production, employee turnover, and safety. However, this satisfaction-profit correlation is substantial. As cited earlier, in conducting utility analyses on the individual company data included in the meta-analysis, Harter et al. (2002) found the effect sizes represent substantial practical value to business. Applying standard utility analysis (see Box 2.2) to the effect sizes for companies in the meta-analysis, profitability was from 6 percent to 20 percent higher (1 percentage point to 4 percentage points higher) for top- versus bottom-quartile business units (on an index of employee satisfaction). Differences in sales dollars, customer loyalty, and employee turnover were also substantial.

Box 2.2   Utility Analysis

Standard utility analysis, as applied in industrial psychology (Schmidt, Hunter, McKenzie, & Muldrow, 1979), has four basic components:

1. The relationship between the predictor and the performance variable (as represented by the correlation, r)
2. The standard deviation of the performance variable in units of measurement that reflect practical values
3. The number of standard score units' growth or difference in the predictor (independent variable in z-score form)
4. The cost of implementing the change effort required (measuring and increasing the predictor = c)

This basic formula is as follows: Utility $(U) = r \times s \times z - c$. Utility is usually computed on a per year basis.

In a financial institution with over eight hundred bank branches, employee satisfaction in year 1 was compared to employee turnover in year 2. The top satisfaction quartile in year 1 realized 34 percent employee turnover in year 2. The bottom satisfaction quartile in year 1 realized 45 percent employee turnover in year 2, almost a third higher turnover. Most estimates of turnover cost are substantial (taking into account both direct and indirect costs), and the above differences represent millions of dollars in direct cost alone. Observed effect sizes (r's) of .20 can result in substantial utility.

For example, in one retail organization with over five hundred stores, comparisons were made between stores that had and had not improved satisfaction levels. After controlling for location variables (such as socioeconomic area and competitive proximity), the difference in profit growth between stores that had and had not significantly improved in satisfaction represented over $200,000 in profit increase per store per year. For every one hundred stores that had grown in satisfaction, this represents $20 million per year. If it costs each store $2,000 to make changes that increase satisfaction based on the employee survey, the return on investment is 100 to 1 per year.

Early individual-level job satisfaction research (Iaffaldano & Muchinsky, 1985) estimated the satisfaction-performance relationship at .17. Researchers considered this correlation low, without considering the practical utility that this relationship would have if job satisfaction were actually the cause of performance. Although the true relationship at the individual level has now been found to be .30 (Judge et al., 2001), had researchers studied the practical effect of .17, they may have found substantial utility. Applying effect sizes from satisfaction-performance meta-analyses frequently results in utility that far exceeds cost.

Another frequently used method of summarizing size of effect is percentage variance accounted for, or r^2. A satisfaction-profit correlation of .20 is then represented as 4 percent of the variance accounted for. However frequently it is referenced, r^2 has no direct interpretation in the context of practical utility (Schmidt et al., 1979). An effect size with great practical meaning can then appear diminished if one focuses only on r^2. The surface-level interpretation of r^2 may impede the advancement of our understanding because it encourages the recipient of the information to discount the importance of many meaningful relationships (Hunter & Schmidt, 2004).

Translating unit-level effect sizes into practical meaning is essential to creating positive change through satisfaction surveys and programs. Unit-level research gives many more options to present research in a way that is meaningful to key stakeholders, such as executives, who often focus on outcomes measured at the unit level (such as profit).

Where Science and Practicality Merge

Employee surveys cost money. Depending on economic situations, companies often run on lean budgets. Executives need to see return on investment. Validation research and utility research can help decision makers see the value in investing in measuring and improving facets of employee satisfaction.

In addition to better understanding the return on investment in improving satisfaction facets and related constructs, unit-level measurement has other benefits. Practitioners want efficient measures. Scientists want measures with strong psychometric characteristics. Since unit-level measures of satisfaction are summaries of many respondents, item-level scores are more reliable than they would be if we were reporting individual-level satisfaction.

Most satisfaction research focuses on individual-level responses. This is most likely due to the luxury of large sample sizes at this level. However, measurement error is much higher for individuals than it is for the sum or average across individuals. We generally need many items to reliably measure a dimension at the individual level (for instance, the coefficient of equivalence reliability, such as coefficient alpha, is a function of number of items and average inter-item correlation). With unit-level measurement, each unit-level survey item score is an average across many different individual-level item scores, making single items quite reliable.

Accumulating across individuals also averages out individual personality differences and other dispositional idiosyncrasies that can distort individual-level satisfaction-performance correlations. Individual items, then, in unit-level research have reliabilities similar to multi-item dimensions in individual-level research. Using two different methods, Wanous and Hudy (2001) found reliability of .80 for individual items with unit-level data. Harter et al. (2003) found reliability of .77 for a single satisfaction item at the unit level (using test-retest reliability). These findings have implications on the length needed for surveys reported at the unit level.

It is not unusual to find employee satisfaction surveys of fifty to one hundred items or more. Such length should be justified by practical utility. Shorter surveys that measure the most critical and performance-related issues may serve all parties in the long run. Employees are then not burdened with surveys that are too lengthy and redundant, managers can more quickly digest what they need to focus on, and researchers have more opportunity for longitudinal studies since the end user has a more useful experience.

As meta-analytical designs continue to become used in unit-level research, investigators will begin to narrow down the number of facets necessary to capture performance-related information. The number of items needed to capture performance-related information may be fewer than originally thought.

Finally, the items used in unit-level reporting must be actionable. They must be based on issues the managers and employees can understand and act on in response to the survey feedback. For instance, the Likert-scaled items, "I understand what I am supposed to do at work" or "My manager has listened to me recently," are more actionable than the items, "I am proud to work here" or "I am satisfied with my company." The former are more concrete and actionable, and the latter more abstract. One could argue the latter are important in the testing of some theories, but it is important that a survey also include actionable items if the intent of the survey is to become part of a change process.

Conclusion

In this chapter, we have discussed the importance, complexity, and practicality of unit-level research when studying the satisfaction-performance relationship. Unit-level research is important because it is the level at which employee survey data are generally reported and at which many important outcomes are measured (profitability, sales, customer loyalty, safety, turnover). High response rates are necessary to increase unit-level reliability and thus reduce error in estimating the size of effect. Once the investigator clearly identifies relevant outcomes, it is important to assess the reliability of the outcome metrics, ensure the outcome is not biased by other external factors that may confound a relationship that is really present, and assess practical utility.

We encourage investigators to increase the number of unit-level studies. Unit-level research has many practical benefits that should stimulate even more interest among researchers, practitioners, and managers in the satisfaction-performance relationship.

References

Batt, R. (2002). Managing customer services: Human resource practices, quit rates, and sales growth. *Academy of Management Journal, 45*(3), 587–597.

Brayfield, A. H., & Crockett, W. H. (1955). Employee attitudes and employee performance. *Psychological Bulletin, 52,* 396–424.

Broberg, J. C. (2001). *Employee engagement differences by time of response* (Tech. Rep.). Washington, DC: Gallup Organization.

Denison, D. R. (1990). *Corporate culture and organizational effectiveness.* New York: Wiley.

Harter, J. K. (2000). The linkage of employee perceptions to outcomes in a retail environment—cause and effect? *Gallup Research Journal, 3*(1), 25–38.

Harter, J. K., Schmidt, F. L., Asplund, J. W., & Killham, E. A. (2004). *Employee engagement and performance: A meta-analytic study of causal direction* (Research Rep.). Omaha, NE: Gallup Organization.

Harter, J. K., Schmidt, F. L., & Hayes, T. L. (2002). Business-unit-level relationship between employee satisfaction, employee engagement, and business outcomes: A meta-analysis. *Journal of Applied Psychology, 87*(2), 268-279.

Harter, J. K., Schmidt, F. L., & Killham, E. A. (2003). *Employee engagement, satisfaction, and business-unit-level outcomes: A meta-analysis* (Technical Rep.). Omaha, NE: Gallup Organization.

Herzberg, F., Mausner, B, Peterson, R. O., & Capwell, D. F. (1957). *Job attitudes: Review of research and opinion.* Pittsburgh, PA: Psychological Service of Pittsburgh.

Hunter, J. E., & Schmidt, F. L. (2004). *Methods of meta-analysis: Correcting error and bias in research findings* (2nd Ed.). Thousand Oaks, CA: Sage.

Iaffaldano, M. T., & Muchinsky, P. M. (1985). Job satisfaction and job performance: A meta-analysis. *Psychological Bulletin, 97*(2), 251–273.

Johnson, J. W. (1996). Linking employee perceptions of service climate to customer satisfaction. *Personnel Psychology, 49,* 831–851.

Judge, T. A., Thoresen, C. J., Bono, J. E., & Patton, G. K. (2001). The job satisfaction–job performance relationship: A qualitative and quantitative review. *Psychological Bulletin, 127,* 376–407.

Koys, D. J. (2001). The effects of employee satisfaction, organizational citizenship behavior, and turnover on organizational effectiveness: A unit-level, longitudinal study. *Personnel Psychology, 54,* 101–114.

Locke, E. A. (1970). Job satisfaction and job performance. A theoretical analysis. *Organizational Behavior and Human Performance, 5,* 484–500.

Organ, D. W. (1988). A restatement of the satisfaction-performance hypothesis. *Journal of Management, 14,* 547–557.

Ostroff, C. (1992). The relationship between satisfaction, attitudes, and performance: An organizational level analysis. *Journal of Applied Psychology, 77*(6), 963–974.

Petty, M. M., McGee, G. W., & Cavender, J. W. (1984). A meta-analysis of the relationships between individual job satisfaction and individual performance. *Academy of Management Review, 9,* 712–721.

Reynierse, J. H., & Harker, J. B. (1992). Employee and customer perceptions of service in banks: Teller and customer service representative ratings. *Human Resource Planning, 15*(4), 31–46.

Roethlisberger, F. J., & Dickson, W. J. (1939). *Management and the worker.* Cambridge, MA: Harvard University Press.

Ryan, A. M., Schmitt, M. J., & Johnson, R. (1996). Attitudes and effectiveness: Examining relations at an organizational level. *Personnel Psychology, 49,* 853–882.

Schmidt, F. L., & Hunter, J. E. (1996). Measurement error in psychological research: Lessons from 26 research scenarios. *Psychological Methods, 1,* 199–223.

Schmidt, F. L., Hunter, J. E., McKenzie, R. C., & Muldrow, T. W. (1979). Impact of valid selection procedures on work-force productivity. *Journal of Applied Psychology, 64*(6), 609–626.

Schmitt, M. J., & Allscheid, S. P. (1995). Employee attitudes and customer satisfaction: Making a theoretical and empirical connection. *Personnel Psychology, 48,* 521–537.

Schneider, B. (1991). Service quality and profits: Can you have your cake and eat it too? *Human Resource Planning, 14*(2), 151–157.

Schneider, B., Ashworth, S., Higgs, A. C., & Carr, L. (1996). Design, validity, and use of strategically focused employee attitude surveys. *Personnel Psychology, 49*(3), 695–705.

Schneider, B., & Bowen, D. E. (1992). The service organization: Human resources management is crucial. *Organizational Dynamics, 21,* 39–52.

Schneider, B., Hanges, P. J., Smith, D. B., & Salvaggio, A. N. (2003). Which comes first: Employee attitudes or organizational financial and market performance? *Journal of Applied Psychology, 88*(5), 836–851.

Schneider, B., Parkington, J. J., & Buxton, V. M. (1980). Employee and customer perceptions of service in banks. *Administrative Science Quarterly, 25*, 252–267.

Schneider, B., White, S., & Paul, M. (1998). Linking service climate and customer perceptions of service quality: Test of a causal model. *Journal of Applied Psychology, 83*(2), 150–163.

Schwab, D. P., & Cummings, L. L. (1970). Theories of performance and satisfaction: A review. *Industrial Relations, 9*, 408–430.

Ulrich, D., Halbrook, R., Meder, D., Stuchlik, M., & Thorpe, S. (1991). Employee and customer attachment: Synergies for competitive advantage. *Human Resource Planning, 14*(2), 89–103.

Wanous, J. P., & Hudy, M. J. (2001). Single-item reliability: A replication and extension. *Organizational Research Methods, 4*, 361–375.

Wiley, J. W. (1991). Customer satisfaction: A supportive work environment and its financial cost. *Human Resource Planning, 14*(2), 117–127.

Zohar, D. (1980). Safety climate in industrial organizations: Theoretical and applied implications. *Journal of Applied Psychology, 65*, 96–102.

Zohar, D. (2000). A group-level model of safety climate: Testing the effect of group climate on micro-accidents in manufacturing jobs. *Journal of Applied Psychology, 85*, 587–596.

CHAPTER 3

Employee Experiences and Customer Satisfaction

Toward a Framework for Survey Design with a Focus on Service Climate

William H. Macey
Benjamin Schneider

Customer satisfaction has become an increasingly important focus for many organizations. This is true because it has been clearly shown that improved customer satisfaction yields increased customer loyalty, revenues, and profits. In the world of marketing, customer satisfaction measurement has become big business. The problem for marketing has been that once the customer satisfaction measurement is in hand, the changes necessary in organizational design to affect those measurements are not clear. In this chapter, we provide a framework for the design of employee surveys that can be used to illuminate the organizational issues that are reflected in customer satisfaction. The framework will organize a number of different approaches to employee surveys and show how they meaningfully relate to each other—and how they logically get reflected in customer satisfaction.

Our approach will be to ask and answer the following question: What are the ways information from employees about their firms can be used to diagnose and inform those organizations about ways they can promote customer satisfaction? Within this question, we focus on the types of employee surveys used to gather such information, with a specific emphasis on service climate surveys.

Types of Employee Surveys

Industrial/organizational (I/O) practitioners use a variety of organizational surveys (attitude, opinion, engagement, climate, culture) to diagnose employee experiences in the workplace. In the typical organization, some combination or all of such survey programs may be used for different, though sometimes overlapping, purposes. These range from simple pulse taking as part of the executive scorecard to integrated parts of an ongoing change management effort—as a basis for change or as a monitoring for how the change is going, or both. But what kind of survey should a practitioner use? Interestingly, little exists to guide the practitioner in making choices with regard to the appropriate kind of employee survey to use and the potential subsequent use of the survey.

Not surprisingly given the various purposes for which they might be used, employee surveys draw on a variety of concepts and item types. The item content in such a survey will reveal the practitioner's implicit theory of what the employing organization needs, desires, or wants and the practitioner's causal model of the key issues related to an outcome or outcomes of interest. Our intent in this chapter is to provide a structure that can guide practitioners in choosing from among various research traditions in designing a well-crafted organizational survey. In doing so, we ultimately present a single unifying framework that integrates what we know about employee satisfaction with the job and the organization, organizational climate, and what has come to be called employee engagement. Thus, we locate the focus of this chapter—service climate—within the larger traditions of employee opinion research and present a framework that reveals the kinds of choices it is necessary to consider if the administered employee survey is going to maximally meet the needs of an organization. Looking forward, we conclude that service climate is sometimes neither what first needs to be assessed nor last needs to be assessed to understand the causes of customer satisfaction. This is because important antecedents and consequences of service climate should be included as part of the diagnostic model. Our working framework will permit identification of the issues and choices that are appropriate for a given situation. First, to provide some essential background, we discuss the different traditions in employee opinion research, how they relate, and how they contribute to our understanding of organizational effectiveness.

The Typical Employee Survey

We begin the discussion of survey types with a brief introduction to the usual or typical employee survey. The typical employee opinion survey (EOS) item is attitudinal, wherein respondents rate agreement with a variety of statements measuring different facets of the organization and the quality of the employee-employer relationship. Most survey items tap global attitudinal and affective constructs, including satisfaction with supervision, the job, career opportunities, and the organization as a whole. While some of the items used in these surveys ask respondents the extent to which they agree or disagree with global descriptive statements about jobs, pay plans, supervision, career management practices, and so forth, the surveys are implicitly, if not explicitly, asking for opinions, reactions, and affect, if not outright satisfaction ("I am satisfied with my pay"). Some survey items lean toward a higher degree of specificity, particularly when targeted toward measuring a specific organizational or work characteristic of interest to a specific client (for instance, a focus on opinions with regard to quality improvement or Six Sigma programs).

More recently, surveys have been focused on a notion generally termed *employee engagement.* A term that seems to have captured the fancy of the moment, *engagement* defies consistent definition, although it seemingly implies what the typical individual would think "motivated" people do. Given the very broad interpretation such a definition might be given, I/O practitioners tend to interpret and use the term in varying ways. In perhaps the most public use of the term, the Gallup organization has designed a survey focused on twelve items (the Gallup Q12) that collectively assesses various facets of employee opinions and satisfaction and collectively is termed *engagement* (Harter, Schmidt, & Hayes, 2002). Precisely how these twelve items assess something different from the more traditional employee surveys described earlier is not clear.

But what is clear is that the items focus in on issues directly or indirectly controlled by the work unit immediate supervisor and seem to be modestly related at the work unit level of analysis to such issues as unit turnover, profits, productivity, and customer satisfaction (Harter et al., 2002).

We propose that a conceptually more direct assessment of engagement is with a focus on organizational commitment or organizational citizenship behavior (OCB), or both. In the former case, research has focused on the degree to which respondents report feeling attached to the organization (Meyer & Allen, 1997). Regardless of the antecedents, we will term these feelings of commitment *attitudinal engagement*. With regard to OCB, especially in more recent work targeted on group and organizational effectiveness (Podsakoff, Ahearne, & MacKenzie, 1997), respondents report on the level of OCB behaviors that characterize their work units, with higher rates seen as indicating more commitment, yielding what we will call *behavioral engagement*.

Regardless, the typical EOS is likely to have a smorgasbord of some or all of these kinds of items. The hope is that analyses of the resultant data will yield insights into needed action planning. Indeed, the Gallup approach focuses on the immediate supervisor precisely because of the action implications. That is, there has been an explicit decision made to focus their twelve items of engagement (Q12) on issues over which the immediate supervisor has relatively direct control (Harter et al., 2002). Especially when the EOS results for a specific organization can be benchmarked against the results from other organizations, the action planning can have a comparison database as a frame of reference for change. That is, when data norms are present, action planning can be based on normative contrasts of the organization to other organizations, so plans for change can be made based not only on item or scale means but on comparative data. And as we achieve additional data sets that cut across work units and even organizations where relationships are established for EOS data against important organizational outcomes (Harter et al., 2002; Schneider, Hanges, Smith, & Salvaggio, 2003), organizational surveys will be increasingly useful as a basis for change.

This is a point worth emphasizing because our experience in working with organizations is that they wish to see their EOS data arrayed by items that have high scores and items that have low scores, but this is an inefficient, if not ineffective, way to look at data. Much more useful is to look at data where *in comparison to relevant norm groups,* high and low scores are shown and/or the items are identified that have statistically significant relationships to outcomes of interest like employee turnover or absenteeism and/or customer satisfaction and then the high and low scores are shown on those items.

In summary, EOS work ranges across a diverse set of issues with the typical survey addressing a very broad range of employee experiences with the workplace. While some surveys (Harter et al., 2002) begin with a notion of change in mind, most surveys, we would argue, tap a variety of diverse issues without a specific plan for change or a specific target of interest in mind. Surveys that have normative or validity data associated with them would seem to be more powerful sources of potential information to use as a basis for change. We will return to the kinds of surveys just described because we can organize the different kinds of surveys into a framework that has both conceptual and validity bases and we want to present another kind of survey first, the service climate survey, for which external validity data exist.

The Items in Service Climate Surveys

In contrast to the typical EOS with its focus simultaneously on a broad range of human experiences at work, climate surveys focus on some specific set of attributes that fit a single underlying strategic construct or family of constructs, for example, service. Fundamental to the notion of focusing surveys is the idea that there exists a key set of practices or conditions that characterize climates of more effective organizations with regard to specific strategically important outcomes. That is, climate surveys reflect an explicit theory about causal mechanisms and the importance of setting priorities in organizations if specific strategic goals are to be achieved.

The explicit assumption behind such surveys is that employees have the knowledge of how the strategy is being played out on the shop floor. To that end, service climate surveys are dominated by items that focus directly on service and also focus on the conditions in the workplace necessary for a service quality initiative to have success. Schneider and his colleagues, who have been working in this arena for twenty-five years, have shown that employee experiences of the service climate in which they work will significantly predict customer satisfaction. Schneider and others have found what Wiley (1996) calls this "linkage effect" to be robust across industries as diverse as banks, insurance companies, supermarkets, automobile financing offices, retail, hotels, and restaurants (see Schneider & White, 2004, for a summary of this work).

In this long-term program of research, the facets of organizational life that constitute a service climate for employees have been fairly well documented (Schneider, White, & Paul, 1998):

- Leadership focuses on goals and planning for service.
- There are recognition and rewards for service excellence.
- There is internal support from others on whom service deliverers depend.
- Adequate tools and equipment to deliver service quality are present.
- Employees report working in an environment where customer needs are considered when decisions are made.

Note in this description that the issues mentioned all refer explicitly to service quality or customers, or both—and so do the items in the service climate survey. This is one distinguishing characteristic of the climate survey: the emphasis is not on planning or goal setting in general, but planning and goal setting for service quality. The same is true for rewards and recognition: not any kinds of rewards and recognition but expressly for service quality.

A second distinguishing characteristic of the well-designed climate survey is the explicit measurement of causal factors relevant to the climate construct. For example, the framework Schneider and his colleagues use suggests that good fundamental human resource management provides a foundation on which a service climate can be built. In this work (see Schneider et al., 1998), service climate does not exist in a vacuum but rests on a foundation of overall superior human resource management practices. Service climate, then, concerns not only how the organization works to promote service excellence but how the organization works to provide for its own human resources. The metaphor of a house is useful here: strong houses are built on strong foundations, and service climates are built on a foundation of superior management, including, but not limited to, human resource management practices. So the typical service climate survey asks employees of service units, such as bank branches and departments in supermarkets, to respond to items describing both the general management practices under which they work and the more specific management practices they experience with regard to the production and delivery of service quality.

For general management, the items tap into such issues as the availability of training and equipment and resources, information sharing, and the supportive nature of leadership—like items in a traditional EOS. The main difference between traditional EOS items and climate items is that the former focus on employee opinion and employee satisfaction, while the latter focus on organizational and unit practices. Indeed, directions in service climate surveys tell respondents to be reporters of what happens to them and around them—to report, not just to give their opinions or feelings. (The dichotomy presented here between EOS and service climate items is for expository purposes. Obviously many EOS items ask for reports on specific organizational practices, but they are presented along with opinion, that is, agree-disagree items, and explicit satisfaction items, making the general set one of feelings and opinions.)

For the specific focus on service, items tap into the extent to which rewards focus on service quality, planning and goal setting focus on service quality, measurement of processes and outcomes focus on service quality, and so forth. In addition, there are items regarding such issues as the attention paid to customer feedback and the customer orientation that upper management is perceived to practice.

All of these issues related directly to service climate are assessed using employee surveys, and each unit studied (bank branch, supermarket departments) is given a series of scale scores on the specific service climate dimensions as well as a summary global service climate indicator (Schneider et al., 1998). With data from this diverse set of items, it is possible to not only diagnose general impressions employees may have of the service climate in which they work, but the specific practices and procedures that constitute that climate.

In summary, although the traditional employee survey has a very broad range of issues assessed, the service climate approach operates from a more strategic perspective. This perspective provides an opportunity for survey researchers to implement a theory about the organizational design issues that collectively are the likely causes of the specific outcome of interest and then to design survey items around those hypothesized causal issues. The question is how to integrate the more traditional generic approach to survey design with the more strategic focus of the service climate approach.

A Conceptual Framework

Service climate researchers have demonstrated robust linkages between such climate measurements and customer satisfaction (Schneider & White, 2004). This linkage research tradition in service climate is deeply established. On one level, this reflects in large part the fact that service organizations tend to have many organizational units (examples are bank branches and hotels), facilitating the exploration of data at the unit level. More important, it reflects the fact that climate research has a particular theoretical orientation toward the role of front-line employees as a useful source of input in describing how the organization actually functions and what constitutes organizational effectiveness. This latter point bears repeating: climate research is not possible without a clear understanding of strategic focus. Although the approach is diagnostic, it is not exploratory. It is built on an explicit model, if not theory, of effective organizational functioning and by definition has strategic relevance.

The linkage between more usual EOS data and organizational outcomes has also recently been explored (Harter et al., 2002; Schneider et al., 2003). However, these results have not been explicitly targeted to specific organizationally relevant outcomes, so the findings, while significant, have not been as robust as those in the service climate tradition. The question facing us is how to use what we know based on both of these survey traditions to maximize the amount of information we can provide organizational decision makers that is simultaneously of value for understanding employee morale and diagnosing organizational success in customer satisfaction. The answer rests on illuminating the conceptual bases of the traditional EOS and understanding that good management practices provide the foundation necessary for the achievement of strategic objectives. In other words, we propose that if the traditional EOS had a firmer conceptual foundation, then the measurement of it and service climate would be more easily integrated and would also provide clear choices in the design of employee surveys.

It is very important to point out that the framework to be presented rests on the notion that employee reports on their work experiences are valid and, given recent findings, potentially of competitive advantage. The findings by Harter et al. (2002), Schneider et al. (2003), and others (for example, Denison, 1990; Huselid, 1995; Lawler, Mohrman, & Ledford, 1998) in this growing literature at group and organizational levels of analysis reveal that employee reports from the front lines of where the work gets done relate to important strategic objectives of the firm. Thus, it is often forgotten that in earlier times, managers could claim that employee surveys were useful only for "taking the human pulse" or "getting a feel for morale." But we now know that if we want the most valid data at the level where change can result in real competitive advantages in the marketplace, we must turn to front-line employees for knowledge about how the strategy is working. Strategic human resource management used to be about finding the best talent and developing it. Today strategic human resource management can also be about the collection of useful survey data from employees and then taking appropriate action. Thus, contemporary management consultants (Kaplan & Norton, 2004) stress the importance of using surveys to evaluate the alignment of organizational characteristics (typically referenced in general terms as culture) with the corporate strategy.

Figure 3.1 shows the framework we have been working with. Note that the figure has two conceptual foci. The first focus concerns what we call *foundation issues* (general management practices, general attitudinal engagement, and general behavioral engagement). The second focus concerns the *strategic objectives* of the firm (service leadership practices, service climate, service behavioral engagement, and customer satisfaction). Note further that the foundation issues are seen as supporting the service and customer satisfaction strategic objectives and not likely to be reflected immediately in customer satisfaction. In other words, foundation issues are a base on which specific practices promoting customer satisfaction can be built and that, in the absence of such foundation issues, such strategic practices are unlikely to occur and that customer satisfaction is therefore also unlikely to occur.

Figure 3.1. A Long-Linked Model of
Some Antecedents of Customer Satisfaction

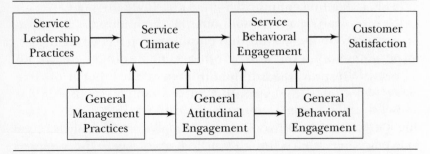

Note: General management practices provide a foundation for service leadership and service climate rather than causing them directly. The same is true for general attitudinal engagement in relation to service climate and service behavioral engagement. The idea is that without good management practices and attitudinal engagement, the potential for service leadership and a service climate are depressed. In what follows, we work from right to left in the figure to explore the linkages pictured, beginning with the relationship between behavioral engagement and customer satisfaction.

The Behavioral Engagement—Customer Satisfaction Link

Recall the distinction we made between attitudinal engagement and behavioral engagement, the former conceptualized as attitudinal commitment and the latter as OCB. Figure 3.1 shows two kinds of OCB: those focused on supporting the organization in the abstract and those focused on customer service. In other words, like the work on service climate—with a focus always on service—we propose that OCB also be conceptualized and measured both in general and with a focus on customers. We do so for three reasons. First, OCB were originally offered as the missing link in understanding the relationship between job satisfaction and individual performance (Organ, 1988). Second, citizenship behavior is regarded as largely discretionary. Third, OCB are directed toward specific targets (for example, coworkers, the organization, the supervisor, and customers); it therefore becomes possible to distinguish the focus of engagement behavior on the basis of relevance to corporate strategy. Thus, in the world of customer service, customer-oriented engagement behaviors are strategically relevant (Bettencourt & Brown, 1997). This suggests that companies whose employees consistently show such behaviors should have a competitive advantage over those companies that do not.

Some of our recent research provides data to this point. As part of a larger research effort, we recently surveyed individuals employed by twenty-seven companies in various sectors (banking, airlines, and retail) of the service industry. As part of the design, we included questions regarding both general OCB behaviors like conscientiousness (for example, "Employees in my work unit give an honest day's work for an honest day's pay") and customer service OCB behaviors (for example, "Employees in my work unit help customers even when it is not part of their job description"); we call these Engagement-Conscientiousness and Engagement-Customers. On the surface, it would appear that both forms of engagement are desirable and should be important to organizational success. However, in service industries, we would expect that customer-relevant engagement behaviors would be more strongly related to competitive success in regard to customer satisfaction than would conscientiousness-oriented engagement behaviors.

Fortunately, a measure of competitive success on customer satisfaction exists in the form of the American Customer Satisfaction Index (ACSI, 2004; Anderson & Fornell, 2000), and we were able to relate the two forms of OCB to it as shown in Figure 3.2.

Figure 3.2. Expectancy Table Showing the Relationship Between Two Forms of Engagement Behavior and the American Customer Satisfaction Index

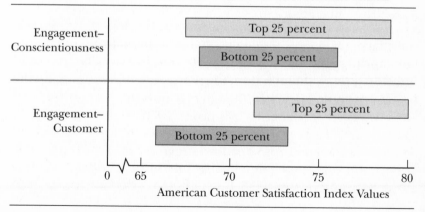

Based on the scores for Engagement–Conscientiousness, companies were segmented into the top 25 percent and the bottom 25 percent of companies; there were seven companies in each of the top and bottom quartiles based on Engagement–Conscientiousness. Based on the scores for Engagement–Customer, companies were again segmented into the top and bottom 25 percent, again with seven companies in each of those extreme quartiles. The ranges of ACSI scores for each of the quartiles so identified were then calculated. So for the Engagement–Conscientiousness top quartile, we calculated the range of the ACSI scores for those companies and contrasted them to the range of Engagement–Conscientiousness scores for the bottom quartile; the results are shown in the top portion of Figure 3.2. We did the same for the top and bottom quartiles of the companies based on Engagement–Customer, and the results are shown in the bottom portion of Figure 3.2. *Note:* To obtain the bar graphs, we calculated the confidence intervals around the mean ACSI scores of the companies in the top and bottom quartiles as determined by employee reports on Engagement–Conscientiousness and Engagement–Customer. Confidence intervals are a statistical method for determining a range of values in which there is a very high probability (.95) that the "true mean" score falls in the range of scores shown. By *true mean,* we are referring to the mean score that would be obtained if we had based our analyses on all possible service companies. Finally, the statistical correlation coefficient between Engagement–Conscientiousness and ACSI was not significant, while that between Engagement–Customer and the ACSI was. The results in Figure 3.2 are compelling and clear: customer service engagement behaviors differentiate companies on customer satisfaction much more strongly than do the more general measure of conscientiousness engagement behaviors.

It is important to note that one cannot reach the conclusion that engagement or OCB of the conscientiousness sort is unimportant. It is just that this form of OCB is conceptually and, on this sample of companies, less immediately important in understanding customer satisfaction. It is probably already clear that in a causal sense, certain themes measured in employee surveys are more closely related (proximal) to organizational outcomes than others and that the chain of cause and effect involves multiple links. For example, in the Schneider et al. (1998) research, general management practices as reported by employees are less strongly related to customer satisfaction than are service climate reports, but the general management practices are important for service climate itself. The issue of whether a driver of important strategic outcomes is near (proximal) or far (distal) in the causal sequence of events is an important issue, and one that Figure 3.1 makes clear.

For now, we stress two important points. First, some forms of behavioral engagement—in the case here those focused on customers—are more immediately useful as correlates and drivers of customer satisfaction. Second, the constructs measured in employee surveys represent different links in the sequential chain of relationships that likely determine important business outcomes. To anticipate a bit, if an organization wished to improve customer satisfaction, these data say that it should focus on supporting customer service behavioral engagement, not just general behavioral engagement, as the former is closer (more proximal) to customer satisfaction than the latter. The latter is conceptually and empirically further removed (distal) from customer satisfaction than the former, and Figure 3.1 shows the former will more likely link to the very customer service behaviors desired.

Antecedents of Behavioral Engagement

How can we understand what it is that promotes the behavioral engagement we see reflected in customer satisfaction? Figure 3.1 proposes that three factors directly affect service behavioral engagement: general behavioral engagement, general attitudinal engagement, and service climate. These proposals are based on both theory and research.

Social Exchange and the Norm of Reciprocity

Out of the extraordinarily rich research tradition within our profession, we now have considerable understanding of what drives engagement. This tradition suggests not only what is important to include in a well-crafted organizational survey. It also provides the opportunity to capitalize on the body of knowledge offered within our profession to create significant organizational change—change that can drive employee engagement and create competitive advantage.

The particular constructs we focus on here are the notion of reciprocity and social exchange. Specifically, we know that when a person is treated well, there is a natural obligation to return or reciprocate the favorable treatment. This is the well-accepted principle of social exchange (Blau, 1964; Coyle-Shapiro & Conway, 2004). Central to this view is that employees differentiate among their obligations, and they choose to reciprocate in ways that they believe are appropriate and on how they believe others would like them to behave. The norm to reciprocate can exist separately in relation to individuals (the manager), groups (the team), and the organization. Most important for our purposes is that this norm to reciprocate is driven by a reliably consistent set of factors, including organizational support, relationship with the manager, and perceived fairness within the organization. These are all classic, if not typical, factors measured within the context of the organizational survey and collectively constitute what we call general management practices in Figure 3.1.

In our view, three social exchange processes are relevant to the development of employee engagement:

- Perceived organizational support (POS) represents the quality of relationship between the employee and the organization (Eisenberger, Huntington, Hutchinson, & Sowa, 1996).
- Leader-member exchange (LMX) represents the relationship of the employee and his or her immediate manager (Graen, Novak, & Sommerkamp, 1982).
- Coworkers on teams (TMX) represents the relationship among team members (Shore et al., 2004).

POS and LMX have been widely studied with relationship to each other and to a variety of antecedents and consequences. TMX has received much less attention, although more recent research by Colquitt (2004) has explored the complex nature of justice in teams.

Emerging from these related lines of research is a clear set of interrelated constructs that, not surprisingly, are often represented in organizational surveys. Some of the more significant of these are fairness, trust, the presence of developmental opportunities, inclusion and involvement in decision making, and contingent rewards. This body of research points to some specific areas requiring attention in survey design to capture the specifics of these processes so that data are available to use as a basis for organizational interventions to enhance their formation and development (Skarlicki & Latham, 1997). Most important, these threads of research have been explicitly linked to both the behavioral and attitudinal definitions of engagement introduced earlier. Thus, a rather complete set of relationships has been defined and explored, in terms of both antecedent and outcomes, in a mediating chain (Schneider & White, 2004). This mediating chain comprises a major part of the sequence of cause-and-effect relationships that explain why workplace perceptions relate to organizational performance. The result is a blueprint for making informed choices about the types of items to include when designing employee surveys. This framework makes it possible to design an organizational survey that is truly diagnostic precisely because the questions represent the major linkages in the cause-and-effect sequence, showing just where in that sequence the organization should direct its efforts to develop and maintain competitive advantage. We turn next to the issue of service climate, a key issue in this causal chain leading to customer satisfaction.

Service Climate

While the norm of reciprocity is useful in understanding engagement, it does not specify toward what ends such behaviors are likely to be targeted. This is where the idea of a specific strategic climate—in the case here, a service climate—becomes important. So if OCB are largely discretionary, how does an employee know to what ends those behaviors should be displayed? He or she knows this based on the kind of environment in which he or she works. As noted in detail earlier, employees who are surrounded by many cues and clues about what is important to their organization are likely to behave in accord with the climate they conclude exists.

It is important to note here that previous work on service climate has revealed a direct link between it and customer satisfaction, yet Figure 3.1 shows this link to be mediated by service-focused engagement behaviors. This is logical because it is not the climate that directly relates to customer satisfaction but the behavior customers encounter that has the effect (Schneider, Ehrhart, Mayer, Saltz, & Niles-Jolly, in press).

The Role of Leadership

Every employee survey has items on it about leadership. Most of such items focus on the relationship between the leader and the employee, as in the LMX measure. The implicit and sometimes explicit theory that survey designers work from is that leadership is important for both employee morale and organizational effectiveness. Our own thinking is that this is correct but that surveys must contain at least two kinds of leadership items for them to be useful. The first kind of item would be of the usual sort found in EOS work: general descriptions or evaluations of both the relationship and task focus of the leader. The second, less common, sort would be of the strategic focus of the leader—in the case here, the service quality focus of the leader. The evidence is beginning to accumulate that when leaders focus their time and effort on specific organizational objectives, this is a sign to employees that this objective is valued and one to which they should devote time and effort. Such research exists in both the service climate arena (Schneider et al., 2004) and other areas of research like safety (Hoffmann, Morgenson, & Gerras, 2003). This line of thinking about the strategic focus of the leader has a number of implications:

- Not just any kind of leadership is required to produce a focus on strategically important issues. Service leaders plan for, set goals for, and organize around service quality (Schneider et al., 2004).
- Service leadership alone does not affect service climate, as shown in Figure 3.1. Service leadership is facilitated in its effects on service climate when employees report they experience generally satisfying management practices (one characterized for example by POS, LMX, TMX, and so forth).
- Service climate is both directly and indirectly controlled by the leader. The leader directly controls the climate by his or her focus on service quality and indirectly by his or her focus on ensuring availability of necessary service-relevant training, resources, staffing, and attention to employee feedback on service quality issues. As Schein (1992) has noted, if one wants to know what employees focus on, look at what their leader focuses on.

Summary: The Overall Framework

Figure 3.1 summarizes the model as a long-linked model beginning with traditional issues assessed using traditional EOS and moving through the service climate created by the leader to customer-focused employee engagement and then customer satisfaction. Note in Figure 3.1 that we would not predict that employee satisfaction (as assessed using the traditional EOS focused on general management practices) is likely to be directly related to customer satisfaction. We would also not predict that service leadership is likely to be reflected in customer satisfaction unless a strong foundation for it is established first through superior general management practices and the resultant attitudinal engagement.

We have already noted that sometimes service climate is not the first thing that needs assessing and attention, and here we see why that is true. Unless attitudinal engagement is established in organizations, a service climate—or any other strategic climate—is not likely to exist. We also noted that service climate may not be the last thing that needs to be measured and, again we now see why: behavioral engagement regarding customers is something that we conceptualize as emerging when a service climate exists.

On the Use of Survey Data: Issues of Levels in Employee Surveys

It must be recognized that we have presupposed throughout this discussion of surveys that for the most part, organizational surveys are actionable to the degree that the data generated are related to the accomplishment of organizational objectives. To do this, one or both of two circumstances must exist: (1) the data for any one organization must be compared to relevant norms from other organizations, and (2) the data must have been shown to be statistically related to the organizational strategic objective of interest. With regard to point 1, it is beyond the scope of this chapter to describe how to develop norms for employee surveys, but we are convinced that at a minimum, organizations must have norms against which they can compare their own data prior to using such data for making change. A more certain scenario exists when norms are available as a frame of reference, and there has also been statistical documentation of the relationship between the survey data and customer satisfaction. This documentation may be at the organizational level of analysis (as in the data we show in Figure 3.2) or it can occur for a single organization across multiple units (as described in the work by Schneider et al., 1998, in bank branches). It is these kinds of data that provide a real basis for change, and when the survey items used are structured around Figure 3.1, it is clear where to put emphases for change and how likely it is that change will yield relatively immediate effects on customer satisfaction.

Our bottom line here is that employee survey data with no frame of reference for interpretation in relation to organizational strategic objectives will not be seen as actionable by anyone in management—nor should these data be.

Recommendations

Our argument thus far has been that converging lines of evidence dictate the importance of simultaneously measuring several key constructs in organizational surveys. These flow from the social-exchange processes model underlying employee engagement and the climate research that encourages a focus in surveys on important organizational objectives. Schneider and White (2004) describe in detail the kinds of questions best represented in climate surveys. Ehrhart (2004) provides examples of questions that capture employee judgments regarding OCB. In what follows, we focus on the kinds of questions that should be included in surveys to represent two of the more significant social-exchange constructs underlying the long-linked model shown in Figure 3.1: organizational justice and trust.

Organizational Justice

Colquitt, Conlon, Wesson, Porter, and Ng (2001) summarized twenty-five years of research in organizational justice, including the role of justice as an antecedent of OCB, POS, and LMX. What is important about their review is that a reading of it makes it clear that survey researchers have had a very narrow interpretation of justice, focusing almost exclusively on the fairness of pay decisions. We strongly urge the design of surveys that focus on the different manifestations of justice, most important, distinguishing procedural from interpersonal, distributive, and informational justice. For example, relevant diagnostic content might include an assessment of whether opportunities exist to appeal unfair outcomes, whether procedures are applied consistently, and whether employees have a voice in decisions that affect them. In addition, relevant survey content might address issues as to whether management provides adequate explanations for its decisions. In an example of a specific instance regarding the effects of organizational downsizing, a relevant item might read, "Management has provided adequate explanations for their decisions regarding workforce reductions" as opposed to "The workforce reduction decisions are fair."

Trust

Consistent with the observation that the employees form different relationships within the organizational setting, Dirks and Ferrin (2002) differentiated between trust in senior leadership and trust in direct supervision. Trust is a key component of LMX and is often used as a surrogate for the quality of the relationship between employees and their managers (Ambrose & Schminke, 2003). It is thus an essential touch point in the long-linked model. As with organizational justice, contemporary survey practice tends to avoid appropriately differentiating between sources of trust and thereby provides insufficient diagnostic information. Furthermore, questions of trust are largely expressed in terms of credibility, rather than in terms of the quality of relationship. Thus, typical survey content includes questions such as, "I feel confident that senior management will make the decisions necessary to ensure the future success of the company." An example of a question intended to reflect trust in the employee-organization relationship might read, "I can approach management with concerns or bad news without fear of retribution" as a means of capturing the deeper meaning of trust. Obviously, trust also includes confidence in management's competence, consideration, and consistency.

Conclusion

We might seem to argue that organizational surveys necessarily become long and involved, of a length that would invite nonresponse. This is not the case. Rather, we believe that a well-designed employee survey should include the content necessary to monitor the conditions known to precede a service climate (trust, fairness, and other facets of attitudinal engagement), service leadership, service climate, and service-focused behavioral engagement. A survey containing four to six items for each construct deemed important in a specific setting would not be burdensome and would yield scale scores with acceptable internal consistency reliability. If carefully chosen, the scale scores would correlate in ways that would·indicate changes that would promote customer satisfaction.

What Figure 3.1 tells us is that a focus on just general management practices (fairness, trust, LMX) or even on just service leadership is likely to yield an incomplete portrait of the set of issues simultaneously operating in a firm to yield customer satisfaction. What Figure 3.1 also reveals is that there are clear choices that survey practitioners can make about what they wish to focus on. Survey practitioners make these choices implicitly now anyway, and we hope the figure reveals the implications of those choices for the eventual implications the survey data will have for organizational change.

Organizational surveys are conducted for a variety of reasons, more often than not as a general diagnostic intended to meet multiple agendas. In contrast, this chapter was about strategically focused surveys that have a very specific purpose: to determine the capacity of the organization to provide a high-quality service experience to its customers. Our goal in this chapter was to describe how strategically focused surveys provide a superior diagnostic method for driving organizational change and creating competitive advantage. We have chosen service climate because it fits our specific personal interests, there is a substantial relevant body of research, and it is a topic of general interest to those whose business success depends on satisfying customers. Nonetheless, a point that we want to emphasize is that our specific foci, service climate and customer satisfaction, are exemplars of a more general approach to survey development and use that we think is important. The framework, logic, and much of the content we presented are directly transferable to other strategic imperatives, including innovation, ethics, safety, and production efficiency. We believe this strategic survey emphasis would meet both the diagnostic needs of the practitioner and the management information needs of the executive, achieving an objective often not realized with contemporary organizational surveys.

References

Ambrose, M. L., & Schminke, M. (2003). Organization structure as a moderator of the relationship between procedural justice, interactional justice, perceived organizational support, and supervisory trust. *Journal of Applied Psychology, 88,* 295–305.

American Customer Satisfaction Index. (2004, Sept.). *The voice of the nation's consumer.* http://www.theacsi.org.

Anderson, E. W., & Fornell, C. (2000). The Customer Satisfaction Index as a leading indicator. In T. A. Swartz & D. Iacobucci (Eds.), *Handbook of services marketing and management* (pp. 255–267). Thousand Oaks, CA: Sage.

Bettencourt, L. A., & Brown, S. W. (1997). Customer-contact employees: Relationships among workplace fairness, job satisfaction and prosocial service behaviors. *Journal of Retailing, 73,* 39–61.

Blau, P. (1964). *Exchange and power in social life.* New York: Wiley.

Colquitt, J. A. (2004). Does the justice of the one interact with the justice of the many? Reactions to procedural justice in teams. *Journal of Applied Psychology, 89,* 644–646.

Colquitt, J. A., Conlon, D. E., Wesson, M. J., Porter, O.L.H., & Ng, K. Y. (2001). Justice at the millennium: A meta-analytic review of 25 years of organizational justice research. *Journal of Applied Psychology, 86,* 425–445.

Coyle-Shapiro, J. A-M., & Conway, N. (2004). The employment relationship through the lens of social-exchange. In J. A-M. Coyle-Shapiro, L. M. Shore, M. S. Taylor, & L. E. Tetrick (Eds.), *The employment relationship: Examining psychological and contextual perspectives.* New York: Oxford University Press.

Denison, D. R. (1990). *Corporate culture and organizational effectiveness.* New York: Wiley.

Dirks, K. T., & Ferrin, D. L. (2002). Trust in leadership: Meta-analytic findings and implications for research and practice. *Journal of Applied Psychology, 87,* 622–628.

Ehrhart, M. G. (2004). Leadership and procedural justice climate as antecedents of unit-level organizational citizenship behavior. *Personnel Psychology, 57,* 61–94.

Eisenberger, R., Huntington, R., Hutchison, S., & Sowa, D. (1986). Perceived organizational support. *Journal of Applied Psychology, 71,* 500–507.

Graen, G., Novak, M. A., & Sommerkamp, P. (1982). The effects of leader-member exchange and job design on productivity and satisfaction: Testing a dual attachment model. *Organizational Behavior and Human Performance, 30,* 109–131.

Harter, J. K., Schmidt, F. L., and Hayes, T. L. (2002). Business unit relationship between employee satisfaction, employee engagement, and business outcomes: A meta-analysis. *Journal of Applied Psychology, 87,* 268–279.

Hoffmann, F. P., Morgenson, F. P., & Gerras, S. J. (2003). Climate as a moderator of the relationship between leader-member exchange and content specific citizenships: Safety climate as an exemplar. *Journal of Applied Psychology, 88,* 170–178.

Huselid, M. A. (1995). The impact of human resource management practices on turnover, productivity, and corporate financial performance. *Academy of Management Journal, 38,* 635–672.

Kaplan, R. S., & Norton, D. P. (2004). *Strategy maps: Converting intangible assets into tangible outcomes.* Boston: Harvard Business School Press.

Lawler, E. E. III, Mohrman, S. A., & Ledford, G. E. Jr. (1998). *Strategies for high performance organizations: Employee involvement, TQM, and reengineering programs in Fortune 500 corporations.* San Francisco: Jossey-Bass.

Meyer, J. P., & Allen, N. J. (1997). *Commitment in the workplace.* Thousand Oaks, CA: Sage.

Organ, D. (1988). *Organizational citizenship behavior: The good soldier syndrome.* Lanham, MD: Lexington Books.

Podsakoff, P. M., Ahearne, M., & MacKenzie, S. B. (1997). Organizational citizenship behavior and the quantity and quality of work group performance. *Journal of Applied Psychology, 82,* 262–270.

Schein, E. A. (1992). *Leadership and organizational culture.* San Francisco: Jossey-Bass.

Schneider, B., Ehrhart, M. G., Mayer, D., Saltz, J., & Niles-Jolly, K. (in press). Understanding organizational-customer links in service settings. *Academy of Management Journal.*

Schneider, B., Hanges, P. J., Smith, D. B., & Salvaggio, A. N. (2003). Which comes first: Employee attitudes or organizational financial and market performance? *Journal of Applied Psychology, 88,* 836–851.

Schneider, B., & White, S. S. (2004). *Service quality: Research perspectives.* Thousand Oaks, CA: Sage.

Schneider, B., White, S. S., & Paul, M. C. (1998). Linking service climate and customer perceptions of service quality: Test of a causal model. *Journal of Applied Psychology, 83,* 150–163.

Shore, L. M., Tetrick, L. E., Taylor, M. S., Coyle-Shapiro, J.A-M., Liden, R. C., Parks, J. M., Morrison, E. W., Porter, L. W., Robinson, S. L., Roehling, M. V., Rousseau, D. M., Schalk, R., Tusi, A. S., & Van Dyne, L. (2004). The employee-organization relationship: A timely concept in a period of transition. In J. Martocchio & G. Ferris (Eds.), *Research in Personnel and Human Resources Management* (pp. 291–370). Greenwich, CT: JAI Press.

Skarlicki, D. P., & Latham, G. P. (1997). Leadership training in organizational justice to increase citizenship behavior within a labor union: A replication. *Personnel Psychology, 50,* 617–633.

Wiley, J. W. (1996). Linking survey results to customer satisfaction and business performance. In A. I. Kraut (Ed.), *Organizational surveys.* San Francisco: Jossey-Bass.

CHAPTER 4

Strategic Surveys
Linking People to Business Strategy

William A. Schiemann
Brian S. Morgan

Strategic employee surveys are focused on the people issues that make the greatest difference in business performance. The items on strategic surveys ask whether people understand the strategy and their role in achieving business objectives, whether they are engaged with these objectives and with the company itself, and whether they have the resources they need to get the job done. These surveys are clearly very different from traditional employee surveys that focus primarily on issues related to employee satisfaction. This chapter defines strategic surveys and their potential value for senior management, describes their content and the unique aspects of the strategic survey process, and reviews the factors that determine their effectiveness.

Jim Barkley, the head of a financial services organization that we will call Cashco, must have felt gratified that the favorable readings of his leadership team on the employee survey had improved by nineteen percentage points. Of course, the big news, and the reasons that Jim and his team were beaming, were the strong financial growth, increased market share and client retention, and faster cycle time that had occurred over the prior three years. This should have been no surprise: their strategic employee survey results had predicted strong operating, customer, and financial performance.

The story had begun four years earlier with the development of a strategy map (Kaplan & Norton, 2004; Schiemann & Lingle, 1999) and scorecard that provided a highly focused set of concepts and metrics to capture the critical assumptions, results, and drivers of their business strategy. (Throughout, we define *strategy* as an organization's overall business goals and the key elements of its plans for achieving these goals. It often includes its product and market focus, its competitive advantage or value propositions, and the core competencies required to achieve the overall goals.) Within that strategy map were a set of people drivers (factors presumed to have influence on an outcome, whether alone or in combination with other factors) that leadership believed were essential to executing the business strategy: issues related to leadership, performance management, values, innovation, and excellence. A number of these important people drivers, such as values, leadership, and alignment of performance management and rewards, were best captured through the eyes of associates in an employee survey.

One key to their success was ensuring that they had good measures of these critical drivers—that their employee survey focused on these strategic drivers, going beyond more traditional employee satisfaction items—so that the survey had business meaning to the top team and the measures could be used as leading indicators of business performance. Another key was prioritizing issues and addressing strategic gaps indicated by the survey. The company's success was largely a tribute to management's relentless focus on the critical few issues and closing performance gaps. The survey became a key strategic tool to identify those gaps and validate their beliefs about the people drivers of the business strategy.

Cashco was one of the first to truly use employee surveys strategically, but it is no longer alone. Strategic surveys represent the most recent evolution of management's ongoing quest to understand the impact of the workforce on the company and on key stakeholders such as customers and shareholders. Surveys have evolved through several phases, as shown in Table 4.1, beginning with surveys focused solely on taking the temperature of the organization, with a focus on satisfaction and morale, up through today's more business-focused surveys. The work of Higgs and Ashworth (1996) describes a similar course of development in organizational surveys over time.

Table 4.1. Evolution of Employee Surveys

Temperature-Taking Surveys	Employee Entitlement Surveys	Tactical Issues Surveys (Engagement, Safety, Quality)	Strategic People Equity Surveys
Focused on issues awareness	Focused on satisfaction, morale, pay, benefits, job security, and other employee relations issues	Focused primarily on employee commitment and engagement and their drivers	Addresses all three human capital components—engagement, alignment, and capabilities—and their drivers or enablers
No linkage	Limited linkage to employee relations outcomes	Linkage to employee engagement, turnover, performance	Strong linkage to customers, operations, and business outcomes
Low action	Action frequently aimed at corporate HR initiatives to improve morale, stem turnover	Feedback and action aimed at issues, managerial skills, and HR processes that influence employee commitment, engagement, and turnover	Enterprise and local action aimed at human capital effectiveness
Low management commitment	Commitment to action is often low or narrowly focused	Commitment varies across levels and functions; greater emphasis on middle management or unit themes	Strong leadership ownership and action; high middle management involvement
Few resources allocated to address issues	Follow-up resources (time and funding) targeted defensively	Follow-up resources targeted tactically	Follow-up resources targeted strategically
Assumptions			
"It's better to know than not know"	"Happy employees are productive employees"	"Surveys help us improve people and people processes"	"Human capital management is a critical strategic challenge"

Development of a strategic survey begins with strategy. In the course of developing a strategic survey, three questions are posed to the leadership team:

1. What are the most important business goals for your organization to achieve?
2. What people results are critical for the organization if it is to achieve these goals?
3. What people drivers (for example, communication of strategy, leadership, professional development, diversity, performance management) have an impact on performance on these people results?

Guiding management through these three questions leads to articulation of what the leadership team believes are the critical people components required to execute its strategy. Strategic surveys have these advantages over other surveys:

- A strategic survey captures the attention of the leadership team. It is directly linked to business imperatives and outcomes and is a tool for strategy execution. It generates a high level of executive interest in the results and a strong commitment to action.
- Because of the linkage to business outcomes, the results tell management where to invest to add value. Rather than leading to scattered investment in a wide array of tactical programs, these surveys help guide management to the most critical issues that warrant investment, as they are focused on the people issues that make the greatest difference in business performance.
- The results provide early warning signals of impending trouble, as strategic people issues are often leading indicators of business performance.

The next two sections focus first on the strategic content of the survey and second on three elements of the survey process—design, analysis, and implementation—that have the potential to be far more strategic.

Strategic Content

One of the critical gaps in creating strategic surveys has been a lack of strategic content. Over the years, we have seen survey reviews or feedback sessions in which the leadership team was truly engaged and others in which they appeared to be going through the motions. Often the type of survey content was at the root. Although most executives express empathy for employee relations issues and the need to motivate the workforce, they often do not see the connection between traditional employee survey content and their most important business goals.

The two are not mutually exclusive. There is a well-documented connection between employee satisfaction, good morale, a positive culture, and business outcomes (Heskett, Sasser, & Schlesinger, 1997; Kowalski, 2004; Rucci, Kirn, & Quinn, 1998; Schiemann, 1996; Wiley, 1996), as well as many proprietary studies in individual companies that have reinforced the validity of these linkages.

A more strategic approach to survey content is beginning to emerge. We discovered the value of this approach through our work in the area of business strategy measurement, including the development of strategic people metrics. Rather than using a bottom-up approach to employee measurement based on what will make people happy, this approach begins with a focus on the business strategy and the requirements for executing it. Approaching the issues from the perspective of strategy and what will be needed to achieve strategic business goals places the focus on human capital requirements along with requirements for technology, information, and financial resources. This line of thinking creates the platform for defining what should be measured in each area. Consideration of measurement requirements in turn points toward the elements of strategy execution on which employees will be able to provide valuable feedback. Employees have a unique vantage point for providing intelligence regarding business processes, the effectiveness of the current structure, teamwork across functional units, customer concerns, barriers to innovation, ethics, and technology deployment. So why not ask them?

Capturing Management and Employee Attention

How do we capture both senior management and employee attention? The answer lies in blending the strategic business issues with the issues that will create workforce engagement. Over the past decade, we have conducted hundreds of surveys with a variety of content areas and have arrived at a model that seems to capture this blend. The approach captures three areas that make up a concept we call *people equity*—a concept that is closely linked with shareholder equity and customer equity (Rust, Zeithaml, & Lemon, 2000). Shareholder equity—an important topic for senior management—is created by carefully developing customer equity in most businesses, and customer equity is enhanced by developing people equity. Many of the elements of customer equity—such as strong customer relationships, service recovery, and enhanced product and service value—are built on employee behaviors. Even elements that are heavily technology driven are often complemented by key employee behaviors.

People equity has three elements: employee alignment with the business strategy, capabilities to deliver customer value, and employee engagement. Together, these elements represent a three-legged stool of value—value that becomes meaningful to the executive team as an aid to reaching their strategic business objectives. Business leaders with whom we work have come to realize that they need employees who are focused on the right things (alignment), are capable of delivering the value proposition to customers (talent, information, and technology), and are engaged—truly committed to the mission, goals, and values of the organization. Without any one of these legs in place, performance will be at best mediocre.

The people equity framework makes sense to most managers, but to develop a framework for action, we also need to understand the levers that control people equity. How is people equity increased or decreased? We have adopted a heuristic model to define how people equity works. Over the past twenty years, we have conducted scores of correlation, regression, time-series, and cross-lagged studies for corporations that have examined the relationships among various people factors (typically based on factor analyses of survey content into components such as leadership, supervision, respect, performance management, teamwork, commitment, and alignment), or the relationship between these people factors and various outcomes such as employee turnover, customer satisfaction, or financial performance. The people equity models explored in this chapter are based on our judgments across many studies of the consistent relationship that occurs between business outcomes; the three people equity concepts of alignment, capabilities, and engagement; and a set of drivers and enablers that have been the most fruitful predictors of people equity and employee and business outcomes.

We have identified nine elements that frequently seem to drive performance across organizations in study after study: four driver categories, four enabler categories, and a company's unique strategy elements.

As shown in Figure 4.1, drivers are assumed to have a direct influence on the three people equity factors, while enablers are assumed to have a more indirect influence. For example, supervision, considered an enabler, often influences the way various drivers, such as rewards, innovative practices, or person-job skills, are matched on a day-to-day basis, while the leadership team and broad organizational values often influence how reward systems, innovation policies, and competency investments are prioritized. Taken together, these elements frequently influence the three people equity factors.

Figure 4.1. People Equity Drivers and Enablers

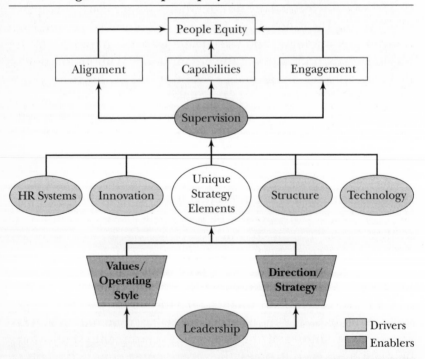

The four drivers are:

- Human resource systems, including talent acquisition and development, performance management, and recognition and reward
- Technology and business processes, including operating effectiveness, business process improvement and effectiveness, adequacy of tools and technical resources, and effectiveness of knowledge management and information use
- Innovation, including production and use of ideas, creativity, and adaptability
- Structure, including deployment of staff and cross-functional information flow

The four enablers are:

- Supervision, including people, technical, coaching, and communication skills and practices of immediate managers
- Leadership, including confidence in senior management and its ability to set, guide, and create a passion for the organization's direction
- Strategic direction, including clarity of direction and presence of a strategic measurement system
- Values, including such areas as respect, diversity, and teamwork

Unique strategy elements are aspects of business strategy implementation that are specific to a given organization.

Our experience has confirmed that these drivers, enablers, and unique strategy elements have considerable heuristic value. They are frequently the leading indicators of the three people equity elements and are often linked to turnover, customer loyalty and retention, and some aspects of operating effectiveness. Most are controllable by senior management, so management can see how changes in these people issues can influence important business outcomes. Finally, the drivers and enablers are closely connected to resources and initiatives in which the leadership team has invested. For example, management approves budget dollars for training, which in turn influences capabilities and resources. Or management invests in rewards with the goal of engaging or focusing employees through the performance management system.

Or management invests in diversity programs to change the values of the organization in a way that will lead to a more productive and valuable workforce. In summary, strategic surveys are outcome driven. They are built on the business strategy and the key employee outcomes (turnover, people equity), drivers, and enablers that allow the strategy to be implemented effectively.

A Mind-Set, Not a Mountain

At first, a strategic approach may seem daunting, but it is quite workable. After much experimentation over the years, we have realized that it is less important to cover each set of drivers and enablers comprehensively than it is to have broad coverage of most of the factors. The reason is that management needs to see the big picture rather than delve too far into specific areas. We find that leadership teams are more likely to connect to a survey of broader issues rather than a few areas in depth. A broad survey allows them to strategically prioritize areas of focus and then explore as needed in the follow-up phase to uncover the root causes of critical performance gaps. A survey that captures employees' perspectives on the core people equity questions, the drivers and enablers, and business outcomes such as turnover intention, productivity, customer focus, and operational excellence can be captured in forty to fifty survey items. An abridged version with only key marker items can capture this content with as few as twenty items. This is enough to focus management's thinking and action about critical people issues.

There are compelling reasons to be less than comprehensive in identifying all of the root causes in a broad survey. First, it would require too many items. Today senior executives and employees have limited tolerance for long exercises. Second, there are complementary vehicles for capturing root cause information. Finally, using findings from a broad survey as a springboard for exploring root causes forces senior executives to come to grips directly with the nuances of the issues being addressed. This approach often leads to better understanding and ownership of issues than one in which the causes or solutions are artificially spoon-fed through quantitative data.

Based on identification of competitive differentiators, the organization can create survey items that will reflect whether the strategy is being executed. These items fall into two categories:

- Standard items from core people driver or enabler areas that are related to one strategy versus another
- Custom items that capture unique strategic issues

Consider an example. If the strategic area of emphasis is uncompromising service, we might go into the "values" enabler and use values items that relate to customer focus, such as, "In our organization, there is a premium placed on delivering outstanding customer service." Or we might select from within the "leadership" enablers an item such as, "Top management walks the talk when it comes to customer service." Alternatively, one might create unique items for strategic initiatives or programs to ensure that they are understood, accepted, and being used—for example, "Associates in my unit strongly support the Customer One program," or "Customer One has helped us understand and deliver better service to our customers." In a broad-based survey, we find that best practice organizations allocate 15 to 30 percent of their survey content to these unique items and use the remaining items to capture the important people issues that typically cross organizations, such as the engagement items or performance management items within the alignment area. Box 4.1 outlines the case of a successful user who built a strategic survey from the people measures on the organization's balanced scorecard.

**Box 4.1. A Strategic Survey
in a Financial Services Organization**

After completing a balanced scorecard that defined the important financial outcomes and customer, operational, and people drivers of their business, a financial services organization needed to capture information on the people drivers of success. Management realized that employees would be the best source of information about most of the drivers. An employee survey provided an ideal mechanism to capture performance on these drivers and to track their improvement to reach targets they had set for these drivers over time. Among the drivers were these:

- Several critical values that management believed were essential to their business, including self-assurance, integrity, and proactivity.

(Continued)

- Leadership. Again, who would be better to evaluate leadership than the followers, especially given the areas of leadership that had been prioritized, such as "providing clear direction on the strategy" and "high accessibility"?
- An aligned performance management system, referring to a clear line of sight from the strategy to department goals to individual goals to team and individual rewards. This area was again appropriate for an employee survey.

The organization also developed items on the employee survey that would directly connect to customer ratings on important issues that market research had confirmed were related to buying behavior and customer retention. For example, customers had already confirmed that one of their most important issues was problem resolution and rapid quotes for new financing. It was straightforward to evaluate employee perceptions on these issues to find out how in touch employees were with customer perceptions. By building this type of survey with strategic targets, this organization was able to increase its performance dramatically.

Survey Process

Strategic focus results from both survey content and survey process. Survey process can be thought of as having six phases: planning, questionnaire design, information gathering, analysis, reporting, and implementation. While we could argue for increased strategic value in all six phases, for purposes of this chapter we have focused on the three that typically have provided the most strategic leverage: planning, analysis, and implementation.

Making the Planning Phase Strategic

During the planning phase of a survey, the objectives for the initiative are set, and issues for coverage in the questionnaire are identified. These objectives and issues define the strategic content of the survey. But the processes by which objectives are set and issues are defined are also critical elements of a strategic survey. The notion of getting executive buy-in is as old as the survey process itself. What is different in a strategic survey is the focus of initial dialogue with executives. At the outset of a strategic survey, the leadership team is engaged in a discussion of their goals, critical people results, and drivers of those people results. This discussion focuses the leadership team's attention on the people issues that make the greatest difference in business performance. Of course, this information is corroborated from multiple sources to create a set of hypotheses about what drives business results. Drawing the leaders into this type of thinking early in the process is helpful in creating a mind-set that is different from their traditional views of employee surveys and is also helpful in creating anticipation for the strategic findings.

The process of inquiry at the outset of a strategic survey is different for employees as well. In employee focus groups conducted in the design phase of a strategic survey, employees are often asked questions such as these:

- What do you believe to be the organization's strategy and its business objectives?
- Do you believe that employees generally buy in to the strategy?
- Do you understand how the work of your department and your own work contribute to the company's achievement of its business objectives?
- Does your unit have the resources and talent you need to meet customer requirements? If not, what are the gaps?

Then the discussion shifts to people drivers and enablers such as leadership, supervision, HR systems, technology, and values. When completed in the right context, this type of group session engages employees in a discussion of strategy and the people issues connected to it, signaling a different focus for the employee survey, and it provides additional information to guide the development of custom survey questions related to the unique strategy of the organization.

Making the Analysis Phase Strategic

Once the survey has been conducted, unique analyses are used to help identify strategic business issues for action.

Providing an Overview

What does the leadership team want to know? The first, and often the most captivating, step in a strategic survey is giving leaders a snapshot of the entire organization. How does the organization look on alignment, capabilities, and engagement at the enterprise, business unit, and perhaps major geographical or functional group levels? Using an alignment-capabilities-engagement (ACE) tree diagram like the one displayed in Figure 4.2, the organization can see (1) its overall performance in the three areas and whether there are areas of consistent strength or concern across all units, and (2) the performance of each unit on these issues to identify both pockets of concern and high-performing areas that can serve as best practice.

Figure 4.2. Alignment-Capabilities-Engagement Tree Diagram

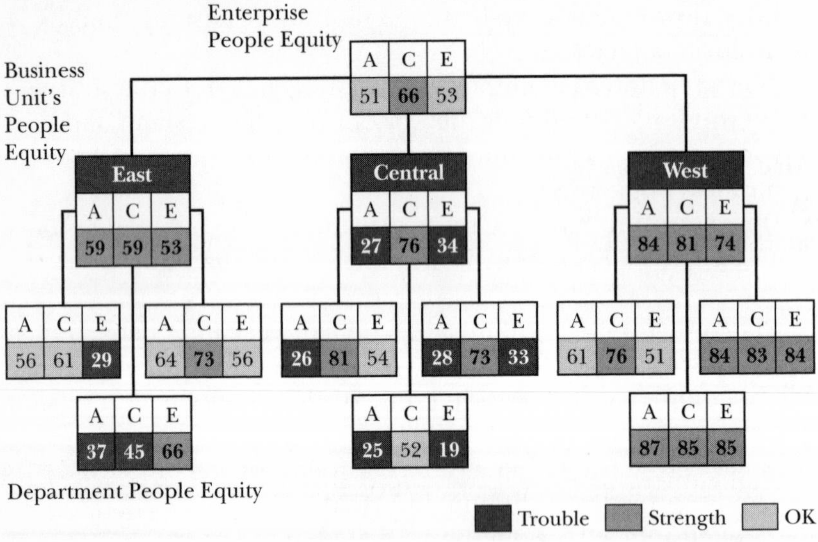

Note: The numbers in the boxes are composite index scores of items within the categories of alignment (A), capabilities (C), and engagement (E). They can range from 0 to 100 (high) and typically represent the "strongly agree" and "agree" (favorable) responses to items in the questionnaire. In this example, strength was defined as 65 or better, okay was defined as 51–64, and trouble was defined as 50 or below. Since this is only a sample of an organization of many more units, the scores for a particular box are not necessarily the average of the subboxes below them.

Are There Systemic Issues?

From the CEO's perch, what is the next most frequent question? Management wants to know if there are a few critical items that need organizationwide attention. The leadership needs to know if there are systemic issues that they control that are pervasive throughout the company. A thorough examination of the variation in ACE scores across units can provide these answers to both the senior team and groups at various levels throughout the organization. As you can see from the tree diagram in Figure 4.2, there are no systemic issues that pervade all major geographical divisions, but the issue of alignment is pervasive throughout the Central Division.

High levels of variation from unit to unit and from manager to manager within units often provide warning signals of flaws in strategy implementation. Are managers across various units aware of and engaged with the company's strategy and direction? Are they conveying the right messages to employees? Are unit objectives consistently aligned with business objectives? Do employees across units understand how their work contributes to achievement of overall business objectives? Or are there pockets of misalignment?

Modeling Approaches

What is typically referred to as driver or linkage analysis—modeling the relationships between outcomes and variables hypothesized to be leading indicators of those outcomes—is also used at this stage, with the objective of providing additional information that focuses management action on the critical few people issues. These analyses can be used to:

- *Validate a company's theory of the business.* If data for business outcome measures (such as operational excellence, customer loyalty and retention, and employee retention) are available, modeling tools such as path analysis, multiple regression analysis, and cross-lagged correlations can be used to identify the impact of people issues on business outcomes.
- *Identify the most critical performance gaps.* Using driver analyses in which survey measures are linked to each other (such as identifying drivers of alignment scores), a few key issues typically emerge as having the strongest relationship to a given

outcome. If performance is poor on these issues, they become high-priority action items.

Once the findings have been analyzed and it is time to begin survey follow-up, management will be armed with the following information to help guide follow-up activities:

- Its own identification of strategic people issues as articulated in the survey development process, now supplemented by actual findings on the issues thought to be keys to business success
- The ACE tree, which identifies both overall organizational and unit-specific strengths and concerns
- The results of linkage and driver analyses that identify the highest-impact people drivers of business performance

This information can be used to focus problem-solving and action planning activities.

Making the Survey Action Implementation Phase Strategic

While many organizations are able to complete the survey planning and analysis phases of the process well, failure often occurs at the survey action implementation phase. Among the factors causing this failure are:

- Lack of prioritization (often tied to lack of strategic context)
- Lack of a disciplined process to complete action outcomes
- Poor implementation skills among managers
- Weak or nonexistent impact evaluation and analysis

In this section we address the implementation issues that can derail a survey even when content and analysis are strategic. We will examine ways to address these issues through the application of more strategic thinking and approaches.

For a moment, we step back and look at why things often break down even after good survey information has been collected, strategically analyzed, and fed back to senior management. Why do we hear so many organizations lament that they do not achieve the impact from the survey that they would like? Why are so many survey managers frustrated that they cannot get senior or middle managers to select critical issues or to follow through on the issues selected? Why do so many good plans seem to fade?

Prioritization

Without prioritization, there will not be enough focus, resources, or managerial energy to drive improvement. Even with traditional surveys, we have found that by focusing management on strategic objectives and what they need from their people to reach those objectives, we can channel executive and managerial action more effectively toward business improvement and organizational transformation (Schiemann, 1992).

Organizations with strategic survey content and processes are in an excellent position to prioritize issues based on strategic priorities (discovered in the development phase), knowledge of the most important drivers of business outcomes (from the strategic analysis phase), and identification of issues that are systemic across the organization. For example, in a medium-sized bank, technology gaps on several fronts were hindering high productivity and customer satisfaction—a capabilities gap. Coupling this information with poor implementation of a major bankwide focus on cross-selling loan products to customers, low customer satisfaction ratings, and employee reporting of technology blunders, the employee survey information on technology use was of major value to senior management.

For organizations that have already created strategic maps (Kaplan & Norton, 2004; Schiemann & Lingle, 1999), the process is much easier. We began using strategic maps in the early 1990s to help translate business strategy into a cause-and-effect model that showed the linkage of employee, operational, and environmental (supplier, safety, regulatory, and community) drivers with customer and financial outcomes. A sample map appears in Figure 4.3.

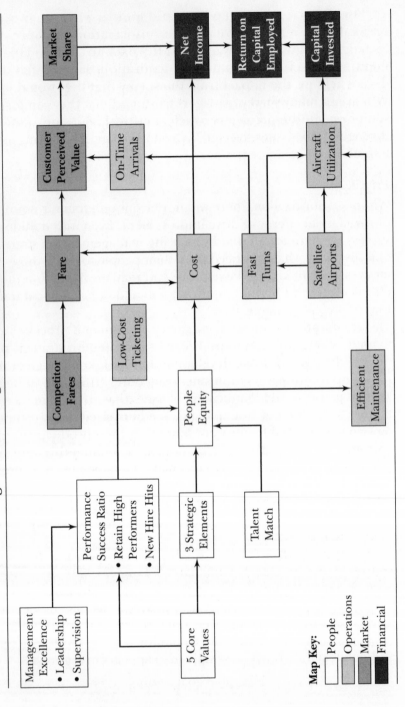

Figure 4.3. Strategic Business Map for an Airline

Management Excellence
• Leadership
• Supervision

Performance Success Ratio
• Retain High Performers
• New Hire Hits

5 Core Values

3 Strategic Elements

Talent Match

People Equity

Competitor Fares

Low-Cost Ticketing

Fare

Cost

Fast Turns

Satellite Airports

Efficient Maintenance

Customer Perceived Value

On-Time Arrivals

Aircraft Utilization

Market Share

Net Income

Return on Capital Employed

Capital Invested

Map Key:

People
Operations
Market
Financial

In this business map for an airline, financial outcomes such as return on capital employed require certain market outcomes (such as high customer perceived value), defined levels of operating performance (for example, on-time arrivals and fast turnarounds), and strong people performance (for example, high people equity, talent utilization, and management excellence). Through a strategic planning process, management of this airline identified six critical people outcomes (people equity), drivers (for example, talent match), and enablers (for example, management excellence) that it believes are most important to implementing its strategy. In this case, survey measures can be used to assess people equity, employee understanding, and buy-in to three key strategic elements, management excellence, and the extent to which the organization is living its five core values. Surveys in this case provide management with critical indicators to let them know whether they are hitting their targets in each of these areas. In this example, the map is a clear guide to defining survey content, conducting the appropriate analyses, and then examining resource deployment to each of these areas.

These maps provide a view of the theory of the business—how senior management believes that value is created for shareholders or key stakeholders. Employees are a critical ingredient of that value equation and often seen as a leading indicator in the value chain. By understanding how employees connect to the business strategy—that is, what outcomes employees drive that are important—it becomes far easier to focus management attention on the important drivers of those outcomes. While maps are typically constructed at the enterprise or business unit level first, a similar thought process can be applied to functional units or departments.

Disciplined Implementation Process

Stakeholder feedback and action planning have been fixtures in postsurvey best practices since the late 1970s, a result of some of the excellent application of good behavioral science at IBM and a few other leading organizations at the time. These organizations realized that there was a crucial linkage needed to move from survey information to organizational action. They recognized the motivating nature of good feedback and the importance of specific, controllable, and measurable goal setting.

The leading applications that emerged from this period included survey processes that fed the survey information down the organization in a cascade fashion, with each level reviewing the information that pertained to it and then creating action plans that were reverse-cascaded up the organization. This process, although cumbersome and requiring exacting execution and skills, had the potential to get information to many levels of the organization and involve each level in the interpretation of the information and the building of plans to ameliorate the gaps in areas of their control, while passing recommendations up the organization in areas that required higher levels of authority to resolve.

While this process had many merits and succeeded in creating buy-in from employees and many managers when executed well, it has declined in use and effectiveness over the past decade for a number of reasons. First and foremost, such surveys often evolved into "entitlement" surveys in which the primary outcome was a list of actions that the senior management team should take to increase employee satisfaction. Management soon became wary of the employee survey as a tool that simply increased the length of its to-do list, often with little impact on their ability to reach their goals or to enhance organizational performance.

Second, in an era of increasing competitive pressure, speed, focus, and agility are becoming competitive requirements. In such an environment, a high premium is placed on rapid flow of information. In this environment, the comprehensive and lengthy cascading survey feedback and action planning processes of the 1970s and 1980s were soon becoming too cumbersome, and their effectiveness had diminished.

Third, the approach produced too much bottom-up information that cluttered the strategic picture. While some of that information was important to building organizational health and dealing with dominant issues (such as unionization at the time), in today's fast-paced, information-clogged, rapid-decision-making environment, information that is strategic and focused provides more value. This requires top-down prioritization of issues that are most strategic, coupled with rapid feedback from the workforce.

While a number of alternative approaches have been developed over the past two decades, the strategic feedback and action planning processes that seem to work best in the emerging competitive environment have the following characteristics:

- Senior management has viewed the survey information from a strategic perspective—that is, they understand which areas are most crucial to executing their business strategy and in which of those areas the most significant performance gaps reside.
- Information is fed back to the relevant stakeholders rapidly so that decisions and solutions can be implemented quickly.
- Stakeholders are almost always employees but are beginning to include others as well, such as board members (on governance issues), suppliers (on supply chain or outsourced labor issues), strategic partners (on joint venture issues), and customers (on service themes).
- Action planning includes elements of quality management, such as cause-and-effect thinking, that helps employees identify root—rather than superficial—causes through such techniques as fishbone diagrams, cause-and-effect thinking, variance analysis with tools such as Pareto analysis, impact analysis with techniques such as cost-benefit analysis, and target setting, including both incremental and stretch targets. Organizations that already have embedded such thinking have a distinct advantage because these tools help managers and their teams clearly identify a limited set of likely root causes of prioritized issues, that, when addressed, will have a positive impact on key outcomes. Of course, root cause analysis is used in more traditional surveys as well. The difference in strategic surveys is the starting point, which is senior management's effort to understand and address a few critical people issues that have been identified as important to reaching strategic objectives.
- Accountability has shifted more from action planning to implementation. In fact, the best practices organizations hold managers and employees accountable for changes in the outcome—not just executing action plans. Best practice organizations most typically avoid punishing managers for low scores in areas under their control the first time, but place much higher accountability on those managers for addressing and improving those areas.
- In support of this, action planning has become more visible in many organizations. This visibility has several beneficial consequences. Sharing gaps and intended solutions enables others who have traveled the same path to share helpful information on the efficacy of intended solutions and to offer alternatives that have worked better. And others who have similar issues can watch and learn if an individual unit's efforts are closing the targeted gaps.

Furthermore, visibility allows managers and third-party evaluators such as organizational effectiveness groups and coaches to scrutinize the quality of the root cause analysis (Did they select the right issues?) and the effectiveness of implementing solutions (Did they execute well?). The action planning process is often a great early indicator of managers' comfort with strategic and quality thinking, as well as their ability to focus to solve business issues.

• Tracking of action plan execution is imperative in a well-executed strategic survey process. Best practice organizations typically have efficient and often technologically driven (for example, Web-posted) systems for collecting action plans. Although there still appears to be wide variability in the level to which action plans are scrutinized at a local or organization level, new technology is making it easier and easier to gather, collate, and integrate such information to draw conclusions on which actions are most productive in different circumstances (for example, a given solution to a particular gap works well for all or certain job groups or for all or certain regions).

Implementation Skills

To execute the previous processes effectively, managers and employees must have the requisite competencies. This is not a given. In our experience, up to 30 percent of managers, regardless of formal training, will find a way to use the survey information to make effective changes. Ten to 20 percent will have trouble, even with sound training. The remainder—about half the managers in most firms—will become substantially better at managing improvement with the right skills. Most of these are the critical skills that make up a well-rounded managerial skill set: strategic thinking, business acumen, prioritization and decision making, giving and receiving feedback, knowledge of root cause analysis and other quality tools, team decision making, building effective action plans, and evaluating change.

The only requisite skill that should be unique to the survey process is "interpreting survey information." While the other skills should be part of a rounded managerial skill set, we typically find a good deal of variance across them. This is one of the biggest gaps in many survey follow-up processes. And many organizations lack the commitment to developing these skills, which are nothing more than the raw ingredients of effective group problem solving.

Most often these gaps are simply made relevant and visible during the survey follow-up process.

Training in these areas can take various forms when done in conjunction with the survey process. We have found it effective to focus on three sets of skills:

- Interpreting the data and prioritizing issues in a strategic framework
- Conducting strategic feedback sessions with employees, identifying root causes and potential solutions, and building strong action plans that are bought into by both management and employees
- Securing resources, implementing the action plans, and tracking results and impact

Impact Evaluation

The final area is determining the impact that the initiatives or intended solutions have on strategic business outcomes. This sounds obvious and reasonably easy to do, but it is the most frequent failure of everything that has been discussed thus far. Partially this is because it is the terminal stage in the overall survey process; those who cannot complete the earlier stages well rarely have the opportunity to evaluate the impact. But those who reach this stage too often settle for anecdotal evidence of improvement or use weak criteria. And because many survey efforts are spaced so far apart, they can move on to other business and only be reminded of these issues again in one or more years.

In our experience, organizations that succeed with strategic surveys implement the following actions more often:

- Changes in survey scores in high-priority targeted areas are reviewed much more frequently than in low-performance organizations. Today it is not uncommon to track changes in areas targeted for improvement by using quarterly pulse surveys. It has been our experience, and we have seen research over the past several decades suggesting it, that if scores in targeted areas for improvement do not change within 90 to 120 days, they are unlikely to change over longer periods of time, with a few exceptions such as longer technological or complex process improvement solutions.

- Improvements in strategic scores are more frequently linked to executive and managerial rewards, with the increasing recognition that if the people metrics have been designed effectively, they represent leading indicators of performance on key business outcomes such as customer retention, operating efficiency, and financial performance.
- Survey feedback and action planning processes are evaluated for their effectiveness on a regular basis. After all, these processes should provide a strong return on investment. While many organizations have reduced the complexity of their survey efforts, they do not want to reduce their impact in identifying and ameliorating key business gaps. This is a delicate balancing act. While many organizations have arrived at the conclusion that their prior survey efforts were becoming their life's work, as they increase the efficiency and effectiveness of these processes, they need to be careful not to lose the impact that the processes were intended to create. Others, in contrast, have never infused their survey processes with the power they deserve. They conduct the survey on faith, and senior management learns some interesting things if they are lucky. Then they get back to work assuming that the information will seep into the organization through osmosis. It rarely does.

The survey process is no different from other competing tools in the business, and it should demonstrate a return on investment. We have documented a link between both return on assets and return on investment, on the one hand, and effective use of surveys and people measures, on the other (Morgan & Schiemann, 1999). For example, organizations in which executives say that their employee surveys provide information that is valuable in guiding decision making have achieved a 65 percent higher return on investment over a five-year period. Survey cost can easily be computed by totaling the hard costs such as survey processing and consulting assistance, dedicated staff time, and the indirect costs of managers and employees throughout the survey process. But the benefits are rarely tracked as part of the process. Part of the reason is the traditional focus on employee satisfaction and a failure to connect satisfaction to business outcomes. But even surveys that have primarily focused on employee satisfaction and a positive work climate have shown impressive results. In recent research reported by Feuss, Harmon, Wirtenberg, and Wides (2004) and Kowalski (2004), the researchers found that a small improvement in work climate and employee satisfaction resulted in substantial financial impact on the cost of patient care and claim processing.

When surveys are based on more direct people drivers and business results, it should be even easier to estimate the value of improvements. For example, changes in certain people drivers will result in improved retention of high performers, higher customer buying or retention, or faster cycle times. If the organization has good measures of these business outcomes, it should be able to estimate the return on investment in the people drivers.

Finally, we have observed that the best practice organizations do not allow these plans to sit. They often incorporate the action planning evaluation into impact reviews in which they evaluate the subsequent changes to key milestones or indicators on a regular basis. Some firms have instituted quarterly surveys that track a limited number of marker items from a baseline survey—either key tracking items or ones that were targeted for high-priority action. These surveys provide timely feedback that enables the plan owners to either declare victory or quickly adjust their plan and execution of those plans to achieve more effective results. Others, who do not conduct pulse surveys with such frequency, look for other indicators of performance improvement. These may be surrogate indicators that would be expected to move if the fixes are working. For example, low scores on customer focus that triggered efforts to give more time and attention to customers would be expected to improve customer satisfaction, retention, or buying behavior. Actions in response to low diversity ratings would be expected to reduce complaints or filed actions by minorities or protected classes. The key is looking for the best available indicators that real change has occurred.

Best Practices

In the end, these are the defining characteristics of a strategic survey:

- The surveys focus on the people issues that make the greatest difference in business performance.
- These issues are defined through dialogue with senior leadership that focuses on the answers to three key questions:

What are the most important business goals for your organization to achieve?

What people results are critical for the organization if it is to achieve these goals?

What people drivers have an impact on performance on these people results?

- Development of content is guided by inquiry into three areas that together constitute people equity: alignment, capabilities, and engagement.
- The survey itself is of moderate length—long enough to provide adequate coverage of the issues but not so long that it either overloads respondents or overburdens those tasked with translating the findings into action.
- Results are analyzed to highlight pockets of strength and concern across the organization in terms of alignment, capabilities, engagement, and related drivers, with a focus on improving overall performance and identifying and reducing variation across units by making improvement in poor-performing units.
- Survey findings are linked to business outcome measures to test senior management's business model and identify key performance gaps for action.
- Priorities are set so that action is focused on a limited number of strategic people issues.
- Action is driven from the top down, with results cascaded to the workforce so that solutions can be developed quickly.
- Managers are provided with the requisite skills for conducting strategic action planning sessions as well as defining and implementing specific actions.
- Implementation is a highly visible activity and is monitored at all levels.
- The impact of action implementation on key strategic indicators is monitored, measured, and documented within one to two quarters of implementation.

The key is to understand the critical impact of people management on achievement of business objectives, focus measurement on the people issues that have the greatest impact on business results, and focus action on the critical few issues that will generate the greatest benefit to the organization's key stakeholders, including shareholders, customers, managers, and employees.

References

Feuss, W. J., Harmon, J., Wirtenberg, J., & Wides, J. W. (2004, Jan.–Feb.). Linking employees, customers, and financial performance in organizations. *Cost Management, 19*(2), 12–22.

Heskett, J. L., Sasser, W. E., & Schlesinger, L. A. (1997). *The service profit chain: How leading companies link profit and growth to loyalty, satisfaction, and value.* New York: Free Press.

Higgs, A., & Ashworth, S. (1996). Organizational surveys: Tools for assessment and research. In A. I. Kraut (Ed.), *Organizational surveys: Tools for assessment and change* (pp. 88–114). San Francisco: Jossey-Bass.

Kaplan, R., & Norton, D. (2004). *Strategy maps: Converting intangible assets into tangible outcomes.* Boston: Harvard Business School Press, 2004.

Kowalski, R. (2004, Apr.). *Employee satisfaction, customer satisfaction, and the bottom line.* Paper presented to the Nineteenth Annual Conference, Society for Industrial and Organizational Psychology, Chicago.

Morgan, B., & Schiemann, W. (1999, Jan.). Measuring people and performance: Closing the gaps. *Quality Progress,* (pp. 47–53).

Rucci, A., Kirn, S., & Quinn, R. (1998, Jan.–Feb.). The employee-customer-profit chain at Sears. *Harvard Business Review,* 82–97.

Rust, R. T., Zeithaml, V. A., & Lemon, K. N. (2000). *Driving customer equity: How customer lifetime value is reshaping corporate strategy,* New York: Free Press.

Schiemann, W. A. (1992). Organizational change: Lessons from a turnaround. *Management Review, 81*(4), 34–37.

Schiemann, W. A. (1996). Driving change through surveys: Aligning employees, customers and other key stakeholders. In A. I. Kraut (Ed.), *Organizational surveys: Tools for assessment and change* (pp. 88–114). San Francisco: Jossey-Bass.

Schiemann, W. A., & Lingle, J. H. (1999). *Bullseye! Hitting Your Strategic Targets Through High-Impact Measurement.* New York: Free Press.

Schiemann, W. A., & Morgan, B. S. (1984). *Supervision in the 80s: Trends in corporate America.* Princeton, NJ: Opinion Research Corporation.

Wiley, J. W. (1996). Linking survey results to customer satisfaction and business performance. In A. I. Kraut (Ed.), *Organizational surveys: Tools for assessment and change* (pp. 330–333). San Francisco: Jossey-Bass.

CHAPTER 5

The Importance of Taking Action, Not Just Sharing Survey Feedback

Allan H. Church
David H. Oliver

1. Feedback is a gift.
2. Taking action from that feedback is what makes the difference.
3. Letting employees know exactly what actions were taken and why closes the loop.

These concepts are simple enough. However, it is often disconcerting to survey practitioners when they realize that their leaders and managers do not fully understand or model these concepts when it comes to taking action from their own organizational survey efforts.

The purpose of this chapter is to demonstrate the critical importance and impact of taking action from organizational survey results. After an overview of the factors driving increased attention on survey action planning, the chapter focuses on the results of an applied research study conducted at a multinational consumer products company that clearly demonstrates the linkages between actions taken by managers and the resulting changes in employee attitudes and business outcomes over time. Implications of these applied findings for survey practitioners and recommendations for driving action planning execution are discussed.

Before moving forward, it is important to underscore the difference between the role of the senior leader and manager in the survey action planning process. Throughout this chapter, we often refer to senior leaders and managers as having separate roles and accountabilities in driving positive change from survey results. The point is to distinguish between roles in situations (usually in larger organizations) where senior leaders such as executives need to sponsor a given survey program and drive accountability regarding the importance of taking action, while midlevel managers typically assume the internal execution (or client) role and become the actual face of the survey to their employees at local levels. In smaller organizations, the leader and manager roles are likely to be one and the same individual. In either case, both roles need to be filled effectively to ensure a successful outcome.

Survey Program Assumptions

Many senior leaders and managers suffer from two flawed assumptions regarding survey efforts. First, they sometimes assume that simply conducting the survey itself is the change intervention (Church & Waclawski, 2001)—that somehow employees will become spontaneously more positive over time simply by asking them about their attitudes and behaviors.

Alternatively, they want to get a read on the organizational issues for their senior team without considering the impact of not sharing results and taking action from them on the broader employee base. However, it is quite possible that just surveying employees and doing nothing at all with the results may actually lead to more negative responses over time: expectations are raised, but no action is taken or changes made.

As survey practitioners, an important point to remember is that by conducting a survey, we are entering into a social contract where expectations are generated on the part of employees that management cares about their issues and is willing to do something about them. Moreover, this contract regarding taking action exists whether the organization in question has 400,000 employees across the globe or 20 employees in a single location. While the process and depth (in the system) of driving a feedback and action planning process may differ based on a combination of resources, experience, readiness for change, and prior exposure to other change efforts (Church & Waclawski, 2001), nonetheless, *some form of action and accountability* must be ensured in order to drive positive change. In addition, different organizations leverage different resource models to drive this type of process (some use dedicated organization development professionals, others use locally empowered human resource generalists working with line clients, and some drive this accountability directly through line managers). Although there is no one best approach, whatever the resource model applied, it is important that the appropriate training, tools, tool kits, and tracking mechanisms are implemented to ensure success.

The second flawed assumption in many survey efforts often shared by senior leaders and managers is that simply sharing the results with employees will automatically lead to improvements in scores over time. This could not be further from reality. Employees already have heightened expectations since they were asked their opinions on the survey, so sharing results increases those expectations (and it creates energy for change). When no action follows, employees are left waiting for something to happen. It is like grilling a steak, putting it on a plate, and then not eating it—unsatisfying, to say the least. In fact, many survey efforts fail for this very reason—results are presented at a town hall type of meeting and then the binder of data is put on the shelf or in a drawer, never to be reviewed again.

Often so much effort goes into administering the survey that little energy or appetite is left for action planning. While sharing results with the people who completed the survey is an important part of the contractual obligation of a survey effort (and the right thing to do from a consulting ethics perspective), the only way to drive improvements in organizational culture, managerial behavior, or workplace dynamics is to take concrete action with the survey results.

Leaders and managers need to identify an appropriate action plan and then execute that plan and make changes in how the organization functions. Failing to do so damages the survey process and survey practitioner and senior leader credibility, and it creates an employee base skeptical that future change will occur from surveys in general. Over time, it is likely that employee apathy toward the survey (and possibly the broader organization as well) will grow and participation rates will decline.

Unfortunately, and largely as a result of the assumption that simply asking the question is enough (which translates to a lack of action ever being taken), leaders and managers are often surprised at the lack of progress made in their scores over time. This also tends to make them even more cynical about the survey process in general. In some organizations, this trend can lead to the death or massive reduction of a corporate survey program. For example, this might result in a survey questionnaire being cut down to only ten to twenty key items (on the assumption that this is all we *really* need to know to track change) or a survey process being reduced to a focus on only a random sample of employees rather than a broader census model (on the assumption that the right sample can represent the action planning needs of all local populations). These decisions are not inherently wrong, but they can shift the purpose of the survey (from a focus on deep action planning to a focus on broader cultural trending, for example) and thereby limit the ability to take action from the survey in future administrations. While it is true that surveys have been a core tool for industrial/organizational (I/O) and organization development (OD) practitioners for decades (Kraut, 1996; Nadler, 1977), and one of the most powerful means we have for driving and measuring organizational change (Church & Waclawski, 2001), positive change can occur only if leaders and managers take action from the results they receive. Sharing results but taking no action will result in the same outcome as doing nothing at all.

The Shift to Taking Action

While some individuals may see our emphasis on taking action from an organizational survey as relatively new, particularly those who see surveys as primarily a tool for trending employee satisfaction levels over time, the concept of driving change from survey results has been around for decades. We can trace its roots to the original work of Kurt Lewin (1946) and his action research model, which heavily influenced the evolution of the field of OD. In fact, one of the fundamental tenets of OD is that data—whether from an organizational survey, 360-degree feedback instrument, set of focus groups or interviews, or a one-on-one assessment—are used to catalyze individual and organizational change (Waclawski & Church, 2002). From this perspective, all feedback is designed to allow an individual or group to unfreeze from their existing state of dissatisfaction, create the opportunity for movement by taking action to reach a desired future state, and finally refreeze that new state. This is why organizational surveys have been one of the primary tools OD practitioners use to drive large-scale systemic change initiatives (Burke, Coruzzi, & Church, 1996; Nadler, 1977). In the OD consulting model, taking action (termed the *intervention stage*) is a critical component to being successful in these efforts.

Despite these roots, not all survey practitioners or consultants have an OD background or a systemic model of organizational dynamics, and there is a real need in the field for greater consistency in practice (Church, 2001). Traditionally, many corporate survey programs have been led by individuals with other types of professional experiences, in I/O psychology, human resources (HR), or business administration. As a result, there has often been more of a focus on psychometrics, modeling trends over time, and providing data only to senior executives for their consideration rather than taking action at various levels, for example, with both senior leadership and managers at different plants or locations. Even organizations that are good at cascading results and distributing extensive action planning tool kits and templates are not always the best at following through to ensure that changes actually did occur. This trend is now shifting.

In general, the importance of taking action from organizational surveys has been receiving considerably more attention over the past decade in both professional conferences and practitioner publications (Church & Waclawski, 2001; Hinrichs, 1996; Kraut & Saari, 1999). Although the availability of new technology-enabled action planning tools and self-service analysis programs has clearly contributed to this trend by placing more power in the hands of the client, the increasing capability inherent in these tools themselves is the outcome, not the driving force behind this new emphasis on taking action.

There are three primary reasons that this shift in emphasis is occurring among both internal survey practitioners and survey consulting firms: (1) the changing role of the survey practitioner,

(2) the increasing popularity of pulse and other related ad hoc surveys, and (3) an overall enhanced focus on HR metrics.

Changing Role of the Survey Practitioner:

While organizational surveys have always played an important role in helping leaders and managers gain a better understanding of the thoughts, feelings, and interests of their employees, only in recent years has the emphasis shifted from conducting surveys for their own sake (for example, to monitor overall trends for senior leadership) to surveys designed specifically to deliver actionable insights at all levels of analysis—from plant manager to senior function heads or division leaders. Practitioners are using employee surveys more now than ever before to assess (and in some cases predict) individual behavior such as turnover intentions or manager quality, as well as to measure attitudes and attitude change.

A number of tactics are employed to drive actionable data-based insights from surveys—for example:

- Follow-up diagnostic questions and additional mini surveys in response to a specific item (for example, if the respondent responded negatively or neutrally) or series of items in succession that assess a specific type of pattern or attitude structure.
- Delivering reports down to each individual manager or group (given a certain cut-off level to protect anonymity) to drive unique accountability for action planning. This can also involve removing items and data from individual reports that are relevant only from an action planning perspective to more senior leaders or functional roles (for example, does each region need to know how its employees feel about the executive compensation or benefits programs when these might be centrally controlled from a corporate group anyway?).
- Including items that are of particular interest to action planning for the company CEO, even if they are of less interest to other groups in the organization (for example, because they are not in action planning scope for local units).
- Providing a section specifically focused on managerial behavior so managers receive direct, actionable feedback. For example, a company might take items from its 360-degree feedback

process and include those same behavioral questions on the organizational survey. This would help ensure that consistent company messages are being conveyed regarding manager quality and leadership excellence and would serve as another means for assessing and action planning against individual behaviors.

• Using paired comparisons (say, year to year) and various types of assignment tools and ranking formats (for example, lists of the Top 10 and Bottom 10) to help drive prioritization of issues and concerns at the time of survey completion.

• Linking data to other types of measures (for example, performance management ratings, prior 360-degree feedback results, talent management data) and profiling specific groups of employees (for example, high-potential employees with three to five years of tenure or retention risks) so that targeted interventions can be developed.

• Incorporating items that allow external benchmarking with other highly reputed or perhaps directly competitive companies to get a broader perspective on the issues being raised (Johnson, 1996).

• Including questions in the survey regarding whether a manager shared results and took action based on a prior survey (and asking, "If not, why not?").

While the method of reporting survey results (and showing ways of prioritizing results and issues) is clearly a critical component to ensuring an effective action planning process, determining the appropriateness of a specific report format is more directly tied to other factors. Some of these include the level and sophistication of the end user who has to do the action planning (for example, front-line managers may have different skill sets in reading and interpreting data compared with senior executives), prior survey experience, HR or OD resource capability to provide analytical and interpretive support, and the organization's culture (Church & Waclawski, 2001). For example, an organization with a culture heavily influenced by scientists and engineers will want very different types of statistics and report formats from a company that is less focused on data and looking for a "one-page solution." Solving the reporting question is really more about knowing the client than any general rule of thumb.

Much of this change in focus is the result of a parallel shift in the role of the survey practitioner from one of content expert to one of change agent (Church & Waclawski, 2001). For example, many corporate survey programs are now being used to drive organizational change using internal and external consulting efforts. No longer content with focusing primarily on execution (such as achieving high levels of participation rates or avoiding double-barreled items at all costs—though that is still good practice), more and more survey practitioners are being asked to behave like consultants: produce tangible outcomes from the results of their surveys (Kraut & Saari, 1999) and demonstrate the linkages to business outcomes and key performance indicators.

Although being able to tell a compelling story based on data-based insights is still a critical skill to have, it is important to remember that the story itself does not lead to tangible outcomes. The next step in the OD model is working with the clients to help them focus on the interventions or actions that need to be taken. In this regard, consulting skills are increasingly needed to help the client determine the best set of follow-up actions and go about implementing these to drive positive change. As survey practitioners begin to leverage these skills, either internally or through external consultants, this emphasis reinforces the importance of taking action from the survey results.

Increasing Popularity of Pulse and Ad Hoc Surveys

There has never been an absence of poorly executed surveys with badly worded items and unbalanced scales, but the rise of the ubiquitous pulse survey has introduced a new sense of urgency regarding taking action from surveys among some practitioners. While large-scale surveys focus on the overall health of an organization, pulse surveys are meant to be short, more focused efforts on a particular topic and usually administered online (for more, see Chapter Eleven, this volume). They are typically inexpensive surveys, often conducted on a sample of the population, and, perhaps not surprising given the Internet, can be created and distributed by anyone—even line managers with little or no survey expertise. A quick scan of the Internet will generate a large list of online survey tools (see Table 5.1 for a sample list). Of course, anyone can use these same tools to create their own one-off or ad hoc surveys as well, which can easily suffer from the same issues.

Table 5.1. Sampling of Online Survey Tool Products

CoolSurveys
EZSurvey
InfoPoll
Inquisite
PollPro
SurveyGold
SurveyMonkey
SurveySage
SurveySaid
SurveySite
SurveyView
Zoomerang

Note: This listing does not imply endorsement of any particular product or service. We strongly recommend a thorough review of each product before making a purchasing decision.

While empowerment is generally a good thing and an inherent OD value, having a plant manager create and administer his or her own survey is like having an I/O psychologist create and manufacture his or her own new line of potato chips. Unfortunately, the pulse survey trend has resulted in more and more organizations seeing a rise in one-off surveys that are poorly designed (for example, with items that are not actionable) and implemented, with no real outcomes or actions being generated from the results. Furthermore, although there are some crude analysis tools included with many of these tools, the action planning support (from a consultant, HR generalist, or OD practitioner, for example) and the importance of accountability for actually doing something effective with the results are typically lacking in these smaller efforts. In fact, in some cases, we have seen pulse and ad hoc surveys conducted where the HR function was never even involved—until the survey created an issue resulting in litigation. That is not the kind of action planning any organization wants.

Pulse surveys and many related ad hoc surveys are typically created and administered online, which allows respondent confidentiality to be compromised (due to the combination of Internet tracking ability and the lack of understanding of the differences between confidentiality versus anonymity by many nonsurvey experts). Many of these surveys are done using employee samples, which tends to prohibit local action planning in small departments, functions, or locations. While the data might be fine for trending, local action planning could be compromised. Finally, these types of surveys are so easy to create and administer online that they can easily be overused or even, as we have seen, conducted during the primary survey administration, increasing response burden, confusing participants (for example, "Didn't we just complete that survey?"), and driving participation rates down over time.

In the end, it takes only two or three ineffective surveys to damage the credibility of more serious action-oriented programs. While pulse surveys and many ad hoc surveys can be used as effective tools in the hands of a survey practitioner (see Chapter Eleven), they can cause considerable damage to broader, more action-focused survey programs as well. Their ease and availability make taking action even more important for survey practitioners. In other words, the survey practitioner needs to differentiate his or her survey effort by designing and executing surveys that lead to positive organizational change or else run the risk of being labeled "just another survey" or "check the box" activity.

Enhanced Focus on HR Metrics

The third and final factor driving an increased focus on taking action from organizational survey efforts concerns the increasing focus on measuring and quantifying all aspects of the HR function. As Hronec predicted years ago (1993), we are increasingly focused on using information (that is, metrics) as our "vital signs" in both driving and evaluating interventions. In fact, surveys do provide the organization with a certain type of internal metrics (and can provide diagnostics on themselves by asking questions about prior survey-related actions taken or optimism regarding the current administration). However, many leaders and managers think of surveys as providing only soft data that are less important than hard metrics based on business performance. Ignoring such soft data from surveys can have significant consequences, such as when employees start leaving for jobs with other companies because of their attitudes about the current organization or its senior leadership.

Nevertheless, it is a business reality that we sometimes need to justify why we do surveys, and taking action from a survey to drive positive change is one such means of providing that justification. If we can point to specific actions taken in an effort to improve employee satisfaction or commitment, we are demonstrating the power of that tool to employees as well as to leaders and managers. Better yet, if we link the results of these actions to actual positive outcomes, we have demonstrated the power, relevance, time, and resource commitment needed for action planning. This is why applied research studies that link various interventions to specific outcomes (Rucci, Kirn, & Quinn, 1998) are so popular among practitioners. Although historically not a core competency of many organizational practitioners (including those in OD), the ability to demonstrate the impact of a change effort on the business, such as reducing turnover, increasing sales or market share, or improving productivity, is receiving increasing attention in actual practice, and managers are being asked more and more frequently to justify their investments in OD, HR development, and various related training interventions (Cummings & Worley, 1997; Ulrich, 1997).

While external consultants are quite familiar with pricing their intellectual property, tracking time, cost structures, deliverables, and demonstrating (or at least attempting to demonstrate) value based on their goods and services, justifying internal HR processes and programs is still a relatively painful process for many organizations, particularly those with large-scale efforts or large internal consulting functions. As with any other function, large survey programs are fair game when it comes to identifying costs and measures related to return on investment. Consider, for example, a global survey conducted in an organization where access to the majority of employees still requires large amounts of paper and optical scan forms in multiple languages. Compound that with multiple versions of the survey content (due to different sets of supplemental items for each division or country, for example), and it is clear this is likely to be an expensive, complicated effort. In this situation, a lack of action orientation from either senior leaders or the HR function would probably result in the dismantling of the entire survey agenda.

However, if the expectation is such that leaders and managers will be held directly accountable through their performance management system for sharing their results with employees, building detailed action plans, and taking action on those plans, then the effort is worth pursuing and has real teeth. Or more optimistically, if managers can be convinced (with data) that acting on survey feedback is in their best interest—that it leads to improved employee satisfaction and team performance—then they may be more inclined to act on the results. One important note that should be made, however, is that taking accountability for survey results too far, perhaps by building in a specific percentage point increase target in favorability on the next survey into a detailed performance objective, can also lead to problems, such as managers' gaming the survey system to get the results they want. This is not the type of change in attitudes or survey ratings that we want to be driving as organizational survey practitioners. Rather, the accountability and measurement process should be around sharing results and the actions that were taken to drive improvement.

Nonetheless, as with most other change efforts, the challenge is in training, encouraging, and ultimately incenting individual leaders and managers to see the need inherent in their results and then do something about it (whether individually or through action planning teams). Ultimately if people do not take action from surveys, surveys will cease to exist in that social system as a powerful tool for change.

The Impact of Action Planning: A Research Study

Many survey practitioners are familiar with senior organizational leaders asking for bottom-line justifications for their programs. In today's competitive business environment, large-scale survey programs are expected to provide more than a pulse of employees' perception of the organization. They are expected to be instruments for driving positive organizational change across a wide range of levels and fronts. The most effective action planning programs are those where multiple layers of action are being taken (for example, by senior leaders, functional leaders, and local line managers) in an integrated manner. It also helps to have a culture and performance management process that support and drive the notion of taking action. The following case study describes our effort to demonstrate to the organization through applied linkage research that acting on survey results is a catalyst for positive change at the local level and for the organization as a whole.

Overview of the Company and the Survey Program

The company is a large, multinational consumer products company with over 140,000 employees worldwide, spanning several divisions and a corporate office. The company operates in a competitive environment, and its corporate goals are focused on driving growth, innovation, and ensuring high integrity. Over a ten-year period, the company's survey program has evolved from smaller surveys, administered periodically and driven from the department or division level, to a comprehensive, corporate-driven survey program that is administered every other year. This more centralized survey approach is aligned with other change initiatives (including a renewed focus on employer branding or marketing the company's employment offer, new corporate values, increased cross-divisional career development, and more and better talent management tools) and represents a shift in strategic focus from being largely a holding company of distinct divisions to a company with a shared corporate identity.

Today the survey program is well established as one of the core HR processes, with dedicated staff in each division supporting the effort. The survey is sent to every employee, and participation rates are extremely strong (about 80 percent overall). Survey results are distributed in a top-down fashion, with action planning efforts driven at both local levels (for example, down to individual supervisors in plants with six or more respondents) and among senior functional and business leaders, including a complete organization CEO review. Individual line managers are often held accountable for their groups' survey results, as well as for taking action from the survey results through an independent "People Results" rating in the annual performance management process. In short, performance evaluation is based on both business results—driving the business forward—and people results—improving organizational health in a given department, group, region, or function.

The primary purpose of the company's organizational survey is to help teams understand their issues, work together to develop and implement action plans, and make real improvements in employee opinions. It is also designed to help senior management understand broader opportunity areas in the culture and take action against larger organizational issues, such as setting broader agendas; implementing new tools, policies, and programs; or making changes in systems or structures.

The content of the survey is organized based on a relatively straightforward internally developed conceptual model (see Figure 5.1), which links perceptions in five major areas (company, manager quality, work environment, job and career, and compensation & benefits) to the two critical outcomes of overall satisfaction and commitment (defined as turnover intentions).

Figure 5.1. Sample Organizational Survey Model

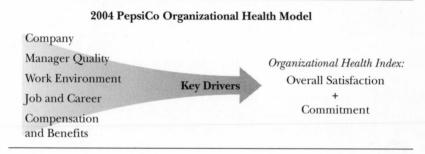

2004 PepsiCo Organizational Health Model

Company
Manager Quality
Work Environment   **Key Drivers**
Job and Career
Compensation
and Benefits

Organizational Health Index:
Overall Satisfaction
+
Commitment

By administering the same core set of items and using a conceptual model for framing the survey content, managers are able to quickly absorb the results (Church & Waclawski, 2001; Kraut & Saari, 1999), as well as track perceptions over time. Through the evolution of the survey program, this core HR process has become a powerful and integrated tool for learning about strengths and opportunity areas throughout the organization, and driving organizational change over time.

A critical component of any successful survey program is strong commitment throughout the organization for the survey itself and for taking action from the survey results. Just as poor action planning can damage a survey's credibility, poor execution during administration can as well. Support for the entire survey process must start at the top with senior leadership visibility. Managers throughout the organization must see the importance of acting on results and be held accountable through formal reward and recognition mechanisms. In the case presented here, these needs are compounded by the fact that there are literally thousands of local sites responsible for action planning, which makes it difficult to monitor and enforce action planning efforts. Instead, the survey practitioners have to ensure that the organization supports the survey process and understands that subsequent action is required to lead to positive change. Then they rely on the organization's HR generalists, OD practitioners, and in some cases the local line managers to see it through to the end.

Purpose of the Study

Although the survey program in question is well supported, it is always helpful to have additional ammunition to drive the action planning process. To this end, the goals of this research were really twofold. The obvious and primary goal was to justify the value of the survey to senior leaders as an effective tool for driving organizational change. By linking the survey results to key organizational outcomes, the intention was to demonstrate to senior management that taking action from the survey results was making an impact on employee perceptions and attitudes, as well as the bottom line of the organization.

The second goal was to provide new insights and leverage the results of the research through internal communications to continue to encourage local managers and their HR generalists to recognize that the action planning process is critical to their change efforts. As most survey practitioners know, in a busy and highly complex work environment, getting managers even to share their survey results with employees takes effort. Getting them to actually act on the results is a significantly bigger challenge. By providing a data-driven story to internal clients demonstrating that leaders and managers who took action against their surveys' results made a significant impact on employee opinions and the working environment over time, other managers would be more likely to act on their results as well.

With these two goals in mind, research was conducted to model the value of sharing results and taking action against opportunity areas. The focus was on how the survey results and, more important, the actions that followed from these survey results were instrumental in driving organizational change across the business.

Methodology

For many years, this organization had included two key questions in its survey related to sharing results and taking action. During each survey administration, respondents were asked the following two key questions:

"Results from our last company survey were reviewed with my work group/location." The choices for answers were yes, no, don't know, and not applicable (for example, "I was not here for prior survey").

"Based on these results, my work group/location has taken action on our opportunity areas." The choices for answers were yes, no, and don't know.

These two questions afforded the ability to classify respondents into one of four groups:

- Results were shared, and action was taken.
- Results were shared, but action was not taken.
- Results were not shared, and no action was taken.
- Results were not shared, but action was taken.

These two questions (and the four resulting groupings) have provided internal practitioners the ability to explore several important questions related to the value of this survey program. Three key questions were explored:

1. *Are satisfaction scores higher for locations that report that the previous years' results were shared and acted on?* The research effort started by showing that locations that shared results and acted on opportunity areas also had higher satisfaction scores. Since these data were collected in the same survey administration and therefore had obvious methodological concerns, they were also looked at from two different survey administrations.

2. *Are satisfaction scores higher for locations when the prior year's survey results showed that results were shared and acted on?* Here, the data used were from two separate survey administrations to show that sharing

results and acting on opportunity areas led to greater improvements over time. In other words, those who shared results and took action had a greater impact overall on employee satisfaction than if they just shared results or did nothing at all. Those results were well received, but senior management wanted more proof that the survey efforts were good for the bottom line of the organization.

3. *Is there a link between higher satisfaction scores and important bottom-line outcomes?* For this question, the researchers sought out standard business metrics, including local turnover numbers, lost time by employees, and number of plant-related safety incidents, that are tracked and used at the front line. These outcome measures were compared with action planning efforts to show that taking action from survey results in impacts on the bottom line.

Results

Next we will discuss the key findings and implications for each of our three research questions based on our analyses.

Question 1: Relationship of Satisfaction and Taking Action

After grouping locations based on average responses into one of the four categories described above, the researchers looked at differences in overall employee satisfaction scores for each of the four groups. The results are shown in Table 5.2.

Table 5.2. Impact of Survey Action Planning Outcomes on Employee Satisfaction (Percentage Favorable)

		Took Action from the Organizational Survey	
		No	Yes
Reviewed Survey Results with Employees	Yes	51%	78%
	No	51%	71%

The locations (or business units, functions, or divisions) that shared results *and* took action had the highest average percentage favorable scores (78 percent favorable). In locations where employees said that action was taken but results were *not* shared, satisfaction scores were 71 percent favorable. This category assumes, of course, that employees did not see the data but understood that some action was taken based on the survey data (for example, a change could have been implemented and tied back to feedback from the survey).

Consistent with overall expectations, employees who said that results were not shared with them and that nothing happened from the survey (no action taken and nothing whatsoever was done) were much lower in overall satisfaction, at 51 percent favorable. Even more interesting was the finding that employees who said that the survey results were shared with them but action was not taken reported equally low satisfaction scores (also 51 percent favorable and 27 percentage points lower than employees who said results were acted on). In short, the groups that took action based on their survey results were substantially more positive in their satisfaction overall than those that did not. (Of course, it should be noted here that communication is critical: employees must realize that the actions taken were the result of feedback from the survey; otherwise, they are unlikely to tie the actions to feedback from the survey.) Furthermore, just sharing survey results with employees but taking no action yielded absolutely no difference in satisfaction from those who said their manager, group, or function did nothing at all. These results alone truly highlight the importance and significance of taking action from survey data.

As might be expected, this trend in group scores and overall favorability was consistent across all the major dimensions of the organizational survey model (see Figure 5.2). The areas that are likely more influenced from a local level (such as recognition and manager quality) showed greater differentiation by groups reporting that action was or was not taken. However, areas less affected by local practices (for example, regarding company strategy) were relatively stable regardless of the level of action planning activity. This differentiation in results suggests that the action planning set of questions noted above is not simply a substitute for overall satisfaction levels but rather does relate to changes in employee attitudes across various dimensions of the survey.

**Figure 5.2. Differences in Various Dimensions
by Action Planning Group**

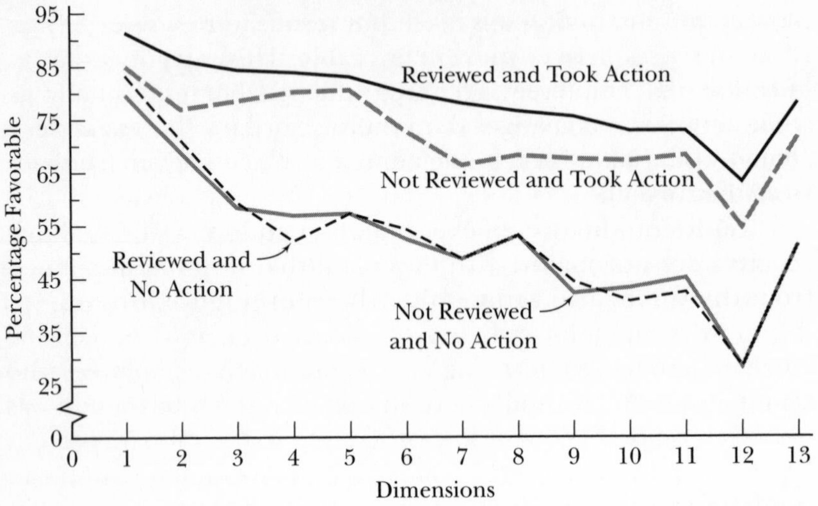

The findings from this stage of the study support the notions that taking action on survey opportunities has an impact on satisfaction scores and that doing nothing at all (or sharing results and doing nothing with them) is associated with lower satisfaction scores. In other words, sharing results is not enough. Managers must take action against survey results to have an impact on employee satisfaction. However, because the results (satisfaction scores and reports on whether action was taken) were from the same survey, methodologically it is difficult to claim causation.

Question 2: Changes in Satisfaction Scores over Time

Although the results from question 1 were intriguing, the researchers wanted to provide the organization with additional data-based proof that the organizational survey and action planning process that follows were truly creating improvement over time—not just linked to current levels of satisfaction. After all, although driving current satisfaction with the company is important, change in satisfaction scores over time is more compelling. If taking action from an organizational survey truly makes a difference, we should be able to see it in positive change scores over time among work groups that said they actually did something from the prior survey administration two years earlier.

To explore this question, the researchers went back to the historical files and matched data by individual business unit, location, function, and group (where intact groups of similar composition still existed), thus creating a longitudinal data set. This allowed them to compare change over multiple survey administrations to determine if taking action had an impact on subsequent survey results. Since some locations administered the survey in 1998 and 2000 and the other locations administered it in 1999 and 2000, the comparisons were either 1998 versus 2000 or 1999 versus 2000. In total, they were able to create approximately 850 matched sets of findings over time—about evenly split based on the timing of prior surveys across business units. Given the consistency of the results from question 1, the data set for this analysis was narrowed to only two groups: those that took action and those that did nothing.

Consistent with expectations, locations where the majority of employees said that they took action from the prior survey effort were significantly more likely to see their survey results improve over time (see Figure 5.3). Furthermore, the groups with a two-year window between administrations yielded stronger correlations in change scores on overall satisfaction than did those with only one year to plan and take action from their results ($r = .32$ versus $.24$).

**Figure 5.3. Impact on Taking
Action from Survey Data on Change over Time:
Relationship Between Change in Satisfaction and Taking Action**

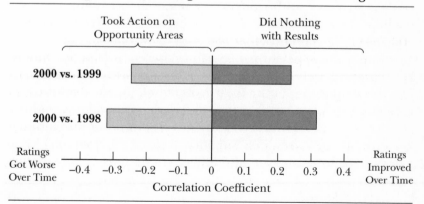

One possible explanation is that the locations with a two-year window had more time for action planning to take place and improvements to be made. Relatedly, locations whose employees indicated that they did not take action from their prior results saw a decrease in overall satisfaction scores over time.

Although the strength of the correlations in change scores is not where many survey practitioners would like to see, it does at least suggest that about 10 percent of the variance in scores swinging more positively or negatively over time is tied to employee perceptions of whether something was done with their prior survey effort. Considering all of the other potential factors that can influence survey results at any given time (for example, external conditions, timing or reward and recognition cycles, changes in leadership, or structural moves downsizing activity), this relationship speaks to the viability and potential impact of taking action from survey results. The results also provided data to reinforce to local managers that taking action leads to positive changes in employee opinions over time.

Question 3: Business Impact of Satisfaction Scores

Although the previous findings were meaningful and certainly supported the overall survey agenda, one question remained unanswered. In the classic tradition of linkage research and in an effort to truly catch the attention of the organization to drive local action planning efforts, the next question was whether one could link taking action to hard bottom-line metrics. To this end, the final phase of the research was to go deep with the analysis into a single division of the organization that had relatively stable performance metrics and structure at the time so the researchers could investigate the impact of taking action there. In this case, this division had several key business metrics that were well known throughout the organization. These performance standards were part of an existing HR scorecard. Leveraging these data, the researchers were able to link three outcomes at the local group level: (1) incident rates of accidents on the job, (2) lost time in days due to accidents, and (3) actual turnover. The research also looked at turnover intentions, a key variable measured in many surveys since the dot-coms. (For more on turnover and survey findings, see Chapter Nineteen, this volume.)

First, the focus was on investigating the relationship between taking action and three key metrics: accidents, safety violations, and lost time days. Locations where the majority of employees (based on the average response for that location) reported they took action against survey results had incident rates that were 50 percent lower than locations that did not take action. Not surprisingly as a result, locations that took action also had 48 percent fewer lost time days due to accidents. (Questions around facility safety, safety training, and managers' role modeling of safe behaviors are a significant component of the survey.) These results were compelling because they have a real financial impact for the organization.

Next, the researchers focused on employee turnover. Turnover intentions have been used as a type of leading indicator of the percentage of employees likely to leave the organization. Although there is limited research indicating the exact percentage of employees who actually follow through with their stated intentions, some external research combined with internal estimates suggests that approximately 50 percent of employees who "say they want to leave" the organization eventually do leave for another opportunity. Following this analysis, the researchers learned that when no action was taken at a given location, turnover intentions as measured by the two items above were significantly higher. When no action was taken, employees were three times more likely than employees where action was taken (based on results to the specific survey question noted above) to say they intended to leave the organization within the next year (24 percent versus 8 percent). They were also nearly two and a half times more likely to say they intended to look for a job in the next year (28 percent versus 12 percent). Although this finding may reflect a common method variance issue given that employee perceptions were collected in the same survey (as may be the case in several of the initial findings regarding overall satisfaction as reported in question 1 of this research), it nevertheless sends a strong message to managers regarding the need to take action.

Finally, for those who might question the value of turnover intentions, the research also looked at true front-line turnover for the past year. In locations where the majority of employees said that action was not taken on their prior survey results, actual turnover was 31 percent higher than in those locations where employees said they took action. While causality is always difficult to determine in these types of efforts and there was no longitudinal information available on front-line turnover, this applied study does demonstrate that at a very basic level, locations where employees at least perceived that action was being taken (based on survey results where employees said that action had been taken) were less likely to leave or want to leave the organization. In short, the strong relationships between taking action and turnover are compelling arguments for managers to take action against their survey results—something no survey practitioner would argue against. For this organization, this was powerful enough to drive our ongoing process.

Overall Results

In summary, the findings from this applied internal study were clear:

- Managers and work groups that review results and take action against their opportunity areas are more likely to see positive changes in employee opinions and attitudes at their locations.
- Managers and work groups that simply review results and do nothing else will probably be just as ineffective as those that do nothing at all.

Whether anyone can definitively prove that these effects are directly linked to taking action or due to other potential moderating factors (such as the overall quality of the manager in question, which probably is a related variable—that is, better managers are probably more proactive about acting on their survey results), they do clearly make an important statement. The results of this study provide a compelling argument for all managers that an organizational survey is a valuable tool for driving organizational change—as long as employees perceive that managers act on the results.

In the end, these findings reinforced the organization's strategic agenda, the organizational survey, and the value of the action planning process to drive improvement. In addition, results from the next survey showed the same pattern of findings with even larger differences. Overall satisfaction levels for employees who said results were shared and action taken was at a high of 80 percent favorable overall; those who only shared data or did nothing at all were both at only 42 percent favorable.

Whether due to survey practitioners' efforts to focus the organization on taking action or not, two years later there is also evidence that employee optimism for positive change occurring as a result of our organizational health survey process (based on another new survey item asked of employees) has significantly increased an average of 11 percentage favorable points across the entire organization worldwide. And as might be expected, the favorability of this item also shifts depending on whether employees perceived if action was taken from the survey two years ago.

Recommendations for Taking Action in Practice

Although the importance of taking action from an organizational survey should now be quite clear (from both a philosophical and an applied data-based perspective), and many of the other chapters in this book focus on different aspects of this process in greater depth than we can address in the remaining space here, we did want to end this chapter with some additional practitioner-focused suggestions for helping leaders and managers do something with their survey results.

In general, these fall into three major categories, from the more strategic to quite tactical in nature (Church & Waclawski, 2004):

- Framing—by providing connectivity between the organization, the business, the survey effort, and the HR processes
- Linking—by building metrics and systems that allow preferences, attitudes, behaviors, and outcomes to be linked together so that relationships among them can be identified
- Designing—by developing flexible interventions, options, and arrangements to meet the differential needs and concerns of specific groups of employees that are critical to the success of the business: high potentials, diverse talent, new employees, and experienced professionals in highly technical jobs, for instance

Framing

The first recommendation is to ensure that the entire organizational survey process is well framed for employees. This involves several different components. First, all communications, tools, templates, and other aspects of the action planning process, as well as leader and manager behaviors, should clearly demonstrate the importance of taking action from the survey—including how accountability for this outcome is linked to other internal reward and recognition systems. This includes holding individuals accountable for taking action (not necessarily improving individual item scores per se) from an organizational survey through integration using various people processes such as a performance management process.

Second, framing involves ensuring that employees understand how the survey is organized and the content structured in a way that supports interpretation of the results and the strategic direction of the business. While we have used our own internal model to drive this message, other more strategic survey efforts have used a host of different models, including the Burke-Litwin model (for more examples, see Burke et al., 1996; Waclawski & Church, 2002; and Kraut & Saari, 1999).

Finally, the last aspect of framing involves ensuring that employees receive communications from multiple media that describe what activity (such as roles and responsibilities) to expect from their leaders and managers, what actions they or their action planning teams have planned, and, later, what changes were ultimately made from an organizational survey effort. Remember that even if action was taken from a survey, if employees do not perceive that any positive changes were made, they are less likely to be positive or optimistic in the future regarding the survey process.

Although there are many ways to do this, we have seen such tactics as companywide brochures describing various key findings and changes being made to address them, delivering results and obtaining suggestions through online interactive presentations, and formally distributing action plans and conducting short follow-up surveys in between broader organizational survey administration windows. These approaches are effective means for determining if managers have actually taken action. The last is a particularly effective means for communicating and driving the importance of taking action as results from this type of action planning check-up survey. This type of pulse or ad hoc survey can be used as an input into determining a manager's performance results for the year. As always, the things that managers are held accountable for are the things that get done.

Linking

The second recommendation involves linking various data sources across different types of processes and outcomes. Although this notion has been raised earlier here and is discussed in greater detail elsewhere in this book (see Chapters Two, Three, Four, and Seven), the importance of using linkage analyses to demonstrate the impact of survey efforts and changes in employee attitudes and behaviors on hard organizational outcomes cannot be overstated. This is the reason behind our survey action planning research as well many other studies that attempt to connect various I/O and OD interventions to tangible performance metrics. Although these types of linkage efforts are often difficult to research due to shifting structures and performance cycles, identifying appropriate levels of unique identifiers and external forces, and isolating the center of causality for a given set of scores, the payoff when they do work is significant for many types of internal change efforts, including survey processes.

This is one of several ways in which HR professionals, including, but not limited to, I/O and OD practitioners, can demonstrate their ability to add value to the business besides the standard execution of HR processes—that is, by providing unique data-based insights. This is why some practitioners have placed a premium on the ability to tell a compelling story from data as a core skill set for all organizational practitioners (Waclawski & Church, 2002) and why this ability is included in the most recent HR functional competency model in use across PepsiCo (Church & Herena, 2003). The other way in which linkage research proves useful is in allowing specific groups of individuals to be identified (with the help of an external vendor in order to protect the confidentiality of individual survey responses) so that their unique skills, attitudes and behaviors, and preferences can be profiled. This leads to the final area of recommendation, termed *designing*.

Designing

Designing involves making sure that survey action planning and the interventions that follow are targeted specifically at those groups that really need them. Clearly not all employees need or want the same set of changes (nor do all managers behave in the same way), which is why localized action planning is so important. Ensuring that broad-based policy and programmatic changes are taken from a survey at senior levels in the organization is critical for demonstrating organizational commitment to the effort. Still, in many instances, additional action steps may need to be taken at more strategic and targeted levels among specific groups. Some of these groups might include highly skilled professionals in critical functions (such as corporate tax) who, if they left the organization, would be extremely costly and difficult to replace. Similarly, there might be a need to focus efforts across functions and divisions on all front-line sales supervisors to help encourage more balance in their work-life efforts. Or perhaps newly minted M.B.A.s hired in marketing need much quicker career progression and support tools than do most other functions.

The best way to drive change effectively for a specific group is to identify and isolate their results, and then engage in the action planning process around their specific needs and preferences. For example, if we linked prior performance history (say, from performance management records) to perceptions of compensation fairness (say, from an organizational survey) to individual motivation-related behaviors (a 360-degree measure), we might find that future leaders are significantly more driven to excel when greater differentiation exists in their reward and recognition program. This insight would allow us to design our compensation plan accordingly.

Although there are many ways to get at these types of groups, some of the best approaches include the tactics noted earlier regarding advanced survey item methodology, which are typically technology driven, given their complexity of administration. For example, advanced item technology includes the immediate generation of new sets of items based on profiling sets of response patterns, providing diagnostic follow-up choices and write-ins following specific types of responses, or using conjoint item sets to force individuals to make choices among various combinations of item groupings (for an example of the latter regarding employment offer preferences, see the Corporate Leadership Council's report on its Compelling Offer Survey, 2002). Considering the value of these types of analyses, it should be clear that the ability to link various data sources together is critical to targeting survey interventions to a specific group of employees. In the end, by designing targeted action plans for specific groups of employees based on their unique needs, we are in a better position to make an important impact from our actions.

Conclusion

Every survey administered is a chance to take action from the results. As social scientists and survey professionals, we have a professional responsibility to ensure that the surveys we work on have content with these characteristics:

- Well grounded empirically
- Focused enough to be action oriented
- Relevant to both senior leaders and local line clients
- Integrated (linked) with other internal processes to ensure they can be true drivers of organizational change
- Created in such a way as to ensure sustainability and measurability over time
- Supported by an effective survey process and action planning strategy

Unfortunately, far too many organizations (whether from lack of interest, lack of skilled practitioners, lack of resources, a poor survey administration process, simply bad items, or a total lack of energy following an arduous administration process) engage in survey efforts only to shelve the results after the initial review. Given the rise of easy-to-use online, ad-hoc survey tools in the hands of people who have never been trained in how to write items or analyze data, this is unacceptable. As OD professionals and survey practitioners, we need to leverage our data-based skills to create insights for senior leaders and managers that will truly drive positive change in organizations. The primary goal of this chapter has been to engage leaders, managers, and practitioners in the importance of doing something with survey results and to demonstrate through our own applied research that taking action following an organizational survey can and does make a difference in a number of employee attitudes and business outcomes.

References

Burke, W. W., Coruzzi, C. A., & Church, A. H. (1996). The organizational survey as an intervention for change. In A. I. Kraut (Ed.), *Organizational surveys: Tools for assessment and change* (pp. 41–66). San Francisco: Jossey-Bass.

Church, A. H. (2001). The professionalization of organization development: The next step in an evolving field. In W. A. Passmore & R. W. Woodman (Eds.), *Research in organizational change and development, 13* (pp. 1–42). Greenwich CT: JAI Press.

Church, A. H., & Herena, M. R. (2003). The PepsiCo HR career framework: A data-driven approach to career development. *OD Practitioner, 35*(4), 27–33.

Church, A. H., & Waclawski, J. (2001). *Designing and using organizational surveys: A seven step process.* San Francisco: Jossey-Bass.

Corporate Leadership Council. (2002). *The Compelling Offer revisited: Changes in employee preferences across time.* Washington, DC: Corporate Leadership Council. www.corporateleadershipcouncil.com.

Cummings, T., & Worley, C. (1997). *Organization development and change* (6th ed.). St. Paul, MN: West.

Hinrichs, J. R. (1996). Feedback, action planning, and follow-through. In A. I. Kraut (Ed.), *Organizational surveys: Tools for assessment and change* (pp. 255–283). San Francisco: Jossey-Bass.

Hronec, S. M. (1993). *Vital signs: Using quality, time, and cost performance measurements to chart your company's future.* New York: AMACOM.

Johnson, R. H. (1996). Life in the consortium: The Mayflower Group. In A. I. Kraut (Ed.), *Organizational surveys: Tools for assessment and change* (pp. 285–309). San Francisco: Jossey-Bass.

Kraut, A. I. (Ed.). (1996), *Organizational surveys: Tools for assessment and change.* San Francisco: Jossey-Bass.

Kraut, A. I., & Saari, L. M. (1999). Organizational surveys: Coming of age for a new era. In A. I. Kraut & A. K. Korman (Eds.), *Evolving practices in human resource management: Responses to a changing world of work* (pp. 302–327). San Francisco: Jossey-Bass.

Lewin, K. (1946). Action research and minority problems. *Journal of Social Issues, 2,* 34–46.

Nadler, D. A. (1977). *Feedback and organization development: Using data-based methods.* Reading, MA: Addison-Wesley.

Rucci, A. J., Kirn, S. P., & Quinn, R. T. (1998). The employee-customer profit chain at Sears. *Harvard Business Review, 76*(1), 83–97.

Ulrich, D. (1997). *Human resource champions: The next agenda for adding value and delivering results.* Boston: Harvard Business School Press.

Waclawski, J., & Church, A. H. (Eds.). (2002). *Organization development: A data-driven approach to organizational change.* San Francisco: Jossey-Bass.

CHAPTER 6

Organizational Surveys as Leverage for Organization Development and Change

W. Warner Burke

When I was a doctoral student a long time ago at the University of Texas in Austin, I loved Southwest Conference football. Under Coach Darrell Royal, UT had some great teams. Vivid in my memory is sitting in the stadium on a sunny Saturday afternoon in October and, along with 75,000 other rabid fans, cheering the Longhorns to victory. As odd as it may sound, what also stands out in my memory was the urgent desire at half time to administer a questionnaire. Think about it: an N of 75,000!

This malady of mine continues to this day. But I am not alone. Industrial/organizational (I/O) psychologists are, after all, data-centric. We love questionnaires and analyzing all those data. Moreover, in the world of organization development and change (ODC), I have urged practitioners over the years to be data based. Any proposed action needs to be grounded in data provided by members of the organization. I am not alone with this admonition. Argyris (1970), for example, has been a prominent proponent of basing organizational interventions on valid data.

While by no means the only intervention that ODC practitioners today use, organizational surveys have nevertheless become a major tool for change work. We refer to this type of work, or an ODC intervention, as survey feedback. A critical component of ODC practice is not only to gather valid data but in this case to get these survey results back into the hands of organizational members (the respondents to the survey) as soon as possible. Why? To ensure that (1) the data are current (things change rapidly these days) and (2) action is taken—but action that is data-based.

The purpose of this chapter is to explain the importance of using surveys in ODC work, provide suggestions for how to use surveys as leverage for organization change, and include case examples of such use. But first, a little history is useful. What we now refer to as survey feedback is a significant and highly used method for diagnosis and intervention in ODC practice today. Where did this use of surveys as leverage for organization development and change originate, and how? Answering this question of origination will help us to see how the integration of early I/O psychology and ODC practice became such a natural outcome.

Origins of Survey Feedback

One of the first organizations (and maybe the first) to conduct organizational surveys was the Institute for Social Research (ISR) at the University of Michigan. Rensis Likert, the first director of the ISR, also started the Survey Research Center as part of the institute in 1946. At about the same time, Kurt Lewin founded the Research Center for Group Dynamics at MIT. With his untimely death in 1947, the center was moved to the University of Michigan later that year. These two centers initially constituted Likert's institute. The two primary thrusts of these centers, questionnaire surveys for organizational diagnosis and group dynamics, combined to give birth to the survey feedback method. As early as 1947, questionnaires were being used systematically to assess employee morale and attitudes in organizations.

One of the first of these studies, initiated and guided by Likert and conducted by Floyd Mann, was done with the Detroit Edison Company. From working on the problem of how best to use the survey data for organization improvement, the method we now know as survey feedback evolved. Mann (1957) was key to the development of this method. He noted that when a manager was given the survey results, any resulting improvement depended on what the manager did with the information. If the manager discussed the survey results with subordinates, particularly through group discussion, positive change typically occurred. If the manager did not share the survey results with subordinates, however, and failed to plan certain changes for improvement jointly with them, nothing happened—except perhaps an increase in employee frustration with the ambiguity of having answered a questionnaire and never hearing anything further.

Briefly, the survey feedback method involves, first, the survey—data collection by questionnaire to determine employees' perceptions of a variety of facilitators, most focusing on the management of the organization; and second, the feedback—results of the survey reported back systematically in summary form to all people who answered the questionnaire. *Systematically,* in this case, means that the feedback occurs in phases, starting with the top team of the organization and flowing downward according to the formal hierarchy and within functional units or teams. Mann referred to this flowing-downward process as the "interlocking chain of conferences."

The chief executive officer, the division general manager, or the bureau chief, depending on the organization or subunit surveyed, and his or her immediate group of subordinates receive and discuss feedback from the survey first. Next, the subordinates and their respective groups of immediate subordinates do the same, and so forth downward until all members of the organization who had been surveyed hear a summary of the survey and then participate in a discussion of the meaning of the data and the implications. Each functional unit of the organization receives general feedback concerning the overall organization and specific feedback regarding its particular group, and the boss and his or her subordinates then jointly plan action steps for improvement. Usually a consultant, either internal or external, meets with each of the groups to help with data analysis, a group discussion, and plans for improvement.

Since most organizations are structured hierarchically, following this procedure and process makes sense. For organizations that are not particularly hierarchical, more like a network, for example, the feedback process can begin almost anywhere, say, with a node or cell in the network.

In any case, this rather orderly and systematic way of understanding an organization from the standpoint of employee perceptions and processing this understanding back into the organization so that change can occur, with the help of an independent resource person, not only is a direct precursor to and root of organization development, but it is an integral part of many current ODC efforts today.

With this brief historical statement as background, let us move immediately to the present and begin outlining some important reasons for using organizational surveys, particularly in ODC practice.

Importance of Using Surveys in ODC Practice

I have over the years urged ODC practitioners to be data based. Often they are not, relying mostly on facilitation skills, process consultation, and off-site meetings as their tools of practice. While useful tools, they may be no more than using ODC techniques rather than really doing ODC. ODC means focusing one's efforts on the larger system and attempting to deal with the organization as a whole. Beckhard's original definition (1969) of organization development emphasized the larger system: "Organization development is an effort (1) planned, (2) organization-wide, and (3) managed from the top, to (4) increase organization effectiveness and health through (5) planned interventions in the organization's 'processes', using behavioral science knowledge" (p. 9).

To deal effectively with the larger system, the practitioner needs information that is systemic, reflecting what the organization looks like as an entity, that is, a totality. Relying on interviews and focus groups is useful but not sufficient for developing the big picture. An organizational survey administered to the entire population, or to a representative sample of the total organization, helps the practitioner to see the larger system and, depending on the nature of the questions in the survey, have at hand both quantitative and qualitative data to work with.

The previous statement was not meant to position interviews and focus groups as an either-or to surveys. Data from interviews and focus groups can be very helpful at the front end to construct the survey, that is, to ask the right questions to find out what is on people's minds. Data from interviews and focus groups can also be useful on the back end as well, that is, to help embellish and clarify what the results from the survey actually mean. The point is that surveys help ODC practitioners to be data based at the total systems level.

Another point of importance for using surveys in ODC practice is that they help to establish an internal benchmark for comparisons over time. Surveys are very useful—maybe the most useful process for a source of data for tracking progress in an overall organization change effort. Comparing time 2 data with time 1 data, say, after a year of intensive work on organization change, helps to determine if the change goal is being achieved.

A final point about the importance of surveys is that they help to provide direction for next steps in a change effort. The process of analyzing comparative data over time can provide considerable clarity about what a next initiative needs to be. It may be (and this is often the case) that when time 1 and time 2 data are compared, people's understanding about the revised or new organizational strategy at time 2 is clear, but their understanding of the revised or new structure to support the strategy is anything but clear. The next change initiative becomes quite clear, however: to work on the organizational structure and get it right.

It is probably not especially difficult to convince I/O psychologists, ODC practitioners, human resource (HR) specialists, and others about the importance of conducting an organizational survey to provide solid data, establish internal benchmarks, and help with determining next steps in an organizational change process. Convincing line managers and executives of the importance of conducting organizational surveys is not quite the same.

Selling the Survey as an Action Tool

Organizational surveys serve as highly useful levers for organizational change. But they do not represent *the* leverage point for successful change. While not desirable in my judgment, it is quite possible to significantly change an organization without the use of an organizational survey. An example from the United Kingdom stands as a prime example.

I served as a change consultant to an airline in the UK from 1985 to 1990, the five-year period when most of the culture change of the organization occurred. Try as I might, and I tried mightily several times, to convince top executives at the airline to administer an organizational survey to track progress of and provide further focus for the change effort, they steadfastly refused. To be honest, I never could quite figure out why. When it came to collecting marketing and customer data, the airline's executives were zealots. But with respect to collecting perceptual and opinion data from their employees, as we say in Brooklyn, "forget about it." My initial reaction was that maybe this was a cultural difference: compared with Americans, they simply do not believe in the efficacy of employee perceptions based on a survey. But later I realized that this cross-cultural hypothesis was anything but true. Another British company in the media world as of 2001 had completed time 5 of its organizational survey process (Burke, 2002). And as I understand it, it has recently completed a sixth survey. So the British are not anti-surveys.

But it was a local cultural thing at the airline. There had been some bad history regarding surveys. Getting over this historical hurdle was next to impossible. Organization change, most of it successful, did occur at the airline, nevertheless (see Burke, 1994, 2002, and Goodstein and Burke, 1991).

So gaining acquiescence from executives to conduct an organizational survey is not always easy. And some organizational executives are a tougher sell than others. For example, I have found senior executives in a highly technological organization to be receptive. Being scientists and engineers, they are believers in data (even from a psychologist). The same is true at the British media organization. Although they are not scientists and engineers, executives at a large retail consumer business in the United States authorize immense amounts of data collection. Like individuals, organizations differ with respect to their receptivity. Regardless, a sell usually needs to be made. Regarding conducting a survey in the context of organization change, here are a few selling points:

• Although a survey by definition is a set of questions, the content of the questions contains a message. A survey is an opportunity for senior management to send a message to all organizational members. For organization change purposes, the content of questions would emphasize change goals, behaviors required to reach those goals, and what particular initiatives will likely be launched.

- A survey helps to focus organization members' attention on the change effort.
- Senior executives typically want results, so anything (a measure) that will help them to determine whether the results they desired have been achieved will get their attention. Explaining that a survey can help with determining the degree of progress toward a change goal or set of goals is an effective selling point. A survey helps to track progress, especially when future times of measurement are compared with earlier times.
- The final selling point concerns the advantage of a survey for targeting next steps for action. In addition to wanting results, senior executives like action—not action that is willy-nilly but action that is appropriate and focused. Survey findings where items are rated low, for example, can help to focus attention and energy on problems that need fixing and on issues that need further exploration and understanding.

Finally, it may be helpful to include in the presentation a framework or model for how survey results would be organized and categorized. When I was in the entry stage with the CEO of a newly merged pharmaceutical company and we were exploring the possibility of my consulting with him and his colleagues (the new top team of the merged company), we discussed an array of potential initiatives and change activities, such as team building for the top group of executives, a new mission statement, clarifying the role and responsibilities of the chairman and president-CEO, communication strategies, and changes within the HR function to facilitate support for the merger. Included in our discussion was my brief presentation of the Burke-Litwin model shown in Figure 6.1.

This entry stage rapidly moved to contracting, and I was off and running for over three years as an external consultant to help with the merger. I learned later that what turned out to be a key selling point for me as a consultant was the Burke-Litwin model. The CEO not only was attracted to the model, he particularly liked the fact that I had a point of view, that is, that I used the model as a way of explaining how I thought change should be planned and conducted.

Figure 6.1. Burke-Litwin Model of Organizational Performance and Change

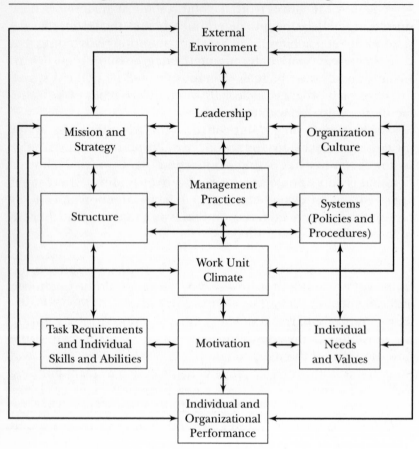

Source: Burke and Litwin (1992).

A brief rationale for using the Burke-Litwin model or one like it is appropriate at this stage of addressing the importance of using a model to help with the survey "sale."

In addition to the assumption that all organizations are open systems with the external environment as input, the organization itself as throughput, and performance as output, a fundamental premise of the Burke-Litwin model is that change can be considered in terms of transformation (discontinuous, episodic, and revolutionary) and as transactional (continuous, evolutionary, and operations). In the model, the transformational factors are those at the top of the diagram most directly influenced by the external environment—mission and strategy, leadership, and organization culture—and the remaining factors are more transactional (structure, management practices, and systems, for example).

Large-scale change, then, begins with the transformational factors and gradually cascades down through the system (for example, strategy work preceding structural change), eventually having a significant impact on performance and demonstrating the effects of change. The final points regarding the model are that (1) the order of what comes first, second, and so forth is critical, (2) the boxes in the model are primary categories for diagnosis and levers for change, and (3) the arrows are more important than the categories (understanding how subsystems interact and affect one another is crucial to effective management of change in a large, complex organization). Thus, a model that is more than mere description of an organization and has a point of view may help with the sale of conducting a survey. (For more on the use of the Burke-Litwin model, see Burke, 2002, and for the full story on the merger of these two pharmaceutical firms—one American, the other British—see Bauman, Jackson, & Lawrence, 1997.)

Preparing the Organization for the Survey Process

Using focus group meetings comprising a cross-section of organizational members helps to generate the right kind of questions for constructing the survey in the first place, or revising it if we are at time 2 or later. The "right kind of questions" means that work with focus groups ensures that the survey will be timely and relevant to what is on people's minds. The focus group process needs to be guided, however, so that extraneous questions are eliminated and that emergent themes fit within an overall conceptual framework or model. Moreover, from the perspective of using the survey as leverage for ODC, focus group work beforehand helps to build commitment. With this involvement of numbers of organizational members, commitment to the survey process is significantly strengthened.

Preparation for the survey process also includes communicating to organizational members the purpose for the survey. An example of such a statement (this one for a bank located primarily in the northeastern United States) follows:

> This survey is intended to establish a baseline measurement for determining our progress toward our strategic plan, in other words, to create a way to see how we are doing over time. It will also serve as a starting point for making improvements to our business. Your participation in the survey therefore is very important, so please take the time to complete it.
>
> The questions in the survey concern your business unit as well as the entire organization. The questions cover many aspects of the Bank and are intended to measure progress in key areas of performance, leadership, customer service, and employee satisfaction.

This statement comprised page one of the survey.

Administration of the Survey

Clearly there has been a shift to online administration of organizational surveys—but not exclusively. In a recent survey project aimed at organization change at the ground level of a large conglomerate, for thirteen of the fourteen sites my students and I surveyed, we had to use a paper-and-pencil version since most respondents did not have access to a computer or were not sufficiently computer literate. This slowed the feedback process and lessened the potential impact of the survey results for change.

Including an opportunity for survey respondents to provide write-in comments can also slow the feedback process, but responses beyond the typical five-point Likert scale can help to clarify the meaning of overall survey responses and priorities for action steps regarding change. Here is one example of write-in questions used in a large-scale change effort with a bank:

- What is exciting about your job? What makes you want to come to work each day?
- What are the blocks, hindrances, barriers that you experience in attempting to do your job?

- If you were in charge and could change one thing to improve the effectiveness and satisfaction people experience at work, what would it be?
- Think about the changes that have occurred over the past few years as a result of the mergers. What are some of the things the bank has done in the recent past that have been helpful and should continue to do?
- What would you suggest in order to make changes go more smoothly in the future?

The Feedback Process

Feedback of survey results can be a significant intervention in ODC work. First, it is highly important for the consultants to get the data feedback right (that is, make certain that the data are accurate), provide full disclosure of the data, and format feedback in such a way that understanding the results will be as user-friendly as possible.

Working with a CEO and his head of HR a few years ago, we arranged an initial meeting for me to go over the survey results with the two of them. When the CEO began to press for changing the feedback report for his top team and then for all of the organizational members, alarm bells began to ring in my head. My quick assumption was that he wanted to change the data feedback in some way to prevent full disclosure. I began to argue strongly for "my results" and for the feedback to be presented the way I had planned it. We went back and forth. Finally I began to realize that he did not want to change the data, which was my biggest concern, but simply to modify the format I had created for the feedback, that is, which set of data should be presented first, which second, and so forth. I then relaxed and went to work on changing the format.

I have had experiences in the past when clients did not want full disclosure, and I had to fight for what I thought was right, so I was somewhat conditioned to see a value clash. Although I thought I saw a problem in the example just summarized, such a clash fortunately did not exist. The point here may be obvious, but it is worth declaring to make sure. Meeting with the CEO, and perhaps with the senior team at the same time, helps to ensure that the data will be understood, that they can explain the results and respond to questions from organizational members, that they believe in the veracity of the data, and that they are committed to working with their people to take appropriate action.

Second, after the initial meeting with the CEO and top team, it is wise to present the feedback simultaneously to as many organizational members as possible. For a large organization with thousands of members, the initial feedback may need to be in a quick summary form sent by e-mail. Then as quickly as possible, face-to-face (and perhaps with video-conferencing) meetings need to be held so that dialogue can occur.

In another example, with a bank consisting of several thousand people who were geographically dispersed, after the initial meeting with the CEO and the head of HR, we conducted a large group intervention with the top echelon of the organization—approximately three hundred people. At the outset of the meeting held at a nearby hotel, the survey data were presented to all three hundred together. Then business unit heads met with their teams to pore over their own data and compare their results with the results of the overall organization and plan corrective action. Following this one-day meeting, an overall summary of the survey results was sent to everyone else. As soon after as possible, the chairman, president, and I held a number of "town meetings" with one hundred employees at a time in their respective locations to discuss the survey results. In the meantime, business unit heads continued to cascade feedback and action planning down through the system hierarchically. Two activities were transpiring simultaneously: business unit heads were planning action steps based on their data (much as Mann suggested fifty years ago), and all employees, one hundred at a time, were hearing from the top leaders. It was a matter of getting the big picture and working within their business units at the local level.

A second example was with an agency of the federal government. After a feedback meeting with the agency director and his top team, a large group meeting was held with all first-line supervisors—some five hundred people meeting together in a ballroom at a nearby location. Hotel space near the agency was either not available or their rooms were not large enough. We settled for a large facility that catered to weddings, bar mitzvahs, and other celebrations. The decor was a bit gaudy and not especially conducive to a survey feedback process, but we needed a very large room. Fortunately it worked in spite of our initial reactions, which were followed soon with jokes and related comments.

The purpose of this meeting was twofold: to provide the feedback and opportunity for questions and discussion and to help with how the supervisors would follow up with their people. What helped to make this large group intervention work was the back-and-forth process of the large group to the small group and back to the large group. After the initial large group data feedback presentation, the five hundred supervisors were asked to meet in small work groups to discuss the data, clarify issues, and raise further questions. Then back in the large group session, a small group representative would summarize the group's discussion and present further questions. These questions were responded to by either the center director or me in the consultant role. Also following the meeting, the center executives held meetings with their work units.

Finally, regarding the feedback process for effective OD work, it is critical to move back and forth between the large group and the work unit (the smaller group sessions). Large group sessions are used primarily to ensure that a consistent message gets to as many people as possible as quickly as possible and at the same time, and to provide opportunities for organizational members to understand the message as thoroughly as possible through dialogue. Small group sessions in the work unit configuration are used primarily to understand the data as thoroughly as possible for their part of the larger system and to plan and implement change based on what the data indicate. While a bit difficult to articulate regarding just how to do it, let me simply point to the importance of attending to a rhythm of when large group work is beneficial and then when the shift should be made to the small group and then back to the large group, and so forth.

A Survey Feedback Example

The example in Box 6.1 illustrates how the language of a feedback report might be stated at time 2 of a large-scale organization change effort. The full feedback report for all employees was over thirty pages and provided considerable detail, including the comparative ratings from time 1 with time 2 on each survey item.

Box 6.1. Example of a Survey
Feedback Summary Statement at Time 2

Four years ago the Bank committed itself to the vision of becoming the financial services institution our customers choose first for all their financial needs. By offering customers the products and services they require along with highly personal service, we have made considerable progress towards achieving this vision. Moreover, the organization survey reveals that people are clear and excited about the vision, and feel confident in their contribution to our continued success.

So how have we changed over the past year since we took our first survey? Where do we continue to do well and where do we need to improve? As you may remember the organization survey asked you to rate 150 questions ranging from progress toward change, vision and strategy, leadership style and company culture; to how people are organized, managed and rewarded; to people's individual jobs, motivation, needs and values—all of which affect individual and company performance.

Almost half of those questions were asked of you last year and we can gauge how much progress has been made in the past year and what areas still need attention.

The strides we have made in focusing the entire Bank on the customer are reflected in our key business accomplishments. We are a stronger, more customer-focused and customer-responsive organization than a year ago.

Since last year's survey, we have also made some headway on issues that you identified as areas of concern. More than 35 "back office" functions have been removed from the franchises and transferred to the Central Processing Center, thus giving franchise staff more time to spend meeting their customers' needs. During 1994, more than 8,000 employees received in-house training on a variety of subjects, including sales and service skills, operational issues, Bank products, systems issues, critical thinking and management development. Still, many of you report that time constraints keep you from getting the training you'd like.

From a combined data analysis of the organization survey results with shopper surveys collected at the branches and quarterly financial performance indicators, we have found that the biggest impact we can have on performance are in the areas of:

Managerial Practices, particularly in the areas of:

- Recognizing people and giving praise
- Developing authority

- Encouraging people to develop new approaches
- Communicating changes—both what and why
- Listening openly to criticism and suggestions
- Actively supporting change through employee participation

Systems Improvements, particularly with regard to using more advanced technology along with the appropriate training. We need computer upgrades and new and more useful software. These changes will significantly enhance our customer service capacity.

[Many other topic areas were summarized and reviewed in the original thirty-page document. Only a few excerpts are shown in this example.]

Next Steps

The task the Bank faces now is to use the survey results in helping the organization thrive in the next decade. There is a saying "you treasure what you measure" and the survey results are just one way of measuring progress in achieving the vision of "First Choice." The work ahead is formidable, the gains unquestionable.

Organization Change with a Merger

This example provides a synopsis of an extensive ODC effort that was the consequence of a merger. Survey feedback in this case was one among several interventions and illustrates how action follows from the feedback process. Due to a shrinking market in the savings bank industry, two such banks in the same metropolitan area decided to join forces. Three initiatives were launched at the outset of the merger. First, a strategic planning process was put into place. Second, an organizational survey was developed to determine the state of employee morale; assess organizational members' understanding of the new strategy, the new desired, "merged" culture, top executives' goals and mode of leading, and the new structure; and establish an internal benchmark for future survey comparisons to track progress regarding change. The third initiative was to write a mission statement for the newly merged savings bank.

The initial organizational survey showed that most members of the bank were positive about the merger, top leadership, and the business model and strategy, and they believed the new mission was appropriate. However, organizational structure was perceived to be unclear, information technology inadequate, and management below the senior executive team poor.

Action was taken based on the results of the time 1 survey. Systems were improved particularly in the areas of information, compensation and reward, and communication. The structure was modified yet again, and starting with the top 125 executives, a significant initiative was launched to improve leadership and management. This initiative consisted of training and multirater feedback based on behavioral practices that reflected key values embedded in the bank's mission statement. This leadership program began at the time of the second survey, some eighteen months after the time 1 survey.

These surveys were based on the Burke-Litwin model (Burke & Litwin, 1992) with questions being categorized according to the twelve boxes of the model: external environment, mission/strategy, leadership, culture, structure, management practices, systems, climate, job-person match, individual needs and values, motivation, and performance. Feedback for both time 1 and time 2 was conducted with a combination of large and small group sessions.

An additional unique feature of the time 2 feedback was to incorporate the survey results into the leadership development program. As a significant part of the program, the top executives received two forms of feedback: (1) the multirater process based on self-ratings and ratings from the individual's boss, peers, and direct reports and (2) the survey results for his or her business unit. With these two forms of feedback, the executives, with coaching assistance, were able to interpret their individual ratings in the context of their business unit survey results.

There was much for them to sort through, but with the help of the program faculty, we were able to combine the two sets of feedback to help with action planning that was strongly connected to the business and their respective organizational units.

Summarizing the survey results from time 2 compared with time 1, it seemed clear that the action steps taken for ODC had paid off. On 123 of the 125 survey items, higher ratings were realized at time 2. It is difficult to declare unequivocally that the desired changes realized were indeed valid and successful, but it was clear that the executives, managers, and employees believed that positive change had occurred. (For a more comprehensive description of this change effort, see Burke, 2002.)

Conclusions

The purposes of this chapter were to provide some principles to follow and suggest further ways with examples of how to use an organizational survey as an intervention and leverage for ODC. At the outset of deciding whether to administer an organizational survey, it is very important to ask whether the survey is to be used as an annual or biannual checkup or as a lever for organization change. If the latter, then the content of the survey questions will need to be somewhat different from questions typically used for the former. In other words, if the survey is change oriented, the survey questions will need to emphasize perceptions about the change goals, rate of progress toward those goals, and the degree to which initiatives and interventions are helping. And, finally, the survey questions need to be constructed and categorized according to a sound and theoretically grounded organizational framework or model. (For further rationale regarding using a model to undergird a survey, see Burke, 2002.)

An organizational survey can serve as an important lever for change. Feedback from a survey, as Nadler (1977) has pointed out, can energize organizational members, and this new energy can help staff achieve enhanced progress toward change goals. With feedback, organizational members can see that their voices were heard and believe that they may indeed have an important impact on the organization. (For examples and further recommendations for effective use of surveys in an organizational change effort, see Burke, Coruzzi, & Church, 1996.)

Building on the belief that survey feedback is a powerful ODC intervention, both the use of data and the process of feedback, particularly with respect to the action steps outlined by Mann (1957) many years ago, can help to ensure that this kind of intervention leads to positive change. Mann's guidelines and the relevance of the work of his colleague Rensis Likert (1967) regarding the use of surveys for organization change and renewal have stood the test of time. Their admonitions are just as pertinent today regarding survey feedback for effective ODC practice as they were back then. Yet these guidelines are typically not followed sufficiently if we are serious about the use of survey feedback for change. We tend to stop short of complete action and follow-through. As internal and external consultants to such a process, our behavior seems to be based on the assumption that if we provide accurate data and put the information in the hands of unit managers, they will make positive change happen. In other words, we can leave them alone. We believe they will take the ball and run with it.

This rarely happens. Receiving survey feedback at the local work unit level, for the manager at least, is not unlike receiving feedback from a multirater-multisource process. It is personal. Resistance builds up. Competent consultant help is needed, if not required, for change to occur (or research that points to the importance of coaching for effective follow-up action concerning multirater feedback; see, for example, Luthans & Peterson, 2003; Seifert, Yukl, & McDonald, 2003; and Smither, London, Flautt, Vargas, & Kucine, 2003). The same need is present when a manager has to deal with survey feedback regarding his unit members' perceptions about how things are going, some of which, whether positive or negative, is a direct reflection on his or her leadership and managerial effectiveness. It is typical for a manager faced with negative feedback not only to become resistant but immobilized regarding action. Sometimes if action occurs, it can be rather punitive for a manager's direct reports. Competent coaching and consulting by a third party is needed especially regarding the attainment of commitment to follow through on change.

Argyris (1970) provided useful criteria for determining whether an intervention for organization change would be effective as opposed to a waste of time or even making matters worse. The three criteria for an effective intervention were (1) valid information (the data are a true reflection of how people think and feel), (2) choice (no singular action is imposed; there are options from which to choose), and (3) commitment (people are motivated to take action and bring about positive change). Too often in survey work, only the first criterion is met; choice and commitment remain untouched. ODC consultants must help to ensure that choice and commitment are reached. It does not happen as a matter of course. Following Mann's guidelines as a consultant will help.

References

Argyris, C. (1970). *Intervention theory and method.* Reading, MA: Addison-Wesley.

Bauman, R. P., Jackson, P., & Lawrence, J. T. (1997). *From promise to performance: A journey of transformation at SmithKline Beecham.* Boston: Harvard Business School Press.

Beckhard, R. (1969). *Organization development: Strategies and models.* Reading, MA: Addison-Wesley.

Burke, W. W. (1994). *Organization development: A process of learning and changing* (2nd ed.). Reading, MA: Addison-Wesley.

Burke, W. W. (2002). *Organization change: Theory and practice.* Thousand Oaks: CA: Sage.

Burke, W. W., Coruzzi, C. A., & Church, A. H. (1996). The organizational survey as an intervention for change. In A. I. Kraut (Ed.), *Organizational surveys: Tools for assessment and change* (pp. 41–66). San Francisco: Jossey-Bass.

Burke, W. W., & Litwin, G. H. (1992). A causal model of organizational performance and change. *Journal of Management, 18*(3), 532–545.

Goodstein, L. D., & Burke, W. W. (1991). Creating successful organizational change. *Organizational Dynamics, 19*(4), 5–17.

Likert, R. (1967). *The human organization.* New York: McGraw-Hill.

Luthans, F., & Peterson, S. J. (2003). 360-degree feedback with systematic coaching: Empirical analysis suggests a winning combination. *Human Resource Management, 42,* 243–256.

Mann, F. C. (1957). *Studying and creating change: A means to understanding social organization.* Ann Arbor, MI: Industrial Relations Research Association,

Nadler, D. A. (1977). *Feedback and organization development: Using data-based methods.* Reading, MA: Addison-Wesley.

Seifert, C. F., Yukl, G., & McDonald, R. A. (2003). Effects of multisource feedback and a feedback facilitator on the influence behavior of managers toward subordinates. *Journal of Applied Psychology, 88,* 561–569.

Smither, J. W., London, M., Flautt, R., Vargas, Y., & Kucine, I. (2003). Can working with an executive coach improve multisource feedback ratings over time? A quasi-experimental field study. *Personnel Psychology, 56,* 23–44.

CHAPTER 7

Using Linkage Research to Drive High Performance

A Case Study in Organization Development

Jack W. Wiley
Bruce H. Campbell

Linking employee and customer survey results burst onto the landscape of organizational science approximately twenty-five years ago. The seminal work of Benjamin Schneider and his colleagues (Schneider, Parkington, & Buxton, 1980; Schneider & Bowen, 1985) demonstrated that employee views of customer service policies and practices were significantly and positively correlated with measures of external customer satisfaction. Jack Wiley and Walter Tornow (Wiley, 1991; Tornow & Wiley, 1991) were the first to extend this original employee-customer concurrent research design to incorporate measures of business performance as well. Several other studies by a variety of authors were then presented or published. In the first literature review of this topic, Wiley (1996) labeled this emerging body of research *linkage research*. The following definition and purpose were provided: "Linkage research involves integrating and correlating data collected from employees with data in other key organizational databases. The purpose of linkage research is to identify those elements of the work environment—as described by employees—that correlate or link to critically important organizational outcomes such as customer satisfaction and business performance" (p. 330).

This seminal review produced the Linkage Research Model. This model, since retitled the High Performance Model (see Figure 7.1), integrated all previously published linkage research findings to produce an understanding more comprehensive than could be provided by the results of any single study. The model suggests that the more visible and present certain organizational values and leadership practices are in a given work environment, the more energized and productive the workforce is. In turn, the more energized and productive the workforce, the greater the satisfaction and loyalty of customers, and with a time lag, the stronger the long-term business performance of the organization.

Figure 7.1. High Performance Model

Leadership Practices
Customer orientation
Quality emphasis
Training
Involvement

Business Performance
Sales growth
Market share
Productivity
Profitability

Employee Results
Communication
Teamwork
Engagement
Retention

Elapsed time

Work characteristics

Customer Results
Responsiveness
Product quality
Overall satisfaction
Loyalty

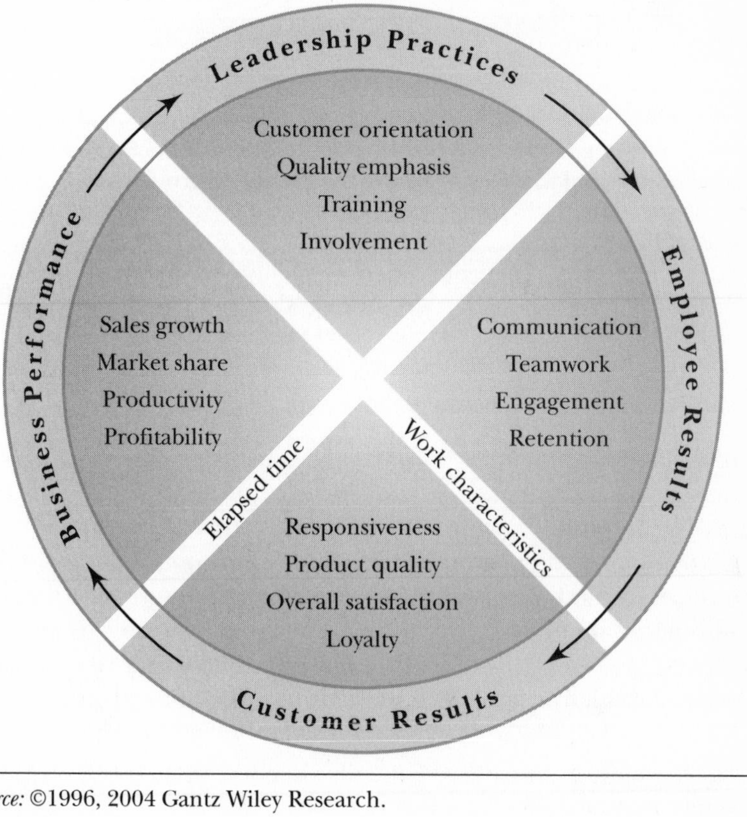

Source: ©1996, 2004 Gantz Wiley Research.

A second major literature review (Wiley & Brooks, 2000) summarized newly published studies, many of which were longitudinal in nature and thus allowed the migration from findings that were merely correlational to a more fruitful understanding of causation in the employee-customer-business performance linkage. These new studies not only demonstrated general consistency with original linkage research conclusions but also helped produce a taxonomy of the high-performance organizational climate. This taxonomy (see Table 7.1) describes with greater clarity how higher-performing units differ from units within the same organization that produce lower levels of customer satisfaction and business performance.

Table 7.1. Characteristics of High-Performance Organizations: The Employee Perspective

Leadership Practices

Customer orientation

> Employees see a strong emphasis on customer service and in fact believe their organization does a good job of satisfying customers.

> Customer needs are attended to quickly, whether in initial delivery of products and services or in the resolution of problems.

Quality emphasis

> Senior management is committed to quality and demonstrates this priority in day-to-day decisions. These values are effectively translated and implemented by lower-level managers.

> Employees can see that quality is a priority over cost containment, and especially over meeting deadlines.

> Employees believe their work groups do quality work, as judged by clear quality standards, and are able to improve continuously.

Employee training

> Employees have written development plans to take advantage of the formal and informal skill improvement opportunities that exist within the company.

> Whether on-the-job or formal, employees say they have the training to perform their current jobs well. This can include specific training on products and services or explicitly on customer service.

> New employees are oriented and able to come up to speed quickly, without undue burden on existing staff.

**Table 7.1. Characteristics of High-Performance
Organizations: The Employee Perspective, Cont'd**

Involvement and empowerment

Employees have the authority and support they need to serve their customers.

Employees are encouraged to participate in decisions affecting their work and, perhaps more important, to innovate.

Management solicits and uses opinions of employees in such a way that employees can see the connection.

Employee Results

Information and knowledge

Management creates and communicates a compelling vision and direction for the company.

Employees understand their role in the organization—how their goals fit into overall company objectives.

Employees report having enough information to do their jobs, including company information, advance warning of changes, and information from other departments.

Teamwork and cooperation

Employees both within and across departments cooperate to serve customers and get the work done.

This teamwork is actively supported by management.

Workload is managed effectively within a given work group. The load is divided fairly, and short staffing is not a significant barrier.

Overall satisfaction

Employees derive intrinsic satisfaction from their work and see a good match among their jobs, their interests, and their skills and abilities.

Employees are satisfied with and proud of their organization.

There is confidence in the company's ability to succeed, leading to long-term stability for the employee.

Employee retention

Employees value their relationship with the organization and have no short-term interest in leaving.

Longer-tenured employees are more efficient and create more value for the organization and its customers.

Source: © 1999 Gantz Wiley Research. Reprinted by permission.

The purpose of this chapter is not to update or more fully explain past linkage research. Rather, consistent with the overall intent and purpose of this book, this chapter aims to demonstrate how linkage research can inform and drive organization development (OD) efforts to produce higher levels of organizational performance. What follows is an illustrative study that integrates employee, customer, and business performance measures and demonstrates how linkage research can provide the framework for discovering best practices. The best practices can then be deployed throughout the organization to elevate the performance of the overall system.

Phase I: Starting with Linkage Research

The study setting was a large automotive credit branch system in North America. The leadership team of this organization was convinced that their overall system performance could be, and needed to be, improved. They also believed intuitively in the employee-customer-business performance linkage. However, despite possessing various databases, no effort had been extended toward their integration. We worked with this leadership team to examine these linkages and provide recommendations for enhancing system performance.

The stated objectives of this initiative were to:

- Identify the relationships that exist between management practices, employee opinions, dealer satisfaction, and key operating measures on a branch basis.
- Determine the key cultural and work environment drivers of dealer satisfaction and branch operating performance.
- Identify and recommend action planning and OD efforts aimed at driving higher branch-level dealer satisfaction and operating performance results.

All three databases to be integrated—employee survey, customer survey, and business performance—existed. They were part of an overarching measurement system whose purpose was to track the organization's success in operating against its core beliefs and values. We were not involved in designing or administering the questionnaires that had been used to collect the employee survey data or the customer satisfaction data. Our role was that of integrating these databases, analyzing and illuminating their interrelationships, and using the linkage research results as a framework for OD initiatives.

It is important to acknowledge the timing of the three measurements. Both the employee and customer surveys were administered simultaneously in June, which coincided with the last month of the organization's second quarter reporting period. As a result, we decided to use business performance measures that were also drawn from this same time period. This provided us with concurrent measures for all three databases. Indeed, the High Performance Model suggests stronger relationships will emerge when there is a time lag between employee and customer data and business performance measures. However, the leadership team was eager to move forward quickly, unwilling to delay the linkage research study in order to incorporate business performance measures that would not be available until the year's end.

Employee Survey

The design of the employee survey had been guided by the objectives of assessing the organization's culture—with special emphasis on practices that support the delivery of outstanding customer service—and providing an internal evaluation of a recently installed customer service initiative. The corporate human resource research function of this organization's parent company had developed and administered the survey. Across the system of eighty-five branches, 2,016 employees completed the survey. Based on factor analysis and internal consistency analysis that we performed, we determined that the eighty-four items contained in the employee survey reliably measured twenty themes. The themes could be categorized into two major clusters:

Customer Service/Quality	*Employee Relations*
Customer Service/Satisfaction	Senior Management
External Customer Feedback	Supervisor

Internal Customer Feedback

Senior Management Quality Emphasis

Supervisor Quality Emphasis

Work Group Quality Commitment

Resources for Quality/Service

Recognition for Quality/Service

Use of Measurements

Best in Class Emphasis

Goal Awareness

Job Satisfaction

Company Satisfaction

Coworker Relations

Interpersonal Climate

Training

Career Development/ Advancement

Survey Utilization

Customer Survey

The branches provided automotive credit directly to auto dealer-ships and their retail customers. In order to assess how the fi-nancing needs of the dealers were being met and monitor the success of the quality service initiative, the leadership team au-thorized a branch-level dealer satisfaction survey that was designed and administered by another outside firm. The key measure that was available from this survey, and on which we focused our analy-ses, was the Dealer Satisfaction Index (DSI) score. According to the agency that collected the customer satisfaction data, the DSI composite score contained the most potent and reliable predic-tors of overall dealer satisfaction. The DSI scores were used as a critical ingredient in the branch manager reward system. DSI scores from 2,390 completed surveys across the eighty-five branches were available for inclusion in our analysis.

Business Performance

A wide array of business performance measures was available. Inter-views were conducted with selected branch managers to under-stand better the performance measures and solicit their opinions regarding which of these measures provided the best reflection of branch performance and were most under the control of branch personnel. After discussion with credit company executives and other internal subject matter experts, we decided to focus on four key measures:

Wholesale market share. More technically known as field stock penetration, this is a measure of the percentage of all new vehicles on dealers' lots within the geographical market of the branch for which the credit company has provided wholesale financing.

Retail market share. More technically known as retail volume penetration, this is a measure of the percentage of the dealer's new vehicles that are financed or leased by end customers through the credit company.

Loss to liquidation. Technically this is the ratio of dollar losses to dollar liquidizations. A loss occurs, for example, when a repossessed vehicle is sold for less than the balance due on a loan. This ratio in effect measures the quality of the credit analysis in determining to whom retail credit should be extended. The lower the ratio is, the better the credit decisions are.

Productivity. This is a ratio of the number of open retail accounts divided by the number of full-time equivalent employees per branch. The higher the number is, the busier the branch is.

Linkage Research Results

The correlational analyses show significant and consistent linkages between employee survey ratings and dealer satisfaction and between employee survey ratings and measures of business performance. However, these relationships are not always in the expected direction.

Employee Survey Linkages: Theme Level

The means and standard deviations of the employee survey themes, the DSI, and the business performance measures are presented in Table 7.2.

Table 7.2. Employee-Customer-Business Performance Linkages

Employee Survey (Mean/SD)	Dealer Satisfaction Index (838.3/47.4)	Wholesale Market Share (80.0/18.2)	Retail Market Share (22.8/8.0)	Loss to Liquidation (.95/.46)	Productivity (1,249.7/212.5)
Customer Service/Quality Themes					
Customer Service/Satisfaction (3.65/.30)	.31		.20		
External Customer Feedback (3.79/.25)	.27			−.19	−.21
Internal Customer Feedback (3.59/.29)	.22			−.19	−.27
Senior Management Quality Emphasis (3.56/.39)					
Supervisor Quality Emphasis (3.55/.35)		−.19		−.21	−.20
Work Group Quality Commitment (3.44/.39)	.26			−.26	−.25
Resources for Quality/Service (3.16/.41)					
Recognition for Quality/Service (3.02/.46)	.20				−.26

Use of Measurements (3.16/.33)	.30		
Best in Class Emphasis (2.95/.40)	.21		-.23
Employee Relations Themes			
Senior Management (3.36/.44)			
Supervisor (3.35/.33)			
Goal Awareness (3.64/.31)			-.25
Job Satisfaction (3.66/.26)	.21		-.31
Company Satisfaction (3.66/.32)			-.29
Coworker Relations (3.79/.31)	.26		-.22
Interpersonal Climate (3.55/.35)	.19		
Training (3.18/.35)	.30		-.33
Career Development/ Advancement (2.44/.34)		-.22	
Survey Utilization (3.29/.36)			
Dealership Satisfaction Index	.31	.28	

Note: Means computed on the basis of branch averages. Correlation coefficients are presented only when they achieve statistical significance. Correlations ≥ .19 significant at $p \leq .05$. Correlations ≥ .25 significant at $p \leq .01$, by two-tailed significance test.

Correlations between the employee survey themes and the DSI show a generally strong positive relationship. Of the twenty possible correlations, all are positive, and eleven are statistically significant. Consistent with the High Performance Model, the pattern of positive correlations to the DSI is generally stronger for the set of Customer Service/Quality themes than for the Employee Relations themes. The employee survey themes emerging as the strongest predictors are Customer Service/Satisfaction, Use of Measurements, Training, External Customer Feedback, Work Group Quality Commitment, and Coworker Relations. Employee survey themes that achieve more moderately positive though still significant correlations with the DSI are Internal Customer Feedback, Best in Class Emphasis, Job Satisfaction, Recognition for Quality/Service, and Interpersonal Climate.

In general, the employee survey themes do not correlate as strongly with the business performance measures as they do with the DSI. The Wholesale Market Share and the Retail Market Share measures show relatively little evidence of relationship to the employee survey themes. Both the Loss to Liquidation measure and the Productivity measure, by contrast, are significantly related to a number of the employee survey themes, but these correlations are consistently negative in sign.

For Loss to Liquidation, negative correlation coefficients would be expected, since lower scores on Loss to Liquidation reflect better credit decisions and thus better branch performance. The significant employee survey predictors of Loss to Liquidation are Work Group Quality Commitment, Supervisory Quality Emphasis, External Customer Feedback, and Internal Customer Feedback. Interestingly and quite understandably, the two employee survey themes most strongly correlated with the quality of a branch's credit decisions (as reflected in its Loss to Liquidation score)— Work Group Quality Commitment and Supervisor Quality Emphasis—measure the local branch's emphasis on quality from both the supervisory and peer group perspectives. The other two significant correlates—External Customer Feedback and Internal Customer Feedback—highlight the extent to which branches that make higher-quality credit decisions see themselves as listening to and acting on customer feedback, whether the feedback comes from internal or external customers of their services.

Eleven culture survey themes correlate significantly with the productivity ratio. These correlation coefficients are also always negative in sign. In other words, the productivity ratio tends to be higher in branches where employees describe the work environment in consistently less favorable terms. In fact, the themes with the strongest inverse relationship to the productivity ratio are Training, Job Satisfaction, and Company Satisfaction—measures that are central to the basic employee-employer relationship.

This pattern of findings was not only surprising to us but also perplexing in the light of past research. However, the inverse relationship between employee satisfaction and the productivity ratio came as no surprise to the credit company executives with whom we were working. Rather, this finding confirmed a strong belief they held: that the formula for head count addition was too stringent. Justification for branch-level head count additions required branches to demonstrate over a sustained period of time that they were averaging over 1,250 open accounts per employee. Only when this criterion was met would requests for additional head count be approved. Our clients at the credit company felt this approach put too much emphasis on cost containment and was counter to the recently installed strategy of providing superior customer service as a means of achieving long-term success. They believed that increasing productivity levels was valuable up to a point, but beyond that point became destructive to the work environment.

The results lend support to that interpretation. The highest productivity branches were the leanest staffed. As that condition prevailed, overtime hours and stress levels increased. This eventually resulted in employee dissatisfaction as well as frustration with this perceived barrier to successfully implementing the initiative aimed at delivering improved customer service.

Employee Survey and DSI Linkages: Special-Item-Level Analysis

As a starting point, theme-level correlations can be very informative, particularly if themes are built in a psychometrically sound manner and properly titled. However, in-depth analysis at the item level can significantly enhance the understanding of theme-level dynamics. Table 7.3 lists the items contained within the employee survey that produce the strongest positive correlations with the overall measure of dealer satisfaction. This more detailed analysis reveals that branches achieving higher levels of customer (that is, dealer) satisfaction are those where employees are more likely to:

- Believe that dealers are satisfied, and that their concerns and issues get resolved quickly
- Receive enough training to improve their job performance and to be effective team members
- Use feedback from customers and other measures to improve quality and customer service
- Believe their work group is committed to and produces high-quality work and that individuals are recognized for serving customers well
- Indicate that plans have been established and are being followed to continuously improve—to achieve best in class

Table 7.3. Strongest Predictor Items
of Dealer Satisfaction

Employee Survey Theme	Item	Correlation to DSI
Customer Service/Satisfaction	Overall, our dealers are satisfied with our products and services.	.44
Recognition for Quality/Service	Where I work, individuals are recognized for serving their customers well.	.32
Customer Service/Satisfaction	Where I work, dealers' concerns/issues get resolved quickly.	.32
Use of Measurements	My organization tracks measurements to evaluate progress in customer service and quality improvement.	.31
External Customer Feedback	My work group receives adequate feedback from external customers.	.29
Training	I receive enough training to help me continually improve my job performance.	.29

**Table 7.3. Strongest Predictor Items
of Dealer Satisfaction, Cont'd**

Training	I have received the training I need to be an effective team member.	.29
External Customer Feedback	My work group uses feedback from our external customers to improve the quality of our work.	.27
Best in Class Emphasis	My work group is following plans to become the "best in class" at what we do.	.26
Work Group Quality Commitment	How would you rate the overall quality of work done in your group?	.26

Note: Correlations presented are significant at $p \le .01$, one-tailed significance test.

Dealer Satisfaction–Business Performance Linkage

The correlations for the remaining linkage, dealer satisfaction and business performance, are also presented in Table 7.2. Of the four business performance measures, the DSI reliably and significantly predicts two: Wholesale Market Share and Retail Market Share. That higher branch-level DSI scores are related to higher Wholesale and Retail Market Share is totally consistent with expectations. These results confirm that dealers who are more satisfied with the products and services provided by the branch do in fact finance a higher percentage of their wholesale purchases through the branch and also have a higher percentage of their end customers who finance their vehicles through the credit company.

Linkage Research Summary Conclusions

The results of the linkage research study were presented to the credit company leadership team (see Figure 7.2). Although the results produced considerable discussion, they were accepted as an accurate reflection of the employee-customer-business performance cycle for this organization. In simple terms, the findings indicate that the quality of business decisions and the satisfaction of customers are higher in branches where employees have more favorable opinions of key aspects of their work environment. In turn, branches that produce more satisfied customers also achieve greater wholesale and retail market penetration.

Figure 7.2. Employee-Customer-Business Performance Linkage Research Summary

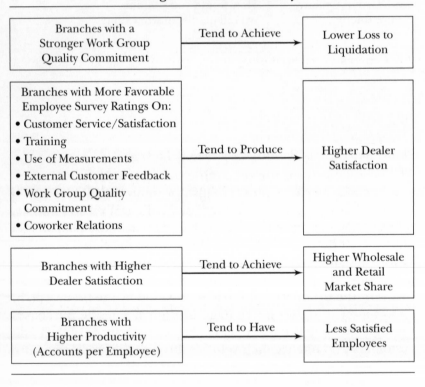

However, the branches considered most productive, in terms of number of open accounts per employee, are branches where employees are most disgruntled. Employees in these branches see management as sending conflicting messages about what matters most. In particular, the messages that they see as conflicting have to do with the value placed on cost containment (restricting head count) versus service quality (improving dealer satisfaction and thus gaining increased market share). Interestingly, the concise manner in which the results were summarized in Figure 7.2 aided the acceptance of the main conclusions from the linkage research. With the results fully accepted by the leadership team, the next step was to convert this understanding to actions that branch managers could take to improve overall branch-level performance.

Case Study Phase II: From Linkage Research to Best Practices

The initial phase of this research demonstrated meaningful linkages within the employee-customer-business performance cycle. The goal of the second phase was to identify specific management practices that drive the desired branch outcomes. We proposed a series of site visits to high- and low-performing branches as a qualitative data-gathering technique for identifying best practices. The credit company leadership team accepted our proposal.

The Branch Ranking and Interviewing Processes

To identify high- and low-performing branches, we ranked all branches on three sets of measures: the employee survey themes most predictive of dealer satisfaction and business performance, DSI scores, and the four business performance measures. Although very few branches were uniformly high or low across all measures, we were able to identify four branches clearly considered high performing and six branches considered relatively low performing overall. An eleventh branch was also included for a site visit because it had mixed results: very high dealer satisfaction but very low scores on the employee survey predictors.

Two researchers visited each of these branches. In addition to interviews with branch managers, we conducted from two to five small group interviews (depending on the size of the branch). This allowed us to collect data from each employee level and job function in the branch. We conducted 37 group interviews, involving over 125 employees across the 11 branches. The group interviews typically lasted 90 to 120 minutes.

In each interview, we sought to uncover underlying causes of the linkages among employee opinions, dealer satisfaction, and operational performance that we had discovered and documented during phase 1. We posed a series of questions designed to identify practices that may drive high versus low scores on each of the employee survey predictors of dealer satisfaction. We also asked questions designed to explore management and employee beliefs about contributors to dealer satisfaction and business performance. Finally, we asked specifically for ideas about what can or should be done to improve the work environment, dealer satisfaction, and business performance. Sample interview questions are presented in Table 7.4. It is important to note that branch personnel were not aware that their branches were, for the purposes of this initiative, labeled as a high-, mixed-, or low-performing branch.

Table 7.4. Sample Branch Personnel Interview Questions

Customer Service/ Satisfaction	What are the biggest obstacles or barriers to providing truly excellent service to dealers? To customers?
	What one or two changes would do the most to increase the satisfaction of your branch's dealers?
Training	How do you feel about the adequacy of training at your branch?
	To what extent are employees fully cross-trained to do other jobs?
Coworker Relations/ Interpersonal Climate	How would you describe the level of teamwork and cooperation among people in the branch?
	In what specific ways, if any, does your branch manager affect the amount of teamwork in the branch?

Table 7.4. Sample Branch Personnel Interview Questions, Cont'd

Work Group Quality Commitment	How much commitment to doing quality work exists among your coworkers?
	What are the biggest obstacles to doing quality work at your branch?
Use of Measurements	To what extent does your branch manager emphasize the use of measurements or statistics to monitor how well the branch is doing?
	Does your branch manager regularly share measurements about branch performance with employees? If so, how is this done?
Customer Feedback	What, if anything, is your branch doing to actively solicit feedback on branch performance from dealers?
	What would help your branch to do a better job of responding effectively to feedback from dealers?
Overall Employee Satisfaction	How would you describe the overall level of employee satisfaction and morale at your branch?
	What are some things that have a positive impact on employee satisfaction or morale at your branch? Negative impact?
Dealership Satisfaction	Why do you think your branch ranked where it did on the most recent DSI measurement?
	What, if anything, is your branch doing to try to increase dealer satisfaction and raise your DSI score?
Workload/ Resources	How do you feel about the adequacy of staffing at your branch?
	What additional resources would most help you to handle your own workload effectively?
Business Performance	What specific strategies or practices does your branch use to try to increase retail volume penetration? Field stock penetration?
	What changes or improvements do you think it would take to significantly increase your branch's retail volume penetration? Field stock penetration?

Practices Separating High- from Low-Performing Branches

By comparing and contrasting the information we obtained from the eleven branches, we were able to identify fourteen factors that contribute to highly effective branch performance. These "best practices" in some cases have to do with very specific, tangible behaviors the branch management team displays or specific standards or expectations they have successfully established. In other cases, the best practices appear to have more to do with personal characteristics or personality attributes of the management team members or with the group dynamics they have been able to establish and maintain. In all cases, however, the best practices appear to originate in the values and leadership style of the branch managers themselves and to be supported and reinforced by other management team members.

These practices can be clustered into three major categories: Employee Communication, Orientation toward Employees, and Dealer Orientation.

Employee Communication Best Practices

One group of best practices had to do with how effectively branch management communicated with employees, both in sharing information and in demonstrating enthusiasm and confidence of success.

Understanding of the Big Picture

The management teams of branches that exemplify this best practice characteristically believe that it is important for all employees to have a clear understanding of branch operations as a whole and to know how their specific jobs relate to and affect the work of the other job functions, and ultimately to the success of the branch. Moreover, these management teams have apparently worked hard to impart a clear understanding of this big picture to every employee.

Employees in branches lacking this best practice often commented on a feeling of being isolated in their own narrow job function. These employees are likely to describe the branch as having two distinct "sides" and to admit that they have little knowledge or understanding of what happens "on the other side." They also typically feel that their personal efforts and contributions are unnoticed or unappreciated by those outside their own job function.

Clarity of Branch Goals and Service Standards

Management in some branches does a much better job of setting clear goals and service standards and of obtaining employee buy-in and support. Employees in branches characterized by this best practice typically know the goals their branch is striving to achieve, and they understand how specific service standards (for example, "no credit application sits on the fax for more than 1 minute") will contribute to the accomplishment of those goals.

Employees in other branches often indicated a lack of clear goals for the branch as a whole and lack of uniformity or consistency in service standards. Frequently it appeared that whatever goals or standards they were aware of had been given to them from "on high," without much, if any, explanation or rationale. Consequently, employees often viewed the goals and standards as being unreasonable or unattainable and showed little evidence of personal buy-in.

Sharing of Measurements and Branch Awareness of Results

Employees in some branches appear to be much better informed about specific branch results than their peers in other branches. The credit company routinely measures and reports a vast array of branch performance statistics. What differentiates branches characterized by this best practice from others is that branch management has found ways to distill from this mass of complex and detailed reports the critical numbers that truly provide meaningful feedback. These managers have also educated their employees about the meaning and significance of these performance indicators.

Managers in other branches receive the same types of reports but evidently make relatively little effort to share the information with employees or create an understanding of the most critical numbers and their significance. In some cases, employees indicated that the raw reports are routed and that employees are required to initial the reports. This, however, does little good, as these employees appear to have only a limited understanding of the most critical indicators and what they really mean.

Positive, Can-Do Attitude

Managers who exemplify this best practice characteristically have a positive, can-do attitude that some employees describe as "infectious." They appear to be enthusiastic about their own work, the branch, and the company as a whole and to be confident about their own abilities and the abilities of their employees. They apparently make a conscious effort to "leave a bad mood at the door" and to display a positive, upbeat attitude even in adverse circumstances. These managers appear to have the ability to use humor effectively to lighten up tense or stressful situations. Perhaps most important, their positive outlook, eagerness to tackle challenges, and confidence of success influence their employees, who appear to be much more energized, optimistic, and goal directed than their peers in other branches.

Orientation Toward Employees' Best Practices

A second group of best practices had to do with branch management's orientation toward employees. This included their emphasis on cross-training, their ability to foster teamwork and to empower employees, and their attention to employees as individuals and to the interpersonal climate at work.

Extent and Effectiveness of Cross-Training

Among all the best practices we were able to identify, perhaps the one that stood out most clearly was the extent and effectiveness of cross-training that some branches have managed to attain. In branches exemplifying this best practice, it is common for employees to have attained true proficiency in doing two or three different job functions. No individual job function hinges on the presence or absence of any one person (or, often, even any two people) for its successful completion.

In branches lacking this best practice, by contrast, employees often describe the level of cross-training as "inadequate," or "lacking," or even "nonexistent." Although both management and nonmanagement employees in these branches typically appear to recognize the advantages that effective cross-training would bring, they have not been able to make it happen. Lack of time is almost unanimously given as the reason.

Teamwork and Cooperation

Branches where this best practice is evident have an exceptionally strong spirit of teamwork and cooperation. Both management and nonmanagement employees say the entire branch truly pulls together as a team and in some ways resembles a "big, happy family" more than a simple collection of coworkers. Employees describe their coworkers as being more than willing to spontaneously pitch in and help one another whenever the need arises. This occurs despite the lack of corporate-sponsored team reward policies.

Branches where this best practice is absent, by contrast, are often described as having a level of teamwork that is only "generally good" or "okay for the most part." These employees are likely to indicate that there are "a few people" who do not want to help out or to be team players or that teamwork within their own function is good but lacking across functions. Complaints about uneven distribution of work across areas appear to be common.

Empowering Management Style

Employees typically describe managers who exhibit this best practice as having a participative, empowering management style. These managers appear to truly believe that their employees are intelligent, responsible, trustworthy people who may often have better ideas than they themselves have and who can be counted on to "do the right thing" if they are given sufficient guidance and understanding of goals and objectives.

Managers who do not exemplify this best practice appear to have much more of a command-and-control style of management. They appear to have an "I know best" attitude, tend to make decisions independently, and give orders or instructions that they expect to be carried out, often without providing any explanation or rationale.

Caring About Employees

Employees in branches where this best practice is evident feel their managers truly care about them as individuals and are concerned about their well-being. They described their managers as being friendly and approachable and as taking the time to get to know them personally. These employees feel valued and described their managers as showing recognition for their accomplishments and appreciation for their efforts.

Employees in branches lacking this best practice, by contrast, are much more likely to have the impression that their managers are unconcerned about them as individuals. Their managers apparently make much less effort to get to know employees or to be friendly toward them. These managers tend to be seen as aloof and unapproachable. They are likely to be described as giving negative feedback liberally, but as rarely saying thank-you or showing genuine appreciation.

Attention to Interpersonal Climate

Managers who exemplify this best practice appear to be far more attentive to the overall interpersonal climate in the branch than managers at other branches. They appear to actively monitor how well people are getting along and do not allow interpersonal clashes or frictions to fester and grow. Managers in branches lacking this best practice, by contrast, seem much less in tune with and less skillful at managing the interpersonal atmosphere at work.

Branch Management Pitches In

Managers who illustrate this best practice are both willing and able to "roll up their sleeves" and "pitch in" to help accomplish whatever kind of task needs to be done to keep the branch's performance on track. Typically these managers were described as being integrally involved in all aspects of branch operations and as knowing how to do virtually any task.

Managers who fail to demonstrate this best practice, by contrast, were more likely to be described as being uninvolved in day-to-day operations. These managers were often described as not knowing how to do many branch tasks or even as not understanding the work of certain functions. They clearly do not see it as part of their job to pitch in and help with mundane tasks, and they are likely to be seen by employees as having a "that's beneath me" type of attitude.

Willingness to Bend the Rules

According to their own reports as well as those of their employees, managers who illustrate this best practice seem much more willing to bend the rules, to "make waves" with higher management, and to "stand up" for their branch and their employees. These managers appear to have a strong, clear sense of what is best for their branch and for their employees, and are willing to buck the system to make things happen that they believe are in the best interests of their branch and will contribute to their branch's success. Managers who fail to demonstrate this best practice, by contrast, are much more likely to be described as "going by the book" and as unquestioningly conforming to and implementing the instructions and wishes of their superiors.

Dealer Orientation Best Practices

A third group of best practices had to do with branch management's orientation toward dealers, including their efforts to make themselves accessible to dealers and their insistence on effective telephone answering practices.

"Dealers Come First" Attitude

At some branches, it became apparent within just the first few minutes that branch employees have truly internalized the attitude that "the dealer comes first." Their comments typically indicated a clear understanding that the success of their branch and, ultimately, their own job security depend directly on their ability to serve their dealers responsively and to satisfy their dealers' needs. They described their branches as being truly committed to "go the extra mile" and to do "whatever it takes" to keep their dealers happy.

In branches lacking this best practice, by contrast, this type of attitude, if expressed at all, typically came across as less genuine and enthusiastic. It was not unusual for employees in these branches to describe their dealers as being "unreasonable," "overly demanding," "disloyal," or even "big babies."

Branch Managers' Accessibility to Dealers

Other managers may spend more time visiting dealers than do managers who exemplify this best practice. Those who employ this best practice appear to make themselves far more accessible to dealers by phone, fax, and other means, on an as-needed basis. They appear to place a greater priority on personal responsiveness to dealer needs than do other branch managers.

Managers who do not employ this best practice seem likely to have a set of preferred dealers with whom they are willing to

interact directly and another set of dealers to whom they are re-
luctant to devote much time or energy. Managers who illustrate
this best practice, by contrast, seem to make a conscious effort to
make themselves equally accessible to all dealers, and not to give
up on even those dealers with whom it is difficult to do business.

Telephone Answering Standards

The last best practice is a very specific but important one. Some
branches appear to have much higher standards for answering telephones than do other branches. Perhaps more important, employees in branches characterized by this best practice appear to
truly believe in the importance of maintaining their telephone answering standards and work very hard at doing so.

Branches characterized by this best practice generally have an
explicit standard regarding the answering of incoming calls (for example, calls will be answered by a human being on or before the
third ring). They also have procedures or practices in place, and a
level of employee buy-in and support for these procedures, that
allow them to meet their standards most of the time. Their employees understand that responsiveness to the telephone is a critical success factor, and they display true teamwork by willingly providing
telephone coverage and picking up each other's telephones.

Branches lacking this best practice, by contrast, have at least
some employees who look on providing telephone coverage as a
nuisance and on incoming calls as annoying interruptions that prevent them from getting their "real" work done. Our casual observations suggest that it is not uncommon for telephones to be
allowed to "ring off the hook" (in some instances, up to thirteen
rings before being answered based on our own observations) in
branches where this best practice is not employed.

Additional Observations
Regarding Best Practices Branches

Besides the fourteen practices described, there were two additional
ways in which branches that exemplify all or most of these best practices appeared to differ fundamentally from branches that do not.
These seem to be essentially outcomes of the types of best practices
described above rather than specific practices or behaviors.

Alignment of Management and Employee Perceptions

In branches where most or all of the best practices prevail, the viewpoints expressed by management were highly similar to and aligned with the comments we heard from nonmanagement employees. In fact, in these branches, the consistency between what management had to say and what their employees had to say was quite remarkable. This was not generally true of branches where few of the best practices prevail. In these branches, management often expressed much more favorable assessments of teamwork, morale, and employee participation than did their employees.

Employee Motivation and Morale

Managers who enact a majority of the best practices described typically have employees who display a much higher level of energy, positive motivation, esprit de corps, and morale than do their peers in other branches. One could almost literally see and feel the difference by observing the behavior of branch employees for even a short time. And the differences in what employees told us about motivation and morale in branches characterized by a majority of the best practices versus branches lacking these practices clearly supported our direct observations.

Case Study Phase III: Deploying Best Practices to Drive High Performance

We chose to provide a detailed description here of the best practices in order to convey the depth and richness of the qualitative data that emerged from the interviews. In fact, it was this detailed description and the real-life examples of branch life that helped convince the credit company leadership team that the results were indeed valid and truly descriptive of what separated high- from low-performing branches.

Given the leadership team's acceptance of the catalogue of best practices, they were open to our recommendations for action plans.

Action Recommendations

We recommended a number of actions the leadership team should take that specifically addressed:

- Communicating the credit company's big picture to branch-level personnel
- Reducing staffing shortages, both chronic and acute
- Providing needed training and cross-training at the branch level
- Streamlining and increasing the relevance and understanding of operational reports
- Increasing employee recognition and appreciation
- Empowering branch managers through relaxing tight centralized controls

While these actions were offered as tangible, data-responsive techniques for improving branch performance, it was clearly recognized that most of the identified best practices arose from the personalities, attitudes, and personal value systems of the managers themselves. This led to a bundled set of recommendations that addressed branch manager selection, promotion, training, compensation, and reward systems. It was these recommendations that were regarded as the most vital to lifting the performance of the overall branch system.

Process Recommendations

In addition to specific actions, we provided recommendations regarding the process for using the best practices interview results:

- Concept testing: Involve a representative set of branch managers in a review of the results, asking for reactions and ideas for how to best use the information to drive change.
- Coaching: Provide more coaching to branch managers on how to use employee, customer, and business performance results with branch employees to build responsive action plans.
- Use quotations: In upcoming and ongoing communications with managers and branch personnel, liberally quote from the results to increase acceptance of new programs and initiatives and to demonstrate how they connect to real-life branch-level challenges and issues.
- Parceling out responsibility: In a more general sense, recognize that because many of the issues raised are system issues, it

will be tempting for participants to think it is someone else's responsibility to take action; therefore, working through a process of parceling out responsibilities and assigning executive "champions" to oversee follow-through will be critical.

Evaluations of Actions Taken

The initial reaction to the recommendations was very positive. Both internal subject matter experts and members of the leadership team could understand the logical flow from the integration of archival data, to the establishment of employee-customer-business performance linkages, to the cataloguing of best practices that drive higher-level performance, and finally to a set of recommended action steps. As a result, these actions were implemented with the explicit expectation that doing so would raise overall system performance.

An obvious way of measuring the impact of the actions taken would be to monitor results of future employee and customer surveys and to track business performance metrics. Unfortunately, however, subsequent employee survey data and business performance data were collected internally by the credit company. Customer (that is, dealer) satisfaction data were collected by another provider. Given that the work of our consulting group was considered complete, we relied on internal subject matter experts to gauge the success of the actions taken. Through personal communications with our internal contacts, we learned that the organization was indeed making noteworthy progress toward its performance goals. The actions taken, along with the retooled customer service initiative, were seen as important contributors to their drive for continuous improvement and the goal of becoming best in class.

Even so, we were disappointed that we were not involved in tracking and analyzing the critical metrics that would more closely calibrate the quality of our recommendations. As behavioral scientists, we naturally seek valid and reliable data before feeling confident in drawing conclusions about the success of our activities. As this case illustrates, executives by nature are often more willing to take a leap of faith and to forgo the more rigorous data-based approach to making such judgments. When faced with the choice, as they were in this case, executives decided to expend their limited financial and human resources on implementing the decided-on actions as opposed to the further and more detailed evaluation of individual elements of the overall action plan. Compounding our difficulty in obtaining the data we desired were changes within the leadership team of the credit company. Our executive sponsor, who selected us to perform this work, moved on to another, and more demanding, assignment. In addition, there were changes in the personnel of the project team with whom we interfaced. New team members were operating with a different set of priorities. Those priorities focused on taking action, and taking action with a sense of urgency.

The Overarching Model

The central theme of this book is about getting action in response to organizational survey results. The central theme of this chapter is about introducing a nontraditional OD model that starts with survey results but also incorporates both linkage research and best practices analysis. This model is presented in Figure 7.3.

Figure 7.3. Using Linkage Research to Drive High Performance

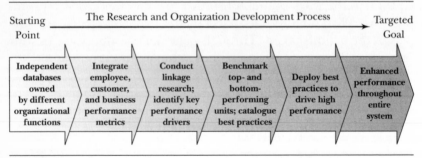

Linkage research is indeed a powerful framework for organization development and provides many advantages:

• Linkage research tells us about the nature of the interrelationships among the employee, customer, and business performance measures. It provides us with an understanding of the strength of those interrelationships and, in the best examples of the technique, the directionality as well.

- Linkage research suggests which measures to track among the many that are often available. For example, some topics within a typical employee survey are consistently more potent predictors of organizational success than others (Brooks, Wiley, & Hause, in press).
- Linkage research can serve to illustrate important and perhaps previously hidden trade-offs. The case study reflects that point by highlighting the trade-off between cost containment (a productivity objective) and the service quality initiative (a strategy for increasing market share). Bringing this trade-off into the light forced policy changes that led to increased organizational effectiveness.
- Linkage research helps create a road map. By identifying the predictors of the desired outcomes, it focuses attention on those soft measures that if improved, lead to higher performance on the more objective hard measures of business success.
- Linkage research gives executives a focal point for communication to employees about survey results. It illustrates how the interests of all three critical stakeholders of profit-seeking organizations (employees, customers, and financial stakeholders) are intertwined and therefore why taking action on the results of a properly designed employee survey is a business matter, not just an employee happiness concern.

Adding the internal benchmarking step to the OD process is also powerful. In this case study, it clearly identified local-level practices that supported and interfered with effective functioning. The cataloguing of best practices also provides a solid framework for building both individual manager development plans and broader-scale organizational development initiatives.

There is a potential danger, however, with this technique. A quick review of the sample questions used in the internal benchmarking interviews (Table 7.4) is instructive. The best practices that emerged from the interview data—employee communication, orientation toward employees, and dealer orientation—are indeed a reflection of what we asked about. This can lead to the erroneous conclusion that the fixes to the system are primarily human resource oriented when in fact there can be no doubt that changes to other elements of the system (such as marketing, operations, or information systems) would also lift overall organizational performance.

Even so, this approach to organization development holds great promise. Simply linking employee survey results to outcome measures alone has added greatly to the perceived value of survey feedback-based organization development. Combining linkage research techniques with internal benchmarking processes and best practices analysis advances our understanding even further while simultaneously increasing the potential impact of surveys to drive high performance.

References

Brooks, S. M., Wiley, J. W., & Hause, E. L. (in press). Using employee and customer perspectives to improve organizational performance. In L. Fogli (Ed.), *Customer service delivery.* San Francisco: Jossey-Bass.

Schneider, B., & Bowen, D. E. (1985). Employee and customer perceptions of service in banks: Replication and extension. *Journal of Applied Psychology, 70,* 423–433.

Schneider, B., Parkington, J. J., & Buxton, V. M. (1980). Employee and customer perceptions of service in banks. *Administrative Science Quarterly, 25,* 252–267.

Tornow, W. W., and Wiley, J. W. (1991). Service Quality and Management Practices: A Look at Employee Attitudes, Customer Satisfaction, and Bottom-Line Consequences. *Human Resource Planning, 14*(2), 105–115.

Wiley, J. W. (1991). Customer Satisfaction: A Supportive Work Environment and its Financial Cost. *Human Resource Planning, 14*(2), 117–128.

Wiley, J. W. (1996). Linking survey results to customer satisfaction and business performance. In A. I. Kraut (Ed.), *Organizational surveys* (pp. 330–359). San Francisco: Jossey-Bass.

Wiley, J. W., & Brooks, S. M. (2000). The high performance organizational climate: How workers describe top-performing units. In N. M. Ashkanasy, C.P.M. Wilderom, & M. F. Peterson (Eds.), *Organizational culture and climate* (pp. 177–191). Thousand Oaks, CA: Sage.

PART 2

New Technologies

Part Two, on new methods, looks at innovative techniques with an impact, and sometimes a great one, on survey practice. These include the use of Web-based surveys, improved computer programs for creating reports and dealing with write-in comments, innovative statistical approaches, the use of pulse surveys, and elegant data presentation approaches. The chapters in this part present new and better ways of dealing with surveys and the data they produce.

Kristofer J. Fenlason and Kathleen Suckow-Zimberg in Chapter Eight use their experience and skill to describe the benefits, challenges, and pitfalls in doing Web-based surveys. They compare online methods favorably to paper surveys and take us through the steps to ensure that Web-based surveys work smoothly. They dispel the illusion that online surveys are simple to do and give a checklist of ways to avoid problems.

Karen M. Barbera and Scott A. Young describe in Chapter Nine the processes and choices that must be faced when online survey data are reported. They show how Web technology can be leveraged to report results the same way: online. Confidentiality, time pressures, and user sophistication are among the considerations that influence the mode and options for reporting, such as self-service and real-time reporting.

In Chapter Ten, Patrick Kulesa and Ralph J. Bishop put us in touch with the latest ways to handle write-in comments. Sophisticated computing routines now use lexicons to quickly and accurately compile and count write-in comments. They show how flexible and customized write-in categories can lead directly to actions to support an organization's strategic goals.

Joe Colihan and Janine Waclawski review in Chapter Eleven the growing practice of pulse surveys, which are more frequent, narrow, and sample based than traditional census surveys. Pulse surveys help management to make decisions quickly on hot issues, but they have significant limitations, including that action taking is less likely at lower organizational levels than at higher ones.

Sara P. Weiner and Anthony T. Dalessio note in Chapter Twelve that oversurveying is a concern in many organizations. The growing desire for special studies and pulse surveys is among the reasons for the frequent use of surveys. Drawing on their experience at IBM, they explore the causes and consequences of this phenomenon and suggest potential cures.

Steven G. Rogelberg in Chapter Thirteen helps us understand how to increase response rates and understand the meaning of failures to resond to our surveys.

Kyle M. Lundby and Jeff W. Johnson present in Chapter Fourteen a new statistical method that seems particularly well suited for survey data analysis. The technique of relative weight analysis uncovers the relative importance of different measures in a survey, in a way that allows action to be directed at the highest-payoff issues.

William H. Macey and Larry D. Eldridge deal in Chapter Fifteen with the mounting issue of using data norm comparisons. They look at the value of such "benchmarking" and conclude that data norms often energize and motivate action. They also review how to judge the quality of norm data, and they note situations where direct comparisons require caution.

Sarah Rassenfoss Johnson guides us in Chapter Sixteen through the essential steps in preparing a direct and appealing data presentation to higher management. She shows how a careful consideration of the message and the audience can lay out a clear set of next steps. To do that, she gives a set of practical suggestions to create clear and powerful reports for any audience.

Ingwer Borg and Matthias Zimmermann give an additional, complementary view in Chapter Seventeen of how to prepare a stimulating presentation of survey data to top management. (The criticality of a good presentation merits the additional chapter.) They position the presentation within the overall process of a survey's action follow-through. Various statistical techniques are illustrated, and they imagine various dialogues with management that can stimulate action taking.

CHAPTER 8

Online Surveys
Critical Issues in Using the Web to Conduct Surveys

Kristofer J. Fenlason
Kathleen Suckow-Zimberg

Online technology offers one of the most versatile survey administration methods ever available to organizations. Although early electronic surveys were conducted using e-mail, diskettes, or mainframe systems, the widespread use of online surveys began with the World Wide Web in the mid-1990s. As Kraut and Saari (1999) noted, as organizations connected their employees via e-mail, the Internet, and corporate intranets, the use of online surveying increased. This was not surprising given that such surveys offer several advantages over paper-and-pencil surveys, including increased speed, the potential for lower cost (Kraut & Saari, 1999), and a greater degree of control over the flow of the survey, such as through branching questions (Dillman, 2000).

In the early to mid-1990s it was cutting edge to administer organizational surveys online; it is now relatively commonplace. Online surveys are now designed and deployed as custom-developed systems within corporations and offered as standard products by survey research firms, and they are available as stand-alone self-service software or a hosted service through self-service Web sites. Perhaps because online surveys are so prevalent, it is easy to take the technology for granted. Yet administering an online survey is neither a trivial task nor simply a technical execution issue. For organizations to make full use of surveys, these online systems must function well, and employee reactions and responses to the system must be understood and managed. System problems, whether real or perceived, can have tangible effects on the survey process. Incorrectly captured data can call into question the credibility of the survey system and those associated with it. Barriers to completion such as difficult navigation controls or needlessly complex instructions can reduce response rates and lower employee commitment. In short, practitioners need to understand both where and how to avoid pitfalls in design, development, and deployment to ensure the maximum utility of the survey system and the data it yields.

This chapter provides an overview of five key areas of online survey systems: comparing and merging paper and online methods, enhancing surveys with online capabilities, improving the user experience, system testing, and ensuring privacy and security. Given the variety of ways online surveys can be delivered, we chose topics that should apply broadly regardless of the survey delivery system. For instance, whether one is developing a system, working with a professional survey firm, or using an off-the-shelf self-service software package, one would always want to check item content and the basic functioning of the survey system. Nevertheless, certain sections may apply more than others, and it is assumed that practitioners will exercise common sense and apply time-tested practices to ensure survey success. Although the primary focus in this chapter is on survey administration, many points also apply to the broader survey system used to report or act on the survey results. In these cases, we use the more inclusive term *survey system*. We also use the term *practitioner* to encompass researchers, degreed professionals, and others charged with executing surveys in organizations. Finally, the term *online* is used to refer to electronic surveys that are conducted over the Internet/Web or on a company's intranet.

Comparing and Merging Methodologies: Online and Paper

Although today's survey practitioners have a wider variety of survey administration options at their disposal than ever before (telephone, paper, online, e-mail, personal digital assistants), it is likely that paper and online methods will account for a substantial proportion of organizational surveys in the foreseeable future. As Macey (1996) commented, paper-and-pencil surveys have been the dominant method of organizational surveying, and this is likely to continue for some time. Reasons for the persistence of paper include infrastructure (for example, PCs are not universally available), employee readiness (for example, confidentiality concerns, lack of PC training, comfort with paper and pencil), and organizational culture (such as commitment to offering a choice). Consequently, not all organizations can use online surveys exclusively, and some may be in a permanent state of dual-method surveying due to the issues noted.

Research on the effects of administration methods is not new (see Kiesler & Sproull, 1986; Schuman & Presser, 1981), and it is being updated to focus on online surveys (see Church, 2001; Stanton, 1998; Thompson, Surface, Martin, & Sanders, 2003). A literature review and our own professional experiences indicate four areas about which practitioners should be aware.

Measurement Equivalence

A central question in dual-method surveying is measurement equivalence, that is, whether responses collected using one method are psychometrically equivalent to responses collected using another method. The implication is that when equivalence can be established, results can be interpreted with the confidence that any observed differences are likely due to real differences between groups being compared and are not due to the two methods measuring different things. It should be noted that simply examining how mean scores or percentages differ from one method to another is not a sufficient test of measurement equivalence. For instance, when trending results for a given group, one cannot simply assume that similar mean scores indicate there is no difference between present and past-year results if different collection methods were used in the two years. It is possible that employee responses changed from one year to the next but that this change was erased by method effects.

Definitive research on the measurement equivalence of dual-method surveys has tended to employ analyses using item response theory or structural equation modeling. A review of studies that used these approaches indicates that there is likely no difference between data collected using paper and those collected using online methods (Donovan, 2000; Donovan, Drasgow, & Probst, 2000; Fenlason, 2000; Magnan, Lundby, & Fenlason, 2000; Stanton, 1998; Young, Daum, Robie, & Macey, 2000). Although encouraging, these findings do not necessarily mean that paper and Web survey measurement equivalence can be assumed in all cases. These conclusions are based on a handful of studies, and practitioners should continue to examine equivalence until the findings have been replicated across a broader variety of settings and instruments.

Item and Scale Score Differences

The central concern with this issue is that if one method yields more or less favorable responses than the other, appropriate interpretation and use of the results may be unclear or inaccurate. Early studies of (pre-Web) electronic surveying studies found some differences between paper and electronic surveying, but did not indicate a compelling, broad-based pattern of differences on items or scales (for example, see Rosenfeld et al., 1991; Lautenschlager & Flaherty, 1990; Booth-Kewley, Rosenfeld, & Edwards, 1993).

More recent studies focusing on a direct comparison of online and paper administration methods found some differences, but taken together there does not appear to be a consistent or compelling method effect on quantitative results. (Interested readers are referred for details to Church, 2001; Magnan et al., 2000; Stanton, 1998; Yost & Homer, 1998.) One interesting finding across several of these studies is that score differences between groups often disappeared when controlling for job type. This appears to be due to differential access to the Web or paper surveys. For instance, one group of employees (such as production personnel) may tend to use paper surveys because they lack access to PCs, while other groups (such as office professionals) may have PC access on their desk and be more likely (or even required) to use an online survey version. In this case, if one examines survey results purely by administration type (online versus paper), one would expect to see a difference, but it is more likely due to the group differences rather than the administration method. Consequently, practitioners should exercise caution about interpreting score differences without first determining if significant demographic differences exist that could have influenced the responses.

Comments

To date, much of the published literature on written comments within Web and other types of electronic surveying has focused on comment length. Overall, one emerging finding is that online comments tend to be longer than those on paper. Fenlason (2000) and Mehta and Sivadas (1995) found online comments to be about one-third longer, while Kiesler and Sproull (1986) and Yost and Homer (1998) found online comment length was double that of paper. There could be several reasons for longer comments, but one is that online surveys often place no limit on comment length, while paper surveys have a finite amount of space available. Another reason might be that respondents receive less feedback about the amount they are writing (for instance, text boxes often show only part of what is typed without scrolling).

Completion and Response Rates

Another potential concern when comparing online and paper surveys is a possible method effect on item completion and response rates. Both incomplete surveys and differential response rates can affect the quality and validity of the data obtained.

There are few published studies about online item completion rates, so it is difficult to reach firm conclusions. While Stanton (1998) found that online surveys tended to have a lower percentage of items that were not completed, Fenlason (2000) found no differences in the percentage of missing item responses. Similarly, Church (2001) found no difference in item completion rates within two surveys.

However, when examining item-level completion rates, practitioners should be aware of possible differences in employee use of Don't Know/Not Applicable responses versus skipping questions. For instance, Church (2001) found that the online method yielded seven times as many skipped items as paper in one study and five times as many in another study. In contrast, Church found in one study that Don't Know responses occurred slightly less often in the online method than the paper method (the ratio of online to paper occurrences of Don't Know responses was 1 to 1.29). Church found no significant differences in the occurrence of Don't Know responses in a second study.

Church's dissection of completion rates (2001) by examining Don't Know responses separately from skipped items is an important example to follow. Future investigations should consider analyzing Don't Know or Not Applicable responses separately where possible because indiscriminately combining them with skipped items could mask potentially important differences. Until a larger body of empirical work has been developed, generalizing about completion rates should be done carefully and should explicitly spell out what constituted item nonresponse.

It appears that the question of whether there are overall differential response rates between online and paper surveys has not yet been fully answered. While some (especially early) studies have found lower response rates with electronic compared to paper surveys, practitioners should differentiate between earlier electronic formats, typically e-mail, and more recent Web-based inputs. For instance, both Schaefer and Dillman (1998) and Mehta and Sivadas (1995) found lower response rates for online surveys than paper surveys, but these studies used an e-mail format.

In several more recent studies, it is not possible to ascertain meaningful overall response rates for the two methods. This has occurred for several reasons, including employees not having a true choice of method due to lack of PC access, management assignment to a method, or lack of tracking of response rate within groups (for more detail, see Spera & Moye, 2001; Stanton, 1998; and Young et al., 2000).

Moving Forward with Dual-Method Surveys

It is a business reality that dual-method surveying will likely remain a necessity for some organizations. It is therefore encouraging that the research to date does not indicate troublesome differences between responses collected using the two methods. The implication is that (all other things being equal) practitioners can use paper and online results interchangeably. Nevertheless, it would be prudent for practitioners involved in such efforts to remain aware of potential differences, including the areas examined in this section, and incorporate future research findings into their practice choices and decision making.

Enhancing Surveys with Online Capabilities

Online surveys can essentially replicate paper-based surveys, or they can take advantage of a range of additional function, format, and feedback options not available on paper. Such enhancements can lead to an improved experience for the survey taker and greater control and data yield for the survey practitioner. The range of such enhancements is virtually unlimited; we provide six illustrations of this potential and related risks.

Text Substitution

Organizational surveys often contain questions about various referent groups (one's work group, division, location). The traditional paper approach has been to provide generic forms of these questions, such as, "Rate how well your division communicates about strategic plans." An online alternative is to substitute specific text for these generic names (in this example, "the logistics division" in place of "division"). The specific substitute text can be determined by previous questions or demographic information that acts as a switch.

Potential advantages include reducing ambiguity about the referent group, increasing rating accuracy, and moving employees through the survey more quickly because they do not have to refer to a list of terms. A potential disadvantage is that if a switch question is answered incorrectly (by employee mistake in the demographics or database error when demographics are precoded), employees would then be answering questions that contain incorrect text substitution. Text substitution may also create the impression that the survey is not confidential. This is a particular concern when employee demographics are precoded into the system rather than being self-reported. In this case, even if practitioners have crafted communications that inform employees about this approach, it is likely that a percentage will not read or remember these communications and as a result may react negatively.

System-Managed Branching

The extent of branching can vary widely in organizational surveys, from none to multiple and highly complex skips, depending on several responses. When executed on paper, branching requires the survey taker to read the branch instructions and correctly execute the action. In that case, the branching is manual or respondent managed. In contrast, online surveys can be designed with system-managed branching such that the employee is automatically advanced to the next appropriate question based on prior answers. A system-managed branch (especially when branching complexity increases) reduces burden on the employee, lowers the probability of answering incorrect question sets, and reduces completion time.

As with text substitution, a concern about system-managed branching is that if employees supply incorrect answers to initial branching questions, they will be subsequently directed to sets of questions that may not apply to them. Also, because designers can now craft increasingly complex branches, there is a greater potential for error due to flaws in the logic or execution of the branches. Such cases require that all possible permutations of branching are considered and tested.

Real-Time Response Validation and Feedback

Error correction of invalid or out-of-range responses in paper surveys typically occurs after a survey has been completed, while online surveys can validate and provide feedback on responses in real time. The system compares responses to a reference list, out-of-range values are identified, and a pop-up error message is provided. This probably applies most to items for which employees must enter a response value (for example, a four-digit code) versus choosing from among closed-ended responses. Although this sort of check may be most prevalent at the individual item level, it is also possible to place such validation checks throughout a survey to detect and flag inconsistent or contradictory answers (such as indicating that one belongs to a combination of department and division that does not exist). Practitioners using this option need to decide how and how often survey takers are informed of possible mistakes.

Item Completion Reminders

In contrast to paper, online surveys can provide real-time reminders that questions have not been answered, either immediately before moving to the next item or as a summary list at the end of the survey. Reminders have the potential advantage of bolstering item completion rates and thereby ensuring higher data quality. They also have the potential disadvantage of seeming to force people to respond. To avoid this, reminder text and instructions should indicate that responding is optional and that this is just a friendly reminder. For example, if an employee leaves several items blank in a survey section, the following reminder might appear in a pop-up box when the employee clicks on the "Next Page" button: "These items were not completed: 2, 5, 11. You may complete any or all of these items or, if you would like to leave the items as is, you may click 'Next Page' again." We can think of no circumstances under which employees should be forced to provide an answer before moving on in the survey. Employees have always had the option of not responding to all items with previous survey methods, and this should be preserved with online methods.

Precoding of Demographics

Along with the increasing integration and standardization of systems and databases comes an increased ability to precode demographic information. That is, information from an HR database (for example, one's location or group code) can be sent to the survey database prior to employees' receiving the survey. Precoding can lower the effort and time it takes to complete the survey, enable text substitution, allow the use of demographics that employees may not be able to report (such as designation as a high-potential employee, if the company does not alert people to this designation), and in some cases increase the accuracy of demographic coding. However, this approach requires uniquely identifying the employee within the HR database and when the employee enters the survey to respond. Depending on security levels and whether the survey is hosted on site or by a third party, this can increase employee concerns about being more identifiable than with a paper survey. In addition, prepopulated demographics could be incorrect, or the employee may believe they are wrong. Consequently, if practitioners are interested in using this feature, they should decide whether and how to allow employees to change the data. In an informal benchmarking exercise on the topic of precoding in 2004 (with nineteen large companies with ongoing survey programs), we found that most companies that use precodes do not offer employees the opportunity to edit the demographics.

Regardless of whether employees can edit their precoded information, it is probably ethically and practically prudent to inform employees about the use of precoded data and provide assurances about response confidentiality. This information can be communicated to employees in various ways, such as within the survey invitation, within the survey instructions, or over an intranet Web site. The practitioner can also choose to display the actual data in the survey itself. In our experience (and based on the previously mentioned benchmarking) it appears that most companies that use precodes disclose to employees how the data are being used but do not typically display the precoded data within the survey.

Content Creation and Change

Making changes to a survey is much easier and faster when it is online. Practitioners can quickly make changes and have them uploaded into the system within a short period of time. Comparatively, paper surveys require reprinting and redistributing the surveys, which takes much longer. Online surveys also streamline version control; practitioners can completely replace previous versions, removing the possibility of outdated versions being used. Online capabilities also enable practitioners to field a survey quickly to capture current reactions to a recent event or change. Testing new content is also facilitated. Without the constraints of paper length and physical space, insertion of items for pilot testing is a relatively low-cost option. Of course, because of the relative ease of content change, practitioners may also need to be on guard against increased pressure for last-minute content changes—changes that may not receive the full consideration they should if more time to review and debate were available.

These examples highlight just some of the enhancements available in online surveys. As the number and type of enhancements continue to grow, practitioners should ensure that good research and practice decisions are made.

Improving the User Experience: Usability and Accessibility

The formats and functions available with online surveys have the potential to enhance the user's experience (such as lowering the level of effort required), but they can also degrade user experience (for instance, by supplying cryptic error messages or making it more difficult for those with disabilities to access, navigate, and answer the survey), resulting in negative outcomes such as lowered participation rates. Usability testing provides survey practitioners with a method to identify and assess the effect of these online design choices across users. Designing specifically for disabled users (accessibility is discussed at the end of this section) helps ensure participation by a group of employees whose needs are sometimes overlooked and typically creates a better experience for all users.

Usability and Usability Testing

Usability is broadly synonymous with the concept of user friendliness. In the survey context, usability generally focuses on the look and functionality of an online survey tool as it appears to end users. In an attempt to define the term more specifically as applied to surveys, Lundby and Mack (2003) adapted an existing definition (from the International Organization for Standardization; ISO 9241–11), in which *usability* is defined as "the extent to which a product can be used by specific users to achieve specified goals with *effectiveness, efficiency* and *satisfaction* in a specified context of use" (UsabilityNet, 2003, italics added). In the organizational survey context, the users are employees; the overall goal is to collect survey responses while maintaining participation in the process. *Effectiveness* is the extent to which the survey is fully and accurately completed and how well employees understand how to use the survey. *Efficiency* is how quickly, easily, and clearly employees can navigate through the survey. *Satisfaction* focuses on the overall online survey experience as well as specific survey sections or tasks.

Usability testing is essentially a practical evaluation approach to identifying "problems in time to fix them" (Dumas & Redish, 1999, p. xiv). The intent is not to catch all potential problems or to create a perfect survey system, but rather to improve system functioning so it facilitates rather than hinders the actions of the end user.

Practitioners should be aware that usability testing and system testing are not the same. The latter focuses on the functioning of the system independent of a given user (Couper, 2002). Although usability testing may incidentally identify system issues, it does not systematically assess for software and hardware problems and so cannot substitute for system testing. In a sense, usability testing is analogous to some of the pretesting that practitioners have done for years with paper-based surveys, in that we are looking for user reactions to the content, instructions, and so on. In contrast, system testing does not typically involve end users and focuses on how well data are captured and reported.

The Importance of Usability Testing

The online survey experience is dynamic. The interaction of employee factors (such as PC knowledge) and system factors (such as browser configuration and connection speed) can make assessing user reactions to online surveys difficult, but it is also why it is so important (Dillman & Bowker, 2001). Usability testing enables practitioners to understand these dynamic reactions better.

Specific reasons for investing in usability testing of online surveys include maximizing positive and minimizing negative experiences, ensuring high data quality (for example, higher completion rates due to lower user frustration) and cost control (for instance, by limiting the time employees must cope with confusing navigation; see Lundby & Mack, 2003). More usable systems also promote self-sufficiency, which is critical because employees are typically expected to complete online surveys without outside aid. Finally, usability testing can increase practitioner awareness of user knowledge gaps and concerns and enable subsequent adjustments to communications or training.

Usability Testing Techniques

Although there are many usability testing techniques, this section highlights five techniques that are likely to be the most approachable for survey practitioners.

Heuristic evaluation involves a small group of experts (such as programmers or survey practitioners) who review the system and compare it against established usability guidelines, or *heuristics*. Reviewers independently use the system and document conflicts with the heuristics. The reviewers then meet as a group and, with the guidance of a facilitator, discuss their findings (Levi & Conrad, 2002). Examples of heuristics (adapted from Nielsen, 1994b) are presented below as applied to a survey system. Practitioners should examine to what extent the survey system:

- Provides feedback on user progress/location.
- Uses symbols, actions, or phrases consistently throughout the survey (for example, the action for moving to the next page should be identical).
- Offers users who make a mistake a clear exit or path backward (such as being able to navigate to previous questions and change answers).
- Ensures that error messages and possible solutions make sense to the typical user.
- Provides helpful information for users who might want or need assistance.

The *cognitive walk-through* technique involves a small group of designers and developers who work through a set of task-based scenarios created to emulate a user's experience. The group role-plays the part of the user, relying on available system cues to navigate and accomplish tasks. At each decision point, the group determines if the user would have chosen the correct path or understood the task. The group documents possible reasons for problems and where they occurred (for more detail, see Dumas & Redish, 1999, or Spencer, 2000).

The *think-aloud* technique asks end users to verbalize their thoughts while completing a task in the presence of an observer. Nielsen (1994a) advocates that for most uses, simply observing the user live and taking notes throughout the test is sufficient.

Another option is *focus groups,* in which a group of five to twelve users are asked to engage in a survey system task and then to discuss their experiences. *Questionnaires* can also be administered after users work with a survey system, capturing ratings of overall experience and feedback regarding specific system features.

Applying Usability Testing

In general, it is better to use multiple techniques in order to avoid the blind spots that can occur by applying a single method. Different techniques have been found to identify different types of problems and levels of severity (see Dumas & Redish, 1999; Jeffries, Miller, Wharton, & Uyeda, 1991), and multiple methods help ensure adequate coverage of the three usability components of effectiveness, efficiency, and satisfaction, emphasized by Lundby and Mack (2003).

Usability testing can be used at any point in the life cycle of an online survey program, but applying it early and repeatedly allows more time to address issues and evaluate the effectiveness of changes (Marquis, Nichols, & Tedesco, 1998; Rosenbaum, 2000). Early testing can also help reduce costs because system changes tend to cost less when executed earlier rather than later in the process (Bias & Mayhew, 1994; Levi & Conrad, 2002).

Practitioners should consider testing when making major system changes, such as switching to a new online survey system or adding features or functions within an existing system. While isolated and relatively minor changes might not merit testing individually, practitioners should consider testing when a collection of such small changes is being made. Also, because user interaction with a system depends in part on the mix of employee experience, knowledge, and skills, changes in the user population may also merit testing (such as after a merger).

A guiding principle in deciding who and how many people to involve in testing is to ensure representation of the user population. For early system design and development work, survey staff or others closely involved may be sufficient to catch problems that would affect a wide range of users. However, involving end users is key to comprehensive improvement because techniques involving end users are likely to identify a higher percentage of severe problems than other methods (Jeffries et al., 1991; Dumas & Redish, 1999) and because different people tend to find different problems (Nielsen, 1994b). If the user population is sufficiently represented, many techniques will detect the majority of issues with only a few users (Nielsen, 1994b; Mayhew, 2002). While the recommended number of subjects for usability testing is somewhat debatable, the usability literature typically advocates obtaining data from five to ten individuals within a technique.

Practitioners should not be deterred from testing because their situation does not seem to neatly fit the techniques described or because of lack of time or access to usability professionals. Usability methods are flexible, can be combined and modified to fit the situation, and often require only a modest investment of resources. If applied judiciously, using multiple techniques at multiple times, usability testing should catch the majority of and the most severe usability issues.

Designing for Accessibility

When thinking about designing survey systems using the many enhancements available with online surveying and when thinking about designing a system with high usability, it is important to remember those with disabilities. Nearly one-fifth of the U.S. population has a disability of some form (Bohman, 2003; U.S. Department of Commerce, 2000). Of course, not all disabilities affect an individual's ability to interact with an online survey system. For some, however, particularly those with sight and mobility impairments, the design of surveys and associated tools can determine the extent to which these individuals can independently complete surveys and other tasks.

A few key design principles will increase the accessibility of the survey and associated tools for those with disabilities and will, in fact, improve usability for all users (Bohman, 2001; Brewer, 2001). For instance, survey systems should be fully keyboard compatible. With partially or non-keyboard-compatible systems, respondents will be required to use a mouse at some point during the survey. For those with mobility impairments, such as repetitive stress injury, using a mouse may not be possible or preferred. Consequently, it is important to provide a choice that enables users to respond using either a keyboard or a mouse.

In programming the survey and reporting tools, all entities (buttons, graphs, images, tables, and response option check boxes, for example) should be labeled with text. For example, if a table format is used to present survey questions, it should be identified in the programming with text such as "table of questions." This text would not be visible to the majority of participants. For those who are either sight or mobility impaired, however, this will ensure that adaptive technologies, such as screen readers, are able to describe the survey component to the user. In this example, the screen reader tool would read "table of questions" aloud so the user would be able to interpret upcoming survey content.

Another key principle is to avoid the use of color or shading alone to convey meaning, such as when creating graphs. Although color or shading can be used, these should be used in conjunction with text or numerical labels because those who are sight impaired will not be able to distinguish the colors or shading. For individuals with some, but not complete, sight loss, additional design principles should be applied, such as employing high-contrast background and text for surveys and reports (such as black text on white background). In addition, selection and navigation buttons should be consistent in placement or located in positions typical to other Web sites.

To increase accessibility for all users, developers should not hard-code any formatting. Hard coding refers to designing programming code in such a way that limits the user's ability to make changes to what appears (background colors, font sizes), rather than creating flexible code that allows the user to override the default settings. For example, when font size is hard-coded, someone with a visual impairment cannot improve readability by increasing the size of the font. Other design decisions are less about the programming of the tool and more about the content within the tool. For instance, practitioners should number options in a drop-down box for easier selection, avoid the use of sight-related words such as "see below," and describe hyperlinks rather than just displaying the entire hyperlink address (imagine being sight impaired and having to listen to text-reading software provide a character-by-character spelling of an extensive Web site address).

There are a number of other design issues to consider when developing survey systems to be used by individuals with disabilities. The list here provides a solid start, but for more detail, practitioners should speak with an information technology professional and review accessibility-related Web sites, such as www.w3.org, www.usability.gov, and www.Webaim.org.

The Future of Design Improvement

As research and practice experience grows, practitioners will begin to compile more definitive best practices for online system design. However, this does not mean that usability testing or ensuring accessibility will be passing needs. Technology, users, user capabilities, formats, and functions will continue to change, so we will need to continue to study these developments (see Couper, 1999). Practitioners should become familiar with usability testing techniques and the issues associated with designing for disabled users at some level. Some may use the information to conduct testing on their own, while others may use it to interact more effectively with their online survey providers, or to make more informed decisions about which off-the-shelf online survey software to use or when they might want to bring in usability testing or accessibility professionals.

Testing the System: Ensuring Tool Success and Data Integrity

System testing is an important aspect of preparing the survey (as well as reporting tools) for deployment. While usability testing focuses on how users perceive and experience system interactions, system testing focuses on the behind-the-scenes aspects, that is, the system on which the survey and reporting tools are built. While users may directly experience problems with the system (such as during server crashes), other system problems can go undetected by the user and can be identified only by means of a technical review. A thorough technical review ensures that the end-to-end work flow processes and handoffs are executed successfully and as expected and that data are both captured and reported correctly.

There are several important aspects of system testing (Sandora, 2002; Suckow, 2002). Researchers can choose to engage in some or all forms of testing described (as well as others not discussed here). Decisions regarding what types of testing to conduct are typically based on available time, money, and people resources. Testing decisions may also be based on the extent of experience with the specific survey tool; for a tool that has been used repeatedly by the organization, less emphasis may be put on testing than if the tool were new to the organization. As with usability testing, the most important point is that conducting some testing is far better than conducting no testing. This applies for both the survey and any reporting tools and should be conducted whether using a vendor tool, an off-the-shelf tool, or a tool one has built oneself. (Note that the names for the tests described in this section may vary across IT professionals and companies.)

Content Review

Content review involves proofing the content, which is safe to assume that most practitioners do, as this is also common practice with paper surveys. Nevertheless, the reader may benefit from some reminders that can ensure high-quality testing. For instance, conduct a detailed review of all languages of the survey and reports, perhaps engaging colleagues who are native speakers of the language to conduct the reviews. One method for proofing content is to place the original content and the online content into a word processing program. The content from each can then be merged and compared automatically to identify where there are differences in the text.

When conducting content reviews, it is important to remember to review any hover text within the survey. Hover text is text that appears when the mouse pointer is placed over some entity (such as response options) on the Web page. As an example of why this is important, having a response option of "strongly agree" with hover text that reads "strongly disagree" can be a confusing cue for an employee.

Component or Unit Testing

Component or unit testing involves conducting a separate check of each element of the survey system, as well as the connections between the elements in the survey system process. This testing is conducted to verify that the survey system does what it is supposed to, does not do what it is not supposed to, does not break when pushed, and handles errors appropriately. In addition to usability testing (described above), there are at least three important aspects of component testing.

Functionality Testing

Functionality testing involves verifying the basic functionality of the survey system. For instance, it is important to test all hyperlinks within the survey and reporting tools. During functionality testing, the practitioner should also verify that users can navigate through all Web pages as expected and that the Web pages appear in the correct order. Functionality of all questions should be confirmed by verifying that all radio buttons (circles that respondents use to select their response) or check boxes work and that comment fields accept text. Testing should also verify that certain actions do not work. For example, if written comments fields are set up to accept only numerical responses, the field should not accept alpha characters. This aspect of testing involves some creativity in thinking about various ways that users may abuse or innocently misuse the survey system to ensure that they cannot take these actions.

Data Integrity Testing

In this form of testing, also known as pattern testing, the goal is to verify that entered survey responses are correctly captured in the database by entering responses to simulate employees completing the survey. During this testing, it is critical to use all response options (including skipping items and entering written comments) and a combination of responses (different test cases should have different responses). After entering responses for several individuals, the database should be examined to verify that all entries match what is in the database. For example, if the survey is set up such that a response of "agree" is equal to a numerical response of four, each selection of "agree" should yield the number four in the database. This is also a good test to verify that the written comment entry fields can handle a sufficient comment length and any non-English text characters. For example, if a written comment of one thousand characters is entered, does the entire comment appear in the database, or is it truncated?

Accessibility Testing

Accessibility testing verifies that individuals with disabilities will be able to access the survey and reporting tools. There are many ways to test aspects of accessibility, such as practitioners trying to navigate and complete an entire survey (or report) without using a mouse. If a mouse is needed at any point, the tool is not fully accessible. Similarly, practitioners should attempt to resize text within the tool; if it does not resize, it is not fully accessible. To test accessibility better, the researcher could obtain a demonstration version of accessibility software and go through the survey process using the tool. For example, the screen reader tool JAWS for those with visual impairments is available in a demonstration version.

Contacting the IT department to ask for assistance in accessibility testing can also be helpful. Of course, one of the best ways to test accessibility is to engage employees with disabilities to review the survey system. We have found this method to be particularly valuable and rewarding.

Performance Testing

Performance testing helps ensure that the process and system will function flawlessly when accessed by a high number of users. A thorough performance test will verify that response times for loading pages and processing responses are acceptable and that a large number of users can be in the system at the same time (that is, load or stress testing).

One way to conduct performance testing is to create programs (scripts) that simulate having hundreds or thousands of users in the survey at one time. These tests can be designed to confirm that the system can operate flawlessly with the average number of users, the peak number of users, or a much higher-than-expected number of users. The first two options confirm that the system can handle a typical load. The third option puts greater stress on the system, which can be helpful in bringing other system flaws to the surface and ensuring the capacity to handle exceptional system demands. Practitioners should examine historical use patterns to determine targeted user numbers for each of these options.

Full Systems Testing

The final test is the full systems test. During this test, a complete end-to-end test should be run of the entire system to ensure that the full process of accessing the tool, entering any data or responses, and receiving raw and aggregated results all work flawlessly. This level of testing requires simulating users to enter responses into a number of surveys, calculating what the results should be, and then comparing expected results to those produced by the reporting tools. This provides another verification that data have been captured correctly and will ensure that aggregation and any data rules (such as minimum number of respondents for creating reports) are working appropriately.

When thinking about testing survey tools provided by a vendor, it is ideal to conduct at least some of this testing directly within the organization where the survey will be used rather than relying on the vendor to conduct all of the testing (this applies to both customized systems and off-the-shelf software or hosting services). Because organizations have different rules in place for security and because of differences in technology infrastructure, surveys and reports may behave differently at the vendor's site than within the organization. Therefore, although the vendor can and should conduct much testing, testing should still be done on site as well to ensure the tools function as expected.

Some readers might question whether it is worth the time and effort to understand and engage in the testing steps described, particularly if a professional vendor or IT team has designed the survey or reporting tools. Although technology is a deeply integrated part of our lives and work, it is not error proof or fully predictable. Human errors do occur. Therefore, work should still be verified and systems should still be tested for the sake of the credibility of the survey and process, to ensure a positive user experience, and to guarantee accurate data. A few hours or days invested in systems testing can provide huge payoffs if it prevents problems with the survey system or process.

Addressing Privacy and Security in Online Surveys

Awareness and concern about data privacy and security have grown as regulations for protection of personal data have been implemented, systems have been compromised, and user trust has eroded. In this section, we outline several privacy and security concerns and provide suggestions for addressing these issues.

Data Privacy and Trust in the Survey System

Data privacy has been a longstanding concern of survey practitioners, independent of administration method. Online administration presents many of the same concerns as paper but also raises some new concerns. To manage and protect data privacy and employee trust in the system, practitioners should have a firm grasp of the applied ethical issues and obligations that apply to surveys in general. Sashkin and Prien (1996) and Lowman (1998) provide excellent general guidance in this regard. Practitioners should also consult with their organization's legal resources, exploring how current regulations, such as the European Privacy Directive, might affect the survey process. Finally, practitioners should be aware of at least two additional issues that apply to online surveys.

Managing Perceptions

Managing employee perceptions about anonymity and confidentiality can be critical in online surveys. Kraut and Saari (1999) noted this as a potential concern in 1999, Fenlason and Suckow (2004) reconfirmed this as a continuing concern, and Thompson et al. (2003) noted this may particularly apply when organizations initially switch to online. Employee reactions to such concerns have the potential to result in dishonest or socially desirable responses (Sashkin & Prien, 1996), reduced participation in future surveys (Thompson et al., 2003), and general distrust of management and the survey program itself. Of course, practitioners need to manage the actual privacy of the data, but it is equally important that they manage the communications directed at employee perceptions.

Our experience indicates that there are several actions practitioners should consider to manage employee perceptions effectively. Practitioners can conduct interviews, focus groups, or usability testing to understand employee concerns regarding privacy. Once concerns are known, appropriate messages or training materials can be developed. Another action is to collect and maintain only a minimum amount of personally identifying information in the survey system. In some organizations, practitioners may address concerns about the security of entry into the system by offering options, such as not requiring passwords, allowing employees to swap passwords, providing a paper-based option, or using an outside party for data collection. Finally, practitioners should communicate about the specific mechanisms used to protect anonymity and confidentiality (for example, minimum group size for reports). This helps reassure survey takers that safeguards are in place, publicly commits management to these guidelines, and reminds potential system abusers that rules are in place. Because each organization has its own set of norms about employee privacy and each has a unique history of surveying, practitioners will need to inform their actions based on each organization's culture and needs.

Tracking Responses

Online survey technology offers the unique ability to track, at a high level of detail, who, when, and in what ways individuals interact with a survey system. Although such detailed information may seem generally useful, practitioners should carefully consider these administration options. Perhaps the most common use is to monitor response and completion rates for a survey. Organizations often want to know how many surveys were accessed, begun, or completed so that groups with low participation could be encouraged to complete the survey. Although such tracking requires individual-level identification in the system, it is typically reported at only aggregate levels to protect anonymity and confidentiality. Even so, it is critical that access to this information be carefully restricted to authorized users, who should receive training and communications about the proper use of this information.

A less common use of response tracking is to obtain information about how to improve the survey itself (in fact, this is another usability testing method). Examination of session log information can identify possible user problems. For example, if survey instructions are unclear, log information may show respondents changing response options or returning to previous pages on multiple occasions. Ethical guidelines (see Lowman, 1998; Sashkin & Prien, 1996) allow collection of this information if individual identity is protected (for instance, reported by group) and used for legitimate research questions. However, potential damage to the reputation of the survey process is great. Even if confidentiality is ensured, employees may perceive that the company is tracking every keystroke. Consequently, practitioners would be wise to use this option only when others have been exhausted. Practitioners who elect to track individual responses in this way would be prudent to restrict data gathering to subsets of individuals who have been specifically informed of the logging and the purpose of this data gathering.

Survey System Security

Thanks to widely publicized attacks, it is difficult not to be aware of the impact of computer viruses and hackers on the use of computers around the globe. What we may be less aware of is that technology security needs extend far beyond these highly visible attacks and include the need to secure the survey system itself.

Survey system security should be viewed from at least three perspectives: the physical area, people, and the technical system itself. Security from the physical perspective includes such actions as ensuring that data servers are housed in a locked, secure area; making backups of all systems; and securely storing hard copies of data or reports. From the people perspective, security includes considering strict permission rules for access to data and systems and ensuring that employees engage in safe behaviors such as using complex passwords (combinations of unpredictable alpha characters, symbols, and numbers) and locking their workstations before leaving them unattended.

Ensuring the security of the survey system from a technical perspective is more complicated and specialized than actions under the other perspectives. Consequently, while practitioners can take some actions on their own, creating strong security typically requires partnering with an IT professional. The practitioner's role in this process is to work with the IT professional to develop possible scenarios and identify possible threats to the system, so that the IT professional can work to ensure these threats can be countered. Typical events or threats include individuals' assuming the identity of another to access or view a survey or report within the system; inserting code into a survey that then corrupts the survey, database, or larger system; and gaining access to sensitive data (for example, individuals' survey responses or personnel data).

There are several fundamental considerations from the technical perspective to address such threats. For example, practitioners and IT professionals should ensure that all responses are sent in a secure manner (such as by using encryption); all sensitive documents are password protected with complex passwords (using text, numbers, and symbols); documents are shared using a secured server rather than through e-mail; different servers are used to house the survey and respondent data (Naglieri et al., 2004); and demographic information and survey responses are stored in separate (secured) databases. These fundamental practices limit the opportunity for unauthorized individuals to gain access to the survey system and confidential information.

To demonstrate the importance of security, one specific type of security breach, code injection, is described here. Code injection occurs when someone is able to insert programming code or language, such as HTML, directly within a survey or reporting tool that then runs within a specific tool or within the larger survey system. For example, if proper precautions are not taken, it is possible to insert HTML or other programming codes within input fields in a survey (such as comment spaces and check boxes). Such code can be designed to disable the survey for users, corrupt the database with fake data, erase the database, or create other havoc within the larger system.

To protect against this risk, the survey system should be programmed to convert all entries to text so they cannot run as executable commands. Similarly, unless the code language is relevant to the specific survey, programming should convert standard code commands to other characters, which would also prevent any code from running. An example of a code change would be if the user had entered "<script>alert(hi)</script>," the program should change this to read, "<script>alert(hi);</script&gt." This conversion changes executable programming code to characters that cannot be run but that can still be interpreted (at least by those who know what characters were used to replace the code). This should be done for any point where a user can provide text input.

To provide comprehensive coverage of survey system security, the physical area, people, and technical perspectives should be addressed. While practitioners can manage a number of these security issues on their own, to offer the strongest protection, practitioners should work closely with IT representatives who have a deep understanding of security issues and the specific organization's standard protocol. While the approaches and safeguards may vary, the critical issue is that the survey system is secured. This protects the integrity of the process and the data collected and provides peace of mind for all involved in the process, including the employees completing the surveys.

Conclusion

This chapter has provided an overview of considerations for online survey systems. The following points are offered as key actions practitioners should consider applying to the online survey systems for which they are responsible, whether they are using tools developed themselves, tools purchased from professional survey firms, or off-the-shelf self-service tools:

- When using paper and online surveys, practitioners can largely assume equivalence, but should verify this and examine the data for possible group-based differences.
- Practitioners should explore online survey enhancements to improve the user experience and data gathering, but should also assess the effect of such enhancements.
- When developing a survey or reporting tool, consider all audiences who will use the system, including those with disabilities. Creating a more positive experience for these individuals will invariably also improve the experience for others.
- Test the survey and any reporting tools. Usability, accessibility, data integrity, component, performance, and full system testing can greatly improve user experiences and ensure a successful survey and accurate data.
- Critically examine how to protect, improve, and communicate about survey system privacy and security.
- Leverage employees and IT professionals. Employees can provide important perspectives on the experience of using the survey system and can provide suggestions for improvement that will have a direct, positive impact on them. IT professionals will be able to provide expertise on the details and nuances within the technology that many industrial/organizational professionals do not have.

Online technology is a powerful addition to the survey practitioner's toolbox. It can enhance the process for both employees and practitioners. Change will undoubtedly continue to occur, with systems becoming more secure, accessible, feature rich, user friendly, and robust in functioning. Nevertheless, as these changes progress, practitioners should inform their decisions by continuing to apply the practical experience and guidelines of the past in the light of research and practical experiences of the present. Such a balanced approach will ensure that online organizational surveys will continue to be a positive force in organizational improvement and change.

References

Bias, R. G., & Mayhew, D. J. (1994). *Cost-justifying usability.* Orlando, FL: Academic Press.

Bohman, P. (2001). *Section 508 Web accessibility checklist.* http://www.Webaim. org/standards/508/checklist?templatetype=3.

Bohman, P. (2003). *Introduction to Web accessibility.* http://www.Webaim. org/intro/?templatetype=3.

Booth-Kewley, S., Rosenfeld, P., & Edwards, J. E. (1993). Computer administered surveys in organizational settings: Alternatives, advantages, and applications. In P. Rosenfeld, J. E. Edwards, & M. D. Thomas (Eds.), *Improving organizational surveys: New directions, methods, and applications* (pp. 73–101). Thousand Oaks, CA: Sage.

Brewer, J. (Ed.). (2001). *How people with disabilities use the Web.* http://www. w3.org/WAI/EO/Drafts/PWD-Use-Web/.

Church, A. H. (2001). Is there a method to our madness? The impact of data collection methodology on organizational survey results. *Personnel Psychology, 54,* 937–969.

Couper, M. P. (1999). *Usability evaluation of computer assisted survey instruments.* www.asc.org.uk/Events/Sep99/Pres/couper.ppt.

Couper, M. P. (2002, May). *Designing effective Web surveys.* Paper presented at the American Association of Public Opinion Research Conference, St. Pete Beach, FL.

Dillman, D. A. (2000). *Mail and Internet surveys: The tailored design method.* New York: Wiley.

Dillman, D. A., & Bowker, D. K. (2001). The Web questionnaire challenge to survey methodologists. In U. Reips & M. Bosnjak (Eds.), *Dimensions of Internet science.* Lengerich, Germany: Pabst Science. http:// survey.sesrc.wsu.edu/dillman/zuma_paper_dillman_bowker.pdf/.

Donovan, M. A. (2000, Apr.). Web-based attitude surveys: Data and lessons learned. In N. J. Mondragon (Chair), *Beyond the demo: The empirical nature of technology-based assessments.* Symposium conducted at the annual conference of the Society for Industrial and Organizational Psychology, New Orleans, LA.

Donovan, M. A., Drasgow, F., & Probst, T. M. (2000). Does computerizing paper-and-pencil job attitude scales make a difference? New IRT analyses offer insight. *Journal of Applied Psychology, 85*(2), 305–313.

Dumas, J. S., & Redish, J. C. (1999). *A practical guide to usability testing.* Portland, OR: Intellect Ltd.

Fenlason, K. J. (2000, Apr.). Multiple data collection methods in 360 feedback programs: Implications for use and interpretation. In T. Anselmi (Chair), *Current issues and challenges in the use of survey-based data.*

Symposium conducted at the annual conference of the Society for Industrial and Organizational Psychology, New Orleans, LA.

Fenlason, K. J., & Suckow, K. (2004, Apr.). *Leveraging technology in organizational surveys: Critical issues in the on-line process.* Preconference workshop presented at the annual conference of the Society for Industrial and Organizational Psychology, Chicago.

Jeffries, R., Miller, J. R., Wharton, C., & Uyeda, K. M. (1991). User interface evaluation in the real world: A comparison of four techniques. In S. P. Robertson, G. M. Olson, & J. S. Olson (Eds.), *Proceedings of the ACM CHI 91 Human Factors in Computing Systems Conference* (pp. 119–124). New York: ACM Press. Available online http://portal.acm.org/citation.cfm?id=108862&coll=portal&dl=ACM&CFID=5326 6630&CFTOKEN=21447832.

Kiesler, S., & Sproull, L. (1986). Response effects in the electronic survey. *Public Opinion Quarterly, 50,* 402–413.

Kraut, A. I., & Saari, L. M. (1999). Organization surveys: Coming of age for a new era. In A. I. Kraut & A. K. Korman (Eds.), *Evolving practices in human resource management* (pp. 302–327). San Francisco: Jossey-Bass.

Lautenschlager, G. J., & Flaherty, V. L. (1990). Computer administration of questions: More desirable or more social desirability? *Journal of Applied Psychology, 75*(3), 310–314.

Levi, M. D., & Conrad, F. G. (2002). *Usability testing of World Wide Web sites.* www.bls.gov/ore/htm_papers/st960150.htm.

Lowman, R. L. (Ed.). (1998). *The ethical practice of psychology in organizations.* Washington, DC: American Psychological Association.

Lundby, K. M., & Mack, M. (2003, Apr.). Usability research: Introduction, review, and implications for I/O survey practitioners. In K. M. Lundby (Chair), *Usability research in Web surveying: Introduction, examples and practical implications.* Symposium conducted at the annual conference of the Society for Industrial and Organizational Psychology, Orlando, FL.

Macey, W. H. (1996). Dealing with the data: Collection, processing and analysis. In A. I. Kraut (Ed.), *Organizational surveys: Tools for assessment and change* (pp. 204–232). San Francisco: Jossey-Bass.

Magnan, S. M., Lundby, K. M., & Fenlason, K. J. (2000, Apr.). Dual media: The art and science of paper and Internet employee survey implementation. In T. Anselmi (Chair), *Current issues and challenges in the use of survey-based data.* Symposium conducted at the Annual Conference of the Society for Industrial and Organizational Psychology, New Orleans, LA.

Marquis, K., Nichols, E., & Tedesco, H. (1998). *Human-computer interface usability in a survey organization: Getting started at the Census Bureau.* www.census.gov/srd/papers/pdf/sm98–04.pdf.

Mayhew, D. (2002). *Usability testing: You get what you pay for.* www.taskz. com/ucd_usabilty_testing_indepth.php.

Mehta, R., & Sivadas, E. (1995). Comparing response rates and response content in mail versus electronic mail surveys. *Journal of the Market Research Society, 37*(4), 429–439.

Naglieri, J. A., Drasgow, F., Schmit, M., Handler, L., Prifitera, A., Margolis, A., & Velasquez, R. (2004). Psychological testing on the Internet. *American Psychologist, 59,* 150–162.

Nielsen, J. (1994a). *Guerilla HCI: Using discount usability engineering to penetrate the intimidation barrier.* http://www.useit.com.

Nielsen, J. (1994b). *How to conduct a heuristic evaluation.* http://www.useit. com/papers/heuristic/heuristic_evaluation.html.

Rosenbaum, S. (2000, Aug.). *Not just a hammer: When and how to employ multiple methods in usability programs.* Paper presented at UPA 2000, Usability Professionals Association, Asheville, NC.

Rosenfeld, P., Giacalone, R. A., Knouse, S. B., Doherty, L. M., Vicino, S. M., Kantor, J., & Greaves, J. (1991). Impression management, candor, and microcomputer-based organizational surveys: An individual differences approach. *Computers in Human Behavior, 7,* 22–32.

Sandora, L. (2002, Apr.). Testing web-based systems: A framework for getting started. In K. J. Suckow (Chair), *Protecting your data and your job: Testing your technology.* Symposium conducted at the annual conference of the Society for Industrial and Organizational Psychology, Toronto, Canada.

Sashkin, M., & Prien, E. (1996). Ethical concerns and organizational surveys. In A. I. Kraut (Ed.), *Organizational surveys: Tools for assessment and change* (pp. 381–404). San Francisco: Jossey-Bass.

Schaefer, D., & Dillman, D. (1998). Development of a standard e-mail methodology: Results of an experiment. *Public Opinion Quarterly, 62,* 378–397.

Schuman, H., & Presser, S. (1981). *Questions and answers in attitude surveys: Experiments on question form, wording and context.* Orlando, FL: Academic Press.

Spencer, R. (2000). *The streamlined cognitive walkthrough method, working around social constraints encountered in a software development company.* http:// reed.cs.depaul.edu/peterwh/Class/eval/articles/p353-spencer.pdf.

Spera, S. D., & Moye, N. A. (2001, Apr.). *Measurement equivalence between paper and Web survey methods in a multinational company.* Poster presented at the annual conference of the Society for Industrial and Organizational Psychology, San Diego, CA.

Stanton, J. M. (1998). An empirical assessment of data collection using the Internet. *Personnel Psychology, 51,* 709–724.

Suckow, K. (2002, Apr.). *Protecting your data and your job: Testing your technology.* Symposium conducted at the annual conference of the Society for Industrial and Organizational Psychology, Toronto.

Thompson, L. F., Surface, E. A., Martin, D. L., & Sanders, M. G. (2003). From paper to pixels: Moving personnel surveys to the Web. *Personnel Psychology, 56,* 197–227.

U.S. Department of Commerce. Bureau of the Census. (2000). *Census 2000.* http://www.census.gov/main/www/cen2000.html.

UsabilityNet. (2003). UsabilityNet homepage. http://www.usabilitynet.org/home.htm.

Yost, P. R., & Homer, L. E. (1998, Apr.). *Electronic versus paper surveys: Does the medium affect the response?* Paper presented at the annual conference of the Society of Industrial and Organizational Psychology, Dallas, TX.

Young, S. A., Daum, D. L., Robie, C., & Macey, W. H. (2000, Apr.). Paper versus Web survey administration: Do different methods yield different results? In M. Sederberg & S. Rogelberg (Chairs), *Improving the survey effort: Methodological questions and answers.* Symposium conducted at the annual conference of the Society for Industrial and Organizational Psychology, New Orleans, LA.

CHAPTER 9

Online Reporting
Real Time, Real Impact, Real Opportunities

Karen M. Barbera
Scott A. Young

For many organizations, the question of whether to incorporate online processes into survey programs is no longer the relevant one. Instead, the question is how best to leverage the technology to enhance the overall value of the survey program. Rather than rely on Web technology solely for survey administration, organizations are increasingly using the Web to manage all aspects of the survey process, from specifying and verifying organizational structures to generating and distributing reports and subsequent action planning activities.

This chapter focuses on the use of Web technology for reporting and disseminating results, a practice that in many respects is still in its infancy but evolving rapidly. Historically, survey practitioners have had the responsibility of deciding who will receive which types of reports. Enhancements in Web technology as well as corporate infrastructure now allow organizations to decentralize the process of deciding on the content and format of the reports delivered to key stakeholders. Referred to as a *self-service model,* this approach allows managers and other authorized personnel to request reports specifying the type of report that they want and the data that they want to include.

In a self-service model, with a simple click of a button, executives may delve into their results in more detail by switching from an executive summary to a detailed report, and managers in Switzerland can choose to generate their reports in English, German, French, or Italian, depending on their native tongue. Not only can managers have a broad range of options available to them, they can use them in a self-service environment around the clock. This self-service capability can greatly reduce the amount of coordination required of survey practitioners to produce reports— something that likely will become even more important as organizations continue to outsource a greater proportion of human resource (HR) services (Babcock, 2004).

The flexibility afforded by online reporting, particularly when results are generated in real time, also allows late-breaking requests to be accommodated with relative ease. Imagine the following scenario where the survey practitioner is relying on a sophisticated system for report generation: the practitioner receives a last-minute request to prepare an executive presentation on the results for one of the organization's major business units. While working on the presentation late at night, the practitioner becomes curious whether the written comments might shed light on some gender differences in the quantitative data, but no previously generated report allows this comparison. Having access to a real-time reporting system, the survey practitioner is able to immediately run separate comment reports for men and women, without any time delay.

This chapter specifically addresses online reporting. A significant portion of this chapter describes the amount of flexibility and control that system users may have over the report style used and specific groups displayed within a report. We also discuss the factors that are important to system users' level of control and review system features that help to minimize user error. In addition, we describe different online reporting strategies, what reports managers request when given the choice, how reports may be distributed, and implications of online reporting.

Although confidentiality and anonymity concerns are addressed, general reporting issues such as what information should be displayed in reports and how reporting should be managed throughout an organization are outside the scope of this chapter. Interested readers are referred to Church and Waclawski (2001) for a discussion of these issues.

Managing the Process of Requesting Reports

Because a great deal of flexibility can be provided to users of an on-line system, a fundamental question to address is who has access to what types of reports. Authorized system users may include managers who receive reports, survey liaisons or other HR professionals who coordinate and support the survey process, the survey practitioner and team, external vendors, and other third parties as appropriate (for example, other executive coaches who are not part of the survey vendor). Furthermore, our discussion is not meant to be limited to situations where a company's survey reporting is completely outsourced to an external firm. Some companies have developed software for their own internal survey needs, and others use commercially available software that allows survey practitioners to create online surveys and generate reports completely on their own. The decisions and trade-offs that we address are applicable to any system that contains the features and functionality discussed.

The privileges granted to each type of user in a self-service model should be determined in advance because these rules often guide how the system is designed, customized, and implemented. In this section, we discuss the factors that influence the reporting options provided to system users, define different types of control that users may be permitted, and explain the trade-offs associated with these.

Factors That Influence Options Provided to System Users

Advances in survey reporting technology enable companies to provide managers and HR professionals with tremendous flexibility in the types of survey reports they can generate. The amount of decision-making authority granted to system users should be considered carefully. A key responsibility of the survey practitioner is to find the middle ground between imposing too much structure, which can limit the usefulness of the reports, and imposing too little structure, which may overwhelm system users with a complex process that requires too many decisions and takes too much time. This middle ground may differ from company to company and even from survey to survey within the same company.

An important caution is that for some organizations, an electronic self-service model may not be appropriate regardless of how it is structured. In some cases, not all managers have their own computers, and those who do may not have Internet access. Assuming that a self-service model is feasible, we recommend that survey practitioners consider the following factors when deciding how much flexibility or control to provide to system users:

- *Users' level of sophistication.* This is an important consideration when deciding how much flexibility to provide. User sophistication refers not only to experience in using computers, but also experience working with quantitative data. Users who are comfortable working with computer software and the Internet are less likely to have difficulty navigating through the report generation process. Similarly, if users have generated their own reports in previous survey administrations, then it may be appropriate to increase their levels of flexibility or complexity of reports in subsequent years. In addition, users who have experience working with quantitative data are also more likely to understand the various types of statistics that may be available to them. When users are less data savvy, practitioners may want to consider preventing users from exercising certain reporting options such as displaying standard deviations or from including too much information in a single report.

- *Number of expected users.* Typically, as the number of users rises, so does the need for practitioner consultation, especially when users have higher levels of flexibility in report design. One way to manage this potentially high demand on the practitioner's time is to ensure that the process is relatively simple and structured or to provide users with default report options.

- *Number of reports requested per user.* This can influence decisions regarding the sophistication of the reporting process. Users who will be requesting dozens or hundreds of reports (such as when report generation is handled exclusively by members of HR) are much more likely to invest the time needed to learn a more complex system. Users who will be requesting only one or two reports expect a simple process with few decisions required of them.

- *The extent to which users' needs vary.* In some organizations, job levels may differ by division, which may require flexibility in terms of combining job levels for reporting. These differences can be even more critical in companies in which different business units or functions have been allowed to customize processes in the past. In situations like these, imposing a common set of report rules may not be realistic. However, if the exceptions are few, it may be that the survey practitioner can handle those requests separately.

• *Degree to which users have the time needed to generate reports.* Managers at all levels and in all functions frequently report that bureaucracy and internal initiatives distract them from their core job responsibilities, especially in large organizations. In addition, workforce reductions in the past few years have left many companies leaner, resulting in greater demand on managers' time. Although empowering managers to generate their own reports may reduce the time demands on survey practitioners, it may also create more work for hundreds or thousands of managers. Therefore, it is critical to make decisions based on what is most efficient for the organization as a whole and with input from the users themselves.

• *Rate of structural change in the organization.* This rate at times requires that users be given flexibility to define and choose the groups to be included in their reports. In some organizations, constant change means that it is impractical for the survey practitioner to maintain an up-to-date representation of the organizational structure. By allowing users to define their own groups based on low-level units such as work groups or cost centers, which remain intact through structural changes, report definition does not have to rely on an outdated organizational structure. The disadvantage of this approach is that generating reports for higher-level groups can be more cumbersome because it requires combining many lower-level groups.

• *Confidentiality.* This is an important consideration in determining the amount of flexibility to permit. For instance, access should be more restricted when it may be possible to identify individual respondents through a comparison of results from different reports.

• *Cost implications.* Survey practitioners should carefully consider all factors that might contribute to higher costs. Much depends on the specific nature of the project. For example, while a system that provides users with many reporting options may have higher development costs, a more standardized process may require a high number of customized reports to be generated through alternative means, which can drive costs up considerably. An important part of this analysis should be to examine the internal labor costs for both the system users who generate reports and the survey practitioners consulting with them.

Levels of User Control over Reporting

The number and types of possible choices made available to users of report generation systems continue to increase, with systems ranging from minimal to extensive flexibility. One way to discuss the access given to users is to describe their level of control over report style and group specification (that is, which groups are included in a report). We discuss control over reporting style and group specification in terms of three different levels (see Table 9.1). We then examine the implications of these levels along four facets of online reporting: flexibility, complexity of the user interface, risk to confidentiality and anonymity, and cost. We present this as one possible framework in an effort to illustrate the relevant choice points and trade-offs.

Control over Report Style

At the first or lowest level of control, managers may be given access to reports that were preordered and generated for them. However, they may also be given the opportunity to select an alternative report style for their groups (for example, spreadsheet format or executive summary) from a limited number of report styles. This may include requesting the same report style but in a different language. Although alternative styles exist, these styles provide basically the same type of information but present it in different forms or in a trimmed-down version (for example, an executive summary versus a detailed report). This allows managers to view results in the format most useful to them and in some cases (for example, spreadsheet format) to extract or sort results that enable them to more easily develop presentations for sharing results and developing action plans.

Users at the second or moderate level of control may be allowed to select alternative report styles from a broader array of options. The options provided may allow new types of information to be included in reports rather than simply displaying the same

Table 9.1. Levels of User Control over Reporting

	Level 1: Low Control	Level 2: Moderate Control	Level 3: High Control
Definition	*User can generate reports for predefined groups to which user has access. Report options limited to a few styles, all containing essentially the same type of information.*	*User has limited flexibility to define groups and can select from a broader array of default styles.*	*User has complete control over group specification; user has the ability to mix and match report styles to produce or define custom reports.*
Flexibility	Limited flexibility. However, flexibility is probably viewed in relative terms. For managers who have been provided with default reports in the past, without the opportunity to select styles, even limited flexibility may be well received.	Limited to moderate flexibility, depending on the number of report types available.	High degree of flexibility. In all likelihood, the level of flexibility provided at this level is far greater than what most managers want or need. However, survey practitioners' needs may best be met with this level of flexibility. Even if survey practitioners do not generate reports on their own, they appreciate knowing that they can do so to meet an urgent need.
Complexity of user interface	Simple. A point-and-click interface is all that is necessary. On-screen text is sufficient to convey what needs to be done.	Simple to moderate. May require more extensive instructions or a help document to support full use of available options, or both.	Moderate to high in complexity. Often requires training to properly define groups.

(Continued)

Table 9.1. Levels of User Control over Reporting, Cont'd

	Level 1: Low Control	Level 2: Moderate Control	Level 3: High Control
Risk of user compromising confidentiality and anonymity	Little to none.	Some, depending on sizes and types of groups that may "roll up" to a particular manager. Requires foresight and planning to ensure confidentiality is maintained.	Could be significant if managers have this level of control over group specification. Potential users should be educated about the impact of reporting choices on confidentiality. In practice, this level is often provided only to the survey practitioner.
Cost	The cost to develop an online reporting system or to customize a commercially available one is lowest when flexibility is limited. However, if the system is too limited in its offering, costs for handling ad hoc or unusual requests may offset these savings.	Development costs for a system providing a moderate level of control are likely to be closer to level 1 than level 3. However, the number of unique report styles offered may influence this.	Costs to develop a system that allows this type of power are significant. Ongoing costs need to consider any external fees associated with use of a commercially available system (for example, licensing or per report fees) and internal costs (such as cost of staff time to generate reports).

information in an alternative style. The types of reports allowed here may extend to include other report types, such as demographic reports or special benchmarking reports.

Complete flexibility over the type of report generated and specific style options within these reports may be allowed at level 3, the highest level of control. For example, users might select the specific report sections they desire from an available list of styles (for example, most and least favorable items, item detail, dimension summary) and specify the order in which they want these to appear to create a custom report style. Furthermore, users may be given additional control over style options within sections (for example, select ascending or descending order, portrait or landscape format, whether to include historical data, and whether to report results as percentages or mean scores).

Control over Group Specification

In addition to control over report style, users may be given the ability to select and define groups for which results will be displayed. However, in practice, group specification sometimes dictates the use of a specific report style.

At the lowest level of control over group specification, users might be permitted to generate reports only for groups created for them and to which they have been given access (for example, all groups that hierarchically roll up to the manager). At this simplest level, manipulation of these groups is not permitted in any way, even to simply combine groups.

The moderate level of control may allow users limited flexibility in specifying groups to be displayed in a report. Often users are allowed to specify which groups to include or exclude from among those groups for which they have viewing privileges (for example, create a report that shows only a subset of departments that roll up to a particular manager). This can be extended to allow group specification based on organizational unit and responses to a single demographic item at a time. For example, a report could be created that contains results for all minority employees within a particular division.

At the highest level of control, users might be given complete control over how groups are defined for a report, provided that confidentiality rules are not violated within the report. Users can create new groups not previously defined. These groups may be defined based on responses to survey questions or based on data extracted from organizational databases and preloaded into the reporting system (for example, job level or tenure). As one example, the user might reclassify responses to a question about the respondent's race into a new variable that classifies respondents as minority or nonminority. A more complex report might display results for all female minorities with less than a year of service in a particular division. In essence, such highly customized reports can function as an alternative to manipulating data in other commercially available statistical software.

Trade-Offs

Clearly, there are many options in terms of how an online reporting system is structured and implemented. As the flexibility afforded by the system increases, the user interface typically becomes more complex, and a simple point-and-click interface may no longer suffice. Similarly, as flexibility increases, so does the risk of compromising the respondents' anonymity and confidentiality. For this reason, what we have described as the highest level of control for defining new reporting groups is generally restricted to survey practitioners and their teams.

System Features That Minimize User Error

When access to online reporting is broad, it is especially important for the system to be easy to use and designed to minimize user error. In this section, we review some system features that can facilitate the report generation process. These features may be important to consider when evaluating a platform for use or developing one in-house.

One way that a system can ensure that users receive the information they expect in their reports is to provide them with feedback about their report requests throughout the process. This is particularly important when the report system allows a great deal of flexibility in defining groups and selecting report styles. A basic level of feedback could be to provide users with a list of reports already generated and to alert users to duplicate entries for report titles or group specifications across their own report requests. Similarly, before finalizing a report request, the user could be shown a list of all reports they have previously requested that include the current group of interest.

More specific information can also be provided by the system to ensure that users receive the reports they truly need. Ideally, the number of respondents and corresponding population size would be displayed once a group is defined or chosen but before the request is finalized. This would allow the user to confirm that the report was defined as intended. For example, if a report is supposed to include only one particular job level within HR but shows two hundred more respondents than all of HR, this is an immediate red flag that an error in specification has been made. For commonly used groups such as overall company or operating group, it may be best to pre-define the group to limit the possibility of error further. In addition, information might be provided in the form of help screens with step-by-step examples of how to create different kinds of reports. In more complex systems, this may even extend to formal training.

Another desirable system feature is an intuitive display of the company's organizational structure. User confusion can be minimized if a user's view is customized such that the password entered determines which portion of the organizational structure is displayed. This may be particularly important for lower-level managers or employees who are not well versed in the entire organizational structure.

For organizations with matrix structures, ideally the system would allow users to view the structure through the two different organizational perspectives (for example, by function and by management structure) and to define groups using either or both perspectives. For example, the system would allow a group to be created that consists of employees who work in the marketing function and who work in a particular line of business.

Next, it is helpful if the system shows users their group definition in a format that is different from how they specified it, so that a mistake in specification may be more evident. Similarly, in organizations with rapidly changing organizational structures, it is helpful if the system provides users with a list of all employees invited to participate in the survey in the groups that they defined for the report. Of course, this approach may not be appropriate for very small groups in which anonymity is more of an immediate concern.

Finally, perhaps the best way to help users determine whether they are defining reports properly is to provide an actual preview of reports, possibly populated with group sizes but without displaying actual data. Often users are better able to articulate their needs once they see an actual report. Previews provide users with a concrete example that they can use to think through how they will use the data and to confirm they have correctly specified the report. If they do not recognize a specification error until they see the report with actual data, they may find themselves in a situation in which they are not allowed to generate the report that they truly need due to safeguards present to protect confidentiality and anonymity.

Real-Time Versus Discontinuous Reporting

Online reporting can mean different things to different people. With self-service online reporting, the actual generation of reports can take place in real time, in a discontinuous manner, or in some combination of the two.

Real-Time Reporting

Real-time reporting, as its name implies, means that when a user requests a report through the reporting system interface, the report is generated automatically at that moment and is available within seconds. Real time, however, does not necessarily mean that results are immediately available at the close of survey administration. There may be a delay for system processing, the length of which is determined by the specific technology used and the size of the data file. In addition, there may be delays for a variety of off-line interventions, including the editing or translation of written comments, the development and incorporation of a model of employee engagement into reports, or matching survey data to other information on respondents extracted from an HR database, if not done in advance due to anticipated changes to the organizational structure.

Although there may be off-line interventions and associated delays, the defining characteristic of a real-time reporting strategy is that once a user is allowed to request a report, the system immediately generates it without further human intervention. Some online systems in fact allow reports to be generated immediately after the close of survey administration; in some cases, reports may be defined in advance so that once the survey administration is complete, they may be generated automatically by the system at the moment the survey closes. This may extend to include interim reports that can be created and viewed even while the survey is being administered. For more complex survey projects, a real-time reporting system's ability to provide this extreme flexibility is dependent on system design, for example, its ability to easily integrate data from other sources, such as historical data, or respondent information, such as job level from an employee database.

The main benefit to this reporting strategy is speed. Managers appreciate having immediate access to reports that they generate. Any survey practitioner who has needed to prepare a report for top management likely will appreciate having access to the data even before the survey administration window has closed.

The real-time system also has the advantage of removing human intervention from the data compilation and calculation of results, thereby minimizing the risk of error. However, the quality of real-time reporting depends on the user accurately defining the report and the system having been thoroughly tested for all possible reporting scenarios. In addition, practical issues of how results are rolled out over time (for example, staggered by management level or desire for paper reports) may limit the need for having results available in real time.

This approach also results in a loss of some control by the survey practitioner. For example, some managers or executives might run a series of reports in search of information that can be used to discount their unfavorable overall results. In addition, real-time reporting creates some unique data confidentiality challenges.

Discontinuous Reporting

Under a discontinuous reporting strategy, there is a delay between the user's report request and the generation of the report, with the reports actually generated off-line, often in large batches. This delay in report availability is in addition to other off-line actions, for example, editing written comments.

When a discontinuous reporting strategy is used, the report requests are sometimes centralized, or they are made in what can be described as an online report ordering system. Users may still be given tremendous flexibility in what groups they include in a report and what report styles they use, but the request itself is made in a system independent of the report generation system. The actual specification of the report in the report generation system is performed by the person who receives the request (for example, an HR manager within the organization or a staff member at the survey vendor), not the person who makes the request (for example, the manager whose data are represented in the report).

There are several important implications of the choice between real-time and discontinuous reporting strategies. Discontinuous reporting typically provides greater flexibility than real-time reporting, because these systems are usually intended for a smaller number of highly trained users. Real-time reporting software is typically developed with the goal of providing report generation capability to a relatively wide audience, so simplicity of the user interface is of primary concern. In addition, greater control is usually available in a system designed for discontinuous processes because the person fulfilling report requests has the opportunity to question or modify what is being requested. However, these benefits come at the expense of speed of report generation and delivery. In addition, there may be differences between the two strategies in terms of data and report quality.

Hybrid Reporting

In many cases, a combination of real-time and discontinuous reporting is used. For many large-scale survey projects, hundreds or even thousands of reports are generated. Typically most reports are defined well in advance of the close of survey administration, whereas a smaller percentage of the report requests are made later. Often a discontinuous approach is used for generating the predefined reports. Ad hoc reports are then generated using real-time systems, where the efficiency of running one or two reports is greater.

Confidentiality and Anonymity Concerns

An overarching concern throughout the survey process is how to best protect and maintain the confidentiality and anonymity of individuals' responses. This concern takes on added importance in organizations that (1) have limited experience in administering employee opinion surveys; (2) have a presence in the European Union, where more stringent requirements concerning the confidentiality of employee data exist; (3) have had problems with inappropriate use of survey results in the past; (4) have a high degree of distrust between employees and management; (5) base managerial or executive pay or bonus on survey results; (6) use a low minimum number of respondents for reporting results for a group (generally referred to as the minimum N); or (7) include a large number of demographic questions on their survey, thereby increasing the chances that anonymity could be compromised.

Safeguards

When reports are generated off-line, several provisions are typically put into place to ensure that commitments made to employees regarding the confidentiality of results are maintained during the reporting phase:

- Rules are established prior to launching the survey regarding the minimum N, such as reporting numerical results for a group only if there are ten or more respondents. Sometimes a higher minimum N is applied to reporting comments than to reporting numerical results. These rules are communicated to survey participants and managers, generally as part of their survey invitation as well as through inclusion in the survey's privacy or confidentiality statement, which is often a hyperlink on online surveys.

- Data suppression rules are incorporated into reporting systems to prevent managers from being able to "back out" data within a report—that is, from being able to calculate the results of one group whose results are not shown by comparing the results of other groups whose results are shown. For example, consider the situation where the minimum N is ten, and a report is generated for an overall group of twenty-eight respondents comprising three subgroups that have fifteen, ten, and three respondents each. The subgroup of three respondents is the only one in this report that fails to reach the required minimum N. However, typically results are suppressed for this group of three as well as the group of ten to prevent the results for the three from being backed out of the overall data line containing all twenty-eight respondents.

- The set of reports to be generated for each end user is often reviewed to ensure that confidentiality is not inadvertently compromised by examining results across several reports.
- As part of survey communications, respondents should be made aware if information about them (such as demographic information extracted from an HR database), other than what they will be asked to provide on the survey, will be used as part of the reporting process.
- Typically instructions are provided to respondents cautioning them to avoid compromising their anonymity by the nature of their comments and writing style.
- Comments are often translated into a common language to ensure that the choice of language does not compromise the anonymity of respondents. In addition, comments are often edited to remove references to personal names (generally other than those of senior leadership) to further protect confidentiality. These interventions are possible only with an off-line process.

Some unique challenges exist in protecting the confidentiality and anonymity of results in real-time reporting. The greatest challenge with regard to confidentiality in this situation (or in any other self-service model where individual requests are not monitored) is that of inappropriate requests, particularly across a series of reports. For example, depending on the level of control over group specification that has been provided, it may be possible for a manager with only one direct report with less than one year of tenure to isolate that individual's responses by generating a report for his or her department and then running the same report again but excluding individuals with less than a year of tenure. In addition, most commercially available Web sites that allow full survey authoring and reporting do not provide complex rules that prevent opportunities to back out data when multiple groups are included within a report.

Responsibilities of Survey Practitioners

Real concerns exist with maintaining the confidentiality and anonymity of survey results in any survey program, and these concerns can become intensified with an online reporting system. This should lead practitioners to raise questions about the requirements of the system itself as well as their own role in the process:

• *Should the system prevent inappropriate requests from being implemented?* At a glance, the obvious answer to this seems to be a resounding yes. However, this may not be implemented easily. While it is relatively simple programming to suppress data from being displayed within a single report, it is considerably more complicated to design a system that tracks requests made over time and ensures that confidentiality is maintained across a combination of requests made by a user. Furthermore, designing this functionality into the system does not remove the practical issue of what the survey practitioner should do when a manager needs a report that cannot be generated due to prior reports received. Poor sequencing of report requests could result in managers' not seeing results that otherwise would have been available to them. This is especially a concern when access to these results is of higher priority than reports generated earlier.

• *Should the survey practitioner review all report requests to ensure that only appropriate reports are generated?* This is often done with a discontinuous or an entirely off-line process, but would result in a delay with a real-time reporting system, reducing one of its key benefits. In addition, this policing role may interfere with the survey practitioner's time for engaging in other activities, such as conducting advanced statistical analyses and facilitating data interpretation and action planning. Of course, if requests are not monitored, responding to concerns about confidentiality being compromised could also interfere with the survey practitioner's time for engaging in these types of activities.

• *Alternatively, is the survey practitioner's role only to educate users before launching the reporting system, without any subsequent monitoring of requests?* If monitoring is not done, sufficient time and resources should be dedicated to developing clear and concise communications. Our experience is that opportunities for backing out data across reports frequently emerge, but they are often not recognized by managers and even HR professionals who have a key role in supporting survey programs. Consequently, when a training-only strategy is used, two practices may be advisable. The first is to limit the extent to which a self-service model is used by providing managers with default reports that have been requested for them and made available at the close of data collection. The second is to incorporate system reminders and messages into the report-generation process (for example, a reminder that overall reports for a unit should be requested prior to requesting a specific demographic breakdown). For greatest effectiveness, a list of the reports already generated by the user should be accessible for review.

What Types of Reports Do Managers Request?

Providing managers with control over the style of their reports and the groups included within them holds great potential to better meet the unique needs of individual users. So what do managers request when given this flexibility? Making general conclusions about managers' preferences is extremely difficult for the following reasons: (1) online reporting is relatively new and rapidly evolving; (2) different organizations offer different sets of report options to their users, making it difficult to determine preferences across organizations; and (3) the extent to which managers are required to work with quantitative data differs across companies, which may mean that their preferences for style and level of detail also may differ. However, based on our experiences and those of the clients with whom we have worked, we offer the following preliminary observations:

- Reports in spreadsheet form have gained a great deal of popularity in recent years. Managers appreciate the ability to sort and extract the information in these reports in a way that is most useful to them. For example, managers or HR professionals can copy and paste information directly into presentation software, whereas this is much more difficult in a PDF report. When managers request spreadsheet reports, they often use them as a supplement to, rather than as a replacement for, traditional PDF reports.
- Managers generally want to know how they stack up to others. For top management, the critical comparison is typically an external norm. For other managers, internal benchmarks are generally desired. In some cases, this benchmark might be the results for the entire company, whereas in other organizations, managers may want to be able to compare their results to those of other managers

at their level. If standard reports do not have these types of comparison data embedded in them, managers are likely to request reports that provide this information.

• In organizations with a matrix structure, managers often want reports both with and without their "matrixed" employees included.

• Demographic reports tend not to be requested widely by managers. Rather, these types of reports may be generated by whatever individual, department, or task force oversees diversity issues.

• Often managers are frustrated when their group is too small to receive a report. When this is the case, some managers may want the option of seeing the comparison data that would have been included in their report if their group had been large enough. For example, they may want to see the results of their manager's organization so that they can learn something about the attitudes of the employees in their area.

• Managers often desire a brief report that contains higher-level or summarized information. For example, an executive summary report might show only the percentage of favorable responses for each question and dimension rather than showing the full distribution of responses or mean scores. We have noticed some clients moving toward providing this type of summary report by default and providing a more detailed report to those who request it.

Report Distribution

Many methods for distributing reports are available. An organization's specific choice of method may be driven by past practice, organizational infrastructure, or technological savvy of management, for example. Despite the fact that Web surveys seem commonplace, paper reports still can play a significant role in many survey efforts. However, when electronic distribution can be used, it has the advantage of making distribution easier and generally more cost effective than paper. Distribution by e-mail, report warehouses, and direct file transfers or shared services is described below. The choice of distribution method may be particularly important when an external firm is responsible for survey processing and report generation because of security issues in transferring reports from an external source.

E-Mail Distribution

Reports may be e-mailed to managers or report owners and other appropriate parties. This places minimal burden on report owners to retrieve results because they simply appear in their in-boxes without any action on their part. However, there are some potential drawbacks to this approach, including the following:

- E-mail is not a secure transmission method unless encryption protocols are set between destinations.
- Viruses can be transmitted through e-mail attachments.
- An influx of e-mails with large attachments may tax organizations' servers.
- E-mails may be rejected by spam detection systems.
- Depending on the number and size of files, reports may need to be sent in a compressed file format, requiring the end user to have software to open them.
- Many organizations have restrictions on the size of e-mail boxes and files that can be accepted through their firewalls, which can be a challenge given that PDF and Excel files, often the preferred formats, tend to be large.
- Under this approach, a centralized depository of reports usually does not exist.

Electronic Report Warehouse

Storing all reports in a centralized location (a virtual report warehouse) can offer significant advantages. These online depositories enable reports to be viewed and downloaded on demand. Reports are accessible around the clock, allowing convenient retrieval by managers and survey practitioners. Access is password restricted, with individuals being able to access only reports assigned to them. Extensions of report warehouses can include an e-mailing capability that allows organizations to more easily manage the e-mail distribution of reports, though this introduces the concerns with e-mail distribution addressed above. In addition, report warehouses can be extended to include action planning tools and support.

Report warehouses are generally considered more secure than e-mail and do not place the same types of demands on the organization's e-mail system. As such, they are currently a particularly popular method to distribute reports. However, this method is not without security concerns. Although the reports are not sent by e-mail, access and password information typically is. In addition, report warehouses are less secure than real-time reporting systems in which reports are generated instantaneously on request, and thus are not stored as physical files until generated and downloaded by the user.

Direct File Transfer and Web Services

FTP (File Transfer Protocol) and HTTPS Internet protocols can be used to transfer reports over the Internet directly from one computer (for example, the survey vendor's computer) to another (for example, a computer at the client organization). This is most often done when the organization wishes to have reports available on its own intranet or portal so that managers have a single place to go to access a variety of information, using a single log-on and password. One method to transfer information is direct file transfer. This method provides a number of advantages, including enhanced security from having reports reside on an intranet without exposure to the outside world, a single password to remember (typically one's log-on password), and ease of merging data with other organizational information (for example, customer satisfaction data). However, this method is not without drawbacks. Direct file transfers may require IT support or setup to transfer large volumes of data securely and may result in delays due to transfer time. In addition, employees may have a greater degree of comfort with reports residing on external sites rather than on an intranet due to concerns about the confidentiality of their responses.

When a real-time reporting strategy is used, Web services overcome many of these drawbacks. Web services return results to the organization in a format usable by corporate Web sites for merging with other results. Because information is processed in real time, delays are not experienced.

Implications of Online Reporting

Providing managers and others with the ability to request their own reports based on the style and organizational units that they wish to view is a relatively new concept in survey programs. Potential benefits and drawbacks of this approach are discussed below.

Benefits

Implied in this approach are a number of benefits, though many remain largely untested:

- Providing managers with the specific information they want, when they want it, and in the style and format they want helps enable and motivate managers to use the information for action planning and continuous improvement.
- Interest in the survey process tends to wane the more time that elapses between survey administration and reporting. Online reporting generally expedites report delivery over paper processes and can even allow results to be available in real time, thus providing results to managers when they are most energized to act on them.
- A challenge at times in a global survey process is knowing what specific languages are appropriate for which managers. Often an assumption for companies with headquarters in the United States is that all managers will be comfortable with reports provided in English. At other times, assumptions are made about managers' desired language based on their location, with a single language typically being chosen for each country. The assumptions made in these cases may not always be appropriate. Online systems can allow managers the opportunity to quickly generate their reports in their language of choice. This is advantageous not only in global survey programs but also in domestic survey programs. Consider, for example, a retail organization whose report includes a summary to post for employees. Being able to generate reports in Spanish may be critical for managers to be able to appropriately disseminate results in retail units with Hispanic workers whose primary language is Spanish.

- Overall costs for a survey program could potentially be minimized by allowing managers to request only the reports that they truly want. However, giving managers the authority to request their own reports could potentially increase costs.
- Online reporting more readily allows a self-service model. This may be especially critical given reductions in HR staff and may allow survey practitioners to focus their time and energy more on value-added consultation than on project management and administration.

Concerns

Some potential drawbacks or concerns to this approach include the following:

- At times, managers can be overwhelmed by the wealth of information within a single report, particularly if the organization does not have a strong tradition of using surveys or training managers to use reports. Unfortunately, providing additional report styles and options may contribute to information overload for some users and place added demand on support personnel who work with managers to help them understand their results and develop effective action plans. These concerns can be minimized by clearly articulating the options available and providing rules and recommendations on which options are most appropriate and useful for different types of users (for example, allow demographic reports to be generated only at specified organizational levels). Generally default styles are provided that should meet the needs of the majority of end users. In addition, it may be appropriate to phase in options over survey administrations as people become more sophisticated in using the reporting system and survey results.
- Concerns over confidentiality may be greater with an online self-service system than with other off-line processes. The safeguards that exist when requests are centralized or processed in an off-line process are often lost in this approach. For example, if the minimum N for report generation is ten respondents, a manager may be able to isolate the results for two employees through a series of report requests that define a group in slightly different ways.

Managers may be less likely to request these combinations of reports if they have to justify their requests to the survey practitioner. In addition, even if inappropriate requests are made in an off-line, monitored process, the survey practitioner has an opportunity to prevent them.

• Often managers request reports to address particular questions of interest or concern to them. Sometimes the survey practitioner is able to help managers determine what report will provide the most useful information. In a self-service model, the opportunity for consultation in this area may be diminished.

• Just as the introduction to online surveys and self-authoring survey software can lead to oversurveying employees (Thompson, Surface, Martin, & Sanders, 2003), giving managers complete control to request reports can result in some managers requesting every conceivable report or way of viewing the data. This can create an overwhelming volume of information and lead to "paralysis by analysis." In addition, when such a high volume of information is produced, some managers may spend their time searching for reasons to discount unfavorable results rather than searching for ways to address the root cause of those results.

• Costs for the reporting phase could potentially be higher than would otherwise be the case if costs are based on a per report fee and managers request more reports than they would typically receive under a traditional off-line process. This may be of greater concern in organizations that are very data oriented in nature (for example, organizations with a large number of scientists and engineers) or when report costs are not allocated directly to the requesting manager's budget.

• While the survey practitioner's time may be minimized under a self-service approach to survey reporting, an important question to ask is whether this time savings comes at the expense of overall organizational efficiency.

Conclusions

Online reporting of organizational survey results has expanded recently to include requesting and generating survey reports by employees other than the survey practitioner. These advances have the potential to dramatically change the role of the survey practitioner, such that time previously devoted to managing report requests and distribution may now be spent consulting with managers and executives on results interpretation and action planning. However, implementing online reporting throughout an organization also creates new challenges, from ensuring respondent confidentiality and anonymity to maintaining some control over how the survey results are reported. Despite these challenges, online reporting, especially when reports are generated in real time, has the potential to transform the way that surveys are used in organizations now and in the future.

Acknowledgments

We thank Diane Daum and Mathew Heck for their helpful suggestions on the chapter.

References

Babcock, P. (2004). Slicing off pieces of HR. *HR Magazine, 49*(7), 70–76.

Church, A. H., & Waclawski, J. (2001). *Designing and using organizational surveys: A seven step approach.* San Francisco: Jossey-Bass.

Thompson, L. F., Surface, E. A., Martin, D. L., & Sanders, M. G. (2003). From paper to pixels: Moving personnel surveys to the Web. *Personnel Psychology, 56*(1), 197–227.

CHAPTER 10

What Did They Really Mean?

New and Emerging Methods for Analyzing Themes in Open-Ended Comments

Patrick Kulesa
Ralph J. Bishop

Critics of the use of employee surveys in organizations often argue that if senior leaders want to know what employees think, they should start walking the hallways and shop floors to find out for themselves. Open-ended comment questions in employee surveys have the potential to serve precisely this purpose for management. The analysis of traditional closed-ended survey responses is a valuable tool for identifying the key issues an organization needs to address in order to enhance employee engagement or improve business performance. Yet identifying an issue and knowing what actions to take next are two separate steps on the road to organizational improvement. Responses to open-ended questions can play a crucial role in moving from issue identification to action. The rich and diverse content that can result from the intelligent application of comment questions creates a virtual focus group that management can use to have a virtual conversation with employees on nearly any topic of interest.

For such a virtual conversation to take place, responses to open-ended questions in large-scale surveys with hundreds or thousands of participants must be mined in directed ways to point management to the most critical input from employees. The method of choice for such cases is content analysis, defined as the systematic examination of text, spoken discourse, or visual media to uncover patterns of syntax, word use, tone, and other elements of meaning. In this chapter, we review some of the basic issues associated with using open-ended comment questions in employee surveys and outline several approaches to content analysis of employees' responses. We then turn to specific applications of content analysis in employee surveys to demonstrate the types of insights to be gained through the intelligent analysis of open-ended comment responses. We conclude by discussing some of the practical challenges associated with capturing and using qualitative data and how to meet those challenges.

Question Types

Survey researchers use open-ended questions to gather many kinds of information, from simple one- or two-word answers to short essays filled with opinions and suggestions. The type of question selected certainly influences the answers received and can drive the choice of methods applied to interpret those answers.

Open-ended questions can be distinguished along two dimensions: scope and purpose. Scope can be general or specific; purpose can be to describe a situation or prescribe a solution. Combining these two dimensions generates four basic question types: general/descriptive, general/prescriptive, specific/descriptive, and specific/prescriptive. Examples of each type are illustrated in Table 10.1.

General questions are typically placed at the end of a survey. They do not identify a particular topic area for discussion but instead ask for general information about issues in the workplace or what could be addressed to make the company a better place. General questions can elicit responses that describe conditions within the workplace or provide prescriptive solutions to an issue that management needs to address.

Specific questions may be placed at the end of a survey or may be used as branching questions that are to be answered only when certain responses are made to a previous question. Specific questions

Table 10.1. Open-Ended Comment Question Types

Scope	Purpose	
	Descriptive	Prescriptive
General	"If you have additional comments, please write them in the space below."	"What is the one change that management could make that would most improve your ability to do your job effectively?"
	"Are there any other matters you wish to bring to the attention of management?"	"What one or two things could management do to make the company a better place to work?"
Specific	"If you answered no to the previous question [for example, a question on intention to stay with the company], please give your reasons."	"In your opinion, what is the single greatest barrier to the company's continued success, and what would you do to remove that barrier?"
	"Please describe a difficult situation you feel you handled particularly well, and tell what you did to resolve it."	"What are the three most important issues facing the new CEO in the next 100 days, and how can they best be addressed?"

often ask for information related to a difficult or unusual situation (for example, disputes with a manager or bullying on the job), or they may ask for particular solutions to improve business performance. Questions incorporating branching logic provide unique opportunities to acquire detailed reasons for employees' decisions to make a specific response to a quantitative question, such as indicating an intention to leave the organization. Like general questions, the specific type may elicit descriptive statements about a situation or context or solutions directed toward solving particular business challenges.

Although the four question types differ along the dimensions of scope and purpose, they share a number of characteristics. First, responses to even the most general and nondirective questions are effectively limited to topics covered in the survey, meaning that the responses will be related in some way to the company and the workplace, limiting the topics under study in an analysis of the returns.

Second, our experience indicates that there are a relatively small number of key words and phrases reliably related to the survey topics. To take an obvious example, among U.S. employees, the word *benefits* occurs universally and almost exclusively in the general discussion of fringe benefits.

Finally, responses to open-ended questions tend to be short. Our internal tracking measures show an average range of 40 to 80 words. Responses of over 250 words to a single question are uncommon. Responses of over 1,000 words are rare indeed, typically found in less than one in 5,000 questionnaires. Responses for online surveys tend to be 25 to 40 percent longer than those provided in paper surveys. These commonalities across question types allow researchers to predict the general nature of the returns, which facilitates the next step in the process of extracting insight from responses to open-ended questions: analysis of employees' answers.

Computer-Assisted Content Analysis

Regardless of the type of question asked, the systematic coding and interpretation of text is enormously tedious without the aid of computers. It relies on the judgment of individuals, and when more than one analyst is involved, serious problems with interrater reliability may surface. Computers can read and store vast quantities of information. They can apply coding rules consistently to that information and accurately perform complex statistical calculations related to the frequency and patterns of occurrence of different words and phrases. Moreover, they can do all these things with great speed. The advantages of having so powerful a tool were apparent to practitioners of content analysis as soon as computers came on the scene.

Computer-assisted content analysis of the responses to open-ended questions depends on three main processes: counting, coding, and comparing. The order in which counting and coding occur may differ depending on the research strategy and the software used. Words and phrases are counted, they are coded or assigned to topic areas, and the results of these first two processes are compared with internal or external standard benchmarks. Results are also studied to determine similarities and differences in patterns of occurrence of keywords and phrases.

There are many computer applications available to assist researchers in conducting content analysis of texts. Some applications require a great deal of user input, particularly in coding, whereas others incorporate dictionaries and algorithms that allow them to operate almost independently of human coders. A thorough technical introduction to the theory, tools, and methods that apply to analyzing texts is available in Krippendorff (2004). We focus on highly automated applications that offer a clear advantage for researchers engaged in time-sensitive employee surveys. These applications require little or no manual coding of text, work very rapidly, and fall into two main groups: text mining software and text analysis software.

Text Mining

Text mining applications such as Leximancer from the University of Queensland (information available from www.leximancer.com) and Megaputer's PolyAnalyst (information available from www. megaputer.com) typically use a neuronal network model to analyze proximity of words and phrases to each other in a multidimensional semantic space, sometimes incorporating several hundred dimensions (for a fuller discussion of neuronal and other semantic network models, see Krippendorff, 2004). They usually identify and map concepts that emerge from the text. Text-mining applications work well with very large data sets gathered from multiple sources. Text mining can be useful, for example, in a public health setting to find common ground and points of difference among survey responses, including records of structured interviews and replies from client populations, health care providers, public health administrators, and social workers. An excellent site for current information on data mining and text mining in general can be found at www.kdnuggets.com. This site bills itself as "the leading source of information on Data Mining, Web Mining, Knowledge Discovery, and Decision Support Topics, including News, Software, Solutions, Companies, Jobs, Courses, Meetings, Publications, and more."

Text Analysis

Text analysis software such as Provalis Research's WordStat (information available from http://www.simstat.com) and SPSS Text Analysis for Surveys (information available from www.spss.com/textanalysis_surveys/) uses predefined or user-defined lexicons (that is, lists of words and phrases) as bases for comparing themes within a body of text. Text analysis works particularly well with data from a single source, such as an employee survey or customer survey, situations in which the number of topics is limited and the issues encountered are somewhat predictable.

A useful site for information on text analysis (and to a lesser degree text mining) is Harald Klein's Text Analysis Info page (http://www.textanalysis.info/). CONTENT, an informative Internet mailing list, offers a forum for technical discussion in the field at all levels, from novice to expert practitioner. The list can be reached through the Content Analysis Resources page at the University of Alabama (http://www.car.ua.edu/).

Development and Implementation of Text Analysis Lexicons

In the applications section of this chapter, we present a set of case studies analyzing write-in comments from employee surveys for large multinational corporations. These analyses apply lexicon-based text analysis using WordStat, from which we have developed a standard lexicon of approximately four hundred key words and phrases grouped into thirty major topics covering all aspects of work life and organization culture. For example, the topic "Customer" includes the words "client(s)" and "customer(s)" and the acronym "CRM" (customer relationship management). The use of this standard lexicon allows reliable and valid comparison across responses to similar questions from surveys of different populations, or from surveys of the same population over time.

In the application of lexicon-based text analysis, developing a lexicon is a crucial step. The user creates two lexicons (called dictionaries) that WordStat uses in tandem to analyze text. The program designates one dictionary as an exclusion dictionary and the other as an inclusion dictionary. The exclusion dictionary contains words that are not to be counted, primarily high-frequency, low-content words such as *and, or, the, ever,* and *go*. All other words are counted. We use numerous inclusion dictionaries in our work: the standard, general dictionary covering common workplace issues just mentioned as well as specialized dictionaries modified for specific research purposes.

The amount of time required to develop a dictionary depends on the scope of the research problem. A specialized dictionary covering a limited area, such as a specific training program offered by a human resource department, can usually be created and tested in a day or less. General dictionaries for the analysis of broad domains, such as attitudes toward the organization or other complex entities, take much longer to create, often as long as a week or more. The additional time is required to ensure accuracy in the assigning of key words and phrases to their proper topics. Our standard for a dictionary entry is that 90 percent or more of the text records containing the entry should be correctly assigned to the relevant topic.

Once the user has created a lexicon (or inclusion dictionary) and has tested it to verify that it is retrieving the appropriate material, WordStat analyzes bodies of text in several steps. First, a frequency count of all words present is generated. Next, all the words and phrases in the exclusion dictionary are eliminated from that count. WordStat then applies the inclusion dictionary, coding the material to topic areas and generating the counts that represent the main output from the content analysis. In the process, WordStat can track the frequency of phrases as well as words, a useful step that allows phrases with words in common to be assigned to different topics. For example, consider the word *cost*. "Cost of insurance" can be assigned to the Benefits topic, "cost of living" to the Compensation topic, and "cost cutting" to the Operating Efficiency topic. This feature is particularly important when dealing with words that are strongly affected by context. *Management,* for example, is used in so many different contexts that it appears in our standard workplace issues lexicon only as part of a phrase.

WordStat analyzes text quickly and with a minimum of user intervention. In fact, analysis of even fairly large bodies of text (that is, 10 MB or more) is completed in a matter of minutes. It is therefore unnecessary to assign text to specific categories by hand before proceeding with the analysis, although this step can be taken if desired. Respondents may also be given the option of coding their answers according to a topic list assigned to the comment question. When this self-categorization option is present, a cross-tabulation of the employee choices against the WordStat lexicon adds considerable depth to the analysis.

It is important to recognize that the content analysis lexicons developed for use with WordStat are not static documents. Due to changes in language, dictionaries are never complete. Relevant new words and phrases must be added as they are encountered in data sources. In addition, entries must be dropped or modified occasionally to account for changes in use.

The potential of lexicon-driven text analysis is fully realized when the application of open-ended questions is linked to the specific goals of the survey itself. The next section illustrates several examples of this strategic use of text analysis in employee surveys.

Applications: A Continuum from Exploratory to Strategic

Employee surveys are conducted for a variety of reasons. In some cases, the purpose is primarily to define problematic issues within the culture of the organization (for example, pay scales are not competitive, training is inadequate, or safety concerns are overlooked). In other cases, the survey is conducted with a more strategic goal in mind, such as improving customer focus or efficiency, engaging employees, or enhancing leadership effectiveness. The goal in these contexts is to identify key issues for action planning and generate potential solutions to address and correct those issues. And in some cases, the goals of a survey may incorporate both problem description and solution identification.

This section presents findings from a diverse range of surveys, some focused on describing workplace issues and others on generating solutions. These are not discrete types of surveys but rather can be seen as research tools with a continuum of applications, as illustrated in Figure 10.1.

At one end of the continuum, exploratory focus applications employ comment exercises that use general descriptive questions, as when an exercise at the end of an employee survey asks for any additional comments from respondents. Exploratory analytical

Figure 10.1. A Continuum of
Employee Survey Application Types

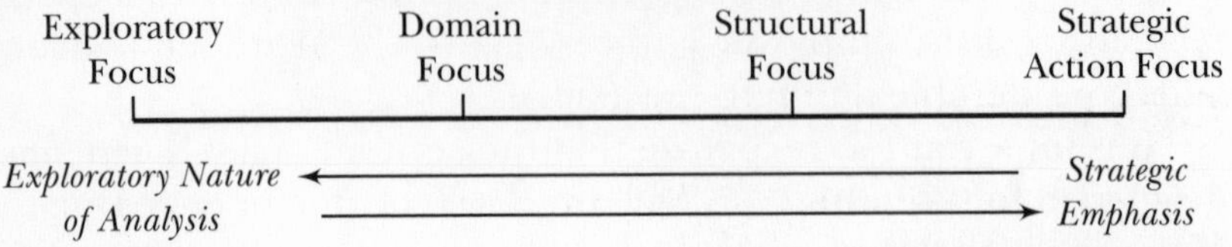

Exploratory Focus	Domain Focus	Structural Focus	Strategic Action Focus

Exploratory Nature of Analysis ←——————————————————— *Strategic Emphasis*
——————————————————→

methods are best suited to the exploratory nature of this type of exercise.

In a domain focus application, a specific topic domain within the responses is singled out for study, as when a survey exercise elicits comments addressing organizational leadership effectiveness. Such applications are still rather exploratory and can use a specific question discussing or describing a particular topic area or a general question asking respondents to prescribe ways to make the company a better place to work.

A structural focus application is particularly relevant when the goal of the survey process is to understand how organization culture affects the success of strategic business objectives, such as producing high-quality products or services. In such cases, specific question types, both prescriptive and descriptive, are typically used, and a lexicon closely tied to key elements of organization culture is applied to map the content of open-ended comments.

When circumstances warrant a narrower focus for a survey exercise, as in the case of a new CEO acquiring feedback from senior leaders, a strategic action focus application may be employed. In these instances, the comment questions used are precisely tailored to solicit input defining urgent strategic imperatives and soliciting recommendations for action on them. Consequently, the lexicon is built exclusively from the responses of the survey population, and the analysis becomes a foundation for generating the action plans that drive survey follow-up.

Two qualities thus distinguish these four application types: extent of strategic focus and the exploratory nature of the analytical process itself. The greater the strategic emphasis of the comment exercise is, the less exploratory is the nature of the analyses used to obtain insight from the responses. In addition, more strategic applications tend to employ more specific and prescriptive question types.

Case Examples of Lexicon-Based Text Analysis

Examples of each application type are considered next. To perform the analysis in each case, we either created a specialized lexicon of key words related to a specific topic or set of topics or we adapted one from prior applications. Open-ended comments from employees were then filtered through this lexicon to obtain counts of specific topic occurrences.

Exploratory Focus Applications

Our first example comes from a global professional services firm. Many surveys simply ask respondents in an open-ended format to list any additional thoughts they have about their workplace, as was the case here. In addition, respondents were asked to assign a code to each comment to indicate the topic area (such as compensation, leadership, or career advancement) that was the respondent's major focus. We combined an analysis of the respondents' categorization of their own answers with a lexicon-based text analysis of the same responses to provide a deeper level of insight than could be obtained from either method alone.

Figure 10.2, often called a "heat map," shows the output from the application of a standard lexicon containing the specific topic areas most often referenced in responses to an open-ended comment question. In this case, the lexicon is used in conjunction with employee self-coding. Along the left-hand side of the figure are the general themes included in the lexicon, which are presented in order of frequency of occurrence in the comments.

The three codes at the top of the figure correspond to the three categories most frequently selected in respondent self-coding: Talent Management, Reward and Recognition, and Work/Life Balance. The lighter the shading in each column of the heat map, the higher the percentage of comments from each category assigned to a particular topic area by the general lexicon. Percentages increase from zero (dark shade) to 20 percent or higher (light shade).

Figure 10.2. Heat Map from Case Example
Applying General Lexicon to Employee Self-Coded Comments

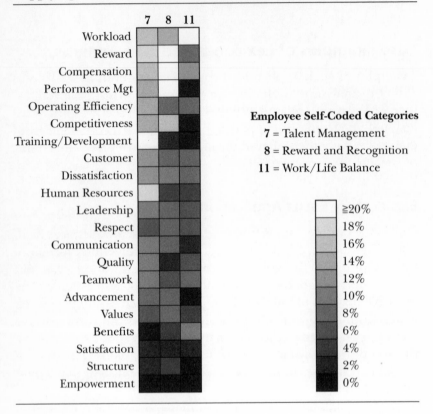

Employee Self-Coded Categories

7 = Talent Management

8 = Reward and Recognition

11 = Work/Life Balance

Without the application of a general lexicon, organization management might have concluded that a high percentage of comments self-coded as Talent Management implied a high level of employee concern with training and development programs. But the frequent appearance of lighter shades under Talent Management indicates that comments in this area address more than just training and development issues; reward and compensation (plus human resources in general) are additional themes frequently mentioned in comments self-coded to that topic. This finding suggests that action planning to improve talent management requires a focus on these additional issues as well as their interrelationships, a key insight that without text analysis might have been overlooked.

Domain-Focus Applications

Employee surveys are often conducted with a specific topic domain in mind as a key focus. Comment questions and qualitative analyses can be tailored to provide insights into a key issue, maximizing the value of the survey returns to the organization. Lexicon-based text analysis serves well as a tool for studying a specific domain. Two examples of such studies are described in this section.

The first study was conducted for a large, fast-moving consumer goods company. Responses to a comment question asking for recommendations to improve the organization were sorted to isolate comments from managers. The comments functioned as a focused upward-feedback mechanism to evaluate organizational leadership effectiveness. A custom lexicon of key words was designed to analyze the responses according to a conceptualization of leadership that distinguishes six types of behaviors. Two of these types concern efforts by leaders to position the company for effective performance:

Direction: Defining a clear strategy and coherent goals and objectives

Values: Codifying what the company stands for and will pursue through its activities

A third type of leadership behavior addresses communication:

Inform: Persuading employees of the importance of direction and values and making clear to employees the impact of these concepts on their work activities, company plans, and, ultimately, company performance

The remaining three types address leaders' abilities to execute, or perform their job-specific functions:

Respect: Leveraging employees' diverse abilities and involving them in key decisions

Role modeling: Displaying appropriate behaviors that are consistent with company goals and values

Energy: Facilitating employee efforts by making decisions quickly and establishing clear, consistent priorities

A set of key words was defined for each of these six types of behaviors, and the open-ended comments were then filtered through the resulting lexicon.

Table 10.2 shows the comment frequencies, from highest to lowest, for each behavior type by three levels of company leadership: line management, middle management, and senior leadership. Comments about direction and energy were most frequent, suggesting that leaders at all levels are most concerned about clarifying strategic direction, but also translating that direction into specific priorities for employees to execute. Consistent with this concern for communicating priorities to employees, comments related to the theme of informing employees were next highest in frequency. Also of note is that the number of comments about the themes of direction, energy, and inform increased at higher levels of leadership. Because senior leaders are in an influential position to set direction and communicate the implications of strategy to all other levels, their high frequency of comments in these areas suggests serious concerns about the effectiveness of top leadership to execute some of its most basic responsibilities.

**Table 10.2. Percentage of Comments by
Leadership Dimension and Level**

Leadership Dimension	Line Management	Middle Management	Senior Leadership
Direction	12	16	18
Energy	13	15	18
Inform	9	10	13
Respect	10	9	10
Values	7	6	8
Role modeling	6	6	5

Note: Because many comments from the survey did not include vocabulary related to the leadership dimensions under study, percentages should not be expected to sum to 100.

Respect, values, and role modeling were considerably less frequent open-ended comment themes and showed little variation in frequency by level, indicating that behaviors in these areas were not a particularly important concern among company leaders.

These findings point the organization to specific leadership behaviors to emphasize in survey follow-up and to stress within leadership training and development programs.

Our second domain focus application comes from a financial services organization whose survey exercise focused specifically on uncovering ways to further engage employees. Qualitative analysis of open-ended comments supported numerous quantitative analyses that were completed to achieve this goal. First, an engagement index developed from a factor analysis of the quantitative data was used as a measure of engagement. Second, multiple regression analysis was applied to uncover the key statistical correlates of engagement, prioritizing issues for action planning to improve engagement. Third, the data were further refined by applying a cluster analysis, which segments employees into subgroups that represent levels of employee engagement. Four clusters were identified in the data. To capture the meaning of the clusters, each cluster was given a name that metaphorically reflects the strength of the relationship between the employee and the organization. Employees in the cluster with the highest levels of engagement were called the Engaged. Employees in the next most engaged cluster were called the Cohabiting, followed by the Separated and the Divorced, who were the least engaged.

Once the issues that best predict engagement are uncovered and meaningful subgroups identified, how can an organization design actions to address the key issues? For this financial services organization, regression analyses showed that the strongest predictor of employee engagement was perception of leadership. The more that employees perceived their leaders as effective, the higher the employee engagement levels tended to be. But a question arises: Does this result imply that a focus on leadership should be the primary issue to address across the entire organization? Is leadership truly first in the minds of all employees, regardless of their extent of engagement?

Qualitative data analysis of open-ended comments was used to address these issues. Employees were asked to list ideas to improve the company and to self-code their comments into predetermined categories. To combine the qualitative data with insights from quantitative research, comment frequencies were examined for each engagement cluster. This analysis identified whether the issue of leadership is top of mind for employees, regardless of engagement level. The resulting rank ordering of comment frequencies by cluster is shown in Table 10.3.

**Table 10.3. Rank Order of Frequency of
Comment Topics by Employee Engagement Cluster**

Comment Topic	Company Overall	Engaged Cluster	Cohabiting Cluster	Separated Cluster	Divorced Cluster
Leadership	1	5	2	1	1
Pay and benefits	2	2 (tie)	1	2	2
Workload and pressure	3	2 (tie)	3	4	4
Training and career management	4	2 (tie)	4	3	3
Operating efficiency	5	1	5	5	5

Note: Shown are the top five categories by frequency in self-coded, open-ended comments.

Leadership, the top statistical correlate of engagement, was in fact the issue raised most often overall and by employees in the Divorced and Separated clusters and was second in frequency in the Cohabiting cluster. This pattern of results clearly points to leadership as a major source of critical comments among the least engaged employees, consistent with its role as a top predictor of engagement. The comments of employees from the Divorced, Separated, and Cohabiting clusters serve as an important source of ideas for action planning to improve leadership effectiveness.

The analysis of comment frequencies by cluster revealed one additional insight: In the Engaged cluster, operating efficiency was the category with the highest frequency, and Leadership was fifth in importance. This finding makes management aware that the issues to be addressed in efforts to increase engagement are not necessarily the same ones required to maintain high engagement levels. Ignoring concerns about the operating efficiency of the workplace runs the risk of eroding already established engagement levels. Comments from employees in the Engaged cluster may also be studied to identify steps to streamline and simplify the work environment for these employees. A dual focus on increasing engagement by improving leadership effectiveness and maintaining established engagement levels through improved efficiency served as the main message from this combination of cluster analysis with the qualitative study of open-ended comments.

Identifying the most frequently mentioned comment categories yields useful insight, but it is also important to understand what respondents are saying, and how. In this instance, a simple reading of random samples of leadership comments by cluster revealed clear variations in tone by cluster membership. Specifically, comments among employees in the Engaged cluster focused on concern over some managers' abilities (for example, "some managers need to be better trained"), whereas comments among employees in the Cohabiting, Separated, and Divorced clusters revealed strong feelings of discontent about management in general (for example, "no support," "no real care for us," "no respect for employees"). This sharp contrast in tone of responses is further evidence of the depth of dissatisfaction with leadership among the least engaged clusters.

Structural Focus Applications

As human resource departments gain stature as strategic partners within organizations, surveys are more often used as tools for understanding what aspects of a company's culture may be facilitating or inhibiting the attainment of strategic goals. The next example shows how analysis of responses to open-ended comments helps leaders identify cultural factors that distinguish companies consistently successful in meeting their strategic priorities from those that are less successful.

Just asking general questions and reading the answers clearly is inadequate for maximizing qualitative data in this context. Rather, creating a more strategic application of qualitative analysis requires a unique approach to studying employees' responses to open-ended questions. In particular, a different approach to defining a keyword lexicon is required—an approach that aligns the content of employees' expressed ideas with the strategic goals of the business.

To meet this objective, we developed a text analysis lexicon linked to the results of an unpublished research study that we conducted on the aspects of organization culture that distinguish companies successful at meeting one of five business strategic priorities: company image, customer service, efficiency of operations, innovation, and quality products or services. This separate research study compares the opinions of employees from organizations highly successful at achieving their strategic priority, as defined by superior financial performance, with those of employees from less successful organizations. In general, employees from highly successful organizations have more favorable opinions across the board. The topic areas showing the largest gaps in opinion between employees in highly successful organizations and those in less successful organizations are defined as cultural differentiators of success.

The specific differentiators vary markedly by priority. For instance, companies successful under an efficiency mandate provide good working conditions, adequate training, and a clear focus on priorities, whereas companies pursuing innovation support diversity of thought, reward for risk taking, and the sharing of information across functions. Other differentiators are more similar to each other, but are nuanced in terms of how they apply to a particular strategic priority. For example, successful customer service cultures stress positive working relations, ensuring that strong employee morale translates into courteous, professional behavior toward customers. Working relations is also important under a quality mandate, but the key focus in this context is the sharing of best practice procedures that help reduce error rates and promote product quality.

This model of cultural differentiation served as a guide for creating tailored text analysis lexicons for each strategic priority. These lexicons include key words linked to each of the differentiators; examples are provided in Table 10.4. For instance, key words such as *creativity, ideas,* and *innovate* capture content relevant to the theme of innovation. Open-ended comments are then filtered through this lexicon to determine the frequency with which content related to each of the strategic priorities occurs within the open-ended returns.

Table 10.4. Sample Lexicon Key Words by Strategic Priority

Strategic Priority	Sample Lexicon Key Words
Company image	Brands Principles Values
Customer service	Client Customer
Efficiency of operations	Efficiency Overtime Priorities Workload
Innovation	Creativity Ideas Innovate
Quality of products or services	Error Quality Scrap

To illustrate the value of this strategy-specific lexicon, consider the example of a large financial services company. The organization designed a companywide employee survey to assess how well its culture is aligned with its strategic priorities of customer service and efficiency. As part of the survey, employees were asked an open-ended question seeking ideas to improve business performance. The second column in Table 10.5 shows the frequency of comments related to each of the five strategic priorities included in the text analysis lexicon. The lexicon identified customer service and efficiency as the two most frequent areas referenced within employee comments. Classifying the comments through this lexicon showed that the suggestions from employees are indeed aligned with the strategic priorities of the business. The program that generates the frequency data also creates a key word-in-context file that can be studied easily to find specific suggestions on how to improve in any of the strategic priorities listed.

Table 10.5. Percentage of Comments by Strategic Priority for Five Industry-Specific Case Examples

Strategic Priority	Financial Services	Pharmaceutical	Research and Development	Telecommunication	Fast-Moving Consumer Goods
Company image	6	8	4	7	18
Customer service	25	11	11	23	17
Efficiency of operations	24	25	30	14	26
Innovation	13	26	34	13	33
Quality of products or services	3	7	6	8	9

Note: Since many comments from the survey did not include vocabulary related to the strategic priorities under study and because many comments referred to more than one priority, percentages should not be expected to sum to 100 and may exceed that figure.

Table 10.5 also reveals how the frequencies differ within three other organizations with distinct strategic priorities. In each case, the most frequent response categories matched the strategic priority of the business. Specifically, the pharmaceutical and research and development organizations, although from different industries, face similar business challenges: to innovate by developing new products and efficiently deliver goods to market. Comments from employees in these organizations more often addressed the themes of innovation and efficiency than the other three themes. The telecommunications company referenced in Table 10.5 is focused on the goal of effective customer service, a priority clearly evident in the relatively high frequency of ideas to improve this aspect of the business. In each case, analysis of the comments confirmed that employees tended to respond most often in content areas aligned with the strategic priorities of the organization, providing senior leadership with a significant source of recommendations tied to key business issues.

The final result shown in Table 10.5 illustrates how changes over time in the opinions of employees are often reflected in their survey comments, allowing the comments to serve as a data source that can explain emerging trends in employee opinion and the business model itself. The organization profiled is a large, fast-moving consumer goods company that has traditionally stressed the efficient delivery of products to market. The annual companywide survey regularly asks employees to assess company competitiveness on a range of areas, including responding to new market trends and developing new products, issues that speak to innovation more than efficiency. Recent survey results showed significant declines in the percentage of employees satisfied with company competitiveness in these two areas, suggesting a concern among employees that the business model is slow to react to market developments calling for an emphasis on innovation in addition to efficiency.

To explore the reasons behind this change in employees' opinions, the strategic priority lexicon was used to analyze the open-ended responses. Results shown in Table 10.5 indicate that innovation was the most frequent response category mentioned by employees offering suggestions to improve business performance, followed closely by efficiency. These comments serve as a rich data source for understanding the scope and sources of employees' concerns regarding shifts in the marketplace. They also address, from the perspective of employees performing different functions at different levels, steps the company needs to take to improve its competitive position.

Strategic Action Focus Applications

In our final case, a large pharmaceutical firm hired a new CEO who sought immediate feedback on a range of issues from the top one hundred leaders. Any survey must be designed and administered quickly in order to obtain critical insights. The application used here needed to be specific enough to address the strategic business requirement and flexible enough to provide fresh insights fast.

A comments-only survey was created that addressed a set of five questions drafted in large part by the CEO: the most urgent business priorities to handle in the first six months, the top priorities to address for long-term success, the greatest opportunities achievable under the existing business plan, the greatest barriers to achieving those opportunities, and the opportunities most easily implemented from a cost and efficiency standpoint. To analyze the results, a lexicon was developed in which key words tied to one of ten topic areas were defined. Results for each question were filtered through this lexicon to determine the highest-frequency issues within respondents' comments. The lexicon provided an effective way to map the themes in the 1,388 returned comments that would not have been possible from a casual reading of the information.

Results showed strong differences by question on the issues most frequently mentioned. Table 10.6 ranks the topics by frequency for all questions and separately for the question concerning most urgent business priorities. The overall results indicated that four topic areas were most on the minds of corporate senior leaders: research and development, competitive issues, strategy, and products. Despite these overall trends, topic ranks for the question on immediate priorities showed significant variation. In fact, not one of the top five issues from the analysis of all comments appeared among the top five priorities for immediate action, which instead included regulatory issues, company image, leadership, culture, and quality. In other words, in the view of senior leaders, the most immediate needs of the business were quite distinct from the topics that needed to be addressed to ensure long-term success, achieve the business plan, and do so easily from a cost and efficiency perspective. The tailored, specific nature of the feedback and the text analysis lexicon allowed these distinctions to emerge from the senior leadership survey exercise.

Table 10.6. Rank Order of Frequency of Comment Topics

Comment Topic	All Questions	Question on Most Urgent Business Priorities
Research and development	1	10
Competitive issues	2	9
Strategy	3	8
Products	4	7
Operating efficiency	5	6
Regulatory issues	6	1
Leadership	7	3
Culture	8	4
Quality	9	5
Company image	10	2

Note: Shown are the top ten categories by frequency in open-ended comments.

Returning to Figure 10.1, it is evident that there are many different ways to apply computer-assisted text analysis to the study of open-ended survey questions. Consistent with the wide array of purposes driving surveys in organizations today, the types of lexicons used in our examples are necessarily quite diverse. Although it is difficult to obtain firm estimates, many organizations use open-ended questions at the end of a survey and require more exploratory than strategic applications. Fewer organizations make use of strategic open-ended comment studies, although these applications are gaining popularity. As the potential strategic focus of open-ended comments attains wider acceptance and use among practitioners, we might expect to see strategic applications used as often as exploratory approaches.

Practical Considerations

The analysis of qualitative data from open-ended survey questions provides valuable insights that inform the conclusions drawn from quantitative data obtained through closed-ended responses. The two data streams are in many ways separate, but when combined, they have the potential to generate greater insight than each could yield individually. Gathering qualitative data has unique practical challenges, however. Among these challenges are issues related to mode of administration, confidentiality, and multiple languages.

Mode of Administration

Managing the returns from open-ended questions in paper surveys can be very costly. The responses are often expensive to process, particularly if the survey design includes branching questions and if targeted questions are scattered throughout the survey. Paper surveys, of course, produce handwritten replies, which are not machine readable and must be transcribed before data analysis, a process made even more complicated and expensive when the returns are provided in multiple languages.

The solution to high transcription costs is simple: use an online survey data collection mode instead of paper surveys as often as possible. Online survey returns require no transcription and are easily retrieved from online survey data capture programs. The accessibility of online survey collection may be limited in some organizational contexts, particularly in a manufacturing environment, but the use of online surveys is clearly growing, and most organizations are able to collect at least a portion of survey returns online. A requirement for multiple languages presents technical challenges for online data collection. Characters for most languages are incorporated in the Unicode character set, but some (for example, Khmer, a Southeast Asian language) are not and therefore require special fonts.

Online data collection has other advantages. Specifically, branching questions are easier to apply in an online rather than paper mode, as directing select employees to an open-ended question is accomplished through simple branching protocols in the data capture program. In addition, based on our experience, online surveys tend to elicit longer responses than paper surveys; consequently, the survey design must allow sufficient capacity in the response boxes to accommodate employees who have much to say.

Confidentiality

If the responses are to be reported verbatim, confidentiality and anonymity are of great concern. Verbatim reporting is common practice with employee surveys, but there are a number of contexts in which verbatim reports must never be issued (for example, responses to public health or substance abuse studies). Care must also be exercised when an external third party is used to provide verbatim comment feedback. No matter how carefully the responses are vetted, it is impossible for an outsider to determine whether a given response contains enough clues for an employer to positively identify or, perhaps even worse, falsely identify the writer. Often, analytical reports that include examples of typical verbatim comments are provided by a third party. In such instances, it is essential to avoid providing examples that mention specific situations, individuals, named departments, or other potentially identifying information.

When permissible, if a survey's open-ended responses are to be reported verbatim, respondents should be informed with a clear notice placed at the beginning of the comment section, such as this example: "Your comments will be collected, typed [for paper surveys only], sorted into groups, and reported to management exactly as written. Please do not sign your name or include in your comments any information that might directly identify you." The use of such a notice may discourage some individuals from responding, but based on our internal tracking, its presence does not have a significant impact on comment response rates. Indeed, in some cases, respondents appear to want to be identified and sign their names anyway.

Multiple Languages

In addition to the challenges already discussed, multiple languages provide further issues for lexicon-based text analysis. Clearly, the application of a lexicon in the presence of multiple languages requires that the key words be available in all relevant languages.

Translating lexicons for use in multiple-language contexts is an iterative process that requires native speakers who are familiar with not only the business issues to be captured by the lexicon but also with the situational uses of the specialized vocabularies involved. Text mining applications such as Leximancer that are based on neuronal network technology may be a better choice in multilingual projects because they do not require translation of employee responses or predefined dictionaries. Even so, analysis of comments in some languages may require special software to deal with their individual character sets and formats.

Conclusion

There is more to the written word than meets the eye. Ever since the first Bible concordances (indexes of words displayed in context) were published in the twelfth century (Eslinger, 2004), scholars and researchers have sought ways to analyze the content within written material to extract more information than can be obtained from even the most careful reading. That challenge echoes through time and is evident today in the difficulties often faced by management when an employee survey includes open-ended comment responses.

This challenge is important to solve because employees have a firsthand understanding of the issues they face in the workplace and are uniquely positioned to provide specific recommendations for action to enhance organizational effectiveness. As described in this chapter, computer-assisted content analysis is a powerful tool for extracting employees' knowledge and maximizing the value of open-ended comments. Many types of applications exist, and the selection of question type and analytical method is thus critical to the successful use of open-ended questions. The best general advice we can give management is to consider carefully the purpose of the survey exercise and then tailor the choice of questions and analytical options to suit that specific purpose.

What future developments might be expected in the application of open-ended survey questions? No doubt as computer technology continues to advance, so too will the techniques available to study open-ended comment returns. In addition, as open-ended questions and qualitative analysis techniques become more standardized, the opportunity to benchmark comment frequencies emerges.

From an organizational perspective, such advances provide many tangible advantages. Specifically, the ability to find the root of a new idea within a body of comments is greatly enhanced. Often the best new ideas to push a company forward come from the minds of its people. Furthermore, if benchmarking can tell managers that employees at their key competitors are concerned with aligning their roles to the strategic priority of the business, whereas their own people are mainly worried about their pay, this insight can shape the nature of future discourse between managers and employees. As the challenges of doing business in a complex, global economy continue to multiply, the clear line of sight into the experiences of employees in any corner of the business provided by open-ended survey questions represents a largely untapped source of competitive advantage.

References

Eslinger, L. (2004). *Concordances: History and uses.* http://www.ucalgary.ca/~eslinger/genrels/Concordance.html.

Krippendorff, K. (2004). *Content analysis: An introduction to its methodology* (2nd ed.). Thousand Oaks, CA: Sage.

CHAPTER 11

Pulse Surveys

A Limited Approach with Some Unique Advantages

Joe Colihan
Janine Waclawski

The use of employee attitude or organization surveys (as they are often referred to) as a tool for measuring employee attitudes, perceptions, and behaviors has been well documented (Church & Waclawski, 2001; Kraut, 1996; Waclawski & Church, 2002). More important, though, surveys have become an important part of running the business in many large organizations. In particular, feedback from employees on their workplace climate, job satisfaction, intentions to stay with the business, leadership practices, and business processes, among others, all help feed into day-to-day decisions that help drive the business. When making decisions about which programs to support, which ideas to implement, and which problems to focus on, accurate representations about the perceptions of employees on these issues is critical. This is why surveys have become so commonplace in contemporary organizations.

The importance and popularity of these kinds of surveys has led to the emergence of a relatively new form of organization survey that has been called a *pulse survey*, so named because it is designed to take the pulse of an organization. Exploring the medical analogy further, a traditional survey, which typically measures many broad factors in an organization from morale, satisfaction, and commitment to more specific topics such as feelings about one's manager, the company's senior leadership, and even benefits and compensation, can be thought of as assessing the overall organization's health. In fact, at PepsiCo this is what the biannual organization survey is called: the Organization Health Survey. This type of survey is like a full medical exam for an organization.

In contrast to a thorough survey approach like the Organization Health Survey, a pulse survey represents a slimmed-down version of the traditional survey. By sacrificing one or more of the characteristics of a traditional survey, an organization can get some critical information more quickly than it could through a traditional approach. The medical analogy describes it well. While a traditional survey represents a full annual physical assessment of a person by his or her regular doctor, a pulse survey represents a neighborhood clinic where this person could stop in for a quick check on blood pressure or blood sugar level.

A pulse survey, then, is a technique for gaining limited information about an organization's workplace climate quickly. The information would be limited, relative to a traditional survey, on one or both of the following dimensions: content and generalizability. A pulse survey that is limited in content, also called a special topics survey, focuses on a limited subset of workplace climate (for example, diversity). A pulse that is limited in generalizability focuses on a subset of the organization based on demographics (such as executives), clusters of employees (such as new employees), or random sampling. Results from such a pulse would be limited to the demographic group in question or to only very high levels of the organization where sampling produces enough data for a representative view.

The limitations of a pulse survey also provide unique opportunities for an organization. Because a pulse is smaller in scope than a traditional climate survey, the pulse can be used to get a quick reading about a particular issue. Another option made possible through a pulse is multiple measurements. For example, while it would not be practical to conduct a traditional full-blown traditional survey on a monthly basis, a more limited pulse survey could be and has been used to take a reading of the workplace climate twelve times in a single year. A typical pulse survey program of this type, where measures are taken monthly, quarterly, or semiannually, would be limited in generalizability through random sampling and may also be limited in content (perhaps with four key questions from the full-blown workplace climate survey).

Pulse surveys are typically considered complementary to a traditional survey approach. In fact, many companies augment their annual survey processes, designed to measure overall health, with pulse surveys designed to gain more limited information more quickly. This chapter presents an overview and definition of pulse surveys, how they are used, and how they are similar to and different from traditional organization surveys. In addition, advantages and disadvantages of using pulse surveys are discussed, and several applications of pulse survey technology are highlighted.

What Is a Pulse Survey, and How Has It Evolved?

Until recently, organization surveys have typically been described in the literature as taking one of two forms: either census (a survey of the entire employee population of a given organization) or a sample (a survey of a portion of the entire employee population of a given organization). To a large extent, the way organizational practitioners have thought about and implemented surveys has been tied to the technology that has been available.

Until the late 1990s, most organizations used paper-and-pencil technology or interactive voice response systems (telephone surveys) to survey their employees. Data collection devices like optical scan forms and even simple paper instruments where employees were asked to "check the box" (often in group administrations) were commonplace. This typically required a great deal of manual work for the survey practitioner in terms of printing, distributing, scheduling, collecting, and scanning or entering data. For a large corporation, the administration of the survey would often require weeks, if not months, of preparation (just to shuffle all the paper), in addition to the development of the actual survey content. To a large extent, this meant that for many companies, it was practical to survey no more frequently than once per year if a census or large sample was being conducted, especially for organizations with a large population of employees who do not have access to computers and must complete paper questionnaires.

Technological advances have changed not only the way and speed with which we process information as a society but also as organizational survey practitioners. Because of these advances in technology, clients' expectations about the method of administration (today surveys are expected to be conducted online) and the speed of communicating results (clients typically want to get results in days, not weeks) have been shaped by their experiences outside the survey arena.

Specifically, the business world and the information that drives it (through Personal Digital Assistants, Internet, instant messaging, cell phones, and other devices) has created a landscape where receiving instantaneous information is the norm. Surveys are not immune to this expectation. Moreover, our increased reliance on computers, and the Internet in particular, has made new modes of survey administration more possible and popular. This change has had an impact not only on how most companies conduct their employee surveys (online data collection) but the nature of surveys themselves as well. One example of the changing nature of organizational surveys can be seen with the advent of the pulse survey.

Key Elements of a Pulse Survey

Given their recent entry into the survey practitioner's tool kit, pulse surveys remain in their infancy with regard to measuring organizational employee attitudes. In fact, little research exists on organizational pulse surveys. A search of the American Psychological Association's PsychINFO database conducted in September 2004 produced no relevant journal articles with the terms *pulse* and *survey*. An expanded search including Web sites and conference presentations produced a few references to pulse surveys in such applications as election polling, housing starts, industry evaluations, and employee attitude surveys (Berwald, 2004; Colihan, 2004; Lotz-Turner, 2004). Due to the newness of this process, there is still no consistent definition of *pulse survey*. The most common conception of pulse surveys differs from traditional organization surveys in a few key ways:

Mode of administration. Pulse surveys are generally collected online, not through other means, although many companies still survey by paper and pencil, especially to reach employees in the field who may not have access to computers. Pulse surveys are often administered from a Web site because it is much easier to survey this way than by distributing and collecting paper surveys.

Objective of the survey. Pulse surveys are typically designed to get a quick high-level view of the climate as opposed to a comprehensive data collection effort. Often this is the case when only a portion of the organization is being surveyed.

Sampling methods used. Pulse surveys typically are not a census but sometimes can be. A simple sampling approach would involve inviting a random sample of 25 percent of an organization to a quarterly pulse survey. Without replacement and ignoring the dynamic nature of an employee population with some new employees and some employees leaving, an organization could get close to inviting all employees in a given year.

Focus of the survey. Pulse surveys are typically focused on a few specific topics as opposed to traditional surveys, which are often more broadly focused on many topics. That is, a pulse survey is often focused on only one or two topics, unlike a comprehensive organization assessment, which is often focused on a plethora of topics or issues.

Table 11.1 highlights some of the key differences between traditional and typical pulse surveys with respect to several key dimensions: frequency, participants, content, method of administration, ease of administration, promotions/communications, and taking action.

**Table 11.1. Characteristics
of Traditional and Pulse Surveys**

Characteristic	Traditional Surveys	Pulse Surveys
Frequency	Typically annual or biannual, limited opportunity to tap timely or hot topics	Typically monthly or quarterly (more frequently than traditional surveys), greater opportunity to tap timely or hot topics

Table 11.1. Characteristics
of Traditional and Pulse Surveys, Cont'd

Characteristic	Traditional Surveys	Pulse Surveys
Participants	Typically a full census of employees but sometimes a sample; results often available for first-line managers	Typically a sample (for example, 25 percent each quarter) or sometimes a census; often involves a sacrifice of lower-level results (for example, first-line managers)
Process	Typically, measure, analyze, create action plan, and implement actions before surveying again to evaluate impact	Typically, measure and analyze in the short term but act and evaluate on longer-term trends; opportunity to address problems before they get worse
Content	Content typically focused on a wide range of factors and frequently based on an organization model (for example, often a systems approach to organizational diagnosis)	Content typically focused on either a top-line (high-level) assessment of cultural state or a specific area of focus (for example, diversity, a CEO survey, or current organization initiatives)
Length	Varies but typically longer (50 to 150 items is most common)	Varies but typically shorter (10 to 25 items)
Method of administration	Increasingly conducted online, but many organizations still require extensive use of paper-based methods (for example, optical scan or keypunch) as well as voice response methods: to ensure the	Typically perceived to be an online (technology-enabled) process; however, the concept does not preclude other methods

(Continued)

Table 11.1. Characteristics
of Traditional and Pulse Surveys, Cont'd

Characteristic	Traditional Surveys	Pulse Surveys
Method of administration	ability to reach front-line, geographically dispersed, and technology unenabled employees	
Ease of administration	Mixed: some organizations rely on expert survey vendors because of cost efficiencies, experience, scope of the survey, and access to survey norms; others have internal survey groups and/or internal custom online survey programs	Generally self-service (for example, Zoomerang, Surveymonkey, and other "do-it-yourself" simple-to-use tools are often used to build, administer, analyze, and report the survey)
Promotions/ communication	Event-based communications, posters, general marketing, and hype to drive the process and enhance participation, accountability, and action planning	Promotion of actions and success stories rather than the survey event. Ongoing trending and timely results reinforce the timeliness of the process and emphasize real-time nature of data collected.
Taking action	Accountability for taking action is driven to the lowest organization level possible (for example, front-line supervisor/ team level)	Can be as targeted as a traditional survey if taken to the same level of specificity (for example, work group level) when designed, but this is not typical. Pulse surveys are often used to track larger organizational trends over time.

Given these considerations and the fact that very little litera-ture about pulse surveys yet exists, we offer the following working definition: *a pulse survey is a measurement technique that produces timely, quick, but limited information about the health of an organization.* In a pulse survey approach, limitations based on content, sampling, or other characteristics are accepted in return for gains in speed and simplicity. Accepting certain limitations makes it possible to get in-formation about the business in a short period of time. Pulse sur-veys also allow ongoing workplace climate measures on a frequent basis (say, monthly or quarterly).

Reasons for Considering Pulse Surveys

Although there are many reasons for considering alternative ap-proaches to traditional surveying, this chapter focuses on some of the more common ones. A desire for more frequent real-time data is generally accepted as one of the strongest reasons for conduct-ing a pulse survey. Consider the information technologies (IT) in-dustry. At IBM, many managers needed to get more timely information for making decisions or evaluating progress on spe-cific workplace climate initiatives than the traditional survey ap-proach provides. This need was driven in large part by the rapid pace of change in the IT industry. Specifically, the quickly chang-ing competitive environment made survey results that had been collected over a year earlier seem inadequate and dated.

In fact, the number of mergers and acquisitions in IT in the past decade has been tremendous; consider companies like Cisco that built on more than forty previously separate IT companies. Even popular software programs get updated often, in some cases several times a year, reflecting the increasing pace of change. It is interesting to note that the Information Technologies Survey Group (www.itsg.org) recently began providing attitude survey benchmarks to its member companies twice a year rather than once due to the collective feeling in the group that things move very rapidly in IT and more timely benchmarks would better match the business needs of its members. This is just one example of how the pace of business today has had an impact on surveys. One could easily argue that these trends hold for all industries.

Another practical reason for increased interest in pulse surveys is the ease and relatively low cost with which they can be administered if a commonly marketed, self-service, online survey tool is used. If an expert vendor is used, pulse surveys can be more expensive. Self-service survey tools like Zoomerang, Survey Said, Surveysage, and SurveyMonkey have made it easier than ever before for survey practitioners (and even those with absolutely no survey experience) to design, administer, analyze, and report survey results with the touch of a few buttons. This can result in dire consequences, as this enables people with no formal survey training to design and administer them. This point-and-click approach to surveys is very appealing in that it allows not only real-time data collection but real-time design and administration as well. In addition, these tools (in comparison to using an expert survey vendor) are often extremely inexpensive, typically allowing the survey practitioner to conduct large numbers of surveys for a fraction of the cost of conducting one traditional annual survey. Many of these self-service tools cost a few hundred dollars per year for an unlimited amount of surveys.

Still another common use of pulse surveys is to augment the traditional survey process. For example, at PepsiCo, pulse surveys are used in addition to the biannual Organization Health Survey, which is administered to over 140,000 employees worldwide. In this organization, pulse surveys are used to collect data on special topics such as diversity and work/life balance on a quarterly basis instead of measuring these once every two years. This allows PepsiCo to assess change over time and to intervene and develop action plans as needed if the data suggest that it is warranted.

Who Is Using Pulse Surveys?

Trends in professional survey practices indicate increased interest in conducting employee attitude surveys more frequently than one may have seen ten years ago. The most common frequency of surveys among companies in two benchmarking groups, Mayflower (Johnson, 2004) and the Information Technology Survey Group, is still once per year. However, several companies, including Accenture, Dell, Gateway, IBM, Merrill Lynch, Microsoft, and PepsiCo, have been experimenting with pulse surveys. In fact, Microsoft has been conducting its MS Pulse Survey since 2001. According to Kate Suckow, "At that time, we thought we would give the mid-year survey idea a try, not knowing if we would continue to do it. Since then, we have continued to offer it each year because of the high demand for it. Our MS Pulse survey is an optional survey for businesses. Although optional, a large number of businesses do choose to participate in the process, indicating the value they see in understanding employee opinions" (K. Suckow-Zimberg, personal communication, September 10, 2004).

A poll of survey professionals conducted by the Center for Research and Service in July 2004 found fairly widespread belief in the potential utility of pulse surveys. When asked, "How should an organization use pulse surveys?" only 11 percent stated that they "did not recommend pulse surveys." A few more (18 percent) indicated that organizations should invite all employees to either a small subset of the traditional survey or a special topics survey focused on a small set of issues. The majority of survey practitioners (70 percent) indicated that pulse surveys should be applied to gain insights through a small subset of employees, either on special focused topic areas or a set of broader traditional survey questions. Nevertheless, according to this same study, most still recommend conducting surveys annually or less frequently. When asked, "How often should an organization conduct an employee survey?" only 4 percent indicated that a quarterly or semiannual pulse survey was the most appropriate. Most (61 percent) recommend an annual survey. All in all, most survey practitioners see value in a pulse survey approach, but still tend to rely more often on a traditional annual census survey approach.

Some Advantages of Using Pulse Surveys

The main potential benefit of conducting pulse surveys seems obvious: availability of climate results that are more up-to-date than would otherwise be the case. Climate measurements taken only once a year or less can sometimes leave organizations with results that look dated. Consider a traditional census survey project that is conducted once a year. A company may survey employees in September, receive and analyze results in October, and formulate some action plans to begin implementing before year end. The next April, the company begins to reevaluate its action plans and think about measuring progress. However, new results to evaluate progress will not be available for another six months. An executive may receive progress reports from various business units that provide some achievements (such as a 14 percent reduction in time spent in meetings or the fact that 147 managers completed a new training program). However, it is unlikely that this information will help the executive to estimate whether next September's climate measures will be up, down, or stable. In other words, it is difficult to truly know whether changes and initiatives carried out in reaction to the prior survey are on track.

By way of contrast, consider a pulse survey conducted on a sample of employees four times per year. Following a September survey in which the results are available in October, new results would be available perhaps again in January, then again in April, then again in July. If effort and money are invested in some initiative that does not seem to be resulting in gains on a specific question of interest, there is still time to investigate and make adjustments to the program in hopes of increasing its effectiveness. Tom Rauzi of Dell notes a case in point: "Dell has used pulse surveys over the last several years as a means of maintaining a close connection to employee perceptions on key organizational issues. The surveys allow us to conduct more timely linkage research, serve as a checkup on the impact of organizational initiatives, and identify areas of concern at an earlier stage than might otherwise be possible" (T. Rauzi, personal communication, September 13, 2004).

Surveys that are administered more often than once per year (for example, a quarterly pulse survey program) are also, in application, more flexible than traditional survey programs. While an annual survey allows a refresh of the survey content once a year, a pulse survey can evolve quickly within the year. If a new topic becomes hot within a business, questions to measure employee attitudes on that topic can be dropped into the next pulse survey rather than waiting up to a year before addressing it.

Although evidence to date is merely anecdotal, there may be positive effects on workplace climate as a result of a pulse survey's ability to keep the issues on the table. For example, consider a company focused on improving morale among its employees. With a traditional survey approach, there is a big event once a year to generate excitement over participating in the survey and generating new ideas for making the company a better place to work. Activity tends to spike in the one or two months leading up to the survey and maybe for another month or two afterward. For the rest of the year, morale may take a back seat to other issues or crises of the moment. When asked to apply limited resources and energy to improve the bottom line while also improving workplace climate, many managers will admit to feeling far more pressure to improve profit than to improve morale.

Now consider a company with a quarterly pulse survey program that calculates employee and manager bonuses in part based on workplace climate measurements and has a scorecard to track employee morale each quarter throughout the year. Managers in this company have three more opportunities to consider morale among their employees and actions that could improve it. Results can also be tracked against quarterly business performance measures, providing another opportunity to conduct research linking employee attitudes with external objective measures. In this case, the issue of morale has been kept on the table and is part of the day-to-day discussions that get business done. This may also be the case at a company with a less frequent survey that has a disciplined approach to the consideration of morale, but with a pulse survey, the ongoing discussion of morale issues is made more explicit and is more likely to happen, all else being equal.

Disadvantages: Some Cautions About Pulse Surveys

Given the relative ease with which a pulse survey can be carried out (easy relative to decades past, at least), it may seem like a good idea to jump into the development of a pulse survey program. However, there are sacrifices that need to be made to make a practical pulse survey program viable. While the speed of implementation and low cost (if a self-service tool is used) offer many advantages over traditional survey approaches, which are generally more time intensive, there are a few downsides.

Tools That Enable the Inexperienced to Develop Surveys

Perhaps the most important cautions are associated with the fact that self-service pulse surveys provide those who may have absolutely no survey expertise access to advanced survey tools. As the saying goes, a little knowledge is a dangerous thing. For example, with the advent of self-service tools, anyone who can type can design a bad survey item or even an entire survey and send it to hundreds or thousands of respondents in a matter of seconds. In addition, these tools, if not used with care, can violate the confidentiality of respondents. For example, these tools offer the user the ability to publish real-time results online as they come in. However, for some of these tools, unless specific functionality that enables snooping is turned off, results will be linked to individuals. In short, while these tools afford the experienced practitioner additional means to collect organization data, they also extend this opportunity to the inexperienced, thus exacerbating the long-time survey issue of "garbage in, garbage out" if not used judiciously.

Increased Oversurveying in Organizations

Pulse surveys may lead to even more oversurveying in organizations than seen with traditional survey programs. Indeed, the simple fact that technology has made it easier than ever before to conduct an employee survey may be the primary cause of oversurveying that many companies have experienced. Individual managers can now conduct surveys with little outside help, and the proliferation of surveys in some companies has forced them to set up governance processes to ensure quality, avoid redundancy, and involve the right decision makers in a given survey project (Weiner, 2000). One large company found over 150 distinct survey projects in a given year before setting up such a process for governing employee surveys.

Expense

Unless one is using a low-cost self-service tool, expense is an obvious barrier. Even with a streamlined pulse survey program, the costs of conducting a high-quality survey program four times per year will be higher than doing the same survey once using an expert vendor. For example, given the scope of most global survey programs, the costs associated with developing or modifying even one aspect of the survey instrument (for example, translating the survey into multiple languages) can be very costly. Whether the benefits outweigh the costs will depend on the individual business, the competitive environment in which the business operates, and the specific challenges facing the business at a given point in its history. A company in a rapidly changing industry like IT or one that has just undergone a major merger or acquisition may find pulse surveys more useful than, for example, a governmental service center or an insurance company where conditions are more stable in the short term.

Potentially Reduced Response Rates and Lowered Accountability for Results

Moreover, pulse surveys may produce lower response rates than traditional survey approaches. This is because with a single annual event, there is likely to be a lot of promotional activity surrounding the survey. Posters may be hung up in the hallways at company sites, executives may be mentioning the fact that "this year's survey" is rapidly approaching, and brochures and e-mail will be plentiful. Creating a pulse survey may require sacrificing some of these promotional activities to provide a more streamlined, cost-effective method for getting more frequent measurements. Furthermore, if a small sample of employees is invited to a pulse survey, it does not necessarily make sense to use promotional communications across the entire population when many of them will not be invited. Follow-up e-mail participation reminders to invitees may be more appropriate. To protect anonymity, these should not be targeted to only those who have not yet participated, but rather should be sent to all invitees.

A perceived lack of accountability for the results could be another factor serving to keep response rates down. In one large company that switched from a traditional approach to pulse surveys, participation rates dropped from the 60 to 70 percent range with traditional census surveys to the 50 percent range with pulse surveys. Unlike a census survey, sample surveys do not enable representative reports for small units, making it easier for a manager to dismiss the results as not specific to his or her people. (See Youseffnia & Berwald, 2004, for similar findings on pulse surveys and participation rates.)

In addition to the reduced promotional efforts discussed above, the fact that first-line managers no longer receive reports specific to their teams, as was the case with a census survey, may have had the unintended side effect of reducing their perceived stake in the survey project. Increasing accountability at higher organizational levels, which a pulse survey can do, may help to mitigate the effects of a reduced sense of ownership among some first-line managers. Nevertheless, the contrast between an entrenched census survey program and a high-level strategic pulse survey is stark. With the latter, reports are likely to be limited to the highest levels of an organization due to the sampling strategy. The number of responses available for lower-level reports may be too small to provide a representative view, that is, the margin of sampling error will be too high. For example, if forty employees provide responses from an organization of four hundred, the margin of sampling error could be as high as +/–15 percentage points. This would be considered by many researchers to be nonrepresentative, so the report would not be published. Thus, the visibility of results and actions can be significantly diminished. It is possible that involvement or feelings of accountability have decreased among first-line managers simply as a result of not receiving information.

Information Overload and Data of Questionable Value

Information overload is another potential negative outcome of using a pulse survey approach. Assume clients that there are line executives interested in improving their business processes. They make large investments in streamlining operations and hope to see improvements in employee perceptions of process effectiveness. While actual changes in processes may take years to reach fruition, the pulse survey is providing frequent measures of employee perceptions of processes that do not change much from month to month or quarter to quarter. In this case, rather than being motivated by dynamic real-time measurements of employee attitudes, some executives may lament the fourth pulse survey report in a row that shows little movement in answers to the questions of interest. In other words, if the issue being surveyed shows little or no change, then interest in the data may not be very compelling. Sometimes more is not better.

Finally, the notion that employee attitudes may be stable over several administrations of a pulse survey raises an interesting question. If results of most questions were unchanged or nearly so across several pulse surveys, then it makes little sense to measure so frequently. If it is already known that January results are going to be nearly identical to results obtained in November, then why expend resources on conducting that January pulse survey? Pulse surveys may reveal a greater level of stability in results than many leaders hope or expect to see.

Case Example 1: Tracking Culture Change at PepsiCo

At PepsiCo, quarterly pulse surveys have been used since 2000 to measure a myriad of special topics between administrations of the biannual Organization Health Survey. One specific example involves using the pulse survey tool to gauge progress toward the goal of becoming a more diverse and inclusive organization. To this end, since 2003, PepsiCo has been conducting a quarterly pulse survey to track diversity and inclusion efforts. This survey, the Inclusion Pulse Survey (IPS), ranges in length from twenty to thirty questions and is sent to a relatively small sample of employees (approximately two thousand associates in North America). The purpose of this survey is to measure change not only in the organization's culture but also in managerial behaviors with respect to the company's diversity efforts. The sample includes 50 percent of the executive population with an oversampling (100 percent) of the diverse executive population.

In terms of its content, the IPS contains a mixture of core and noncore items. Core items focus on topics such as the effectiveness of PepsiCo's diversity training, how inclusive managers are perceived to be, and if the culture of the organization is becoming more or less inclusive. The purpose of the noncore items is three-fold: (1) to pilot new items for potential use in the Organization Health Survey, (2) to assess any immediate needs on other initiatives that do not warrant their own survey, and (3) to collect interim data on important topics that the company wants to track between administrations of the Organization Health Survey (for example, intent to leave). These are different from the core items because they may be used for only one or two administrations of the pulse survey, not every quarter.

As an example, with respect to pilot testing, fifteen pilot items were added to the most recent IPS. As a direct result of asking respondents a series of questions about these items (via online write-ins), it was discovered that only six actually worked the way in which they were intended. This was a key learning as it enabled the elimination of "bad items" that were not ultimately included in the worldwide survey.

A unique piece of functionality that was built into the design of the IPS was the ability to track individual respondents over time. For example, in 2003, PepsiCo surveyed two sets of employees by repeated measures: group 1 was surveyed in Q1 and Q3, and group 2 was surveyed in Q2 and Q4. This allowed observation of individual change scores over time and for some interventions at the local department level instead of waiting for two years until the next Organization Health Survey.

Case Example 2: Tracking Trends Bimonthly at IBM

Trends from a pulse survey will depend on a host of factors, including what is going on in the business, what changes have occurred recently, and the economic and political circumstances of the times. Trends also vary greatly depending on what topics are being measured. Questions focused on evaluating progress in a new initiative may show very different trend lines from questions on rewards and recognition, which may also be very different from questions about employee satisfaction. Some representative sample trend lines from pulse surveys at IBM can be seen in Figure 11.1, indicating two, and maybe three, different patterns: stable, increasing, and cycling.

Figure 11.1. Sample Trend Lines from Pulse Surveys at IBM

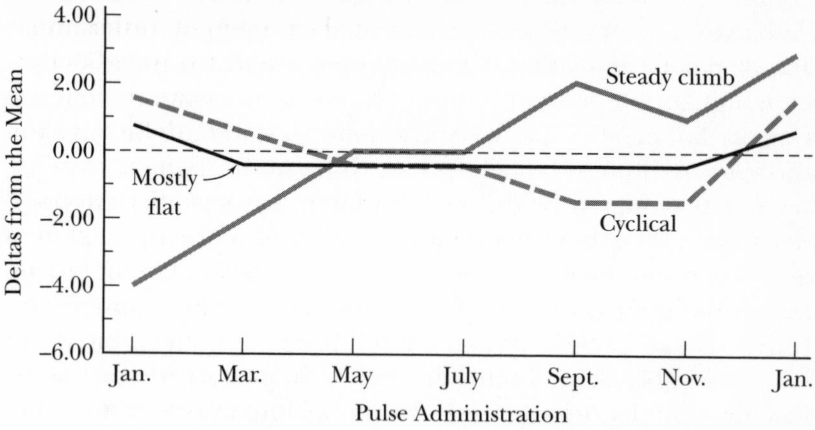

In Figure 11.1, data points are presented as deltas (or deviations) from the mean for that item across all pulse survey administrations.

The "stable" trend line in Figure 11.1, labeled "mostly flat," shows some characteristics of the cyclical trend, though the January spikes are smaller and the entire trend would best be described as stable. This kind of trend reflects questions about opportunities, promotions, lateral movement, and perhaps job security—difficult measures to influence given relatively stagnant economies in many countries of the world.

The most striking trend is labeled "steady climb." Although it shows one slight decline in November 2003, the steady climb trend line generally shows strong improvements starting at four percentage points below the mean in January of 2003 and finishing at three percentage points above the mean the following year. This kind of trend was found to reflect questions regarding understanding of a new corporate strategy. A company finding this kind of trend may decide to declare the objective to have been reached and discontinue use of the question.

The "cyclical" trend in Figure 11.1 shows fairly strong optimism with favorable ratings in January of each year with a gradual drop in between. This kind of trend reflects some questions regarding satisfaction with various elements of the workplace climate (e.g., overall job satisfaction). It is interesting to speculate on the causes behind these seasonal patterns. At least for companies using calendar years as their fiscal years, January represents a fresh start accompanied by new vision statements for the year, executive kick-off meetings, and renewed optimism. There is also some evidence to suggest that people's moods and emotional states can be linked to the seasons, though not always in ways we would expect.

For example, while the most common seasonal affective disorder (SAD) patterns of depression would lead to the prediction of lower scores in the fall and winter months finally returning to normal in the spring, some cyclical trends in workplace climate attitudes instead peak in January and fall throughout the summer before rising back up toward the end of the year. However, at least in some populations, depression and suicide have been found to peak during the spring and summer months (Bradvik & Berglund, 2002; Lambert, Reid, Kaye, Jennings, & Esler, 2003), and some people with SAD show a pattern of depression hitting hardest in the summer months.

Whether there is a statistical link between the seasons and employee attitudes remains to be seen, but it is at least plausible that hours of daylight have an impact on general mood and feelings of well-being that also shows up in measures of job and life satisfaction. Some research on the relationship between personal life events and jobs indicates that perhaps a majority of employees show a spillover effect, with their jobs having an impact on their personal lives and vice versa (Judge & Ilies, 2004). Along these same lines, job satisfaction and life satisfaction also appear to be fairly strongly related, even when controlling for differences in personality (Heller, Judge, & Watson, 2002).

The timing of events, including bonuses, workload, planning cycles, and performance evaluations, may play a role in the seasonality of ratings at many companies. In IBM, many of these events take place at other times during the year and would thus not be likely to play a large role in explaining increased optimism around January.

Given the potential to find cyclical effects in employee attitude surveys, it is important to take into consideration long-term trends as well as short-term views from a pulse survey program. For example, knowing that one could expect a short-term decline from

January to March, it would be misleading to present only the short-term trends during this time. A more accurate portrayal of the employee attitude trends in March of a given year would include March results from the prior year or prior years. This is similar to how financial business results are often reported as a comparison to the same quarter in the prior year.

Cyclical effects in employee attitude trends present some interesting challenges for a survey researcher who is attempting a pulse survey approach, but with proper attention to short-term as well as long-term trends, an accurate picture can emerge describing an organization's workplace climate and progress on various initiatives. It is interesting to note that such cyclical effects found in one large company would have remained invisible had it continued to survey employees only once per year. The emergence of trends within a year can help to pinpoint causes and identify outcomes resulting from organizational policies and programs.

For example, if a performance appraisal process is carried out once a year at the same time every year, it may be possible to identify dips (or improvements) resulting from those activities. In short, pulse surveys can provide additional insights over and above an annual view of results that can serve to embed the measurements into the fabric of the business or at least provide additional context for interpretation of results.

Moving from a Traditional Survey to a Pulse Survey process

Although some organizations use a combination approach of traditional annual or biannual surveys in conjunction with pulse surveys, other organizations have chosen to move toward pulse surveys alone. This move will likely require a hefty dose of streamlining to make the pulse an effective tool while keeping costs down. It involves an exercise in examining all of the elements of the program, from survey length to sampling plans and from write-in comments to promotional efforts. For some companies, this means that many of the features associated with an annual survey will be minimized or eliminated in a pulse survey approach.

To this end, write-in comments are one element of many survey programs that provide a weighty challenge in terms of digesting, summarizing, and making use of verbatim comments. While these comments can provide a very rich source of information, helping to paint the picture of an organization's workplace climate, a pulse survey approach may require placing some limitations on the volume of comments received. Some companies have even decided to forgo write-in comments altogether in their pulse surveys.

For example, a monthly (as opposed to quarterly) pulse survey program will generally require a faster turnaround in getting results reported, and the sometimes overwhelming volume of write-in comments received can be an obstacle to providing feedback quickly. Nevertheless, tools are available to use mathematics and the power of computers to provide an initial structure on a set of qualitative comments. These tools can be a major boon to help digest qualitative data, but they are far from an easy, complete solution to the analysis problem. (See Chapter Ten, this volume, for more on this topic.)

Sampling and Weighting

Pulse surveys generally involve a reduction in the number of employees invited to each survey. For example, one company decided that instead of inviting 100 percent of the employees once a year, they would invite one-twelfth of the population every month. The advantage to this approach is that it limits the response burden on employees because they would not be invited to a survey more than once per year. It also allows the survey practitioner to focus on getting a good response rate from this smaller group of respondents. If such a sampling strategy is followed without replacement (i.e., you can only be invited once), a company could effectively invite all or nearly all employees to at least one pulse survey per year, but it would sacrifice the benefit of tracking individuals over time through repeated measures.

A smaller sample will of necessity limit the number of representative views of the results. For example, with a traditional census survey, many or even most managers might be able to receive a representative view of the attitudes of the people working for them. However, if only one-twelfth of the company was invited to a pulse survey, many of the managers who would have received a representative report for their people with a census survey will not get one because the margin of sampling error would be too great.

A pulse approach may require limiting reports to higher levels of the organization than does an annual census approach.

An effective sampling technique will provide representative data for the larger population of interest even though a small subset of that population will actually be surveyed. Random sampling, though not perfect due to differences in response rates, will help to ensure that sample results generalize to the population of interest. For example, in a company with three thousand employees, a sample of five hundred employees might be randomly selected to participate in a survey. In this case, a random number generator or analogous computer program could be used to ensure true random selection. Without these tools, it would be possible to approximate a random sample by simply selecting every sixth employee from a list of the population. Assuming a 60 percent response rate, we would receive responses back from three hundred employees. A sample of three hundred employees from a population of three thousand would produce a margin of error of about +/−5.4 percentage points (at a 95 percent confidence level). This can be calculated with the following formula, with A as the population size and B as the sample size (see Henry, 1990):

$$\text{Square root of } (((0.25 \times 1.96^2 \times A) - (0.25 \times B \times 1.96^2))/ \\ (A \times B)) \times 100.$$

This formula assumes results near the middle of a distribution (for example, 50 percent favorable). The estimate of variance in this case is .25 ($p \times q$, or .5 × .5). For results that are more skewed positively or negatively, a different estimate of variance could be substituted. For results that are 20 percent favorable, for example, the variance estimate would be .16 ($p \times q$, or .20 × .80). In the example above with a sample of three hundred out of a population of three thousand, the margin of error would be +/−4 percentage points with the lower estimate of variance.

A conservative approach would be to always use the maximum variance estimate to ensure that the margin of error will be no greater than five points, no matter how favorable the results may be. A researcher can also use these formulas in reverse to decide on an acceptable margin of error and then work backward to decide on the size of the sample. It is recommended that information about the margin of sampling error be provided along with any report from a sample survey. In addition, when inviting employees to a sample survey, explaining to them that they were selected at random from a much larger population of employees may emphasize the importance of their views and encourage greater participation.

In certain circumstances, it is advisable to oversample certain groups of employees to ensure that representative results will be available for them. In such a stratified sampling approach, care must be taken to weight the results appropriately when aggregating to higher-level reports (for example, the entire organization). For example, if 10 percent of employees participated but 50 percent of executives participated due to higher sampling rates, the combined results would have to be weighted more heavily toward the nonexecutives to reflect the whole organization accurately. Weights can be calculated by dividing a population by the number of responses received, and applying that weight to all responses within that sample. This will ensure that the weighted results best reflect the population value you would get if you had responses from everyone in the population. (Many sources exist with further detail on survey strategy, sampling, and weighting techniques, including Best, Krueger, Hubbard, & Smith, 2001; Fife-Schaw, 2000; Krosnick, 1999; Rust & Johnson, 1992; Smith, 1989.)

One approach to this problem of weighting is to weight each case as a function of its proportion of the entire population. For example, if there are one hundred executives in a company and you have survey responses from fifty of them, you could weight each executive case by a factor of 2 (100/50). If you had one thousand nonexecutives and data from one hundred of them, you could weight each nonexecutive by a factor of 10 (1,000/100). With such a weighting scheme, you could combine data from executives and nonexecutives to get an estimate of what the results would have been if you had responses from all eleven hundred employees. This approach could be applied to sampling approaches stratified by job level, divisions of an organization, countries, or any other variable where large differences in group sizes make stratification attractive.

Aggregating Results Across Sample Surveys

Is there any hope for the lower-level managers to receive reports using a pulse survey approach that is based on a sampling methodology as opposed to a census? The answer may lie in aggregation of the pulse survey data across administrations. While it is debatable whether a pulse survey approach with aggregation can come up with, for example, a single set of results for a full year, it is at least technically and theoretically possible to aggregate across pulse surveys to provide an estimate of what one would get with a single annual survey approach.

In the best of programs with attention to quality and other issues raised in this chapter, it should be possible with a pulse survey program to get the short-term trends that only a pulse can offer, along with the long-term trends available by aggregating across different pulse surveys. It is recommended, nevertheless, that reports from each sample pulse survey be representative of the population of interest on its own, without the need to aggregate across surveys. In other words, any reports produced should have an acceptable amount of sampling error. For example, a margin of error of no greater than +/−5 percentage points for each pulse survey will ensure that not only are the short-term views of the data representative of the population, but that aggregations across those surveys will also be representative.

While aggregated pulse results may not be exactly equivalent to results received through a more traditional annual census survey, it could also be argued that the annual survey approach is biased due to limitations of applying a measurement only once per year. If there were natural cycles in the data, then the time of year one chooses will set the average levels of results that would be found. The cycles found by some of the companies using pulse surveys would suggest that the most favorable views of results could be attained by conducting employee surveys in January, when results tend to be more favorable, rather than July.

A more representative reflection of company performance on workplace climate measures may be provided by measurements conducted across a series of pulse surveys rather than a single snapshot of performance during one month of the year. It is also possible (and recommended) to provide equal weighting to results from each pulse survey so that the aggregated annual view reflects results across different months of the year equally. For example, with six pulse surveys, you take a simple average of any given result by adding them and dividing by six. With different numbers of employees responding to each survey, such a weighting scheme would provide the only way to ensure that the annual aggregated total reflects a company's performance across the entire year rather than being more heavily influenced by pulse surveys with greater numbers of employees responding.

Making It Work: Getting Action from Pulse Surveys

With today's technology making pulse surveys possible within many organizations and knowing that some potentially useful insights may be derived from a pulse survey that a traditional survey program cannot offer, the next logical question involves whether pulse surveys are useful as a catalyst for organizational improvement. Certainly the availability of more timely information on employee attitudes will, in itself, have no impact, either positive or negative, on the business. Just as with a traditional survey approach, the magic is not in the measurement process. Although one could argue that simply asking employees how they feel about various issues could have a positive effect (just asking the question changes the nature of the response), the real benefit can be gained by focusing energies on group problem solving and innovation in the workplace. Measurement for measurement's sake is antithetical to a profit-based business, so conducting pulse surveys where change is not apparent in the data may seem like a waste of time and effort and even exacerbate problems that are continually asked about but not resolved. However, most survey professionals would acknowledge that one of the most difficult parts of creating a successful survey program is linking results and actions to organizational improvements. This ability to create links has been hampered by the long stretches of time between collecting survey data, reporting results, and action planning that often coincides with an annual or biannual survey process. Pulse surveys serve as a means to mitigate this problem as the time between these steps is greatly shortened.

Action Planning with Pulse Surveys

A typical development and subsequent action planning process for a more traditional annual survey is a complex and often time-consuming process with many steps (Church & Waclawski, 2001) that can take from several months to up to a year to complete. Such a comprehensive approach can hardly be squeezed into the time frame of a typical pulse survey. When conducting a pulse survey, even on a quarterly basis, there is not enough time for a complete follow-through to implementing actions before the next pulse is scheduled to begin.

Taking action on the results to a pulse survey requires a longer-term view than the immediate comparison of one pulse survey's results to the next pulse. Although measuring in the short term, organizations need to react in the long term. Reacting in the short term may be possible for small organizational problems, but most workplace climate issues are not amenable to short-term quick fixes. Relatively unfavorable results on an issue across two or three pulse surveys may confirm the existence of a problem, and plans can be formulated and implemented across a long-term time frame. Progress can best be measured year over year rather than pulse to pulse, but short-term trends can at least alert decision makers about potential problems that may or may not be confirmed in long-term trends.

Pulse Survey Action Planning: A Case Example

Consider an organization developing a new corporate strategy. Part of the task will be to educate employees about the strategy, how it affects them and links to individual jobs, and why, if executed properly, the strategy will be helpful in attaining success for the business. In one large company, the strategy was particularly complex, involving new models for how service is provided that could affect an entire industry. Early employee measures indicating that fewer than half understood the strategy led to a need to act more decisively in educating employees and managers about the strategy, promoting the strategy, and defining how the strategy links to employees' jobs. A series of executive "road shows" was put together spanning many countries of the world from May through September. High-level executives traveled to many different cities and spent two hours or more with groups of employees and managers discussing and promoting the strategy.

Because the organization conducting the strategy road shows had a pulse survey approach to workplace climate measures, several important outcomes took place:

- Executives were alerted early on that the new strategy was seen as very complex and not well understood, giving them time to react with a new approach.
- The organization was able to include specific measures tied to understanding the strategy and linking it to jobs. This was useful not only for evaluating progress but editing the content of the strategy sessions based on pulse survey feedback.
- Each strategy session included pulse results specific to that area of the business, giving leaders from those areas real-time information about where their own efforts at training and promotion might be most needed.
- Concrete and objective measures of success became available not only in the form of before and after measures, but trends during the execution of the road shows themselves.

In the end, results indicated a steady increase in understanding of the strategy that involved a nearly 10 percentage point gain in overall favorability. Could the same improvement have been gained through an annual survey? It is entirely possible, but conversations with executives involved indicated that objective measures from employees about the strategy in real time led to an enormous amount of energy being applied across the globe to tackle a specific business need. Having consistent pulse measurements showed little employee understanding at first but was followed by gradual and steady gains. This information provided the foundation and incentive to gain buy-in and direct involvement of many managers to "keep the train moving" regarding the traveling strategy road shows.

Conclusions

A traditional survey approach may make it seem easier to tie up loose ends and view a survey program as a self-contained package of measurement plus actions followed by additional measurements. A pulse survey approach is not quite as clean and serial. It requires a shift in mind-set on how a survey program can and should be carried out. Then a pulse survey can provide some unique benefits that may lead to greater organizational improvements. Pulse surveys may:

- Help keep issues on the table as part of the ongoing daily discussions and decisions about running the business.
- Enable the timely measurement of issues that are hot for executives.
- Give an organization time to react to emerging problems before they get worse.
- Remove some excuses for not acting on results that are seen as dated or irrelevant.

All of these potential benefits can be subsumed under the umbrella of embedding an organization survey program into the fabric of the business. By making timely employee attitude measurements available to decision makers, focusing on topics that are important to executives today, and building measurements into organizational scorecards and linking them to business performance (typically reported on a quarterly basis), pulse surveys make it possible to strengthen the link between what is happening in the business and the people research that supports that business.

Pulse surveys, though not nearly as popular as traditional employee attitude surveys, have many unique advantages. They offer an organization the ability to quickly respond to changing circumstances without sacrificing employee input into key decisions. They offer an organization a way to adapt or make changes to a new program or initiative midway through its implementation rather than waiting until completion and hoping for positive results.

This transition toward greater availability of timely information for running a business parallels that seen in other forms of communications. Many clients in charge of various business activities are demanding more information in real time, on demand. Just as traditional mail using the postal system evolved toward e-mail before evolving again toward instant messaging, pulse surveys may be the next wave in the world of surveys: nimble, on-demand applications that help business leaders make better decisions based on real-time information.

Nevertheless, an organization must be prepared to balance the benefits of pulse surveys with potential problems that include oversurveying and lowered response rates. However, if pulse surveys are used judiciously, organizations can make use of them as an additional tool for organizational improvement to make full use of the views of employees, so critical for the ultimate success of an organization. In the political arena, the era of modern polling has given citizens of some countries almost weekly snapshots of likely voter responses to an upcoming election. Organizations that are savvy about the pros and cons of pulse surveys and understand how to apply them can reap the benefits of more frequent "polling" on workplace climate issues while avoiding the information overload that makes people tune out a constant barrage of messages. By using pulse surveys wisely, these organizations would presumably have a competitive advantage over others that let this rich source of critical information on the business languish for another year or two before the next survey.

Acknowledgments

Thanks to Wayne Kromrey, Mathian Osicki, Tom Rauzi, Lise Saari, and Kate Suckow for their helpful contributions to this chapter.

References

Berwald, M. (2004). *Pulse surveys in organizations: useful or waste of resources?* Paper presented at practitioner forum conducted at the 19th annual meeting of the Society for Industrial and Organizational Psychology, Chicago, IL.

Best, S., Krueger, B., Hubbard, C., & Smith, A. (2001). An assessment of the generalizability of Internet surveys. *Social Science Computer Review, 19*(2), 131–145.

Bradvik, L., & Berglund, M. (2002). Seasonal distribution of suicide in alcoholism. *Acta Psychiatrica Scandinavica, 106*(4), 299–302.

Center for Research and Service. (2004, July). *Organizational surveys best practices results.* Chicago: Illinois Institute of Technology. http://www.iit.edu/~psyccrs/.

Church, A. H., & Waclawski, J. (2001). *Designing and using organization surveys: A seven-step process.* San Francisco: Jossey-Bass.

Colihan, J. (2004, Apr.). *The IBM Global Pulse Survey: Making the move toward frequent, small-sample surveys.* In K. Lundby (Chair), *Perspectives on pulse surveys.* Practitioner forum conducted at the 19th annual meeting of the Society for Industrial and Organizational Psychology, Chicago, IL.

Fife-Schaw, C. (2000). Surveys and sampling issues. In G. Breakwell & S. Hammond (Eds.), *Research methods in psychology* (2nd ed., pp. 88–104). Thousand Oaks, CA: Sage.

Heller, D., Judge, T. A., & Watson, D. (2002). The confounding role of personality and trait affectivity in the relationship between job and life satisfaction. *Journal of Organizational Behavior, 23*(7), 815–835.

Henry, G. T. (1990). *Practical sampling.* Thousand Oaks, CA: Sage.

Johnson, H. (2004, Aug.). All in favor, say benchmark! *Training Magazine,* 30–34.

Judge, T. A., & Ilies, R. (2004). Affect and job satisfaction: A study of their relationship at work and at home. *Journal of Applied Psychology, 89*(4), 661–673.

Kraut, A. (Ed.). (1996). *Organizational surveys: Tools for assessment and change.* San Francisco: Jossey-Bass.

Krosnick, J. (1999). Survey research. *Annual Review of Psychology, 50,* 537–567.

Lambert, G., Reid, C., Kaye, D., Jennings, G., & Esler, M. (2003). Increased suicide rate in the middle-aged and its association with hours of sunlight. *American Journal of Psychiatry, 160*(4), 793–795.

Lotz-Turner, A. (2004). *Industry pulse survey shows open source is becoming part of mainstream IT strategy.* CATAAlliance, http://www.cata.ca/ media_and_events/press_releases/cata_pr04210402.html

Rust, K., & Johnson, E. (1992). Sampling and weighting in the National Assessment. *Journal of Educational Statistics, 17*(2), 111–129.

Smith, A. (1989). Evaluating the products of alternative sampling methods. *Social Indicators Research, 21*(2), 175–191.

Waclawski, J., & Church, A. H. (Eds.). (2002). *Organization Development: A data driven approach to organizational change.* San Francisco: Jossey-Bass.

Weiner, S. P. (2000, Apr.). IBM's Worldwide Employee Survey Registry. In E. M. Papper (Chair), *Managing the madness: Getting survey volume and quality under control.* Paper presented at practitioner forum at the 15th annual conference of the Society for Industrial and Organizational Psychology, New Orleans, LA.

Youseffnia, D., & Berwald, M., (2004). An exploratory look at the response rates of sample, census, special topic, and broad-based surveys. Paper presented at Annual Conference of the Society for Industrial and Organizational Psychology, Chicago, IL.

CHAPTER 12

Oversurveying

Causes, Consequences, and Cures

Sara P. Weiner
Anthony T. Dalessio

Employee attitude or opinion surveys are an extremely valuable strategic tool to diagnose organizational issues and identify actions needed to improve employee performance and business effectiveness. As surveys have increased in popularity, the potential for excessive surveying has also increased. A major challenge for survey professionals is to ensure high-quality surveys for achieving organizational goals while avoiding an unnecessary survey burden on employees. What is the definition of *oversurveying*, and what are its causes and consequences? This chapter addresses these issues and provides recommended solutions for curbing oversurveying in both large and small organizations.

Defining Oversurveying

What are the key factors that contribute to an impression by employees that they are being oversurveyed? A definition of oversurveying has three major components: the survey burden rate (the number of surveys that an employee receives during the year), survey timing (the amount of time between surveys), and survey length (the number of questions or amount of time that it takes to complete the survey). Although there are no absolute values for these parameters, reasonable guidelines will be presented along with specific examples from the IBM Corporation survey program.

Regarding burden rate, a range of no more than three to five surveys per employee per year is suggested to avoid an impression of excessive surveys. If the survey burden rate for an organization is near to the upper end of this range, then a stronger emphasis should be placed on clearly communicating the business value of each survey to the invitees, along with actions taken based on previous surveys and follow-on communications about the actions taken as a result of the current survey. When clear actions from previous surveys are taken and communicated, there should be a greater willingness of employees to participate in future surveys. Although these are important survey practices to follow in general, in conditions of higher burden rates, they become even more critical to help employees clearly understand the important business reasons for the survey and why they are being asked to make responding a priority.

The timing of surveys is also an important factor in defining oversurveying. The overlap in the administration of surveys is one aspect of the timing issue. For example, even when the survey burden rate for employees is at the lower end of the range of three to five per year, an employee who receives three surveys in the period of five business days is likely to feel oversurveyed.

A second aspect of the timing issue is considering the cycle of workload for various employee groups during the year. As an example, if an employee receives only two surveys in a year but both are sent during a high workload period, the employee may feel oversurveyed. High workload times are obvious for some groups of employees, such as the end of a quarter for sales employees who are working hard to close deals. In addition, the fourth quarter of the year is a time when workload is high for many employees. Sending surveys during holiday periods also may result in feelings of being oversurveyed, because employees are either working to complete projects before taking vacation time or catching up on work afterward.

A final component in defining oversurveying is the length of the typical survey. As the business environment has become progressively more streamlined and competitive, with shorter product and services cycles, and a corresponding increase in workload, the length of employee surveys needs to follow suit and become more efficient. In this environment, a suggested guideline for the length of employee surveys is in the range of twenty to forty questions in mostly multiple-choice format, with a few demographic questions, and a minimal number (one to three) of open-ended questions. This guideline assumes a reasonable target of about thirty minutes to respond to a survey, including time to read instructions and approximately one minute to answer each question. Some empirical support for the thirty-minute target is provided by Sharp and Frankel's study (1983), which found that interviewees were more willing to participate in a follow-up interview when their initial interview was twenty-five versus seventy-five minutes long. IBM's surveys once were routinely over one hundred questions and now most typically have fewer than half that number. According to information we have from colleagues, many other companies are following a similar trend.

There is no one consistent definition of *oversurveying* that will apply to all companies. The unique business environment and history of the culture regarding surveys in each company need to be considered in defining and addressing oversurveying. As an example, IBM has used the following guidelines: no more than five surveys per year per employee, limited to approximately one survey per quarter with consideration of workload cycle and global holidays, and a recommendation not to exceed twenty to thirty questions per survey.

Causes of Oversurveying

Causes for oversurveying can be organized into four major categories: advances in survey administration technology, a desire to make data-based business decisions, lack of centralized oversight, and "other than survey" invitations.

Advances in Survey Administration Technology

The growing ease of conducting Web-based surveys versus the more labor-intensive and costly paper-based approaches of the past encourages surveys as a data-gathering tool of choice. There are many excellent survey Web tools that skilled survey administrators can use to put a survey on the Web, ready for administration to samples of any size within days. Preparation of the survey data for analysis becomes merely part of the Web administration process.

Besides administration of surveys on the Web, other technology allows distribution of surveys to individuals using automated phone systems or at kiosks at convenient locations. Even surveys sent to a cell phone screen with responses keyed in from the cell phone pad are possible (within Federal Communication Commission regulations). All of this technology allows easy administration and response, which has led to technology outpacing careful evaluation of each survey's values.

Desire to Make Data-Based Business Decisions

One primary cause of oversurveying is an organizational culture that recognizes, believes, understands, and supports the value that surveys can bring to the decision-making process. In such a culture, the well-intentioned desire of senior management, ad hoc committees, and lower-level management teams to obtain data that add value in making decisions about workforce issues can contribute to the proliferation of surveys and consequently result in employees' feeling they are being oversurveyed.

The tracking of metrics has also contributed to a greater quantity of surveys. The balanced scorecard (Kaplan & Norton, 1992) proposed that companies use a critical few measurements that provide a comprehensive current view, along with future projections, of performance. The importance of including employee satisfaction and motivation measurements in scorecards was later highlighted (Kaplan & Norton, 1998). As human resources (HR) has assumed its role as a strategic partner in the business, measurements have increased in popularity (Becker, Huselid, & Ulrich, 2001). Employee surveys provide softer data on components of workplace climate that complement harder business measures such as financial data, hiring, and attrition figures. Linkage research demonstrating relationships between workplace climate and business outcomes (see Schneider & Bowen, 1985; Wiley, 1996) has further driven the desire for these measurements. Even if formal scorecards of employee metrics are not established, new management at the highest level of a company (the CEO or a new executive or management team in a division) may want a survey of the organization as a baseline from which to move forward and measure the effectiveness of changes they implement.

Lack of Centralized Oversight

A poorly managed survey program with little or no oversight can also contribute to oversurveying, as the number of surveys going to employees may not be tracked. Lack of communication among business units within an organization regarding survey content or timing can result in a greater number of surveys and multiple surveys sent to the same employees in a given time frame. Lack of survey oversight can also result in inviting larger samples than are necessary to obtain results with a reasonable margin of error. For example, without some professional guidance on sampling methodology, census surveys are often conducted when a smaller sample survey would provide sufficient information.

Another cause of oversurveying, related to lack of oversight, is when alternative data collection methods or alternative sources of data are not considered, and surveys become the default methodology of choice for gathering information from employees. A central coordination point for all organizational survey activity would track the survey data available on various populations of employees in the organization. Duplication of surveys, and therefore duplication of work effort, could be avoided if existing survey data can be provided to answer the same questions as a proposed survey. Alternatively, under some circumstances, qualitative research may be more appropriate than quantitative. For example, when only a very small number of people are the target of the data-gathering effort, focus groups or interviews are the logical method of choice rather than a survey.

Other Invitations Contributing to Perceptions of Oversurveying

Previously discussed factors are not the only causes of a perception of excessive surveying. Other requests, outside the control of the employee survey profession, may also produce a sensitivity or predisposition on the part of employees to feeling oversurveyed. Employees may not see a difference in the many types of invitations they receive to participate in opinion or customer satisfaction surveys, 360-degree feedback requests, or training evaluations. Even required participation in training, other business requirements (such as review of business conduct guidelines or submission of forms to track company assets), or off-the-job surveys (such as for telemarketing or political purposes) may be lumped together into a general category in the eyes of an employee, and all may contribute to a perception of oversurveying on the job.

Consequences of Oversurveying

The consequences of oversurveying include unnecessary costs to the organization, lower response rates and other response quality issues, confusion among employees about the surveys they are receiving, and irritation of employees that under some circumstances may color or produce less favorable responses about the company and the work environment.

Increased Costs

When unnecessary surveys are conducted, the organization incurs additional costs: staff time to develop and field the survey, employee time to respond to the survey, server time to host the survey, and possibly the cost of external consultants, along with all the resources needed to analyze, interpret, and act on the results. Surveys that serve no real business purpose or gather redundant information can result in large losses of employee productivity. Eliminating these costs may be well worth the investment of other resources put in place to reduce oversurveying.

Lower Response Rates and Other Survey Response Quality Issues

One of the most likely consequences of oversurveying is a lower response rate. "Survey fatigue" seems the logical result of numerous survey requests outside of regular job tasks, which can lead to fewer responses (see Stanton & Rogelberg, 2002). Another quality issue is skipping items, which may also be a consequence of survey fatigue. An exact estimate of the number of lost respondents or skipped items due to oversurveying is hard to pinpoint.

Research indicates that the attitudes of those who skip items (both closed- and open-ended) are less positive about the value of surveys in general (Rogelberg, Fisher, Maynard, Hakel, & Horvath, 2001). Following survey directions well is also related to a higher perceived value of surveys by invitees (Rogelberg et al., 2001).

Who are the people who do not respond to surveys, and what effect do they have on the data? Active and passive nonrespondents have been described in recent research (Rogelberg, Conway, Sederburg, Spitzmuller, Aziz, & Knight, 2003), with active nonrespondents identified as those who make a purposeful choice to not complete a survey and passive nonrespondents identified as those who do not respond to a survey for external reasons rather than a conscious choice (for example, they did not remember in time, their workload was too high, or they were away during survey administration). In their research, Rogelberg et al. (2003) found that passive nonrespondents did not differ significantly from respondents on a number of variables. In contrast, active nonrespondents have been found to be less satisfied with the sponsoring organization, have a higher intention to leave the organization, and be less agreeable. Active nonresponders comprised about 15 percent of nonrespondents and therefore had minimal effects on the statistical accuracy of the results (Rogelberg et al., 2003). The number of passive nonresponders is likely to increase under conditions of oversurveying. In addition, the percentage of active nonresponders may also increase due to their irritation with multiple requests. Empirical research is needed to determine the effects of oversurveying on both passive and active nonresponse and the subsequent statistical representativeness of the data.

Even if the nonresponders do not affect the representativeness of the data, lower response rates as a result of oversurveying can affect both the perceived and actual integrity of the survey results. Regarding the perceived integrity, it may be more difficult to convince management clients about the accuracy of the survey results even if a lower response rate is statistically accurate, that is, within a reasonable margin of error. For example, management is likely to question the accuracy of a response rate of 30 percent more than they would with a response of 60 percent. Regarding actual integrity, when the response rate becomes too low, an unacceptable margin of error will result, and using the survey results to draw conclusions even at the total level may not be possible or meaningful. Furthermore, as response rates drop, the ability to gain additional insights by analyzing data using demographic (for example, tenure or gender) or background questions (for example, division or geography) is more limited due to higher margins of error for these data breakdowns.

Survey Triage

Oversurveying may also lead to a conscious judgment about the surveys to which one will respond. Similar to a medical triage model, only surveys meeting certain criteria will receive attention. When the number of requests exceeds the available hours to respond, then only surveys of greatest importance or of particular interest to the invitee will warrant a response. In a study that manipulated interview length, Sharp and Frankel (1983) found that when the topic was of high interest to interviewees, the length of the initial interview was not a factor in their willingness to participate in a follow-up interview. Conversely, when the topic was of little interest to the interviewees, interview length was a major factor. Employees who have expertise in a particular area of the business or are members of a certain profession may be in high demand as survey respondents. Feelings of being oversurveyed, and therefore engaging in "survey triage," may be most prevalent for these populations.

Creation of Confusion

Lack of coordination in surveying can easily cause confusion. One practical example highlighting this issue was when a reminder note for one survey was sent the day before an invitation to a different survey. Many of those who received both notes mistakenly deleted the invitation to the second survey. Simple oversight at a higher level in the organization could have prevented this undesirable outcome.

Irritation

Oversurveying may produce irritation among employees that results in less favorable feelings about surveys in general or about the organization, or both. An example of one situation where this outcome was avoided was when the leader of the business organization sent a note to all senior executives emphasizing the importance of focusing all their resources on having a strong close to the quarter. After sending the note, the leader realized that an important survey of the senior executive team in the organization had been scheduled a week before the end of the quarter. To avoid frustration and a confusing message to the senior team, the survey was postponed until after the start of the next quarter.

Not all leaders take this type of action. In fact, in another example, a sales employee received three surveys during the last week of the quarter. The employee complained to the senior vice president of the organization. It is likely that other invitees who experienced this level of frustration either did not respond at all or responded less favorably about some aspects of the business.

Consequences of Undersurveying

A discussion of the consequences of oversurveying begs the question: What are the consequences of undersurveying? Due to the multiple benefits of surveys, an organization that undersurveys employees not only loses the opportunity to gather valuable information on important business issues and act to improve employee and business performance, but also may communicate to employees a lack of interest about employee views. Therefore, a balance is needed: surveys should be used to achieve business objectives and communicate to employees that their views are valued. Impressions of both over- or undersurveying can lead to detrimental consequences.

Solutions

Ensuring that surveys provide business value and are of high quality in conjunction with monitoring the "flow" of surveys in the organization are key ways to reduce oversurveying.

Ensuring Survey Quality

The consequences of oversurveying may be mitigated to some extent when surveys are high quality: they have strong business value that is well communicated, have well-constructed and organized questions, are administered in a professional manner, and have clear actions that are taken based on the results. Taking visible actions based on survey results is likely to have the strongest effect on the perceived value of surveys and the perception of whether subsequent surveying is excessive. In organizations in which expenses are carefully controlled, administration of a survey could appear frivolous if it is not positioned as anticipating a demonstrated business benefit. Clearly presenting the business value of the survey is important not only for justifying the commitment of resources to the survey project, but also for influencing response rates and the quality of the information that respondents provide. For example, Roberson and Sundstrom (1990) found that arranging survey topics in an order that matched the business priorities of employees resulted in higher return rates (96 percent) compared with any of five random orderings (average response rate, 78 percent). These researchers also found that when demographic questions were placed at the end of a survey, return rates were higher (85 percent) than when placed at the beginning of the survey (77 percent), most likely because the demographics distract from the business purpose of the survey when they are at the beginning.

Given that well-constructed survey instruments can improve response rates (Roberson & Sundstrom, 1990), this effect may be amplified in an environment where employees find an increasing number of survey invitations in their e-mail in-box. Research is needed to address empirically the issue of oversurveying and determine the extent to which the quality of the survey can affect the limits that respondents have for higher survey loads, overlapping surveys, and longer surveys. For example, two poor-quality surveys a year or ones that do not result in action may be perceived as oversurveying, whereas five surveys of the highest quality that do result in action that is then communicated may be perceived as acceptable and result in higher response rates. These and other related hypotheses need further exploration.

Continuum of Solutions for Oversurveying

There are a number of solutions to oversurveying that organizations may adopt, ranging on a continuum from less to more comprehensive. Figure 12.1 provides a brief description of this continuum. Although each solution is associated with some resource investment, that investment may be well justified and reduce the costs that can result when employees are oversurveyed, which include the cost of survey administration, analysis, and losses in productive work time when unnecessarily large samples of employees are invited to participate.

Figure 12.1. Continuum of Solutions for Oversurveying

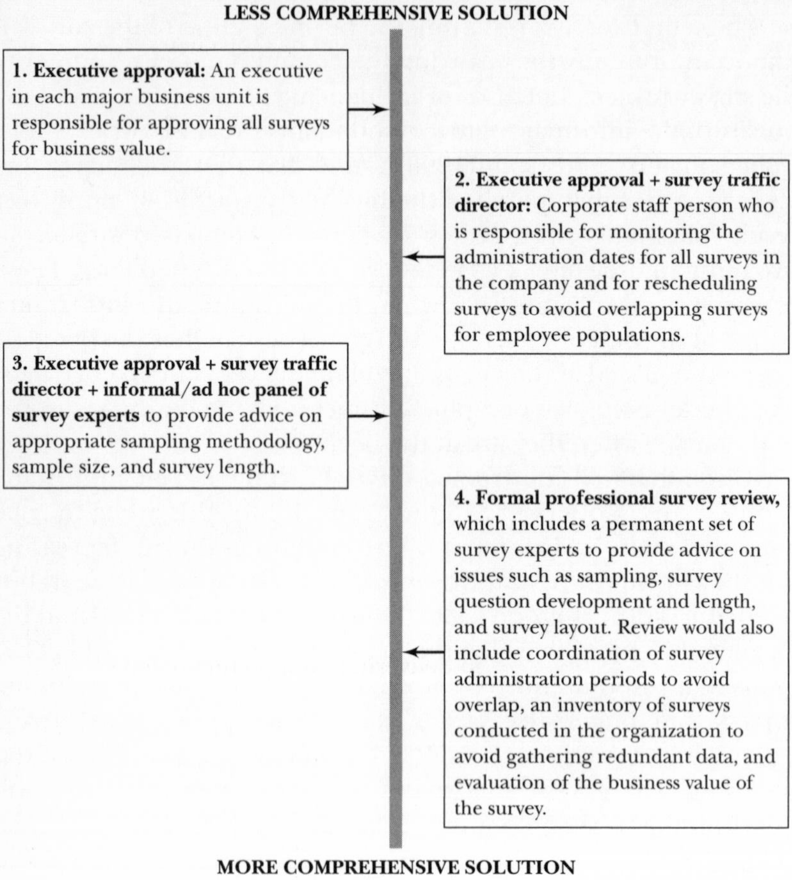

LESS COMPREHENSIVE SOLUTION

1. **Executive approval:** An executive in each major business unit is responsible for approving all surveys for business value.

2. **Executive approval + survey traffic director:** Corporate staff person who is responsible for monitoring the administration dates for all surveys in the company and for rescheduling surveys to avoid overlapping surveys for employee populations.

3. **Executive approval + survey traffic director + informal/ad hoc panel of survey experts** to provide advice on appropriate sampling methodology, sample size, and survey length.

4. **Formal professional survey review,** which includes a permanent set of survey experts to provide advice on issues such as sampling, survey question development and length, and survey layout. Review would also include coordination of survey administration periods to avoid overlap, an inventory of surveys conducted in the organization to avoid gathering redundant data, and evaluation of the business value of the survey.

MORE COMPREHENSIVE SOLUTION

Executive Approval

At the less comprehensive end of the continuum, an organization might establish a process whereby an internal survey sponsor would submit a clear written statement of the business value and objectives of the survey to the executive of the targeted business unit. The executive for each business unit would be required to review and approve the project for business value. This process would eliminate surveys that do not benefit the company and reduce the survey burden rate on employees. Table 12.1 provides some examples of such statements for three types of surveys: a regional work group survey, a special topic survey, and an internal client satisfaction survey.

Table 12.1. Examples of Clear Statements of
Survey Objectives and Business Values

Type of Survey	Statement of Objectives
Regional work group survey	Significant organizational change has taken place in the region over the past year as a result of the acquisition and reintegration of several business units. The employee survey will provide the opportunity to gauge the current status of these integrations directly from employees, address work climate issues, and progress on our business and cultural objectives.
	The survey will also provide the opportunity to provide survey results and create action plans at the first-line manager level, which has been identified by the executives as one key to addressing climate change.
Special topic survey	The survey objective is to determine which global initiatives the sales force is most familiar with and which of these initiatives they feel are most helpful to them in delivering value to their clients.
	The survey will obtain ideas from the sales force about how the initiatives can be improved in both content and implementation.
	The sales team senior leadership will use the results to take action on improving the communication and effectiveness of the global initiatives for addressing the business needs of our clients.
Internal client satisfaction survey	The objective of this annual survey is to determine the effectiveness of IT services delivered to the end user employees in our company. This survey will determine the areas that require improvement and facilitate development and refinement of action plans and prioritization of IT deployments to improve employee productivity. This worldwide sample survey provides an opportunity to reach a broad audience in sufficient numbers to draw conclusions and take actions.

Add a Survey Traffic Director

The next level in a review process would be to add a centralized corporate staff member to "direct traffic," that is, monitor the timing of surveys to the same invitees and encourage sponsors to alter dates if necessary to avoid overlapping surveys sent to the same populations. A guideline would need to be established for the amount of time suggested between survey administrations for the same group of employees. An additional feature for this solution is to institute a limit on the amount of time that surveys would be available to the invitees, so that no single survey dominates a long time period for a particular population of employees. For example, surveys could be made available to respondents for a maximum of ten business days, with an employee being invited to no more than one survey per quarter. When surveying worldwide, consideration of specific country holidays is critical in survey scheduling. Guidelines such as these would facilitate scheduling surveys at reasonable intervals for various populations of employees. A system would need to be established where survey sponsors could submit the dates that their survey would be available to the population of interest, and the survey "traffic director" could determine where there is overlap and serve as the coordinator to adjust the scheduling of the surveys accordingly.

Add an Informal or Ad Hoc Expert Survey Panel

If an organization is interested in a more comprehensive solution, an informal review of the survey sampling methodology and length can be added to the executive review for business value and "traffic director" review for timing. Large organizations may have survey expertise within the company and could identify an informal or ad hoc panel of experts who would agree to review proposals and provide suggestions on issues related to oversurveying, including whether a survey is the best method to answer the research question and how to ensure the sample size and the survey length are the minimum needed to reach objectives. In smaller organizations, this informal panel may need to be made up of contractors from an external consulting firm or survey experts at a university.

Add a Formal Professional Survey Review

At the most comprehensive level, a formal review procedure would include a dedicated staff of professional survey researchers who would coordinate the timing and content of surveys, provide consultative assistance on the quality of the survey and research approach, and establish an inventory of surveys conducted in the organization that could be used to eliminate redundancy in survey efforts. This so-called survey competency center could be a small corporate group within a large organization that would not "own" surveys across functional areas but would provide professional consultative services to internal clients to manage oversurveying while increasing the quality and the value of research conducted. The data from all surveys conducted need not be stored by the competency center; alternately, data requesters could be referred directly to the data owners (for example, survey project leaders in business units). Alternatively, a one-stop-shopping competency center could also be developed where experts would not only monitor but also administer surveys. For organizations that do not wish to establish any in-house group, an external professional consultant or a survey expert at a university can be excellent resources for accomplishing the same goals.

If an organization wishes to establish a formal review for approving all employee surveys, the procedure should be clearly delineated and easily accessible (for example, using the company intranet). Survey requesters will need to understand the necessary steps, such as getting an executive to sponsor the study, confirming it will add business value to the organization, being flexible in choosing survey dates to avoid overlapping surveys, and determining the appropriate number of employees who will be surveyed and from what business units and locations. Specific guidelines could be set for limiting the number of minutes per year an employee would be asked to spend taking surveys, and coordination of timing, sampling (for example, mutually exclusive samples within specified time periods), and content of surveys helps to achieve this goal.

Limits on communications also assist in controlling impressions of oversurveying—for example, one invitation and one reminder along with a maximum of a ten-business-day survey administration period over three work weeks. Guidance can also be provided on postsurvey communications of findings and actions taken so employees see that the time they took to respond to the survey was well spent. Consistently providing feedback on survey actions taken to improve the work environment is an important way to communicate to employees the value of participating in future surveys.

Guidance could be offered for determining whether conducting a survey is the best method for answering the research question or whether another method is more appropriate, thus reducing oversurveying. Finally, a dedicated competency center can create an inventory of surveys conducted in the organization to avoid gathering redundant data and so reduce the propensity for oversurveying.

One example of a functioning survey review procedure comes from IBM and includes all the prior elements discussed plus some additional features. HR generalists and industrial/organizational (I/O) psychologists who rely on an extended global team for consultative assistance oversee the IBM Employee Survey Review (ESR). Every survey intended for IBM employees worldwide must go through the ESR for formal approval. The ESR was established as a result of employee perceptions of oversurveying at a time of increasing focus on obtaining measurements of internal client satisfaction and workplace climate. Prior to the ESR, the ease of electronic administration of surveys also contributed to an unreasonable increase in the number of surveys.

The two main objectives of the ESR are to control the volume of employee surveys and ensure that professional survey standards are upheld. HR leaders and global partners provided substantial input in designing the ESR. The senior vice president of HR issued a "corporate instruction" (an official internal directive), and the ESR was launched in January 1998. There were broad communications using internal media emphasizing the criticality of ensuring that surveys meet professional standards to provide value to the organization, explaining the process for obtaining approval for internal surveys, and encouraging employees to take only surveys bearing an ESR approval number.

In IBM, the survey requester must obtain an executive sponsor who attests to the business benefit of the survey. A form is completed and sent to the ESR describing the research, along with a note confirming the executive's support. The form requests information such as a description of the project, to whom the survey will be sent, how many employees will be invited and from which business units and locations, and whether the HR issues have been evaluated.

According to their subject matter expertise, HR professionals and I/O psychologists review projects. These reviewers ensure the following conditions:

- The method will answer the research questions.
- Use of a survey is indicated.
- Questions adhere to professional standards on clarity, response scale appropriateness, length limits, and HR cultural and legal considerations.
- The sampling plan or census approach is viable and will meet the research needs.
- Dates avoid overlap with other research efforts in the same population.
- The administration method follows guidelines, for example, on anonymity.
- An extended global team reviews surveys for any HR implications in their countries including Works Council approvals (groups established in some countries to represent the interest of employees).

The ESR approves surveys based on worldwide volumes and professional survey standards and provides an approval statement with a registration number that sponsors must publish on each survey. Any changes to dates, sample size, questions, or method must be approved.

Diplomacy and responsiveness are two critical elements in establishing successful relationships with survey requesters in IBM. The advantages and disadvantages of different approaches have been documented so ESR consultants can provide requesters with sound, proven, and consistent advice. Care must be taken to ensure the ESR remains efficient and does not become a protracted, bureaucratic process. Forms need to be concise. Feedback must be timely, clear, and to the point. The information provided needs to be framed as advice and counsel. Absolute requirements should be limited to a few critical issues, such as approval of schedule or method changes, anonymity of responses, and setting a maximum margin of error standard for reporting results. In this way, the consultative assistance provided will be generally appreciated as adding business value to the project.

A by-product of establishing a review procedure similar to the ESR is that survey quality can be improved by the expert input, in addition to curbing oversurveying. For example, professional guidance can be provided on question and response scale construction; anonymity and confidentiality issues; HR, cultural, legal, and labor considerations; and data analysis and interpretation. Another advantage of a survey competency center is the opportunity for the company to develop a survey database that would include survey items developed internally by the organization as well as any items from external benchmarking groups in which the company may be a member. Regular use of items in the database could lead to the development of internal benchmarks, along with easier access to items with known external benchmarks, for the purposes of better data interpretation and improved decision making.

Conclusions

The number of surveys an employee receives in a year, the timing of the surveys, their length, the amount of time to complete the surveys, and the perceived value of surveys are all aspects of whether employees feel oversurveyed. Oversurveying in an organization is likely to be the result of good intentions on the part of management to track employee attitudes and acquire data for making informed business decisions. The ease of survey administration, lack of oversight, and the preponderance of requests for all types of information can contribute to employees' impressions of being oversurveyed. Oversurveying employees may result in higher costs to the company, lower response rates, confusion among employees about the surveys they are receiving, and the irritation of employees, which can result in less favorable survey responses about the company and the work environment.

Organizations can implement solutions for oversurveying that involve a relatively small investment in resources that can reduce some occurrences of overlapping surveys as well as eliminate surveys that provide little value to the business. With the investment of additional resources, companies can also limit survey length, control the size of employee samples, avoid redundant surveys, and have the added benefit of ensuring a high-quality survey program. Organizations will need to consider their specific business environment and survey culture in defining oversurveying and determining the best solution for controlling oversurveying.

Acknowledgments

We gratefully thank Meridith Pease for her invaluable assistance providing important background information for this chapter and

Allen Kraut and the anonymous reviewers for their insightful comments on earlier drafts of this chapter.

References

Becker, B. E., Huselid, M. A., & Ulrich, D. (2001). *The HR Scorecard: Linking people, strategy, and performance.* Boston: Harvard Business School Press.

Kaplan, R. S., & Norton, D. P. (1992, Jan.–Feb.). The balanced scorecard—Measures that drive performance. *Harvard Business Review, 71*–79.

Kaplan, R. S., & Norton, D. P. (1998). *The balanced scorecard: Translating strategy into action.* Boston: Harvard Business School Press.

Roberson, M. T., & Sundstrom, E. (1990). Questionnaire design, return rates, and response favorableness in an employee attitude questionnaire. *Journal of Applied Psychology, 75*(3), 354–357.

Rogelberg, S. G., Conway, J. M., Sederburg, M. E., Spitzmuller, C., Aziz, S., & Knight, W. E. (2003). Profiling active and passive nonrespondents to an organizational survey. *Journal of Applied Psychology, 88*(6), 1104–1114.

Rogelberg, S. G., Fisher, G. G., Maynard, D. C., Hakel, M. D., & Horvath, M. (2001). Attitudes toward surveys: Development of a measure and its relationship to respondent behavior. *Organizational Research Methods, 4*(1), 3–25.

Schneider, B., & Bowen, D. E. (1985). Employee and customer impressions of service in banks: Replication and extension. *Journal of Applied Psychology, 70,* 423–433.

Sharp, L. M., & Frankel, J. (1983). Respondent burden: A test of some common assumptions. *Public Opinion Quarterly, 47*(1), 36–53.

Stanton, J. M., & Rogelberg, S. G. (2002). Beyond online surveys: Internet research opportunities for industrial-organizational psychology. In S. G. Rogelberg (Ed.), *Handbook of research methods in industrial and organizational psychology* (pp. 275–294). Cambridge, MA: Blackwell.

Wiley, J. W. (1996). Linking survey results to customer satisfaction and business performance. In A. I. Kraut (Ed.), *Organizational surveys: Tools for assessment and change* (pp. 330–359). San Francisco: Jossey-Bass.

CHAPTER 13

Understanding Nonresponse and Facilitating Response to Organizational Surveys

Steven G. Rogelberg

Surveys possess enormous potential for effectively initiating and driving organizational change. In order to realize this potential, however, careful attention must be given to the topic of survey non-response. Low response rates are a cause for significant concern among survey users:

- They often mean smaller data samples. Smaller data samples decrease statistical power and increase the size of confidence intervals around sample statistics. In general, this limits the number of statistical techniques that can effectively be applied to the collected data.
- They can serve to undermine the perceived credibility of the collected data in the eyes of the stakeholders (Luong & Rogelberg, 1998). For instance, a manager who is displeased with the obtained results can discount the findings by attributing them to low response rates (Macey, 1996).
- They can undermine the validity and generalizability of the collected data because they may lead to biased samples of organizational respondents (Fowler, 2002). As a result, the survey data may stimulate inappropriate organizational changes while leaving the real problems intact.

This chapter discusses typical response rates, the nature of non-response, the implications of nonresponse, and how to increase response rates. Although a great deal of literature exists on these topics, most of it has been generated using polling or consumer surveys. This literature is only somewhat applicable to organizational survey researchers, the focal audience of this chapter. Namely, an organizational survey differs from other survey types along subtle dimensions. Potential respondents to organizational surveys have a relatively close connection to the survey sponsor, their organization's management (Youssefnia, 2000). A perceived track record of inaction or action with past organizational survey data typically exists for the survey sponsor. Potential respondents may also perceive greater psychological risk associated with completing an organizational survey as opposed to a polling or consumer survey (for example, possible repercussions). Finally, results of an organizational survey are usually shared with participants to some degree; this is not typically the case with other types of surveys. This chapter highlights the nonresponse literature using organizational surveys.

Response Rates

Response rate is a ratio of total number of surveys returned (the numerator) to the total number of surveys distributed (the denominator). The resulting proportion is then multiplied by 100 to obtain a response rate percentage. Occasionally researchers adjust the numerator by including only fully completed surveys or adjust the denominator by subtracting the number of surveys that did not appear to reach the person sampled (such as due to a bad address).

Baruch (1999) found that the average response rate of studies in five leading organizational journals in 1995 was 48.4 percent. Regarding organizational surveys in practice, Church and Waclawski (1998) reported that response rates vary from 30 to 85 percent (these are employee rather than customer surveys; customer surveys typically receive lower response rates). Youssefnia and Berwald (2003) examined fifty-eight organizational surveys conducted over five years by two consulting firms. Organizational surveys were classified into four types. The first type, broad-based, such as general employee attitude surveys, census surveys received an average return rate of 67 percent. Broad-based sample surveys received an average return rate of 46 percent. Special topic (for example, a survey on work/life balance) surveys based on samples had a slightly higher return rate (47 percent) than those using a census approach (42 percent). Weiner (personal communication, August 1, 2004) outlines typical response rate information from the Information Technology Survey Group (http://www.itsg.org), a benchmarking and best practices nonprofit consortium for workforce surveys that counts as members some of the world's major information technology companies (Accenture, Cisco, Dell, EDS, EMC Corporation, HP, IBM, Intel, Intuit, Microsoft, SAP, Siemens, Sun Microsystems, T-Systems, Unisys, and Xerox). Most of the member companies agreed to share response rate information on their employee surveys (assessing issues on culture, climate, and satisfaction issues). Twelve of the thirteen companies providing information conduct census surveys regularly; for this group, the response rate range was 50 to 97 percent, with a mean of 78 percent. One of the thirteen organizations conducts a sample survey multiple times throughout the year, with an average response rate of 47 percent.

These response rates were typically generated from an online survey administration (for example, Intranet). As summarized by Thompson, Surface, Martin, and Sanders (2003), however, no consistent differences in response rates across modalities have been found. Some studies suggest that online surveys receive higher response rates, and others suggest that they receive lower response rates than their paper equivalents.

Although external benchmarks on typical response rates are useful, internal benchmarks (for example, how an obtained response rate compares to the rate achieved in the previous administration of the same survey) often prevail when interpreting a response rate. A 75 percent response rate celebrated in one organization will be lamented and scrutinized in another organization that traditionally achieves 85 percent response rates. There is no agreed-on standard for a minimum acceptable response rate (Fowler, 2002). Anecdotal reports and conventional wisdom reported in survey "how-to" books (for example, Church & Waclawski, 1998) suggest that rates above 65 to 70 percent are generally considered acceptable and "good" by most standards; rates lower than 50 percent are generally perceived as being questionable from both an analytical perspective and a credibility perspective.

Nonrespondent Characteristics

As the statistics above indicate, nonresponse will be an issue in every survey effort despite the best-laid plans. Consequently, researchers are concerned with learning about the characteristics of nonrespondents so that the potential impact of an obtained response rate is understood.

Research on nonresponse generally focuses on individual sociodemographic variables. The amount of education consistently differentiates respondents from nonrespondents (Gannon, Northern, & Carroll, 1971). Specifically, nonrespondents tend to have lower education levels than do respondents. Less consistently, research suggests that females respond more readily than males (Pucel, Nelson, & Wheeler, 1971). Other characteristics, such as age, organizational tenure, socioeconomic status, race, marital status, and occupation, are related to nonresponse in some studies but not others (Gannon et al., 1971; Pucel et al., 1971).

With regard to other types of nonrespondent characteristics, interest in the survey topic is consistently related to survey response; individuals most interested in the topic respond more readily than do those with little or no interest (Martin, 1994). Individuals' attitudes toward the act of filling out a survey and their attitudes toward the value of surveys in general relate positively to willingness to participate in survey research projects (Rogelberg, Fisher, Maynard, Hakel, & Horvath, 2001). Recent research profiles nonrespondents' characteristics after considering the nature of the nonresponse.

Creating Profiles of Nonrespondent Groups

Survey nonresponse may occur for many reasons, but a number of researchers have proposed that there are actually just two main classes of nonrespondents (Rogelberg, Luong, Sederburg, & Cristol, 2000). The first class of nonresponse is passive in nature. Failure to respond is not necessarily based on a conscious or overt decision by the survey recipient. In fact, the nonrespondent may have wanted to return the survey, but due to various circumstances such as work demands or losing the survey could not or did not. The second class of nonresponse is active. In this case, the active nonrespondent has made a conscious decision not to respond to the survey.

Population profiling has been used to study the two principal classes of nonresponse. The approach involves creating an archival database on potential respondents that contains attitude and personality information along with names. The database would also contain information on these individuals' intentions to participate in upcoming survey work. Because the database contains identifiers, future surveys can be administered with code numbers linking back to the identifiers. Therefore, the organizational researcher can determine who does not return the survey by examining the code numbers. Respondents and nonrespondents to these subsequent surveys can then be compared on the comprehensive information contained in the archival database.

Because the archival database contains information pertaining to individuals' intentions to participate in the survey work that was actually conducted, classes of nonrespondents can be studied. For example, passive nonrespondents are those indicating positive intentions to participate in a survey that they did not actually respond to. Population profiling represents a nearly ideal way of studying nonresponse. Practically, however, it can be implemented only in limited and unique circumstances—for example, a controlled field experiment involving some deception (see Rogelberg et al., 2003, for an example).

Rogelberg et al. (2003) used population profiling to create personality and attitudinal profiles of active and passive nonrespondents for two organizational surveys. Hypotheses for this study were based on prior research and theory on organizational citizenship behavior. Those who are satisfied with the organization, conscientious (the extent to which individuals are organized, dependable, and persevering), and agreeable tend to engage more readily in helping behaviors (Organ & Ryan, 1995). In this case, completing a survey is considered a helping behavior.

Although students served as the respondent groups in this research, these were not simulated surveys. The surveys were administered by institutional research as part of a university's efforts to assess student satisfaction and retention. Their results are summarized below.

Active Nonrespondents

Rogelberg et al. (2003) found that the active nonrespondent group was relatively small (approximately 15 percent of the total population), and this fraction is consistent in size with other research (Sosdian & Sharp, 1980; Rogelberg, Luong, Sederburg, & Cristol, 2000; Youssefnia, 2000). Active nonrespondents differed from survey respondents along meaningful dimensions. They were not as satisfied as were respondents with the organization sponsoring the survey and were generally not as conscientious. Some evidence suggests that active nonrespondents had greater intentions to leave the organization and were less agreeable.

Passive Nonrespondents

Rogelberg et al. (2003) found that the vast majority of nonrespondents can be classified as passive. Considering that individuals who make up the passive nonresponse group seem, as a general rule, willing to participate in filling out the survey (as indexed by the response intentions recorded in the archival database), it is not surprising that they do not differ from respondents with regard to job satisfaction or intentions to leave the organization. Passive nonrespondents were nearly identical to respondents in terms of these work attitudes. They were found to be less conscientious than respondents.

These data suggest that passive nonresponse does not appear to be planned or based on disdain or dislike for the survey sponsor or survey effort. Instead, passive nonresponse may be understood by considering extraneous or situational factors. For example, passive nonrespondents may not have actually received the survey (unbeknown to the researcher), might have forgotten about it, mislaid it, were ill, or just did not get around to doing it (Peiperl & Baruch, 1997).

Data Generalizability

Arguably of most interest to applied survey researchers is whether nonresponse leads to nonresponse bias. Nonresponse bias can be operationalized with the following heuristic formula (Rogelberg & Luong, 1998):

$$\text{Nonresponse bias} = P_{NR} \, (\overline{X}_{Res} - \overline{X}_{Pop}), \qquad (13.1)$$

where P_{NR} refers to the proportion of nonrespondents; $\overline{X}_{Res}$ is the respondent mean, and $\overline{X}_{Pop}$ is the population mean, if it were actually known. Overall, the impact of nonresponse on survey statistics depends on the percentage not responding and the extent to which those not responding are systematically different from the whole population on survey relevant variables (Fowler, 2002). Based on this equation and definition, we can make a few observations:

• When response rates are low, the potential for error due to nonresponse is very large. As Fowler (2002) illustrates, suppose a sample of 100 is drawn and 70 respond (response rate of 70 percent). Of those 70, 35 say yes to a particular question; the other 35 say no. There are 30 people (the nonrespondents) whose opinions are unknown. If these nonrespondents had responded with a yes, the true figure for the population would be 65 percent yes. If they had responded with a no, the true population percentage would be 35 percent yes. As seen here, the possible range of error is directly tied to response rates.

• Although the potential for error increases, nonresponse bias is not a forgone conclusion in the case of a low response rate. To illustrate this point, consider a job satisfaction survey. Assume the mean job satisfaction score for respondents was 4.50, and the mean for nonrespondents, if obtained, was also 4.50. In this case, no bias exists even for a response rate as low as 1 percent.

• If a response rate is exceptionally high (around 95 percent), sample estimates will be accurate even if nonrespondents are distinctively different.

• The phrase "systematically different from the whole population on survey relevant variables" is important to consider when examining bias. Bias exists when nonrespondent differences are related to standing on the survey topic of interest such that respondents and nonrespondents differ on the actual survey variables of interest. In the case of most employee surveys, attitudinal differences are the fundamental variables to examine when considering bias. Respondent differences on noncentral variables, such as demographic variables, are relevant only to the extent that they are strongly related to the topic of study.

Data on the Existence of Bias

Research examining how respondents to an organizational survey differ from the population on attitudinal variables that comprise the organizational survey is close to nonexistent. Rogelberg et al. (2003) ran a series of analyses comparing respondent attitudinal data to data from the population. None of the satisfaction variables, such as satisfaction and intentions to quit, indicated nonresponse bias. They found that most of the mean differences were close to zero (the two largest differences were no greater than 0.1 on a five-point scale).

The lack of nonresponse bias for these satisfaction variables is not surprising given the following equation adapted from equation 13.1. When nonrespondents are broken into active and passive nonresponse groups the equation becomes:

Nonresponse bias =

$$(P_{NR} \times \overline{X}_{Res}) - (P_{ANR} \times \overline{X}_{ANR}) - (P_{PNR} \times \overline{X}_{PNR}), \qquad (13.2)$$

where the subscript ANR refers to "active nonrespondents" and PNR refers to "passive nonrespondents." Equation 13.2 shows that each nonresponse group's potential to create bias is limited by its size (n) in relation to the total sample size. If a group represents a small proportion of the total, then even if its mean is substantially different from respondents, the group will not create much bias.

The active nonrespondent group, where differences were found for satisfaction and intentions to quit, was a small proportion of the total population (15 percent of the population). It was not large enough to significantly alter the mean of the entire nonrespondent group. Bias would have occurred if they found that passive nonrespondents, with a much larger proportion of the population, differed from respondents on relevant satisfaction variables. This was not the case. Passive nonrespondents did not differ attitudinally from respondents.

Given the relatively small number of active nonrespondents, bias was not likely to be introduced by this group. Unless the active nonrespondent group increases dramatically in proportion, the passive nonrespondents represent the larger group. Variables related to passive nonresponse such as conscientiousness are the ones most susceptible to bias.

Practical Applications Stemming from the Nonresponse Research

Survey researchers should consider estimating the magnitude of anticipated active nonresponse to a proposed survey effort. One way to estimate active nonresponse is having a third party conduct interviews or focus groups to ask employees confidentially their response intentions to the specific survey situation. Those who explicitly state that they will not participate in future survey research can be thought of as active nonrespondents. If it seems that the percentage of active nonrespondents will be over 20 percent (resulting in a potential bias), the organization should consider three options:

1. Consider postponing the survey and instead analyze (and work to remedy) the reasons that purported active nonresponse is so high.
2. If the data are still needed, try more personal data collection approaches, such as interviews.
3. Allocate a specific time of day for survey completion, and gather potential respondents into a group setting such as an auditorium or cafeteria. In these types of captive settings, pressures to participate exist, and thus response among those likely to be active nonrespondents can still be secured.

Efforts to minimize potential active nonresponse are best done in a proactive manner. The strongest correlate of noncompliance in Rogelberg, Luong, Sederburg, & Cristol's research (2000) was participants' beliefs regarding their organization's handling of survey data. Organizations that show a commitment to acting on survey data, provide feedback regarding survey findings and potential action plans, and execute changes based on survey data (or at least explain why they did not make changes) may be able to minimize future survey noncompliance.

Another way to reduce noncompliance is to prevent oversurveying. This idea is consistent with the work of Goyder (1986), who found a negative relationship between attitudes toward surveys and the number of survey requests received by the potential respondent. The following guidelines suggested by Edwards, Thomas, Rosenfeld, and Booth-Kewley (1997) may be useful when deciding on whether to survey employees: (1) Does an actual and important need exist? (2) Is a survey the best way to address the need? and (3) Are the stakeholders committed to acting on the results of the survey efforts (or at least committed to explaining why they did not act)? Finally, consider managing your efforts by creating a survey registry within your organization. Decreasing "survey mania" in a company can increase response rates for surveys that are mission critical.

Response Facilitation

The best way to mitigate against nonresponse bias is to encourage high rates of response. Achieving a high response rate requires great thought and effort on the part of the survey researcher.

Where appropriate, a survey researcher can consider implementing the following facilitation approaches (Dillman, 2000; Fowler, 2002; Fox, Crask, & Kim, 1988; Heberlein & Baumgartner, 1978; James & Bolstein, 1990; Luong & Rogelberg, 1998; Yammarino, Skinner, & Childers, 1991; Yu & Cooper, 1983):

1. Actively publicize the survey. Communicate information about the purpose of the survey and how the information collected will be used (for example, action planning). The internal communications department may be able to assist in spreading the word, creating posters and internal newsletters, advertising the Web link, and in other ways.
2. Personally notify potential participants that they will be receiving a survey in the near future. The notification can occur one to two weeks in advance.
3. Provide incentives, if appropriate. Inexpensive items such as pens, key chains, or certificates for free food or drink can increase responses. Including the incentive with the survey is more effective than the promise of a later reward (Church, 1993).
4. Keep the survey to a reasonable length. No magic number exists for determining the correct length. Church and Waclawski (1998) suggest that a survey should contain up to but no more than 150 content-related items. Rogelberg and Waclawski (2000) recommend that the survey not take longer than fifteen minutes to complete. A survey does not have to measure and assess all possible topics. A theory-driven approach to survey design helps determine what is absolutely necessary to include in the survey instrument.
5. Be sensitive to the physical design of the survey. For example, how questions are ordered may have an impact on respondent

participation. A study by Roberson and Sundstrom (1990) suggests placing the more interesting and easy questions first and demographic questions last. The physical layout should be clear. The questions should be attractively spaced, easy to read, and uncluttered.

6. Send reminder notes. Remind individuals in the data sample to complete and return their surveys after an appropriate (three to seven days) amount of time has passed. Response rates may bump up 3 to 7 percent with each reminder note, but keep in mind that there is a point of diminishing returns when people who have chosen not to participate become irritated.

7. Give everyone the opportunity to participate by such means as using paper surveys where required and scheduling time off the telephone in the call centers. At IBM, for example, most surveys run for ten business days and span across three workweeks. This ensures exposure to invitees who may be out of the office for one reason or another in a regular workweek.

8. Track response rates so that HR generalists or the survey coordinators can identify units with low response rates and contact the responsible manager to increase responses. These indexes are updated as people complete surveys online; paper surveys can be scanned every few days. Friendly competition among divisions for the best response rates can assist collection efforts as well.

9. Assure individuals that their participation is important. Let them know, for instance, that their participation is beneficial to research or that this is a valuable opportunity for them to express their opinions.

10. Foster commitment to the survey effort. For example, you can involve a wide range of employees (across many levels) in the survey development process. Link the content of the survey to important business outcomes, such as increased profit or production or lower turnover, and compelling strategies or initiatives. Then top management (the most senior leaders) can hold division and unit leaders accountable for the survey results, noting, for example, that survey results will bear on their performance ratings.

Whereas passive nonrespondents may be influenced by all of these response facilitation techniques, individuals who purposefully withhold their participation are unlikely to be affected by the majority of them. For example, reminder e-mails will most likely have little effect on an active nonresponder. It may be the case, however, that the facilitation techniques 9 and 10 may serve to reduce active nonresponse. These techniques communicate a genuine interest in the employees and their perceptions and a desire to improve the organization.

A final approach to facilitating response occurs after the survey data are collected. This approach influences future survey efforts rather than the present survey by positive use of the survey results. Provide respondents with survey feedback after the project is completed. Besides general feedback of the survey's findings, action plans and follow-up work should be shared, and there should even be explanations when no action is to be taken. Be careful not to abandon participants once you get the data you wanted from them. Their experience with the survey will affect the likelihood that they will participate in future surveys. The approach may be the single best way to manage and potentially decrease future active nonresponse (Rogelberg, Luong, Sederburg, & Cristol, 2000).

Conclusion

Understanding typical response rates, the nature of nonresponse, the implications of nonresponse, and how to increase response rates enables survey researchers to better realize the strengths and minimize the limitations of the most common data collection technique, the questionnaire.

References
Baruch, Y. (1999). Response rate in academic studies—A comparative analysis. *Human Relations, 52*(4), 421–438.

Church, A. H. (1993). Estimating the effect of incentives on mail survey response rates: A meta-analysis. *Public Opinion Quarterly, 57,* 62–79.

Church, A. H., & Waclawski, J. (1998). *Designing and using organizational surveys.* Aldershot, England: Gower.

Dillman, D. A. (2000). *Mail and Internet surveys: The tailored design method.* New York: Wiley.

Edwards, J. E., Thomas, M. D., Rosenfeld, P., & Booth-Kewley, S. (1997). *How to conduct organizational surveys: A step-by-step guide.* Thousand Oaks, CA: Sage.

Fowler, F. J. (2002). Challenges for standardizing interviewing. *Contemporary Psychology: APA Review of Books, 47*(4), 405–407.

Fox, R. J., Crask, M. R., & Kim, J. (1988). Mail survey response rate: A meta-analysis of selected techniques for inducing response. *Public Opinion Quarterly, 52,* 467–491.

Gannon, M., Northern, J., & Carroll, S. (1971). Characteristics of non-respondents among workers. *Journal of Applied Psychology, 55,* 586–588.

Goyder, J. (1986). Surveys on surveys: Limitations and potentialities. *Public Opinion Quarterly, 50*(1), 27–41.

Heberlein, T. A., & Baumgartner, R. (1978). Factors affecting response rates to mailed questionnaires: A quantitative analysis of the published literature. *American Sociological Review, 43,* 447–462.

James, J., & Bolstein, R. (1990). The effect of monetary incentives and follow-up mailings on the response rate and response quality in mail surveys. *Public Opinion Quarterly, 54,* 346–361.

Luong, A., & Rogelberg, S. G. (1998). How to increase your survey response rate. *Industrial Organizational Psychologist, 36,* 61–65.

Macey, W. H. (1996). Dealing with the data: Collection, processing, and analysis. In A. I. Kraut (Ed.), *Organizational surveys: Tools for assessment and change* (pp. 204–232). San Francisco: Jossey-Bass.

Martin, C. L. (1994). The impact of topic interest on mail survey response behavior. *Journal of the Market Research Society, 36,* 327–338.

Organ, D. W., & Ryan, K. (1995). A meta-analytic review of attitudinal and dispositional predictors of organizational citizenship behavior. *Personnel Psychology, 48,* 775–802.

Peiperl, M. A., & Baruch, Y. (1997). Models of careers: Back to square zero. *Organizational Dynamics, 35*(4), 7–22.

Pucel, D. J., Nelson, H., & Wheeler, D. (1971). Questionnaire follow-up returns as a function of incentives and responder characteristics. *Vocational Guidance Quarterly, 19,* 188–193.

Roberson, M. T., & Sundstrom, E. (1990). Questionnaire Design, Return Rates, and Response Favorableness in an Employee Attitude Questionnaire. *Journal of Applied Psychology, 75,* 354-357.

Rogelberg, S. G., Conway, J. M., Sederburg, M. E., Spitzmuller, C., Aziz, S., & Knight, W. E. (2003). Profiling active and passive-nonrespondents to an organizational survey. *Journal of Applied Psychology, 88*(6), 1104–1114.

Rogelberg, S. G., Fisher, G. G., & Maynard, D. (1997). *Good data, bad data: The role of attitudes about surveys.* Paper presented at the annual convention of the Society for Industrial and Organizational Psychology, St. Louis, MO.

Rogelberg, S. G., Fisher, G. G., Maynard, D., Hakel, M. D., & Horvath, M. (2001). Attitudes toward surveys: Development of a measure and its relationship to respondent behavior. *Organizational Research Methods, 4,* 3–25.

Rogelberg, S. G., & Luong, A. (1998). Nonresponse to mailed surveys: A review and guide. *Current Directions in Psychological Science, 7,* 60–65.

Rogelberg, S. G., Luong, A., Sederburg, M. E., & Cristol, D.S. (2000). Employee attitude surveys: Examining the attitudes of noncompliant employees. *Journal of Applied Psychology, 85*(2), 284–293.

Rogelberg, S. G., & Waclawski, J. (2000). Instrument design. In D. Bracken, C. Timmreck, & A. Church (Eds.), *Handbook of multisource feedback* (pp. 79–95). San Francisco: Jossey-Bass.

Sosdian, C. P., & Sharp, L. M. (1980). Nonresponse in mail surveys: Access failure or respondent resistance. *Public Opinion Quarterly, 44,* 396–402.

Thompson, L. F., Surface, E., Martin, D., & Sanders, M. (2003). From paper to pixels: Moving personnel surveys to the Web. *Personnel Psychology, 56*(1), 197–227.

Yammarino, F. J., Skinner, S. J., & Childers, T. L. (1991). Understanding mail survey response behavior: A meta-analysis. *Public Opinion Quarterly, 55,* 613–639.

Youssefnia, D. (2000, Apr.). *Examining organizational survey response quality with OCB related job attitudes.* Paper presented at the annual convention of the Society for Industrial and Organizational Psychology, New Orleans, LA.

Youssefnia, D., & Berwald, M. (2003, Apr.). *An exploratory look at the response rates of sample, census, special topic and broad-based surveys.* Paper presented at the annual convention of the Society for Industrial and Organizational Psychology, Chicago, IL.

Yu, J., & Cooper, H. (1983). A quantitative review of research design effects on response rates to questionnaires. *Journal of Marketing Research, 20,* 36–44.

CHAPTER 14

Relative Weights of Predictors

What Is Important When Many Forces Are Operating

Kyle M. Lundby
Jeff W. Johnson

In the current business climate, where human and capital resources are limited, those engaged in survey research—whether the focus is internally on employees or externally on customers—are increasingly being held accountable for using their survey results to drive tangible change. As Kraut and Saari (1999) noted, there has been a strategic shift away from the traditional purpose of organizational surveys, which was simply assessing employee satisfaction. Although satisfaction is still included in many employee opinion surveys, that construct is now accompanied by others, such as customer orientation and employee engagement, that have a more direct impact on important business outcomes like productivity and revenue. A similar shift has occurred in market research. Organizations are no longer content with measuring customer satisfaction; instead, the focus is on identifying customer actions or product features that are more directly related to customer behaviors, such as long-term repeat business (that is, loyalty). Tying it all together is linkage research, with its primary aim of modeling the statistical relationships among organizational survey results, customer survey results, and bottom-line financial measures.

Whether it is employee attitudes or customer attitudes, there is a clear shift toward making the data we collect more actionable, and therefore more valuable, to the end user. One way to do this is through the application of key driver analyses, a general term that describes a variety of procedures (statistical and nonstatistical) for identifying priorities from among a larger set of issues. Employee opinion surveys, for example, typically comprise a number of items, with each question rolling up into a theme or topic area. A frequent challenge for organizations wishing to take action on their data is the process of determining which items or themes warrant the greatest attention. Assuming the survey is well developed and taps into the issues that are important to the organization, a key driver analysis can answer this question. By determining the relative impact of various items or themes on a desired outcome, such as employee satisfaction or retention, the key driver results suggest where attention should be focused in order to have the greatest impact on that outcome. Again, this assumes that the survey is well developed and measures factors important to the organization.

There are a number of ways to conduct a key driver analysis, and each has its own set of advantages and disadvantages. In this chapter, we review several of the more common approaches and introduce readers to relative weight analysis (RWA). RWA is a relatively new procedure that appears to overcome many of the problems inherent in other key driver analysis procedures such as stated importance, correlation, and multiple regression. We view RWA as an important new tool for survey researchers. In addition to comparing and contrasting RWA with other procedures, we provide a case study to help make some of these concepts more concrete. In addition, we have provided SPSS syntax (see the chapter appendix) so that interested readers can gain firsthand experience in the application of the RWA procedure.

Before we begin, we look at a large organization that we refer to as Service, Inc. (For the purpose of illustrating RWA's application in an applied setting, we created Service, Inc., a fictitious organization, from various consulting experiences in the private sector.) Service, Inc. was recently confronted with the issue of encroaching competition from other low-cost providers. Although the company could not necessarily go head-to-head on price, management did believe that it could beat the competition in terms of service quality. Having just collected data in a companywide employee opinion survey, they turned to their results for some ideas on how to improve the service being delivered to their customers. However, a quick scan of the results provided no clear direction. Like other organizational surveys, their survey included a number of questions about many different topic areas, such as employee satisfaction, training and career opportunities, organizational commitment, senior leadership, engagement, teamwork, and customer orientation. Although all of these issues were important, it was not clear from the data which areas to focus on in order to enhance the service that customers were receiving. In fact, a rational argument could be made for just about any of the topics. For instance, one could reason that satisfied employees are more pleasant to be around and therefore more likely to treat customers well. Training would have to be a critical component in delivering quality service, and surely customer orientation must play a role. Given all the potential drivers of service quality, where should a manager focus attention with limited time and resources? Which areas are most likely to have the greatest impact?

A key driver analysis can supply the missing link. We know that employee perceptions of service quality are highly correlated with actual customer service, a link that is well established in the literature (see Lundby & Fenlason, 2004). A key driver analysis can provide a rank ordering of the survey items or topics in terms of their relationship to employee perceptions of service quality. Taking appropriate actions to improve scores on the items or topics that are most highly associated with service quality—the key drivers of service quality—should ultimately enhance the experience of customers. Using a key driver analysis to determine priorities would increase the overall return on investment of Service, Inc.'s survey program by helping it identify the issues that are likely to have the greatest impact on customers and drive meaningful change for the entire organization.

There are several common approaches currently being used to identify key drivers, and each has its own set of advantages and limitations. One recent approach to determining the relative importance among multiple items or topics to an overall evaluation, RWA (Johnson, 2000), overcomes the limitations of other approaches.

In the next sections, we review RWA and compare it to stated and derived importance procedures such as correlation and multiple regression.

Common Methods of Determining Importance

Traditionally, two approaches have been used to determine relative importance—direct or stated importance or statistically derived importance. Both approaches and their advantages and limitations are described in this section.

Direct (Stated) Ratings of Importance

Some surveys ask employees to rate the importance of different organizational attributes. While the direct method is easy to explain and allows importance to be measured at the individual respondent level, it has several limitations. First, direct ratings may not reflect reality. For instance, most survey researchers who have asked for direct ratings of importance will note that the responses tend to cluster around the high end of the scale, with very little variability. Although a certain proportion of these ratings are likely to be accurate (they really are important to the employees), it is unlikely that everything really is important. In addition, people may base their rating on what they believe they should say rather than what they truly feel. They may rate pay as less important because it is not socially appropriate to be overly concerned with pay; conversely, they may rate quality as most important to their satisfaction because it is in the organization's mission statement, when in fact it is not their own most important criterion. In the end, it is impossible to be certain about the extent to which direct ratings are influenced by individuals' true opinion of the importance of an attribute relative to external considerations that may influence the rating.

Second, research has shown that people have trouble actually rating how important they think something is in contributing to an overall area like job satisfaction (Hobson, Mendel, & Gibson, 1981; Slovic & Lichtenstein, 1971). Making an overall evaluation is a complex process, and it is difficult for people to accurately report on how they weight each individual attribute to arrive at the overall judgment.

A third limitation of direct importance ratings is their impact on the length of organizational surveys. There was a time when surveys with as many as one hundred items were acceptable. Increasingly, however, organizations seek shorter surveys that still yield actionable data on important topics. Direct importance ratings increase the length of the survey, especially if both a satisfaction and an importance rating have to be made for every item. This tends to lower the response rate and decrease the degree to which respondents pay attention to what they are doing.

Derived (Statistical) Measures of Importance

The limitations of direct ratings have prompted many survey researchers to choose derived, or statistical, procedures for determining relative importance. The most popular methods have been zero-order correlations and standardized regression coefficients (although many other methods have been applied; Johnson & LeBreton, 2004). Correlation and regression coefficients have the advantages of being easy to compute using standard statistical software packages and they are familiar to those with a basic knowledge of statistics.

When predictors are uncorrelated, zero-order correlations and standardized regression coefficients are equivalent. The squares of these indices sum to R^2, or the proportion of variance in the overall attribute that is explained by the specific attributes, so the relative importance of each variable can be expressed as the proportion of predictable variance for which it accounts. When predictor variables are correlated (there is high multicollinearity among predictors), however, these indexes have long been considered inadequate (Budescu, 1993; Green & Tull, 1975; Hoffman, 1960). In the presence of multicollinearity, squared correlations and squared standardized regression coefficients are no longer equivalent, do not sum to R^2, and take on very different meanings. Correlations represent the unique contribution of each predictor by itself, whereas regression coefficients represent the incremental contribution of each predictor when combined with all remaining predictors.

The following example illustrates the concept of relative importance and the inadequacy of correlation and regression as measures of relative importance. A bank conducts a customer satisfaction survey. Once data are in, the researcher wants to determine how each specific aspect of bank satisfaction (for example, teller service, loan officer service, phone representative service, the convenience of the hours, and the interest rates) contributes to customers' overall satisfaction with the bank, that is, which attributes are most important to overall satisfaction. Regression coefficients are inadequate because customers do not consider the incremental amount of satisfaction they derive from each bank aspect while holding the others constant. Zero-order correlations are also inadequate because customers do not look at each bank aspect independent of the others. Rather, customers consider all the aspects simultaneously and implicitly weight each aspect relative to the others in determining their overall satisfaction.

Because neither derived index tells the full story of a predictor's importance on its own, Courville and Thompson (2001) recommended that both regression coefficients and correlations (or the equivalent structure coefficients) be examined when interpreting relative importance. However, examining two different indexes in order to determine a relative ordering of importance is highly subjective, hence the ongoing search for a single meaningful index of relative importance.

As a result of this search, a rich literature on determining the relative importance of predictors has developed in statistics, psychology, marketing, economics, and medicine (Azen & Budescu, 2003; Budescu, 1993; Gibson, 1962; Goldberger, 1964; Green, Carroll, & DeSarbo, 1978; Healy, 1990; Johnson, 2000; Kruskal, 1987). Johnson and LeBreton (2004) reviewed many alternative statistical measures of importance and found that almost all of them have significant shortcomings in either the logic behind their development or the apparent sense of the results they provide. Besides correlations and standardized regression coefficients, other importance methods that have been found lacking include:

- Unstandardized regression coefficients (Lane, Murphy, & Marques, 1982)
- The increase in R^2 associated with adding a predictor to the model (Darlington, 1968)
- The semipartial correlation and its associated t statistic (Bring, 1994; Darlington, 1990)

- The product of the standardized regression coefficient and zero-order correlation (Hoffman, 1960; Pratt, 1987; Thomas, Hughes, & Zumbo, 1998)

The primary problem with most of these indexes is that they often provide nonsensical results such as negative or zero importance for attributes that should be important under conditions that are common in survey research (for example, high attribute intercorrelations).

Two alternative procedures that Johnson and LeBreton (2004) recommended as the best available measures of the relative importance of predictor variables are Budescu's dominance analysis (1993) and Johnson's RWA (2000). These indexes do not have logical flaws in their development that make it impossible to consider them as reasonable measures of predictor importance. Both yield importance weights that represent the proportionate contribution each predictor makes to R^2; both consider a predictor's direct effect and its effect when combined with other predictors; and both result in estimates of importance that make conceptual sense. They also produce almost identical results despite being very different approaches to evaluating predictor importance (Johnson, 2000; LeBreton, Ployhart, & Ladd, 2004).

For the purpose of evaluating survey data, RWA has two notable advantages over dominance analysis. First, relative weights can be computed much more quickly than dominance analysis weights in terms of both researcher time and computer processing time. RWA takes the same amount of time regardless of the number of predictors, but the time required to run a dominance analysis increases exponentially as the number of predictors increases. Dominance analysis requires that regression analyses be conducted for all possible combinations of predictors, so a ten-predictor model requires 1,023 separate regression analyses and a fifteen-predictor model requires 32,767 separate regression analyses. Even with high-speed computers, this can take significant computer processing time. Code must also be written or edited to generate dominance analysis output given the results of these regression analyses. The RWA syntax requires only that the variables to be included in the analysis be input. Choosing RWA over dominance analysis could therefore result in considerable cost and time savings, especially when multiple analyses are required. Second, dominance analysis is very difficult with more than ten predictors because it requires a statistical software package that can do all-subsets regression (SAS has a procedure to conduct all-subsets regression for up to ten variables; SPSS does not have this type of option). Given that employee opinion surveys often contain more than ten themes and certainly more than ten items, this is a serious disadvantage.

Relative Weight Analysis

Relative weight analysis is based on the observation that almost all statistical measures of predictor importance yield the same results when predictors are uncorrelated. The first step is to transform the predictors (the specific attributes measured on the survey) to their maximally related orthogonal counterparts. In other words, a set of new variables is created that is as highly related as possible to the original set of predictors but the new variables are uncorrelated with each other. This is a relatively simple mathematical process, described by Gibson (1962).

Conceptually, the process could be likened to a principal components analysis in which the same number of components as number of predictors is extracted and rotated to the point where no other rotation would yield higher correlations between each original predictor and its associated orthogonal variable. The criterion (some overall evaluation measured by the survey such as overall customer satisfaction or overall employee satisfaction) is then regressed on the new uncorrelated variables. The squared standardized regression coefficients unambiguously represent the relative importance of the new variables.

The relative importance of the new variables is an approximation of the relative importance of the original predictors. To arrive at an estimate of the relative importance of the original predictors, there must be some mechanism by which information on the relationships between the new variables and the criterion is combined with information on the relationships between the original predictors and the new variables. Johnson (2000) showed that the appropriate way of doing this was to regress the original predictors on the orthogonal variables. Because regression coefficients are assigned to the uncorrelated variables, the relative importance of the uncorrelated variables to the original predictors is also unambiguous.

By combining the indexes representing the relative importance of the uncorrelated variables to the criterion and the indexes representing the relative importance of the uncorrelated variables to the original predictors, we can compute an index representing the relative importance of the original predictors to the criterion (that is, relative weights). In practical terms, the output of RWA is a weight for each predictor that represents its relative contribution to the dependent variable. Larger weights indicate a stronger association with the outcome. (See Johnson, 2000, 2001, for mathematical formulas detailing the derivation and calculation of relative weights and see the chapter appendix for sample SPSS syntax.)

Relative weights partition the predictable variance (represented by R^2) in the criterion variable among the predictor variables, so they are interpretable as the percentage of predictable variance associated with each predictor variable. Expressing relative weights as percentages of R^2 is a convenient way of communicating the relative importance of each survey attribute compared to the other attributes in explaining scores on the criterion variable. For example, suppose one objective of an employee opinion survey program is to improve overall employee satisfaction. RWA can be used to determine which of several employee opinion themes have the greatest impact on overall satisfaction. The output of this procedure is a list of each predictor (survey theme) along with its relative weight (expressed in both raw terms and as a percentage of R^2). Predictors with larger weights (higher percentages) would be likely areas to address in order to improve employee satisfaction.

An approach that uses a similar philosophy as RWA is principal components regression. In principal components regression, the original predictors are reduced to a smaller number of uncorrelated principal components. The criterion is regressed on the principal components, and the resulting squared standardized regression coefficients represent the relative importance of the principal components to the criterion. The problem is that the principal components are just approximations of the original predictors, so no conclusions can be reached about the relative importance of the original predictors.

By contrast, RWA overcomes this problem by linking the uncorrelated variables back to the original predictors. Also, the principal components may not have any intrinsic meaning because they are required to be uncorrelated even though the original predictors are highly correlated. Even if there are the same number of principal components as original predictors (such that the principal components explain 100 percent of the variance in the original predictors) and the principal components are rotated so they are maximally related to the original predictors, Green et al. (1978) showed that the principal components may not be close representations if two or more original predictors are highly correlated. This phenomenon would be exacerbated as the number of predictors increases.

Service, Inc.: A Case Example

To illustrate the application of various derived importance procedures, let us take another look at Service, Inc. Although it has enjoyed a fair amount of success over the years, it was not as large as many of its closest competitors, which increasingly were trying to take away Service, Inc.'s share of the market. Although Service, Inc. was not prepared to go toe-to-toe on price or number of locations, it did believe that it could compete effectively, and actually surpass the competition, in terms of service and the resulting customer loyalty. And although the human resource (HR) team members did not consider themselves experts in customer loyalty research, most felt they had a good idea of what kept customers coming back. They believed customer loyalty was predicated on having satisfied, committed employees, so they built an employee opinion survey focused on six key topics (satisfaction, training, customer orientation, teamwork, pay and benefits, and career development) that they thought would provide critical information to help them drive employee satisfaction, and therefore customer loyalty.

The HR team was quite satisfied with the employee opinion survey. Each topic contained multiple items, and all were measured using the same five-point Likert scale (1 = Strongly Agree, 5 = Strongly Disagree). In a typical administration, Service, Inc. would obtain a decent response rate (approximately 68 percent, or thirty-five hundred completed surveys, and each topic in the survey had acceptable levels of internal consistency reliability (Cronbach's alpha in excess of .70).

While the survey itself seemed to be a good instrument, Service, Inc.'s HR team found itself in a bit of a quandary after several administrations. Results had consistently shown that employees were least satisfied with two areas—pay and benefits, and career development—so HR had focused efforts on improving scores in these two areas. First, they reviewed Service, Inc.'s salary structure. They found that pay was comparable to what other organizations offered but that their overall benefits package could be improved. As a result, they switched to a new benefits provider. They also conducted a series of focus groups to determine what sort of career development opportunities employees felt they were lacking. This led to the implementation of a job rotation program and tuition reimbursement for attending courses at a local community college. Despite the success of these new initiatives, however, Service, Inc. failed to see any significant movement in customer loyalty.

Once again, the HR team turned to its employee opinion survey results for answers. In the past, they had assumed that fixing topics with the lowest scores would naturally lead to greater customer loyalty. However, no one had actually tested the statistical relationship between the employee survey topics and actual customer behavior. The HR team asked a data analyst to conduct a set of statistical analyses to determine the relative impact of each employee opinion survey topic on customer loyalty, as measured within each of Service, Inc.'s locations. The data analyst combined the data from the most recent employee opinion survey with customer loyalty data from a separate but ongoing customer feedback study by aggregating both to the location level ($N = 150$ locations).

First, the data analyst created a correlation matrix that included all of the employee opinion survey topics and customer loyalty. This matrix is displayed in Table 14.1. As expected, they found that some topic areas were more strongly related to customer loyalty than others. Interestingly, pay and benefits and career opportunities were not among them, although these were highly correlated with the other survey topics. For that matter, all of the survey topics seemed to be highly correlated with one another. This made it difficult to determine which topic was the most important to customer loyalty. Some members of the HR team wondered if some topics were related to customer loyalty simply because they were related to other topics that were more strongly related to customer loyalty.

Table 14.1. Correlations Between Customer Loyalty and Employee Survey Themes for Service, Inc.

Theme	1	2	3	4	5	6	7
Customer Loyalty	–						
Pay and Benefits	.34	–					
Career Opportunities	.40	.58	–				
Satisfaction with Training	.45	.55	.46	–			
Teamwork	.48	.59	.48	.46	–		
Overall Satisfaction	.52	.68	.59	.59	.62	–	
Customer Orientation	.52	.49	.51	.46	.53	.58	–

The data analyst then reanalyzed the data using multiple regression, which assigns weights to predictors based on their incremental contribution beyond the other predictors. The HR team reasoned that this would provide a clearer picture of where to focus attention in order to enhance customer loyalty. Standardized regression coefficients from the regression analysis are presented in Table 14.2. Unfortunately, the results again proved somewhat ambiguous. Pay and benefits, which had been positively correlated with customer loyalty, emerged with a large negative regression coefficient. This would be difficult to explain to management, because cutting pay and benefits would clearly be unlikely to improve customer loyalty. Again, no clear direction emerged from this derived approach to determining importance.

Table 14.2. Correlation, Multiple Regression, and RWA Results for Predicting Customer Loyalty

Theme	Correlation	Standardized Regression Coefficient	Relative Weight
Pay and Benefits	.34	−.206	5.4%
Career Opportunities	.40	.067	10.3%
Satisfaction with Training	.45	.179	17.2%
Teamwork	.48	.201	19.5%
Overall Satisfaction	.52	.240	21.2%
Customer Orientation	.52	.258	26.5%

Note: R^2 = .40. Relative weights are presented as percentages of R^2.

Finally, recognizing that there was a high degree of predictor multicollinearity, the HR team turned to RWA as an alternative. The results are shown in Table 14.2 along with the zero-order correlations and the standardized regression coefficients. The relative weights showed that customer orientation had the greatest impact on customer loyalty, followed by overall satisfaction, teamwork, and satisfaction with training. Pay and benefits was the least important driver of customer loyalty.

The RWA results have several advantages over the correlation and regression results. Because relative weights consider both the relationships with the criterion and the intercorrelations between predictors in proportionately distributing the predictable variance among the predictors, they are better able to distinguish between predictors with similar correlations with the criterion. The correlations made it appear that overall satisfaction and customer orientation were equally important, but the relative weights show that customer orientation is more important. Similarly, while the correlations made it appear that pay and benefits had a fairly substantial level of importance, the relative weights show they made almost no direct contribution to customer loyalty. Meanwhile, the regression coefficients made it appear that pay and benefits was one of the more important contributors to customer loyalty, but in a *negative* direction. Clearly, the RWA method gave Service, Inc., the direction it needed.

In the end, Service, Inc., refocused its efforts on the areas that RWA revealed as having the greatest impact on customer loyalty. They still felt that all of the survey topics were important to employees and to the organization. However, in terms of prioritizing actions to improve customer loyalty and ensure their competitive position in the marketplace, Service, Inc., focused on what appeared to matter most: customer orientation. Over time, redirecting their attention to bolstering customer orientation in the units that appeared to be lagging seemed to have the intended effect. Through additional customer service training, an increased emphasis on service delivery, and elimination of barriers to delivering quality service, employee ratings of customer service quality improved, as did customer loyalty at those same locations. This translated into greater retention of skilled workers and valued customers, fewer headaches for managers, and less time wasted.

Technical Considerations in RWA

In this section, we review a number of important considerations for those interested in conducting RWA themselves, including the types of variables that can be used (such as interval versus dichotomous), how to choose appropriate criterion variables, required sample size, and significance tests.

Types of Variables

In general, the types of variables that are appropriate for RWA are the same types that would be appropriate for any kind of correlational analysis. In other words, variables should be measured at the ordinal level or higher—preferably an interval or continuous scale. This means that scores can be rank-ordered meaningfully. A survey item on a scale that has its most favorable point in the middle (for example, *too much, about right, too little*) is not appropriate for RWA because it is not monotonically increasing. Correlational analyses assume that the variables are on at least an interval scale, but analyses of ordinal variables are common when the intervals between scale points can be assumed to be approximately equal. So as not to violate the interval-level assumption too much, however, survey items should have at least four scale points to be included in a relative weight analysis. Note, however, that dichotomous items, such as yes/no, can be used as predictor variables.

Criterion Variable

Relative weight analysis assumes a causal relationship between the predictor variables and the criterion variable. Therefore, the criterion variable should be something that could reasonably be expected to be influenced by the predictor variables. With surveys, we usually apply RWA to see how respondents' opinions about specific issues influence some overall evaluation. For example, a measure of overall satisfaction with the company is an appropriate criterion variable if the predictor variables are measures of satisfaction with specific aspects of the company; we can assume that company satisfaction can be influenced by things like satisfaction with career development, job security, pay, supervision, training, and work group.

It would not be appropriate to use a criterion variable for which the assumption of causality is not reasonable. A survey question or a composite of survey questions that all measure very specific things (for example "I am informed of changes that affect my work," "I am satisfied with the quarterly company newsletter") would not be suitable criterion variables, because opinions about other things measured by the survey would not be expected to influence the responses to these questions. In addition, the criterion variable cannot be dichotomous. Ordinary multiple regression is not appropriate with a dichotomous criterion variable because the assumption of linearity is violated (techniques such as logistic regression may be used). RWA would also violate the linearity assumption with a dichotomous criterion, although the extent to which RWA is robust to violations of this assumption has not been examined.

Predictor Variables
Predictor variables should be aspects that can reasonably be assumed to influence the criterion variable. With surveys, these should be specific, actionable survey topics—issues over which the organization has some control, such as pay, supervision, training, and career development opportunities. These are issues that could be changed by the organization in order to influence the criterion variable, which is not directly controllable by the organization, such as overall satisfaction.

Items versus Dimensions or Topics
It is tempting to use individual survey items as predictor variables because they are so specific, but this approach is not recommended when the number of survey items is greater than about fifteen. There are several reasons for this. First, results tend to be less reliable as the number of predictor variables increases. Using dimension scores rather than item scores helps to keep the predictors to a more manageable number. Second, items tend to be less reliable than dimensions. If a set of items measures aspects of the same topic, a composite of those items will more accurately reflect an individual's opinion than can any single item. Third, dimension scores are more continuous than item scores, so the assumption of interval-level measurement is not violated as blatantly with dimensions.

Finally, and most important, relative weights for single items can be misleading if there are differing numbers of items measuring similar topics. Because the importance of highly correlated items is spread out more or less symmetrically among them, a large number of items measuring one topic would tend to get smaller relative weights than a small number of items measuring an equally important topic. As a simplified example, consider two survey dimensions that each account for 10 percent of the predictable variance in the criterion variable: supervision and training. Suppose supervision is measured by five items, and training is measured by two items. If RWA were run at the item level, that 10 percent of the predictable variance would be spread out among five items for supervision, so the average importance weight for each item would be about 2 percent. For training, the 10 percent is spread out among only two items, so the average importance weight for each item would be about 5 percent. Both of the training items would appear to be much more important than any supervision items, so the conclusion would be to work only on training issues. In actuality, however, supervision is as important as training, so equal emphasis should be given to both topics.

To report on the importance of single items, a two-step procedure should be used. RWA should be applied to dimension scores to determine the relative importance of general survey topics. Then separate RWAs can be applied to the items within each dimension. For example, if supervision is the most important dimension to overall satisfaction, RWA can be run on just the items composing the supervision dimension, with overall satisfaction as the criterion variable. The result would be a set of importance weights for each of the supervision items. Again, the weights would sum to 100 percent, and scores with higher values could be interpreted as having a greater impact (influence) on the criterion variable (overall satisfaction). Using this two-step procedure, the supervision items that are most important to overall satisfaction are determined in step 2, and then actions can be taken on these specific areas.

RWA may be applied in either of the following two situations: (1) when all predictor variables are conceptually distinct (for example, different survey dimensions) or (2) when all predictor variables are measuring the same general topic (for example, items composing a single dimension). It should not be applied when some predictor variables are measuring the same thing and others are measuring something different.

Sample Sizes

Another factor that limits the application of RWA is the available sample size. The sample size for running RWA should not be smaller than that appropriate for conducting ordinary multiple regression, but there is no minimum sample size appropriate in all situations. Lindeman, Merenda, and Gold (1980) suggested that a useful rule of thumb for multiple regression is a sample size of at least one hundred, or at least twenty times the number of variables, whichever is larger. More recently, Maxwell (2000) pointed out that rules of thumb are generally inadequate and presented equations for determining sample size based on desired power to detect significant effects and estimated effect sizes. We recommend a minimum sample size of about twenty times the number of variables. Note, however, that it is possible for smaller samples to yield acceptable standard errors, which we discuss in the next section.

Standard Errors and Significance Tests

Because RWA is usually conducted on a sample from a population, it would be nice to have a measure of the stability of the relative weights. For example, how confident can we be that one survey attribute is actually more important than another? Is the relative importance of an attribute significantly greater in group A than it is in group B? There is no sampling error theory for relative weights, but Johnson (2004) showed that confidence intervals can be estimated using a bootstrap approach. Bootstrapping is a nonparametric procedure for estimating standard errors. Rather than making assumptions about an underlying population distribution, the standard error is estimated on the basis of repeated random samples (with replacement) from a sample (Efron, 1979). Between five hundred and a thousand such subsamples are taken, with the relative weights calculated within each subsample. The standard deviations across subsamples represent the standard error of each relative weight. A confidence interval of a given size can be constructed around a relative weight by multiplying the standard error by the appropriate z value from the normal distribution. For example, a 95 percent confidence interval is constructed by multiplying the standard error by ± 1.96 and adding the results to the relative weight. Confidence intervals around relative weights may be used to make confidence statements about the value of individual relative weights in the population. Note that it is not possible to test whether a relative weight is significantly different from zero, because confidence intervals around relative weights will never include zero. Negative relative weights are not possible, so the value in each bootstrap subsample will always be zero or greater.

When comparing relative weights within a sample (for example, to determine if one predictor is significantly more important than another), confidence intervals must be computed around the differences between relative weights (Johnson, 2004). The null hypothesis is that the difference between relative weights is zero. Johnson (2004) recommended computing confidence intervals around all pairwise differences between relative weights and adjusting the critical value to take into account the number of significance tests.

When comparing the importance of a predictor relative to the importance of other predictors in the model across populations, the bootstrapping procedure is not necessary (Johnson, 2004). Instead, confidence intervals should be constructed around the difference between two independent proportions (Moore & McCabe, 1989). This requires that relative weights be expressed as proportions of the predictable variance, which is recommended to control for differences in R^2 across samples (Johnson, 2004). Differences should be interpreted as differences across populations in the importance of a predictor relative to the other predictors in the model.

Magnitude of R^2

R^2 is a measure of the proportion of variance in criterion variable scores that can be accounted for by a weighted linear combination of predictor variable scores. Relative weights represent the relative percentage of this predictable variance that is accounted for by each predictor variable. The magnitude of R^2 should always be considered when interpreting relative weights. If R^2 is small compared to what is expected, then even the most important attribute could be considered unimportant in an absolute sense. For example, if survey dimension scores account for only 20 percent of the variance in overall satisfaction scores, 80 percent of the variance is still left unaccounted for. This probably means that there are other important attributes not being measured by the survey.

The minimum size of R^2 that is necessary for interpretable results depends on what variables are involved. With ten or more survey dimensions, an R^2 of .50 is an acceptable minimum because of the large amount of method variance that is usually associated with survey responses. Method variance refers to the tendency for people to give similar responses to questions on the same instrument, which tends to artificially increase correlations, which affects the level of R^2. An R^2 between .50 and .70 probably indicates that some attributes that affect the criterion variable are not included but the most important attributes probably are. An R^2 below .50 may indicate some very important attributes are not being included. The upper limit of R^2 is most likely about .80, because there will always be some error in measurement. Anything above .80 could indicate that the predictor variables are measuring the same thing as the criterion variable, or there is a very large amount of method variance.

A poorly constructed survey will also affect the level of R^2. If survey dimensions are not being measured reliably, they will account for less variance in the criterion variable than would the same dimensions on a better constructed survey. (See Johnson, 2004, for a discussion of how differential predictor reliabilities may influence the magnitude of relative weights.)

Another consideration is that R^2 is often different for different groups of people. For example, higher R^2s are usually obtained in analyses of data from employees at higher organizational levels. This can mean that either surveys tend to cover topics that are more important to employees at higher organizational levels, or there is more method variance in the responses of employees at higher organizational levels.

Finally, R^2 resulting from RWA will always be exactly the same as the R^2 obtained from an ordinary multiple regression analysis. If there is a discrepancy, it is most likely due to different data being used in each analysis. A common mistake occurs when pairwise deletion of missing cases is used for RWA, but listwise deletion is used for multiple regression. Different correlation matrices are being used as input, so different R^2s will result.

Conclusion

Over the years, the uses of employee and customer opinion surveys have changed. Increasingly, survey research is being evaluated based on its ability to have an impact on meaningful outcomes such as customer loyalty or bottom-line revenue. Employee and customer opinion data are also being married to relevant measures in the form of balanced scorecards (Lundby, Fenlason, & Rasinowich, 2003). While the goal of making surveys more strategic is an important and necessary step forward for the field, it has raised some challenges. A past criticism of employee opinion surveys was that they were simply feel-good measures that dealt with interesting issues but did not necessarily contribute to such real business outcomes as customer retention or revenue growth.

In response to these criticisms and because the field is evolving, more and more survey researchers are building their survey content around complex models of organizational functioning. For example, Wiley's High Performance Model (Wiley, 1996) is founded on linkage research (see Lundby & Christianson DeMay, 2003; Schneider, White, & Paul, 1998), an evolving field whose primary emphasis is on identifying the statistical linkages between employee attitudes, customer attitudes, and business outcomes such as customer loyalty and financial metrics. Out of this research has come a better understanding of what employee issues are likely to have the greatest impact on customer and financial measures. Constructing employee or customer opinion survey content on the basis of this sort of research is a significant step forward in making survey data more actionable and therefore more valuable to users of those data.

Although such models have helped practitioners build better surveys, the point comes when the data are collected and the organization must decide what to do with the results. Typically this involves some sort of prioritization process in which a larger set of potential issues (or "opportunities," as they are commonly referred to) is narrowed down to a smaller set of priorities for action. In the absence of information about the relative importance of each issue with respect to a specified outcome (for example, customer loyalty or employee retention), one common strategy is to focus on items or survey topics with the lowest scores. The problem with this strategy is that some issues (for example, satisfaction with pay) rarely receive high scores. Despite a significant investment of time and resources, focusing on these issues may yield only marginal improvements and may not, in the end, have any significant impact on what really matters to the organization.

To help focus follow-up efforts, most survey researchers have turned to a variety of methods for determining relative importance. By uncovering issues that are more likely to have an impact on a targeted outcome, whether employee satisfaction, customer loyalty, financial outcomes, or some other measure, the survey becomes a tool for driving meaningful change. Stated importance is probably the easiest method to understand and compute, but it suffers from a number of limitations. As an alternative, many have turned to derived importance procedures such as correlation and multiple regression. Relying on statistically derived importance is an effective way to avoid many of the problems associated with stated importance, such as rating everything as important).

In this chapter, we have focused on three approaches to deriving relative importance: correlation, multiple regression, and RWA. Squared correlations, squared standardized regression coefficients, and relative weights are equal when predictor variables are uncorrelated. As experienced survey researchers know, however, survey items or dimensions are rarely uncorrelated, making zero-order correlations and standardized regression coefficients impractical for determining relative importance. Correlations consider a predictor's direct effect on an outcome variable, and regression coefficients consider a predictor's incremental effect in the context of the other predictors. To fully reflect the relative weight of a predictor, the direct effect should be combined with the joint effects it has with other predictors (Green & Tull, 1975). Relative weights appear to successfully combine these different types of information to provide a reasonable estimate of the relative importance of highly intercorrelated predictor variables (Johnson & LeBreton, 2004).

In the quest to make surveys more strategic, the RWA procedure appears to be an important development. By overcoming the limitations of stated importance and other derived importance procedures, survey researchers who employ RWA can offer recommendations that are more likely to support change in the areas that are of greatest importance to the organization. Moreover, by incorporating this approach into a linkage research methodology in which employee attitudes are the predictors and customer opinions or some other appropriate external outcome measure serves as the dependent variable, the information can take on an even greater relevance (for an application of the RWA procedure using customer loyalty as a dependent variable, see Lundby & Fenlason, 2004). This further solidifies the role of organizational surveys as tools for strategic change and promotes the value of survey research as a field.

Appendix 14A

The syntax that follows can be used to conduct the RWA procedure using SPSS. The material within the asterisks is information intended to help the user conduct the procedure.

```
* * * * * * * * * * * * * * * * * * * * * * * * * * * * * *
*                                                          *
*    This program takes a correlation matrix with one dependent variable   *
*    and any number of independent variables and determines the relative   *
*    importance of each independent variable to the dependent variable.   *
*    The correlation matrix may be of any sort as long as it is symmetric and   *
*    positive definite.                                    *
*                                                          *
*    See Johnson (2000) for an explanation of how the relative weights are   *
*    derived.                                              *
*                                                          *
*    This program is set up to calculate relative weights from a correlation   *
*    matrix provided by the user, in which the first column is the dependent   *
*    variable and the remaining columns are the independent variables.   *
*                                                          *
* * * * * * * * * * * * * * * * * * * * * * * * * * * * * *


* * * * * * * * * * * * * * * * * * * * * * * * * * * * * *
*                                                          *
*    The user must input the names of the variables and the correlations   *
*    between the variables. The first column should contain correlations   *
*    with the dependent variable.                          *
*                                                          *
* * * * * * * * * * * * * * * * * * * * * * * * * * * * * *
```

```
NEW FILE.
MATRIX DATA VARIABLES=ROWTYPE_ overall x1 x2 x3 x4 x5 x6 x7 x8 x9 .
BEGIN DATA
  CORR   1.0000
  CORR    .1746 1.0000
  CORR    .2064  .6681 1.0000
  CORR    .1403  .2137  .3026 1.0000
  CORR    .1523  .3113  .4252  .5493 1.0000
  CORR    .1218  .2365  .3051  .5942  .5982 1.0000
  CORR    .1497  .1805  .3169  .4371  .4744  .4083 1.0000
  CORR    .0851  .1661  .2903  .2920  .3071  .2205  .5473 1.0000
  CORR    .2045  .1903  .2756  .2855  .4035  .3376  .3008  .2088 1.0000
  CORR    .2962  .0999  .2547  .2995  .4125  .3731  .2965  .1960  .5608 1.0000
END DATA.
MATRIX.
```

```
*  *  *  *  *  *  *  *  *  *  *  *  *  *  *  *  *  *  *  *  *  *  *  *
*                                                                      *
*     The user can provide variable labels for the output here, if desired.    *
*     Labels are limited to eight characters.                          *
*                                                                      *
*  *  *  *  *  *  *  *  *  *  *  *  *  *  *  *  *  *  *  *  *  *  *  *
```

```
COMPUTE LABELS = {'x1';'x2';'x3';'x4';'x5';'x6';'x7';'x8';'x9'} .

MGET
        / TYPE = CORR.

COMPUTE R = CR.                 /* CR is default name of matrix */
COMPUTE N = NCOL(R).            /* Number of variables */
COMPUTE RXX = R(2:N,2:N).       /* Correlations between the X's */
COMPUTE RXY = R(2:N,1).         /* Correlations between Y and the X's */
CALL EIGEN(RXX,EVEC,EV).        /* Begin singular value decomposition */
COMPUTE D = MDIAG(EV).          /* Diagonal matrix of eigenvalues */
COMPUTE DELTA = SQRT(D).        /* Square root of eigenvalues */

* Create the matrix of correlations between the original X variables
  and the new orthogonal variables.
COMPUTE LAMBDA = EVEC * DELTA * T(EVEC).
```

```
COMPUTE LAMBDASQ = LAMBDA &**2.        /* Square the correlations */
```

* Use the inverse of LAMBDA to find the regression
  coefficients of Y on the orthogonal variables.

```
COMPUTE BETA = INV(LAMBDA) * RXY. /* Regression coefficients */
```

```
COMPUTE RSQUARE = CSSQ(BETA). /* Calculate R-square */
```

* The next two steps multiply the squared LAMBDA elements by the squared
  betas, sum across variables, divide by R-square, and multiply by 100 to
  create the importance weights.

```
COMPUTE RAWWGT = LAMBDASQ * BETA &**2.        /* Raw importance weights */
COMPUTE IMPORT = (RAWWGT &/ RSQUARE) * 100.  /* Rescale to % of R-square */
```

* Print the relative weights. The number of decimal places can be controlled
  by changing the format.

```
PRINT RSQUARE /FORMAT=F8.3.
PRINT RAWWGT /FORMAT=F8.3
    /TITLE = "Raw Relative Weights"
    /RNAMES = LABELS.
PRINT IMPORT /FORMAT=PCT8.1
    /TITLE = "Relative Weights as Percentage of R-square"
    /RNAMES = LABELS .
```

```
END MATRIX.
```

Acknowledgments

We thank several anonymous reviewers for their valuable suggestions on earlier drafts of this chapter, and we greatly appreciate the assistance of Sally Blecha in helping us communicate a complex topic as clearly as possible.

References

Azen, R., & Budescu, D. V. (2003). The dominance analysis approach for comparing predictors in multiple regression. *Psychological Methods, 8,* 129–148.

Bring, J. (1994). How to standardize regression coefficients. *American Statistician, 48,* 209–213.

Budescu, D. V. (1993). Dominance analysis: A new approach to the problem of relative importance of predictors in multiple regression. *Psychological Bulletin, 114,* 542–551.

Courville, T., & Thompson, B. (2001). Use of structure coefficients in published multiple regression articles: β is not enough. *Educational and Psychological Measurement, 61,* 229–248.

Darlington, R. B. (1968). Multiple regression in psychological research and practice. *Psychological Bulletin, 69,* 161–182.

Darlington, R. B. (1990). *Regression and linear models.* New York: McGraw-Hill.

Efron, B. (1979). Bootstrap methods: Another look at the jackknife. *Annals of Statistics, 7,* 1–26.

Gibson, W. A. (1962). Orthogonal predictors: A possible resolution of the Hoffman-Ward controversy. *Psychological Reports, 11,* 32–34.

Goldberger, A. S. (1964). *Econometric theory.* New York: Wiley.

Green, P. E., Carroll, J. D., & DeSarbo, W. S. (1978). A new measure of predictor variable importance in multiple regression. *Journal of Marketing Research, 15,* 356–360.

Green, P. E., & Tull, D. S. (1975). *Research for marketing decisions* (3rd ed.). Upper Saddle River, NJ: Prentice Hall.

Healy, M.J.R. (1990). Measuring importance. *Statistics in Medicine, 9,* 633–637.

Hobson, C. J., Mendel, R. M., & Gibson, F. W. (1981). Clarifying performance appraisal criteria. *Organizational Behavior and Human Performance, 28,* 164–188.

Hoffman, P. J. (1960). The paramorphic representation of clinical judgment. *Psychological Bulletin, 57,* 116–131.

Johnson, J. W. (2000). A heuristic method for estimating the relative weight of predictor variables in multiple regression. *Multivariate Behavioral Research, 35,* 1–19.

Johnson, J. W. (2001). The relative importance of task and contextual performance dimensions to supervisor judgments of overall performance. *Journal of Applied Psychology, 86,* 984–996.

Johnson, J. W. (2004). Factors affecting relative weights: The influence of sampling and measurement error. *Organizational Research Methods, 7,* 283–299.

Johnson, J. W., & LeBreton, J. M. (2004). History and use of relative importance indices in organizational research. *Organizational Research Methods, 7,* 238–257.

Kraut, A. I., & Saari, L. M. (1999). Organization surveys: Coming of age for a new era. In A. I. Kraut & A. K. Korman (Eds.), *Evolving practices in human resource management* (pp. 302–327). San Francisco: Jossey-Bass.

Kruskal, W. (1987). Relative importance by averaging over orderings. *American Statistician, 41,* 6–10.

Lane, D. M., Murphy, K. R., & Marques, T. E. (1982). Measuring the importance of cues in policy capturing. *Organizational Behavior and Human Performance, 30,* 231–240.

LeBreton, J. M., Ployhart, R. E., & Ladd, R. T. (2004). A Monte Carlo comparison of relative importance methodologies. *Organizational Research Methods, 7,* 258–282.

Lindeman, R. H., Merenda, P. F., & Gold, R. Z. (1980). *Introduction to bivariate and multivariate analysis.* Glenview, IL: Scott, Foresman.

Lundby, K. M., & Christianson DeMay, C. (2003). Leveraging employee-customer linkages to build customer loyalty. *Quirk's Marketing Research Review, 17,* 46–52.

Lundby, K. M., & Fenlason, K. J. (2004). Service climate and employee satisfaction in linkage research: Which matters? When and why? In A. Buono (Ed.), *Research in management consulting: Current trends in management consulting.* Greenwich, CT: Information Age Publishing.

Lundby, K. M., Fenlason, K. J., & Rasinowich, C. (2003, Winter). Using linkage research to make your scorecard more actionable. *Marketing Research,* 14–19.

Maxwell, S. E. (2000). Sample size and multiple regression analysis. *Psychological Methods, 5,* 434–458.

Moore, D. S., & McCabe, G. P. (1989). *Introduction to the practice of statistics.* New York: Freeman.

Pratt, J. W. (1987). Dividing the indivisible: Using simple symmetry to partition variance explained. In T. Pukilla & S. Duntaneu (Eds.), *Proceedings of Second Tampere Conference in Statistics* (pp. 245–260). University of Tampere, Finland.

Schneider, B., White, S. S., & Paul, M. C. (1998). Linking service climate and customer perceptions of service quality: Test of a causal model. *Journal of Applied Psychology, 83,* 150–163.

Slovic, P., & Lichtenstein, S. (1971). Comparison of Bayesian and regression approaches to the study of information processing in judgment. *Organizational Behavior and Human Performance, 6,* 649–744.

Thomas, D. R., Hughes, E., & Zumbo, B. D. (1998). On variable importance in linear regression. *Social Indicators Research, 45,* 253–275.

Wiley, J. W. (1996). Linking survey results to customer satisfaction and business performance. In A. I. Kraut (Ed.), *Organizational surveys: Tools for assessment and change* (pp. 330–359). San Francisco: Jossey-Bass.

CHAPTER 15

National Norms Versus Consortium Data
What Do They Tell Us?

William H. Macey
Larry D. Eldridge

Imagine for the moment that a manager, Alice Jones, has just received her employee survey report. Like the typical report, results are reported in terms of the percentage of employees giving favorable, neutral, or unfavorable responses to each survey question. As she looks at the results, she finds that 40 percent of the people in her unit rate their pay in favorable terms and 40 percent express satisfaction with their opportunity for a promotion. She notes in passing that 68 percent say their supervisor treats them with respect. Alice wonders how to interpret these findings, and whether they are good, bad, or merely typical, and where she should start in taking action based on her survey findings. As we will show, high-quality normative data (referred to as *norms* in this chapter) can help her answer these questions and also help her make good decisions about where to invest time and resources in preparing an action plan.

In this chapter, we first discuss the value of benchmarking, then turn to where norms can be found, and finally examine what is important to consider in evaluating the quality of benchmarking information. Where relevant, we distinguish between the client, or user of benchmark information (our manager in the example), and the survey analyst, who might be an industrial/organizational

(I/O) psychologist or other professional with responsibility for survey design and interpretation. Although we focus primarily on external norms, internal data and historic comparisons can often serve the same purpose, particularly for subunits of the business.

The Value of Norms: Getting More and Better Action from Employee Surveys

Organizations conduct surveys to get candid feedback from their employees and use this information as they identify where they should devote energy and resources to create an effective work environment. Norms serve the following purposes:

- *Norms provide context for interpreting survey findings.* Survey data are often summarized using the percentage who answered each question favorably—the percentage favorable. Looking just at this number, there is a tendency to rank items from most to least favorable and work on the lowest-scoring items. However, different items have very different average scores across the general population. Comparing the scores to the norms allows the manager to quickly identify the relative strengths and weaknesses for the organization.
- *The norm distribution can give the organization its relative ranking.* Of particular importance is the fact that the distribution of scores across organizations is quite narrow. Based on the distribution of survey results observed across many companies, 50 percent of organizations will fall within 5 percentage points of the norm "percentage favorable" and 80 percent of organizations will fall within 10 percentage points of the norm (see Figure 15.1). This distribution does vary somewhat depending on the size of the organization, the specific question, whether the norm score is in the middle range or the extremities in percentage favorable, but the rule of thumb is a reasonable first estimate.

From Figure 15.1, you can see that an organization scoring about five points higher than the norm will rank at the seventy-fifth percentile, while one that scores ten points lower will fall at the tenth percentile, and so on. Knowing the organization's relative ranking allows the manager to gauge how easy or hard it will be to make improvements. If the organization scores low relative to

**Figure 15.1. Typical Empirical
Distribution of Organizations on an Item**

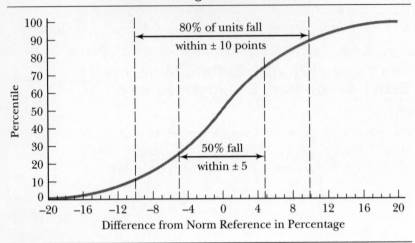

Source: © Genesee Survey Services, Inc.

others, the manager can talk to others, find best practices, and adapt them to the organization, a strategy that is fairly easy to implement and would be supported in most organizations. If the organization already scores very high, the manager knows that copying others is unlikely to help; an entirely new approach may be required—a much more difficult and risky task in most cases.

• *The ranking creates energy for action.* Relative standing drives managers to take action. The direct comparison to the norm average is useful, but when given just this one number, managers may substitute this for the goal and settle for achieving the average. In contrast, when the manager is given the organization's ranking against others, it tends to put the survey results on par with financial or product leadership results, and the manager wants the organization to be among the top performers, not just average. Ranking also encourages action by making it clear that such goals are achievable. The consequence is that the manager tends to set stretch targets that are still achievable.

It should be noted that blindly making a comparison to the norms and then focusing strictly on the areas where the organization has the lowest relative scores is not the most effective approach, although it is preferable to ranking items from most to least favorable and working on the lowest-scoring items. Not all items are of equal importance to the organization in meeting its strategic objectives. The manager needs to determine which areas are critical, but after this is done, the norms provide an essential context for interpretation.

• *Knowing the ranking guides action.* It helps to eliminate doubt about where and how to invest scarce resources. The norm ranking helps managers avoid two potentially costly mistakes as they take action based on survey results: focusing on areas that have little potential for improvement and copying others' business practices when they are really a model organization. As noted earlier, without the comparison to the norm, the only assumption the manager has to work on is that a higher score is better and all items could reasonably achieve the same target score.

In general, the organization will find it most productive to focus on items where the organization scores low compared to others. However, in some cases, an organization will need to continue to focus on an area where it is already a leader. For example, an organization may have a strong competitive advantage based on its exceptional customer service and the survey may show that it is already a leader in this area. To maintain this competitive advantage, the organization may choose to continue to focus on this area. Even in this case, knowing the organization ranking provides guidance in selecting appropriate action. If the organization scores low, it can search out best practices inside or outside the company and adapt them for its use. If it ranks very high, it must find creative new solutions and take the risks to implement them. It would be very costly to spend the time, energy, and money to implement the less effective practices of its competitors!

• *More detailed norm comparisons provide insight.* Comparing specific demographic groups to equivalent norm groups provides still more insight, which the organization can use to refine its action plans further. For example, it is well known that managers tend to be much more positive than production workers in describing their work environment. A group composed mostly of managers should compare its results to managerial norms. If this group compared itself to production workers, it would probably score very well and take no action. But if it used a managerial norm for comparison, it could easily find that it lagged behind and action would be a priority.

• *Norms provide an excellent basis for goal setting.* Using benchmarks, the organization can set goals and recognize performance in constructive ways. It is well known that having concrete goals helps organizations achieve greater results. Too often, in response to survey findings, the top manager will establish an improvement target for the whole organization, say 5 percentage points in favorable response, and then generalize this to all subunits in the organization, saying everyone needs to improve by 5 percentage points. The consequence of this action is to penalize the top performers and reward the lowest performers. For a unit that is already a leader, scoring in the ninetieth percentile, it will be a challenge just to maintain this high score, and a five-point increase is likely to be impossible. The manager of such a unit should be sharing what makes it successful and continuing to innovate to maintain the high score. For a low-scoring unit, a five-point improvement is likely to be very easy. For this type of unit, the target should be higher.

A more effective strategy for goal setting is to use the normative distribution to set an overall organizational target (for example, the ninetieth percentile). For subunits that already meet the goal, the expectation is that they share their best practices and seek to maintain their score or improve by a modest margin. Units that score below the target might select a goal of moving halfway to the corporate target from their current score. Over a period of three to four years, the total organization will reach its ultimate goal.

Realistic goal setting is even more important if the organization elects to compensate managers on their employee survey scores. If a manager sets a target that everyone should improve by 5 percentage points, top-scoring managers would be penalized because improvement would be very difficult, while managers of low-scoring units could reach their goals with little effort.

Consider the dilemma of Alice, our hypothetical manager:

As Alice quickly reviews the results, she is concerned that only 40 percent of the people in her organization express satisfaction with their opportunity to get a better job and the same percentage rate their pay as good or very good. From a national normative database, we can tell her that on average, about 49 percent of people rate their pay as good or very good and about 35 percent express satisfaction with their opportunity to get a better job. This normative comparison helps put the results in perspective. What she finds particularly interesting is that her results place her organization in the top quartile on opportunity but in the bottom 10 percent of organizations on perceptions of pay.

Alice notices one other issue as she continues to compare her results to the norms. She is a little surprised to find that so many people in the normative results say their supervisor respects them: 76 percent. This raises a question in her mind about the fact that only 68 percent of the people in her group feel their supervisor respects them. At first, she was ready to celebrate her results, but now she recognizes that these results also place her organization in the bottom quartile. In fact, supervisory respect should be a focus of her survey action planning efforts, particularly since supervisory relations are a key part of her personal responsibility.

Making the comparison to the norms has helped Alice make much better decisions about what issues to work on and what actions to take. She realizes she has the greatest opportunity for improvement in the two areas where she ranks very low, pay and supervisory respect, even though the absolute scores for these two issues are quite different. After all, the norms show that others are able to achieve much higher scores. At the same time, she understands that it would be much more difficult to make improvement in the perceptions of opportunity. The low-norms score shows that this is clearly a difficult issue for most organizations. Few have figured out better ways of dealing with this issue than she has.

Third, the comparison has given her energy to take action. Knowing that she lags well behind others in perceptions of pay and supervisory fairness activates her competitive spirit and nurtures it with the understanding that better scores are really achievable. Fourth, she has a better idea of how to generate ideas for improvements. Where she lags behind the norms, she can look to other companies and import or adapt best practices, but if she adopted this strategy with the issue of pay, she is likely to invest a lot of time discovering practices that are worse than her own. To make improvement in this area, she would need to invent new approaches. Finally, Alice has a better idea of the goals she might strive to achieve. In the first year, she might seek to move up eight or nine percentage points on pay and supervisory respect, achieving an average score. She might aspire to move up another five to six points the following year and four to five points in the next year, ultimately achieving a leadership position in these areas. In the area of opportunity, she might seek to move up three to four points to a real leadership position in this area.

Typical Forms of Benchmark Data

In general, norms are reported at the item level, and the specific measures mirror what is reported in the typical organizational survey report, including item response averages, response distribution (for example, strongly agree, agree), and consolidated distributions (favorable, neutral, unfavorable). As aggregate data, norms are calculated by summarizing cases pooled across organizations or by summarizing organizational data points at the organization level of analysis. (The importance of these differences is discussed later in this chapter.) Benchmark reports typically include means and medians as summary measures, but may also provide distributional information such as quartile and decile values. Interestingly, some consulting organizations provide organizational survey feedback only in the form of percentile ranks, implying that raw summary statistics are of no value. Obvious problems with such an approach include the inability to track actual results over time and an assumed precision and stability in benchmark composition. We mention this practice here only to advise readers to practice careful due diligence in selecting their source of normative information.

In some instances, benchmark data may allow comparisons at the overall organization level (for example, company means) and also by certain demographic categories (for example, gender, ethnicity, payroll level). Norms may be available by industry subgroups and even by job title or category. However, the finer the cut is, the lower is the precision in the norm comparison for any given data set, as either the number of organizations represented in the norm will be diminished or the sample sizes will be reduced. (Issues regarding norm quality are addressed later in this chapter.)

Sources of Benchmark Information

Benchmark data are generally available from three external sources as well as through internal comparison.

Consortium Norms (Public or Private Sector)

These norms are summary data based on aggregation of responses from member organizations. Membership is generally selective, and the consortium operates according to policies established by the members. Data in the norm base are aggregated from survey data collected by consortium members in their separate, distinct organizational survey efforts.

Perhaps the best-known private sector consortium is the Mayflower Group (R. Johnson, 1996; H. Johnson, 2004), with a history of nearly thirty-five years of benchmark data gathering and information sharing. In the past dozen years or so, a number of other consortia have been developed based on a similar model. For example, the Information Technology Survey Group includes firms in the information technology industry, and the MIDAS Group is a consortium of financial services organizations. Gowing (1999) describes the operation of a government consortium organized by the Office of Personnel Management. Morris and LoVerde (1993) provide an overall perspective on consortium norms, describing the operating procedures and policies of the now dissolved Telecommunications Employee Survey Consortium in considerable detail.

How Consortia Work

Survey consortia share one essential purpose: to provide benchmark information on a core set of survey items for the benefit of their member organizations. Benchmarking is made possible because each member submits data on a regular basis to the consortium, usually following a rigorous set of operating procedures. These guidelines specify which items can be selected and the flexibility that can be applied; when, what, how, and to whom data are to be submitted; and the nature and procedures for generating benchmark reports. Membership in a consortium also provides other benefits, including information sharing on survey best practices, but these are not considered further here.

The stringency of the guidelines governing data submissions varies across consortia. Some establish strict criteria on item wording and use a rigorous auditing process to ensure that members follow the policy. Other consortia may permit variability, in both item wording and response scales. Policies may also govern how often data must be submitted, as well as the number of cases that must be included. Submissions are typically made to an independent vendor that aggregates the data on an annual or semiannual basis. The vendors providing these services apply complex rules to ensure that confidentiality cannot be compromised.

Strengths and Weaknesses of Consortia Norms

Consortium benchmarks have several benefits:

- The norms represent a stable group of organizations and items. This makes it easy to plan for regular survey administrations by knowing what benchmark data are likely to be available.
- Consortium procedural requirements minimize some of the risk in drawing inferences about the representativeness of the data.
- Consortium member companies are usually similar in size and industry group, reflecting the common interests of the members.
- Consortium members tend to be larger organizations (the Mayflower Group requires a minimum of seventy-five hundred U.S. employees for membership) with diverse operating environments, often operating in multinational, if not multicultural, environments. Because large differences can exist around the world, consortium norms may report international as well as domestic U.S. norms, giving the members the capacity to delve into differences based on geographic region or country.
- Consortium norms typically provide considerable depth in terms of the number of demographic, sector, and organization breakouts. Larger consortia can offer breakouts by factors such as sector, ethnicity, and gender. They may even be able to show results broken down within a subgroup, like job responsibility within sector.
- Norm reports often display rank-ordered individual organization results (identity not disclosed) on the basis of percentage favorable or other summary metric. This allows the members to compare themselves to others within the consortium and also provides an indication of where best-performing organizations stand.

Despite these significant strengths, there are several clear limitations to consortium benchmarks:

- Consortium members submit results for the specific questions they use, and this varies from member to member. Thus, two companies might each submit data on twenty questions, but there may be only ten questions that are common. As a result, the benchmark composition floats. This makes comparisons difficult, particularly when the number of individual companies submitting data for any one item is relatively small. This also introduces complexities in conducting research requiring inter-item correlations. Schneider, Hanges, Smith, and Salvaggio (2003) describe an interesting approach to addressing some of these issues, but the complexities in conducting such research are significant.

• The available norms may only partially address the issue of interest to the survey analyst. For example, it is not uncommon for only twenty of fifty questions on an organization's survey to overlap with the consortium norm. To overcome this, the analyst may rely on different sources of benchmark information, if he or she can find them. Several consulting firms offer norms directly for sale to nonclients. However, this creates additional problems with interpretation. This can be partially alleviated through effective report design, such as by clearly distinguishing between the sources of benchmark information.

• The item norms available through the consortium norm are unlikely to reflect any specific theory of employee motivation or engagement. They represent the inherent compromises necessary to define an item pool acceptable to all members.

• Consortium norm reports often disclose only some of the available data, typically distribution summary statistics for each survey item and the percentage of favorable, neutral, and unfavorable responses. Item means are often not reported. As Rogelberg, Church, Waclawski, and Stanton (2002) argue, much of the richness in the survey data is lost by reporting in this manner. They concisely demonstrate the danger in interpreting comparisons on the basis of recoded response scale information. However, for ease of interpretation by their clients, most organizational survey consultants rely on the item response and recoded response distribution statistics.

• Items measuring organizationwide themes assume some degree of consensus within the organization. To test whether such agreement is present typically requires analysis of within-organization agreement. Nonetheless, measures of within-company agreement are not usually reported.

• Individual members may use different survey strategies for collecting the data they submit to the consortium. Some, for example, may submit census survey data, while others may submit samples. Thus, the representativeness of the individual submissions may vary.

Population Samples

These data are gathered from a survey conducted with the express purpose of creating a norm. The respondent sample is typically selected from some larger survey panel (such as a list of individuals willing to participate in surveys) chosen to be representative of a defined population (such as all employed individuals in the United States). The sponsor of the data collection effort is typically a consulting firm.

These norms are distinguishable from consortium and similarly constructed roll-up norms primarily on the basis of the sampling unit. Thus, samples are typically formed by first selecting individual respondents based on important demographic or occupational characteristics. Norms are then generated by summarizing individual responses. In contrast, consortium and other roll-up norms are created by first identifying the organizations to be included, sampling from those organizations, and generating norms by summarizing company averages. In population samples, each case may be weighted equally or by demographic category. In consortium norms, each organization is weighted equally; individual cases are therefore weighted inversely proportional to the number of employees for each respective company.

There are several unique advantages to benchmarking against national panel data:

• All survey respondents complete a single defined instrument. The sample on which norms are based is consistent from item to item.

• Because of the large number of items included in the survey, it is likely that the issue of interest will be addressed.

• Population sample surveys permit consistent reporting on the basis of theme or dimension.

• National panel data facilitate both research and analysis on the resulting norm base with respect to both historical trends and potential factor structure.

• Properly designed national sample surveys are representative of a defined population. Some match U.S. census demographics. Other samples represent a more selective population, such as companies on the *Fortune* "best to work for" or "most admired" lists.

There are also limitations inherent in the population sample approach:

- Respondent motivation is different from that of the employees completing a survey where they have a vested interest in the outcome (creating change within the organization). In the consortium and roll-up models, the data are typically collected as part of an internal company research or organizational change effort. Respondents in population sample norms are typically told that their data are being used for research purposes. It seems reasonable to assume that respondent motivation may bear on survey results as the benefits from responding are of a very different kind in the different situations. For example, less motivated respondents may be more susceptible to response order effects or fail to differentiate among items (VanBeselaere, 2002).
- Population samples may represent a different kind of organizational membership than desired, though often a subset of the population sample can be selected to match what is needed. For example, 51 percent of respondents in one national survey (Towers Perrin, 2003) represented employers with under $50 million in annual revenue and 500 or more employees. Employee opinions in companies of such (relatively) smaller size may differ in systematic ways from employee opinions in larger, Fortune 500 companies. The one-hundredth largest company in the 2004 Fortune 1000 had 34,000 employees and $22 billion in revenue; the five-hundredth largest company had 13,400 employees and $3.2 billion in revenue; and the one-thousandth largest company had 6,600 employees and $1.2 billion in revenue.
- Respondents tend not to be representative of the employed population as a whole, but rather reflect those who express an interest in completing surveys, such as part of the membership requirement for inclusion on consumer survey panels. Moreover, these biases are not necessarily equivalent for different demographic groups represented in the population.
- The comparison point of interest in benchmarking studies is the organization, not the average individual in the population. Of course, statistics based on population samples are summary measures of individual case data. The importance of this issue is discussed later.

Samples of Convenience

These are data gathered from independent survey efforts over a common pool of items. They differ from consortium norms in that the organizations included selectively represent the data available to the sponsoring organization, typically a consulting firm. These norms vary widely in their manner of construction and availability. Although a relatively few consulting firms offer norms based on national sampling, most offer norms reflecting their client base. As such, these are samples of convenience. Regardless of the breadth of the consulting base, the organizations represented in the norm base are those that choose to work with the consulting company and permit their data to be included as an anonymous part of the norms. As a result, they reflect whatever biases are inherent in that choice.

There can be significant advantages to using norms compiled in this manner:

• The item pool is often designed to reflect a specific consulting or business model (for example, Harter, Schmidt, & Hayes, 2002). This facilitates understanding of the data within the context of the broader initiatives that may be in play, including business strategy, recruitment processes, and management education.
• While not unique to samples of convenience, consulting firms may offer a high-performance norm based on specific best-in-class organizations, identified by some external metric such as corporate reputation or financial standing.
• A consulting firm may specialize in a particular industry, such as health care, and provide a more focused comparison.

There are disadvantages to this benchmarking approach as well. These include:

• A client's access to the benchmark data may be confined to the duration of a consulting engagement. Benchmark data are valuable assets, and their owners are likely to treat them accordingly.
• The composition as well as the stability of the benchmark data may change over time as the roll-up of individual companies

represented in the norm changes. In many norms, the organizations are not identified, leaving questions of representativeness unanswered. This becomes a particularly significant issue if data are aggregated at the case level, as the addition or deletion of one particularly large company in the data set can significantly change the benchmarking data.

With some notable exceptions, few consulting firms offer comprehensive multinational norms. Arguably, comprehensive multinational and representative norms may not be available from any single source.

Internal Norms

These refer to aggregate data collected as part of the organization's own survey. Comparisons can be made from a historical perspective or from a current comparative perspective. Internal comparisons are nearly always desirable, regardless of whether external comparisons are available. While current differences between groups may be enlightening, a lack of difference between groups provides little guidance regarding the overall interpretation of results. Nevertheless, certain internal comparisons can be particularly useful, such as when the norm is a larger parent company. While survey content may change over time, most organizations that survey regularly make content decisions with the value of making history comparisons in mind.

Reality Check

Consortium membership is inherently restrictive and thus open to only a relative few. Reflecting the value in their intellectual property, many consulting firms provide access to their norms only through client engagement. Indeed, many consulting firms believe (or at least behave as if) their norms represent a significant competitive advantage. Thus, it is often the case that the survey analyst accepts what is available. That said, the following section discusses the threats to validity that should be considered when making comparisons to normative data.

High-Quality Norms: Threats to the Validity of Benchmark Comparisons

Norm comparisons are typically made at the item level and under certain conditions at the theme level. All of the extraneous factors that introduce bias or measurement error in opinion survey responses also serve as threats to the validity inferences resulting from benchmark comparisons. These threats are often compounded by the fact that the survey analyst may often have less information about how the benchmark data were constructed than about his or her own survey data. We next look at some of these threats.

Lack of Equivalence Between Question Wording

The practical need for benchmarking leads many analysts to draw comparisons among items that do not have identical wording. In some cases, the differences may be nearly trivial. For example, substitution of company name for the words "this company" is one often considered to fall in this class. (However, the question of whether "the company" means the corporate entity or a subsidiary can result in significant debate.) In many other cases, differences may seem minor but may be significant. For example, consider the two items, "I am confident in the fairness of management" and "My manager treats employees fairly." In the second, the referent is to a specific person; in the first, the referent is (perhaps) to a larger group that may include many individuals or even the entire organization. It may be tempting at times to make comparisons in the absence of any directly equivalent benchmark item. However, the practical experience of most survey professionals is that even minor variation in wording content can have a significant impact on responses. As Schwarz (1999) suggests, it is not possible to predict how a question will be interpreted; questionnaires not only elicit information, they also provide cues that respondents use to frame the judgment task so that they can cooperatively answer.

Lack of Equivalence Between Response Scales

The benchmark data may be collected using a different response scale from the one used in the organizational survey. Obvious differences are apparent when scale anchors vary. It is particularly common that the midpoint definitions vary, even in commonly used scales. Less obvious problems exist when one response scale allows five response options (such as Strongly Agree, Agree, Neither Agree nor Disagree, Disagree, Strongly Disagree) whereas another allows those same five plus an additional "Does not apply." Common practice would be to treat the "does not apply" category as equivalent to a nonresponse in the original five-alternative scale. However, such comparisons are clearly made at risk. Minimally, the survey analyst should examine the frequency with which the "NA" response scale option is chosen relative to the frequency with which nonresponses occur in the other. This said, the analyst is clearly assuming equivalence in the absence of direct experimental confirmation of response scale equivalence.

In some instances, survey data are gathered and reported on a seven-point scale yet compared to benchmark data gathered and reported on a five-point scale (or vice versa). Here, comparisons are typically made by comparing favorable responses. For example, on a seven-point scale, the favorable responses would include scale points 1 (Extremely Good), 2 (Very Good), and 3 (Good), and on a five-point scale, the favorable response would also include points 1 (Very Good) and 2 (Good). The logic is that for the seven-point scale, the first three scale points are all "favorable" responses, and the logical equivalent of "favorable" are the first and second scale points on the five-point scale, with the middle response category considered "neutral." The same logic would be applied to the remaining scale points. Thus, the five- and seven-point scales are each transformed into two three-point ordinal scales. Unless there has been a controlled study comparing the responses across scales that differ this widely, any observed difference could be attributed to the differences in scales, making the comparison virtually useless. More subtle problems exist when the reader of the survey report is unaware of these conversions (perhaps because reporting is at the theme level aggregated over multiple items) and their implications. This would seemingly beg the question as to why such comparisons might be made at all. Simply put, the analyst is faced with the choice of being unable to attach a referent to the organizational survey results. General wisdom would argue that such comparisons should not be made, for they are more likely to lead to incorrect conclusions than add the value that proper norm comparisons can provide.

Differences in Context Effects and Item Placement

It is generally well known that where an item is placed within the context of other items in the survey can influence responses. For example, it has been shown that placing the question, "How would you rate your overall satisfaction with your company as a place to work?" at the beginning of a long survey will result in a higher score than if the same item is asked at the very end of a survey (Kraut, Wolfson, & Rothenberg, 1975). As suggested by Rogelberg et al. (2002), differences in context effects work against reliable interpretation of comparisons between organizational survey responses and norms. The issue is that variability within the norm can be attributed in part to differences in context effects, usually to an unknown degree. To the extent that data are collected across very diverse questionnaires, it might be argued that local context effects are washed out. However compelling an argument, we are not aware of any evidence corroborating this hypothesis. Regardless of such compensatory effects, comparisons to organizations that fall at the extreme ends of the norm distribution are most susceptible to this interpretation problem; the further the organization is from the mean, the more likely the deviation represents some form of measurement error.

Unclear Company Representation

Consortium norms and norms based on convenience samples are created by aggregating data across companies conducting very different surveys. Different companies use different items, so the norm for one item may be based on a very different group of companies from the norm for another item. Even if the companies remain stable from item to item, some companies may have submitted data from a census survey or a carefully selected random sample to reflect their organization, while others may have collected their data from a unique subset of people within the company—for example, just one division or just the exempt population. The comparison benchmark thus floats from item to item. This issue causes particular concern when data are differentially represented in terms of payroll level, supervisory status, or other factors known to have an impact on the mean response level. Because of such concerns, some consortia separately report "representative" and "nonrepresentative" data based on criteria defined by their members. The distinction between the two is typically made on the basis of member self-determination as part of the data submission process.

Representativeness is a cause for concern with population sample norms as well. Specifically, these norms are often based on sampling from national panels. These panels may not be equally representative of socioeconomic groups. They also may not be representative of organizations that are of interest to the client. For example, if the sampling scheme is intended to reflect employed Americans, many individuals included in the sample would necessarily be employed by smaller organizations. In particular, an analysis of data reported by the U.S. Census Bureau (2004) indicates that of approximately 115 million employed by U.S. businesses in 2001, about half (57 million) were employed by firms of fewer than five hundred employees. Significant differences would be expected in certain content areas (such as benefits) between smaller organizations represented in the sampling frame and those of Fortune 500 or larger organizations. Furthermore, many executives would question the relevance of population norms, arguing that industry or competitive factors make them different from the population at large, even if there is no evidence suggesting systematic differences across these boundaries. It is important to note that significant differences are typically found in comparing unionized employees to nonunionized employees or across payroll levels. These issues may be of lesser concern when the benchmark comparison is within an industry group, where common business and HR practices may apply.

History

The benchmark data may reflect surveys administered at different points in time or collected at times very different from when the client survey was taken. As such, economic trends and major events, for example, may account for some differences between the norm and the organizational survey results. Some consulting firms have noted differences in national survey responses before and after the terrorist attacks of September 11, 2001. While others have found no differences with respect to this specific historical event (Ryan, West, & Carr, 2003), it is clear that differences in the timing of survey data collection can create variability within a norm base, a factor that may be unknown to the survey analyst. Certain consortium norms are constructed more frequently than others. Again, it might be argued that including a wider data collection window might tend to average out unimportant differences. Indeed, experience suggests that most norms remain remarkably stable over time. However, as consultants, we have often found ourselves addressing the question of a "freshness guarantee" from our clients.

Respondent Motivation

Conventional wisdom suggests that the purpose of the survey can influence the survey outcome. Survey practitioners also feel that threats to anonymity will cause results to be more positive. This may be one reason that more favorable responses are found for telephone-based surveys (Kraut, 1999). Perhaps a more subtle effect may play a role when respondents in national surveys respond from a very different motivational basis than do employees who have a vested interest in the outcome of the survey. For example, some organizations reward managers on the basis of employee satisfaction, clearly raising the potential for biased outcomes. A similar point can be made for companies that administer special surveys used for supporting their candidacy on "best-to-work-for" lists.

Data Collection Across Different Methodologies

Web- and paper-based data collection methods were the dominant mode of data collection when this chapter was written. Most survey administrations assume equivalence of survey administration methods, a finding corroborated for Web- and paper-based surveys (Church, 2001; Kraut, 2001; Stanton, 1998). However, few data exist to support a similar inference for other data collection methods, and Kraut (1999) has demonstrated significant concern for the equivalence of telephone-based surveys.

Mismatch Between Levels of Analysis

Benchmarking implies a comparison of a single organization to other organizations. Thus, the unit of analysis is the organization, not the individual case. Nonetheless, some benchmark data are available only as an aggregate of individual case-level data. To the extent that individual case-level data are weighted to reflect organizational membership, this may not be an issue of concern when comparing simple averages. However, without using alternative approaches like the rules of thumb included here (see Box 15.1), it is not possible to draw inferences about where an organization might fall in comparison to other companies using aggregated individual data.

Box 15.1. Estimating the Organization's Relative Standing

Organizations find it valuable to know where they stand compared to others, but if the normative data are collected from a random sample of individuals, there is no distribution of organizations and therefore no guidance on the relative standing of the organization that can be gained directly from the norms. As already noted and illustrated in Figure 15.1, the empirical distribution of survey results across organizations can be combined with the mean value from the norm to estimate the organization's relative standing. Empirically, about 50 percent of organizations will fall within 5 percentage points of the normative percentage favorable, and 80 percent will fall within 10 percentage points.

Knowing the difference in the percentage favorable between the target organization and the norm, it is possible to estimate the percentile ranking for the target company. For example, if the target organization scores ten points lower than the norm, it is likely that it falls among the lowest-scoring 10 percent of organizations. If it scored five points higher, it is likely that it is among the top 25 percent. This is an area that needs to be refined, for the distribution varies depending on the organization size as well as the concept measured by the question, but this general rule gives management considerable additional insight and enhances the ability to make good decisions.

The substantive issue is whether an interpretation based on individual-level responses is appropriate. The degree to which this is problematic depends in part on the construct represented by a specific item. For example, norms representing organization-level constructs such as service climate or safety climate assume aggregation at the organizational level. This is because the construct being measured is intended to reflect a shared perspective. However, consensus requires verification, which is typically done by analyzing within-group (organization) agreement. Unfortunately, this type of evidence is seldom reported as part of the benchmarking practice. We see this as a significant opportunity for improvement in benchmarking practice. Issues regarding the appropriate level of analysis are complex (see Kozlowski & Klein, 2000, for far greater detail on the levels of analysis issue).

Conclusions

Our focus in this chapter has been on demonstrating the role that quality norms can play in helping organizations get more and better action from their surveys. We are not arguing that normative comparisons should be the only consideration in deciding on what action to take. Indeed, a thoughtful analysis will include identifying the most and least important attributes of the work environment based on the organization's mission, vision, values, and strategic plan and considering the absolute percentage favorable and unfavorable scores. With that caveat, norms are essential in giving the organization an understanding of its relative standing compared to others, answering the question of whether this particular score is "good" or "bad."

Of course, if the organization aspires to just be "as good as others," the comparison to the norm can sometimes be an excuse and lead to inaction. However, if the organization truly seeks to excel, knowing that its score is average or below, or knowing that it is a bit above average when it aspires to be an industry leader, is a strong motivator for change. The comparison to norms also enhances the quality of action selected. If the organization falls well short of the norm, it can adopt a strategy of looking to others for best practices and tailoring them as needed to fit its culture. If the organization scores high compared to others, it knows it is going to have to look for creative solutions and take the risks associated with being a pioneer. Of course, these benefits can be realized only when quality norms are available.

We have described four common normative references or sources for norms. For subunits, the reference that is virtually always available is the internal comparison: the total organization or a major business unit within the organization. Besides being readily available, this reference contains most, if not all, of the questions the subunit has used, so it is consistent across questions and available not only at the question level but also at the theme level. In addition, the method for data collection is usually the same, and the context for the questions is the same. All of this makes the internal comparison an excellent reference for subunits. Of course, the internal norm really does not give the manager a comparison to the larger world. For the top managers of the company, the total company numbers are the numbers they are concerned about, and the internal norm provides no comparison at all.

To get a broader reference, most organizations turn to a consulting firm that maintains a normative database. Consulting firms create their norms either by aggregating results across surveys they have done with their clients or conducting population sample surveys. Norms built on client data often contain large numbers of respondents and large numbers of questions. They may contain international norms and may reflect a particular theoretical model of organizational functioning espoused by the consulting firm. At the same time, because different clients usually use different questions, the norm reflects different groupings of companies from question to question. To get large samples, sometimes the data have been collected over a long period of time, so they may not reflect current opinions. Because the data are collected from organizations that have done business with a particular consulting firm, they do not represent a random sample of all companies, a bias that may be positive in that it might reflect a particular industry of interest or it may be negative in that the level of bias is unknown to a large extent.

When data are collected through sample surveys, the same questionnaire is administered to all respondents. This means that the base of reference stays consistent from question to question. While the sample size is usually smaller than aggregated databases, respondents fairly represent the population because they are usually obtained using scientific sampling procedures. Typically norms are available for many questions, allowing comparison for a wide range of potential workplace issues and perhaps comparisons at the theme level. Also, the data have usually been collected recently. At the same time, the motivation of the respondent is different from employees who are completing their company's survey, an organization in which they have a personal stake. The target population may be different from what the company would most like to have (for example, they would like to know about retail operations in the United States rather than the total U.S. working population), and nonresponse may lead to interpretive issues.

Some organizations turn to their peer companies or consortia for benchmarking purposes. The quality of these norms depends on the requirements the members agree to meet and the willingness of organizations to fulfill these requirements. At its best, a consortium will have stringent requirements for equivalent wording on a core set of questions and for the representativeness of the data submitted to the common database. When this is true, the data will reflect the opinions of the people working in the consortium companies and provide an excellent reference regarding the ranking of the member company within that consortium. Because the consortium members are often from similar industries and are similar in size and diversity of operations, these norms are of most interest to management. Consortium norms may also be available for multiple regions and countries. At the same time, because the questions themselves are agreed to by the consortium members, there may be relatively few in the core survey, and it may be difficult to change the core to get information on more recent issues of concern. Depending on the internal requirements, the companies that submit data on any particular question may vary, so the reference may vary by question. There also may be tolerance for wide variations in representativeness of the submissions made to the consortium.

Whatever the choice of norms, some limitations may limit the validity of the conclusions that can be drawn in making comparisons. It is important that practitioners communicate to their clients, in layman's terms, any flaws in the norm comparisons so that conclusions are properly tempered. When appropriately used, norm data are a great help in putting one's own survey results in perspective and thus leading to appropriate action.

References

Church, A. H. (2001). Is there a method to our madness? The impact of data collection methodology on organizational survey results. *Personnel Psychology, 54,* 937–969.

Gowing, M. K. (1999, Apr.). *Identifying needed change in organizations through the organizational assessment survey.* Symposium presented at the Fourteenth Annual Meeting of the Society for Industrial and Organizational Psychology, Atlanta, GA.

Harter, J. K., Schmidt, F. L., & Hayes, T. L. (2002). Business unit relationship between employee satisfaction, employee engagement, and business outcomes: A meta-analysis. *Journal of Applied Psychology, 87,* 268–279.

Johnson, H. (2004, Aug.). All in favor say benchmark! *Training Magazine,* 31–34.

Johnson, R. H. (1996). Life in the consortium: The Mayflower Group. In A. I. Kraut (Ed.), *Organizational surveys: Tools for assessment and change* (pp. 285–309). San Francisco: Jossey-Bass.

Klein, K. J., Conn, A. B., Smith, D. B., & Sorra, J. S. (2001). Is everyone in agreement? An exploration of within-group agreement in employee perceptions of the work environment. *Journal of Applied Psychology, 86,* 3–16.

Kozlowski, S.W.J., & Klein, K. J. (2000). A multilevel approach to theory and research in organizations: Contextual, temporal, and emergent processes. In K. J. Klein & S.W.J. Kozlowski (Eds.), *Multilevel theory, research, and methods in organizations: Foundations, extensions, and new directions* (pp. 3–90). San Francisco: Jossey-Bass.

Kraut, A. I. (1999, Apr.). *Want favorable replies? Just call! Telephone versus self-administered surveys.* Paper presented at the Fourteenth Annual Meeting of the Society for Industrial and Organizational Psychology, Atlanta, GA.

Kraut, A. I. (2001). "An e-mail to a friend (on Web versus paper surveys)." *TIP (The Industrial-Organizational Psychologist), 38*(4), 37–39.

Kraut, A. I., Wolfson, A. D., & Rothenberg, A. (1975). Some effects of position on opinion survey items. *Journal of Applied Psychology, 60,* 774–776.

Morris, G. W., & LoVerde, M. A. (1993). Consortium surveys. In P. Rosenfeld, J. E. Edwards, & M. D. Thomas (Eds.), *Improving organizational surveys.* Thousand Oaks, CA: Sage.

Rogelberg, S. G., Church, A. H., Waclawski, J., & Stanton, J. M. (2002). Organizational survey research. In S. G. Rogelberg (Ed.), *Handbook of research methods in industrial and organizational psychology* (pp. 141–160). Cambridge, MA: Blackwell.

Ryan, A. M., West, B. J., & Carr, J. Z. (2003). Effects of terrorist attacks of 9/11/01 on employee attitudes. *Journal of Applied Psychology, 88,* 647–659.

Schneider, B., Hanges, P. J., Smith, D. B., & Salvaggio, A. N. (2003). Which comes first: Employee attitudes or organizational financial and market performance? *Journal of Applied Psychology, 88,* 836–851.

Schwarz, N. (1999). Self-reports: How the questions shape the answers. *American Psychologist, 54,* 93–105.

Stanton. J. M. (1998). An empirical assessment of data collection using the Internet. *Personnel Psychology, 51,* 709–725.

Towers Perrin. (2003). *Working today: Understanding what drives employee engagement.* Stamford, CT: Towers Perrin.

U.S. Census Bureau. (2004). *Statistics of U.S. businesses.* http://www.census.gov/csd/susb/susb01.htm.

VanBeselaere, C. (2002, July). *Survey response quality: Shirking behavior in telephone and Internet surveys.* Pasadena, CA: California Institute of Technology. http://survey.caltech.edu/ComparePhoneNet10.pdf.

CHAPTER 16

Preparing and Presenting Survey Results to Influence Audiences

Sarah Rassenfoss Johnson

The survey process finally seems to be at an end. After many long months of planning, designing, testing, administering, and processing, the survey data reports are finally being sent to supervisors so they can conduct their employee feedback meetings. The survey team may be breathing a sigh of relief: the work is almost done. But another critical step remains: preparing a presentation that summarizes the key findings of the survey. That is the subject of this chapter.

Many survey professionals view this as a daunting task. Making a presentation to a large audience is not something a lot of us like to do. And the thought of taking stacks of survey data and transforming them into a relatively small number of slides seems nearly impossible. Can so much information be reviewed in so little time? Isn't it enough to provide managers with their data and let them work with this material?

In fact, the presentation of survey results provides the survey professional with unique and valuable opportunities and, despite the amount of work that must go into a presentation, is not an opportunity to be missed. The presentation allows the survey professional to influence the players, the message, and the next steps.

The *players* are the audience for the presentation. Typically they are also individuals who play a critical role in making the survey a

377

success by acting on the results and reinforcing the value of employee surveys in the organization. They could include the senior leadership of an organization, the board of directors, leadership within a subunit of the organization, or a group of supervisors or employees. The presentation provides the survey professional with the focused attention of key, select people in the organization. The presentation is an opportunity to create thought, dialogue, and debate among the players, engaging them in the topic. If planned correctly, the key player, be it the CEO, president, or business unit head, can be prepared to model his or her support and endorsement of the results and how the survey data should be used.

The *message* is the story of the survey results, or what it all means. This is the survey professional's opportunity to interpret the data, distilling a lot of numbers into a handful of pithy insights. Since the key players are in the room, these critical and focused messages can be shared in such a way that they can be further disseminated by the audience. To engage the players in the process further, the message in the presentation ideally should be constructed so the players feel they have discovered the message on their own. This enhances ownership of the data and deepens their understanding.

Finally, the presentation can spark next steps, or what happens next with the survey results. The presentation and the reaction of the players create momentum for the dissemination of survey results, action planning, and action taking. If the presentation is engaging and well constructed, it sparks interest in the survey process. The players will discover that the results are not just numbers on a page but information that is user friendly, timely, interesting, and valuable for managing the business.

How Not to Present Survey Data

The presenter plugs the laptop into the projector and begins the presentation. As more and more slides are presented, the audience begins to notice a pattern, or perhaps the lack of a pattern: no objectives for the presentation have been stated, and there is no agenda; data are being presented without any clear order; and it seems as though the presenter is showing full results for every question on the survey, regardless of whether that information is relevant to the members of the audience. There are so many slides and they are being shown so quickly there is no chance to glean any information from them. There are so many numbers! Where is the color? Where are the graphics? How can fourteen trend lines fit on the same graph? Just when the audience thinks the end is near, the presenter begins a review of all questions by every demographic included in the survey, reading the numbers directly off the chart. Where is the interpretation? What does it all mean? What is the point? When will it stop? There is an ominous sound of foreheads hitting the conference room table.

A bit far-fetched? Perhaps, but we have all sat through presentations that fit some or even all of the descriptions above. It is easy to present survey data badly, and the key words here are "present survey data." A run-through of just data is dull and tedious. But a review of key findings based on careful analysis and interpretation, geared toward the interests and needs of the audience, can be engaging and informative.

To begin, the survey presenter must resolve four basic issues:

- Who is the audience?
- What is the most effective way to uncover the "what" and the "so what?" in the data?
- What is the best approach to presenting the message and supporting data?
- What are the next steps?

Who Is the Audience?

One of the most important steps in preparing an effective presentation is to understand who the audience is and what their information needs are. Is it a group of senior executives or human resource (HR) professionals? Are they business unit leaders or colleagues in other organizations? The challenge for the presenter is to anticipate what the audience needs to know and how best to provide that information. Talking effectively to the audience requires the presenter to consistently see things from the other person's point of view and anticipate how the audience listens (Green, 2004).

Generally senior executives need information focused on organizationwide issues such as organization strategy, most likely in the context of why the survey was run in the first place. They may wish to see only data for the whole organization. Because they receive so much information on a wide variety of topics daily, they need information that is succinctly stated, summarized as opposed to detailed, and easily translatable into action.

HR staff may want to focus more on the demographic categories in the survey or questions that focus on HR programs such as compensation, benefits, or empowerment. Business unit leaders may want to focus on their individual unit's data, using organizationwide data to create a context.

The point is that different audiences have different information needs. They have interests that might not be shared across audiences. Furthermore, the type and amount of data that they are used to seeing and prefer to have will vary. Some groups want to have handouts of the presentation; others do not. Some audiences are loaded with numbers jockeys who want to see lots of detail on the data; others want only top-line summaries of the results. This is a case where one size clearly does not fit all. By understanding the needs of the audience, the presenter can tailor the program to meet those needs. This will result in an enjoyable and effective presentation.

It is also beneficial to consider how the messages of the survey link to ongoing organizational initiatives of interest to that audience. If the organization is undergoing significant change, the focus should be on survey data that will help the audience understand how that change is going. If leadership is an issue in the organization, try to tie survey findings to that. Linking the survey to critical organization initiatives creates continuity and adds relevance to the survey results. It enhances the use of the survey data and can even strengthen the organization's commitment to future surveys. The preparation of the survey content in the survey planning and survey design phase is critical to meeting such expectations.

Different audiences may prefer to listen to specific types of presenters. Depending on the culture of the organization, different types of presenters, such as external consultants or business unit or staff executives, may be deemed to have greater credibility than an internal survey professional. Identifying the appropriate presenter is as important as presenting the right data; a presenter who is viewed as highly credible by the audience will be more capable of convincing them of the veracity of the data interpretation and moving them quickly to action.

Presenters must be flexible and prepared. Sixty minutes on the agenda can be cut to fifteen minutes at the last minute. Be prepared to pick the five or six charts that most clearly convey the message. If the audience and the message of the data are well understood, it will be easy to winnow down the presentation and identify that handful of charts.

The Heart of the Presentation: The "What" and the "So What?"

The presentation of survey results should not be seen as an opportunity to show slides of pages from the survey data reports. An effective presentation goes beyond the numbers to present analysis and insight that the audience may not have reached independently. As such, the role of the presenter cannot be separated from the story of the data.

The role of the presenter is to tell the story of the survey, not to drop data on the audience. Ideally, the presenter has led or played a key role in the analysis of the survey data and has been active in distilling the mountains of data into the most useful conclusions and messages. The presenter is the face of the survey program and the subject matter expert. He or she not only presents the slides but facilitates discussion, clarifies issues, and leads the audience to the conclusions and next steps. If the presenter has done this job well, a change in the audience has been effected, and they have been convinced of the importance of the actions that must be taken.

The "What"

The "what" is the story of the data that will be highlighted in the presentation. A single survey may generate multiple presentations, each presentation focusing on a different story or aspect of the results. The data analysis process, coupled with a good understanding of key organizational issues, uncovers the "what" of the survey.

Understand the Critical Issues That Preceded the Survey

What was the reason for the survey? Some organizations conduct general surveys of the entire population on an ongoing basis. Other surveys are narrowly focused on a specific topic or slice of the organization's staff. Generally surveys are designed around issues that already exist in the organization. Use these issues as a guide to create an analysis plan. Examine the results of the most recent prior survey (if available) to make a list of subjects that need follow-up. Identify any critical events or changes in the company where it is important to gauge employee reaction. Anticipate the questions that constituencies in the company, especially top management, might need answered. What do they need to know? Focus on questions or dimensions that represent these issues and can serve as dependent variables in the ensuing analysis.

Examine the Basic Numbers First

Although they may seem humdrum to a professional experienced with multivariate analyses, percentages are a valuable place to start the analysis. Most survey summary reports group individual item responses into three categories: percentage favorable (the combination of the positive response categories), percentage neutral (the midpoint of the scale), and the percentage unfavorable (the combination of the negative response categories). Review the percentages looking at categories, dimensions, and indexes first, and then the individual items for the most and least favorable items, and differences between demographic groups or subunits. If history data are available, examine the trends over time.

Use normative data from a nationally representative survey, a consultant's database, or a survey consortium to provide a context for the results. Norms can help determine if the organization's results are typical or significantly higher or lower than what is common. Normative data can also shed light on which topics usually receive low favorable ratings (such as compensation) and which receive higher favorable ratings (such as the job or work itself).

Survey results are often available as the arithmetic mean of responses to each of the survey questions. Ultimately, means and percentages provide the same information, that is, which end of the response scale most respondents choose. The difference between the two, however, is how easily this information is conveyed to the audience. When hearing employee survey results, most managers want to know what the majority of employees think about a topic. Their interpretation becomes very literal: Of their total group of employees, how many think one way and how many another way? Percentages communicate this information clearly and unequivocally.

They can easily determine what proportion of the group is favorable and what proportion is unfavorable. But although most managers are comfortable with the mean as a statistic, it does not convey the same depth of information about their people as a group.

As the review of the basic numbers continues, start looking for themes. Is there a common thread in the items that changed the most from the previous survey? For example, do they focus on specific employee programs, or are they reflective of employees' concerns about the future of the company? Once a theme has been identified, examine it by demographic variables or subunit. Do women, but not men, view this as an issue? Is the rank and file concerned about change, while supervisors do not see this as an issue?

Distill the Data Further

There are also many sophisticated statistical analyses that can be performed on survey data, including correlations, factor analysis, cluster analysis, structural equation modeling, and content analysis of written responses to open-ended questions. Although it is beyond the scope of this chapter to explain these processes in detail, it is worth commenting on them from the perspective of the value they have in distilling the data further and the ease a presenter would have in describing their outcomes to an audience.

Correlation analysis. A correlation coefficient describes the relationship between items in the survey and can provide some insight into how constructs in the survey are related. Correlations can also be useful in understanding the relationships between demographic categories and survey items (for example, the relationship between years of service and satisfaction with benefits). Managers generally understand correlation coefficients, but the results are most effectively displayed through a cross-tabulation between two survey items. Displaying a cross-tabulation in bar chart format creates a visual impact that a correlation coefficient cannot. Figure 16.1 shows how a stacked bar chart of a cross-tabulation provides more information to an audience than a simple correlation coefficient.

In this example, a reasonably strong correlation ($r = .35$) is well illustrated by the differences in the chart's bars. Respondents who understand how their pay is determined are more satisfied with pay than respondents who do not understand how their pay is determined.

Figure 16.1. Stacked Bar Chart of a Cross-Tabulation

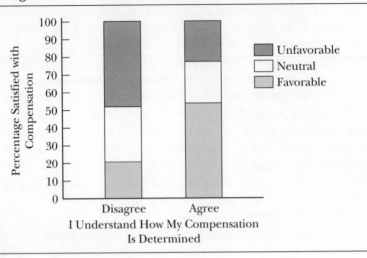

Note: $r = 35$.

Factor Analysis. This procedure is commonly used in the analysis of survey data to create themes. Based on the correlations among items, factor analysis reduces the many survey items to a relatively smaller number of homogeneous factors or themes. Sample themes include opportunity for development, compensation, understanding of company strategy, teamwork, or confidence in the future of the company. The value of themes created by factor analysis is that they create groupings of items that survey respondents perceive to be similar. As such, the grouping of items can provide a broader understanding of an issue than can a single survey question.

Examining a group of questions on a topic will provide a more detailed understanding of the issue and can begin to point the data analyst in the direction of what action needs to be taken. It is often easier for an audience to remember conclusions based on categories of data rather than on individual items.

Factors are often used as a way to structure the survey reports. Survey reports that are provided to supervisors and others in the organization are most useful when the data are grouped into categories. Most survey reports also create a category score, usually an average of the percentage of employees choosing each response option. So in addition to looking at the most favorable and unfavorable questions in the survey or the questions that have changed the most since the previous survey, examine the most and least favorable survey categories, as well as the categories that have changed the most. (These categories may also be called *dimensions*.)

Factor analysis is an important tool because it can detect nuances in the data and simplifies the presentation of the data. It provides links between survey items based on employees' associations. Often these factors stretch across any survey categories that were used in the development of the survey content. This will shed light on emerging themes in the survey and the linkages between constructs. Figure 16.2 illustrates how the results of a factor analysis provide new insight into the data.

Figure 16.2. Factor Analysis Provides New Insight into the Data

Categories Based on Questionnaire Structure	A Category Based on Results of Factor Analysis
Communications • My supervisor keeps me well informed. • My role here is very clear to me. • I understand my contribution to our goals.	**Advancement Opportunities** • My supervisor keeps me well informed.
Career Development • I know what I must do to be promoted here. • Promotion decisions are fair and equitable.	• I know what I must do to be promoted here. • Promotion decisions are fair and equitable.
Immediate Supervisor • I trust my boss's assessment of my work. • My supervisor treats me in a respectful manner. • Our work group is well run.	• I trust my boss's assessment of my work.

Grouping items into categories based on content seems logical to most audiences, and there is virtually no need to explain factor analytic techniques to help the audience understand how you derived the categories or why this is a useful exercise. A statement as simple as, "We grouped survey questions into themes based on employees responses," usually suffices. The results of the factor analysis (the questions in their groupings) will make intuitive sense to most audiences, resulting in very few, if any, questions on the steps taken to get there.

Cluster Analysis. This is a statistical technique that creates groupings of individuals who responded to the survey rather than groupings of survey questions. Cluster analysis provides insight into factions within the company, identifying groups of employees who share a common set of opinions. This technique has been used successfully in organizations that are undergoing dramatic change (Johnson, 2000). In this case, managers and executives responding to the survey were assigned to clusters based on their responses to a subset of survey items that focused on organizational change and organizational culture. The results of the analysis identified a number of clusters that, on examination, revealed the percentages of the management and executive population who supported the changes in the organization, those who opposed the changes, and those who were taking a wait-and-see attitude. The presenters gave the clusters eye-catching labels, such as "Turned Off and Tuned Out" and "Disgruntled, But Not Lost Yet," as a way to grab the attention of the audience and engage them in discussion. Ultimately the information was very useful in helping the senior leaders of the organization determine what additional actions needed to be taken to get the management team onboard with the changes the organization was trying to put in place.

Like factor analysis, the notion of grouping individuals into categories or market segments will make sense to most audiences. After all, marketing analyses often focus on the buying behavior or decision-making processes of customer segments. Many companies are comfortable with the notion of customer demographics and how those demographic groups differ from one another. Using the analogy of understanding the opinions and behaviors of customer groups may facilitate the audience's understanding of cluster analysis in the interpretation of survey data. "We grouped employees who took the survey into groupings based on their responses. These groups comprise employees who share similar opinions on key issues in the survey" is a good way to begin to explain the results of a cluster analysis.

Structural Equation Modeling. This analysis technique goes beyond correlation coefficients by establishing evidence of cause and effect between variables in the survey. Variables used in structural equation modeling (SEM) are typically established using factor analysis, and alpha coefficients are then calculated. Models may be proposed and tested, or the analysis can be run to see which models emerge (Kline, 1998).

SEM models must establish an outcome variable, which in employee opinion surveys is often Employer of Choice, Employee Engagement, Overall Satisfaction, or some other variable that has meaning for the organization. These become the dependent variables initially incorporated within the survey. "Actor" variables (such as supervisor, work group, or senior management) and "process" variables (such as compensation and benefits, organization strategy, the work itself, and opportunity for growth and development) are then tested as predictors of the outcome (Kline, 1998). A useful way to create these models is to identify the impact actors have on processes and ultimately on the outcome variable, such as that shown in Figure 16.3.

Figure 16.3. General Structural Equation Model Format

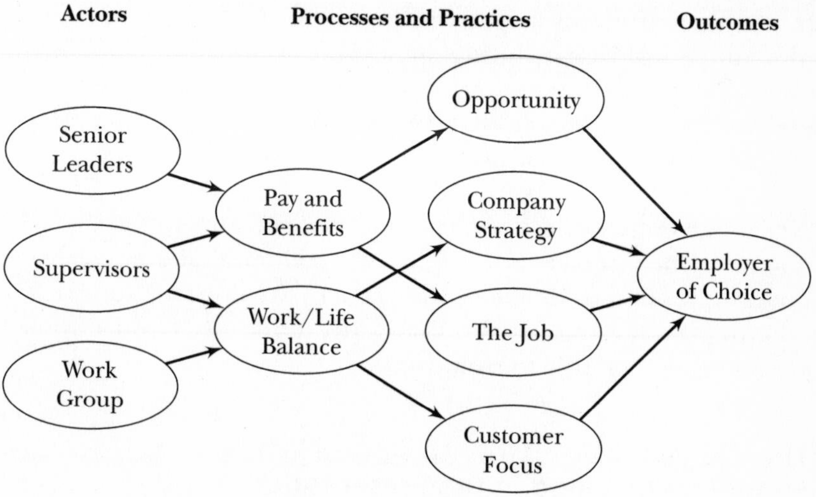

Note: Paths are for illustration purposes only.

SEM can be a powerful tool for uncovering the linkages among actors, processes, and outcomes, but it can be difficult to explain to an audience unfamiliar with statistics. Often SEM diagrams are a maze of arrows, circles, and numbers; without careful editing of the chart and a straightforward explanation from the presenter, SEM results can leave the audience confused and disengaged. Think carefully about the audience and the message to be conveyed when deciding to include the results of a SEM analysis in a survey presentation. How critical are SEM results to the message? Consider a graphic presentation of only a segment of the SEM model, or eliminate the boxes and arrows that fall below a statistical threshold. The results of SEM require simplicity in their presentation. If the model presented is too complex or does not pass the "So what?" test, it could easily derail the presentation.

Content Analysis of Written Comments

Most surveys provide an opportunity for respondents to comment in their own words, and content analysis of written comments can provide powerful results. A summary of written comments can support the results from the data-based questions or provide additional depth of information on an issue. There are a variety of ways that content analyses may be conducted, and results may be reported through a simple frequency across content categories. Selected verbatim comments can be added to a presentation to illustrate employee opinions on a topic. Very often hearing an opinion expressed in an employee's own words can make an impression on an audience that numbers alone cannot. (See Chapter Ten, this volume, for more on written comments.)

Caution must be exercised, however, when using employees' verbatim comments in a presentation. Some comments are so eloquently written or so emotional in their content that they can overpower other data and take center stage in the presentation. When creating the message of the survey presentation, choose to use comments judiciously to support the message.

The "So What?" or How to Decide What Should be Included in the Presentation

Any survey will produce a significant amount of data, particularly if the analyses listed above have been run. What should be the focus of the presentation? The survey reports and the data analyses have produced the "what," that is, the data. The individual responsible for creating the presentation must determine the "So what?" Just because the data are available does not mean they should be included in the presentation. Too many presenters make the mistaken assumption that their audience has to be told everything in order to understand anything (Weissman, 2004). Instead, ask why the audience would want to hear or need to hear about the results. Determining the "So what?" is the most difficult task in preparing the survey presentation. Three criteria can help to assess the "So what?" of the survey data:

Relevance. Are the data relevant to the organization and the audience? Senior leaders in the organization probably do not need to hear details about issues that are relevant only at local levels of the organization. Include results that have meaning for that particular audience, and touch on issues or initiatives that are important to them.

Clarity. Is there clarity in the results? Often survey data hint at an emerging issue or provide results that are equivocal. To avoid confusing the audience or leading them to erroneous conclusions, present data that are clear and easily explained and communicated.

Importance. Are the data important to managing the business going forward? There is a difference between information that is interesting to have and information that is necessary to have. Of course, necessary information can be and often is interesting, but the point here is to give the audience information that they need to run the organization. Focusing on the topics they are able to influence encourages action planning and reinforces the relevance of the survey program in providing critical business information. Their time is valuable. Give them what they need to know.

At this point, move from data analysis to data interpretation. What is the thread that connects the results of all the analyses? Is there a theme that pops up across analyses? Themes could include (among many others) lack of communications, a strong belief in the company's future, frustration over organizational changes, or commitment to the job.

After poring through the data, write several sentences that provide a high-level summary of all the results. Use complete sentences written clearly, and without using jargon. Identify the themes that link the sentences together. Test these sentences against the "So what?" criteria listed. When the sentences have passed that test, note the data that support each sentence. These notes will serve as the basis for outlining the structure of the presentation. At first, it will seem as though a lot of data are being left out of the presentation. But if the data have been carefully analyzed and the sentences constructed well, most of the survey data can be attributed to one or more of the sentences.

Presenting the Message and the Supporting Data

Once the sentences are written, it is time to use them to create a story line, supplemented with data that support the points.

What to Leave in and What to Leave Out

A popular piece of advice in many guides to preparing presentations is, "Tell them what you're going to tell them, tell them, and remind them what you told them." The point is for the audience to understand the message of the survey results; therefore, construct the presentation so that this message is clearly communicated and understood.

Outlines are as valuable for developing presentations as they are for writing research articles or book chapters. The exercise of creating the outline will help present the data in a logical order and build the case for the conclusions and proposed actions. The outline does not need to be detailed, and preparing it does not take much time.

A useful tool for creating the outline is the storyboard, which allows the presenter to map the presentation visually. There are a number of ways to create a storyboard, including simply jotting notes for each slide on individual pieces of paper or sticky notes and arranging them sequentially on a wall or table. Another way is to complete a basic form like that in Figure 16.4.

Figure 16.4. A Storyboard to Map the Presentation

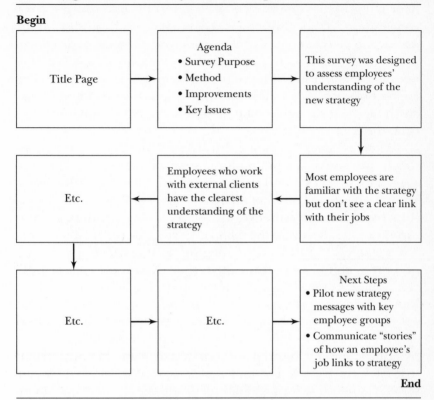

Each box on the storyboard represents one slide in the presentation. Jot down a few notes describing each slide in the boxes. Once the presentation has been mapped out, check the flow, the logic, and the sequence in which information is presented. Reviewing the storyboard can reveal where details need to be added to the presentation and where there is redundancy that needs to be cut back.

Effective presentations have identifiable components such as an agenda, a short description of the survey process details, a series of charts describing the key results, a summary page, and recommended next steps (Plavetich & Kleiner, 1992). Keep these components in mind as the survey presentation is laid out. The messages need to be consistent across all of these components.

When presenting the story of the survey, build a case for the interpretation. The analysis should support the interpretation and conclusions. As slides are developed, evaluate each one against the message to be conveyed. If it does not support the message, leave it out of the presentation. Just because the information is available does not mean it needs to be included in the presentation. The content of each slide builds on the previous one, creating a story based on the data. As the slides progress, the full message emerges from the data.

When building the message, it is useful to triangulate the data, that is, provide data from multiple sources that support the message. The sources could include results of the multiple-choice items in the survey, content analysis of open-ended comments, results from previous surveys, as well as nonsurvey data such as turnover rates, trends in the company's stock price, or results from other employee initiatives. Showing supporting data from a variety of sources builds support for the interpretation that will be difficult to discount or ignore. Confirming data culled from multiple sources underline the message and solidify the conclusion.

Identify a graphic look for the presentation, and carry this look consistently across all the charts. The graphic look should be simple, clean, and uncluttered and not detract from the information that will be presented. The look that is selected should make it easy for the audience to locate and understand the key information on the chart.

Each chart must be titled in some way to distinguish one chart from the next but also to briefly summarize the contents, much like newspaper headlines. Copies of presentations are often circulated throughout an organization, so the content needs to be understandable without the presenter's physically being there to talk the reader through the data. For this reason, the use of headlines for titles can provide a record of the interpretation of the data.

The data presented in Figure 16.5 support the interpretation stated in the headline. The lower headline provides more information to the audience than would the title above it that simply identifies what is on the chart. Headlines are also easier for audiences to recall. They may not be able to remember the percentages, but they will remember that senior managers have a very different view of the company from the rest of the employees. If the messages in the survey data are clearly identified, the headlines may be written in such a way that the audience can simply read the headlines from each chart and understand the key findings and conclusions. The headlines can stand on their own apart from the data and represent "sound bites" that the audience can easily recall and use themselves in subsequent communications.

**Figure 16.5. Using Headlines to
Provide Information to the Audience**

Headline choice 1:
  Comparison of Leaders vs. Employees on Overall Satisfaction

Headline choice 2:
  Senior Managers See the Organization Through a Different
  Lens from the Rest of Employees

	Percentage Favorable		
	Senior Managers	All Employees	Difference
Satisfaction with information from management	86%	48%	+38
Overall satisfaction with the company	76%	46%	+30
Management outlines a credible future	67%	38%	+29
I feel valued as an employee of this company	80%	54%	+26
This company has a sincere interest in its employees	62%	37%	+25

The headlines should follow a logical progression. There are any number of progressions that can be used and no single way that is best. Many presenters like to start with results that are positive, move into results that are more negative, and end on a positive note with upbeat results.

Other presenters like to start with data that are controversial or startling as a way to grab their audience's attention up front.

Consider the total message of the survey. If the results point to serious issues in the company, it may be best to address those issues right away so the audience is not distracted or lulled into complacency by relatively more benign results.

Another approach is to create an action orientation tone. Start with positive results that reflect management actions or results that call for a straightforward management response. This builds the audience's confidence that they can take (and in fact have taken) appropriate and effective actions. Proceed through the more complex and nuanced issues, which will challenge the audience to devise inspired actions and ideas.

Order the presentation of results and issues in such a way that the case is built for whatever actions or next steps are proposed. Go back to the storyboard, and try out a couple of alternatives for the organization of the data. It may be useful to review several alternative storyboard sequences with a few trusted colleagues to get their feedback on which version best communicates the message and proposed action plans.

If one goal of the presentation is to generate debate and audience participation, it can pay to be provocative in the way the headlines are worded. Challenging long- or widely held beliefs is one way to get the audience to react to what they are being presented. Presenting an interpretation that is provocative can break the audience out of a sense of complacency, making them pay close attention to what you are saying. It alters their perception of what the survey is all about and the significance of the results. This can be a risky venture, so make sure there is a clear understanding of the audience and the data. Test the plan with valued colleagues and key players before presenting it to the intended audience.

Graphical Presentation of Data

Visual depictions of the data go a long way in effectively communicating the message of the survey. Slide after slide of numbers can be mind-numbing for the audience and does little to achieve the objectives of the presentation. Well-thought-out graphics communicate complex ideas with clarity, precision, and efficiency. The graphical display of data should encourage the audience to focus on the substance of the findings rather than on the methodology, graphic design, or the technology used to create the graphic design (Tufte, 1983).

Simple graphics such as stacked bar graphs and line graphs to illustrate trends are an effective way to illustrate points visually. Pie charts should be used infrequently and only for categorical or nominal data. Select colors carefully when preparing graphs. Not only do certain colors hold meaning for most people (for example, red means stop or danger; green means go or prosperity), certain colors have meanings within a company. In one company, green could not be used in graphics because it was the color associated with the company's chief rival.

Once the colors are selected, use them consistently through the presentation. If percentage favorable data are presented on many charts, always use the same color to represent these data. Choose colors that are distinctly different from one another so as not to confuse an audience member sitting at a distance from the speaker. Shades of a single color may not be easily distinguishable (Werts, 2004). Print all color presentation materials on a black and white printer. Examine the charts to confirm that all shading, text, and patterns are still distinguishable.

Slides should contain one or two messages at the most. And if using a graphic, try to limit it to five to seven data points. The more information there is on the slide, the longer it will take the audience to process it. If a slide is overloaded with information, the audience runs the risk of falling behind the speaker; while the speaker is moving on to the next slide, the audience is still grappling with the information on the previous slide and is not paying attention to the speaker. According to Tufte (1983), outstanding graphics give the viewer the greatest number of ideas in the shortest time and in the smallest space. This is no small task.

Plan on spending about two minutes presenting each slide. That means in a sixty-minute presentation there should be no more than thirty slides, and probably fewer. Budget some time to respond to questions and facilitate discussion of the results. The impact of the presentation will be compromised if there is too much material for the time allowed and the presenter feels forced to move through it too quickly or cannot make it through many of the slides.

In spite of good planning, unexpected and extended audience input happens, and the presenter must be prepared to end protracted discussion when it threatens the integrity of the presentation. An effective technique, artfully applied, is to listen attentively and, when an opening appears, summarize the points of the discussion briefly and then move on quickly to the next slide. If the discussion is veering off in a direction away from the content of the presentation, gently suggest that the discussion be continued later.

In addition to considering the perspective of the audience when designing slides, the presenter must keep in mind his or her own biases. Recent research (Tractinsky & Meyer, 1999) suggests that presenters show a greater tendency for gratuitous use of visually complex graphics when they are trying to make a favorable impression on the audience than when they want to facilitate decision making. Presenters also show a tendency to use simple graphs when they are presenting favorable information but revert to gratuitously complex graphics when the information is undesirable for the presenter. Tufte (1983) writes that that every object or bit of color on a chart requires a reason, usually to present new information. Otherwise it is merely clutter and creates little interest for the audience. Keep things simple and straightforward so that the message does not get lost in the graphics.

The Role of the Charts and the Role of the Presenter

One of the goals as a presenter is to establish trust and confidence in the presenter's interpretation of the data and subject matter expertise. This goal will not be achieved if the charts consist of little more than the text of a speech projected on the screen. Charts and graphics also do not replace a speaker. They should complement the spoken word and the speaker rather than make them redundant. If too much detail is included in the graphs and charts, the audience spends most of their time with their eyes glued to the screen and ignoring the speaker. If the audience reads ahead faster than the presenter can get the words out, they will lose track of what the presenter is trying to say (McMaster, 2002). By simply reading numbers or words, the presenter becomes unnecessary (Abernathy, 1999). Presumably the audience can read for themselves.

If too little information is included in the graphics and charts, the audience may lose track of the message and have difficulty assimilating what could be complex information. Handouts of skimpy information can be uninterpretable later on to others. Visuals reinforce the speaker's key points, help the audience stay with the message, and provide a visual cue as to when the speaker changes topics or dives deeper into a topic.

Studies indicate that an audience will remember only 20 percent of what they hear and 30 percent of what they see but 70 percent of what they hear and see (Waxman, 1999). Charts and graphics should periodically summarize the key points and serve as a reference for the audience to keep track of the progression of the presentation agenda. Data should be represented simply to support interpretations. The presenter's words should add to what is on the chart, providing insights beyond what can be gleaned from the visual alone. The combination of visuals and the presenter should create an impact greater than either on its own.

The Closing: Next Steps

If the presentation is constructed properly, the proposed next steps, or actions that need to be taken based on the survey results, should flow naturally and logically. A well-persuaded audience may even arrive at these conclusions before the presenter does, and it is a powerful moment when it happens. The audience has made the connection between data and action, and this experience enhances their understanding and ownership of the survey. They feel they have made a critical discovery.

When drafting proposed actions, it is helpful to seek the input of other experts in the organization. Depending on the issues that have emerged in the presentation, input may be required from organization development specialists, the training and development organization, communications, the head of HR, or the information systems group, as well as heads of the business units or divisions. Engaging these experts serves multiple purposes, such as briefing them on survey results, collecting ideas for actions, and gaining their support for what comes next.

The survey results that have been presented need to build an effective case for these actions and support their implementation. These actions need to be described in enough specificity to be well understood by the audience, but not so much that the audience feels that they cannot make suggestions and recommendations. The recommended actions should engage the audience by demonstrating that actions will be taken as a result of the survey and inviting their participation in creating the actions. If the senior leader in the audience has been effectively briefed prior to the meeting, he or she can reinforce the proposed actions and begin to make assignments and set deadlines for action.

It makes good sense to propose actions that can be taken at multiple levels of the organization. This avoids the perception by the audience that only some individuals have responsibility for taking action; accountability needs to be shared. It also makes the point that there is no single action that will resolve the issues identified in the survey. Organization issues are typically complex, and multiple actions at multiple levels of the organization are the most effective way to address them.

If the survey results have been presented as critical information for running the business, then accountability for actions will be spread throughout the organization rather than centered in any single unit, such as HR. The audience needs to feel ownership of the results in order to feel ownership of the actions.

Often one of the proposed next steps will be additional organization research. This could initiate discussions of and planning for the next employee survey. The presentation would be a good opportunity to propose changes to the survey content or the procedures recommended for following up on the issues that were presented. Other research that could be proposed may include a follow-up survey of a specific population, such as company leadership or other employee subgroup, or a survey designed to probe deeply into a single issue.

A critical objective of the survey presentation is to persuade the audience that the interpretation of the data is logical, valid, and important information for making organizational decisions. Another objective is to gain consensus among the members of the audience that appropriate action needs to be taken. The structure of the presentation will build the case for acceptance of the results and commitment to action.

Salespeople carefully construct their sales pitches to present an airtight case for action on the part of the customer. They are trained to ask for the sale at the end of their pitch to gain the customer's agreement to move forward as proposed.

The survey presenter should also ask for the sale before the presentation is over. Ask the audience for their agreement with what has been presented and proposed. If they cannot give a definitive answer, identify a date when an answer will be available. Agree on the individuals who will discuss these actions at a later time, and make a decision. Get a commitment to action, be it small or large.

In some cases, it may be appropriate to review proposed actions with key decision makers in advance of the presentation. In addition to providing useful feedback, this approach can streamline the next-steps discussion during the presentation, moving the group more quickly to action. And by all means, clearly specify the role of the presenter in the next steps. Who will review these results next? What role will the presenter play in making action happen? When will this group reconvene for an update on the issues?

And in Conclusion . . .

Action happens when the right person gets the right information in the right format at the right time:

- The right person is the audience. Make sure the survey results are presented to the people who can make things happen.
- The right information is data that are relevant to the audience's interests and responsibilities, clear, and just enough needed to take action—no more, no less.
- The right format is information presented in the way the audience likes to listen. The flow of the presentation is logical. The message is easily identified, and the relevant supporting data are clear and concise.
- The right time is getting the information out quickly after the project has closed, when interest is high and managers are ready to take action.

Surveys are effective tools for initiating action in organizations. Presentations of survey results can focus those actions in ways that are most beneficial for the organization.

References
Abernathy, D. J. (1999). Presentation tips from the pros. *Training and Development, 55*(10), 19–23.

Green, D. (2004, April 4). Talking "up" to management without flaming out. *Human Resource Department Management Report,* p. 7.

Johnson, S. R. (2000). *Sharpening the follow-up focus at Eastman Kodak.* Paper presented at the Fifteenth Annual Convention of the Society for Industrial/Organizational Psychology, New Orleans, LA.

Kline, R. B. (1998). *Principles and practice of structural equation modeling.* New York: Guilford Press.

McMaster, M. (2002). Missing the point: How PowerPoint may be sucking the life out of your sales presentation. *Sales and Marketing Management, 154*(9), 23–25.

Plavetich, R. G., & Kleiner, B. H. (1992). How to be an effective public speaker. *Training and Development, 46*(11), 17–20.

Tractinsky, N., & Meyer, J. (1999). Chartjunk or goldgraph? Effects of presentation objectives and content desirability on information presentation. *MIS Quarterly, 23*(3), 393–409.

Tufte, E. R. (1983). *The visual display of quantitative information.* Cheshire, CT: Graphics Press.

Waxman, M. (1999). Tips for giving presentations with pizzazz. *Business Journal, 17*(10), 13.

Weissman, J. (2004). *Absolute beginner's guide to making winning presentations.* Indianapolis, IN: Que.

Werts, C. E. (2004) Before-and-after magic: Creating effective graphs for data presentation. *Information Outlook, 8*(3), 21–24.

CHAPTER 17

How to Create Presentations That Spark Action

Ingwer Borg
Matthias Zimmermann

If everything works well, the presentation of an employee survey's results to management succeeds in (1) informing management about the empirical results so that they see the big picture as well as important details and do not get lost in statistics; (2) arriving at valid interpretations that go beyond simple good-bad categorizations and relate to business goals; (3) making management aware of the opportunities that the data provide to promote their goals; and (4) motivating and empowering management to grasp these opportunities.

Presentations of survey results rarely pursue these goals systematically. Rather, they often do little more than show statistical results in an item-by-item sequence. Interpretations remain limited to sorting the items into good-neutral-bad categories defined by benchmark values. Moreover, the design of the follow-up processes and management's roles, leverages, and time lines in these processes are not stated explicitly.

Under these circumstances, it is not surprising that management, when seeing the results of an employee survey, feels pressure to deliver some visible responses quickly. After all, if no action is taken, employees may conclude that management does not value their feedback, with negative consequences for organizational citizenship behavior and change management, for example. The survey seems to imply a psychological contract: your feedback for our consideration and action. However, managers often do not know how to arrive at sensible actions on the basis of survey data, and so they may resort to defensive or even mock activities. Examples are delegating all further activities to lower-level management or deciding to conduct lots of workshops to clarify and discuss the findings. Executives in particular are often glad that they can free themselves with such decisions from an uneasy topic and get back to things that "count" and where they have more expertise.

Positioning the Presentation Within the Follow-Up Processes

To make the survey presentation effective, one should first position it within the follow-up processes. The flow of the follow-up processes, with its roles and deliverables, must become clear so that management understands its role in them. Textbooks often recommend beginning "at the lowest level possible" (Edwards, Thomas, Rosenfeld, & Booth-Kewley, 1997, p. 144), but this means that things must later be consolidated at higher levels, a laborious task in practice. Moreover, suggestions from below often lack a common direction, which makes it difficult to align them to generate strategic impact. Most organizations therefore proceed, implicitly or explicitly, in a top-down fashion similar to what is shown in Figure 17.1. We recommend following not only the sequence but also the contents of the various steps. For example, top management should interpret the results (with the help of survey experts) and sort the issues in terms of priorities, define certain topics that the organization must pay attention to or act on, decide on particular responses or actions to the survey results, and discuss the results with their respective direct reports.

Lower management always wants to know how higher management assessed the survey results. Implicitly, they ask for some guidance on how they should frame the data. The best way to deliver this guidance is for top management to define certain areas of focus or even fields of action. That is, higher-level management states that it expects all lower-level managers and their teams to closely study the outcomes in a few well-defined substantive domains. For ex-

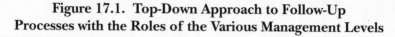

Figure 17.1. Top-Down Approach to Follow-Up Processes with the Roles of the Various Management Levels

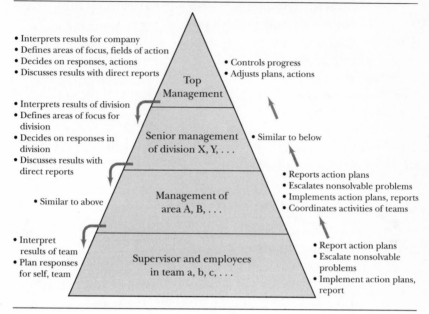

ample, the survey may have shown that the employees feel they "could be much more productive given certain changes in their work environment." Declaring this issue an area of focus legitimizes higher-level management to later ask lower-level managers what their results were, what they have done or not done on that issue, and why. A stronger form is to declare this an action field and ask all lower-level managers to design, report, and implement actions on that issue.

The usual problem with a top-down approach for the follow-up processes is that higher-level management never delivers any guiding input to lower-level management. Top management, in particular, is often slow to decide on an official interpretation of the survey results, let alone strategic guidelines in the form of areas of focus or fields of action. Executives typically first want to have a chance to study their own data in depth and then later revisit the general findings for decision making. Lower-level managers then either wait in vain for guiding input or proceed, against the rules, in a "preliminary" fashion. Consequently, the follow-up processes fall apart.

To avoid this problem, it is crucial that managers be given enough time to respond to the survey. A good approach is to assign a certain time slot to a particular management level. The next-lower management is asked to wait with follow-up activities until they get input from above or until the end of the time slot, whichever comes first. If no input has been given at the end of the time slot, they are allowed—indeed expected!—to move on with their activities. Upper management may still feed decisions into the hierarchy at a later date, even though these decisions may require some adjustments in the action plans of lower management.

Using a Wide Notion of Action

Textbooks as well as practitioners usually conceive of actions as planned patterns of activities (Edwards et al., 1997; Trost, Bungard, & Jöns, 1999; Church & Waclawski, 2001). We propose that is it is more useful to think of actions as responses to the survey—any response, from decisions to projects, from overt to covert, from individual responses to one-on-one discussions and officially communicated activity patterns. All of these responses should be systematically considered, because each can have tremendous impact on the behavior and the decisions of managers and non-managers—for example:

- Reflecting on and adjusting one's own behavior in view of the survey results
- Influencing subordinate managers directly (in one-on-one discussions or in workshops with groups of managers)
- Deciding on particular issues (including deciding not to act on an issue) and communicating these decisions
- Defining substantive areas of focus that guide further follow-up processes at lower levels of the hierarchy (possibly as task assignments)

Along with a wider notion of action, one should also adopt a wider scope on the issues that should be considered. Actions are often problem oriented, intending to solve or repair a bad state of affairs. Indeed, identifying the issues where action should be taken is often accomplished by finding the items or indexes that are a certain amount below the respective benchmark target. This may be a useful first approximation, but it may also lead to overlooking opportunities for positive improvement.

For example, employees often indicate that they have concrete ideas on how to do things more efficiently. Strong agreement could be classified as a problem, but if one actually discusses with the employees what can be done and then implements proper actions, the next survey typically shows that the endorsement of this item goes up. So there really is not a problem. Rather, employees feel encouraged to think in terms of improvements, not in terms of fixing something wrong. Hence, a "problem" may very well be low endorsement of this item in the survey. What is a problem and what is an opportunity is not that easy to say, and so a more useful approach would be to look for issues that serve as springboards for responses that promote operational and strategic goals.

Presenting a Story

Effective presentations are not simply reporting number after number. Rather, they weave the statistics into a coherent story where the various details become meaningful. To build such a story, however, is not without risk. In particular, the expert must take great care not to overinterpret the data or the statistics. We have seen presentations that use structural equation modeling, for example, to interconnect many variables in one statistical model. This is fine, but when reading the annotations, it became clear that the model was described in causal terms: if you boost variable X, then Y will go up. Yet without strong theoretical arguments, such relations are dubious foundations for powerful actions. The same is true for interpretations such as simple comparisons of the results with benchmarks that pay no attention to sampling and context. Hence, the expert should not present a full and final story but offer various approaches that support each other, build on data and theory, and invite the recipients of the presentation to become active partners in interpreting the results.

Interpretation, in any case, is going beyond the data by linking them to prior knowledge or to databases that belong to the expert but also to management. Four such approaches are particularly important in employee survey research.

Benchmarking

The typical first approach to interpretation is gauging the survey results on external benchmarks. Relevant benchmarks, of course, are difficult to obtain, and they are hardly ever representative in terms of industry, time of survey, context, or strategy. Nevertheless, some external benchmarking is always requested by management. One mostly benchmarks against averages, although one may argue that comparing with the best is more interesting (Dale, 1994). One may also benchmark against the worst or against a normal range, for example. One may even benchmark against management's own prognoses of results. And, of course, one can benchmark within the organization, comparing different organizational units among each other, or comparing the results with those from previous surveys.

The many ways to benchmark show that benchmarks need to be discussed. In one case, a manager who was naive about benchmarks remarked: "Ah, here we made the benchmark. Great!" When we explained that this meant, "Here, you are average," an intense debate was set off about whether being average is good enough, where it might indeed be good enough, and where not.

In another case, the CEO of a large company was much more goal oriented and political. He asked us, ahead of time, to use demanding benchmarks comparing against the best, because if the results of his organization looked "too good," he would have problems getting real action from his executives. Benchmarks therefore are potentially springboards for a fruitful discourse and for motivating responses. In a presentation, they should be used for a first gauging of the results, but most of all as a starting point for setting intelligent targets, not as a device that prescribes what must be done.

Substantive Theory

Presentations often remain exploratory and explain the data without noticing the speculative nature of the theorizing. The only criterion is whether the interpretation appears to make sense. A better approach is a more theory-guided analysis and interpretation of the survey data wherever possible. For example, if employees complain about insufficient feedback on their performance, if they cannot tell how well they are doing, it is clear that a central element of most motivation theories is damaged. Without proper feedback, realistic expectancies about the consequences of performance cannot develop. Learning also becomes impossible, self-efficacy beliefs cannot develop properly, and self-confidence cannot be derived from success, among other things. The many consequences of deficient feedback need not be rediscovered time and again. They are known and can be used to guide interpretation.

Figure 17.2 interconnects what is known from motivation research (Porter & Lawler, 1968; Mealiea & Latham, 1996; Muchinsky, 2002) in one comprehensive theory (which Borg, 2003, calls the satisfaction-performance motor). In practice, one can simplify this theory and show, for example, just its backbone with the effort-performance-feedback-rewards connections, although it is usually worthwhile to point out that there are several forms of performance (such as results and organizational citizenship behavior) and several forms of satisfaction (such as outcome satisfaction and system satisfaction). Managers are usually quite interested to see that psychological sciences have solid laws and well-tested theories to offer, not just simple assertions such as, "Satisfied employees lead to satisfied customers." They also see that "there is nothing more practical than a good theory" (Lewin, 1951, p. 169) when it comes to deriving what should be done.

Strategy and Scorecards

Another way of interpreting the survey data is to view them in the context of the organization's strategy. One approach in this regard is to use survey items or construct indexes that relate to the measurement fields of a balanced scorecard (BSC). Figure 17.3 illustrates the idea. In the middle column are the four measurement fields of the standard BSC (Kaplan & Norton, 1996). The left-hand side shows some typical indicators for these fields. For example, the company's financial strength is measured by cash flow, return on investment (ROI), and earnings before interest, taxes, depreciation, and amortization (EBITDA). The right-hand column shows a set of corresponding indicators from an employee survey. For example, almost all surveys contain items that ask about the employee's satisfaction with pay.

Figure 17.2. The Satisfaction-Performance Motor

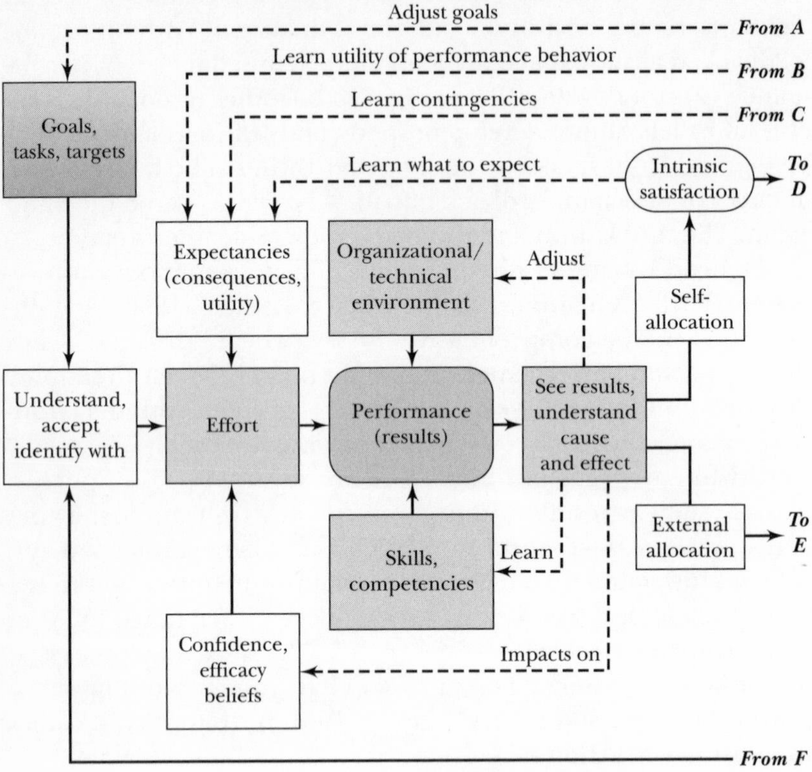

From an investor's point of view, a low score on pay satisfaction should generally be negative news for the financial strength of the company, because it suggests that the company's earnings are threatened by the employees asking for more money. (Exceptionally high pay satisfaction would be equally dubious from the investor's perspective.) If the employees indicate that they are used to assessing all their activities and decisions in terms of business costs and business benefits, then we have a positive indicator for financial strength. The BSC is a useful vehicle for linking hard and soft indicators. Soft indicators, moreover, point more strongly toward the future. Once presented in such a way, managers are quick to realize this and then view the survey results with considerable interest.

Figure 17.2. The Satisfaction-Performance Motor, Cont'd

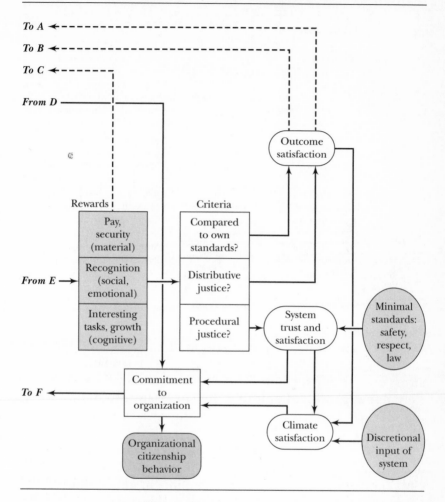

Structure and Dependencies

One can easily get lost in the data that result from an employee survey. Theory is one way to structure the data. Multivariate statistics is another one. A particularly useful technique is multidimensional scaling (MDS; see Borg & Groenen, 2005), because it often leads to simple maps that can be further explored by eye. Figure 17.4 shows an example that exhibits the intercorrelations of twenty-seven items and indexes from an employee survey in a high-tech

Figure 17.3. Two Sides of the Balanced Scorecard

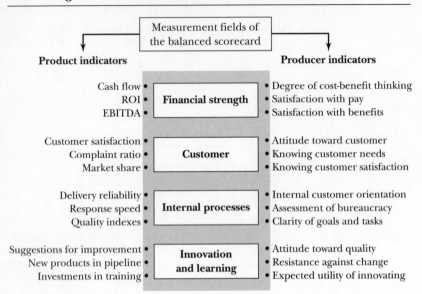

	Measurement fields of the balanced scorecard	
Product indicators		**Producer indicators**
Cash flow • ROI • EBITDA •	**Financial strength**	• Degree of cost-benefit thinking • Satisfaction with pay • Satisfaction with benefits
Customer satisfaction • Complaint ratio • Market share •	**Customer**	• Attitude toward customer • Knowing customer needs • Knowing customer satisfaction
Delivery reliability • Response speed • Quality indexes •	**Internal processes**	• Internal customer orientation • Assessment of bureaucracy • Clarity of goals and tasks
Suggestions for improvement • New products in pipeline • Investments in training •	**Innovation and learning**	• Attitude toward quality • Resistance against change • Expected utility of innovating

company. The plot is a simplification of an MDS configuration with fifty-five variables, representing 1,485 correlations with a stress of .19, an excellent fit to the data. Since all correlations were nonnegative, it holds that the closer any two points are in the MDS configuration, the higher the correlation of the variables they represent.

The white regions are derived from theoretical considerations about domains of job satisfaction. The point with concentric circles represents an organizational commitment index, a variable of particular importance for management in this company. Managers quickly learn how to interpret such a plot (but need guidance to avoid lavish causal interpretations). For example, in Figure 17.4, one easily notes what goes with commitment and what not, and this stimulates ideas about what can be done to boost commitment.

Adding Punch to the Presentation

The considerations already noted lead to solid presentations and interpretations within a transparent process framework that shows

Figure 17.4. MDS Representation of Twenty-Seven Items from an Employee Survey at an International IT Company

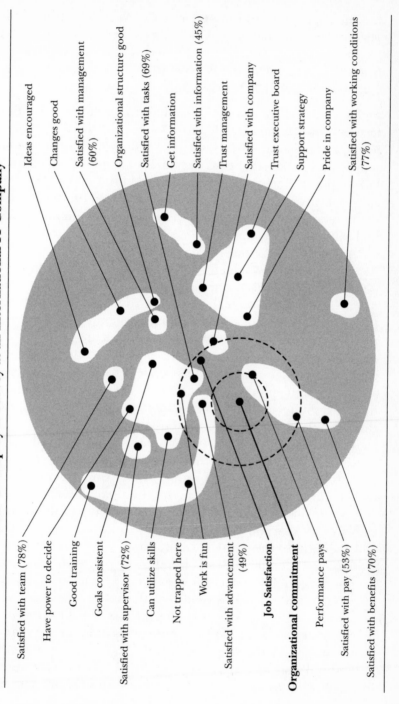

how management can respond and act. We now discuss a number of considerations that help to motivate managers to actually do that.

Showing the Variance Below the Surface of Central Tendencies

One recipe that always works is to show the variance below the surface of central tendencies. Figure 17.5 displays this not in the usual form of a statistical index value or a histogram, but in a plot that represents each of seventy-six organizational units in company ABC by one point. The points are not labeled here to protect the managers' anonymity. The work groups are sorted on the abscissa by the percentage that their employees endorse the item, "I am satisfied with my direct supervisor."

A display like the one in Figure 17.5 immediately leads to questions such as these: "Which team is this here at the bottom? Who is the manager of this team? Should I fire him or her?" Then some discussion sets in about the teams with the 100 percent scores ("Too high?"), and often even about the context of these results ("How comparable is this? What other data are there?"). In any case, the plot makes the managers eager to get their own reports to check how their respective teams rated their supervisors or managers. Thus, the plot motivates them to act and discuss these findings with the respective subordinate managers. The survey expert then should show how such discussions can be conducted efficiently and effectively and what mistakes should be avoided (Borg, 2003). The best approach to act on these results, in our experience, is for the manager to conduct one-on-one dialogues with his or her subordinate managers about the survey results of their respective teams. If such dialogues start at the top of the hierarchy, they usually cascade down all the way to work group managers, which energizes the entire organization.

Figure 17.5 illustrates a general principle: averages are often boring; analyzing the data for variance and comparing teams are exciting. Yet comparisons yield sensitive information and should be handled with care. The guiding principle is that the responsible manager should be present when it comes to his or her team and should be given a chance to explain the context of the data. He or she should also see the results for the unit before the superior manager does to have a chance to digest this report. Otherwise

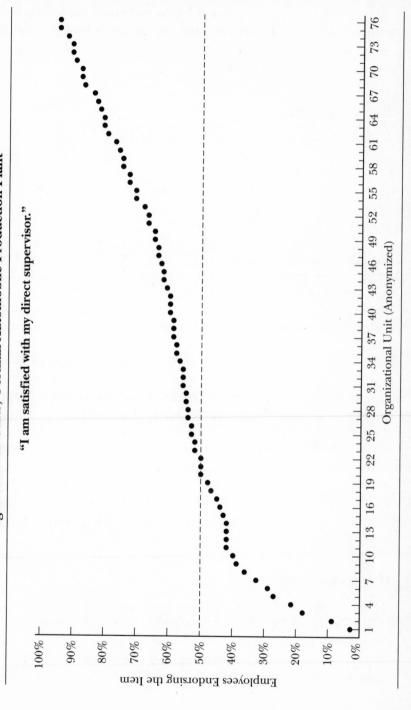

Figure 17.5. Percentage Satisfied with Supervisor for Seventy-Six Organizational Units, German Automobile Production Plant

"I am satisfied with my direct supervisor."

comparisons can easily lead to defensive behavior and to bitterness ("unfair") that stalemates all further processes. If these conditions are not satisfied, then comparisons should be made without identifying the units (as in Figure 17.5).

Showing Examples

A similarly powerful element in a management presentation is to show at least one example that relates survey results to hard business data. For example, in one production site, we had access to the sickness rates of some 180 work groups. We then correlated these rates, item by item, with the average item ratings of the employees in each work group to find the items that best "predicted" sickness. It was found that items that described to what extent the work itself was enjoyable were the best predictors (with correlations up to –0.50), confirming what is known from the literature (Johns, 1994). We demonstrated on the scatter plot and its regression line that if one interprets the statistical relation causally, boosting satisfaction with work itself by 20 percent over all work groups would reduce sickness rates by 3.4 days on the average. Such relationships can be made even more impressive if they are formulated in terms of dollars (known as behavioral accounting; Cascio, 1999). As one manager remarked: "This is when I realized that soft is hard!" He also knew what to do: go to the various teams, find out what they did in the high and low teams, and then act on what he had learned.

To find hard data that can be used to demonstrate such relationships is typically not easy, because survey data cannot be broken down to the individual level and because performance data are rarely available for smaller teams. However, it usually suffices to demonstrate the soft-hard relations with just one example to convince management that the survey data are serious information.

Using Prognoses

A third recipe to generate punch is using prognoses. We always ask top managers before the survey to predict the results of the survey for some important items ("At what percentage level will the employees in your organizational unit endorse this item?"). We later compare these predictions with the actual results. Typically some of the predictions are quite off the mark, and this leads to discussions and, thus, involvement. But even if the predictions are more or less accurate, their scatter is always substantial, and this finding usually makes an even bigger impression on managers.

The main purpose of predictions is that they reduce the "problem of obviousness" (Lazarsfeld, 1949). Survey findings typically appear trivial; the recipients believe "I knew it all along," a problem closely related to a common cognitive fallacy: the hindsight bias (Fischoff, 1977). Borg and Hillenbrand (2003) have shown experimentally that making predictions—or, indeed, just seeing the predictions of other persons—has the effect that survey results appear more interesting and less obvious. They are also better remembered by those who make predictions.

Confronting Management with Results They Can Influence

Another motivator in survey presentations is to confront management with some of their own results. As an example, see Figure 17.6, which shows the results for two items, broken down over different levels of the hierarchy. Almost all employees, on all levels, agreed that they personally do everything that is possible for the customer. The assessments of the company's behavior in this regard are much less positive—even for top management. When this findings was presented to management, the question came up, "Who is the company?" This led to intense discussions. In the end, it was concluded that the root problem was poor cooperation among teams and functions. This conclusion was corroborated by other survey items that directly assessed cooperation. The motivator here was to show management a disturbing finding where they noticed, "This is us! This is what we said!" and one that shook complacency (such as the proverbial, "It's all middle management's fault").

Avoid Wasting Time on Side Issues

The time allotted to a survey presentation is always too short. Yet a long presentation would not necessarily be more effective either. The solution is focusing. The presenter must avoid getting sidetracked with marginal issues. A typical time waster is the return rate

Figure 17.6. Endorsement of Two Survey Items by Managers of Different Hierarchical Levels and by Nonmanagers, Respectively, German Logistics Group

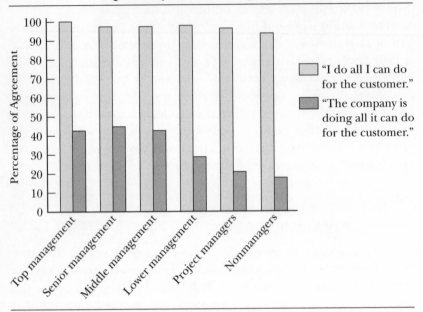

of the survey. If return rates are low, they always lead to the question whether the results are biased. Comparing the sample's demographics with the demographics of the population partially answers the question. Yet what one really wants to know is whether respondents and nonrespondents differ in their attitudes and opinions. Research shows (Rogelberg et al., 2003) that most nonrespondents are simply too passive to participate, but do not differ in the attitudes and opinions assessed in the survey (not even in organizational commitment). Only some 15 percent of the nonrespondents are purposeful ("active") nonrespondents. And only they differ somewhat from respondents (their attitudes are slightly more negative, and they are slightly less conscientious, for example). Also, early respondents do not differ from later respondents (Borg & Tuten, 2003). Since later respondents are almost nonrespondents, this too indicates that biases, if they exist, are likely to be small.

Item nonresponse is a related problem. Indeed, employees who skip some of the demographic items in a mail survey assess their supervisors more negatively, for example (Borg, 1991). Yet although the differences are significant, they are also small. Item nonresponse in content items shows no systematic relation to other content items (Borg & Treder, 2003). Thus, from what we currently know, the bias induced by nonresponse is not large enough to warrant lengthy discussions.

There is also no simple interpretation of the return rate. To see this, consider two opposing interpretations from one company. The CEO took a low response rate as a sign that the employees are highly satisfied ("There was no reason for them to participate"), while the works council concluded just the opposite ("Voting by refusing to vote"). It should suffice to point out such findings, and then proceed with the presentation, concentrating on the data one has, not speculating on the meaning of data one does not have.

Comparing return rates across organizational units is not that simple either. What must be taken into account are the mode of the survey (different modes such as a mail survey sent to the employee's home address versus a survey administered in a group session have different typical response rates; Borg, 2003; Borg & Faulbaum, 2004), the type of employees (blue or white collar, education, gender, country, tenure), but also technical matters such as correcting for net return rates or psychological factors such as the respondents' experience with previous surveys or their personalities (Dillman, 2000).

Another element that tends to consume too much time in a survey presentation is benchmarking. Initially benchmarks are often interpreted rather naively. First, there are many types of benchmarks (averages, top scores, averages of best-of-class scores, thresholds, minimal values, and others). Second, what matters a lot are the samples on which these values are based (what companies, which industries, what countries, when surveyed). Benchmarks in organizational surveys are never representative in a survey sampling sense, even if based on very large samples. Once such issues are pointed out to management, benchmarks are typically taken for what they are worth: they yield a first and simple way to approach data interpretation.

Overcoming Typical Psychological Barriers

Few managers are experts on psychology. It is normal during presentations that they pull all kinds of counterarguments that challenge the results and their interpretation, in particular if the results are "negative." If the expert does not succeed in answering them well, the presentation will have no effect. Here are some common examples, together with generic answers:

- *Argument:* "What the employees said is objectively wrong!" (or: "The employees do not know what really counts."). *Answer:* "Maybe so, but perception is reality. Survey data allow one to reliably predict what people actually do. Also, if the employees do not understand, you may have to do a better job explaining things."
- *Argument:* "The employees did not understand the items!" *Answer:* "They did. We tested that." (We hope you did a pretest and documented its results.)
- *Argument:* "The employees did not take the survey seriously. They randomly checked the answer boxes." *Answer:* "Not likely. The data interlock systematically. [See an MDS plot like the one in Figure 17.5.] Random data show no such structures."
- *Argument:* "Trivial. I could have told you this in advance." *Answer:* "Not likely. The typical hindsight bias. We can compare your predictions with the results." [We hope you collected predictions. If not, let them predict some results on the spot.] And besides, even if your predictions are correct, they were just hypotheses. Now you know."
- *Argument:* "More analysis is needed!" *Answer:* "Do not fall into the paralysis-through-analysis trap. We have seen this often in practice: The main issues are usually clear, and more and more analyses do not change the picture." But also show some typical data breakdowns ahead of time, such as men versus women, tenure groups, or functions. This information is useful to know for managers to avoid simplistic comparisons.
- *Argument:* "There is nothing we can do. It's the circumstances, the market, and other things beyond our control." *Answer:* "It is important to see the whole picture, but it is hardly ever true that management cannot do anything."

- *Argument:* "The employees' responses are extra negative on purpose, so that we give them what they really want: More money." *Answer:* "Survey responses predict future behavior. They are usually quite consistent, fit into a theory [as shown in Figure 17.2] with many variables and dependencies. Material rewards are just one element in this system, and the amount of pay is only one aspect of how material rewards are assessed. Perceived fairness, for example, is at least as important. Also, what often happens is that employees *think* that other companies pay more, even though that is not true. If so, HR management has to make this more transparent."

- *Argument:* "I'd like to know who said that! Can you identify these persons?" *Answer:* "We just focus on trends, not on single individuals. A few outliers do not affect the trends very much. Also, remember that we guaranteed to treat the data confidentially. All statistics are based on at least N persons."

- *Argument:* "It is all so terrible. I am deeply depressed." *Answer:* "Do not get stuck in depression. Focus on what you can do. The employees are less interested in your feelings than in your actions."

- *Argument:* "There is an error in your Table X. How can we know that there are not more errors? Come back some other time with a more professional analysis!" *Answer:* "Attacking the messenger is no solution. We checked everything, but the presentation slides are made by hand, and so minor errors may occur. The computer-generated reports are 100 percent error free." We recommend that you check and double-check everything. Even minor formatting or spelling errors can massively damage the effect of the presentation. What counts, in the end, is your credibility and your track record with the company. If they are good, minor errors become exceptions of no significance.

The Role of Recommendations for Actions

Survey presentations always implicitly suggest or discourage certain fields of action by way of the analyses, the interpretations, and the theorizing that they make or that they do not make, respectively. The most obvious such approach is to classify certain issues in a good-to-poor fashion by relating the survey results to certain internal or external benchmarks. Being more than a certain predefined amount below the norm indicates a need for action. But should one also make an explicit suggestion on what to do?

Explicit recommendations in this regard are sometimes requested by management. In the simplest form, they come at the end of the presentation: "What would you recommend doing?" The expert should be prepared to answer this request. In our experience, what works best is to present something rather informally, possibly on a flip chart rather than with overly sleek PowerPoint slides, so that it leaves much room for discussion.

When asked ahead of time to conclude the presentation with recommendations, the expert should be cautious. He or she is not a manager, and recommendations should promote specific operational and strategic goals that are, in the end, known to the managers only. To reduce the risk of recommending something that is not fitting, the expert should discuss his or her recommendations with the CEO, the survey sponsor, or the HR director before presenting them to the entire management group. The recommendations can thus be made more differentiated, possibly supported with more data analysis, and better linked to the particular business objectives. But then the recommendations become, at least in part, the recommendations of the respective managers, and it would be proper for the expert only to present the analyses and then hand over the discussion to these managers. It is quite risky for the expert to present these recommendations as his or her own conclusions because they never follow directly from the survey results.

What the expert can do, though, is to support management in arriving at meaningful decisions. First, the expert should always attempt to identify issues that promise to yield real effects if acted on. Second, what is most useful and stimulating in presentations to managers at all levels is to point to what others (other companies, other plants, other managers) have done when they encountered similar situations, if possible. Such cases always lead to a more concrete discussion. Managers check whether the reported solution is applicable for them too, or how it could be fitted into their context. Or they find reasons that this solution does not work for them, but this too helps them to focus on proper actions. Third, one recommendation that the survey expert can always make is on the process that should be used to review and digest the data and turn them into actions. If the presentation has been introduced in the context of systematic follow-up processes, closure can be achieved by returning the audience to specific recommendations that address how important findings can be highlighted in staging the management response.

Conclusion

Presentations of survey results can be quite boring, reporting one percentage value after another. They can also be a firework of gimmickry, showing impressive statistical modeling in animated multimedia displays. In both cases, little is typically accomplished in terms of enabling and motivating management to set up a set of effective responses to the survey. We have described a few rules that have been developed and tested successfully in numerous presentations. What is important is to:

- Clarify management's roles within the follow-up processes and give them the time to influence all further activities with proper decisions and actions.
- Present the survey results using multiple approaches to data interpretation, and invite management to participate in this interpretation to identify opportunities for responses that serve their goals.
- Add punch to the presentation by showing variance, reducing the impression of obviousness, shaking management's complacency with some of their own survey results, or showing some cases that link the survey results to hard data.
- Minimize speculations about nonrespondents and discussions about benchmarks.
- Support management in defining actions, for example, by referring to what others have done in similar situations.

In an effort to motivate management to do something with the survey data, one must also take care not to overinterpret the data in statistical models that are fitted to the data with many free parameters. Substantive know-how is essential, and any survey story should be supported by scientific theory.

References

Borg, I. (1991). Sind Personen, die sich in Umfragen nicht identifizierbar machen, besonders kritisch? [Do persons who make themselves unidentifiable respond more negatively to survey items?]. *Zeitschrift für Sozialpsychologie, 22,* 123–129.

Borg, I. (2003). *Führungsinstrument Mitarbeiterbefragung.* [Employee surveys in management]. Göttingen, Germany: Hogrefe.

Borg, I., & Faulbaum, F. (2004, Apr.). *Comparing four modes of administering an employee survey.* Paper presented at the Sixth International German Online Research Congress, Duisburg, Germany.

Borg, I., & Groenen, P. (2005). *Modern multidimensional scaling* (2nd edition). New York: Springer.

Borg, I., & Hillenbrand, C. (2003). Prognosen als Methode zur Reduktion der Offensichtlichkeit von Umfragebefunden: Ein Pilotexperiment. [Using prognoses to reduce the apparent obviousness of survey results: A pilot experiment]. *ZUMA Nachrichten, 52,* 7–13.

Borg, I., & Treder, C. (2003). Item-nonresponse in Mitarbeiterbefragungen. [Item nonresponse in employee surveys]. *ZUMA Nachrichten, 53,* 77–95.

Borg, I., & Tuten, T. (2003). Early versus later respondents in intranet-based, organizational surveys. *Journal of Behavioral and Applied Management, 4*(1), 134–147.

Bungard, W., & Jöns, I. (Eds.). (1997). *Mitarbeiterbefragung: Ein Instrument des Innovations- und Qualitätsmanagements.* [Employee surveys: An instrument of innovation and quality management]. Weinheim, Germany: Beltz.

Cascio, W. F. (1999). *Costing human resources: The financial impact of behavior in organizations.* Boston: Kent.

Church, A. H., & Waclawski, J. (2001). *Designing and using organizational surveys: A seven step approach.* San Francisco: Jossey-Bass.

Dale, B. G. (Ed.). (1994), *Managing quality.* Upper Saddle River, NJ: Prentice Hall.

Dillman, D. A. (2000). *Mail and Internet surveys: The tailored design method.* New York: Wiley.

Edwards, J. E., Thomas, M. D., Rosenfeld, P., & Booth-Kewley, S. (1997). *How to conduct organizational surveys.* Thousand Oaks, CA: Sage.

Fischoff, B. (1977). Perceived informativeness of facts. *Journal of Experimental Psychology: Human Perception and Performance, 3,* 349–358.

Johns, G. (1994). How often were you absent? A review of the use of self-reported absence data. *Journal of Applied Psychology, 79,* 574–591.

Kaplan, R. S., & Norton, D. P. (1996). *The balanced scorecard.* Boston: Harvard Business School Press.

Lazarsfeld, P. F. (1949). The American soldier—an expository review. *Public Opinion Quarterly, 13,* 377–404.

Lewin, K. (1951). *Field theory in social science: Selected theoretical papers* (D. Cartwright, Ed.). New York: HarperCollins.

Mealiea, L. W., & Latham, G. P. (1996). *Skills for managerial success.* Chicago: Irwin.

Muchinsky, P. M. (2002). *Psychology applied to work: An introduction to industrial and organizational psychology.* Belmont, CA: Wadsworth.

Porter, L. W., & Lawler, E. E. III (1968). *Managerial attitudes and performance.* Homewood, IL: Irwin.

Rogelberg, S. G., Conway, J. M., Sederburg, M. E., Spitzmüller, C., Aziz, S., & Knight, W. E. (2003). Profiling active and passive nonrespondents to an organizational survey. *Journal of Applied Psychology, 88,* 1104–1114.

Trost, A., Bungard, W., & Jöns, I. (1999). *Mitarbeiterbefragung.* [Employee surveys]. Augsburg, Germany: Weka Verlag.

New Applications

Part Three covers a variety of new applications in which surveys play an exciting and important role: managing mergers and acquisitions, dealing with turnover, coping with the special needs of complex, global organizations, and helping to drive change and organizational effectiveness.

Mitchell Lee Marks and Daniel Baitch describe in Chapter Eighteen how surveys can assess and guide the progress of mergers and acquisitions. They lay out the techniques that can lead to success or failure in doing surveys on such sensitive, high-profile topics. Specific measurement issues are illustrated with case examples and sample questions.

Michelle A. Donovan and Scott M. Brooks take a fresh look in Chapter Nineteen at the perennial problem of employee turnover and retention. They show different methods to diagnose the underlying problems that lead to turnover and offer ideas on how to truly understand and get action on the relevant survey data.

John C. Scott and Paul M. Mastrangelo write on the special challenges for complex and global organizations that use surveys to gauge employee attitudes and use the data to achieve strategic objectives. They show in Chapter Twenty how global firms must take account of cultural and local factors when doing surveys and dealing with the results.

Robert J. Quinn describes in Chapter Twenty-One an extraordinary case where employee surveys, over several years, became the cornerstone of a huge cultural change in a financial organization. Using a systemwide approach, key middle managers were designated to communicate and foster a culture of inclusion. Surveys stimulated and showed that these actions, bolstered by a consistent reward system, had a strong positive effect.

Sharon F. Parker, Michael J. Schroeder, J. Thomas Bowler, Jr., and Patricia L. Muldoon recount in Chapter Twenty-Two the use of an organization survey as a vital part of an organization's revitalization while it coped with major stress and change. They recount the tools and strategies used to improve employees' morale and engagement and the favorable effect on the firm's effectiveness.

Norman D. Costa and Peter Bachiochi review in Chapter Twenty-Three the issue of "best company" lists. They look at who compiles these lists, and the role that survey data play in getting on them. Many firms covet the prestige conferred by these lists, but the processes used to create the lists raise several issues about their objectivity and meaning.

Tracey Carsten Roll tells a personal story in Chapter Twenty-Four of her attempt, as a relative newcomer to surveys, to improve organizational effectiveness in one firm. Despite a well-prepared survey and a strong conceptual model, her efforts languish until a new executive champion comes along. Then the combination of good survey tools and strong executive support creates a year-round dialogue for organizational improvement.

CHAPTER 18

Measuring Employee Opinions During Mergers and Acquisitions

Mitchell Lee Marks
Daniel Baitch

Mergers and acquisitions (M&A) have become entrenched in the repertoire of contemporary business executives. M&A has the potential to accelerate the execution of business strategy by rapidly helping a firm expand its product or service mix, move into new regional or international markets, capture new customers, or even eliminate a competitor.

Although the terms *merger* and *acquisition* often are used interchangeably, they actually are two distinct events. A merger is the integration of two previously separate entities into one new organization, while an acquisition is the taking over and subsequent integration of one firm into another. Of course, there are various shades of gray here; there are very few mergers of equals, and a lead firm may adopt key components of the acquired target. We will use the terms *M&A* or *combination* to represent the full range of mergers and acquisitions.

Despite their popularity, the reality is that 75 percent of all mergers and acquisitions fail to achieve their strategic or financial objectives (Bruner, 2002). Many reasons have been suggested for this dismal track record, including buying the wrong company, paying the wrong price, or making the deal at the wrong time. However, research findings repeatedly reveal that the factor that matters most in eventual merger or acquisition success is the process through which the partner companies are integrated (Stahl & Mendenhall, 2005; Schweiger & Goulet, 2000).

Integrating organizations in a productive manner requires the collection, interpretation, and use of valid information. This information helps leaders in ways such as translating theorized synergies into real gains, recognizing and dealing with unintended consequences spawned by well-intentioned actions, and capitalizing on various approaches to managing the transitions. In this chapter, we describe how employee surveys can play a role in informing the executives and managers who plan and implement mergers and acquisitions. We begin by examining the dynamics of M&A that make these events far more difficult to manage than other forms of organizational change. We then discuss the benefits of using employee surveys to guide the successful integration of organizations and share some of the lessons we have learned regarding how to successfully achieve those benefits. We conclude with a case example of a survey process in a major financial services acquisition.

The Difficulties of Merging or Acquiring

The very ways in which mergers and acquisitions are executed make these events difficult to manage (Marks & Mirvis, 1998). To begin, deals must be shrouded in secrecy. For legal and competitive reasons, executives cannot openly discuss their M&A intentions. This obviously impairs efforts to communicate a deal's purpose or implications to employees. In addition, most buyers do not really know what they have acquired until after a deal is done. The "diligence" in due diligence is lacking in many cases (Cartwright & Cooper, 2000). So executives cannot discuss their vision for the new company or offer a road map for the integration until after legal closure and they have had some time to collect and digest reams of additional information. And it is very difficult to "drive in two lanes at one time": especially in this era of downsized corporations, there is not much bench strength for senior executives to call on to properly manage the competing demands of running regular business operations while managing a complicated transition like a merger or acquisition (Marks, 2003). As a result, something has to fall through the cracks, and typically it is careful management of M&A.

Unintended Impact on Individuals

These characteristics of practically every merger or acquisition accentuate the need to gain insight about what is being integrated and how the process is proceeding, especially from an employee perspective. However, the experience of living through a merger or acquisition produces a set of responses that interfere with the articulation and assessment of employee viewpoints. Importantly, these responses are exhibited throughout the workforce, even in work areas that seemingly are unaffected by the integration (Marks & Mirvis, 1985).

There is always a groundswell of anxiety and confusion in the early stages of a merger or acquisition. People focus on the potential downside costs rather than the upside benefits. With rumors swirling around the workforce, they worry about what they might lose as a result of the transition: employment, security, organizational identity, career opportunities, rewards, status, informal perks, relationships with superiors and coworkers, and so on.

People predictably settle into a defensive self-protection mindset, consumed with concerns about security. They crave information about the impact of the merger or acquisition on their workplace ("Will we be shut down?"), their careers ("Will my new boss know my track record?"), and their culture ("Will the new firm be committed to diversity?"). Despite their managers' attempts to keep them informed, answers to many of employees' questions come too slowly. And when answers are forthcoming, they tend to be incomplete and spawn even more questions. As a result, morale and commitment decline while frustration and anxiety rise (Marks & DeMeuse, 2002). Employees who deny their vulnerability in a merger or acquisition are just that—in denial.

Unintended Impact on Work Groups

At the work group level, M&A can have a dramatic impact (Mirvis & Marks, 1986). Integration activities suddenly get imposed on top of regular job responsibilities, throwing priorities into disarray and causing confusion about what work should be delayed or even discontinued. Simple, everyday processes can become more arduous compared to prior to the integration. A lack of role clarity hinders people's ability to get work done in a timely manner, especially when they are not sure to whom to turn with their requests and needs for resources to get the job done. And decision making can become excessively bureaucratic as people from both partners need to be involved.

As layoffs, reassignments, and voluntary turnover occur, work groups are suddenly charged with maintaining output with fewer resources. Groups can slip into a reactive, management-by-crisis mode as deadlines become more difficult to meet. Critical management processes—like performance reviews, coaching, project planning, goal setting, and feedback—often fall by the wayside. In addition to adding to the critical mass of uncertainty, this blocks important channels of two-way communication between superiors and subordinates.

The Communication Imperative

Amid all the real and perceived threats to their work situation, employees watch carefully for cues that the merger or acquisition is being well managed and that care is being taken to treat people in a respectful manner. Often, however, what they find are signs that leadership is not being responsive, that superiors are not providing sufficient direction, and that the integration is veering off course. Even when leadership has done a good job of communicating, the high degree of stress and uncertainty, exacerbated by the many rumors and worst-case scenarios engulfing the workplace, interfere with employees' ability to accurately hear the messages being sent (Schweiger & DeNisi, 1991).

Upward communication from employees to top management is as crucial as downward communication in M&A. Since people respond to mergers and acquisitions in differing ways, leadership needs an accurate mechanism for understanding how key messages are being received and for tracking the impact of the event on organizational effectiveness. This is important not only for employee well-being and work team performance, but also for customer interactions. Customers have their antennas up during integration (Bastien & Hostager, 2002). Many turn to their employee contacts to make sense of the event and develop a sense of what the short-term consequences and long-term implications may be. Some customers, especially those who experienced poor service levels in previous mergers or acquisitions, will be ready to bolt at the first sign of inattentiveness. Leadership needs to know not only if employees have heard merger-related messages, but also how employees are conveying them to those outside the company.

The high level of stress that accompanies M&A impairs perception and judgment. Although a moderate amount of stress increases people's vigilance in gathering information, a high level leads many to simplify and distort what they hear (Lazarus & Folkman, 1985). Even among the best listeners, there can be information overload. As a result, important information is often overlooked or misinterpreted.

Why Conduct Employee Opinion Surveys During M&A?

The purpose of conducting employee surveys during a merger or acquisition is to assess how the merger or acquisition is progressing: Do people understand why the event is occurring? Do they support the changes? What are early impressions of the combined organization? How is implementation proceeding, and what could be done to improve it? How are people coping with uncertainty and stress? Is commitment to the new organization developing?

Knowing What Is Going On

Integrating successfully benefits not just from skilled management but also from informed management. M&A has the potential to affect employee morale and productivity, work processes and quality, group and intergroup relations, customer service and satisfaction, and practically every other aspect of organizational life. Thus, it is helpful to monitor the impact of the transition and the effectiveness of the integration process. Valid information also directs attention and resources to the issues that matter most in eventual integration success.

Of course, managers frequently think they know what is going well and what is not. But when they consult exclusively with their peers and direct reports, which typically is all they have time for when confronted with the simultaneous tasks of running the business and managing the transition, what managers hear is often censored and self-serving. This gives them a distorted picture of progress and false assurance that problems will pass so long as they stay the course. Months later, the picture is clearer: transition trauma hits the bottom line, and executives have no recourse but to shift into damage control mode.

Benefits of Using Surveys in Mergers and Acquisitions

Choosing to be proactive in managing a merger or acquisition, executives in several organizations we have worked with have benefited in many ways from using employee surveys:

- *Determining if the integration is proceeding according to plan or veering off course.* The survey process provides decision makers with feedback on how the transition is affecting people and the business. In one high-tech acquisition, questionnaire results revealed that unclear work charters, timetables, and financial targets were preventing integration planning task forces from coming to decisions about the design of the combined organization. When briefed on the survey findings, the CEO met with each task force to clarify its situation.
- *Identifying hot spots before they flare out of control.* In an acquired manufacturing firm, the secrecy of precombination negotiations created an air of distrust between employees and management. An employee survey conducted a few months following the acquisition showed morale eroding among production workers. Attributing this to postmerger stress, management initially downplayed the data. However, when follow-up interviews showed that employees felt neglected by management and were agitating for union representation, senior management moved swiftly to open communication channels and respond to aggrieved employees.
- *Ensuring a good flow of upward communication.* Bad news does not easily rise to the top of the organization in a merger or acquisition. A formal survey process gives employees the chance to communicate to upper management and provides a mechanism for top echelons to hear from those closest to the action. Often managers are dismayed to learn of the discrepancy between actions and words. In one case, for example, management of two combining

sales forces ballyhooed the benefits of cross-selling each other's products. Salespeople were eager but had no updated sales literature, no demos, and no idea what to charge customers or when products could be delivered. Busy with all the red tape involved in processing employee transfers, setting up office space, and servicing existing orders, sales managers downplayed these complaints. Once senior management learned of these problems through survey results, however, they barged through the bureaucracy, and sales aids soon flowed to the branches.

• *Demonstrating interest in the human side of change.* The survey process has tremendous symbolic value, demonstrating that management is interested in the human dimensions of the transition. The acquisition of one publisher by another was held up for several months by lawsuits blocking the deal. Senior leaders truly had little news to convey to employees during this extended period, yet commissioned an employee survey both to generate data to discuss and show that they had not lost sight of the plight of employees.

• *Sending a message about the postcombination culture.* How the merger or acquisition is managed starts to define the new organizational culture. A formal survey process signals the importance of two-way communication and conveys management's genuine interest in people's problems and perspectives. By comparison, the absence of any formal feedback channels can imply that leadership does not care about what people think or feel now during the transition and later in the combined organization.

Resistance to Using Surveys in Mergers and Acquisitions

Despite the many benefits of conducting employee surveys during a merger or acquisition, there always will be some resistance. Early in the process, managers fret that nothing positive has happened yet, so employees will cite the downside only if asked their views. As integration planning begins in earnest, managers object on the grounds that the time taken to collect, analyze, feed back, and work with data detracts from attending to business opportunities. And as planning gives way to implementation, some managers argue it is "too late" to assess employees' attitudes since the event is almost "over," while other managers assert it is still "too soon," claiming that their organization and people have not yet settled into a normal routine. These arguments have some validity: there is no ideal time to conduct an employee survey during a merger or acquisition. However, this is not an excuse for putting off a survey effort.

Managers' resistance clearly may be motivated by fear of being assessed or by negative recollections of poorly managed employee research efforts in past mergers or acquisitions. It is important, then, that a developmental tone is established. The data are being collected to understand and focus on key issues influencing integration success, not to be used as a scorecard for sizing up individuals.

Success Factors for Employee Surveys During M&A

Given the sensitivity that naturally surrounds mergers and acquisitions, it is important to clear a path for the survey process to increase the likelihood that results are actually used. Often the decision regarding whether to conduct a survey during integration becomes a political football. One precombination organization may have a history of using employee surveys, while the other does not; executives from one side may support it, while those from the other side actively oppose it or even passively sabotage its effectiveness.

Measurement of employee views must be conveyed as a core component of the integration process. A few key actions can greatly enhance leadership's—and the rest of the organization's—acceptance of the survey process.

To begin, identify an appropriate sponsor who can build a base of support for the survey process and can allocate the necessary resources. This is typically the CEO, but may also be the head of a business unit to which an acquisition is reporting or the head of the transition team. If the CEO or leadership team of the combined organization cannot or will not act as the sponsor, then it is better not to conduct a companywide effort and instead look for a business unit leader or department head who would like to conduct a survey in their part of the organization.

Next, convene a measurement team to oversee the development and use of the survey. The team should include members from both organizations and include business leaders to demonstrate the organization's seriousness about doing a survey, along with technical specialists to aid in the implementation. In one recent acquisition in the telecommunication industry, the measurement team included the chief operating officer and a business unit president from the lead organization, the head of HR and senior marketing executive from the acquired entity, and two HR generalists with solid quantitative skills.

Then make a strong business case for conducting a survey during the integration. Much like groupthink, momentum builds in the boardrooms of acquiring organizations for doing a deal. Making the deal work, however, is another matter. Someone has to step up and educate executives—and the overall workforce—on the realities of a 75 percent failure rate. Making a clear and compelling business case that links measurement with eventual M&A success is essential for generating support for the process. Tracking the integration process with measures like employee surveys increases success rates by providing timely feedback on how things are going and increases the likelihood of making needed midcourse corrections. Measurement also helps get matters like culture clash, frequently undermanaged in combinations, into the discussions and deliberations of executives, managers, and employees.

The partner organizations may have sharply different experiences with and approaches to employee research. Set ground rules for the survey process up front. Establish specific goals for measurement, and get all involved agreeing on how the results will be communicated and used.

Finally, communicate obsessively. The need to overcommunicate in mergers and acquisitions is a given. Still, most executive teams bemoan that "there is nothing new to say," and employees seem to have an insatiable appetite for news. A survey provides multiple opportunities for executives, managers, and supervisors to communicate with their people. In particular, feedback meetings can go beyond just presenting results and engage employees in exploring and discussing the "why" underlying the survey results. Follow-up actions that may be spawned by the survey provide even more content for communication through multiple channels.

What to Look For

Employee surveys during the integration process diagnose both what is going on and how people feel. They also measure the impact of the transition on morale and expectations for the emerging organization. Our experience is that effective survey programs zero in on the specific dynamics in each phase of a deal.

The precombination phase is the period between the announcement of the intent to merge or acquire and the actual legal closing of the deal (often referred to as "Day One"). During this phase, there is a near-tunnel vision on the financial aspects of the deal and little attention to operational detail. At this early phase, employee measurement assesses the extent to which people understand the purpose and promise of the merger or acquisition, as well as initial impressions of its impact:

- Is the rationale underlying the deal clear?
- What business benefits and costs are anticipated?
- What personal benefits and costs are anticipated?
- How are morale and productivity being affected?
- Do people feel well informed?
- Does the full management team appear in sync regarding the deal?
- Are managers taking steps to minimize negative reactions and build positive impressions?
- What early impressions are being formed of the partners' ways of doing things?

The combination phase commences with the legal approval of the deal. In this phase, integration planning begins in earnest. Here, measurement focuses on the quality of integration decision making:

- Are integration planning teams being pushed for the best possible solutions?
- Are new and better ways of doing things being considered, or are the old ways being carried forward?
- To what extent are politics and favoritism influencing the decision-making process?

- Do people outside the planning process feel well informed?
- To what extent are staffing decisions based on valid criteria?
- To what extent is a truly better organization emerging?

Finally, as planning gives way to implementation, the post-combination phase is entered. Here, the dust begins to settle on the combined organization, and measurement now focuses on assessing the extent to which people are prepared to make their contribution:

- Do people understand their new roles and responsibilities?
- Are reporting relationships clear?
- Do people have the information, equipment, and other resources they need?
- To what extent are new systems running efficiently and effectively?
- What is valued and rewarded in the new organization?
- Is a one-company mind-set developing, or are cultures clashing?

The Survey Process: Gathering Helpful Data

For survey-generated data to be helpful to busy executives managing M&A, they have to be valid, timely, linked to the strategy, and focused on the critical issues that relate to eventual success. Surveys that generate fallacious data are a waste of time and, importantly, misdirect focus from critical areas requiring attention. Moreover, the volume of data coming from all sources is enormous and can overwhelm even the most capable leaders.

The extent to which people are candid in completing questionnaires very much depends on prevailing levels of trust in the combining organizations. Even in organizations with cultures characterized by high trust and open communications, a merger or acquisition thrusts people into a mode of insecurity. Therefore, many executives rely on outsiders to conduct surveys, especially in the early months of a merger. Employees are more likely to speak candidly to an outsider than to an internal professional, especially if that internal person comes from "the other side." Once employees see that there are no personal repercussions for speaking up and that the input is indeed listened to by those managing the transition, then complete responsibility for conducting the surveys can be turned over to internal staff. (This is not a knock against internal professionals. The reality is that HR and other staff are stretched thin during a merger. They have an enormous amount of work to do, ranging from collecting compensation and benefits data to contributing to staffing and outplacement decisions. And they can be distracted by their own concerns about job security or fitting into the postcombination culture.)

One potentially sticky situation is when an external resource has been working with one of the partners prior to the deal and is asked to assist in assessing employee views. People from the other side may hesitate at opening up to someone who is perceived as a spy or, at the very least, having a bias toward the other organization.

Guidelines for Conducting Employee Research in M&A

Some special conditions of mergers and acquisitions should be considered when designing a survey process:

- *Understand the history of survey efforts in the partner organizations.* While the survey process should signal to employees that leadership has a genuine interest in managing the human side of the transition well, there are instances when an acquired firm has had a bad experience with previous surveys, and its workforce will be suspicious of the true motives for assessing their views.
- *Specify that the measurement has nothing to do with the selection process.* In a typical merger, there is little communication, and employees tend to overinterpret management's actions. Specify that the survey process has nothing to do with the selection process for jobs in the combined organization.
- *Maintain confidentiality throughout the process.* While confidentiality matters in all survey efforts, employees engaged in a combination will be particularly sensitive. Especially when using write-in comments, take care to ensure that anonymity is always protected and confidentiality is never compromised.
- *Be aware of language differences between the partner organizations.* Words and phrases may be used differently in the partner organi-

zation. Does "associate" refer to a coworker or subordinate? Is one firm's "region" another firm's "district"? Does "leadership" refer to anyone with supervisory responsibility or just the most senior levels of the hierarchy? Take special care to check for understandability across both employee populations, and where necessary, take the time to use specific language that clarifies meaning rather than rely on jargon. In addition, avoid using acronyms that may be unclear to people from the partner organization (for example, using "ELT" instead of "executive leadership team"). For global companies, be sure to have the survey translated into employees' first language where possible, and if English must be used with people for whom English is not their first language, make sure that interpretive nuances are recognized and adequately elaborated.

• *Separate people from the partner organizations in focus group interviews and questionnaire administrations.* Some consultants urge executives to model a combined organization as soon as possible and act in ways that unify the partners. That advice is a big mistake when it comes to measurement. People are more likely to be on their good behavior and less likely to speak up when sitting in a room with counterparts from the partner organization. These self-imposed pressures are not going to yield high-quality and useful data.

After the Data Are In: Making Sense of It All

Once the results are compiled, the challenge is to explore the data in sufficient detail, identify patterns in answers to key questions, and present the findings in ways that are understandable and actionable. The following recommendations help:

• *Involve people in the analysis and interpretation of their own data.* Surveys are one of the most cost-effective ways to involve all or a large number of employees in the integration process. The more employees are engaged in the process, the more likely they are to support the combination (Marks, 1981). Not only does employee involvement help leaders do a better job of interpreting the results, it increases employee perceptions that their views are being considered as the integration process moves forward. One useful tactic is to structure feedback sessions in a hypothesis-generating manner. Rather than tell a work group, "Support for the acquisition is lower in your area than in other parts of the organization," ask people, "Why do you think results in your area are lower than elsewhere in the organization?" The findings can then be shared with leadership and others with authority to act.

• *Make results and recommendations specific to each constituency.* People are very busy in a combination, and they want results and recommendations specific to their situation rather than general findings. This requires that data be examined by key demographics and the results made relevant for each stakeholder group. The data can help drive a number of processes, such as discussions at special events and retention strategies.

• *Compare organizations head to head.* To the extent possible, try to ensure unit-to-unit comparisons across organizations. One company's HR organization may include certain jobs that reside in the information technology or finance functions in the partner organization. Cost centers may vary between traditionally centralized and decentralized organizations. When analyzing results, always ask, "Does it make sense to compare results across merging organizations?"

Case Example: Financial Services Merger

The combination of two major multinational financial services firms provides insight into both the challenges of integrating two large systems and the impact of using employee surveys as part of the integration process. The purpose of the acquisition was to expand the lead firm's scope of products, customer base, and global reach. While legally structured as an acquisition, the case example presented here comes from one major business unit in the combined organization that was created by the merger of similar-sized operations from the precombination firms. The combining units were large, with over ten thousand employees each. Integration occurred at all levels, with people competing for jobs from the most senior to the most junior ranks.

Purpose of the Survey Effort

The buying company (company A) had a long history of growing by acquisition. Having a relatively strong track record in integration success, its leadership was quite familiar with the challenges of integrating operations in a manner that achieved financial and strategic goals while minimizing undesirable impact on employee well-being, work team performance, and organizational effectiveness. So shortly after the announcement of the intent to acquire company B, leadership convened a measurement team made up of line executives and HR professionals to develop a plan for measuring employee views of the integration process.

The purpose of the survey was to provide senior leadership with feedback regarding employee perspectives on the merger. Specifically, leadership wanted to measure the extent to which employees viewed the integration as achieving its business objectives. A corollary purpose of the survey was to enhance upward and downward communication throughout the integration process.

The measurement team designed a survey based on five building blocks for a successful merger:

- *Defining and executing the business strategy.* How well do employees understand and believe in the business strategy, and do employees know how to execute it?
- *Building the culture.* What type of culture does the firm need to be successful, and how great a shift does this require?
- *Retaining key talent.* What factors will make the new company an attractive place to be, and how can leaders respond to the retention risk?
- *Integrating the organization.* What impact is the integration process having on the business, and is it helping the execution of the strategy?
- *Creating the new organization and new teams.* How is the new organization being built, and what does this tell people about the future of the firm?

The Measurement Plan

A comprehensive understanding of employee opinions required a multimethod, multisource approach featuring a combination of executive interviews, employee focus groups, and employee surveys conducted at three time periods. The combination of quantitative and qualitative data assisted leadership in gaining breadth in covering a wide range of issues and employee constituencies, as well as depth in understanding the "why" behind the "what."

Precombination Phase Measurement

Veterans of previous M&As, the measurement team members were proactive in using the period between acquisition announcement and legal closing to collect useful data. To begin, in the weeks preceding Day 1, external consultants conducted one-on-one interviews with senior executives from both merger partners to gain insight regarding their intentions and critical success factors for the new company. The consultants also used the interviews to elicit any expected roadblocks or resistance to the survey process. This was especially critical to solidifying support for the process in company B, which did not have a history of successful integrations.

Next, external consultants conducted focus group interviews with a sample of employees from all departments, regions, and other demographic groups from both companies. Separate sessions were conducted for officers and nonofficers. The focus groups began with a discussion of initial perceptions of the two heritage organizations. These sessions revealed that company A was seen as younger, more aggressive, and faster acting but also as somewhat arrogant relative to company B. Company B was viewed as older, more traditional, strong, and stable but also far too bureaucratic. Importantly, employees made it clear in the focus groups that friction across cultures would be substantial unless these differences were explicitly addressed.

Participants from both sides also cited their aspirations for the combined company culture. Themes such as integrity, meritocracy, customer focus, innovation, adaptiveness, cross-business cooperation, and high involvement rose to the top of the list. Another set of questions in the focus groups explored key concerns about the integration process and postcombination company. Employees were generally skeptical about the fairness of the integration process (especially regarding the transparency of the process for filling key positions and selecting systems, practices, and policies). They also expressed confusion about the combined organization's strategy, worried about having to get more work done with fewer people, and feared that a large bureaucracy would slow decision making. Many employees, particularly those from the acquired firm, cited fears about being "swallowed up" by the buying company and losing valued aspects of their corporate culture.

Combination Phase Measurement

In addition to providing some immediate feedback to senior leadership, the concerns expressed in the focus groups were used by the measurement team in designing a questionnaire to administer to the overall employee population. Table 18.1 displays the core questionnaire items. Some items were taken from a similar merger survey conducted during another major acquisition made by company A three years earlier, and others were written expressly for the current merger. The measurement team also recommended some basic guidelines for the survey process, which were adopted by the senior executive team: have the effort driven and owned by the combined company CEO, use organizational research staff from both partners to conduct the administration and analysis, invite all employees to participate in the process, and conduct the administration on an external web site.

Shortly after the combination received legal approval, employees were invited to participate in an online survey. About 30 percent of employees from both partner organizations completed usable questionnaires. In several areas, focus groups were conducted to understand issues in depth and identify underlying causes and possible solutions.

Findings from this measurement are reported in Table 18.2. The measurement team summarized findings according to each of the five building blocks for a successful integration:

* *Defining and executing the business strategy.* Nearly two-thirds of employees reported understanding why the merger was occurring and the espoused strategy for the combined company, but fewer than half found the value proposition to be compelling. Importantly, they did not sufficiently understand what they needed to do to deliver the strategy to clients, who were seen as taking a wait-and-see attitude regarding the impact of the combination. The implications of the findings for management included helping each employee see his or her individual connection to the strategy and the new value proposition. Critical to this was communicating specific information about each business in the combined company and how employees could bring the full scope of capabilities in all businesses to bear for each client.

Table 18.1. Roster of Questionnaire Items

Selected Questions for the New Company	Defining and Executing Business Strategy	Building the Culture	Retaining Key Talent	Integrating the Organizations	Creating the New Organization and New Teams
1. The merger will result in a stronger company in the financial services industry.	X				
2. The merger will result in better products and services for customers of the merging companies.	X				
3. For the most part, my clients/customers view the merger as a positive event for them.	X				
4. I understand the strategy for my business unit.	X				
5. Measures exist to help us assess how well we are executing the business strategy.	X				
6. Employees have been treated with fairness and respect during the merger.		X		X	X
7. So far, staffing decisions for the merged company have resulted in equally fair treatment of people from all the merging companies.		X		X	X

8. The policies and procedures in my business/function make it easy to deliver excellent service to my customers.	X
9. The amount of bureaucracy I encounter on my job is reasonable given the nature of my work.	X
10. How do you rate your area's productivity at the present time?	X
11. My work group has a climate in which diverse perspectives are valued.	X
12. Employees in my work unit feel comfortable working with people from different backgrounds.	X
13. Senior management shows by its actions that it has a strong commitment to diversity.	X
14. I am encouraged to speak up when I disagree with a decision.	X
15. I feel encouraged to come up with new and better ways of doing things.	X
16. How satisfied are you with your involvement in decisions that affect your work?	X
17. People have the freedom to take the actions necessary to achieve results.	X

(Continued)

Table 18.1. Roster of Questionnaire Items, Cont'd

Selected Questions for the New Company	Defining and Executing Business Strategy	Building the Culture	Retaining Key Talent	Integrating the Organizations	Creating the New Organization and New Teams
18. Relative to the competition, my business is an innovator.		X			
19. My business/function is oriented to promoting change.		X			
20. My manager is sensitive to the relationship between my work life and my personal life.		X	X		
21. Management in my area has communicated openly and honestly about the merger and merger-related issues.		X		X	
22. People from the merging companies are cooperating with each other.		X		X	X
23. How would you rate teamwork in your area at the present time?		X			X
24. We get a quick response to our needs from other work groups.		X			X
25. The merged company will offer more opportunities to develop my career.			X		

Question		
26. Considering everything, how would you rate your overall satisfaction with your company at the present time?	X	
27. Do you plan to be working for the merged company one year from now? (excluding those who will retire)	X	
28. In the long run, I feel the overall impact of the merger for me will be (very positive to very negative).	X	
29. I have been provided with the tools and resources to effectively deal with change.		X
30. So far, we've done a good job of keeping our customers informed about any changes in products or services resulting from the merger.		X
31. How would you evaluate the pace of the integration efforts?		X
32. How do you rate the communications you receive from your supervisor at the present time?		X
33. From what I can tell, the new company will make the best use of the best practices, procedures, and systems regardless of which heritage company they come from.	X	X

Table 18.2. Initial Measurement Findings

Key Question	Initial Survey and Focus Group Results Revealed	Specific Item Results
Defining and executing business strategy: How well do employees understand and believe in the business strategy, and do employees know how to execute it?	People understand the company's strategy on a high level, but are not excited about it yet and do not know how to personally bring the benefits to clients	Understand business unit strategy (66 percent) Feel the merger will result in stronger company (82 percent) Focus group results add: Difficult to get excited if we don't know how organization will be structured, who will stay; lack understanding of products across businesses and how to bring wider variety of products to clients
Building the culture: What type of culture does the company need to be successful, and how great a shift does this require?	People share a view of the type of organization the company should become. Most acknowledge that it will take considerable work to achieve it—particularly in areas of change and speed	Executive interviews and focus groups described aspirational culture in similar terms Most important aspects: Meritocracy, speed, adaptivity, integrity, customer focus, minimal bureaucracy Bureaucracy, infrastructure, and technology present major challenges to decision making and change
Retaining key talent: What factors will make the company an attractive place to be, and how can leaders respond to the retention risk?	Employees cited factors other than compensation as important to their retention. Face-to-face communication with leaders, career development, and involvement in decisions were critical	Compensation was rated highest as a factor in selection. Key drivers of intent to stay also included involvement in decisions, job opportunity, and enjoyment of the job.

Table 18.2. Initial Measurement Findings, Cont'd

Key Question	Initial Survey and Focus Group Results Revealed	Specific Item Results
		Employees stated being in close touch with senior leaders and their thinking made them more confident about the company's future.
Integrating the organization: What impact is the integration process having on the business, and is it helping the execution of the strategy?	Areas of the business are experiencing mixed impact to productivity. There is a need for more specific information about the integration process and its progress in driving the business strategy	Productivity of work units overall high at 75 percent, but considerable variation across units Many open comments suggest confusion about what was happening with the integration teams and what events are in order
Creating the new organization and new teams: How is the new organization being built, and what is this telling people about the future of the company?	The staffing process was frequently seen as political rather than merit based. Leaders were being counted by side rather than by their contribution to a single new business	29 percent favorable on staffing decisions result in fair decisions across merging companies. Comments showed a high level of skepticism that decisions would result in the most effective placements versus attempts to balance out the merging organizations.

- *Building the culture.* Similar to the findings in the focus group interviews, survey respondents described their legacy companies quite differently: company A employees saw company B as static, with an insular historic senior leadership group and overconfident in its capability to drive change. Conversely, company B employees viewed company A as hungry for change but with an internal organization that was traditional, highly bureaucratic, and far too slow to be competitive. Only 19 percent of respondents from company A and 25 percent from company B saw their current business areas as actively promoting change. However, employees from both partners were aligned in saying that culture change was needed for business success in the combined company. And although respondents viewed the two precombination cultures differently, there was a clear alignment of views about the type of organization the new company must become to be successful.

• *Retaining key talent.* The survey findings provided insight into factors that employees judged to make the combined organization a desirable place to work. In addition to fair compensation, employees cited the importance of belief in the strategy and excitement about the potential of the new company, as well as career opportunities, involvement in decision making, encouragement to innovate, and increased direct contact with senior leaders.

• *Integrating the organization.* The initial measurement provided an immediate heads-up to leadership regarding the impact of the integration process. Three-quarters of respondents from both firms reported that the integration effort was diminishing productivity considerably in key areas, including technology support. Most employees commented favorably regarding initial integration communication efforts, including frequent telephone call-in meetings and in-person appearances by executives, but were anxious to learn specifically how their own work areas would be affected by the integration. Overall, employees reported confusion surrounding the timing and sequencing of integration activities and wanted to know more about integration milestones and how key issues like business models and choice of technology platforms would be determined.

• *Creating the new organization and new teams.* Just half of respondents reported that employees were being treated with fairness and respect during the merger. While this exceeded the previous merger benchmark (39 percent), it still was a source of concern for the measurement team and executives. In particular, many employees regarded staffing decisions as being based on politics rather than merit and that poor communication regarding the staffing process and potential layoffs increased anxiety. About half of the respondents felt that decisions for selecting systems and procedures for the combined company reflected compromise rather than working for an optimal solution.

These findings were first delivered to the combined company's executive committee, which reviewed and discussed their implications and committed to a feedback plan. The president took responsibility for communicating overall company results through multiple channels, and he made the measurement team's reports available to all employees. Business unit leaders followed up with town hall and small group meetings to present and discuss findings specific to their parts of the company. In addition, business leaders took opportunities to discuss the survey results and their implications with employees at a variety of other large and small company events. In this way, the importance and value of the employee survey were repeatedly demonstrated.

Action planning based on the survey findings occurred at the companywide, business unit, department, and work group levels. One major initiative was a strong push to get the entire staff to better understand the new company's strategy and to encourage employees to take personal responsibility for bringing it to life in their own jobs. Another program created opportunities for individuals to meet colleagues from other business units in the company and initiate conversations about how to seek ways to reach across businesses to bring better service to clients. Since this was a major problem in both precombination companies, it became a focal point for demonstrating how the integration could result in an enhanced business.

Postcombination Phase Measurement

The initial employee survey became a baseline measure for subsequent employee research. Six months following the initial survey administration, a follow-up merger survey was conducted. Analyses identified significant trends across the administrations, and the results were disseminated in a manner similar to the first measurement.

As Table 18.3 reports, the follow-up survey showed that the merger was playing to mixed reviews six months into the integration process. Employees continued to notice some good aspects of integration management, such as reporting that leaders were still communicating in an open and honest manner and cooperation between the partner companies was increasing. Leadership's efforts to create a desired postcombination culture, however, had taken a step back in most areas. Fewer employees regarded the business as flexible or felt that the level of bureaucracy was reasonable at the six-month mark than had initially indicated so.

**Table 18.3. Selected Survey Results
Across Administrations (Percentage Favorable)**

Measure	January	June	Change
Keeping customers informed	50	57	+7
People in merging companies cooperate	48	52	+4
Management communicates openly and honestly	67	70	+3
See business as flexible	59	54	−5
Level of bureaucracy is reasonable	46	40	−6
Providing customer service	69	60	−9

The multiple waves of data also provided information on customer reactions to the merger from an employee perspective. For example, at the six-month mark, 57 percent of respondents said that customers reported being kept well informed about the combination, up from just 50 percent at the onset of the combination. In contrast, employees who felt customers were receiving good service—a healthy 69 percent at the start of integration activities—fell to just 60 percent six months later. This was a clear target of attention following the administration.

The overall survey data were used in some creative ways in the combined company. For a presentation to the board of directors, employee survey results from this combination were compared with those from one of company A's previous acquisitions. Sometimes the results were worrisome (initially 48 percent of employees reported good cooperation across the partner companies, albeit an increase from 32 percent in the previous acquisition). Yet in many areas, the survey effort documented for the board how executive leadership was becoming more skilled at the difficult job of combination management (70 percent of employees in the current merger gave their leadership good marks for communicating openly and honestly, compared to just 50 percent in the previous merger). Survey data also were used to track the extent to which the newly integrated company's vision and values were first understood and then actually used and making a difference in processes like performance reviews and rewards.

When well managed, a merger or acquisition can be an opportunity to articulate and create a desired corporate culture. Akin to Kurt Lewin's model of unfreezing-changing-refreezing (Lewin, 1947), a combination has the potential to loosen people's grips on the status quo—that is, their accustomed precombination ways of doing things. A CEO or other business leader who takes the time to make lucid a desired way of doing things in the new organization is casting the mold for desired change. And the extent to which forces ranging from the corporate structure to the staffing and reward processes reinforce the new ways, they will become refrozen as the behaviors aligned with the desired postcombination culture.

At the new company, the CEO articulated a vision and set of supporting values much like those of most other multinational corporations. But he went a step further and followed the measurement team's recommendation to measure understanding of the vision and adoption of the values in the merger survey process. He received direct feedback regarding the extent to which his vision and values were just words on a document or indeed jumping off the page and into the fabric of the postcombination organization. For example, he found out that nearly two-thirds of employees regarded the emerging company as being flexible in carrying out its business, but fewer than half were seeing an emerging climate featuring open discussions of differences.

Conclusion: What to Expect When Measuring Employee Opinions During Mergers and Acquisitions

As beneficial as employee surveys can be in providing feedback on the integration process, the psychological and political realities of combining two previously independent organizations into one makes the measurement process a truly complex endeavor. The best intentions for the survey process inevitably will run up against key obstacles. Being prepared for them will aid the professional who seeks to enhance integration through the employee survey process:

• *Expect different approaches to measurement across companies.* Partner organizations can have very different approaches to the survey process. This may include differences in types of survey systems, the sampling approach, the wording of questionnaire items, the composition of scales, demographic measures, metrics used for analysis, reporting procedures, communication methods, and accountability for action planning. Successful integration requires the new company to either adopt one of the existing systems or create a new system that, ideally, encompasses the best of both legacy systems. There is no "best" approach. But working cooperatively to develop a measurement approach that will meet the needs of the new company may be one of the first cooperative successes for an integration team.

• *Expect technology snags.* The complexity of conducting an employee survey is compounded when attempting to coordinate it across two previously independent organizations. Even something as basic as providing every employee with access to the survey is a major challenge. Meanwhile, IT systems may be changing around the survey process. It is crucial to build in plenty of lead time and to have a strong technology representation on the measurement team.

• *Expect the unexpected.* Despite the best of intentions and planning, just about anything that may be expected—or unexpected—will occur. Be patient. Be flexible. Be secure in your ability and confident in the value of the survey process in contributing to a successful combination.

A survey process assessing views on the progress of the merger or acquisition will not save a deal that was structured on questionable financial terms or one that lacks a strategic grounding. But our experience is that a reliable survey process can do much to help a well-founded deal achieve its financial and strategic objectives.

References

Bastien, D. T., & Hostager, T. J. (2003). Resizing and the marketplace: The response of customers and competitors to reorganization. In K. P. DeMeuse & M. L. Marks (Eds.), *Resizing the organization—managing layoffs, divestitures, and closings: Maximizing gain while minimizing pain.* San Francisco: Jossey-Bass.

Bruner, R. F. (2002). Does M&A pay? A survey of evidence for the decision maker. *Journal of Applied Finance Theory, Practice and Education, 12*(1), 48–88.

Cartwright, S., & Cooper, C. L. (2000). *HR know-how in mergers and acquisitions.* London: Chartered Institute of Personnel and Development.

Lazarus, R. S., & Folkman, S. (1985). *Stress, appraisal, and coping.* New York: Springer.

Lewin, K. (1947). Frontiers in group dynamics. *Human Relations, 1*(1), 5–47.

Marks, M. L. (1981). *Organizational and individual response to corporate acquisition impact.* Unpublished doctoral dissertation, University of Michigan.

Marks, M. L. (2003). *Charging back up the hill: Workforce recovery after mergers, acquisitions, and downsizings.* San Francisco: Jossey-Bass.

Marks, M. L., & DeMeuse, K. P. (2002). The realities of resizing. In K. P. DeMeuse & M. L. Marks (Eds.), *Resizing the organization—managing layoffs, divestitures, and closings: Maximizing gain while minimizing pain.* San Francisco: Jossey-Bass.

Marks, M. L., & Mirvis, P. H. (1985). Merger syndrome: Stress and uncertainty. *Mergers and Acquisitions, 20*(2), 50–55.

Marks, M. L., & Mirvis, P. H. (1998). *Joining forces: Making one plus one equal three in mergers, acquisitions, and alliances.* San Francisco: Jossey-Bass.

Mirvis, P. H., & Marks, M. L. (1986). The merger syndrome: managing organizational crises. *Mergers and Acquisitions, 20*(3), 71–77.

Schweiger, D. M., & DeNisi, A. S. (1991). Communication with employees following a merger: A longitudinal field experiment, *Academy of Management Journal, 34*(1), 110–135.

Schweiger, D. M., & Goulet, P. K. (2000). Integrating mergers and acquisitions: An international research review. In C. Cooper & A. Gregory (Eds.), *Advances in mergers and acquisitions.* New York: Elsevier.

Stahl, G. K., & Mendenhall, M. (2005). *Mergers and acquisitions: Managing culture and human resources.* Palo Alto, CA: Stanford University Press.

CHAPTER 19

Leveraging Employee Surveys to Retain Key Employees

A Means to an End

Michelle A. Donovan
Scott M. Brooks

Most practitioners experienced with employee surveys would probably agree with the following:

- Effective surveys are those that follow through on their promise with action and change.
- Managers generally acknowledge a value to addressing employee concerns.
- However, the ultimate value of a survey is too often undone by lack of follow-through.

Certainly one of the most potentially useful applications of an employee survey is to improve employee retention, and for good reason. First, the data can help explain why employees stay and why they leave organizations. Surveys can easily measure both intentions to quit as well as the factors that predict turnover. Second, and just as important, surveys are often built around action planning processes to help line management act on this understanding. This positions employee opinion surveys as effective tools to help retain employees.

This chapter describes how surveys can serve as useful tools to help minimize the negative impact of employee turnover on organizational performance. Turnover, or its opposite, retention, is a universal and important concern. Beyond a concern to the human resource (HR) profession, it is recognized by CEOs and management as a critical issue (Society for Human Resources Management Research, 2000), especially in the form of strategic staffing and succession planning. As the "war for talent" frenzy of the late 1990s has faded, it is clear that the job market and broader economy can modify the intensity of an organization's concern with retention. Yet even in a "jobless recovery," where organizations aggressively manage labor costs through layoffs and other means, increasingly sophisticated treatment of human capital recognizes the unique competitive edge provided by retaining the right talent.

Initially, organizations may focus on the negative impact of turnover expressed in direct financial costs. According to the Corporate Leadership Council (1998), the cost of replacing a non-IT professional can reach as high as $117,000. More moderate estimates of turnover costs range from 93 to 200 percent of salary (Cascio, 2000).

Potentially more damaging than raw costs is the cost of losing strategic talent. Harder to generalize to dollar figures, turnover among key positions can result in quality problems, the delay of innovation, loss of talent to the competition, or the loss of customers, contributing to increasing costs and decreasing revenue. This line of reasoning casts turnover not as a financial but as a strategic problem.

What Is the Turnover Problem?

Using an employee survey to meet an objective demands that we define that objective. How do we define retention, or its opposite, turnover? While turnover may seem straightforward, it is important to carefully define the "it" that we are trying to manage. *Turnover* in its simplest form is defined as an employee leaving an organization. An organization's *turnover problem* is usually more complicated.

For example, Griffeth and Hom (2001) contrast voluntary and involuntary turnover, functional and dysfunctional (or undesired), and avoidable and unavoidable. An organization's concern typically focuses on turnover that is undesirable, voluntary, and avoidable. That is, a valued employee quits, and something could have been done to avoid that. This suggests refining the definition to focus on voluntary, dysfunctional, and avoidable turnover. While "avoidable" is understandably hard to measure, it does follow that useful models of turnover should exclude terminations due to layoffs, retirement, returning to school, or transfers to other business units.

An organization's goal is typically to address the costs and strategic problems caused by turnover. The goal is not simply to minimize quitting across the board. Cappelli provides insight: "If managing retention in the past was akin to tending a dam, today it is more like managing a river. The object is not to stop water from flowing but to control its direction and speed" (Cappelli, 2001, p. 28).

In other words, the turnover *problem* needs to be carefully defined. The problem reflects why the organization cares about turnover—its most harmful consequences. The turnover problem can be expressed, for example, in terms of cost per voluntary termination, loss of executive potential, or number of long-term client relationships left neglected. Including not just turnover but also measures of the turnover problem will make analyses of the survey data much more potent and relevant. Even if researchers cannot directly measure and analyze the turnover problem itself (as opposed to measuring only turnover), this problem should always be at the front of the researcher's mind as the purpose of the work.

Clearly, these concerns create a demand for understanding and avoiding turnover. In several basic ways, surveys are particularly well-suited tools to help meet this demand. First, they help us understand. As measurement systems and diagnostic tools, surveys provide rich data sets for modeling and tracking the relevant issues. Second, they help us act. As organizational development (OD) interventions, surveys foster dialogue, garner resources, and establish local and organizationwide action planning practices. These two themes of understanding and acting are echoed throughout the chapter.

Using Surveys to Understand Retention

How does an organization go about understanding and eventually managing turnover? We review the role of employee surveys as a diagnostic tool to identify the causes of turnover and provide actionable information to improve retention.

Gather Survey Data

There are a number of different ways to solicit information from employees about how they feel during different stages of their employment life cycle. In this section, we discuss different types of surveys that can be leveraged to help understand retention.

Culture and Opinion Surveys

To understand the drivers of turnover, it is important to begin with the perspective of employees, which makes the general employee opinion survey an effective place to start. Many companies have companywide culture or opinion surveys that are administered on a regular basis. This type of survey is ideal for acting on retention-related data as results tend to be analyzed and shared with managers on a routine basis and the findings can be positioned as leading indicators of how to retain employees. In addition, this type of survey may provide more accurate information than exit surveys, as employees may be more likely to state their true intentions (versus providing misleading results in exit surveys to avoid burning bridges; Griffeth & Hom, 2001). To effectively study retention in a survey like this, it is important to establish agreement among key stakeholders that retention is a key objective of the survey and then build the survey around that objective.

One of the best predictors of turnover behavior is turnover intent. Turnover intentions typically focus on an employee's intent to stay (or leave) and/or job search behavior. For example, WorkTrends (Gantz Wiley Research's annual survey of U.S. workers) uses the item, "I am seriously considering leaving my company within the next 12 months." Interestingly, across the United States, the degree to which employees agree with this item—that they intend to quit—has been remarkably stable over the past decade. Typically 20 percent of the workforce is seriously thinking about leaving at any one point in time (Gantz Wiley Research, 2004).

So why do intentions predict actual turnover? According to Fishbein and Ajzen's theory (1975), "The best single predictor of an individual's behavior will be a measure of his intention to perform that behavior" (p. 369). Accordingly, many models of turnover include turnover intentions as the direct antecedent to actual turnover (Griffeth & Hom, 2001). Beyond the theoretical support, there is strong empirical evidence linking turnover intentions to actual turnover (see Steele and Ovalle's 1984 meta-analysis). In other words, often before an employee actually quits, he or she goes through a period of thinking and intending to quit—and it is these intentions, measured within surveys, that can be used as a surrogate for turnover itself.

Including a few items to assess turnover intentions in a survey can provide a meaningful criterion to better understand retention. But what about predictors? Turnover intentions can identify hot spots of high turnover risk, but by themselves cannot direct an organization toward what to do about them. This is where turnover predictors come in handy. When considering which to include, it may be helpful to review turnover models (Griffeth & Hom, 2001; Mobley, Griffeth, Hand, & Meglino, 1979; Muchinsky & Morrow, 1980; Price & Mueller, 1981) or recent reviews (Griffeth, Hom, & Gaertner, 2000; Hom, Caranikas-Walker, Prussia, & Griffeth, 1992; Maertz & Campion, 1998) with the goal of ensuring that potential predictors identified in the literature have at least been considered. Both turnover models and meta-analyses tend to highlight variables such as satisfaction with work, overall job satisfaction, and organizational commitment as having consistent relationships with turnover.

While it has been well established that job satisfaction and organizational commitment are related to turnover, often both organizations and managers are looking for more actionable predictors. For example, it is difficult to act directly on general dissatisfaction and easier to act on more specific drivers, such as recognition or career growth. Certainly the research points to other important predictors beyond summary attitudes. Common predictors include reactions to the work itself, career development, opportunity, recognition, training, managerial relationships, stress, and pay (Cotton & Tuttle, 1986; Griffeth & Hom, 2001; Price & Mueller, 1981). For example, in Gantz Wiley Research's WorkTrends (a specially commissioned survey of more than ten thousand workers across the United States, with a sample balanced to the most recent census with regard to several demographics), the number one issue most commonly related to intentions to quit is not seeing a promising future for oneself at work. While intriguing, that fact is not immediately useful. When "promising future" is omitted from the analyses, more specific, and more actionable, issues emerge as the top drivers of intentions to quit, such as career development opportunities, confidence in the future of one's organization, sense of accomplishment from one's work, perceptions of pay, and sense of job security (Gantz Wiley Research, 2004).

Often the most meaningful items are unique to one's specific organizational environment—predictability of work schedules, safety, or the ability to work with the latest technology. These can be identified from culture surveys, exit surveys, or focus groups conducted in the organization. So while it is important to be familiar with the turnover literature to ensure a comprehensive survey, it is critical to understand the turnover dynamics unique to one's own organization to create a tailored survey with meaningful predictors.

It is also important to link key job and personal characteristics (such as department, geography, and job level or type) to the survey data, either using demographic questions or linking survey data to a company's human resources information system (HRIS) through a third-party vendor. These demographics allow more targeted analyses of the predictors of retention to be conducted on predetermined groups of employees.

Exit Surveys

In a recent survey of the Mayflower Group, a survey consortium comprising over forty blue-chip companies that share survey data and best practices (Johnson, 2004), 88 percent of the member companies used exit surveys. Here we focus on exit surveys as a potential source of data that can be used to understand why employees left in order to make improvements to retain existing employees.

Typically exit surveys are conducted either just prior to an employee's exit or a few months after departure. Exit survey data are most useful when they are routinely examined at both the local level (by managers or departments) and organizational level to identify trends. When examining the data, it is important to focus on the correct criterion: voluntary, undesired turnover. In addition, analyses focused on specific departing employees of interest (such as a department with a high turnover rate, high-potential employees, or employees from underrepresented groups) can sometimes lead to more targeted actions to retain existing employees, which is why it is important to link key demographic variables to the survey data.

While some research indicates that employees are not entirely honest in exit interviews and surveys to avoid burning bridges (Giacalone, Knouse, & Montagliani, 1997; Griffeth & Hom, 2001), there are several ways to build exit surveys to maximize valid and useful responses. For example, conducting them anonymously (if possible) and confidentially, through HR or a third-party vendor, conducting them after the employee has been away from the organization for a sufficient time (versus at the time of leaving), and taking action (and publicizing those actions) on issues identified in surveys (Giacalone et al., 1997; Feldman & Klaas, 1999) can encourage employees to respond honestly. The typical format of an exit survey includes reasons for the departure and ratings of attributes of the job and organization (for example, pay, manager, work conditions, advancement opportunities, training, and performance management). It also includes open-ended questions about what triggered them to leave or could have influenced them to stay (Giacalone et al., 1997). When designing exit surveys, it is important to remember that they must identify actionable predictors that the organization can use to address undesirable turnover.

One best practice is to build exit survey content around validated predictors of turnover in the organization. For example, when Microsoft revamped its exit survey, it first conducted a study based on the annual employee opinion survey and identified items that predicted actual voluntary terminations. The analyses ensured that not only were hypothesized turnover predictors included in the exit survey, but that empirically based predictors were included, which led to a more customized and meaningful exit survey.

Integration and On-Boarding surveys

Some companies also administer surveys shortly after employees join the company to assess their satisfaction and overall integration. These may be called *integration* or *on-boarding surveys*. Integration surveys typically include ratings of manager support, peer communication, job fit, working conditions, and logistics. Overall satisfaction with integration and turnover intentions can also be assessed, and the findings can serve as a leading indicator for any retention issues early on that can be addressed. For example, if an integration survey identifies that managerial support is key to employees' integration and their early turnover intentions, then this finding can be integrated into managerial training to emphasize the importance of managerial behaviors in retaining new employees. Integration survey data can also complement existing indicators; for example, if new hire turnover rates increase in a given department, then integration survey data from that department can be used to identify possible issues to address.

Special Retention-Focused Surveys

Some companies conduct one-time surveys focused specifically on retention to address a pressing need. This can be particularly useful to assess retention in key groups of employees where, for example, turnover rates are higher than typical or retention is vital (for example, high performers). Another purpose of a retention survey can be to assess the impact of a major retention initiative.

Analyze Survey Data

Typically, generating data to help understand turnover is not the problem. Instead, the struggle is to convert these data into efficient, focused, and compelling messages that motivate and direct improvement efforts. The sections below describe several basic approaches. There are, however, three overarching guidelines for analyses:

- *Start as close to the problem as possible.* Do not blindly accept turnover reduction as the goal. Some turnover is, in fact, functional (for example, that based on low performers). Try instead to define a criterion as close to the presenting problem as possible. For example, if managing turnover cost is the real issue, do not simply predict turnover; predict turnover costs. As another example, if the issue is with managerial turnover, do not spend time fitting models to nonmanagers.
- *Work backward from the problem.* Once the criterion is defined, build a model backward from the problem and into the survey topics—both summary attitudes as well as actionable topics. Then test it. Working backward is not a statistical statement about fishing; it is a reminder that we tend to become overinfatuated with predictors, such as dissatisfaction, and not attentive enough to criteria, such as turnover or turnover costs. It is starting with the end in mind and remaining focused on that goal through analyses.

• *Design analyses with line management in mind.* No matter how valid the model is, if one cannot develop a compelling "elevator speech"—advice that could be shared with the CEO in a two-minute elevator ride—it will not have sustained impact. Always drive toward relatively simple and compelling messages about turnover. And avoid analysis paralysis—the reluctance to draw useful conclusions because there are always more questions to answer.

Linking Turnover Intentions to Actual Turnover

Perhaps the most common—and easiest—statistical analysis is to use multiple regression to identify issues that explain the most variance in intentions to quit (typically a one- to four-item index used as a dependent variable). Presenting management with a simple list of top drivers with example items can go a long way in directing survey follow-up efforts and discussions toward improving retention.

To influence stakeholders to act on the drivers of turnover intentions, it is important first to establish the credibility of those intentions as a surrogate for actual turnover. To do this, researchers have two options: (1) make the conceptual argument, that is, describe the logic and research findings, or (2) make the empirical argument, that is, document linkages with organization-specific survey data.

To make the empirical argument, companies that are able to track individual survey responses (often through a third-party vendor to protect the confidentiality of the data) have the capability to link an individual's turnover intentions to that same individual's actual behavior—whether or not the person quits in the future. For example, Griffeth and Hom (2001) noted that in a study of retail employees, 53 percent who responded "probably yes" and 60 percent who responded "definitely yes" to a turnover intention item actually quit six months later, whereas only 10 percent of those who responded "definitely not" and 20 percent of those who responded "probably not" actually quit. The one caveat to linking an individual's survey results to his or her later turnover behavior is that it is critical to keep all promises of confidentiality to the participants.

If more advanced analyses fit the organization's needs, turnover intentions can be linked to actual turnover after a sufficient amount of time has passed using logistic regressions and t-tests (do stayers versus leavers score significantly different on turnover intentions?). For example, in data collected from over sixty-five thousand employees across eight companies in financial services, manufacturing, and retail, the Corporate Leadership Council Solutions Research found significant differences on its Retention Index (a sum of four items, which ask about intentions to leave and job search behavior with a "strong intention to stay/no intention to leave" = 1 on a seven-point Likert scale and a "strong intention to leave" = 7) for "remaining employees" versus "voluntarily departing employees." Figure 19.1 represents one way to depict this finding: it demonstrates that "remaining employees" scored significantly higher (indicating stronger intentions to remain) than "voluntarily departing employees," which provides evidence that the Retention Index is related to actual turnover behavior.

**Figure 19.1. Employee Retention Index
Related to Actual Turnover**

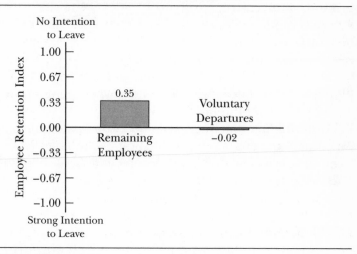

T-test $(65,862) = 33.99, p < .01.$

Source: Corporate Leadership Council Solutions Research (2004).

For companies unable to track survey results at an individual level, it may still be possible to illustrate the relationship between turnover intentions and turnover rates at the group level. For example, even a simple scatter plot of department-level turnover intentions by actual departmental turnover rates can help management see the connection between survey results and important organizational outcomes. While a scatter plot alone (even if described by a statistically significant correlation coefficient) is not enough to create a scientific case, it can be an organization-specific example that gives meaning and credibility to the substantial academic literature available.

Examining Turnover Intentions

Once the turnover intentions have been validated, the next logical step is to examine differences between groups on the intentions and other key variables to answer the key questions: Who is most at risk for leaving? And what differentiates stayers versus leavers or those with low versus high turnover intentions?

To answer the first question, organizations can begin by comparing turnover intentions across key demographic variables, such as department, geography, performance level, gender, ethnic background, and tenure, to identify "pockets at risk." T-tests and ANOVAs can provide statistical evidence of the differences. Sometimes even more important than the analyses themselves is how the results are translated into digestible nuggets of information. Researchers at Intel, for example, created a map of the world and highlighted pockets of risk in red to display geographical differences in turnover intentions.

In addition to the internal comparisons, external comparisons can also be valuable. The Information Technology Survey Group, a consortium of sixteen high-tech companies that share survey data (Deitering, 2003), uses the retention item, "If I were offered a comparable position with similar pay and benefits at another company, I would stay at [insert company name]." Companies such as Intel, SAP, Dell, and Sun Microsystems routinely compare their scores on this retention item against the high-tech norm (or average score from other high-tech companies). Reputable consulting firms may also offer meaningful benchmark data. Benchmark comparisons allow an organization to determine whether employee turnover intentions in their organization (or even in a given department) differ from intentions in other companies. This information can help an organization put their data into context to determine whether their employees intend to leave at higher rates than employees at other companies, which could serve as an indicator that may require an intervention. Comparisons are much more meaningful when benchmark data are from companies in similar industries. For example, it makes much less sense for a high-tech firm to benchmark its turnover intentions against traditionally higher turnover industries, such as retail.

Predicting Turnover at the Group Level

For companies that are unable to track data at the individual level, it is possible to identify predictors of turnover at the group level, such as for work groups or departments. To do this, turnover intentions, as well as attitudes and perceptions of additional variables, can be aggregated at the group level and regression analyses can be conducted. Using regression analyses to identify leading indicators of retention can be particularly useful when they are conducted for targeted groups, such as departments or turnover-at-risk employees.

As an example, researchers at Allstate Insurance Company run multiple regressions based on department-level data. Aggregated responses to individual survey items are correlated with outcomes such as intent to stay and voluntary turnover rate. In one department-level analysis, they found pay was a significant predictor of retention for one department. To follow up on this finding, salary market analyses by geographical location were conducted, and the results revealed potential gaps between Allstate's starting salaries and the market for several positions and locations. This led to the implementation of accelerated merit reviews and increases in selected locations to align salaries with the competition.

The one caution to remember about group-level analyses is that they predict group-level turnover rates rather than individual turnover decisions. The researcher must make sure to interpret both the predictors and criterion at the group level of analysis (for example, how group-level climate relates to group-level turnover rates, not individual-level turnover) and remember that group-level turnover rates can introduce additional dynamics. For example, higher turnover in a department (which often results in many open positions or less efficient new employees) may leave the remaining employees feeling understaffed. This is a clear, alternative explanation to the quick conclusion that the perception of being understaffed is a driver of turnover. As another example, predicting retention by geographical areas can introduce economic factors such as the local job market into the mix. It may be that even the best analyses are unable to fully dissect these issues. In such cases, augment the statistical work with information from multiple sources (as in the Allstate example). This is often required to draw useful conclusions. (See Baysinger and Mobley, 1983, for a more detailed discussion of the individual and group-level issues to consider when analyzing turnover data.)

Predicting Turnover at the Individual Level

For companies able to track data at the individual level, regressions can be used to predict actual turnover of individuals. In other words, what would have predicted whether an individual employee stayed or left the organization? Regressions based on individual-level data can be run after employees have actually left to look back at what could have been improved. This can be especially illuminating when focused on an employee group of particular interest, such as high performers or those from underrepresented groups. A recent technique, relative weight analysis, can overcome some of the deficiencies of multiple regression (for further explanation, see Chapter Fourteen, this volume) to help illuminate important drivers.

Creating Turnover Models

Finally, Maertz and Campion (2004) carefully describe the difference between turnover process models, which focus on how people quit, and turnover content models, which focus on why people quit. Turnover content models are the more applicable for researchers interested in identifying reasons that employees quit. Content models of turnover that take into account predictors, turnover intentions, and actual turnover can be developed to guide survey design, and later evaluated using path or structural equation models. The benefit of modeling is that it allows an examination of the hypothesized direction and weight of each potential predictor, as well as moderators of relationships, and, as we discuss later, valid yet simple models can sometimes be a useful way to encourage understanding and action.

Communicate Results

In most organizations, how the analyses are presented plays a critical role in transforming data into action. Key stakeholders must understand the results before they can act on them.

Researchers at Frito Lay developed a best practice on this front. To explain *t*-tests conducted on "stayers" versus "leavers" (based on scores on their two-item turnover intentions index), they included a written description of the potential leaver group in managers' reports so that they could easily digest areas of improvement. In one report, for example, potential leavers were described as "more likely to say that their managers were not communicating with them, removing barriers, or recognizing and rewarding their work." These descriptions helped managers quickly recognize behaviors they could change and were incorporated into mentor and manager training. It is critical to translate statistical findings into a format that managers can understand and use.

In addition, to emphasize the importance of acting on the data, they translated their findings into future projections of turnover. To do this, they calculated the percentage of employees in a function who responded unfavorably to the turnover intention index and then estimated that 50 percent of those respondents would actually quit. These projections were included in presentations to senior management. Eight months later, the projections for each function were within ±2 points of actual turnover. (For other ideas on how to create presentations that effectively communicate results and spark action, see Chapter Seventeen, this volume.)

Triangulate Multiple Data Sources

One of the best practices in analyzing retention-related survey results is to triangulate survey data with other sources of data before acting on them. Those in the Allstate example follow a clear measurement model of (1) examining multiple sources of data (for example, satisfaction, exit and retention survey data, and HRIS data), (2) identifying root causes through additional analyses (such as salary surveys, interviews, focus groups, and special surveys), (3) developing interventions, and (4) establishing ongoing measurements to track success. In other words, they did not change pay practices solely based on survey data; rather, they used the survey finding as an indicator of a potential issue, then dug deeper using a competitive salary analysis before recommending changes.

The Internal Labor Market (ILM) analysis (Nalbantian, Guzzo, Keiffer, & Doherty, 2004; Nalbantian & Szostak, 2004) represents cutting-edge work on this topic. ILM research follows the tradition of market research where researchers track not only perceptions and preferences through surveys but actual behaviors. As an example, at FleetBoston Financial, survey data indicated pay was a significant predictor of turnover. ILM statistical modeling, which examined external market influences, organizational practices, and employee attributes over time based on HRIS data, further illuminated that it was pay growth over time (and not current pay) that significantly predicted turnover. Therefore, the correct intervention should be targeted at pay growth over time versus providing one-time raises. The lesson here is that it is critical to triangulate survey data with additional data sources before determining actions.

Using Surveys to Act on Retention

Understanding turnover is a prerequisite but insufficient for addressing retention problems. What does the survey professional do once a sound sense of turnover dynamics exists? Ultimately the potency of this effort depends on acting in different ways. This is where the measurement phase of this exercise ends and the organizational development phase begins.

Who Acts on Survey Results?

Who "owns" a turnover problem? It is important to find those within the organization who have a preexisting interest and passion in addressing the issue. In many ways, organizational improvement based on survey results depends on putting directives and motivating information into the hands of people whose job it is to drive improvements. Here we consider three types of stakeholders responsible for action planning: executives, staff functions (most notably HR), and line managers in general. Where a researcher places emphasis may depend on the organization's specific drivers of turnover. Nevertheless, below are some relatively common examples:

• *Executives.* As the most potent owners of an organization's culture, executives (top management) are ideally involved in understanding survey results and championing follow-up. Regarding retention efforts specifically, they become an integral part of action planning when retention has been recognized as a strategic, executive-level issue (for example, when executive bench strength or organizational competencies are of special concern), or when analyses identify executive efforts as a core piece of improving retention (for example, painting a compelling picture of the future in the face of organizational strain). In both cases, the education and direction a survey provides are aimed at helping these executives become stronger leaders.

• *Staff functions.* Staff functions, such as human resources, often have much larger appetites for data and further research. For example, if pay surfaces as an important driver of quitting, the compensation and benefits department will be hungry for more specific information. If executives are interested in high-level perspectives, staff functions are generally more interested in key segmentations that let them easily look across the entire organization for areas of high risk or, conversely, dramatically improved areas to determine best practices.

• *Managers.* Line managers below the executive level may be those least likely to believe survey follow-up is a part of their jobs. Yet if the turnover of key employees has affected their business, they may be more inclined to consider survey follow-up as a way to address retention. With line managers, retention effort follow-up is often interwoven with other forms of survey follow-up efforts (and less likely to be a special endeavor).

To illustrate the impact of each group, consider the case where career development is a primary driver of retention. Executives could highlight the exciting future and new competencies the organization needs to build to meet its five-year strategy. The HR function could create development planning systems to help managers keep in better touch with the career interests of high-performing employees.

Clarify Key Issues and Diagnose Root Causes

Perhaps most important in survey follow-up is a clarification step. Surveys excel at highlighting what employees think, not why they think it. Even if we discover that recognition is related to intentions to quit, we still do not know if the solution requires an overhaul of the performance management and incentives systems or the less expensive, yet much more difficult, task of cajoling managers to personally thank employees for a job well done. The clarification step involves creating opportunities to discuss the issues. Examples of these opportunities include semistructured department meetings for managers to better understand how to improve their own groups or formal, organizationwide focus groups to systematically gather root-cause information.

Create a Message

No matter who acts on the results or what the underlying issues are, success is dependent not just on valid analyses, but on the ability to create a compelling story of retention, what to do to fix things, and why even to bother. This is required to create buy-in on the part of management. Lack of validity can be a showstopper, but so can lack of commitment. In fact, when analyzing and presenting results, often researchers need to trade developing a complex, complete model for a straightforward, less complete model that executives can more easily understand and integrate into their own communications.

Beyond simplicity, compelling stories are crafted from the organization's perspective, not the researcher's. The researcher should already be convinced of the key messages based on scientifically appropriate analyses and statistics. But what convinces management is frequently completely different. Compelling stories require additional work—often hard work—to incorporate numbers, measures, metaphors, and bullet points intuitively grasped by management and the organization at large.

Create Action Plans

Once there is a sense of the central issues and who needs to be involved in the solutions, there are a few broad categories of action that can be pursued—for example:

- Turnover analyses can form the basis for an educational exercise, instructing managers on their role in retaining key talent. Such modules can be inserted into management or leadership development programs or more subtly delivered in executive presentations.

- Organizations often create turnover risk indexes based on the important predictors of voluntary terminations. Such metrics are easily integrated into ongoing tracking frameworks such as balanced scorecards, or measurement systems that benefit from including a leading indicator of talent loss.

- Often the simplest approach to support retention efforts is to incorporate key messages from the analyses into survey follow-up that would occur anyway. Including turnover risk indexes into manager reports or follow-up tools is an easy way to encourage managers to attend to retention. See Box 19.1 for an example of a tool Bristol-Myers Squibb built for just such a purpose.

- Specially chartered projects can follow up on explicitly highlighted issues, such as job security, workload, or job enrichment, to try to improve employee interest in remaining with the organization.

Box 19.1. Turning Survey Data into an Actionable Tool Kit for Managers

One of the biggest challenges with retention-related survey data is how to translate them into information that managers can use. Bristol-Myers Squibb Company has overcome this challenge by creating the Employee Retention Toolkit for Managers. To do this, it determined the most significant predictors of voluntary turnover in employee opinion and exit survey data using regression analyses, and then translated this information into an employee retention risk assessment to help managers identify and manage the strongest predictors of turnover.

The risk assessment contains fifteen questions in four categories: Manager Behavior, Work/Life Balance, Career Development, and Rewards and Recognition—for example: "Does the employee have enough information to establish clear linkages between division priorities and their role?" "Does the employee have a good balance between work and personal time?" "Is the employee acquiring new skills and knowledge in their role?" "Has the employee been recognized for their performance during the past year?" Managers are encouraged to routinely conduct an assessment of these areas for each employee, consulting with the employee as needed. If significant risk is detected, he or she partners with the HR generalist to create a targeted plan to retain the employee at risk.

Like any other organizational change effort, ongoing reinforcement and encouragement are important for survey follow-up efforts to have an impact. A multipronged approach helps. The most successful work includes a mix of centralized and local activities, incentives and other encouragement to live up to the initial good intentions, and regular illustrations of effective retention efforts (both the inspirational and the instructive).

To reiterate, the process of survey follow-up is about putting useful information into the hands of people whose job it is to do something about it. In the end, approaches to action planning are limited only by the creativity and resources of the organization. Eli Lilly has utilized a variety of these and other techniques (see Box 19.2).

Box 19.2. Acting on Retention Data over the Employee Life Cycle

Studying retention at Eli Lilly and Company is not a one-time event. Researchers on the Workforce Research Team consider the retention of employees to be such a priority that they study how to retain employees over their entire life cycle, from when employees initially join Eli Lilly to when they walk out the door.

Like many other companies, Eli Lilly found a spike in turnover for those with short tenure; specifically, they found that nearly a quarter of turnover was occurring within the first two years of employment. To better understand why employees were leaving so early in their careers with Eli Lilly, they created a survey administered to employees within their first year. They learned that key factors, such as not enough supervisor support and not having a job that met their expectations, was leading to turnover in the critical first year. Based on these findings, the corporate orientation process and the "hand-off" from the recruiting organization to line management were improved.

Survey results also indicated that local orientation was much more important to employee integration than the overall corporate programs. As a result, the best practices from the departments conducting more effective local orientation were implemented in other departments.

In an attempt to triangulate data from nonsurvey sources to study the integration of employees, they also found that supervisor continuity (having the same supervisor over time) significantly reduced new employees' intentions to leave. The company had already implemented a guideline that employees should stay in one position for three years, which improves supervisor continuity, and these findings provided evidence to increase the enforcement of that guideline.

Beyond studying employees in their first few years, they also linked their annual survey, the Voice of Employee, to exit survey results and found that employees who reported intentions to leave in the annual survey were dissatisfied with similar issues that the actual leavers were dissatisfied with in the exit surveys (the survey process allows them to track individuals). In other words, employees who intended to leave and actual leavers had significantly lower satisfaction levels than the "stayers," especially on key issues such as supervisor satisfaction and reward and recognition.

Because some of the key dissatisfiers focused on management, some improvements focused on the manager selection process (for example, selecting managers that would be effective coaches). In addition, a retention specialist position was created to manage retention metrics and programs, including a retention workshop for line managers. The key to taking action was to thoroughly understand the experience of employees throughout their life cycle with the company and then to use that information to create action plans to enhance retention.

Challenges

Despite the compelling reasons to act on the leading indicators of retention such as survey data, many organizations continue to rely solely on lagging indicators, such as turnover rates or, worse yet, do not really give retention much attention at all. Why is this?

First, sometimes using survey results to help manage turnover does not deserve to be a priority. Ultimately the point of such an effort is to help an organization maximize its potential and reduce its costs. The point is not to reduce turnover under the automatic assumption that it is a top priority for the organization. If a compelling case cannot be made to address turnover, consider working on something else.

With that said, however, educating the organization with regard to the cost of turnover is important. It becomes the survey researcher's job to define the problem. That means choosing the right criteria and focusing on the right groups.

Analyzing the Data

Once a compelling case has been made to address the turnover problem, the next issue becomes how to predict it. Several challenges can prove difficult in this analysis stage.

Lack of Time or Research Skills

In today's fast-paced environment, finding the time to conduct research on leading indicators of retention can be nearly impossible. One way to tackle this challenge is to clearly link retention research to a current project or problem the organization views as a priority. For example, when Intel was planning growth in several emerging markets, which required substantial skilled human capital, researchers were able to find time to analyze survey data to identify turnover drivers, such as job fit, to identify improvements to retain employees in these key regions.

A lack of research or statistical skills can also impede retention research. To combat this challenge, one option is to work with an external consulting firm. Some companies without the resources to hire external firms have conducted simpler analyses, such as correlations or mean differences, or have partnered with academics to analyze data, and done so with little resource investment.

Measurement Challenges

Once the compelling case has been made to analyze retention-related survey data, the methodological challenges in the pursuit of valid predictors can become the biggest challenge.

- Turnover is an infrequent event with a low base rate. Because of this, there is "vanishingly small variance in the criterion" (Hulin & Rousseau, 1980, p. 66). Strategies to combat the low base rate problem include extending the time period to observe turnover, studying rates at the group (versus individual) level, or expanding the definition of turnover, such as relying on "intentions" or a larger construct, such as "job withdrawal" (Hanisch & Hulin, 1990). It is important to understand the pros and cons of each of these strategies before employing them.

- Level of analysis issues. One must carefully consider the level at which the data are aggregated and ensure that the predictors and criteria align. For example, correlations between survey results and group turnover rates are not necessarily the issues related to an individual's decision to quit. Such relationships may simply reflect the strain in departments of having many open positions or many new employees who need extra support.

- Assessing turnover at one point in time. A survey provides one snapshot in time. A better understanding of turnover as a process can be derived from analyzing survey data collected over time to identify changing trends or the effectiveness of retention interventions.

- Lack of model testing. Correlational and regression analyses are among the simplest analyses to conduct. But a more in-depth look at turnover comes from model testing. In addition to understanding the linkages among numerous variables, model testing can foster an understanding about which variables moderate the prediction of turnover.

- Relying solely on quantitative data. Do not overlook the value of qualitative data. Coding comments or conducting follow-up focus groups can help further diagnose retention drivers and identify possible solutions.

Lack of Action on the Findings

Often the biggest challenge of all is motivating, with a carrot or a stick, managers and leaders to take action on retention-related survey findings. The major barriers to action generally fall into two broad categories: lack of understanding on the part of management and lack of support for acting on the issues. Clearly the biggest benefit to research is when others besides the survey researcher (especially upper management) accept the implications and find meaning in the results. A major problem here includes the failure to translate research findings into a compelling executive-level message: validity can be questioned, implications can be rejected, and, worst of all, retention solutions can be dismissed. It is not unrealistic to expect that half of the survey analysis effort be devoted to creating an easy-to-understand—and use—story of turnover.

An important part of helping an organization understand how a survey can help is education regarding how surveys cannot help. Surveys are great diagnostic tools and can be valid and useful leading indicators of turnover risk. They can point to the issues that demand attention and further dialogue. But it is unrealistic to expect surveys to reveal the exact solution that should be implemented. Deciding how to respond requires some clarification (for example, within focus groups) or convergence with other sources of input.

Once those responsible for acting on the issues have been identified and accept the basic model of turnover, the task becomes one of helping them live up to their good intentions of making sustained organizational change—in other words, genuinely acting on the results. Success at this task involves (1) defining the problem in a manner relevant to those stakeholders charged with acting on results, (2) articulating clear expectations regarding roles and responsibilities, (3) tracking action and process against milestones, and (4) holding others accountable to execute the action plans. With these elements in place, survey follow-up will be much more effective.

To help combat the challenge of management accountability, IBM found that establishing a senior leadership team to hold other managers responsible for making improvements ensured action was taken on the findings. In 1998, IBM conducted a line of internal and external research, including employee surveys, to investigate the factors contributing to the attraction and retention of top technical talent. To ensure action was taken, a team of ten senior line leaders was established to review the findings and implement interventions to improve the attraction and retention of key talent. Interventions based on those analyses, for example, improvement in assimilating new employees, continue to this day. Whatever one's approach, it is important to understand exactly which barriers to acting on survey data, and retention in particular, are at work in the organization in order to effectively address them.

Conclusion

The retention of key employees is critical to organizational success. Surveys are a useful tool to help organizations understand and act on retention-related data. And well-trained survey professionals such as I/O practitioners are uniquely suited to maximize a survey's usefulness.

Although retention is often an explicit organizational concern, garnering the resources to understand and act on employee survey data to address retention can be difficult in today's fast-paced environment. It may seem daunting to design, analyze, and act on surveys to address retention. But the inability to conduct the ideal modeling work should not prevent practitioners from taking steps to apply survey data to retention. Table 19.1 illustrates both more and less time- and resource-intensive approaches. Efforts exemplified by the right-hand column will yield a greater return on what would correspondingly be a greater investment. Yet the easier-to-manage left-hand column is clearly superior than doing nothing.

With an understanding of an organization's needs, time-pressured and budget-constrained survey practitioners can tailor each step of the process to balance the ideal against the easily doable, with the goal of managing the problems that turnover creates more effectively than without the benefit of any research at all.

Table 19.1. Using Employee Surveys to Address Retention

	For Companies with Less Time and Resources	For Companies with More Time and Resources
Understand		
Gather survey data	Use preexisting survey	Survey designed for retention efforts
Analyze survey data	Regressions using intentions to quit as dependent variable	Individual-level modeling with actual turnover or turnover costs as dependent variable
Communicate results	Add turnover risk index to preexisting reporting processes	Index modeled within balanced scorecard; turnover cost highlighted; projections of future turnover; comparisons to external benchmarks
Act		
Clarify key issues/ diagnose root causes	Instruct managers to discuss key retention issues with employees or review open-ended comments for elaboration on turnover	Triangulate multiple sources of data; charter organizationwide program of structured focus groups to clarify causes of turnover
Create a message	Summary of hot spots (groups at risk for turnover) and focus on top drivers of turnover	Retention integrated into larger human capital or employee life cycle framework; educational presentations
Create action plans	Follow-up support focused solely on local-level managers or HR/central efforts or executive level	All levels of action planning are well supported with facilitators and tools

Here are some of the key lessons of this chapter:

- *Plan backward.* Carefully define the turnover problem of interest—whether it is undesirable, avoidable turnover within strategic talent pools, loss of leadership successors, or the training costs for a constantly churning front-line employee. Then work backward to predict and eventually act on the drivers of this problem.
- *Customize research.* Become familiar with general models of turnover and analyses that can be conducted, but tailor the research to the needs of the organization. Often the most meaningful nuggets come from customized research that addresses local issues—for example, studying retention for one job type or segment of employees. What works for a high-tech organization in the Silicon Valley marketplace will not be the same as what works for a business services consulting firm in Minnesota.
- *Understand and act.* There are two distinct phases in the application of surveys to studying retention. Surveys are a tool to help understand retention, but without action on the findings, the research is meaningless. Keep both phases in mind throughout the process to maximize them.
- *Retention is just one application of surveys.* There are numerous applications of surveys. Make sure retention is balanced with other survey objectives and nestles into the larger survey strategy.
- *Surveys are just one tool to address retention.* Surveys are a tool and should be used in conjunction with other tools, such as focus groups, designed to address turnover issues.

Survey data can help organizations understand turnover and guide their action to increase retention. In this way, employee surveys are a proven and valuable tool to improve organizational effectiveness.

References

Baysinger, B., & Mobley, W. (1983). Employee turnover: Individual and organizational analysis. In K. Rowland & G. Ferris (Eds.), *Research in personnel and human resources management.* Greenwich, CT: JAI Press.

Cappelli, P. (2001). *Finding and keeping the best people.* Boston, MA: Harvard Business School Publishing.

Cascio, W. F. (2000). *Costing human resources.* Cincinnati, OH: South-Western.

Corporate Leadership Council. (1998). *Workforce turnover and firm performance: The new business case for retention.* Washington, DC: Corporate Executive Board.

Corporate Leadership Council Solutions Research (2004). Washington, DC: Corporate Executive Board.

Cotton, J. L., & Tuttle, J. M. (1986). Employee turnover: A meta-analysis and review with implications for research. *Academy of Management Review, 11,* 55–70.

Deitering, F. (2003, Apr.). IT survey group: Best practices and challenges in sharing survey data among high tech companies. In M. Donovan (Chair), *Benchmarking employee survey and retention data: The pros/cons of consortia.* Panel discussion conducted at the Eighteenth Annual Conference of the Society for Industrial and Organizational Psychology, Orlando, FL.

Feldman, D. C., & Klaas, B. S. (1999). The impact of exit questionnaire procedures on departing employees' self-disclosure. *Journal of Managerial Issues, 11*(1), 13–25.

Fishbein, M., & Ajzen, I. (1975). *Beliefs, attitudes, intention, and behavior.* Reading, MA: Addison-Wesley.

Gantz Wiley Research. (2004). *WorkTrends 2004—finding the missing piece: Understanding your vulnerability to talent loss* (Tech. Rep.). Minneapolis, MN: Gantz Wiley Research.

Giacalone, R. A., Knouse, S. B., & Montagliani, A. (1997). Motivation for and prevention of honest responding in exit interviews and surveys. *Journal of Psychology, 131*(4), 438–448.

Griffeth, R. W., & Hom, P. W. (2001). *Retaining valued employees.* Thousand Oaks, CA: Sage.

Griffeth, R. W., Hom, P. W., & Gaertner, S. (2000). A meta-analysis of antecedents and correlates of employee turnover: Update, moderator tests, and research implications for the next millennium. *Journal of Management, 26,* 463–488.

Hanisch, K. A., & Hulin, C. L. (1990). Job attitudes and organizational withdrawal: An examination of retirement and other voluntary withdrawal behaviors. *Journal of Vocational Behavior, 37,* 60–78.

Hom, P. W., Caranikas-Walker, F., Prussia, G. E., & Griffeth, R. W. (1992). A meta-analytical structural equation analysis of a model of employee turnover. *Journal of Applied Psychology, 77,* 890–909.

Hulin, C. L., & Rousseau, D. M. (1980). Analyzing infrequent events: Once you find them, your troubles begin. *New Directions for Methodology of Social and Behavioral Science, 6,* 65–75.

Johnson, H. (2004, Aug.). All in favor say "Benchmark!" *Training Magazine,* 30–34.

Maertz, C. P., & Campion, M. A. (1998). Twenty-five years of voluntary turnover research: A review and critique. In C. L. Cooper & I. T. Robertson (Eds.), *International review of industrial and organizational psychology*. New York: Wiley.

Maertz, C. P., & Campion, M. A. (2004). Profiles in quitting: Integrating process and content turnover theory. *Academy of Management Journal, 47*(4), 566–582.

Mobley, W. H., Griffeth, R. W., Hand, H. H., & Meglino, B. M. (1979). Review and conceptual analysis of the employee turnover process. *Psychological Bulletin, 86,* 493–522.

Muchinsky, P. M., & Morrow, P. C. (1980). A multidisciplinary model of voluntary employee turnover. *Journal of Vocational Behavior, 17,* 263–290.

Nalbantian, H. R., Guzzo, R. A., Keiffer, D., & Doherty, J. (2004). *Play to your strengths: Managing your internal labor markets for lasting competitive advantage.* New York: McGraw-Hill.

Nalbantian, H. R., & Szostak, A. (2004, Apr.). How Fleet Bank fought employee flight. *Harvard Business Review,* 1–8.

Price, J. L., & Mueller, C. W. (1981). A causal model of turnover for nurses. *Academy of Management Journal, 24*(3), 543–565.

Society for Human Resources Management Research. (2000). *Retention practices survey.* Society for Human Resources Management Research.

Steele, R., & Ovalle, N. (1984). A review and meta-analysis of research on the relationship between behavioral intentions and employee turnover. *Journal of Applied Psychology, 69,* 673–686.

CHAPTER 20

Driving Change Around the World

Employee Surveys in Global Organizations

John C. Scott
Paul M. Mastrangelo

Global corporations are finding organizational surveys to be increasingly useful for understanding the key drivers of employee behavior and informing their decisions around complex human resource (HR) and business issues. Properly designed employee surveys can be an invaluable guide for achieving key strategic and global integration initiatives. The goal of organizational surveys in this context is to provide the necessary data for making interventions that are aligned with the global vision and at the same time are actionable at the local level. To be effective, surveys must produce results that clearly link to key organizational outcomes, taking into account political, national, regional, and cultural boundaries that may have an impact on these connections.

This chapter addresses some of the key challenges facing organizations that are engaged in global or complex survey initiatives. We have drawn on both research and practice to identify the issues and provide recommendations for successfully translating survey results into meaningful action on a global scale. This chapter is intended for practitioners, researchers, and stakeholders who plan to use organizational surveys for effecting sustainable change on a global scale.

Our use of the term *global* in this chapter refers to both multinational organizations (for example, a U.S. company with subsidiaries around the world that more or less conform to the parent company and culture) and transnational organizations (for example, companies that target international markets and do not distinguish between national borders in product design or operation). Although the focus of this chapter is the global employee survey, the underlying themes apply to any survey process involving more than one business unit, culture, language, or country.

The complexities in administration and interpretation make the global survey different from the domestic survey (Johnson, 1996). These complexities challenge the survey design team and the organization across a number of fronts, from language translation and data collection to interpretation, reporting, and action planning.

Conducting Employee Surveys in Complex and Global Organizations

Worldwide trends within a global company's climate are difficult to detect, and ultimately the improvements that corporate headquarters seek to achieve can be hindered by the increased number of employees, layers of management, and cultural differences. With companies seeking to "off-shore" jobs in efforts to cut costs, the need for organizational assessment across borders, languages, and societies is undoubtedly on the rise. Not only is a global survey difficult to plan and administer, it also presents difficulties in effecting organizational change. A 1993 poll by Management Decisions Systems reported that the leading obstacles to survey practice were the failure to provide feedback, the lack of action planning and follow-through, and poor management commitment at middle and senior levels (cited in Kraut, 1996). Difficult as it is to overcome these obstacles, conducting an organizational survey in multiple locations around the world can only exacerbate these problems.

Characteristics of Global Surveys

The fundamental difference between a global organizational survey and a domestic survey is the tendency toward division throughout the survey process. Global corporations face a continuous conflict between standardization (application of a global strategy) and adjustment (applying multidomestic strategies). This conflict spills over into the design of survey tools. The more global the survey is, the more pressure exists to adopt the planning, administration, interpretation, and action according to each location.

Lingual Challenge

An obvious division in the global survey process occurs when survey items and other content have to be translated into the languages necessary for all employees to respond. Without careful attention to language translations, the validity and reliability of the data may be called into question because certain items "did not make sense" (validity) or "had a different meaning" (reliability) for a particular location. Bad translations that are detected too late or inconsistent or incorrect translations that are not detected at all may result in invalid or unreliable data. Perhaps the best way to guard against survey translation problems is to take the time to have all translations back-translated into the original language in which the survey was written.

Sometimes the complexities of multiple languages do not become apparent until managers are asked to explain differences between their region's survey results and the global findings. Other times languages present insurmountable barriers from the start. For example, some Arabic languages require computer fonts that are not compatible with typical office software or even HTML, which is programming code necessary for posting a Web survey. Even the data themselves may require translation into different languages. Open-ended comments written in respondents' native languages may need to be translated into the native language of corporate headquarters (typically English) or the regional manager. Furthermore, comments may need to be translated for the purpose of providing feedback to a particular set of employees, who may not be fluent in the same language. For example, the English comments read at headquarters may need to be communicated in both French and Flemish for the Belgian location.

Acceptable Survey Content

Another obvious example of global survey division is the conflicting standards among countries for acceptable survey content. Many U.S.-based organizations include a demographic question to record a participant's race or ethnicity, which might include options such as *African American, Asian/Pacific Islander,* or *Native American*. Obviously employees of African descent who work outside the United States will not identify with the term *African American* because it blends the concepts of race and citizenship. In a similar way *Asian/Pacific Islander* ignores the many peoples in the "Far East" (another Eurocentric term in itself). And while consideration for displaced native inhabitants is not a concept unique to the United States, those native peoples are certainly not all "Native American." For example, Australian employers are concerned with equal opportunity for the native Aborigine people, although they may not use the phrase "equal opportunity" in the same way that U.S. managers do. Indeed, many countries make it illegal to ask employees about their ethnicity. Similar differences occur across countries with issues related to gender, religion, and union affiliation. As a result of these various cultures and laws, a global survey either has to reduce content to what is globally acceptable or allow various versions of the survey to accommodate local needs.

Pathway to Action

Given all of the issues that accompany the implementation of a global survey, it can be easy to lose sight of the primary reason for the endeavor: to improve the productivity and work environment of the organization around the world. The survey is merely a means to that end. With increasingly global organizations demanding dashboards and metrics from their strategic HR and organization development (OD) teams, it is no easy task to move from statistics to action—or as one Fortune 50 survey director put it, "moving from data to doing." Fortunately, over the past decade, there have been a number of technical and theoretical developments in the field that have significantly enhanced the survey practitioner's effectiveness when conducting global surveys and effecting change. In this section, we review some of the more recent advances and lessons learned for ensuring that global survey efforts meet the requirements needed for supporting meaningful action. We follow that with specific strategies for translating global survey results into sustainable change.

Recent Trends and Lessons Learned Affecting Global Survey Efforts

A critical goal when conducting global survey initiatives is to obtain technically sound, actionable survey results that will provide a road map for effecting individual and organizational outcomes. While this goal is not unique to global survey efforts, the challenges associated with achieving it are magnified in this context. Advances in technology have rendered many of these challenges more manageable, while advances in survey research have surfaced issues that still need to be addressed. We address six key areas relevant to global surveys that have been affected by recent technology, research, and legislation: survey design and administration, managing response rates, reporting, measurement equivalence, privacy concerns, and stakeholder involvement.

Survey Design and Administration

While it is clear that Web-based administration can greatly facilitate the ease with which surveys are administered and the data captured, there are some lessons learned that might enhance the success of this approach, particularly when conducting surveys globally. A review of the literature and best practice indicates that first and foremost, the design of the survey should be simple so that it can more easily generalize across languages and cultures. In addition, the survey design needs to take into account the following issues:

- *Accessibility.* Since global or complex organizations may not always have the luxury of fully up-to-date or even standardized technology across all locations, it is possible that surveys may look different depending on the respondents' Web browser, operating system, screen setup, and other technical factors (Dillman, 2000; Dillman & Bowker, 2001, Umbach, 2004). The frustration tolerance of respondents may be quite low in cases where they are unable to access the survey on the first try. This can significantly depress response rates and ultimately have an impact on sample representation. It is therefore critical that Web designers test the system on all platforms and versions of the software currently in use within the organization to ensure that the survey looks and operates in the same way with all respondents.

- *Survey length.* It is a good idea to avoid long surveys appearing on a single screen since the task may be perceived as too tedious. Although this is not just a global issue, research has shown that respondents tend to skip questions in longer surveys (Church, 2001). Surveys should be broken into sections and the screens designed so that they are easy to navigate and move from page to page. In addition, it is beneficial to provide respondents with an expectation of survey length or a graphic indicator of their progress toward the survey's end. Experience has shown that managing expectations of completion time counts as much as the screen design in ensuring that the survey is fully completed.

- *Question perspective.* Especially in global surveys it becomes crucial to distinguish questions relevant at the global level (strategic questions), regional level (tactical questions), and local level (day-to-day or operational questions). This framework is necessary for organizing the results into a coherent, actionable model of organizational change by targeting questions (and ultimately interventions) to high-priority, long-term organizational goals as well as local quick-fix concerns. Respondents will be better able to provide the necessary data when the questions are organized in the appropriate context, and the survey team will have a clearer model to follow when determining sampling stratification variables and reporting specifications. In addition, certain of these survey sections can be parceled out and administered on a more frequent basis to track progress on initiatives where immediate action and quick gains can be realized.

- *Multiple languages.* Design issues become even more challenging when dealing with multiple languages. It is especially important to attend to ease of use and navigation across languages and pilot each version of the survey to evaluate this aspect. A strong partnership between corporate and regional information technology (IT) departments will be needed to identify and resolve these and other potential technical issues prior to survey administration. In addition, the survey should be piloted with representative respondents to fully flesh out design issues, language or cultural misinterpretations, coding problems, and other user interface concerns that may not be readily apparent through system testing alone.

Managing Response Rates

Response rates are always a concern when administering a survey where the goal is to capture representative data from multiple groups in diverse, sometimes remote locations. A low response rate throws into question the validity of the findings and reduces the statistical ability (power) to make meaningful comparisons across the groups of interest. Research and experience have shown that response rates are most positively influenced by ongoing, targeted communication from the organization's leadership. The use of online- or Web-administered surveys facilitates this communication by allowing response tracking and efficient delivery of tailored follow-up messages from both HR and business leaders.

The ability of online tools to track response rates in real time and follow up with online reminders offers a clear benefit over paper-based approaches. Some researchers have found that a single e-mail reminder doubles the response rate, and if this reminder is sent two days after the initial invitation, this rate may climb even higher (Crawford, Couper, & Lamias, 2001). To ensure anonymity, e-mail reminders are typically sent to all respondents, regardless of whether they have already completed the survey. While e-mail reminders are an important feature of Web-based surveys, it is important that the content of the initial and follow-up e-mails is clear, describes the purpose and time requirements for taking the survey, and includes an embedded link to the survey. In addition, personalized e-mails have been found to have a positive effect on response rates (Cook, Heath, & Thompson, 2000) and are easily managed with current software packages (Umbach, 2004). Thank-you letters generated from business leaders at the local level can also be effective at increasing response rates.

The use of multimethod approaches to survey administration, such as paper-based combined with Web-based, may also help to increase response rates and should be considered during the survey design, particularly where online access is in question. It should be noted, however, that when both pencil-and-paper and electronic modes of data collection are used, it will be necessary to match the two sets of responses, which requires additional effort for data cleaning and quality checks.

Reporting

Some organizations will want every manager with a minimum number of direct reports to receive a survey report, so that the results serve as a report card for all subunits. Other organizations will want reports issued only to managers of larger divisions, treating the survey more like an organizational assessment tool than a manager performance tool. Still other organizations will want results by demographics and write-in comments to appear in all managers' reports. What makes report specification planning so daunting is not just the sheer number of managers around the world, but also the attempt to accommodate so many stakeholders: corporate headquarters officials, managers of subsidiary companies within the organization, regional and functional vice presidents, midlevel managers, and line supervisors, among others.

Online Survey Reporting Tools. The availability of online, real-time data-slicing tools can be a significant support to global survey teams in responding to ongoing, urgent requests from managers around the company who want their data cut every way imaginable. These sorts of user tools allow the survey team to generate reports against any predefined variable (for example, cut data by location, then by race, then by tenure). This is contrasted with the more manual approach of having to program and run the data to generate customized reports as the requests come in.

In certain circumstances, the survey team may grant access to this function to trained managers who are interested in drilling further into the data to better understand the drivers of their results and create a foundation for action planning with their region, business unit, or function.

While online reporting tools offer a significant benefit to the survey team in accommodating manager data requirements, it is important to place appropriate controls on the flow of data and ensure that the various analyses and data cuts make sense for the situation, do not violate confidentiality, and can be appropriately interpreted. To prevent a free fall from data, it is wise to agree to some clear guidelines and challenge leadership to determine the essential reporting requirements needed to act meaningfully on the results. This should be done prior to the survey administration and be built into the report specifications to the extent possible. The survey leader in a global survey project needs to drive for a standard set of reports and regulate to the extent possible special requests or variations from these standards. While follow-up data requests are to be expected, the bulk of the reporting requirements should be clearly worked out in advance.

Defining Report Specifications. The survey team needs to consider a number of important aspects when designing the reporting and feedback process. Determining the variables or demographics of interest (for example, location, business unit, or tenure) is of paramount importance. Usually these items are built into the survey, and the survey designers rely on respondent self-reported selections. Another option is to hard-code (using human resources information system data) each respondent to an existing database containing demographics for reporting. The latter generally provides more complete data, but is possible only if the organization has data available and the respondents log in under a defined user name, such as an e-mail address. Regardless of the source of the demographic information, controls need to be in place to protect confidentiality. It is essential to ensure that both confidentiality and anonymity are maintained where promised. Respondents should be made aware of how their data will be used and under what conditions, if any, they can be individually identified. To protect confidentiality, a minimum number of respondents is generally required to report data for any selected data cut, say, eight to ten respondents; this restriction becomes even more vital when a data reporting tool is opened to trained managers.

Establishing Report Formats. Report formats should be simple and globally accessible, such as that offered by a PDF (Adobe's portable document format). In general, PDF files are more accessible due to the freeware distribution of Adobe's Acrobat Reader. This is especially important in environments where cost of software is of concern. By producing reports in a globally accessible format, the survey administration divorces itself from retail software. In addition, and perhaps more important, Adobe Acrobat files permit the report creator to set sophisticated security settings. For example, changes to reports can be disallowed, thereby ensuring display of appropriate and unchanged data. In addition, other security measures, including encrypted access, number of times a file may be printed, and number of times a file may be accessed, can be set using third-party "plug-ins." In general, we recommend starting with the globally accessible solution and then considering the capabilities of the organization with the resource costs and purpose of the reports in mind.

As leaders are given responsibility for communicating survey results and developing action plans within their own local organizations, providing report data in a format such as Excel (in addition to a formatted report such as a PDF) may also be a significant benefit when online reporting tools are not available. This allows the secondary users to extract data around specific areas of focus (within defined parameters that ensure confidentiality and appropriate use of the data).

Measurement Equivalence

One of the basic goals in a global survey effort is to make comparisons across countries and cultures with respect to the attitudes being measured. These comparisons are meaningful only to the extent that the constructs being measured are conceptually equivalent across languages and cultures. The construct being measured must mean the same thing regardless of language or culture. Survey scales that are compared across countries without taking measurement equivalence into account can lead to erroneous conclusions and unfounded actions (Ryan, Chan, Ployhart, & Slade, 1999).

Assessing Equivalence.   While there is substantial research on this topic and numerous strategies for assessing measurement equivalence (Candell & Hulin, 1986; Hulin & Mayer, 1986; Raju & Ellis, 2002; Riordan & Vandenberg, 1994; Ryan et al., 1999), the tendency is for survey practitioners to ignore the possibility of nonequivalence and avoid conducting the necessary analyses (Ryan et al., 1999). As a best practice, researchers involved in global survey initiatives should conduct analyses of equivalence that consider both culture and language to avoid misdirected action. While this may seem impractical and a luxury to those who are constrained by tight time lines and resources, a consideration of the impact that inaccurate survey data can have on organizational change efforts should elevate the importance of this activity. It should be noted that it is not enough to simply ensure that the survey has been properly translated. Although accurate translations are necessary, they are not sufficient to ensure that the same conceptual frame of reference is being elicited by the survey across different languages and cultures.

There are obviously realistic limitations for ensuring measurement equivalence across all of the languages and cultures prior to survey administration due to time pressures, resource restrictions, and push-back on the part of the line organization, which may not see the value added for this level of purity. Survey researchers may find it more practical to conduct the measurement equivalence studies as part of their analyses following administration. Also, nonequivalent items can be identified and removed prior to reporting, or the items can be flagged as nonequivalent and the resulting interpretation couched in this context (Ryan et al., 1999).

Indications of Nonequivalence. Questions of measurement equivalence should arise when whole groups of employees from a particular region or country provide consistently lower (or higher) ratings than their U.S.-based counterparts. This commonly observed phenomenon is often interpreted as a characteristic of the group rather than of the survey measure. Unless an analysis of measurement equivalence has been conducted, it will be impossible to tease out whether these results are based on measurement error (such as response biases) or truly reflect actual differences in perception.

When reporting the global survey results, it is extremely useful to understand why the differences in ratings occurred and what role measurement error played. Since interventions will be configured based on ratings and their differences across comparison groups, the analysis of measurement equivalence should be an integral part of the overall ratings analysis.

Reduced-Length Surveys. Measurement equivalence also needs to be considered when using reduced-length, or pulse, surveys, particularly when these shortened surveys are functioning to measure the same constructs as their full-length parent survey. Meaningful comparisons between the two versions require that the psychometric characteristics of the full-length survey be preserved in the shortened version (Stanton, Sinar, Balzer, & Smith, 2002).

Privacy Concerns

New laws and regulations have been enacted in almost every industrialized country to protect the privacy of its citizens. For example, the European Union Privacy Directive is a series of strict privacy laws enacted in 1998 by the fifteen-nation (twenty-five nations as of 2004) European Union (EU) to protect its citizens from privacy invasion and restrict the information collection activities of governments and corporations. Article 1 of the directive requires member states to protect the "fundamental rights and freedoms of natural persons, and in particular their right to privacy with respect to the processing of personal data" (European Union, 1995). Global organizations should closely examine the EU Privacy Directive since they are bound by these laws when collecting survey information from their employees working in EU member countries.

Under the European Privacy Directive, survey respondents are granted, among other things, access to the data, the right to know where the data originated, the right to correct or block data inaccuracies, and the right to withhold consent to use their data. In addition, certain demographic data, such as ethnic or racial origin and trade union membership, can be processed only with the explicit consent of the individual.

Article 25 of the EU Privacy Directive forbids any transfer of personal data outside the EU to countries that do not guarantee or do not have in place adequate safeguards for such data. The U.S. Department of Commerce has developed a set of Safe Harbor Provisions in response to this directive to help U.S.-based organizations avoid interruptions in their data collection efforts and to avoid facing prosecution by European authorities under these privacy laws. Certifying to the safe harbor indicates that the organization provides adequate privacy protection, as defined by the directive.

Certain companies may not be willing to use Safe Harbor Provisions because of the broad restrictions and onerous preparatory paperwork. It is therefore necessary for the survey team to consider all of the relevant laws and regulations when collecting survey data across international borders. Beyond country-specific privacy regulations, there are also state or provincial laws that need to be taken into account (examples are Quebec's differences from the rest of Canada and French and German differences within the EU) when collecting data across borders.

Before embarking on a global survey initiative, the survey team should engage the organization's legal counsel in a review of the survey's content and purpose and solicit direction regarding the organization's compliance with the applicable privacy laws and restrictions. It is also important that the survey leader or the U.S. legal staff check with in-country counsel as well. This generally adds time and complexity to the process and should be integrated into the overall planning effort.

Stakeholder Involvement

Stakeholder involvement is critical throughout all phases of the survey process, from design through implementation of the change. The survey team must identify and involve the organization's key stakeholders (representing all levels, regions, businesses, and demographics) at the beginning of the survey process to cultivate agreement on expected outcomes. Since these stakeholders will ultimately be responsible for using the information and translating the results into action, their input and commitment are particularly critical during the early stages of the survey process. It is necessary to ensure that a thorough exploration of the information needs of these stakeholders is undertaken and agreement is established as to how the survey data will be put to use.

Regional teams, comprising HR and key stakeholders (or their designees), need to be assembled during the survey design phase to review and completely vet the survey questions. As Johnson (1996) points out, certain narrow cultural concepts do not necessarily translate well to other cultures, and an organization's inattentiveness to this fact may be insulting to a country's employees. Not only does this vetting activity help to ensure that the questions are sensible and resonate across languages and cultures, it also serves to engender regional ownership. Regional leaders and other stakeholders who feel ownership of the survey will be more engaged when it comes time to act on the results. This is not a process that can be executed by corporate alone.

Translating Results into Action

We now turn to some of the key challenges confronting the global survey team in its effort to translate survey results into consequential change. As part of this review, we will advance recommendations for creating the support systems needed to implement and sustain survey-based change.

Compared to a relatively simple survey conducted at one location, a global survey is not only more complicated to administer, but it is also more complicated in yielding action. Consider the number of stakeholders present when a global organization conducts a worldwide census. Survey planning at the corporate level has to be tailored to meet the needs of business units, which themselves may span regions and countries. Each business unit is likely to have its own unique organizational structure, led by its own upper management team. And each of these managers likely feels (and maybe is) half a world away from corporate management, who often prescribes survey content, report specifications, and action planning schedules. Frequent and regular communication with representatives from each country or business unit (a global survey team) is recommended to address the communication of expectations, the interpretation of results, and the global accountability for improvements.

Communicate Actionable Results on a Global Scale

The broad communication of responsibilities and performance expectations is a fundamental determinant of the success of a global survey initiative. All levels of the organization need to clearly understand the goals of the survey and their role in supporting the organizational change. Ongoing communication before, during, and after the survey is pivotal for establishing and sustaining the momentum needed to drive results. This requires a solid communication plan that incorporates a unifying vision for change with a clear set of accountabilities.

It is not possible to overcommunicate when attempting to build accountability for action. Representatives from the corporate communications group should play an integral role on the global survey and implementation teams to ensure that consistent and effective messages are delivered across all levels within the organization. This group's expertise should be leveraged to assist the senior-most levels down through first-level supervisors by helping craft the messages and route the communication through appropriate media from informal, formal, face-to-face, "town hall" meetings, audio conferences, newsletters, bulletins, and electronic media. The corporate communications representatives should collaborate with regional communication directors and provide ample time for the global plan to be tailored to fit within each region. The key message here should be leadership's commitment to take action as well as a call to action to all employees. Executing this communication strategy requires strong leadership focus and the continuous engagement of all employees.

The survey leader, in consultation with local survey and business leaders, has the responsibility for determining which managers around the globe should receive a report and what information should be contained in that report. The survey leader must navigate these political land mines by understanding and communicating who ultimately "owns" the data and how the data are to be used. Managers must be properly trained to interpret and translate results into action, and the survey team must be prepared to deliver the results in a timely fashion to sustain momentum.

Train Managers

Leaders and managers should understand their broad accountability for encouraging participation, communicating findings, acting on the results, and providing information about next steps. In turn, employees should be provided with clear expectations that they are accountable for executing the strategy directives that result from the survey's findings.

Managers should be provided with communication directives and the necessary training to ensure effective delivery. A significant part of the training should include what is expected of managers who receive a report. The training should teach managers how to quickly and correctly interpret data. They will need to know how and when to communicate results to their own subordinates. They will want to know when senior leaders will communicate results to employees and when their direct superiors will be viewing the data. The survey leader in corporate headquarters might be able to dictate this course of events, but it is more likely that he or she will present a recommended guideline to the business units or countries. Showing a time line of events (or at least a recommended time line) helps managers move from data interpretation to action. For a global organization, this educational process may need to be repeated several times for multiple audiences. And as wonderful as virtual meetings may be, language and cultural barriers are best overcome by using on-site training, where verbal and nonverbal feedback can ensure complete understanding.

Deliver Timely Results

Many survey leaders talk about "analysis paralysis," where the HR or OD staff spend so much time interpreting results that they stop the momentum toward organizational change. Instead of leveraging the recent survey administration to raise awareness of employees' concerns and management's reactions, there is a tendency to hold on to the data to make sure that no question is left unanswered. If there is a delay in sharing survey results, employees begin to wonder if the survey was just an exercise in futility. To ask for opinions and then put forth no communication of what is going on is probably more damaging than if you never surveyed the employees in the first place. Timely communication of results and subsequent change efforts are essential, especially when that communication must traverse multiple countries through multiple layers of management. It does not take long for employees to wonder, "Does corporate headquarters care about us over here?"

One guideline for postsurvey action is to have all employees receive a basic communication of survey results within thirty days from the end of survey administration. To meet this time line across the globe, reports must be made available quickly, managers have to learn how to look at their data, and the entire management team should understand their responsibilities regarding communication and change efforts. Each of these steps requires advanced preparation and coordination. If it is not possible to communicate survey results this quickly, it is advisable to at least send out thank-you letters from business leaders to respondents explaining when and how results will be shared and the process for determining actions. This approach serves to reinforce and demonstrate business leader commitment to the process.

Interpret Geographical Differences in Results

Organizational change efforts begin after an analysis indicates that something is in need of improvement. How these efforts unfold depends in part on where this need exists. An organization with business units across multiple countries will want to analyze the entire entity, including a comparison among its separate elements. As business leaders look to supplement financial and market data with a "people metric," the organizational survey will be called on to provide this information. However, interpreting survey data across countries and cultures requires consideration of timing, business context, and normative comparisons.

Consider Timing of Administration

Survey data are snapshots in time. Just as a camera can capture the moment when a person has an unusual expression or odd appearance to create an unflattering picture, the survey can capture perceptions that are accurate within the moment but misleading as a lasting record. Unlike financial data, which are aggregated throughout the fiscal year, survey data are typically collected within a matter of weeks, and not necessarily the same set of weeks. Historically, it has been easier for a global organization to create a core survey that has various administration times throughout a survey cycle (say, a year). With this approach, local holidays and norms can be catered to, and there is less need for coordination of events. One negative consequence, however, is that the analysis of separate business units within the organization is confounded by the element of time. The timing of events (a merger announcement or a recalled product, for example) can make it difficult to decipher whether differences among locations are real or chronologically created. In the past decade, Internet technology has made it easier for a global survey to be administered at one time, creating a more timely business metric. Still, events experienced by employees around the world within that same time frame will vary greatly.

It is recommended that the global survey team stay abreast of location-specific events that may affect the interpretation of survey results. This information should be elicited from regional management and global survey team members throughout the survey design and administration phases. Any key issues that would likely affect results interpretation should be reported as such and accounted for when making decisions about postsurvey action.

Account for Business Context

The degree to which each business unit's context should affect the interpretation of survey results depends on the degree to which each unit in the global organization operates as a separate business entity. A "freestanding" company that exists within a global firm must consider its own opportunities and threats to prioritize survey content for action. These local priorities may or may not support changes desired by corporate leadership. For example, new legislation in the European Community might lead a business unit in Europe to seek rapid product development. Therefore, the survey category that focuses on procedural changes and innovation may be the top priority in Europe even though headquarters in the United States is emphasizing something else. Each location should have some voice in determining what action is appropriate given the survey results and specific business context.

Even if business units are given complete freedom in determining postsurvey action, it is generally advisable for this effort to be coordinated with a corporate headquarters survey or OD staff to provide guidance on what analyses, timetables, and documentation should be used as a template for managing change. By centrally coordinating this activity, a common set of guidelines and standards can be applied that takes into account business context while ensuring alignment with the overall goals and vision for the change effort across the organization. The organization realizes efficiencies, and the individual business unit benefits from a vetted set of procedures and a knowledgeable organizational resource. For example, the corporate OD staff could offer change management training for each business unit where the preparation is done just once and shared globally. There is no reinventing the wheel, but the tread can still be modified to match the local pavement. The environmentalist dictum, "Think globally, act locally," provides a useful conceptual model to follow in this context.

Present Relevant Comparisons

Differences between societies and cultures also affect how managers look at and act on their survey results. For example, a global producer of health care products is finding survey scores from Latin America that average nine percentage points higher in favorability as compared to the worldwide average. For this reason, many survey leaders seek out items with preexisting normative comparisons (international norms aggregated by country or region). In an effort to oblige, some survey consulting companies pool data from clients that operate in a given region. However, the degree to which the consultants' client data truly represent a region likely depends on the number of clients with units in that region, the job types represented in each region, the timeliness of the surveys, and so on. Survey consortiums can also be a source of global norms, but the same difficulties apply. The accuracy of their regional norms depends on participating companies' providing timely data that adequately represent all functions in each location. Are those high scores from Latin America due to cultural differences or the existence of only sales employees at this location?

Review the Global Survey Research. There is an increasing need for published research that investigates normative differences in global employee surveys and how these differences vary by the content of the items. Hofstede's landmark 1980 book, *Culture's Consequences,* used IBM's survey data (from 1968 and 1972) to identify four dimensions of work life that differ by society: psychological distance between boss and subordinate (Power Distance), intolerance of ambiguity (Uncertainty Avoidance), importance of individual rather than collective work goals (Individualism), and competitive rather than cooperative environment (Masculinity). His second edition lays out a fifth dimension that addresses long-term versus short-term orientation (Hofstede, 2001). Results from a cluster analysis of these dimensions (with some judgmental modifications) yielded eight clusters of the forty represented countries. These culture areas are summarized in Table 20.1.

The Latin, Asian, and Near Eastern cultures were characterized by a preferred separation between a supervisor and subordinate (high power distance, an authoritarian leadership style). The Germanic and Nordic cultures, and to a lesser extent the Anglo culture, sought more equality from the formal power structure (consultative leadership style where disagreement with a leader can be expressed). The Latin, Japanese, and the Near Eastern cultures showed more of a preference for avoiding uncertainty (adhering to rules, expecting long tenure, and experiencing less stress) than the other culture areas. The Anglo, Nordic, and more developed Latin cultures were characterized by high individualism (more importance attributed to personal time, freedom, and challenge than to use of skills, physical conditions, and training). Finally, Japan and the Anglo cultures showed a high degree of masculinity (more

Table 20.1. Summary of Hofstede's Culture Areas

Culture Area	Power Distance	Uncertainty Avoidance	Individualism	Masculinity
More developed Latin (Belgium and France with Argentina, Brazil, Spain, Italy)	High	High	Medium to high	Medium
Less developed Latin (Mexico, Colombia, Venezuela, Chile, Peru, Portugal)	High	High	Low	Low to high
More developed Asian (Japan)	Medium	High	Medium	High
Less developed Asian (Hong Kong, Singapore, Taiwan, India, Pakistan, Thailand, the Philippines)	High	Low to medium	Low	Medium
Near Eastern (Greece, Iran, Turkey, Yugoslavia)	High	High	Low	Medium
Germanic (Austria, Israel, Germany, Switzerland)	Low	Medium to high	Medium	Medium to high
Anglo (United States, Australia, Canada, Great Britain, Ireland, New Zealand)	Low to medium	Low to medium	High	High
Nordic (Denmark, Finland, Netherlands, Norway, Sweden)	Low	Low to medium	Medium to high	Low

importance attributed to earnings, recognition, and advancement rather than cooperation, working in a desirable area, and employment security).

Hofstede's work can provide survey leaders with some expectations for how their survey scores might differ by country. However, this study may not represent the full range of organizations or job types. Although Hofstede's data were collected from sixty-five countries and fifty occupations, only a few large countries contained all occupations, and only a few occupations (for example, sales representatives and office clerks) occurred in all countries. Furthermore, all participants worked for the same U.S.-based organization.

The more recent and comprehensive GLOBE Study (House, Hanges, Javidan, Dorfman, & Gupta, 2004) surveyed 17,370 middle managers from 951 organizations, using a stratified sample to represent the financial, food processing, and telecommunications industries across sixty-two countries. Only domestic (noninternational) organizations were included, and size per country averaged 251 participants (ranging from 27 to 1,790). A clustering procedure was used to group societies into ten cultural clusters (versus eight culture areas in Hofstede, 2001), which were then compared according to nine cultural dimensions (versus five dimensions in Hofstede, 2001). The GLOBE study also included two sets of survey items: one that asks what "should be" (values) and a matched set asking about perceptions "as is" (practices). (We recommend that leaders of global surveys review Chapter Ten in House et al., 2004, for details.)

These results indicate that Anglo cultures (including the United States, Canada, and Australia) "have mid-level scores on most of the practices and values dimensions of GLOBE" (House et al., 2004, p. 200). Anglo cultures are most similar to Germanic and Nordic Europe and least similar to Eastern Europe and the Middle East. Also, the Latin European and Latin American cultures tend to have scores opposite those of Confucian and Southern Asia cultures. (See House et al.'s metaconfiguration of GLOBE societal cultures, p. 201.) These findings, although not specific to survey content, match our experiences working with survey results from global organizations.

Interpret Global Comparisons with Healthy Skepticism. Although these research efforts provide a starting point for survey professionals to interpret global survey results, there are still a number of research questions concerning the construction of international normative comparisons. Consider one global conglomerate (headquartered in the United States) that recently conducted its worldwide survey and found more favorable responses (averaged across items) for Latin American units and less favorable responses for Asian units. Are the Latin peoples more comfortable making extreme opinions than are Asian peoples? Is this difference partly determined by the perceived prestige of this company (headquartered in the United States) in other countries? Is this a measurement equivalence issue? To what extent would changes in the survey content affect the magnitude of these regional differences? Are these regional differences just a mask for functional differences, such as operations being based in one location while only sales is in another? Business leaders will rightfully ask these methodological questions before investing resources to eliminate gaps. Besides reviewing cross-cultural organizational research, survey leaders should explore available international data from consultants, consortia, or noncompetitive companies as a comparison against their own data.

When considering international norms, we recommend investigating not only the sample size for a given region, but also the accuracy of the sample in representing that region's employers and job options. The ideal source of international norms would be a representative sample of each country's workforce. If an ongoing representative survey existed to provide normative data from employees in countries around the globe, survey leaders would have a far more accurate understanding of cultural differences. Until such time, survey leaders should consider tracking their own company's survey data by country or region to create internal normative comparisons for global locations.

Build Accountabilities for Survey-Driven Change

Even if the development, administration, communication, and interpretation phases of the survey have each been handled well, the ultimate success of the survey still depends on the process of planning and implementing postsurvey action. Too frequently organizations identify so many areas for improvement that they fail to make headway anywhere. Employees fail to see meaningful change, managers become frustrated by the lack of support, and the survey itself is perceived as "just an HR exercise." In these situations, the root problem is the lack of a unified purpose for action. The reader might recall the expression that a horse designed by committee comes out looking like a camel. Given the number of stakeholders in a global survey, the action phase can easily meet a similar fate.

Although there are a number of specific methods for successfully implementing change, the reality is that for large-scale, global initiatives, the CEO and executive team need to be squarely behind the process and willing to invest the energy needed to integrate these initiatives into their organization's strategic and HR planning. It is only through this level of support and commitment that meaningful change can be effected across the organization. Successful strategies for driving global change through surveys must therefore start with ensuring that the top layer of the organization has a common vision for the desired state and is willing to invest in building the necessary foundation to support assessment and change. Without this level of commitment, global organizations will find that the survey process is a complex exercise in wheel spinning.

Establish Roles and Responsibilities to Drive Change Efforts

In a global organization, there are three primary focal points for building the accountability infrastructure: executive leadership, regional management, and employees. Successful survey initiatives that lead to action do so by engaging these three layers of the organization through all phases of the process and link bottom-line results to tangible, personal outcomes such as compensation and bonuses. As a first step in cascading change accountability throughout the organization, the overall survey results should be presented to the CEO and senior leadership team and interpreted around the major issues being surveyed. A commitment to action should be reaffirmed and communicated to the entire organization at this point (Church & Waclawski, 1998).

Assuming that the change effort is communicated as a cohesive message from corporate headquarters, the process (whether mandated or recommended) must still be directed through global constituencies: the heads of the businesses, regions, or countries. For organizations with complex structures, a decision has to be made regarding who is responsible for creating the action plans and implementing them. A regional vice president in Europe, for example, may have "dotted line" authority over a plant in France, but the head of that plant might directly answer to the vice president of manufacturing. Should action plans be developed and filed with the person who has better knowledge of the local landscape or the person who has the formal authority to drive action? In the ideal world, these individuals would work together to formulate a plan that meets the local needs and has the level of needed sponsorship to ensure success. While this would certainly be the recommended course of action, organizational realities may dictate an alternate approach. It is critical, however, that the roles and expectations of all key stakeholders in the change initiative be outlined to ensure that the change initiative is appropriately planned and sponsored.

Once the results have been communicated to the CEO and executive team, it is recommended that regional management take the lead and designate teams (comprising both line and HR) within their respective areas to drill into and interpret the results. These teams would be charged with identifying ways to close the gaps between the actual and desired results. The initial deliverable from these sessions should be the identification of two to three areas that are critical to the entire organization and span regions and businesses. Armed with this information on a global basis, the organization can initiate immediate action that is globally relevant and publicly demonstrates a commitment to taking the results seriously. These immediate actions can then be followed by region-specific interventions that support and are aligned with the overall goals but are tailored and implemented locally.

Line managers and immediate supervisors then have the day-to-day responsibility for keeping the survey results alive through ongoing dialogue with their employees. They are in the best position to notice and communicate improvements and remind their employees of how their actions link to the bottom line. First-line managers should integrate the survey results into ongoing discussions about progress on strategic initiatives and business plans.

This process cascades within each region, relying on teams and allowing tailored action plans based on the specific needs and context of the business and functional units within each region. While the right model for creating actionable areas clearly depends on corporate culture, the degree of autonomy among an organization's business units, and the criticality of a concentrated change effort at a given time, it is generally advisable to allow the planning and execution around these areas to be determined by levels most directly affected by the change.

Link Action to the Bottom Line

Organizations that connect survey-based change management efforts to specific, measurable performance objectives exact greater accountability for desired outcomes. Furthermore, when incentives are clearly linked to explicit performance expectations, the process acquires some teeth. This starts at the top level of the organization, where actions need to be integrated into the strategic plan and specifically tied to performance objectives. Interventions based on survey results should be directly tied to incentives, such as bonuses, starting at the highest levels within the organization. The use of such mechanisms as balanced scorecards (Kaplan & Norton, 1993) or the Management Performance Profile (Church & Waclawski, 1998) can be used to translate strategic change objectives into executives' performance measures, evaluate progress, and provide a link to compensation. This strategy can then be integrated throughout the organization, where organizational, regional, and individual performance objectives are tied to the survey-driven actions.

Church and Waclawski (1998) have also noted that surveys are particularly useful (and more likely to drive change) when their results are linked to other performance outcomes, such as customer satisfaction or profitability. To the extent that survey results can be linked to hard organizational performance outcomes, the results take on increased importance and can serve to target areas for intervention. This information should then be communicated broadly to demonstrate the relevance of the survey and meaningfulness of actions to be taken. There have been numerous studies conducted and published over the past ten years that have analyzed the linkages between employee and customer attitudes and organizational outcomes (Brooks, 2000).

As this linkage research base grows, stable propositions can be made about the relationships between employee attitudes and bottom-line organizational outcomes. Complex organizations generally possess the large number of units necessary to identify stable patterns between survey data and organizational outcomes. It should be noted, however, that complex organizations might also suffer from incompatible HR systems, nonstandard definitions of outcomes, and no one-performance indicator. The key to successful linkage research is careful design and planning.

Monitor Results

No matter what level of the organization is responsible for initiating postsurvey action, the job of monitoring the status of actions and future survey results belongs to management, proceeding up the to the highest levels of the organization. Historically, this is the stage of the survey process when action dies—where more urgent initiatives arise, the survey results are forgotten, and by the time the next survey needs to be administered, the plans are deemed outdated. Yet the success of the survey process will be judged by the improvement that it yields. Ironically, this crucial stage of the survey process is the one that is most removed from the survey leader's control because accountability rests with management.

Following the old adage that what gets measured gets done, it is essential to integrate an evaluation of the survey process (Edwards & Fisher, 2003) and organizational change effort (Church, 2003) into the global survey initiative to ensure that the stated goals are being met and that any necessary course corrections are made during the implementation process. By measuring progress and publicly communicating the results of the evaluation, there emerges a powerful incentive for following through on change initiatives.

Conclusion

Global organizations need their surveys to be not only a record of year-to-year results but also an impetus for change throughout locations. Global and complex organizations are increasingly relying on the employee survey process to help drive their change initiatives. Well-designed global surveys can serve as an invaluable tool for understanding the key drivers of employees' behavior and for identifying and prioritizing areas for intervention across the organization. In this context, surveys can act as a global platform to communicate the organization's vision while measuring progress toward accomplishing its objectives. The challenge when conducting survey-based change initiatives on a global scale is to ensure that the interventions guided by the survey are aligned with the global vision while at the same time actionable at the local level. This requires careful attention to local differences and circumstances when designing, administering, and interpreting the survey.

Accountability for action originates from crafting the survey and change processes around a common vision and holding management and employees responsible for the consequences. Leaders need to be accountable for self-engaging as well as enlisting their employees' commitment to the change. This responsibility emerges through the establishment of clear expectations and is reinforced through a variety of targeted performance management strategies and incentives.

A lot of things have to go right to bring the global survey from administration to effective action. Clearly, the process improves as the survey team gains more experience. Unfortunately, many organizations no longer assign the task of surveying its employees to a dedicated staff of organizational researchers. Increasingly, global surveys are used as developmental projects for young, upcoming HR generalists who may rotate out of the position after the survey administration has ended. This practice damages the survey process not only for the organization but also for the profession. Therefore, it becomes increasingly important to network across organizational boundaries, seek out best practices, and recruit experienced survey practitioners as members of the survey team.

References

Brooks, S. M. (2000). Diagnosing the value chain: A summary of linkage research dynamics. In J. Dietz & S. D. Pugh (Co-Chairs), *A New Time in Service Research: Moving Beyond Main Effects and Isolated Theoretical Perspectives.* Symposium conducted at the Academy of Management Meeting, Toronto, Canada.

Candell, G. L., & Hulin, C. L. (1986). Cross-language and cross-cultural comparisons in scale translations: Independent sources of information about item nonequivalence. *Journal of Cross-Cultural Psychology, 17,* 417–440.

Church, A. H. (2001). Is there a method to our madness? The impact of data collection methodology on organizational survey results. *Personnel Psychology, 54,* 937–969.

Church, A. H. (2003). Organization development. In J. E. Edwards, J. C. Scott, & N. S. Raju (Eds.), *The human resources program-evaluation handbook* (pp. 322–342). Thousand Oaks, CA: Sage.

Church, A. H., & Waclawski, J. (1998). *Designing and using organizational surveys*. Brookfield, VT: Gower.

Cook, C., Heath, F., & Thompson, R. L. (2000). A meta-analysis of response rates in Web or Internet-based surveys. *Educational and Psychological Measurement, 60*(6), 821–836.

Crawford, S. D., Couper, M. P., & Lamias, M. J. (2001). Web surveys: Perceptions of burden. *Social Science Computer Review, 19*(2), 146–162.

Dillman, D. A. (2000). *Mail and Internet surveys: The tailor design method* (2nd ed.) New York: Wiley.

Dillman, D. A., & Bowker, D. (2001). The Web questionnaire challenge to survey methodologists. In U. D. Reips & M. Bosnjak (Eds.), *Dimensions of Internet science*. Lengerich, Germany: Pabst Science.

Edwards, J. E., & Fisher, B. M. (2003). Evaluating organizational survey programs. In J. E. Edwards, J. C. Scott, & N. S. Raju (Eds.), *The human resources program-evaluation handbook* (pp. 365–386). Thousand Oaks, CA: Sage.

European Union Directive 95/46/EC. (1995). *Official Journal of the European Communities of 23 November 1995*. No. L. 281, pp. 31–50.

Hofstede, G. (1980). *Cultural consequences: International differences in work-related values*. Thousand Oaks, CA: Sage.

Hofstede, G. (2001). *Cultural consequences: Comparing values, behaviors, institutions and organizations across nations* (2nd ed.). Thousand Oaks, CA: Sage.

House, R. J., Hanges, P. J., Javidan, M., Dorfman, P. W., & Gupta, V. (2004). *Culture, leadership, and organizations: The GLOBE study of 62 societies*. Thousand Oaks, CA: Sage.

Hulin, C. L., & Mayer, L. J. (1986). Psychometric equivalence of a translation of the Job Descriptive Index into Hebrew. *Journal of Applied Psychology, 67*, 818–825.

Johnson, S. R. (1996). The multinational opinion survey. In A. I. Kraut (Ed.), *Organizational surveys: Tools for assessment and change*. San Francisco: Jossey-Bass.

Kaplan, R. S., & Norton, D. P. (1993). Putting the balanced scorecard to work. *Harvard Business Review, 71*(5), 134–147.

Kraut, A. I. (Ed.). (1996). *Organizational surveys: Tools for assessment and change*. San Francisco: Jossey-Bass.

Raju, N. S., & Ellis, B. B. (2002). Differential item and test functioning. In F. Drasgow and N. Schmitt (Eds.), *Measuring and analyzing behavior in organizations* (pp. 156–188). San Francisco: Jossey-Bass.

Riordan, C. M., & Vandenberg, R. J. (1994). A central question in cross-cultural research: Do employees of different cultures interpret work-related measures in an equivalent manner? *Journal of Management, 20,* 643–671.

Ryan, A. M., Chan, D., Ployhart, R. E., & Slade, L. A. (1999). Employee attitude surveys in a multinational organization: Considering language and culture in assessing measurement equivalence. *Personnel Psychology, 52,* 37–57.

Stanton, J. M., Sinar, E. F., Balzer, W. K., & Smith, P. C. (2002). Issues and strategies for reducing the length of self-report scales. *Personnel Psychology, 55,* 167–194.

Umbach, P. D. (2004). "Web surveys: Best practices." In S. R. Porter (ed.), *Overcoming survey research problems. New Directions for Institutional Research, 121,* 23–38.

CHAPTER 21

Building an Inclusive Culture

The Communicating Managers Program

Robert J. Quinn

People love to be with a winner. Sometimes called the "cocktail party phenomenon," people want to respond to the question, "What do you do?" with pride about not only where they work but about their role in that institution. This chapter describes how one of five diverse businesses at JPMorgan Chase (see Box 21.1) built a culture of inclusion where all staff felt they were a part of something important. Using the strategic intent of the organization as a basis, an organization development (OD) initiative gathered climate information from the annual opinion poll, engaged management around the results, and, based on their definition of the issues, aligned communication, performance management, training, and recognition events to engineer a broad change effort designed to build a culture of inclusion. Particularly important to the success of this effort was the use of employee opinion poll data to establish accountability for change.

Box 21.1. The Businesses at JPMorgan Chase

JPMorgan Chase* is a global organization of approximately 100,000 employees in five distinct and diverse businesses that are bound together by a common purpose and a shared set of values.

The high-powered *Investment Bank* is made up of professionals who have been recruited from the best universities worldwide or have joined in midcareer after highly successful engagements in other elite investment banking organizations.

The *Private Bank and the Venture Capital* businesses are similarly staffed and respected by clients and competitors in those businesses. All of these businesses are team oriented and partner around a deal or customer to deliver high-level and innovative solutions to some of the most elaborate financial challenges faced by high-net-worth individuals, start-up ventures, or established corporations around the world. In acting as financial consultants to these clients, relationships are formed, and JPMorgan Chase has become a valued partner in what makes these clients successful.

On a different scale but with a similar business model is the *Consumer Bank* of JPMorgan Chase. With many more clients, each with varying financial needs, client service personnel bring to bear banking, credit, mortgage, and investment management products to build a relationship with consumers. Just as with the larger clients, the intent is to partner with the consumer to ensure that all financial needs are met in a way that helps ensure success for the goals and aspirations of the client.

The fifth business at JPMorgan Chase is the operating services business, *Treasury and Security Services* (TSS), which consists of approximately 15,000 employees worldwide. More closely aligned to the commercial business than the consumer, TSS provides cash management, securities processing, and trustee services to corporations, fund managers, and government institutions among others. As with the other businesses, TSS emphasizes a client focus, service quality, and innovative solutions to business and financial management needs.

*Data and JPMorgan Chase description were created before the 2004 merger with Bank One.

Strategic Intent at JPMorgan Chase

Despite the diversity in businesses that make up JPMorgan Chase, there are commonalities that transcend the differences and form the basis for the existence of an integrated organization. In fact, the integration of the diverse businesses is seen as a competitive advantage since clients may satisfy a range of needs while dealing with the same organization. This advantage may be realized only if staff from the different businesses work effectively with each other and feel comfortable in referring their customers to other areas of the corporation and the corporation expends significant effort to make that happen.

"One Firm, One Team, Be a Leader"

Each business in JPMorgan Chase is in the service industry. Under the principle of "One Firm, One Team, Be a Leader," JPMorgan Chase extols the values and character that are common to the firm and encourages each employee to be a leader in living that principle. Most important to realizing the strategic intent of the corporation is the belief by all staff that customer service is a common value and that customers who are referred to other areas of the company will receive the highest-quality service.

The human resource department plays a strategic role in creating a culture that supports the "One Firm, One Team, Be a Leader" principle and adopted the service profit chain (Heskett, Jones, Loveman, Sasser, & Schlesinger, 1994) as a guiding philosophy to drive quality service throughout the corporation.

The Service-Profit Chain

The service-profit chain is based on the well-accepted notion that increased employee satisfaction leads to increased employee retention, which is related in turn to higher customer service and, ultimately, higher profitability. The premise is that retained employees come to know the products and services of the firm better, are better able to handle customer inquiries, and are therefore empowered to quickly resolve customer issues; this in turn leads to greater customer satisfaction. Greater customer satisfaction leads to increased customer retention, and longer-tenured customers are significantly more profitable for the firm than are short-tenured customers (Reichheld & Sasser, 1990). The linking of this profitability back to employee satisfaction is the essence of the service-profit chain.

At JPMorgan Chase, the service-profit chain was simplified for employees as the company's intention to be the "Employer of Choice, Provider of Choice and the Investment of Choice." The HR department sought to drive the entire profit chain by focusing on employee satisfaction and being the employer of choice (see also Rucci, Kirn, & Quinn, 1998). Being a geographically dispersed organization and being headquartered in diversity-rich New York City, the firm adopted its diversity initiative as a key program to drive employee satisfaction and be the employer of choice in its markets.

Diversity

The diversity initiative was designed first to increase awareness of the importance of having an inclusive culture and, second, to change behavior at all levels in the organization to ensure that such a culture was indeed being achieved. The employee opinion poll played an integral part in helping to define and measure both the diversity initiative and employee satisfaction so that a focused and strategic set of activities could be developed and tracked.

The Employee Opinion Poll

Every year at JPMorgan Chase (JPMC) an employee poll is conducted to take the pulse on where the corporation is regarding climate and employee satisfaction. This is a worldwide poll in which all employees are given the opportunity to participate. A number of items on the poll relate to, or directly refer to, the firm's diversity initiative. These items are grouped into a diversity index to provide a one-score assessment of how well the initiative is taking hold in each of the major businesses of JPMC.

The success of the initiative within businesses is seen as a combination of the deployment of corporate programs within the business, the initiation of business-specific programs customized to the needs and workforce of that business, and senior management commitment within the business to both these actions. The ability to measure success through the annual poll provides incentive within the businesses to operationalize the initiative in a positive way. Every year, business leaders review their standing on the diversity index with the chairman of the firm and discuss plans to address issues that were revealed.

In 1998 Treasury and Security Services (TSS) was near the bottom of the scale on the diversity index and on overall satisfaction when compared to other businesses at JPMC or to outside norms. Employee focus groups from different levels of the organization confirmed that employees were not happy with the work environment.

One of the key items in the diversity index that engendered the most discussion was the "Respect" item. Only 59 percent of all staff agreed with the statement, "Employees in my area are treated with fairness and respect." In explaining the reason that scores were not higher, staff, especially at lower levels, said they did not feel they were regarded as true colleagues.

Inclusion

Employees related instances of managers walking by their desk every morning on their way to their office and not even acknowledging the employees' existence with a simple "good morning." Many managers two levels up from employees were seen to be aloof or otherwise removed from the staff level. In short, the employees described a traditional, old-school operating environment where employees were treated as "instruments of work." They were told what to do by their immediate supervisors, but not always why. Being shut out of that broader context made the employees feel devalued as individuals.

Career Opportunity

Employees were also concerned about their lack of exposure to others above their immediate supervisors, which made them feel completely reliant on that one individual and cut off from the rest of the firm. They wondered if anyone knew if they were putting in extra effort and seeking to excel in their work and whether that would result in better career opportunities. This in turn made them question if putting in extra effort was worthwhile.

In effect, the staff defined respect in terms of involvement and the implications that had for their ability to contribute. A consequence of lack of involvement was seen to be lack of recognition for what they had to offer, (especially from levels above their immediate supervisor, which limited their growth opportunity).

Relating Respect to Employee Satisfaction

Respect is a firmwide value within JPMC and the cornerstone of the diversity initiative. Further work was done to ensure that diversity and respect were also seen to be critical to employee satisfaction. Using the "overall satisfaction" item on the poll as the target of analysis, the total database of employee responses on all other items on the poll was statistically analyzed through multiple regression to determine the key drivers, or aspects of the work environment that most influenced employee satisfaction. The items that had the greatest influence on satisfaction were "recognition of doing a good job," "involvement in decisions that affected one's work," and "opportunity to get a better job." These items are directly equivalent to the issues discussed in the focus groups.

Both sets of data indicate that staff want to be included as full partners in the business of the enterprise, respected as individuals who could play a role in the business, and recognized for their potential to do more than rote processes. This open and inclusive type of culture was exactly what the corporate diversity initiative was striving to achieve and was evidently where the TSS business had work to do. Efforts to address this issue would have a positive impact in employee satisfaction and, in turn, the service-profit chain. Ultimately these outcomes would move the corporation forward in achieving its strategic intent.

Owning the Issue

Survey results and focus group data gave a fairly clear definition of what employees were feeling and why. Two main challenges needed to be overcome before the problem could be addressed. First, managers needed to believe that each of them was potentially responsible for creating the issue. It is not simply "other managers" driving the results. Second, even if the problem is widespread, that does not mean it cannot be changed.

Within TSS, and more broadly throughout JPMC, there is a problem-solving process called "Workshop" that allows intact management teams, with the aid of a facilitator, to fully define an issue and create a plan for its resolution (see Box 21.2). By involving managers in this problem-solving process, there is a greater chance that solutions will be seen as addressing challenges, ownership of the action will increase, and implementation will be successful.

Box 21.2. Workshop

Workshop is a problem-solving process to be facilitated with intact management teams. It has two distinct parts: issue identification and solution development. Each of these is further divided into three steps.

Issue identification

- Definition/consequences: Why is the current condition of concern? How would you describe the business environment? What is the exposure or potential negative outcome if this issue is not addressed?
- Objectives: What should the objective be? What does the ideal condition look like? Who are the key players, and how must they behave? What kind of behavior maintains the status quo?
- Root cause: What is the root cause or causes of this current behavior or current situation? Why does the cause exist (for example, culture, style, policy, structure)?

Solution development

- Alternative approaches: What different approaches might resolve the issue? What obstacles exist for each approach?
- Preferred approach: Which approach seems the most reasonable with the greatest chance of success? How will the obstacles associated with this alternative be overcome?
- Implementation/Action Planning: How should the approach be implemented? What steps are essential from communication through implementation and follow-up/monitoring. Who will be responsible for each step? What might reasonable timeframes be?

After first presenting the poll data and then relating the focus group information, the "respect" issue in TSS was presented to the management teams across the world as follows: "How can we ensure that staff at all levels feel they are treated as colleagues with a common purpose of achieving the business objective?"

Management teams discussing the issue often went through the expected stages of denial ("we already conduct town halls to go over the strategy", "there now are more e-mails and desk drops talking about business issues than we can expect people to read") or of blaming the victim ("they just want to do their job and go home"; "they are only interested in their paycheck, not with what the business is trying to accomplish").

Strong facilitation of the Workshop discussion enabled the teams to get past these initial reactions and more fully explore and define the issue using the poll data, especially the items identified as key drivers of employee satisfaction (involvement, recognition, and growth opportunity).

The key factor with an impact on employee satisfaction and feelings of respect was seen as one of engagement. Managers agreed that staff received more than enough communication from business leaders (about goals, strategies) and from supervisors (on tasks, objectives), but rarely in forums allowing them to discuss how strategies related to objectives. The people they hardly ever heard from were the middle managers, and those were the people best positioned to engage staff in this type of discussion.

In the traditional hierarchical management structure, the roles at each level are typically defined as represented in Figure 21.1. Whereas leaders establish a vision and strategy, and a structure and systems support to accomplish them, middle managers must interpret that broader direction as it relates to their functional area and integrate that into existing operations (the traditional strategic plan/tactical plan relationship). Supervisors, or first-line managers, should be brought on board with the tactical (and strategic) plan and are charged with translating those into objectives for the staff (Katz & Kahn, 1966; Mintzberg, 1979). The best supervisors would provide context for the objectives but could rarely be as

Figure 21.1. Managerial and Staff Accountability

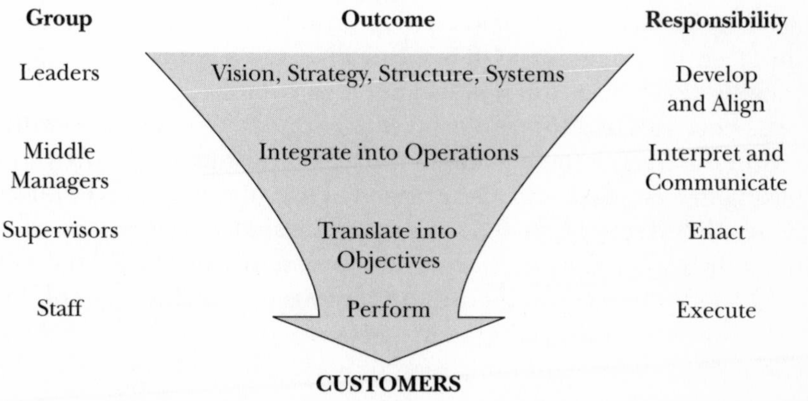

Group	Outcome	Responsibility
Leaders	Vision, Strategy, Structure, Systems	Develop and Align
Middle Managers	Integrate into Operations	Interpret and Communicate
Supervisors	Translate into Objectives	Enact
Staff	Perform	Execute
	CUSTOMERS	

expansive as the middle manager, especially as change or progress occurred over the course of the year. Leaders could, and did, relate broader context issues, but usually in forums too large to allow active engagement by staff.

Getting regular exposure to the middle level of management in small enough groups ensured staff the opportunity to engage in dialogue about what the business was seeking to accomplish and any other issues relating to the company and the work environment. It provided staff a forum to say what they thought and be recognized for how much they knew, and how connected they were to the goals of the business. This addressed not only the "involvement" issue, but also recognition and potential growth opportunity. It was from this discussion by management teams in the Workshop process that the concept of communicating managers was born.

The Communicating Manager

TSS is a business of approximately fifteen thousand people. Communicating managers were defined as individuals who oversaw an area of fifteen to forty people and were usually the manager of a group of first-line supervisors. An examination of the organizational charts within the business determined that there were approximately 750 middle-level managers who should be considered "communicating managers."

In a memo to this population from the head of the TSS business, the managers were informed of their role as communicating managers, which was to "help shape the culture of Treasury and Security Services to be inclusive and proud." The memo described the need for engaging staff around what the business and, more broadly, the entire firm was seeking to accomplish.

Their goal was to make staff feel connected to and a partner within the firm, to take pride in the accomplishments of the business, and to understand their role in achieving those accomplishments. In effect, the goal of engaging the staff was to ensure they had a broader focus than their immediate work area and to encourage them to relate their own thoughts on the direction of the company. Communicating managers were defined as the "critical talent pool" in determining TSS culture.

The Monthly Template

As part of their new responsibilities, communicating managers were asked to hold a meeting of all staff in their area once a month to engage in this dialogue. These meetings were not to replace their own or their supervisors' staff meetings (which typically included only direct reports) but to be in addition to them. Every month a communication template was sent to the communicating manager to help guide the session. The template was not designed to be passed along to staff; it had messages directed to the communicating manager and explicitly stated on the cover of the template that it was not to be distributed.

The format of the template was to provide a headline and some key points to discuss about that headline. Sections existed for corporate-level stories (for example, JPMC in the news, policy changes, community efforts, earnings), TSS-level stories (progress on strategy, earnings, and business events), business-within-TSS-level stories, and finally a blank page for communicating managers to write in news about their own area (new initiatives, progress on existing initiatives, and so forth). The design was meant to encourage the establishment of a line of sight from what the corporation is accomplishing to what each communicating manager's area is accomplishing.

Communicating managers had the freedom to pick and choose how much of the template they used in their meetings. Every template reminded the manager that the intent was to engage the staff, not to simply pass along information. In fact, every story on the template relating to the overall firm or to TSS had been communicated by e-mail or desk-drop memo prior to the release of the template. The communicating manager meeting was an opportunity to engage around those stories and provide a broader context for the story, which could be clarified through dialogue if need be.

A New Responsibility

This communication called for by the template was the responsibility of the middle level of management now dubbed communicating managers. It was not to be delegated to the supervisory level, where meetings already took place to discuss objectives and the work itself. Most of the resistance to this change referenced the fact that supervisors already covered this responsibility and that the call for new meetings by higher-level managers was merely building bureaucracy. It was clear that to convey the intent of the new responsibility and to ensure its execution that the level of management above the middle managers had to be fully on board.

Shared Responsibility

The building of an inclusive culture did involve a change for the TSS world. The management team in Workshop suggested that a culture change could not be effectively attained by focusing on just one population: the middle managers. After all, if managers engaged staff in dialogue but got no response, how long could they be expected to support the new initiative?

If business leaders endorsed the change but were not seen as involved, how long would it be before middle managers slipped back into the more comfortable role of focusing on the levels above them and their direct reports, and remaining invisible to the staff level? In fact, if a change is truly cultural in scope, it has to occur at all levels and, though different by level, be aligned to a common outcome.

The Leadership Role

Business leaders had to visibly demonstrate that managers would be evaluated and recognized based on a balance of financial, client, work quality, and people measures. Typically in such an approach, the balance is tipped toward the financial or client components of the managerial responsibilities, and that is often accompanied by better information flows to leaders as to how managers are performing in these areas.

The creation of the poll indexes as measures of the work climate being established by local managers gave leaders a reliable information system on the people side of the balanced scorecard. Leaders needed to visibly demonstrate the importance they attached to the people agenda through the means by which they made use of poll data. The poll had to be transformed in the eyes of the staff and management from an opinion instrument that was of passing interest to a measurement tool that was an active part of the leadership and management practice in the firm.

Leaders needed to include poll data in their "state of the business" addresses to staff and address how the data were being acted on to effect changes. They then had to ensure that the visibility and impact of those actions were apparent to staff. They had to show that they were actively spending time on their oversight of the people agenda within the firm.

Diversity Councils

Another means by which leaders showed commitment to the people agenda was through their involvement with the diversity initiative. Business leaders had always demonstrated their support for the people agenda by chairing a council of employees within their worlds devoted to improving the work climate around diversity (the diversity councils). Much of this activity had focused on building awareness of and sensitivity to the firm's diversity initiative. Activity that flowed from the councils often involved the staging of events to celebrate diverse groups within the business (for example, Black History Month).

Poll data allowed the councils to broaden their activities beyond awareness. Activities were adopted to engage both managers and staff on ways to change behavior to better build a culture of inclusion. These included brown bag lunches where staff could learn more about the business and roundtable discussions where managers could share best people management practices.

Communicating Manager Role

At the communicating manager level, the share of responsibility was perhaps the greatest. After all, they were designated as the critical talent pool as relates to cultural initiatives. Their role as defined through the Workshop process was not all that new in concept and was generally supported in existing competency model and training programs that were aligned to that population. Still, the results obtained through the poll and focus group process indicated a change was needed in how these concepts were enacted.

Along with competency models to delineate what managers were supposed to be doing, poll indexes were employed. For the communicating manager population, a poll index, "The Employee Engagement Index," was established in 1999 to determine how well each aspect of the responsibilities outlined for the initiative was being deployed. Each of the seven items used in the engagement index conveyed another aspect of the managerial job, but did so in terms of outcome rather than process expected (see Table 21.1).

Table 21.1. Communicating Managers' Competencies and Poll Items

Competency	Employee Engagement Index Poll Item(s)
Represents the strategic direction of the firm to the staff to gain understanding and buy-in	I understand the strategy for JPMorgan Chase.
	How satisfied are you with the information you receive from management on what's going on in JPMorgan Chase?
	To what extent do leaders in your business/function deliver compelling messages about the future of the company?
Ensures all work and activities in the area are aligned to the goals of the business	I see the relationship between my objectives and the goals of my business.
Manages change as needed to maintain satisfaction and productivity	When change is introduced, my manager does a good job of discussing the implications.
Establishes a work environment that is consistent with a culture of inclusion and respect	Sufficient effort is made to get the opinions and thinking of people who work here.
	The management of my business/function demonstrates the JPMorgan Chase Values.

Pull Versus Push as a Development Philosophy

Because the poll index represented a measure, it had a decidedly greater pull effect on managers. Competencies and the behaviors used to describe them, even if represented on year-end appraisal forms, were often hard to evaluate in terms of the outcome engendered.

For example, a behavioral competency such as "represents the strategic direction of the firm to the staff to gain understanding and buy-in" is process oriented and hard to evaluate. As such, managers who were conscientious would attend training and establish communication forums, but that did not ensure the message was being driven down to the employee level.

Managers who had very positive employee scores on the poll item, "To what extent do leaders in your business/function deliver compelling messages about the future of the company?" were easily differentiated from those whose employees were less positive in that regard. Communicating managers who were not performing well on that poll item knew which aspect of their role of creating a culture of inclusion and partnership was in need of further development. Training that was offered to address such issues was therefore sought out by managers ("pulled"), which was expected to have greater impact than training that was offered for general development purposes ("pushed").

The Staff Role

The culture of inclusion would not occur unless the staff also took initiative to make it happen. Staff had already told us they wanted to be included in the workings of the business, as this was a key aspect of respect in their eyes. Still, being given the opportunity to participate would not address the issue if staff were ill prepared to take advantage.

To support the staff for their part in this shared responsibility a number of initiatives were undertaken. A series of events including speakers, lunchtime seminars on the different business functions, and "career expos" were run every year under the umbrella of "Building Your Potential." These efforts were designed to give staff a more comprehensive understanding of the business beyond their immediate workplace and get them thinking about personal growth.

Training programs on taking initiative were also offered to staff. These were designed to not only identify the characteristics of an effective initiative, but to provide guidelines on the best way to establish initiatives for work-related issues and those relating to one's own career.

Finally, the performance appraisal form for the staff level was altered to stress the importance of taking part in the growth of the business. All staff were charged with, at the very least, keeping up with changes that occur naturally in the course of the business as it may affect their job. Employees were evaluated on their ability and energy to participate in the growth of the business.

Establishing Accountability

The efforts of all who shared responsibility for creating an inclusive culture had to be measured, recognized, and rewarded if the initiative was to be successful. The poll indexes were the primary means of measuring outcomes at the leadership and communicating manager level. The challenge was in getting managers to use these measures to establish accountability. In fact, poll results have not traditionally been a force in the performance appraisal process, where accountability is assigned and evaluated. In TSS there was a concerted effort to establish poll data as an important component of the performance management process.

Communicating Managers' Accountability

The performance appraisal discussion is the key component of the performance management process where accountability is assigned and related to reward. Manager and staff often denigrate the performance appraisal as being largely subjective in nature, which leads to vague comments that are hard to translate into distinctive outcomes. The poll, an objective measure of how the management aspect of performance was being handled, needed to be a visible part of the performance appraisal so that accountability could be established and real change could occur.

Total Performance Management

The integration of the poll data with the performance management process would increase the impact and relevance of both organizational tools. Within TSS, performance evaluations are conducted through an online form. As with most other performance forms, there are places to evaluate the accomplishment of job-specific objectives as well as more generic management-related objectives for people and productivity. It was in these latter categories that the poll was used as a targeted information system.

Each communicating manager within TSS would receive poll data for his or her unit on each of the indexes tracked on the poll. These scores (prior and current year as well as a benchmark for the entire business) were put into their online performance form (the Total Performance Management System). The performance evaluation form became a personalized data receptacle so that managers who oversaw communicating managers would have specific information on the work climate being created in each communicating manager's unit. The managers of these broader areas would also have the roll-up data represented on their own forms and be accountable for the climate in their larger organization. This occurred all the way up the line to the business head level.

The fact that the poll data were automatically put on the form (which was available online to both the reviewer and the reviewee) ensured targeted discussion about employee engagement and the climate being created by the local manager as one aspect of the manager's overall performance. Prior year and benchmark data provided objective assessments to gauge the manager's performance. Climate was clearly viewed as having an impact on overall performance ratings and the rewards tied to that.

Target Areas

To heighten awareness of the importance attached to climate scores, business heads would receive a report that rank-ordered all communicating managers in their business from those with the highest average index score to those with the lowest, and how that ranking had changed over the past year. The bottom 10 percent of areas within each business were designated as target areas that would receive support from HR's OD unit to help improve climate.

This had the effect of not only using OD resources most efficiently, but also focusing it on managers who truly wanted or needed support in change management; no managers wanted to be in the bottom 10 percent for two years in a row. Targeted areas received an interim "mini–poll" six months following the full poll to check on progress and impact of action taken.

Senior-Level Accountability

At the more senior levels, poll data were also seen as a key differentiator of talent. Poll scores played a prominent role in annual talent review discussions and in year-end bonus determination. Consistent with the organization's emphasis on leadership, the workplace climate created by a leader was seen as a key determinant of promotions for increased people responsibility.

While the tie between poll scores and outcomes was less crisp at the senior levels than at the communicating manager level, the perception that it played a role was strong and was supported by talent decisions that were visible to the broader population.

Staff Accountability

Finally, there was a need to establish accountability for the staff role in building an inclusive culture. At this level, data were not used; the link between performance and outcome remained somewhat subjective. Still, it was important to communicate the expectation that staff would be held responsible for their action in this process.

The performance appraisal form at the staff level was altered to stress the importance of taking part in the growth of the business. Employees are evaluated on their initiative to stay current with what is going on in the business and their ability to keep up with changes that might affect their job. The supervisor level (generally one level below the communicating manager) was seen to play an important role in making this piece of the inclusive culture initiative happen. A new program, the Supervisor Development Initiative, is being rolled out to fill in this gap and add this important group to the shared responsibility philosophy for any culture change effort.

Support and Recognition

A big part of the communicating managers program was the support and recognition of these middle managers, the target population. The monthly communication template provided to all communicating managers was the most visible and pervasive support tool in the program. The infrastructure to identify, define the roles of, and establish accountability for communicating managers facilitated creation of a delineated community of middle managers. However, the additional role of communicating managers was not readily accepted by all of whom it was asked; if anything, it meant more work and accountability. Thus, JPMC top management realized there was a need to emphasize some of the positive aspects of being a communicating manager.

An important part of the culture change effort was to ensure that the role of communicating manager was perceived to be vital in the organization. This message came in the form of various support and recognition programs. Training sessions developed on communicating effectively with staff and building high-performance teams were offered to the communicating manager population. Group coaching sessions were also offered where communicating managers could meet in groups of ten with an executive coach who would facilitate best practice sharing among managers with a range of poll scores.

On a quarterly basis, business heads would hold meetings of all communicating managers to review business plans, latest results, and upcoming challenges. And at the end of the year, a gala reception would be held mimicking the Oscars Award Ceremony where statuettes called MEAs (for Managerial Excellence Awards) would be presented to the communicating managers who had scored best in each of the indexes tracked in the poll.

The visible recognition of communicating managers had the desired effect of creating a desired and admired new position within the organization.

Outcomes

In order to sustain the effort required to execute against any initiative, managers needed feedback that reliably showed progress and bottom-line impact. Poll data provided feedback on how staff was reacting to management's efforts to build an inclusive culture, and the Service Profit Chain served as the framework to relate that effort to bottom-line impact.

The Diversity Index

The impetus for what became the communicating manager program was the 1998 TSS poll data on diversity. Since 1998, the diversity index of items that is tracked by the corporation has changed as the diversity initiative has matured. Three items have been presented to the employee population each year since 1998, with a rating scale that ranges from Strongly Agree to Strongly Disagree:

"Senior management shows by its actions that it has a strong commitment to diversity."

"Employees are being treated with fairness and respect in my area."

"My manager is sensitive to the relationship between my work life and my personal life."

The average percentage favorable response of all employees in TSS across the three items has been an upward trend (see Figure 21.2).

**Figure 21.2. Diversity Index Outcome,
Treasury and Security Services**

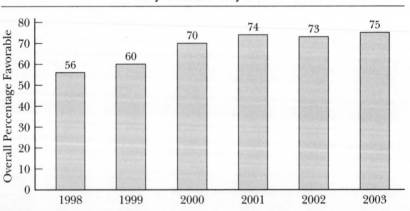

The communicating manager program was initiated in 1999 with a definition of the population, dedicated training, and distribution of a monthly communications template. It was at this time that we also established the Employee Engagement Index of poll items as the measure of communicating manager effectiveness and shared the results with business heads. Within a year, the index measure was further established by linking it to the communicating manager performance review through TPMS. At the end of the second year, we held our first Oscar-like recognition event (the MEA Awards) in all worldwide locations in which TSS had a significant presence. We also began the rank-ordering of communicating managers to identify low performers as target areas. The index results continued to rise year after year (see Figure 21.3).

Figure 21.3. Employee Engagement Index Outcome, Treasury and Security Services

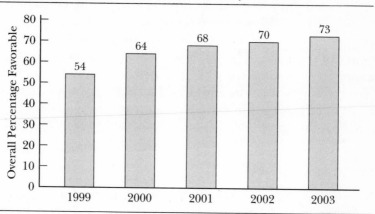

As a result of this success, leadership across TSS businesses increasingly turned to the communicating manager program as the primary means to measure effectiveness in people management. As support became more apparent, the 750 communicating managers increasingly embraced the initiatives. A few of the items in the engagement index are shared by an external consortium of about forty high-profile companies nationwide (the Mayflower

Group). When the most recent scores are compared against this standard, the TSS scores are in the ninetieth percentile. More important, these statistics reveal that most staff within the business now feel like fully included and important participants in the success of the business. The item that states, "Sufficient effort is made to get the opinions and thinking of people who work here," went from 42 percent favorable in 1999 to 69 percent favorable in 2003. Participation rates in the survey went from under 50 percent to 95 percent in that same time period. The poll became recognized as a management tool, and managers clearly became more oriented toward the people agenda within the business.

The Service-Profit Chain

While it is difficult to directly evaluate the outcomes related to the service-profit chain, the data here also point in the right direction. Ratings on overall satisfaction increased from 58 percent favorable in 1999 to 70 percent in 2003; annual turnover dropped from 11.8 to 9.0 percent, and employee ratings on the item, "How would you rate the service your business/function provides to its customers?" went from 62 percent favorable in 1999 to 73 percent in 2003. Customer service ratings from client surveys continued to rise and are rated as the best in the industry. Increasingly more clients and deals were referred to the TSS business from partners in other businesses within JPMC.

Lessons Learned

In working with management to effect the culture change described in this chapter, there were definite take-aways for the organization development function that should transcend all such efforts in the future.

Total Systems Approach

As the success of the communicating managers program became known firmwide, other business units were impressed and sought to adopt the program. This usually involved identifying the middle management population, distributing a monthly communications template, and providing training support for managers in their new responsibilities. This, in and of itself, is enough to have an impact, and all indications from the businesses that adopted it are that it did. However, communicating managers in those businesses have not yet become institutionalized as they have in TSS, and the long-term impact of the program is yet to be determined.

The total systems approach in TSS, which included measurement through the poll, accountability through performance management, and various forms of recognition, is what transformed the initiative in TSS from one of management practice enhancement to culture change. Beyond the changes that occurred at the middle management level, the corollary changes that were made at the leadership and staff levels helped make the change in culture a shared responsibility. It was quickly understood that if a change initiative was to be cultural in scope, everyone would have to take part, and if any group were left out of the initiative, it would lessen the impact.

The Poll as a Measurement Tool

A second lesson learned from the communicating manager initiative was that the survey is not only a climate instrument to help diagnose issues relating to culture, but a measurement tool to establish accountability for change. The integration of survey items, management competencies, and change initiatives that are applied to a target population is a strong catalytic agent of change. It is also a source of information that allows managers at various levels in the organization to evaluate one of the most difficult aspects of management: provide objective evaluations of the people component of the manager's job in a performance evaluation situation. Given the right information and tools, managers will evaluate and provide feedback that emphasizes the people component of a balanced scorecard in a meaningful way.

Institutionalizing Change

Finally, we learned that change initiatives should be thought of in product management terms. The sale and implementation of the initiative is only the start; the operational support and maintenance of the initiative are what determine its ultimate success. As the initiative ages, it requires enhancements to keep it vital, and the way to develop the initiative is to increase market share. Here again the poll became a useful source of information. By examining where the Employee Engagement Index was low within the business, it was apparent where the initiative was not being adopted. By targeting those areas, we were able to convert more managers to the philosophy and practice of communicating managers. This allowed our performance on the index to rise each year.

References

Heskett, J. L., Jones, T. O., Loveman, G. W., Sasser, W. E. Jr., & Schlesinger, L. A. (1994, Mar.–Apr.). Putting the service profit chain to work. *Harvard Business Review*, 164–174.

Katz, D., & Kahn, R. L. (1966). *The social psychology of organizations*. New York: Wiley.

Mintzberg, H. (1979). *The structuring of organizations*. Upper Saddle River, NJ: Prentice Hall.

Reichheld, F. F., & Sasser, W. E. Jr. (1990, Sept.-Oct.). Zero defections: Quality comes to services. *Harvard Business Review*, 105–111.

Rucci, A. J., Kirn, S. P., & Quinn, R. T. (1998, Jan.-Feb.). The employee-customer-profit chain at Sears. *Harvard Business Review*, 82–98.

CHAPTER 22

Reengaging Employees During Turbulent Times

A Case Study

Sharon F. Parker
Michael J. Schroeder
J. Thomas Bowler, Jr.
Patricia L. Muldoon

Anyone who has flown on a commercial airline flight over the past several years or has observed news reports about the failing commercial airline industry knows that the world is a different place. Longer lines in the airports, greater security measures, and fewer flights to choose from have taken their toll on many of us who travel, whether for business or for pleasure. The effects on the airline industry and the organizations that supply parts and services are monumental and have long-term impact. The effects in some cases are causing organizations to redefine their way of life and their core businesses. Many organizations in other industries are under similar pressures. In the end, some organizations will make it, and some will not.

The case study presented in this chapter is an example of one organization and its successful use of an employee survey in a quest to refocus and redefine its business during such turbulent times. In redefining who they are and what they do best, the senior executives of this organization used their employee survey as a tool to measure and increase levels of employee engagement. These executives realized early on that creating organizationwide change could be accomplished only through the engagement and involvement of all employees. As they later learned, it would take a special internal group to make this happen.

The organization, a leader in flight and engine technology for many years, supplies a large share of the engines used in all commercial flights. It designs, manufactures, and services commercial and military jet engines. In the early 1980s, the organization was delivering 65 percent of all new commercial jet engines and powering nearly 80 percent of the Western world's commercial aircraft. Moreover, it produced the engine of choice on every U.S. fighter in service. By 1995, a combination of unanticipated market shifts, quality issues that affected key customers, and intense competition dropped this company's commercial market share to about 20 percent of new deliveries and roughly 55 percent of the installed base. On the military side, deliveries dramatically declined from their peak. The latter half of the decade through today brought additional pressures from the major changes (the general recession in the U.S. economy, the 9/11 terrorist attacks, the Iraq war, severe acute respiratory syndrome in Asia, and others) affecting the airline industry itself. Despite this turbulence, this company has continued to focus on a strategic objective of increasing its revenues and profits by redefining its way of life and core businesses.

In the fall of 1998, the executive committee examined their business strategy and decided they would shift away from low-margin segments of the commercial engine market. As a result, a new strategy emerged that shifted the focus from primarily new commercial and military engine sales to the most profitable segments of those markets and to engine after-market, repair, and overhaul services. This shift created a need to redesign the engineering and business processes throughout the organization.

They were faced not only with the industry dynamics noted, but also a declining number of engines in service as their highest-volume engine models began to retire. The demand for parts for these engine models, which had been a significant portion of the company's revenue stream, was eroding. Concurrent development of new engine models was simply too costly to continue. In light of these developments, as well as the objective to increase the business, the company's president and the executive committee recognized the need to update its strategy. They realized the organization needed to diversify its businesses, focus resources on new engine segments that provided clear growth opportunities, and redirect resources to the engine services market in order to capture sales from the installed engine base. Along with this market strategy shift, the executive committee recognized the need to improve its productivity and cost structure.

This journey, from the early 1990s to today, would significantly change the physical and financial makeup of the company. The number of employees was reduced by 40 percent, all previously U.S. based and now based around the globe to mirror the market more closely. New engine deliveries declined to less than half their peak levels, while revenue from after-market service increased nearly 50 percent. During this time of intense change, customer survey scores suggested the company could do better to satisfy both loyal and prospective customers.

In the face of all this, the company's president recognized the role of employees in its execution of the strategy: "I knew this new direction, which would ensure our continued financial strength while also achieving our growth goals, could only be successful if we engaged the hearts and minds of our employees in the future vision." It was then that he committed to a rigorous, biannual employee survey to gain insight into how employees felt about the company and their work.

The First Global Employee Survey

In 2000, a seventy-eight-item employee survey was developed for the company to assess views of employees from across the globe on a variety of topics, including customer focus, quality, ethics, health and safety, training and development, communications, and management practices. Although the overall survey was designed to primarily measure satisfaction levels with specific functional topics, the survey also provided a means to measure overall job and company satisfaction as well as employee engagement.

For the purposes of the global employee survey, employee engagement was operationally defined as the level of involvement and motivation employees displayed toward the organization, both intellectually and emotionally. Employee engagement goes beyond just coming to work and doing the job. It goes beyond just being satisfied with the job and the company (Howe, 2003). Employee engagement incorporates the head, heart, and hands of the employee. Its measurement assesses the level of emotional involvement and commitment employees have toward the organization and the amount of discretionary effort they are willing to put forth (Bates, 2004; Kowalski, 2003). It measures their enthusiasm for the job and company and their willingness to help the organization achieve its goals.

The results of the first global survey in 2000 collected baseline data from approximately twelve thousand employees, representing 52 percent of the total population. The results of this survey highlighted several areas for improvement across the organization such as communications and management practices.

High levels of uncertainty were revealed within every level of the organization. The survey results showed only 30 percent of employees believed the strategies employed by the executive committee would allow the company to remain competitive. Only one-third believed that the company was making the changes necessary to compete effectively. And less than 20 percent believed that management would follow up on the results of the survey. Baseline results indicated a long road ahead for the organization to engage employees and implement changes necessary for future growth and success.

Traditional methods of management action planning were used to tackle issues identified as opportunities for improvement in the 2000 employee survey. These methods included the dissemination of results to managers and the request for managers to follow up and implement action plans for improvement. Basically managers were left to their own volition to create actions. And as is often the case, some managers identified areas for improvement and implemented action plans, and others did not.

A brief spot survey was conducted in the fall of 2001, using eighteen items from the 2000 employee survey. The eighteen items represented the areas cited most often as opportunities for improvement throughout the organization. The spot survey was administered to a statistically representative sample of the entire workforce. The results revealed these action planning methods were having virtually no effect on survey scores. Results did not improve or even appear to be moving upward.

Launch of the Center of Excellence

As the economy spiraled into a recession and the commercial airline industry went into a tailspin, commercial airlines deferred new engine orders, focusing instead on repair and overhaul of existing engines, to minimize expenditures. The organization's executive committee realized that the only way the organization could shift gears and redesign the business was by redefining the work for all employees.

More than 60 percent of employees within this company were long-service employees—those who had spent the majority of their working lives on the commercial side of the jet engine business. For many, designing, building, and selling the company's traditional products was their life. To redefine their way of life would require significant organizational change. The vice president of human resources (HR) decided it was time for a new approach to employee engagement: "Despite our desires and early efforts toward improving employee engagement, nothing had changed. It was time for us to make some dramatic changes to our methods."

In 2002, a second global employee survey, with eighty items, was conducted to assess current levels of satisfaction and engagement as well as improvements in focus areas, which had been identified as opportunities from the 2000 employee survey. By now, an executive team had conducted focus groups involving hundreds of employees to begin to understand the substantive underlying issues. The results of the 2002 employee survey indicated little to no improvement among the hourly ranks. In fact, some items and categories in the survey were less favorable compared to the previous survey in 2000. A modest 4 percentage point improvement in the overall survey results was beginning to take place among the salaried workforce. While some improvement, that is, higher overall favorable scores, was made within certain departments and locations, cross-organizational improvement was not realized. It was evident to the executive committee that if the employee survey was going to be an effective tool to facilitate and measure cultural change, a new action planning strategy had to be implemented. The committee recognized the value of engaged employees and understood how the cost of disengaged employees could be enough to derail their efforts in implementing the new business strategy.

During an annual senior executive off-site meeting dedicated to strategy development, the vice president of HR proposed and his fellow executive committee members approved the creation of the Center of Excellence (COE). His proposal was straightforward: no incremental cost for creating the COE (the five team members would come from within the organization and not be replaced in their current roles) and a mission of operationalizing employee engagement. He suggested that the rigorous application of ACE (Achieving Competitive Excellence) tools coupled with an improved methodology in prioritizing the survey issues was key. ACE is the organization's fundamental continuous improvement methodology, similar to Six Sigma, a rigorous and disciplined methodology that uses data and statistical analysis to measure and improve a company's operational performance. Through this system, employees are trained, empowered, and engaged in eliminating waste through review and improvement of their processes, all focused on customer satisfaction.

The hand-selected COE team consisted of a manager and four team members with strong, combined experience in HR and organization development (OD). More important, the team manager had more than ten years of line management experience within the organization, and each had demonstrated expertise in ACE initiatives, which included expertise in business process design and measurement.

"Dedicating the resources of the Center of Excellence and creation of a standard business process and metrics for survey action planning were the key decisions that led to the outstanding progress we've realized so far," said the vice president of HR.

Center of Excellence Success and the Four Strategies

From 2002 to 2004, the COE team guided leaders and employees to a new level of engagement. The success of the team and the overall improvements in employee engagement can be traced to four fundamental modifications to their action planning strategy.

Strategy 1: Focus on the Basics

The COE team decided to approach action planning from a new perspective. Instead of focusing action planning efforts on items that scored the lowest (least favorable), they followed an engagement strategy that groups the survey results into three levels of engagement: basic, intermediate, and advanced.

The Employee Engagement Strategy is an action planning strategy that categorizes survey items based on three levels or tiers of employee engagement (Parker, Schroeder, & Fairfield-Sonn, 2002). The levels are based on motivational theories that suggest certain factors need to be met before employees can achieve a level of satisfaction with their job and the company. Models of human functioning and employee motivation, such as Maslow's hierarchical theory of needs (physiological, safety, love, esteem, and self-actualization), Alderfer's ERG model (existence, relatedness, and growth), and Herzberg's Two Factory theory (hygiene and motivators) (Pinder, 1998) have been used to form the basis of the Employee Engagement Strategy. All three models describe different levels of fulfillment starting with basic or necessary-for-survival needs. While the Employee Engagement Strategy employed in this organization does not mirror the theorists' ideas directly and was not deployed as part of an academic or psychological study, it does apply the same principles of a hierarchical structure and the need for fulfillment or satisfaction along different dimensions (Figure 22.1).

The first tier, or basic engagement level, is a categorization of items that address basic needs of the job. Basic items are fundamental to the job and most influenced by the immediate supervisor. Most employees take items and issues embedded within the basic category for granted, but if they are left unmet or unfulfilled, employees become dissatisfied with their job and the company. For example, most employees assume that the work environment will be safe, their supervisor is competent, their team members know their jobs, and they will have tools and training needed to do their jobs.

The second tier, or intermediate level, is a categorization of items that address growth and development needs. Once the basics are met, the supervisor can focus more on intermediate factors. If intermediate factors are fulfilled, satisfaction with the job and the company improves. While factors such as pay and benefits are often viewed as basic needs, the immediate supervisor has less influence on the determination of pay and benefits issues. In most cases, the immediate supervisor facilitates pay and benefits decisions but lacks the ability to influence the amount of pay increases or types of benefits offered. For these reasons, pay and benefits are categorized in the intermediate level.

The third tier, or advanced level, is a categorization of items that address organizational commitment needs, which need to be addressed to exceed employees' expectations and develop a highly engaged workforce. Advanced factors are generally more strategic in nature and most heavily influenced or directed by senior management.

Figure 22.1. Foresight Employee Engagement Strategy

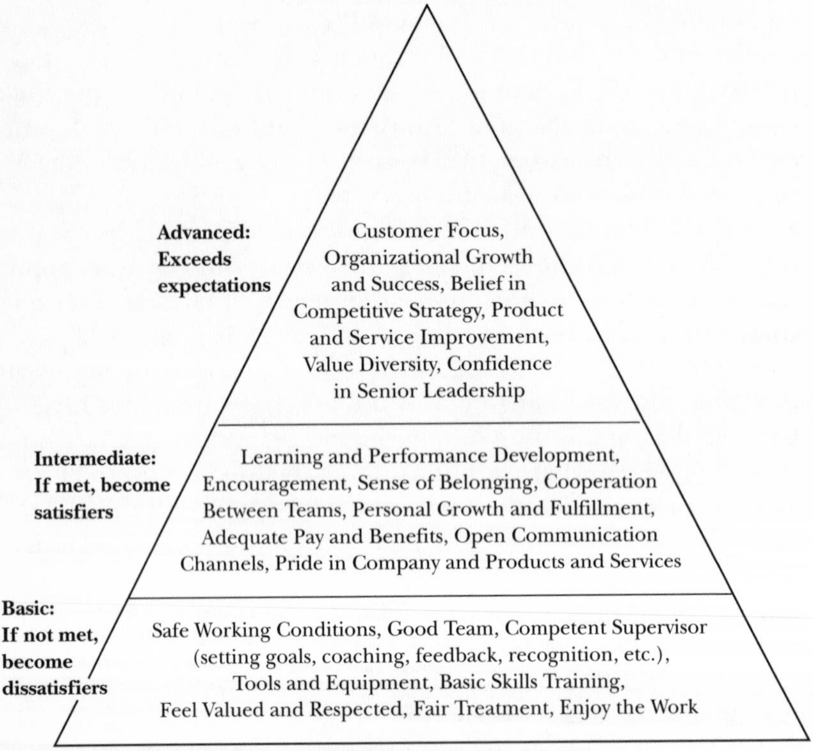

Advanced: Exceeds expectations — Customer Focus, Organizational Growth and Success, Belief in Competitive Strategy, Product and Service Improvement, Value Diversity, Confidence in Senior Leadership

Intermediate: If met, become satisfiers — Learning and Performance Development, Encouragement, Sense of Belonging, Cooperation Between Teams, Personal Growth and Fulfillment, Adequate Pay and Benefits, Open Communication Channels, Pride in Company and Products and Services

Basic: If not met, become dissatisfiers — Safe Working Conditions, Good Team, Competent Supervisor (setting goals, coaching, feedback, recognition, etc.), Tools and Equipment, Basic Skills Training, Feel Valued and Respected, Fair Treatment, Enjoy the Work

Source: Foresight International, Inc. (2001).

The COE team found that the strategy of focusing on low-scoring basic engagement factors first provided a solid foundation and an area of concentration for action planning efforts. The employee survey still measured traditional survey dimensions, such as quality, job satisfaction, environment, health and safety, communications, and management practices, but it also provided an additional focus for managers to better understand and measure the engagement levels of various work groups.

While this engagement strategy follows the hierarchical structure of theories of motivation, one level does not have to be completely fulfilled before a team can work on another level. It simply means that in order to improve survey results, managers must take a look at the basic items and, if low scores are present, begin working on those items. Showing how much the company is doing for the community is positive (advanced item), but overall satisfaction and engagement will not improve if the employee's equipment does not work or the employee lacks competent supervision (basic items). Day-to-day frustrations will continue to build, eventually causing the employee to become disengaged and either leave the company or retreat in some other way, for example, through lower productivity or increased absenteeism.

The use of the three tiers or levels of employee engagement in reports and leadership action planning strategies is designed to enhance the effectiveness of the employee survey by layering the responsibility and action of leadership at all levels. Low favorable scores on basic items are included as opportunities for improvement and should receive a higher priority, greater attention, and focus from an action planning standpoint. Low favorable scores on intermediate items are included as opportunities for improvement as long as all or most of the basic issues have been addressed or resolved. Advanced items should receive priority only after basic and intermediate issues have been satisfied. Organizations with a high number of engaged employees tend to spend more time working on advanced factors because basic and intermediate issues have already been resolved and appear as strengths on survey results.

The results of the 2000 and 2002 employee surveys identified a lack of engagement in the basic issues and among management practices in general. Instead of just working on the lowest-scoring items (lowest favorability) or developing actions based on corporatewide issues, as was historically practiced, managers used the Employee Engagement Strategy to focus action planning efforts on the issues that mattered most to employees and received the greatest return on their investment. Research indicates that the greatest drivers of employee engagement are basic factors, such as recognition, respect, achievement, and integrity (Kowalski, 2003).

Organizations that focus on these basic factors create more engaged employees (Shaffer, 2004). These employees:

- Have lower voluntary turnover
- Have fewer accidents and absenteeism
- Produce higher service and product quality
- Produce more sales per employee
- Are more flexible and open to change
- Voice fewer excuses toward change

The idea of creating a more engaged workforce is not a new one. For more than sixty years, managers have been looking at the organizational factors that engage (or disengage) employees. Research studies have been conducted to determine the link, if any, between an engaged workforce and organizational performance (Bates, 2004; Buckingham & Coffman, 1999; G. Buckingham, 2000; Harter, Schmidt, & Hayes, 2002; Highly engaged employees lead their employers to faster growth, 2004; Teresko, 2004). Although some research remains inconclusive, a continually growing body of work suggests that a correlation between employee engagement and organizational performance factors exists. Research has also found that the immediate supervisor, not the pay, benefits, or perks, was the key in building and sustaining a high-performance workplace (Buckingham & Coffman, 1999; Gubman, 2004).

Strategy 2: Create Standard Rollout Process and Tools

The second strategy was to create a standard process for sharing results with employees and implementing action plans. This involved creating a standard set of instructions and tools for all managers and creating a standard set of expectations. Following an organizationwide process implemented as a strategic quality initiative, the COE created and deployed tools designed to measure and improve employee survey results based on the ACE tools currently in place.

The process model outlined specific actions for each manager and employee team and provided a standardized set of instructions for analyzing the survey results, identifying areas for improvement, and creating follow-up action steps. The ACE tools provided a com-

mon language across the organization and created a simple standardized method for analyzing survey data and verbatim comments.
Efforts were focused on solutions, not methodology. Examples of
tools included:

- Pareto diagramming of comments to create common themes
- Brainstorming activities for problem solving
- Fishbone diagrams of data to get at causes of problems
- Impact and maturity analysis of items to determine items with
  the greatest organizational impact if improved

Accountability for improvement was driven to the work group
level. Each work group's employee team was responsible for creating up to two or three action plans. Company-defined target levels of overall favorability were set for specific items and for the
overall basic level of engagement. Any department or work group
falling below the target levels of favorability on the basic engagement factors was directed to focus action planning efforts on those
items regardless of its scores on other items in the survey. This
shifted the action planning focus away from low-scoring items to
low-scoring basic items.

The first step in analysis was to review the survey results. The
survey administration process was designed to collect results at a
work group level, thus providing a way to drill down into specific
areas of the organization. The COE team realized early on that
to drive management accountability for follow-up down through
to employees required collecting data at the smallest feasible
work group level. The organizational coding and reporting structure was therefore created in such a way as to allow analysis at the
work group level. As confidence in the survey process grew,
the survey's organizational coding structure expanded to provide finer levels of detail. A minimum group size of ten was implemented to ensure the confidentiality and anonymity of all
respondents.

Since most work group results showed scores below the target
levels for favorability, items within the basic engagement category
were then ranked from high to low (most favorable to least favorable). A ranking of the basic engagement items identified areas
that required the greatest focus or opportunity for improvement.

Once the basic engagement items were ranked, they were prioritized based on the impact/maturity matrix (Figure 22.2). Items were assigned to one of four quadrants on a continuum of low to high impact on the vertical axis and low to high potential for improvement on the horizontal matrix. Items identified as having high organizational impact and high improvability were selected as the top priority.

Figure 22.2. Impact/Maturity Matrix

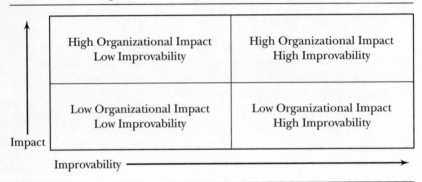

Impact

Improvability

Strategy 3: Increase Employee Involvement and Accountability

Once all basic engagement items were ranked and prioritized, work groups were asked to select two or three items for action planning. They were asked to resist the urge to take on so many action plans that their efforts lacked focus and follow-through. Employee action planning teams conducted the analysis and prioritization of action items.

This third strategy involved dramatically increasing the level of employee involvement and accountability in the follow-up processes by creating action planning teams. The teams were to analyze the data at a department level, interpret the results, identify action items, create solutions, and implement the plans. The follow-up was therefore team focused and team driven. The action planning efforts resulting from the 2000 employee survey clearly identified a need for employee involvement. Earlier action planning efforts, which were primarily management focused and management driven, did not engage the "hearts and minds" of all the employees, with a few exceptions among departments. Given the number of highly skilled, long-tenured employees, the COE team decided to tap into the knowledge of all employees. Employee teams were created to involve employees in the solutions, not just voice their opinions about the problems within the organization.

The COE team created a standard set of instructions for action planning, which identified a method for formulating employee action teams. Employees were selected to participate on the action planning teams through a variety of methods. Employees who were interested in participating could volunteer. Employees were selected by their managers to participate on the action planning teams as representatives for the entire work group. In some cases, employees were selected based on developmental opportunities to work on project teams. Employees were also selected to represent the cross-sections of the organization according to position, level, and length of service. The action planning teams provided a platform for dialogue and input from all employees across the organization. Over one hundred action planning teams were formed in all areas of the company. Managers supported the teams by providing time away from their other work responsibilities to identify and resolve issues. The teams were able to engage in dialogue directly with managers and senior management to better understand issues. Best practices were shared across the organization using an online database. Action teams were given instruction on successful methods for brainstorming, team facilitation, root cause analysis, and appreciative inquiry. An online action planning database was created to assist teams in preparing solutions and recording progress. For the first time, employees felt they had a voice with real influence.

Once each action planning team identified the specific areas for improvement, the members set up a meeting with members of their management team to discuss recommendations for improvement. Action plans were modified in some cases, based on input from managers. In the end, all action plans implemented were done so with employee involvement and management approval. Across the organization, action plans focused on issues such as improving peer recognition, supervisor training, value and respect of all employees, business processes, as well as removing barriers and obstacles that caused frustration on a daily basis.

Over four hundred action plans were entered into the online database. The online action planning tool included follow-up mechanisms and status progress checks. This enabled managers and action planning teams to track their progress and improvements over the next two years. As action items were completed, the teams selected new items and refocused their energies on new opportunities for improvement. Members of the action planning teams rotated throughout the course of the two years between employee surveys. This provided greater involvement and greater opportunities for more employees.

Strategy 4: Provide Research, Coaching, Tools, and Recognition

The fourth strategy implemented by the COE was to provide research, coaching, recognition, and senior management support needed to motivate and sustain team momentum during the change process. As is often the case with most employee survey processes, a great amount of attention and focus was given to the tasks and responsibilities of administering the survey. Those involved in administering the survey spent vast amounts of time and energy. By the time the results were calculated and disseminated, energies were exhausted. The fact remains, however, that the greatest maximum business value is realized once the follow-up activities begin, a fact realized by the COE and the executive committee.

In summary, the COE team was created to help the organization excel at and improve employee engagement and fulfillment. Their mission was to develop processes and tools based on the ACE tools already in place and research-based theory and principles of organizational change processes. The team's ultimate goal was to share this knowledge with all managers in the organization and provide the resources and the expertise needed to drive change. Each COE team member was hand-selected by the senior HR staff. Each team member needed to have demonstrated a high degree of knowledge with current ACE tools and processes, possess leadership development skills, and possess the ability to bridge the gap between research, theory, and real-life work issues.

"I knew selecting the right talent for the COE was critical," the vice president of HR said:

> To have the best chance of success at driving significant change through the entire company, I chose a leader with credibility and a long track record in the organization outside the human resources function. If I wanted the line organizational leaders to get engaged and own this process, I wanted to set the direction that this was not fundamentally an HR functional initiative, it was a company business initiative—that could work and make a huge difference. Staff organizations, to be truly successful in creating real value for the business, need to generate pull from the organization, not just practice push to achieve the big performance improvements.

To identify areas for improvement, the COE team looked first to the survey results. Using the online tools, they created an ad hoc report, which identified and ranked all of the work groups based on overall favorability and overall favorability with basic engagement factors. The work groups identified as the lowest in favorability were allotted more of the COE's time and assistance. The COE team decided to follow a pull approach instead of a push approach in their coaching efforts. In other words, they began coaching and providing guidance to those managers and work groups requesting help. In many cases, those requesting additional guidance and assistance were among the higher-scoring groups. As their reputation grew within the organization, they were better able to pull groups into coaching efforts where they saw a need. The softer approach of being invited into the process earned the team the credibility they needed and created the platforms for implementing further improvements.

The COE team focused on creating and implementing organizationwide action plans. Improved supervisory training was identified as a need across the organization. Working in conjunction with the corporation's learning and development organization and an external consulting firm, a supervisory training program was developed and implemented to specifically address supervisory skill gaps highlighted by the employee survey data, comments, and focus groups. Over two years, all of the eighteen hundred supervisors in the company attended approximately forty hours of training. These supervisors had been promoted primarily through technical and functional ranks, and previously had received little to no investment in supervisory training. Through this training program, primarily focused on the behavioral side of supervising, they learned the basic fundamental skills that are so essential to helping employees perform at their full potential.

The company also focused its energies on improving the performance management process to ensure timely and accurate feedback to all employees. The first goal was to ensure timely feedback by requiring all managers to complete a performance evaluation for every employee once a year. An online tool was created to administer and collect the evaluations. The second goal was to help managers provide high-quality assessments of employees' performance that facilitate development and improve performance. With the assessments now online, HR could audit a sampling of assessments against a set of quality criteria. Through this audit process, they were able to identify the areas of the assessments in need of the most improvement and focus coaching and training in those areas. This effort is ongoing as managers and supervisors continue to use the coaching and feedback skills outlined in the supervisory training program.

The COE team sponsored a Best Practices Event for all action planning team members. This recognition event was promoted as an additional way to share good ideas across the organization and recognize the efforts of all employees thus far who had participated on the action planning teams. Each team was asked to create a poster or display to showcase their action plans. A representative from each team presented the posters or displays to other team members passing by. The event, featuring food, music, and entertainment, was lively and highly interactive and showcased the ideas and efforts already put into place.

Interim Spot Survey

Finally, the COE team decided not to wait two years until the next global employee survey to measure improvement efforts. In the fall of 2003, a spot survey was conducted to measure satisfaction and engagement levels over a reduced and newly targeted set of survey items. A key driver analysis was conducted on the 2002 employee survey data to identify those items most closely aligned with overall company and job satisfaction. A second key driver analysis was conducted to identify the critical issues within the basic engagement category. As a result of the two analyses, twenty-seven items made up the spot survey. Twenty-three items had been identified as key drivers—those items most likely to drive and improve overall employee engagement. Four additional questions were added to the 2003 spot survey to assess the current levels of involvement in the follow-up and action planning activities. The 2003 spot survey was administered to a stratified, random sample of five thousand employees across the organization.

The results of the 2003 spot survey showed trends toward improvement and progress in most areas previously identified as opportunities for improvement. Employee involvement in action planning activities was favorable. Fifty-eight percent of all employees said they participated in feedback sessions where survey results were shared. Almost 50 percent of employees believed action would be taken based on the survey results, a 24 percentage point improvement from the employee survey administered one year earlier. Issues regarding fairness, employee recognition, and involvement were more favorable compared to the previous survey. Overall, the spot survey identified areas where improvements were being made, but it also pointed out several areas that required greater attention and focus.

Action planning efforts were adjusted, and an additional set of work instructions was presented to all managers and employee action planning teams. The 2003 spot survey provided the additional jump-start to reenergize and refocus the action planning teams. The 2003 survey results confirmed the work of the action planning teams and provided options for moving forward.

The COE manager commented on the effect the spot survey had on the organization: "The 2003 spot survey results injected renewed energy in the employee teams across the organization and helped to sustain the momentum. It's been so exciting to see the enthusiasm build and the team membership grow as these dedicated employees see the results of their hard work."

Results of the 2004 Survey

The results of the 2004 employee survey (eighty-one items) showed significant improvement across the entire organization—more than a 5 percentage point improvement overall. The increase in overall results was not only statistically significant but also behaviorally significant. Among the improvements were these:

• Overall survey results showed a 5-percentage-point improvement overall from the hourly populations and a 7-percentage-point improvement overall from the salaried populations from the previous survey.

• The overall job and company satisfaction dimension, which included five items on job and company satisfaction, improved 10 percentage points in overall favorability from 2002 to 2004 where there was no improvement from the previous survey period.

• Employees' satisfaction with their jobs improved 13 percentage points in overall favorability from 2002 to 2004.

• Employees' satisfaction with the information from senior management on what was going on in the company improved 13 percentage points in overall favorability from 2002 to 2004.

• Employees' understanding of the strategy set forth by senior management improved 12 percentage points in overall favorability from 2002 to 2004.

• Belief that something would be done with the survey results improved 16 percentage points in overall favorability over a two-year period (2002 to 2004) and improved 22 percentage points in overall favorability over a four-year time period (2000 to 2004).

• Survey participation rose. Some practitioners believe high response rates are a sign of employee confidence and positive feeling. In this case, participation increased from 44 percent to 76 percent overall.

Change was under way. Visible differences in the way employees interacted with each other, interacted with their customers, and approached their work were noticeable.

As the overall numbers of engaged employees increased (those with the most favorable scores on the engagement factors), the number of disengaged employees (those with the least favorable scores on the engagement factors) decreased. External research studies show the cost of employing disengaged workers is staggering. One large study shows that employees who are disengaged cost the U.S. economy between $292 billion and $355 billion a year (Coffman & Gonzalez-Molina, 2001). Disengaged employees also "cost" employers in many ways (Bates, 2004; Buckingham & Coffman, 1999; Coffman & Gonzalez-Molina, 2001). Disengaged employees tend to:

- Waste more time during the day (estimated by the company to be two hours per day)
- Make poorer decisions
- Produce poorer-quality products and services
- Provide inadequate customer service
- Require more management, coaching, and support
- Turn over more frequently
- Have higher incidents of theft, sick days, lost time, and accidents
- Be less loyal to the organizations they work for
- Be significantly less productive

It is interesting to note that the number of employees in the "neutral zone," neither engaged nor disengaged, remained the same over the four-year period. The increase in the number of engaged employees occurred because the number of disengaged employees decreased. Over the four-year period, the number of employees who were actively disengaged decreased by thirteen hundred. Based on the company's estimate that disengaged employees in their organization wasted approximately two hours per day, it was able to reduce the cost of disengaged employees by nearly $30 million.

The overall profitability of the organization continues to improve. Even in the midst of a commercial airline crisis, soaring oil prices, and rising health care costs, the organization's financial position remains strong. The executive committee's strategic decisions to focus on more profitable businesses and the reengagement of its workforce has provided the right platform for strategic change.

Why It Worked: Six Guiding Principles for Success

The results of this case study indicate that substantial organizational change can occur from the employee survey process even in an organization facing tough competition and difficult times with a workforce steeped in history. Organizations that succeed in realizing measurable improvement follow six guiding principles (Figure 22.3).

Figure 22.3. Six Guiding Principles for Success

Source: Foresight International (2004).

Principle 1: Embrace the Strategic Value of Employee Engagement

Organizations that use their employee survey to improve employee engagement or corporate performance have a strong desire to change and improve. They realize that the only way to instill cultural change, improve customer service levels, improve efficiencies, refocus product offerings, or stay competitive is to truly engage their workforce and reengage those who have become disconnected. It is through the employees that success will be accomplished, not in spite of them. Improving employee engagement becomes a strategic decision, which affects other business outcomes.

The executive committee and senior leadership team of this organization embraced the value that employee engagement would bring to their business. Commitment and focus toward improving the level of employee engagement and employee fulfillment were supported from the top of the organization on down.

Total management focus on employee engagement was a critical component in the overall company business strategy.

Principle 2: Senior Management Involvement

Many survey improvement plans fail due to lack of senior management involvement. Along with the articulated necessity to change and a strong desire to improve, the survey and follow-up activities must have senior management involvement and support. Support must be more than lip service. Support and involvement need to be demonstrated in senior management's behaviors and actions, by the creation of goals and objectives they set for each leader, by the performance mechanisms in place to evaluate the success of each leader, by the compensation systems designed to reward good leaders, and by the way work is conducted on a day-to-day basis. Engaging employees is how work gets done every day. It does not become another activity to be included in the already overwhelming list of management responsibilities.

Principle 3: Ask the Right Questions and Provide the Right Reports

A well-written employee engagement survey can identify the key issues most likely to increase engagement or derail it within the organization. Survey questions need to be actionable and the demographics tied directly to individual work groups. Creating a coding structure that provides distinct data for smaller workgroups as well as larger rollup groups helps leaders identify highly engaged work groups, identify best practices, and identify highly disengaged work groups that require intervention and coaching. Reporting survey results by levels of engagement—basic, intermediate, and advanced—creates the focus that managers need to prioritize action planning efforts. Organizations scoring low in basic engagement factors can begin to build a solid and strong foundation by focusing on the issues most likely to derail engagement efforts. A solid foundation is necessary to ensure that individual goals and objectives align with the strategic goals of the organization. Without asking the right questions and gathering the appropriate department coding, the survey becomes a tool to collect useless information.

Principle 4: Department-Level Data, Coaching, and Accountability

Once the data are collected and results are disseminated to them, managers are faced with the task of interpreting their results and creating action plans. They must have the tools, training, and coaching needed to create effective action plans. Survey results must be reported in such a way as to identify top-priority issues and work groups most in need of follow-up and coaching.

Once action plans have been established, each department manager must take responsibility and be held accountable for implementation of his or her action plan. Creating an action plan is no good if nothing is ever done with it.

Employees expect follow-up actions from the employee survey. This anticipation of action implementation from a survey is highest just after the survey results have been distributed. Experience shows that good managers—those with highly engaged and productive employees—more readily follow up on survey results even if not required to do so, and they continue to improve. Poor managers—those with a higher number of disengaged employees and typically lower performance—tend to do nothing with their survey results unless forced to by corporate edict. If not held accountable, poor managers will continue to create more disengaged employees. Building in accountability structures will ensure follow-up occurs across the entire organization.

Principle 5: Employee Involvement in Action Planning and Implementation

Involving employees in the identification of issues and the implementation of improvement plans can increase the leverage an organization needs to move forward. Involving employees in action planning solutions creates an empowering environment where ideas and suggestions are valued and accountability for success is shared.

The COE dramatically increased employees' involvement and participation in the action planning processes. By involving employees in the solutions, the organization changed the process from a management-owned to a management- and employee-owned process. Accountability was shared across all levels of the organization. The COE was not about improving employee engagement for everyone else; it was about supporting everyone else to improve engagement levels for himself or herself. All initiatives need a periodic recharge to maintain momentum. The COE provided a booster or recharge effect to the organization.

Principle 6: Dedicated Team to Coach, Support, and Recognize

The final principle that fits all of the cornerstones together is a dedicated and focused team whose job is to improve employee engagement. Increasing employee engagement is their mission. This team should be able to develop effective tools to help managers accurately interpret results and create meaningful action plans. They should provide managers with the training and coaching needed to deal with the tough issues and recognize those managers doing things right. They should identify highly disengaged work groups and focus on specific interventions to address concerns. They should observe highly engaged work groups and then document and share best practices across the organization. They should create the spark, drive, and enthusiasm needed to keep the momentum going even when times get tough and employee survey momentum begins to fade. This dedicated team should be experts in change management with access to organizational resources required to make things happen.

Conclusion

The executive committee created a focused and dedicated group in the organization that had the responsibility to facilitate and support engagement: the COE. The results of the 2004 employee survey showed significant improvement across the board. Employees showed greater alignment with the strategies outlined by the executive committee: to diversify the business, focus resources on new engine segments that provided clear growth opportunities, and redirect resources to the engine services. Employee confidence in senior management improved more than 10 percentage points over four years. Forty-four of ninety-five work groups achieved the company-defined target level of 70 percent favorable or higher on basic engagement items compared to seven out of sixty-nine work groups in 2002. As the overall number of engaged employees increased over the four-year period, the number of disengaged employees (those responding unfavorably to survey items) decreased by thirteen hundred, thereby reducing the company's annual cost of disengaged employees by an estimated $30 million.

Overall business results are positive. The organization is on track with continued strong performance. Its successful business performance is clearly attributable to the many changes made and, notably, the widespread culture change driven by the adaptation of ACE. Equally clear is the fact that the employee survey follow-up and action planning processes have played a key role. The vice president of HR commented, "While we cannot attribute the continuously improved company performance to any single item, we know improved employee engagement is a strong contributor with powerful effects on customer loyalty, productivity and cost savings."

References

Bates, S. (2004). Getting engaged—Researchers say employee engagement is lagging badly. *HR Magazine, 49*(2), 44–51.

Buckingham, G. (2000). Same indifference: Uncaring managers lead to staff turnover. *People Management, 6*(4), 44–46.

Buckingham, M., & Coffman, C. (1999). *First, break all the rules: What the world's greatest managers do differently.* New York: Simon & Schuster.

Coffman, C., & Gonzalez-Molina, G., (2001, Mar.). Gallup study indicates actively disengaged workers cost the U.S. hundreds of billions each year. *Gallup Management Journal.*

Foresight International. (2004). *Six Guiding Principles of Success.*

Gubman, E. (2004). From engagement to passion for work: The search for the missing person. *Human Resource Planning, 27*(3), 42–46.

Harter, J., Schmidt, F., & Hayes, T. (2002). Business-unit-level relationship between employee satisfaction, employee engagement, and business outcomes: A meta-analysis. *Journal of Applied Psychology, 87*(2), 268–279.

Highly engaged employees lead their employers to faster growth. (2004). *HR Focus, 81*(7), 8.

Howe, C. (2003). What makes an organization a great place to work? *Employee Benefits Journal, 28*(2), 41–43.

Kowalski, B. (2003). The engagement gap. *Training, 40*(4), 62.

Parker, S., Schroeder, M., & Fairfield-Sonn, J. (2002). *50 tips: How to design advanced online employee survey systems.* Lake Zurich, IL: Foresight Survey Support International.

Pinder, C. (1998). *Work motivation in organizational behavior.* Upper Saddle River, NJ: Prentice Hall.

Shaffer, J. (2004). Measurable payoff. *Communication World, 21*(4), 22–27.

Teresko, J. (2004). Best practices—Driving employee engagement. *Industry Week, 253*(9), 74–75.

CHAPTER 23

Best Company Lists
Using Survey Data to Assess, Recognize, and Reward Organizations

Norman D. Costa
Peter Bachiochi

The drive to be the best can be seen everywhere. Many high school classes have valedictorians. The Super Bowl is not really over until the Most Valuable Player has been named. Organizations also strive to be the best in their market, region, or nation. The Fortune 500 identifies the biggest companies, but biggest does not always mean the best. As a result, several sources have emerged to help identify the "best" companies. The best known is *Fortune* magazine's 100 Best Companies to Work For in America. Levering and Moskowitz (1984, 1993) first produced the list of the "100 Best Companies to Work For in America" in their two books. Since 1998 Levering and Moskowitz have been producing the list with *Fortune* magazine.

Others have developed lists to identify the best companies for working mothers, for various minority groups, and in specific countries, regions, or cities. Some lists use surveys of employees, others use surveys of companies, and some use both. Each list serves different needs and uses slightly different methods, but they all have one thing in common: they all rely on survey data of some kind to identify their best companies.

Being named to a Best Company list (BCL) should be a windfall for a company, but there are many considerations. The application process requires a significant investment of time and resources.

Being named to a list may also create higher expectations among employees and customers. In this chapter, we provide some insight into the BCL phenomenon. More specifically, we describe what a BCL is and then explain the process used to create these lists by providing examples. In addition, we outline what some of the various BCLs reveal about the organizations listed. Finally, we provide some questions to ask and some warnings to companies that may be weighing the benefits and drawbacks of BCL consideration.

What Is a Best Company List?

BCLs are intended to recognize (and thereby reward) companies for exceptional performance on some set of criteria. The criteria can include bottom-line financial measures, family-friendly policies and practices, diversity-related initiatives, and others. A few of the lists have existed for many years. *Fortune*'s Best Companies to Work For list, combined with Levering and Moskowitz's list, has existed since 1984. *Working Mother* magazine celebrated the twentieth anniversary of its Best Companies for Working Mothers in America list in 2005.

In the past five years, however, BCLs have seen explosive growth in the United States and on an international level. At the same time, BCLs are emerging at regional and local levels too. Tables 23.1 and 23.2 list a few examples of the wide range of BCLs in the United States and internationally. An exhaustive search could yield dozens, if not hundreds, of BCLs.

General Characteristics of BCLs

BCLs vary in their objectives, methodology, type of sponsor, and desired influence on organizational behavior and performance. However, we can describe some general characteristics of many BCLs.

Relative Comparisons
A BCL is a process used to assess organizations on any number of factors and then compare the organizations' relative rankings.

Sponsors
There are many different types of sponsors. Examples include print publications, advocacy groups, organization consultants, and nongovernmental organizations (NGOs). Some act alone (*Scientist*

Table 23.1. U.S. Examples of Best Company Lists

Name of Best Company List	Sponsoring Organization or Publication
1 100 Best Companies for Working Mothers	Working Mother Media Incorporated
2 100 Best Companies List	*Hispanic* magazine
3 100 Best Companies to Work For	*Fortune* Magazine
4 100 Best Companies to Work For in Oregon	*Oregon Business* magazine
5 100 Best Places to Work in IT	*ComputerWorld* magazine
6 100 Companies Providing the Most Opportunities for Hispanics	*Hispanic* magazine
7 30 Great Places to Work	*Essence* magazine
8 50 Best Companies for Latinas to Work	*Latina Style* magazine
9 50 Best Companies for Minorities	*Fortune* magazine
10 Best Employers for Workers over 50	AARP
11 Corporate Equality Index	Human Rights Campaign Foundation
12 NAACP Corporate Image Award	National Association for the Advancement of Colored People
13 Top 100 Companies for Working Families in Central Florida	*Orlando Sentinel*
14 Top 30 Companies for Women to Work	National Association of Female Executives
15 Top 50 Companies for Diversity	Diversity Incorporated
16 Top 50 Companies for Hispanic Women	*Latina Style* magazine
17 Top 50 Companies for Minorities	Diversity Incorporated
18 Top 50 Companies to Work For in America	National Society of Black Engineers
19 Top 50 Diversity Employers	*The Black Collegian*
20 Top Organizations for Multi-cultural Business Opportunities	DiversityBusiness.com (formerly 2000div.com)

Table 23.2. International Examples of Best Company Lists

Name of Best Company List	Sponsoring Organization or Publication
1 100 Best Workplaces in the European Union	European Commission of the European Union
2 20 Best Companies to Work for in Germany	VAA, Association of Chemical Industry Managerial Employees
3 25 Great Places to Work for in India	*Businessworld* Magazine
4 40 Great Places to Work in Argentina	*Apertura* magazine
5 50 Best Companies to Work for in Canada	*Globe and Mail's Report on Business* magazine
6 Best Companies to Work for in India	*Business Today* (India)
7 Best Company to Work for in South America	*Financial Mail*
8 Best Place to Work in the Czech Republic	*Prague Post* (Czech Republic)
9 Best United Kingdom Scientific Institution to Work in	*Scientist Journal*
10 Best Workplaces in Austria	*Wirtschaftuniversitat Wien*
11 Best Workplaces in the United Kingdom	*Financial Times of London*
12 Citation for Diversity	*Canadian Business* magazine
13 HanKyung-Levering 20 Great Work Places in Korea	*Korean Economic Daily*
14 New Zealand Top 20 Best Places to Work	*Unlimited* magazine

Journal in the UK, for example), while some act in support of other sponsors (for example, Great Place to Work Institute supports *Fortune* magazine). Others act together as cosponsors, as do the National Association for the Advancement of Colored People (NAACP) and Black Data Processing Associates (BDPA).

Competing Organizations

Companies considered for BCL selection may be a representative sample or merely a sample of convenience. Consideration for a BCL award comes about in a variety of ways:

- Open call for competitors. This process may be public, with solicitation ads placed in print publications. Sometimes the solicitations are limited to organizations within the contact lists of the sponsor. Membership lists and commercial mailing lists are also used.
- Limited call for competitors. Invitations are distributed to a limited pool of organizations. Sponsors may focus on certain industries, such as only organizations in the home building trades. Some require organizations of a certain size (for example, the organization must have at least two hundred managerial employees). Still other BCLs exclude specific organizations, such as charitable institutions and government agencies.
- Prescreening competitors. A consultant group or department within a publication may submit a focused pool of organizations to a sponsor. Competitors may also be prescreened to reduce the competitor pool to a manageable size.
- Self-nominated competitors. Competing organizations usually respond to an invitation with a voluntary self-nomination and provide at least some relevant company information.

Auditors

Only a few BCLs in Europe employ independent auditors as part of the process. Some U.S.-based BCLs use third-party vendors to handle the collection, processing, analysis, and reporting of data. However, it is not known what, if any, independent auditing and data verification are used for sponsors or vendors.

Judges

Some BCLs employ the services of judges to review the data collected on competing organizations and render decisions on final rankings. Generally the judges are experienced professionals who are qualified to make decisions about data given to them. Ideally judges should not have a personal or conflicting interest in organizational rankings on the BCLs. The independence of the judges or whether they are remunerated in any way is not always clear. Some judges assign scores based on their assessment, while others function more like a check on a scoring process that is completed.

How Does the BCL Process Work?

We profile three examples of BCLs selected for their variety, representativeness, and at least one unique issue. The Best Places to Work in the UK is a good example of many BCLs that use the GPTW Institute methodology. The same methodology is used in *Fortune* magazine's The 100 Best Companies to Work For (in America). The methodology has been developed over many years and is used in the United States and in at least twenty countries in Europe, Asia, and South America. The 100 Best Companies [in America] for Working Mothers is profiled as an example of a particularly rigorous BCL process. Third, the Corporate [America] Equality Index (CEI) was selected as an excellent example of a BCL used for highly focused advocacy.

The examples are compared on five factors: eligibility requirements, company input requirements (including employee surveys), verification, evaluation and scoring, and trial by jury. These factors also represent the criteria that any company should investigate when considering application to a BCL.

The Best Places to Work in the UK

The publication *Financial Times* (FT) of London partners with the GPTW Institute United Kingdom and the organization Account-Ability in naming The Best Places to Work in the UK. FT is recognized internationally for authority, integrity, and accuracy in the reporting of business news. AccountAbility is a professional institute that promotes corporate accountability for sustained development and conducts research and public policy advocacy. Also, entries in the UK competition are automatically considered for the European Commission's 100 Best Workplaces in the EU (European Union). The European Commission's objective is focused on raising workplace standards in Europe (European Commission, 2001).

Eligibility to Participate

Eligibility requirements are liberal. Any UK organization with at least fifty employees may enter. Any organization may nominate itself or be nominated by any employee, any nonemployee individual, or any other organization. Targeted invitations are mailed to organizations in FT's contact database for this project and organizations named in other BCLs. Although entry is open to all, the targeted mailing of invitations focuses on likely participant organizations.

Company Input Requirements

Competing organizations are required to provide two types of information. First, information is provided about the company itself. This is supplied in the form of GPTW's Culture Audit, which covers workplace culture, HR practices, policies, and programs. The information in the Culture Audit is supplied by the company's staff. Second, a sample of employees completes an attitude survey. Employee input is assessed with GPTW's Trust Index, a standard survey of employee attitudes. Surveys are usually completed online, but provisions are made for acceptance of hard copy questionnaires if employees do not have access to computers and the Internet. Individual survey responses are kept confidential. Responding employees have an opportunity to provide open-ended comments. It is not known how these are used in assessment and scoring, but they provide colorful additions to the articles that are ultimately published.

Organizations are required to select a random sample of 250 employees to take the Trust Index survey. Competing organizations are given detailed instructions by GPTW on drawing a sample. GPTW also does on-site audits of about 10 percent of the competing organizations, meeting with a small number of employees to verify that proper sampling procedures are used. Neither FT nor GPTW makes it clear whether the sample of 250 employees is the number of invited employees or the yield of surveyed employees.

The content of the Trust Index survey reflects the specific philosophy and emphasis of GPTW. Trust is what makes a company a great place to work, they believe. GPTW believes that trust is the primary relationship between management and labor in the workplace. The Trust Index is a survey questionnaire that assesses trust between management and employees, competence of management, recognition of personal and professional worth, equitable sharing of opportunities and rewards, as well as pride in the job and camaraderie. However, compared to other views on organizational development and assessment, the GPTW philosophy is limited and highly circumscribed. GPTW's employee-centric Trust Index flies in the face of more recent developments that use employee surveys as a means to measure progress toward achieving employee and customer components of strategic business objectives.

Evaluation and Scoring

BCLs that are based on the GPTW methodology are usually described as employee driven because the scoring weights the Trust Index (the employee survey) 70 percent, while the Culture Audit (organization supplied data) is weighted 30 percent in determining an organization's score. We do not know how the individual components of either the Trust Index or the Culture Index are scored or weighted. We do not know if differential weighting of the components (if they are differentially weighted) is constant from year to year.

Trial by Jury

There appears to be no subjective assessment made by an outside panel or judges in arriving at the final ranks. We do not know what influence the management or editors of FT have on the final selection of the list.

The 100 Best Companies [in America] for Working Mothers

Working Mother magazine (WMM) has been published for almost twenty-five years. In 2005, it published its twentieth annual list of The 100 Best Companies [in America] for Working Mothers. WMM proudly considers itself the premier arbiter on best company practices that benefit working mothers and their families. The editors of the publication view themselves as advocates for women in the workplace and devote their publication to that service.

In 1999 WMM partnered with eXpert Survey Systems, a survey consulting organization. The consultant revamped the questionnaire and redesigned it for online administration and objective scoring. It managed the administrative process, collecting questionnaires, processing data, generating reports, and the online interface with competing organizations. The consultant was not part of the judging process and did not make policy decisions for the WMM BCL.

Eligibility to Participate

U.S. companies, corporations, autonomous subsidiaries of companies, and educational institutions of any size were eligible. Companies in child care and work/life research and consulting fields, as well as government agencies, are not eligible to apply.

Participation is through a self-nominating process, usually in response to an invitation from WMM. WMM maintains its own contact database of prior participating companies, companies that expressed interest in the list, and attendees to the magazine's annual Work and Family Congress. It also uses a commercially available mailing list to reach a national audience of HR executives.

Company Input Requirements

Each participating company must complete a comprehensive questionnaire covering the following: company profile, workforce profile, total compensation, mainstream child care, supplemental child care, flexibility, time off and leaves, family-friendly resources, company culture, company essay, and documentation supporting these items.

The total size of the questionnaire changes from year to year. It has ranged from about five hundred to over seven hundred questions. Annual fluctuations in content and numbers of questions reflect changes in editorial preferences and emphasis from cycle to cycle.

Unlike other BCL processes, the organizations' employees provide no independent input through an employee survey. However, WMM used an employee survey for its Best Companies for Women of Color list.

Data Verification

Verification of the questionnaire data is handled at several levels. The WMM questionnaire has been publicly available for scrutiny. The consultant executes appropriate data checks, and WMM has a standard prepublication fact checking process. Finally, the writers assigned to compose company profiles of the winners flag questionable data or information in need of explanation. These issues are resolved directly with the companies.

Evaluation and Scoring

The company questionnaire is the only source of data that is assessed and scored for the WMM BCL. The value system and philosophy of the WMM editors drive the scoring. For example, companies are rewarded not only for having a good work/life program but also for making it available to more employees and tracking the use.

The consultant generates scores for each company and presents a ranking of the companies to WMM. Accompanying this overall ranking are copies of individual company applications and a summary of section scores for each company. Companies are also ranked on each of the composite sections. Annual fluctuations in the scoring and section weights reflect changes in WMM's editorial preferences and emphasis from cycle to cycle.

Trial by Jury

WMM stopped announcing the use of outside judges to review the overall results after 2001. This coincided with a change of management, a new editorial staff, and a restructuring of the company. Since then, only the WMM management and staff review the rankings and supporting data and make the decision on final ranks.

Corporate Equality Index

The Human Rights Campaign (HRC) Foundation of Washington, D.C., launched the Corporate [America] Equity Index (CEI) in 2002. Although it is relatively new, it is an outgrowth of other initiatives and data sources from as early as 1993. HRC is nonpartisan, and its goal is the advancement of equality based on sexual orientation and gender expression and identity. Its workplace project, HRC WorkNet, advises employees and employers by serving as a national source of information on laws and policies. Its publication of the "Corporate Equality Index on Gay, Lesbian, Bisexual and Transgender [GLBT] Social Responsibility"

(2004) is one of the most detailed and comprehensive descriptions of a BCL process that we have seen. In our view, it is a model for any BCL documentation:

> HRC WorkNet was aided in the development of the survey instrument and the index criteria by the HRC Business Council, an advisory group composed primarily of GLBT executives in a variety of disciplines from major U.S. Corporations. The group provides substantial expertise and experience in corporate policy and decision-making to help ensure that the index [CEI] is rigorous and fair. The HRC Council was not involved in administering the survey, tabulating the data or calculating any scores [p. 3].

Eligibility to Participate

The HRC surveys each year's Fortune 500 companies, Forbes's list of the two hundred largest privately held organizations, other organizations that requested a CEI rating, and companies for which they had enough data to generate a CEI score.

Company Input Requirements

Companies are mailed a survey that is addressed to the CEO and HR executive. Follow-up telephone calls are made by HRC to encourage participation and survey completion. A blank copy of the survey questionnaire that is mailed to the organizations and detailed descriptions of criteria are printed in "Corporate Equality Index on Gay, Lesbian, Bisexual and Transgender Social Responsibility." The HRC does not rely solely on this survey. It employs a team of researchers who investigate and check the policies and practices of the organizations. It also reviews Securities and Exchange Commission filings and IRS 990 forms, looks for funding for and connections to antigay organizations or activities, and scrutinizes case law and media reports for relevant information:

> These data were supplemented by HRC WorkNet, which since 1995 has collected information on U.S. employers and maintains the most accurate and extensive database of policies regarding the GLBT community. . . . News accounts, employee resource groups and individuals provided another level of data in determining corporate policies. Companies are not rated until all appropriate information has been gathered and verified [p. 3].

Although we applaud the comprehensiveness of the documentation, we feel HRC could provide more information about the employee resource groups it mentions in the prior quotation.

Evaluation and Scoring

The CEI is a broad-based measure of policies and practices in the organization. It covers issues like nondiscrimination policies, advertising, and event sponsorship. It is a composite of an organization's survey results and other activity over several years. HRC acknowledges that "after scrupulous data collection and careful consideration, assigning a grade . . . involves some degree of subjectivity" (p. 3).

Trial by Jury

The scoring and ranking are done by the deputy director and staff for HRC WorkNet. No outside jury panel is used.

What Do BCLs Tell Us?

Fuller, Gerhardt, and Scott (2003) warn that benchmarking against BCL companies is based on the assumptions that these companies actually have more positive employee relations and that these employee relations have an impact on the performance of the companies. Most BCLs tend to assess the HR policies and practices of organizations, and studies have linked effective HR management to business performance (Harter, Schmidt, & Hayes, 2002; Glade & Livery, 2003). More important from a BCL perspective, HR outcomes tend to influence business outcomes rather than the other way around (Koys, 2001, 2003). Therefore, one could assume that companies doing well on BCLs should also experience better bottom-line performance. However, results of existing research have not been conclusive.

The vast majority of research on BCLs has examined the financial and stock market performance of companies that have been named to the various lists. The results of these studies have been decidedly mixed. Appearing on *Fortune*'s Best Companies list seems to have the most positive impact, but appearing on *Working Mother*'s list of family-friendly companies has been found to have little impact and potentially has negative effects. Although studies do not explain why companies make it onto BCLs, the results shed some light on what may happen to companies after appearing on a BCL.

Fortune's 100 Best Companies to Work For

Fuller et al. (2003) established that companies on Fortune's 100 Best list had positive employee attitudes that were stable over time. In addition, these companies had generally better financial performance and somewhat better stock performance than a matched sample of companies. In the year following the *Fortune* award, the 100 Best Companies outperformed a set of matched benchmark firms in all measures of return (Filbeck & Preece, 2003a).

Fortune's Most Admired Companies

Early studies of *Fortune*'s most admired companies (Filbeck, Gorman, & Preece, 1997; Vergin & Qoronfleh, 1998) found that investors could outperform the market by investing in stocks of *Fortune*'s most admired companies. However, a more recent study found that *Fortune*'s most admired companies did not outperform a sample of matched firms on stock performance (Filbeck & Krueger, 2002). The authors summarized by stating that the most admired companies "may be good companies, but not necessarily good investments" (p. 49). On another publication's list, the *Economist*'s most admired British firms also outperformed the British stock market (Filbeck & Preece, 1995).

Mother Jones and *Working Mother*

The financial performance of the socially responsible companies cited on *Mother Jones*'s list of Better Places to Work and the family-friendly firms on *Working Mother*'s list of Best Companies for Working Mothers have been generally less impressive. A portfolio of companies mentioned by *Mother Jones* had slightly better performance than the S&P 500 but not better than a matched sample of firms (Filbeck, 2001).

There were actually negative returns associated with the announcement of the *Mother Jones* survey results. Similarly, Preece and Filbeck (1999) found that family-friendly firms, according to *Working Mother* magazine, outperformed the market but underperformed a matched set of firms. The market response over two- and ten-day periods was also strongly negative for these companies (Filbeck & Preece, 2003b). The market appears to penalize firms that become known for providing family-related benefits such as parental leave and dependent care assistance.

These findings do not necessarily argue against applying to BCLs because being named to BCLs can have other unanticipated benefits.

Simon (2002) presented unpublished research at *Working Mother* magazine's Work and Family Congress. This study assessed the impact of work/life policies on the firms' customer satisfaction ratings (ACSI, 2001). Simon reported that firms on the *Working Mother* list have higher customer satisfaction ratings than firms that are not on the list. However, Simon is cautious about these findings (personal communication, 2004). Simon feels there may be some artifact influencing the results that is caused by the framing of the research hypotheses.

Who Benefits from BCLs?

The utility of BCLs depends on the players involved. There are a number of stakeholders in BCLs: competing organizations, their employees and customers, publications that sponsor BCLs, NGOs, external advocacy groups, internal advocates, membership groups, HR and management consulting organizations, and service organizations.

Competing Organizations

Competing organizations use BCLs for a variety of purposes. Winning a place on a BCL provides public relations currency. Shellenbarger (1993) mentioned that firms identify the potential publicity as one of the key reasons for submitting an application. Press releases are sent to a wide number of media outlets, and communications are generated for internal distribution and for other stakeholders.

Winning organizations find that their status bolsters recruiting (at least in numbers of applicants) and improves the general image of the organization to the community. Cleaver (2003), in her aptly titled "Lust for Lists," provided the example of Edward Jones, a St. Louis brokerage firm, that appeared as number 11 of *Fortune*'s Best Companies list in its first application in 1998. It has since moved to the top of that list. Before the firm landed on the *Fortune* list, it received approximately 7,000 employment applications a year; that number has ballooned to 400,000 annually since the firm's prominent placement on the list.

Another important use for BCL competitions is benchmarking or normative comparisons against other organizations. Some BCLs provide to their competing organizations, sometimes at added costs, feedback reports that compare them to other competing companies. These reports vary in detail, types of comparison groups, and sophistication. They can cover organization metrics as well as employee survey data.

Finally, winning a place on a BCL amounts to a validation by a third-party entity that is presumed to be unbiased. Fuller et al. (2003) suggested that appearing to be an attractive employer "may create an important intangible asset, positive employee relations, that differentiates firms in a value-producing way" (p. 987). BCLs that reward organizational performance for diversity and women's issues can be extremely desirable to a participating organization. This is especially true for organizations that are the subject of negative allegations and charges or have been recovering from unfavorable publicity or adjudication. In our experience, some highly motivated companies go to great lengths to improve their internal programs, practices, and data management systems to compete better for a place on a BCL.

Employees and Customers

When a BCL competition requires the reporting of extensive company data, the application process itself provides a structured self-audit for the organization even if it decides not to submit data for consideration. Employees and customers then benefit indirectly from BCLs when an organization uses BCL results to improve performance, policies, procedures, or programs.

Sponsoring Publications

Sponsoring publications find that BCLs expand the number of potential feature articles and add legitimacy to their own voice by making them a perceived authority of what is best. More publications seem to be seeking a larger readership, significantly increased circulation, and greater advertising revenues by branching out into BCLs.

Advocacy Groups

Advocacy is a major foundation for the sponsors of many BCLs. Successful advocacy is a significant accomplishment. NGOs such as AccountAbility in Europe are promoting issues like corporate social responsibility. The European Commission of the European Union also promotes better workplace standards (European Commission, 2001). Publications like *Working Mother* and *Business Ethics* magazines are not only sponsors of BCLs but see advocacy journalism as a major editorial role for their magazine. External advocates (external to the organizations participating in BCLs) are using BCLs to benefit their constituents. In the United States, this is principally focused on constituencies based on race, ethnicity, gender, and sexual orientation. The role of internal advocates (employees within the organizations) is overlooked completely in the literature and media. For example, our experience over many years is that staff people in corporate America have had an enormous effect on work-family policies and programs by pushing their employers to enter BCL competitions.

Consulting and Service Organizations

Consulting and service organizations, in the United States and internationally, are constituents of great importance in the BCL phenomenon (examples are Deloitte and Touche, GPTW, Mercer Human Resource Consulting, KPMG, and market research firm TNS and eXpert Survey Systems). Organizational consultants and survey service providers have built substantial businesses, on their own or with the BCL sponsors. Others are developing new practice areas built around the BCL concept. Service businesses are involved in related work such as events, conferences, training, certification, organizational consulting, and the selling of reports.

Should My Company Apply to a BCL?

It would seem that being on a BCL would be good for any company, but there are unanswered questions and some clear warnings to consider.

Who Is on the List?

The first warning deals with what it means to be on a list or, more important, what it means to be absent from a list. The absence of companies does not necessarily indicate decreased performance or employee perceptions that are more negative. Many lists do not include government agencies, and *Fortune* restricts its lists to businesses with five hundred or more U.S. employees (Cole, 1999). Similarly, lists may be focused on a specific region or industry, and the list creator's criteria for selection may not match what you would expect. List creators might espouse explicit criteria—such as employee satisfaction, community involvement, and so on—but the implicit or unintended criteria might be likelihood of purchased advertising or company stock performance. Large NGOs and nonprofits, principally charitable organizations, are typically excluded from lists as well. Therefore, some important competitors of BCL companies may not appear on a list simply based on the selection methods used by the list sponsor.

The Application Process

Many lists require a lengthy application that some businesses choose not to complete. The WMM BCL is a good example. Some of the larger companies report two person-months of effort in order to submit the application questionnaire and supporting documentation. The bottom line is that a company on last year's list may not appear this year not because of a lower evaluation but because it did not apply.

Great Expectations

Making the list creates a "keeping up with the Joneses" phenomenon in that companies feel compelled to provide ever more creative and effective employee benefit programs (Cleaver, 2003). In cases where companies provide information as part of the application, exaggeration of offerings to make it onto a list can create unanticipated fallout. If the portrayal of the organization in the publication of the list is not consistent with the reality that employees see, the recognition could backfire and create a negative response. In our experience, employees have no hesitation communicating their approval or disbelief to BCL sponsors when winners are announced. Therefore, in the same way that conducting an employee survey creates the expectation of postsurvey action, making a BCL creates expectations among current employees and prospective applicants to prove that they are a "best company."

When Good Lists Happen to Bad Companies

It is no secret that some reputedly corrupt and irresponsible companies have been regular winners on BCLs. Three prominent examples are ENRON, KPMG, and Arthur Andersen LLP. It must embarrass and outrage the sponsors when one of their winners is exposed for fraud and ethical deficiencies. To be fair to the BCL sponsors and their partners, issues of management integrity, corporate governance, and professional ethics are not usually part of evaluating HR programs and diversity initiatives. In 2004, the U.S. government–backed mortgage company, Fannie Mae, was found to use inappropriate accounting practices in stating profits. This resulted in the early retirement of the CEO and the departure of the chief financial officer. Nevertheless, Fannie Mae was recognized as a leader in HR policies and practices on a number of BCLs. These are bitter lessons in understanding the uses and limitations of BCLs.

The List Creation Process

The process for many BCLs is described very poorly. Others are produced with proprietary processes and tools that are not disclosed. To have some trust in the validity of the reports, Cleaver (2003) suggests examining the methodology used, specifically the questions asked, the scoring, and the reputation of the publication that is sponsoring the list.

Lists that do not use employee input, for instance, create the potential for creative embellishment on the part of applying organizations. In addition, if the criteria selected by the list creator are not consistent with the organization's goals and mission, using that list as a benchmarking tool may be ill advised.

Given the proprietary nature of the process maintained by many of the organizations and publications that create the lists, one is left to trust that appropriate validation methods have been and continue to be used. However, the changing nature of work and the workplace (such as technology, globalization, and outsourcing) requires regular updating of the criteria used in order to ensure the most valid lists possible.

Finally, the proliferation of BCLs means that nearly every publication and professional organization has created a list. The source of the list should be the first criterion in selecting a list as a benchmarking tool: the list is only as good as the sponsor creating it.

Conflicts of Interest

Multiple forces compete in the creation of lists, such as commercial interests of publishers, the advocacy concerns of many stakeholders, and the need for scientific rigor. There may be conflicts of interests for organizational consultants and public relations firms that promote their own customers as BCL winners. For sponsoring publications, there is the issue of editorial and journalistic independence from the publishers and advertisers.

The publication *Business Today in India* (BTI) is an excellent example of how a sponsoring publication deals openly and honestly with the issue of conflict of interest in the BCL process. BTI has been doing workplace surveys in India since 2000. In its May 9, 2004, publication, it announced the details of an upcoming BCL competition. It discussed the issue of conflict of interest and how it planned to handle this challenge. In our opinion, it was addressing concerns about the role of its prior research partner. In BTI's own words, "The spectre of conflict of interest looms large over all qualitative [BCL] surveys . . . that involve a research partner." Its partner consulting firms "work with the companies participating in the survey, very often in the same [content] areas [that are measured by the BCL]." It continues:

> To cut to the chase, here's the innovation of this year's survey:
> BT's partner in this exercise is . . . an international HR consulting
> firm. However, while [the consulting firm] . . . has developed the
> methodology of the survey and will arrive at a short-list of the best

companies to work for in India, the entire front-end of the survey, and the data collection and aggregation will be managed by [an] international market research [firm]. . . . The research firm will present summary reports for short-listed companies on an anonymous basis to . . . [the consulting firm]. The consulting firm will present a list of proposed rankings to *Business Today* that will put names to numbers, and present these to a jury that will decide on the final ranking [p. 34].

Unlike the three BCL examples that are profiled above, BTI uses a jury panel composed of an academician from one of India's leading business schools, a retired CEO who has become an elder statesman for industry as a whole, a bureaucrat/policymaker who is aware of happenings in industry, an employee of its consulting firm, and an editor from BTI who has covered HR practices across companies for almost a decade.

Manning Pynn (2004), public editor for the *Orlando Sentinel,* raised a serious issue with his own newspaper. This was less than one week after the publication of 100 Top Companies for Working Families in Central Florida in the Florida magazine insert in the *Sunday Sentinel.* Pynn was concerned about the danger of compromising the editorial independence of news reporting from the financial interests of the publication. Specifically, the newsroom was handed the list of winners after the completion of the selection process. At the same time, the list was released to the advertising department. In Pynn's words, "The people who deliver the newspaper and those who sell advertising space have their eyes on the prize: profit. Their siblings in the newsroom, though, contribute to that goal only by producing the best news report they can. They must avoid even the appearance that financial gain could affect their judgment, lest they erode the credibility that prompts readers to buy the newspaper—and companies to buy advertising to reach those readers."

It remains to be seen whether BCL publications will maintain an independent journalistic focus or become advertising-supported catalogues for their winners.

Finally, many companies have turned over the management of their BCL applications to public relations firms. Other companies have created dedicated executive positions with titles like "director of best list competitions." Some corporate executives are evaluated and compensated, at least in part, on BCL standings. All this is understandable and reasonable given the number of BCLs and the importance many companies attribute to winning a place on a BCL. However, it raises concerns about the level of relationship building between companies and BCL sponsors, the packaging of the application information, and the influence of these on the final selection. Clearly the burden is on the BCL sponsor to deal forthrightly with these issues and assure their audience of the objectivity and fairness of the selection process.

Characteristics of a Good BCL

To guide companies weighing the benefits and costs of BCL application, we provide the following list of elements that a good BCL should have. In our view, good BCLs worthy of consideration by organizations should possess the following characteristics:

- The process should be described clearly in terms of eligibility rules, criteria, time lines, sampling, and scoring.
- The process should be clear enough to be scrutinized by other practitioners and professionals.
- The process should have provisions for independent auditing and judging.
- The process should be rational, impartial, and repeatable.
- The organizational characteristics assessed should reflect the role of the organization as an employer.
- The organizational characteristics assessed should be consistent with, and communicate the values, and sometimes advocacy of, the BCL sponsors.
- Data collection may involve methods like surveys and polling, but it may also rely on self-reported data from organizations. The BCL sponsors should produce evidence that their data collection instruments are objective, reliable, and valid.
- Both objective measures and subjective judgments can be used simultaneously in reaching decisions about organizational comparisons.
- The final ranking of organizations should reflect the objectives of the BCL and not be a surrogate measure for something else, like name recognition, financial sponsorship by competing organizations, or stock market performance.

Final Thoughts and Recommendations

The BCL process itself is not a scientific exercise and does not even approach the level of field research. None of the three BCL sponsors profiled in this chapter has proffered its BCL as a scientific research process. Appropriately, none of the three has promoted its BCL as representative of anything more than its own sample of convenience and opportunity. However, all BCLs can improve the level of detail and completeness in describing their BCL process. We need to know more about eligibility requirements, rationale for exclusions, method of nomination, participation rates, sampling error, the sequence of events, the instruments used, the collection of data, the data analysis, the roles of partners, the judging process, and integrity safeguards. In our opinion, this will come about only when participating companies, HR professionals, and social science researchers demand more from the BCL sponsors.

Ultimately, companies need to realize that some BCLs are better than others. We have outlined many of the factors to consider in making that decision. Another important consideration is the benefit of applying (and the possibility of not winning a place on the BCL) versus the investment in time and effort by the organization. The decision to apply to a BCL should not be based solely on the fact that key competitors have made the list. However, if the BCL is from a reputable source, has withstood the test of time, and meets many of the characteristics listed above, the time and effort required for the application process may be well worth it.

References

ACSI. (2001). *American Customer Satisfaction Index Report.* Ann Arbor: University of Michigan Business School.

The best companies to work for in India: The BT-Mercer-TNS study gets off the ground. Here are the details. (2004, May 9). *Business Today in India* (online version).

Cleaver, J. (2003, May). Lust for lists. *Workforce,* 44–48.

Cole, J. (1999, Jan.). "Best companies" lists: What do they mean? *HR Focus, 76*(1), 1–4.

European Commission. (2001, July). *Promoting a European framework for corporate social responsibility—Green Paper.* Luxembourg: Office for Official Publications of the European Communities.

Filbeck, G. (2001). Mother Jones: Do better places to work imply better places to invest? *Review of Financial Economics, 10,* 57–70.

Filbeck, G., Gorman, R., & Preece, D. C. (1997). *Fortune*'s most admired firms: An investor's perspective. *Studies in Economics and Finance, 18,* 74–93.

Filbeck, G., & Krueger, T. (2002). Investment merits of the world's most admired firms. *Journal of Investing, 11,* 45–54.

Filbeck, G., & Preece, D. C. (1995, Fall). Britain's most admired firms: Are they worth it? *Journal of Global Business,* 23–30.

Filbeck, G., & Preece, D. C. (2003a). *Fortune*'s Best 100 Companies to Work for in America: Do they work for shareholders? *Journal of Business Finance and Accounting, 30,* 771–797.

Filbeck, G., & Preece, D. C. (2003b). Announcement effects of the *Working Mother* annual survey of family-friendly firms. *Journal of Investing, 12,* 87–95.

Fuller, I. S., Gerhardt, B., & Scott, K. S. (2003). Are the 100 best better? An empirical investigation of the relationship between being a "Great Place to Work" and firm performance. *Personnel Psychology, 56,* 965–993.

Glade, G. A., & Livery, M. (2003). The impact of human resource management and work climate on organizational performance. *Personnel Psychology, 56,* 383–404.

Harter, J. K., Schmidt, F. L., & Hayes, T. L. (2002). Business-unit-level relationship between employee satisfaction, employee engagement, and business outcomes: A meta-analysis. *Journal of Applied Psychology, 87,* 268–279.

HRC WorkNet. (2004). *Corporate Equality Index on Gay, Lesbian, Bisexual and Transgender Social Responsibility.* Washington, DC: Human Rights Campaign Foundation.

Koys, D. J. (2001). The effects of employee satisfaction, organizational citizenship behavior, and turnover on organizational effectiveness: A unit-level, longitudinal study. *Personnel Psychology, 54,* 101–114.

Koys, D. J. (2003). How the achievement of human resources goals drives restaurant performance. *Cornell Hotel and Restaurant Management Quarterly, 44*(1), 17–24.

Levering, R., & Moskowitz, M. (1984). *The 100 best companies to work for in America.* New York: Penguin.

Levering, R., & Moskowitz, M. (1993). *The 100 best companies to work for in America.* New York: Penguin.

Preece, D. C., & Filbeck, G. (1999). Family friendly firms: Does it pay to care? *Financial Services Review, 8,* 47–60.

Pynn, M. (2004, Aug. 8). All in the family? *Orlando Sentinel.*

Shellenbarger, S. (1993, June 21). Data gap: Do family-support programs help the bottom line? The research is inconclusive. *Wall Street Journal*, R6.

Simon, D. (2002). *Happy employees, happy customers: Understanding the relationship between work-life policies, labor market opportunities, and customer satisfaction.* Unpublished manuscript, Department of Applied Economics and Management, Cornell University, Ithaca, NY.

Vergin, R., & Qoronfleh, M. (1998, Jan.–Feb.). Corporate reputation and the stock market. *Business Horizons*, 19–26.

CHAPTER 24

An Executive and a Survey Model

A Follow-Up Action Success Story

Tracey Carsten Roll

Successful organizational survey programs are not easily achieved and, as a result, not commonplace. When a new internal consultant was given the task of turning a failed survey program into a successful one, there were choices to be made and lessons to be learned. This was particularly true since the consultant was a relative neophyte; indeed, she was fresh out of graduate school with no large-scale survey experience. The most important lesson learned in this instance is that you not only need a survey program—for use in obtaining results leading to organizational improvements—but also a top executive who is ready to support and energize that program in the organization.

This chapter tells the story of the survey-model process and how one president and his team used that process to engage the employees and management of an organization in a year-round dialogue regarding organizational performance needs. It demonstrates that the use of a survey model, coupled with top management support, seems to provide the right combination for successful survey actions and results. The "Lessons Learned" section highlights the key points that led to a successful follow-up action story.

The organization profiled here was the Information Service (IS) Division of ECS, a credit reporting company whose commodity is information and the mining of data. It has two major divisions, the IS Division and the Marketing Division (MS), each with its own president. The IS Division, an organization largely used for marketing information, includes about two thousand employees, generating approximately $700 million in annual revenue. Its business units serve more than twenty thousand business clients by providing insight and capabilities to target, acquire, and develop a customer base and to manage customer relations. The MS Division's mission is to provide information to businesses for the purpose of targeted marketing.

Situation Before the New President Takes Over

In previous years, the IS Division had conducted a number of surveys in an attempt to measure employee satisfaction. These surveys, which had been administered by external survey vendors, were very long (180 items) and cumbersome (separate survey instrument, answer sheets, and coding sheets). Furthermore, the external vendors distributed survey results on a floppy disc and provided little or no instructional or consulting support. Although managers who had had prior experience with surveys or felt strongly about the survey process did provide some minimal follow-through, interpretation of results was inconsistent. Also, since the vendors who conducted the survey owned the survey items and the data, the division's only option was to reengage the same vendors for future surveys in order to have access to its own historical survey data.

Because of the unsatisfactory results using external vendors, it was decided that it would be in the organization's long-term interest to design a new survey model and process it in-house. It was hoped that the model would provide the context within which results could be interpreted and understood, and the administrative process would be user friendly and easy to comprehend.

Survey Design Process

The division's internal organization effectiveness (OE) consultant, an industrial/organizational psychologist, began the design process by looking at survey vendors and software options, weighing internal versus external administration options. An outside consultant, who was considered an expert in the survey field, was retained to assist the internal consultant. This internal/external consultant partnership proved to be beneficial and may have been one of the critical success factors for the process.

In the early stages of the process, managers were interviewed regarding various administrative options, with questions focused mainly on the action phase. The managers expressed their opinions regarding the pros and cons of previous survey administrations and subsequent survey support, both internal and external. Many offered specific suggestions regarding survey administration practices, including the desire for an online survey administration for ease of use, consulting support on action planning from human resources (HR), use of comparative data to help put the survey results into some sort of context, and more communication around survey results, actions, and changes made as a result of survey feedback. They wanted to be able to compare their data to internal and external norms and use the data to engage employees in making the organization a better place to work, increasing organizational commitment, and focusing follow-up efforts where they were most needed.

Once interviews were completed, the consultant team analyzed the information and came up with survey process recommendations, including a survey model, for the senior leaders of the organization. The recommended survey design was a linkage (Heskett, Sasser, & Schlesinger, 1997) type of survey process, where follow-up actions would ultimately drive organizational performance through employee engagement around specific targeted areas identified in survey results.

According to the model, improved customer loyalty is a result of targeted employee performance, which has an impact on organizational performance. Using an action research process (Gustavsen, 2001), which incorporates theory, research, and dialogue, the team developed a model (see Figure 24.1) in which three dimensions of employee engagement—customer orientation, commitment, and recognition—were linked to client experiences and loyalty, and ultimately to organization results (market share, growth, and new ventures). Employee engagement (a dependent variable) results when employees are committed to the company and to their work, oriented toward pleasing their customers, and feel recognized for their efforts. As shown, employee engagement is the desired end result of leadership practices and resources and supports.

Figure 24.1. The Survey Model

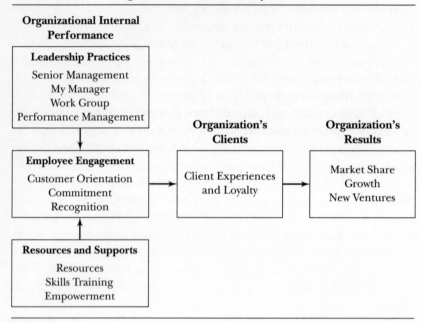

Selected survey items were organized around the three dimensions of employee engagement rather than on employee satisfaction, as in previous division surveys. Each dimension was broken down into several subdimensions, with a half-dozen survey items under each. Many of the items were deliberately chosen to compare with survey results of other companies.

Demographic items were deliberately kept at a minimum to minimize concerns about anonymity and indicate to employees that this new survey was different—not a typical HR satisfaction survey. Items on ethnicity, gender, and other typical demographics were purposefully omitted, as were those regarding compensation and benefits. The demographic items that were chosen were functional unit, department (within the functional unit), tenure (to compare length-of-service differences), and performance rating for the last performance review period. The last item was included to see if high-performing individuals differed from others.

The survey also included two open-ended items, which were specifically focused on business results, as opposed to traditional survey items focused on satisfaction or happiness with the work environment. One item solicited responses focused on "improving the business by better serving customers" and another on "what advice employees would give management to improve the success of the business in 6–12 months." Also, one item asked respondents whether they believed that "management in my organization will act on problems identified by this survey."

The one key factor that could not be designed into the survey process was the commitment and support of senior leadership. The individual serving as president at the time the model was developed did agree to administer the survey derived from the model. However, he did not follow through on the utilization facets, failing to communicate results to employees, except to note vaguely that he would use results to determine the direction in which he would take the organization. Thus, the new survey model, after being launched, rode at anchor in the bay for two years without building up any steam or going anywhere.

The New President

The new president joined the IS Division about two years after the internal survey model and process had been designed. During his first week in office, he asked the internal OE consultant about previous surveys, as well as the linkage-type model that had been created earlier and had been rusting from lack of interest.

Before joining the IS Division, the new president had worked his way up in an organization where he was exposed to a well-entrenched, professionally run, and successful survey program. He had learned how to focus employees' efforts through the survey process. He knew that surveys were not completely successful when they focused mainly on quantitative data rather than on the messages conveyed by employees. He realized that it was important to engage in dialogue with employees and follow up by creating a collaborative plan of engaging employees as part of the solution. He felt that "if it is important enough to ask you, it is equally important for us to have you help us with the solutions."

In his new position at the IS Division, the president had the task of taking a lethargic organization where trust was at an all-time low to a new place. He took the survey information provided by the OE consultant and studied it during his tour of division facilities across the country. Also, he scheduled a follow-up meeting with the consultant to be held two weeks later to discuss administering the next organizational survey.

Once the president decided to move forward with the survey, he met with his senior team members to introduce the survey model and make clear that he would hold them accountable for following through with the entire process. The OE consultant provided a PowerPoint presentation of the model to the team, carefully spelling out the details of each step of the process. The president told team members that survey objectives were to:

- Provide a greater understanding of employees' views, opinions, values, expectations, and needs
- Clarify priorities for change in the organization
- Apply results to client value and financial performance
- Benchmark employee input versus relevant norms
- Improve communication within the organization between managers and employees

He told them that he wanted them to "talk up" the survey in advance and to be "out in front" with employees in regard to survey results.

Top-Down Logic

In the past, there had been no consistent history of management's taking any specific actions after a survey administration. Generally survey follow-up and action planning had been sporadic and inconsistent, depending on an individual manager's level of commitment to the survey process. This survey would be different, since it would use internal support and planned to do something with results. Thus, it was decided to provide the results to senior management (Nadler, 1977) before they were provided to employees and managers. The intent was to have the senior team act as a model for the rest of the organization in implementing action-taking behaviors identified by the survey.

The division's plan was to administer the first two or three surveys over a period of three to five years. In each case, the senior team would receive results first and take action in the organization. Over that same time period, the managers and employees would be trained in interpreting survey data and in how to take subsequent focused actions to drive organizational performance. After two or three survey administrations, the president planned to shift the process; that is, he planned to disseminate survey data to line leadership and line-level employees before senior management. This would allow line management to start working with local survey actions and push recommendations upward to the next level in the organization. This process shift was planned because of the president's belief that line employees are the real drivers of organizational performance.

First Survey Administration

The survey was administered electronically via e-mail. This proved to be a new experience for division employees, although some small surveys had previously been administered in this manner. The president sent employees a memo through their work e-mail addresses, inviting them to participate in the survey process. He explained that such participation was important to all employees, since it would allow them to provide him with data regarding organizational needs and help in making subsequent changes.

Since previous surveys had had little follow-up or accountability, most employees were skeptical about this latest attempt and held a "wait-and-see" attitude. Although the focus of the survey was different from previous ones, trust was still an ongoing issue in the organization. This was especially true with employees in the IS division because of a recently implemented performance management metric system, where employee performance was force-ranked by managers on a bell curve (Welch & Byrne, 2001).

Survey Roles: Internal Organizational Support

In the new survey approach, internal staff would drive the survey process, from administration to rollout of results and action planning. The internal OE consultant provided survey training and backup shadow consulting support for the HR team, since team members were charged with providing help to managers in interpreting results and other support functions. Also, the OE consultant spent several hours providing individualized support for functional and department leaders, depending on their level of survey experience.

The division's internal training department provided managers with courses in basic survey skills that were well attended, even by senior vice presidents. The internal OE consultant helped in-house trainers design these courses and coached them regarding the survey process and basic survey questions that could come up. In these courses, which were conducted before survey results were distributed, the survey model was introduced and explained, along with basic statistics. The trainers taught managers how to conduct survey follow-up, pointing out that it was a critical step necessary to drive organizational performance. Also, trainers advised the managers regarding the president's expectations in their reporting survey actions to him.

Survey communication was coordinated through the IS Communication Department. Throughout the year following the first survey administration, the president took advantage of every opportunity to communicate survey actions and subsequent organizational progress. He not only provided his managers and employees with regular e-mail messages concerning survey progress updates, but also included such updates at his quarterly all-employee meetings (which started as a result of survey feedback from employees). He was so involved in the process that he insisted on crafting his own memos concerning the survey (see Exhibit 24.1). Managers, in turn, reported survey progress in the monthly business reports provided to the president, as well as at departmental and at all-hands meetings.

Because the survey was conducted in-house, the OE consultant was able to obtain real-time survey response rates for each functional unit, which she provided at the end of each business day via e-mail to the president and his managers. This led to a friendly competition among managers, with each vying for the highest response rate. As a result, the final response rate for the IS Division to the first survey administration was an extraordinary 92 percent, with 56 percent indicating that they believed action would be taken as a result of the survey. However, it should be noted that because of management's sometimes overzealous encouragement, some employees suspected that the survey's anonymity had been compromised.

Exhibit 24.1. Survey Model

Memorandum

re: Employee Survey

date: July 5, 2002

to: People of IS

cc: xxxxx

from: The President

Your input matters. I realize that things aren't perfect and we are
not yet where we need to be in order to achieve our stated objectives.
Therefore I am asking that you take the time to complete the attached
Employee Survey. It is shorter than many from the past and it is completely on-line, so it should be easier to do. It specifically focuses on
how we can make ECS more effective in serving our clients and how
we can ensure our future success. It is through increasing our success
that we can make it a better place for all of us.

I have requested the Organization Effectiveness Department, with the
help of a professional survey consultant, to develop this year's survey
with a particular emphasis on driving business performance through
action planning as a result of your input. The team identified particular
organizational characteristics that drive business performance. These
criteria will provide us with an indication of our strengths, and identify
opportunities to improve our performance. The results of this survey
will create a baseline to track our progress as we move forward with
focus, speed and accountability.

The survey is for all of Information Services. To guarantee anonymity
and confidentiality, the survey is being administered by the Organization Effectiveness Department using survey software. The aggregate results will be communicated to you and unit-level reports will be shared
with the staff of the individual units concerned. (To protect confidentiality no reports will be created for groups of less than 12 people.) All
managers will be asked to ensure that there will be unit-specific follow-
up. One important objective of the survey will be to use it as a tool to
link communication between managers and their people. What is important is that I want to hear your input and to get your involvement in
bringing about meaningful solutions. Thank you in advance for participating in this important initiative for our organization.

Analysis the Layperson Can Understand

Survey results were interpreted using a relative weight analysis (Johnson, 2001). This analysis allows the levers, or drivers, from the survey model that are important to employee engagement (the dependent variable) to be examined relative one to another. It looks at all predictors simultaneously and shows the influence each has in the presence of other existing predictors. This process provides a realistic picture of a dimension's impact in an ongoing, fluid organization where other dimensions also have an impact on a particular outcome.

Using the relative weight analysis, the results were put into a context that could translate well to employees and told a story management could understand. One manager made the remark that this was the first time that any survey results made sense to him.

As a result of the relative weight analysis, senior management chose three dimensions—recognition, senior leadership communication, and performance management—on which to drive change through employee focus. The president directed the Finance Department to make sure that money was set aside for each department to focus on local recognition programs. Also, senior management directed managers to hold quarterly performance management meetings with their employees; determined to participate in quarterly senior leadership team meetings with all employees in order to clearly communicate the company's direction and strategy; and decided to investigate employees' recognition needs during the action planning process. They felt that by engaging employees in focus groups, they would find out exactly what employees meant by their survey responses regarding recognition.

A new performance management process had been implemented just prior to survey administration, and employees were quite upset with the new performance management changes. Consequently, employees gave a low rating to survey items pertaining to performance management, probably due to their resistance to the new process. Because of these unfavorable reactions, follow-up actions were focused on increasing the amount of dialogue between employees and managers regarding employee performance.

The analysis of comments from open-ended items, designed to elicit ideas from employees on how to improve the business, was cumbersome to handle internally. However, graduate student helpers worked full time on responses to these items, organizing them around categories or themes.

The use of comparative norms from outside sources provided another source of information, enabling managers to make a contextual comparison (especially for survey one results, given the lack of previous survey data). Normative comparisons were distributed only at the higher business unit levels. However, managers were cautioned that comparisons would best be made with other division business units with similar, if not identical, cultures. This kept managers from making excuses when their data were low compared to outside norms.

Proactive Action Planning

Throughout the first survey process, the action planning had been deliberate and well thought out. Accountability was ensured through active senior leadership involvement and an active communications network supported by the communications team. The president created expectations through frequent survey-focused communications and by demanding monthly reports focused on survey actions from his senior team. His communication to employees when the survey administration was complete was enthusiastic and straightforward:

> Yesterday marked the completion of the survey collection phase in our overall survey process. We reached a participation level of approximately 90%. This is incredible. I want to personally thank you for taking the time to provide input to the survey process. Your involvement is critical to the success of this project and is a demonstration of your commitment to making this the best possible organization.
>
> This is only the first step and I look forward to your continued involvement and commitment in the next steps of the survey process. In these further steps, we will be rolling up our collective sleeves to identify some tangible ways to improve our organizational performance, and move forward in our efforts to achieve the greatness to which we all strive. The following is a general schedule for the next steps in the process. We are all anxious to hear your input and then to select some key areas to work on that will help us move forward. Thanks again for your participation and stay tuned.

Second Survey Administration: Challenges Abound

The second survey was vastly different in size, scope, and senior leadership commitment from the first. First, it was sponsored by the CEO of the organization, whose expectations were high after the success obtained by the IS Division survey. Second, the entire company, consisting of about five thousand employees and several business units, was engaged in the survey process, as opposed to just the IS Division, with six HR generalists serving as consultants. This greatly broadened scope created enormous challenges for the small in-house survey team.

Because of the IS Division president's successful track record with the first survey, organizational leaders looked to him to serve as a leadership role model. For this survey, the president announced to his senior team leaders that he expected 100 percent participation. This created an issue with some employees, as their competitive team leaders were actively, sometimes excessively, encouraging them to complete the survey. Also, competition among managers in regard to survey response rates caught on in other parts of the organization. A couple of senior managers even took informal polls to see who had or had not completed the survey. Since the OE consultant reported response rates to all managers at the close of business each day, some of the managers asked her to identify those who had not yet participated. She advised that since surveys were not linked to employees, it was not possible to fill that request and would not be ethical to do so.

Employees' expectations regarding the second administration were very different from those of the first. The president's memo, which accompanied the survey, acknowledged that this was a new type of survey and that its focus would be on dialogue between managers and employees. The survey results did show that employees' trust had increased, since they felt that something would be done with survey results. However, during the first survey, the bar had been set incredibly high with such a high participation rate. Unfortunately, during the second administration, trust in management within the IT function was at an all-time low, due to a continuing threat of downsizing, outsourcing, and offshoring. Not surprisingly, the response rate fell by almost 15 percentage points.

Cynicism regarding the first survey had been high and was measured by responses to the item that asked respondents whether they believed any action would occur as a result of the survey. Results were very different between the two administrations. Responses to the second survey showed that 62 percent believed action would be taken, as compared to 56 percent for the previous survey. These statistics may not sound impressive; however, an analysis showed that 81 percent of employees who received feedback *and* saw action taken after the earlier survey believed that management would act on problems identified by the second survey, compared to 27 percent of those who had seen no action taken.

This brings up another important consideration for an internal consultant: it is necessary to reassure employees continually regarding the confidentiality and anonymity of survey information. Since surveys were administered online, some employees expressed concern that management might be able to identify particular employees and their responses. This was not possible since surveys were not linked to respondents, but concern continued to exist, particularly among IT employees. To alleviate this concern, the IT senior vice president sent out a memo, pointing out that identifying demographics had purposefully been kept at a minimum and advising employees that it was impossible to link respondents to electronic addresses. Also, he included an explanation provided by the survey vendor that reinforced his statement.

One downside of conducting the survey in-house with a small survey team was the lag time between administration and results dissemination. Both the first and the second surveys were administered in the summer months, and employees were advised that results would be disseminated and survey follow-up actions taken during the fall, before the winter holidays. The survey team and HR scrambled for months to meet these tight deadlines, particularly with the second survey, when the scope of the project expanded to the larger organization.

The survey improvements between the two surveys spoke volumes and provided assurance that the first survey process had paid off. Within the IS Division, all dimensions showed improvement except one, which decreased by an insignificant 1 percentage point. The recognition and senior leadership dimensions improved dramatically, with some of the individual items on "management providing clear direction" and "being encouraged by the direction of the company" increasing by 20 percentage points. Also, the second survey provided internal trending comparisons, based on the IS Division's previous survey data. It was exciting for managers to see how their previous year's efforts had paid off through organizational performance improvement.

The organization's focus on survey action was slightly different between the two surveys. In the first survey, the division's senior management team focused on recognition, performance management, and tools and resources needed to get work done. In the following survey, the division chose the same areas to focus on, although such focus was through the lens of a "client experience" initiative, a companywide effort aimed at focusing on customer needs and providing timely solutions. The items in the second survey were identical to those in the first, but results were organized so that they reinforced the client experience effort and provided another venue through which to focus employee engagement (serving customers, ultimately aimed at increasing customer loyalty). Timing became a sticking point because the survey results rollout preceded the client experience rollout by a couple of weeks. However, the HR team was able to help tie the two initiatives together by coaching managers on how they were related.

After senior team members had received their individual survey results, the CEO held a meeting that included the two company divisional presidents and their senior teams. Prior to the meeting, the CEO encouraged attendees to meet with their managers to discuss their initial reactions to the survey data. He expected them to share their initial reactions with their cohorts and advise what, if anything, they were going to do in response to their survey results. Each leader reported out one by one, beginning with the IS Division president, who advised where his division's initial efforts would be focused and how these efforts supported the client experience initiative. After his report, the other leaders shared their survey efforts with the senior leadership team. As noted, prior to the meeting, the CEO had advised attendees what he expected from them. However, it was apparent that although some took the survey initiative seriously, others had not put much effort behind it. This was apparent when some of them frantically began to scribble notes for use in their report.

After the meeting, the CEO publicly committed to another survey that would be conducted organizationwide next year. Although the CEO did not want to make commitments for the broader organization as a whole, he did advise his team that he expected them to follow up survey results and make changes at their individual units. Also, the fact that he had committed to another survey implied that his team was expected to make changes this year that would reflect on next year's results.

Lessons Learned

The OE consultant and her survey team learned many valuable lessons during each survey administration. They made a point of debriefing the survey process as a team in order to learn from mistakes and best practices and make changes for subsequent survey administrations.

Surveys as a Management Method

As demonstrated by the president and his management team, surveys can be a powerful management method for engaging employees in organizational change. The postsurvey action phase lasts until the next survey administration, provided follow-up actions are taken, followed up on, and communicated widely and frequently. Finally, and most important, role modeling must be demonstrated by the senior leadership team. The IS Division president had learned this through his experiences as a young executive and intuitively understood that employees knew best what was needed to run a successful business. Using the survey process to engage employees in an ongoing dialogue proved to be successful for him at his prior organizations and again at the IS Division.

Developing a Model: Content and Method

Although the OE consultant had conducted small-scale surveys with and without a model, she learned that the model provides a framework for organizing the survey data into a story. It helps the layperson understand what the survey results mean, thus leading to successful application of information and focus to create organizational changes. Prior to creating the model, management and employees were interviewed to find out how they wanted to use employee feedback to drive business performance. Also, employee meetings focusing on past survey applications were conducted. Information gained proved to be helpful in educating management regarding use of survey feedback to increase employee engagement, which leads to increased customer feedback and business performance.

Once the themes had been identified, it was critical to the success of the survey effort to present the model to senior management to make sure they understood it and would give it their full support. Although the model had been created two years before the president arrived at the IS Division, he understood the dimensions of employee engagement around which the model had been organized. A model without senior leadership support, which had been the case before the arrival of the president, is ineffective. The senior team commitment and the survey model created the right combination for successful survey follow-up and subsequent actions.

Advanced planning and a strong survey team were essential elements to surviving a large-scale survey. Conducting the first survey, which included only the IS Division, was simple compared to the next survey. In the first survey, the president championed the entire process, and the OE consultant partnered with the Division HR team, which had been trained thoroughly regarding its role in the survey process. Throughout the time period of the first survey, the OE consultant held frequent meetings with the HR team members to hear their concerns and gain their feedback and suggestions for improvements. Information obtained was especially useful after the first survey's rollout, when plans were being made for the next survey.

The two surveys were vastly different from each other. The IS Division was a little different, and its president's responsibility in the process had been increased. This took some thoughtful planning prior to the second survey administration to account for changes and make sure that trending data would be "apples to apples." Usually this requires repackaging the prior data to fit into the current organizational structure.

Use of Graduate Students

Graduate students have proved to be great resources in supporting various organizational projects. During the IS Division survey process, they were useful in classifying responses to open-ended items, entering data, and doing some of the time-consuming tasks that are easy to get caught up in. Participating in a large-scale organizational survey project gives students a chance to observe the politics, processes, and organizational engagement in reacting to survey results. However, it is important to be fully cognizant of the students' capabilities, as they are often eager to take on exciting projects that may be well over their heads. Thus, they should be supervised when they are working on a large-scale project such as an organizationwide survey.

Use of External Survey Vendors

Although both surveys, conducted after the new president arrived at the IS Division, were developed in-house, previous division surveys had contracted to use external survey vendors. When an organization does use an external vendor, especially in a large survey, there are several factors to consider. For example, in both surveys, it was important to be able to organize the survey data around a model and use the relative weight analysis to support the model and tell a story that management could understand. At the time of this writing, not all survey vendors are aware of this type of analysis.

In addition, it is important that one's own organization (as opposed to the survey vendor) owns the raw survey data, as well as the survey items. If a company decides to switch survey vendors for whatever reason, previous survey results must be available so that longitudinal analyses can be conducted. Many survey vendors hold their survey items as proprietary, and most of the larger vendors use their clients' data as part of a database of normative data. They then turn around and charge their clients for their own data! It should be noted that such databases are representative of only the vendor's own clients and are often not even contemporary. Thus, if you decide to use normative data items, they must be identical or very similar to the normative database items for valid comparison. The decision to use data norms in-house should be determined before the survey is administered. As the organization develops its own survey history, vendor norms will lose their interpretive relevance.

When an organization does contract with an external vendor, representatives of the finance organization and the IT Department should be included when working through the many details of a contract. This will ensure that the company is aware of all the financial and technological details involved in conducting an electronic survey. Firewalls are sometimes an issue, as well as the capability of the server to handle a heavy workload, with or without an external survey vendor.

External Consultant

The external consultant used throughout the five-year survey design and implementation process was invaluable to the internal OE consultant. A survey consultant shadowing the internal consultant (who may be too close to the organization) provides a third party or impartial perspective. A survey expert who is not involved in a survey vendor's direct services might best fill that role.

Recognizing Politics and Enthusiasm

Politics abound in any company. When people jockey for recognition, sometimes what is best for the company becomes secondary to their need for visibility. Although a survey process provides an internal consultant with many opportunities for front-line visibility, his or her proper role is to remain in the background and provide support to management and HR.

It is important for the success of a survey initiative, especially a large-scale survey, to have top-level executive support. Every survey differs, with different or new players for each administration. Thus, when conducting a survey in-house, it is important to consider the degree of enthusiasm that management holds toward the survey process. Lower levels of enthusiasm lead to a much greater challenge for the internal consultant.

Next Steps

Recently the OE consultant asked the IS Division president what he would do differently from the previous two survey administrations. He replied, "Nothing; we'll see what happens this year." For the consultant, this affirmation made the whole effort worthwhile.

When the consultant interviewed the president, he refused to take credit for the survey success; instead, he insisted that the success was due to the dedicated internal team effort. It should be emphasized, however, that a lot of the credit should go to the president and his feelings about employee engagement and dialogue. He was always open to suggestions from the survey team and made the process truly collaborative. Without his leadership support in driving accountability for action, especially after the results were distributed, the survey would never have had the impact that it did.

The president's importance to the survey success was evident to many. When the external consultant came to the CEO's leadership team meeting after the second survey, he wanted to meet the IS Division president. They shook hands, and the consultant declared to the president, "You're my hero!" It was a well-deserved compliment for a successful follow-up action story.

Conclusion

A survey model was very useful in creating a framework within which to tell executives a survey story. The model gives meaning to the survey data that managers can understand and apply to specific targeted actions. However, without executive support, the model would have had little or no impact. A strong model and a supportive executive are a powerful combination in creating action after a survey.

References

Gustavsen, B. (2001). Theory and practice: The mediating discourse. In P. Reason & H. Bradbury (Eds.), *Handbook of action research*. Thousand Oaks, CA: Sage.

Heskett, J. L., Sasser, W. E. Jr., & Schlesinger, L. A. (1997). *The service profit chain: How leading companies link profit and growth to loyalty, satisfaction and value*. New York: Free Press.

Johnson, J. W. (2001). Determining the relative importance of predictors in multiple regression: Practical applications of relative weights. In F. Columbus (Ed.), *Advances in psychology research*. Huntington, NY: Nova Science.

Nadler, D. A. (1977). *Feedback and organization development: Using data-based methods*. Upper Saddle River, NJ: Prentice Hall.

Welch, J., & Bryne, J. (2001). *Jack: Straight from the gut*. New York: Warner Books.

Name Index

Subject Index

A

Accenture, 272, 314

Accessibility: designing online survey, 197–199; global survey, 487; testing online survey, 201–202; Web sites related to reviewing, 198

Accountability: to ensure positive change, 104; global surveys and building in change, 504–508; JP-Morgan Chase managerial and staff, 519*fig*–520, 526–528, 528; pulse rates and potentially lower, 277–278; as reengagement strategy, 545, 546–548, 556; shift to implementation, 95; TSS communicating manager program establishment of, 526–528

AccountAbility (UK organization), 564, 574

ACE (Achieving Competitive Excellence), 540, 544–545, 558

Action planning: designing, 127–129; elements of effective, 95; employee involvement/engagement in, 540–550, 556–557; employee retention survey findings for, 472–475*b*; evaluating, 98; increased visibility of, 95–96; IS (Information Service) survey incorporation of, 593; pulse surveys used for, 288–290; research study on impact of, 113–125; study findings on different dimensions of, 120*fig*; tracking execution of, 96. *See also* Change; Interventions; Taking action

Action planning research study: methodology used in, 117–118; overview of the company and survey program, 114–116; purpose of, 116–117; results of, 118*t*–125; sample organizational survey model, 115*fig*

Active nonrespondents, 316–317, 319

Ad hoc expert survey panel, 306

Ad hoc surveys, 109–111

Administration: computer-assisted content analysis, 260–261; geographical differences consideration for, 499; global survey, 487–488; IS (Information Service) Division [ECS] approach to survey, 589–597; oversurveying due to technological advances in, 296–297; overview of survey, 140–141; pulse survey, 267–268. *See also* Surveys

Adobe's Acrobat Reader, 491

Advocacy groups, 574

Alderfer's ERG model, 541

Alignment-capabilities-engagement tree diagram (ACE), 88*fig*, 89, 90

Allstate Insurance Company, 467

American Customer Satisfaction Index (ACSI), 63*fig*, 64

American Psychological Association's PsychINFO database, 33, 267

"Analysis paralysis," 498

Anglo culture, 501, 502*t*, 503

Anonymity issues: limiting demographic items to protect, 586;

for, 337*t*–338; correlations between employee survey themes
to, 337*t*
Customer research: service climate
survey used in, 57–73; survey linkage research, 156
Customer satisfaction: antecedents
and consequences of service
climate and, 54–55; behavioral
engagement link to, 62–67; increasing organization focus on,
53; key drivers of service quality
enhancing, 328; long-linked
model of some antecedents of,
61–62*fig*; role of leadership in,
68; service climate surveys to research issues of, 57–73
Customers: impact of BCL (Best
Company List) on, 573; linkages
of employees, business performance and, 157, 158*t*–159*t*, 160–
161, 163–165, 164*fig*; loyalty of,
337*t*–338
Customized survey models, 9–11,
10*fig*

D

Data: in comparison to relevant
norm groups, 57; gathering employee retention, 459–463; gathering M&A research, 439–440;
graphical presentation of, 394–
396; how to not present survey,
378–379; linking various sources
of survey, 127; presenting survey
message and supporting, 390–
394; providing relevant employee
engagement, 556; questionable
value of pulse surveys, 278–279;
relevance, clarity, and importance
of, 389. *See also* Information overload; Norms (normative data)
Data analysis: avoiding "analysis
paralysis," 498; benchmark data
validity and mismatched, 371–
372; challenges of employee re-
tainment, 475–478; cluster, 386;

computer-assisted, 241–245; correlations, 337*t*–338, 346, 383–
384*fig*; of employee retention
survey data, 463–468; factor,
384–386, 385*fig*; IS (Information
Service) relative weight approach
to, 592–593; qualitative, 251, 253;
quantitative, 251, 439, 444*t*–447*t*,
477; SEM (structural equation
modeling), 387*fig*–388; text
analysis applications for, 243; text
analysis lexicons for, 243–245;
text mining applications for, 242.
See also Methodology
Data integrity: ensuring online survey, 199–203; testing online
survey, 201
Dealer orientation best practices,
173–174
Decision making: oversurveying due
to desire for data-based, 297; survey data used in, 17–18; survey to
facilitate M&A, 436–437; value of
norms (normative value) to, 352,
353–357
Dell, 272, 274, 314, 466
Deloitte and Touche, 574
Demographic groups: anonymity
concerns limiting survey items
about, 586; ethnic/racial identifi-
cations of, 486; norm comparisons
of, 355–356; online precoding of,
191–192
Derived (statistical) measures,
330–333
Designing: global survey, 487–488;
online survey accessibility,
197–199; recommendations for
action planning/interventions,
127–129
Detroit Edison Company, 132
"Dilbert" cartoon strip, 1
Dimensions (categories), 385
Direct (stated) ratings of importance, 329–330
Discontinuous online reporting,
225–226

applications for, 242; types of, 239–241, 240*t*
"Opinion Surveys: Turning Results into Action" (Kraut), 1
Opinion/culture surveys, 459–461
Organization Health Survey, 265, 272, 280
Organizational culture: M&A post-combination, 433, 449–450, 451–453; PepsiCo IPS (Inclusion Pulse Survey) tracking changes in, 279–280; TSS communicating manager program to build inclusive, 512–534
Organizational outcome measurements, 41
Organizations: BCL (Best Company List) on, 559–580; characteristics of high-performance, 152*t*–153*t*; conducting M&A employee research on partner, 438–439; employee perspective on high-performance, 152*t*; employee surveys in global, 483–509; estimating relative standing of, 371*b*; foundation issues of, 61; M&A integration of, 450; online reporting and structural change in, 217; outcome measurements used by, 41; POS (perceived organizational support) from, 66; prepared for the survey process, 139–140; pulse survey accessing health of, 13, 109, 111, 264–292; reengaging employees during turbulent times of, 535–558; strategic objectives of, 61. *See also* Employee engagement
Orlando Sentinel (newspaper), 578
Outcomes: long-term COE (Center of Excellence), 557–558; modeling relationships between variables and, 89–90; organizational measurement, 41; TSS communicating manager program, 531*fig*–532. *See also* Survey follow-up

process; Survey presentation; Survey results
Oversurveying: causes of, 296–299; consequences of, 299–302; defining, 294–296; pulse surveys leading to, 276; solutions to, 302–310
Oversurveying causes: advance in survey administration technology, 296–297; desire to make data-based business decision, 297; factors contributing to perceptions of, 298–299; lack of centralized oversight, 298
Oversurveying consequences: creation of confusion, 301; increased costs, 299; irritation among employees, 301–302; lower response rates/quality issues, 299–301; solutions to, 302–310; survey triage, 301. *See also* Undersurveying consequences
Oversurveying solutions: adding formal professional survey review, 306–310; adding informal or ad hoc expert survey panel, 306; adding a survey traffic director, 306; continuum of, 303–310, 304*fig*, 305*t*; ensuring survey quality, 302–303; executive approval, 304

P

Partner organization research, 438–439
Passive nonrespondents, 317, 319, 322–323
PDF (Adobe's portable document format), 491, 492
People equity, 81–82*fig*
PepsiCo, 265, 272, 279–280
PepsiCo IPS (Inclusion Pulse Survey), 279–280
Performance: defining, 40–41; deploying best practices to drive high, 175–178*fig*; evaluation of TSS communicating manager,